William Barksdale, CSA

William Barksdale, CSA

*A Biography of the
United States Congressman
and Confederate Brigadier General*

JOHN DOUGLAS ASHTON

McFarland & Company, Inc., Publishers
Jefferson, North Carolina

Frontispiece: Democratic Congressman William Barksdale, Julian Vannerson photograph in McClee's Gallery of the 35th Congress, 1859 (Library of Congress).

ISBN (print) 978-1-4766-8374-4
ISBN (ebook) 978-1-4766-4172-0

LIBRARY OF CONGRESS AND BRITISH LIBRARY
CATALOGUING DATA ARE AVAILABLE

Library of Congress Control Number 2021005085

© 2021 John Douglas Ashton. All rights reserved

No part of this book may be reproduced or transmitted in any form or by any means, electronic or mechanical, including photocopying or recording, or by any information storage and retrieval system, without permission in writing from the publisher.

Front cover artwork "Forward to the Foe"
courtesy Mark Maritato, historical artist

Printed in the United States of America

*McFarland & Company, Inc., Publishers
Box 611, Jefferson, North Carolina 28640
www.mcfarlandpub.com*

This book is respectfully dedicated to my loving wife Susan
who has been my faithful research companion at both
battlefield and reference library over the past thirty years;
and to our two daughters, Laura and Amy, who spent their
vacations at Civil War sites instead of theme parks;
and to those brave Sons of Mississippi whose deeds
of courage and sacrifice on many a battlefield
won fame and honor for Barksdale's Mississippi Brigade,
and for the man whose name it bears.

Table of Contents

Acknowledgments	ix
Preface	1
Introduction	3
Prologue: Gettysburg, July 2, 1863, 7:30 p.m., West of Plum Run Swale	6
One—Beginnings	7
Two—Mississippi: Land of Opportunity	11
Three—Military Service in Mexico: Disease, Deprivation and Death	18
Four—Barksdale Secures His Political Future	31
Five—Turbulent Times in Washington City	41
Six—Epithets, Fisticuffs and the Downward Spiral to Secession	56
Seven—From Quartermaster General to a Combat Command at First Manassas	74
Eight—Charges of Drunkenness, Redemption at Edwards Ferry and a Court of Inquiry	89
Nine—The Seven Days Battles: Barksdale Commands the Mississippi Brigade	104
Ten—Malvern Hill: Barksdale Exhibits the Highest Qualities of the Soldier	118
Eleven—Harpers Ferry and Sharpsburg: Brigadier General Barksdale Front and Center	131
Twelve—Fredericksburg: Dead Yankees on the Pontoon Bridges and in the Streets	149
Thirteen—Second Fredericksburg (Chancellorsville): "We must make the fight whether we hold it or are whipped"	177

FOURTEEN—Gettysburg: A Grim Determination to Do or Die   203

FIFTEEN—Barksdale's Death, Burials, State Funeral and Legacy   236

Appendix: Previously Unpublished/Published Material Concerning William Barksdale   257

Chapter Notes   259

Bibliography   285

Index   293

Acknowledgments

The seed for this book was planted way back in 1980 when I joined a Confederate reenacting group from the "golden horseshoe" bordering Niagara Falls, in Ontario, and New York State. This unit comprised both Americans and Canadians. We accurately portrayed Company B, Benton Rifles of the 18th Mississippi—a regiment in Barksdale's renowned Mississippi Brigade. Despite having studied the Civil War for over 20 years, this marked my first introduction to William Barksdale. I became anxious to learn more about this rather obscure military commander. My quest for additional information began then and finally culminated in this biography—some 36 years later! My research has taken me to many battlefields, libraries, archives, museums, websites etc. I have interfaced with countless helpful and knowledgeable individuals who provided invaluable assistance along the way.

A project of this magnitude cannot be accomplished in isolation and this book is no exception. Therefore, I wish to formally acknowledge the following individuals in recognition of their cooperation, support, and assistance:

Susan Hall of the Mitchell Library at Mississippi State University for providing a copy of Dr. McKee's doctoral dissertation on William Barksdale; Sharon Aughinbaugh, librarian at Texas A & M University; and Diane Jamieson, Burlington (ON) Central Public Library for making accessible Steve Hawley's Master's Thesis assessing Barksdale's military leadership; Jess McLean for his exhaustive compilation, *The Official Records of the 13th Mississippi Infantry Regiment*, and for his kind words of support; John W. Hoopes who provided a copy of the *Abernathy Diary—"Our Mess"* long before it was published; Professor Jason H. Silverman for his words of encouragement; the staff at Broadfoot Publishing Company, in particular Jeannie Register and Page, for ferreting out the transcripts concerning Barksdale's Court of Inquiry and also for providing various compiled service records; and Brian Green, Kernersville, North Carolina, for providing a photocopy of a rare William Barksdale letter from 1845.

Special thanks go to the staff at the Mississippi Department of Archives and History for their assistance, in particular to the late Michael "Mick" Hennen and Alanna J. Patrick concerning Benjamin G. Humphreys' unpublished autobiography. I also extend sincere thanks to the staff at both the Library of Congress and National Archives, including Trevor K. Plante of the latter's Old Military & Civil War Records, and John P. Deeben, Archives Specialist.

The personnel at the Gettysburg National Military Park were always very accommodating and helpful during several visits to their research files. I express my gratitude to Professor Ervin L. Jordan of the Albert and Shirley Special Collections Library at the University of Virginia for providing photocopies of the only two extant and heartfelt letters from the elusive Narcissa Barksdale concerning her family and her husband's death. Sincere thanks go to esteemed Professor Gary W. Gallagher for sharing his original research material regarding the Barksdale-Early feud in the Richmond press following the battle of Chancellorsville, and for his words of encouragement along the way.

Heartfelt appreciation is also extended to R.W. Bro. Christopher M. Reid and the volunteer staff of the Lodge of Research for Mississippi for painstakingly recovering Barksdale's history as a Freemason, to Shawn Kyzer—Adjutant General William Barksdale Camp 1220 Sons of Confederate Veterans in Columbus, Mississippi, and finally to Clay Williams, former Director of the Old Capitol Museum MDAH in Jackson, Mississippi, for information regarding Barksdale's belated nomination and election to the Mississippi Hall of Fame.

Thanks also to prolific Mississippi historian, author, and publisher H. Grady Howell for his kind words of support and permission to quote extensively from *A Southern Lacrimosa*, regarding Barksdale's Mexican war experiences, shared with Surgeon Thomas N. Love. Special thanks to Licensed Gettysburg Battlefield Guide, award-winning author, and Peach Orchard expert extraordinaire Jim Hessler, for critiquing my manuscript and formally endorsing it. And to fellow authors and historians Joe Owen, Edward Alexander, and Alex Rossino for their shared knowledge, resources, support, and words of encouragement.

I wish to acknowledge Hal Jespersen, a true professional, for generating the excellent maps included herein, and talented artist Mark Maritato for providing the striking cover art.

Sincere thanks and appreciation are extended to Dylan Lightfoot and the editorial and production staff at McFarland & Company for finally bringing my dream to fruition.

On a personal note I wish to thank my close friend and computer wizard, Joanne Olenick, for diligently reformatting the manuscript multiple times—always with a cheerful smile!

This marathon labor of love could not have been completed without the loving support and sacrifices along the way by my darling wife, Susie, and our two daughters, Laura and Amy. You three most assuredly share in the final result!

Preface

As a lifelong student of the American Civil War I first became aware of William Barksdale in the early 1980s while reenacting as a member of the 18th Mississippi Infantry, one of four regiments in Barksdale's renowned Mississippi Brigade in the Army of Northern Virginia. With my interest piqued I eagerly sought out more information about this Confederate brigadier general. However, much to my chagrin, I quickly discovered that very little had been written about him. Setting about my task with enthusiasm, determination, and persistence, I began scouring reference libraries and archives from Toronto, Ontario, to Washington, D.C., and all the way to Jackson, Mississippi, together with trips to all the major eastern battlefields where Barksdale and his Mississippians gained fame. After some thirty-odd years, the result is the book that you hold in your hand—the first comprehensive biography of this controversial and larger-than-life statesman and warrior.

Based on exhaustive research and in-depth analysis, this account draws upon a wide array of primary and secondary sources, many for the first time. Importantly the narrative corrects many oft-repeated misstatements and factual errors concerning his political views, beliefs, and actions, and reveals heretofore unknown interesting details about his life.

Orphaned as a teenager, Barksdale was raised by two older brothers and as a schoolboy asserted his independence and challenged authority. As a lawyer, newspaper editor, Mexican War veteran, politician, and Confederate commander he always stood his ground. A dominant and colorful personality, he was no stranger to controversy throughout his life, which makes for a captivating story. Although he reflected Southern heritage and values, his character and innate abilities set him apart.

During four consecutive terms in Congress he was an ardent defender of slavery and advocate for states' rights. Barksdale's speeches and interactions, including an infamous brawl on the House floor, highlight this turbulent period preceding secession.

Aggressive and utterly fearless, his fiery temper and sensitivity to personal insult (real or perceived) resulted in several fisticuffs and three near-duels, gaining him a reputation as a brawler and knife-fighter. Despite his arrest for intoxication and abuse of his men while colonel of the 13th Mississippi, Barksdale survived a Court of Inquiry, regained the loyalty and respect of his men, and became one of the most beloved commanders in the Army of Northern Virginia. Soldiers' diaries attest that Barksdale was a protective father figure to his young soldiers, known affectionately as "Barksdale's Boys." Relations with superiors were often confrontational.

Although a self-taught volunteer officer, as the war unfolded, Barksdale's military reputation soared. Under his capable leadership, "Barksdale's Mississippi Brigade" played a prominent role whenever and wherever it fought. Notably Barksdale's unprecedented defense against the Union bridging of the Rappahannock River and street fight through Fredericksburg are legendary—the first amphibious assault under fire and initial instance of urban warfare on the North American continent. Barksdale's Charge at Gettysburg on July 2, 1863, described by eyewitnesses as the "most magnificent charge of the war," is considered by many to be the true high tide of the Confederacy.

Replete with Congressional transcripts, soldier accounts, original maps, and contemporary photos, this work hopefully will remove "Mississippi's forgotten son" from the historical shadows and restore William Barksdale to his rightful place in history.

Introduction

Why a book about William Barksdale? No definitive biography of him has been published—until now. His life story is compelling and deserves to be told, with a complete account of his political and military careers, his accomplishments and his historical legacy (see Appendix A).

A colorful personality, Barksdale was no stranger to controversy throughout his life. Setting him in his social and political context provides rare insight into the escalating turmoil in Congress leading up to the firing on Fort Sumter. Studying Barksdale's military career reveals the manner in which the American Civil War unfolded in the eastern theater of operations, as the raw recruits and their inexperienced leaders grew into their military roles.

Although a prominent figure before, during, and immediately after the war—first as a colorful United States congressman and later as a Confederate brigadier general—Barksdale subsequently slipped into relative obscurity. References to him are always brief, and occasional articles tend to be superficial and repetitive, focusing on a few incidents in his life. Worse still, they often repeat factual errors and misconceptions. For example, although he believed peaceable secession was permitted under the Constitution, by definition, Southern politician Barksdale was *not* a fire-eater advocating secession. The historical record, including Barksdale's actual words preserved in the official transcripts of congress (extensively quoted herein), simply do not support this mistaken belief.

Authors David S. and Jeanne T. Heidler, in their modern series "The Essential Civil War Curriculum," define *fire-eaters* as "radical southern secessionists who had long been committed to the dissolution of the United States" (see www.civilwarcurriculum.com). In his treatise *The Fire-Eaters* (Baton Rouge, 1992), author Eric H. Walter states: "Origin of the classification 'fire-eater' is nebulous and has been misused and misunderstood. Dating from 1851 fire-eater was applied indiscriminately by northerners and southerners to disparage anyone far outside the political mainstream. Often the terms southern radical and fire-eater have been used interchangeably. However, a precise distinction has been made by some historians, namely that, while all fire-eaters persistently advocated Southern independence, southern radicals, although vigorously promoting Southern rights, did not necessarily champion secession." Thus, William Barksdale falls under the classification of southern *radical* but clearly not *fire-eater*.

Also, Barksdale did *not* actively participate in the caning of Massachusetts Senator Charles Sumner by South Carolina Congressman Preston Brooks in the senate chamber, as is often still alleged today.

The popular impression of Barksdale's political views, motivations, and character has become distorted over time. For instance, a frequently cited reference by a contemporary described Barksdale at Gettysburg as having "a very thirst for battlefield glory." These words conjure up the image of a glory-seeking prima donna—a label attributed by many to George Armstrong Custer. To the contrary, Barksdale's character and actions throughout his life dispel this notion and confirm his primary motivations at Gettysburg were supreme devotion to duty and fervent conviction for the Confederate cause.

William Barksdale reflected his Southern heritage and values. His inherent character and innate abilities, however, rendered him "extra" ordinary. Orphaned at age 13, he nevertheless became a successful lawyer and newspaper editor while still shy of his 25th birthday. Despite no formal military training, through dedication, perseverance, and a God-given aptitude for self-learning, he became one of the most effective "political generals" of the Civil War. Under his leadership, Barksdale's Mississippi Brigade earned the reputation as one of the hardest fighting and most universally respected units within the esteemed Army of Northern Virginia. Moreover, Barksdale demonstrated leadership and prowess equally on both defense (Fredericksburg) and offense (Gettysburg), and on both while arguing his positions on the floor of Congress for nearly eight years immediately prior to secession.

He displayed an aggressive spirit and was utterly fearless in any situation. However, Barksdale had his flaws. A fiery temper and a sensitivity to personal insult—real or perceived—resulted in confrontation and altercation on numerous occasions, including during his time in Congress. His roughneck reputation, while not entirely undeserved, adversely skewed public opinion of him in the North. Overlooked was his lifelong capacity to forgive and embrace his opponents once the heat of the moment had passed. Barksdale also exhibited a strong appreciation for fairness. He maintained the courage of his convictions while often taking unpopular political positions—despite the repercussions. Throughout his time in Congress Barksdale resolutely fulfilled his obligation to earnestly represent his constituents.

Barksdale endured a miserable existence as assistant commissary with the Second Mississippi Volunteer Regiment during the Mexican War—fraught with privation, sickness, and death—but saw no battle action. He finally secured his long yearned-for field command as colonel of the 13th Mississippi in 1861. An early incident illustrates the worst and best aspects of his character. In a serious lapse of judgment, Barksdale became intoxicated and verbally abusive to his men while on march after First Manassas. He was arrested and, in protest, his officers attempted to resign en masse—not once, but twice. When his close personal friend, Confederate President Jefferson Davis, refused to accept these resignations, Barksdale was forced to face a prolonged Court of Inquiry. Through his indomitable spirit, and learning quickly from his mistakes, he retained his command and reestablished his leadership. Over time, through persistent effort, Barksdale regained his soldiers' respect, ultimately becoming one of the most beloved military commanders serving the Confederacy. He became a father figure to his young Mississippi soldiers who were known affectionately as "Barksdale's boys." Barksdale even engaged in a public war of words in the Southern press with a superior Confederate officer (Maj. Gen. Jubal Early) to defend the honor and reputation of his Mississippians—consequences be damned!

Barksdale personally oversaw the determined opposition to the laying of Federal pontoon bridges at Fredericksburg during the first amphibious landing under fire on the North American continent. This outstanding feat of arms was followed immediately by his skillfully conceived delaying action through the streets and alleyways of the town, in the first instance of urban warfare during the Civil War. Both actions garnered universal praise. So too did the unparalleled charge of Barksdale's Mississippi Brigade at Gettysburg on July 2, 1863—regarded by most eyewitnesses, friend and foe alike, as "the most magnificent charge of the war."

As he lay mortally wounded in a Union field hospital at Gettysburg, Barksdale uttered an appropriate motto for his entire life: "Tell them I led my men *fearlessly in the fight.*"

A few final provisos are in order. William Barksdale was a man of his time—reflecting typical Southern beliefs and values. His language was colorful, especially during heated debates in Congress. Barksdale often liberally spiced his remarks with the epithet "nigger" or variations of the same. While this language is obviously unacceptable today, Barksdale is quoted verbatim since this is a factual biography and not revisionist history. However, by doing so, no acceptance of this terminology is implied or intended. Barksdale was also a white supremacist, a slave owner, and an ardent defender of slavery, which epitomized his position within Southern society during the mid-nineteenth century. No attempt has been made to conceal these facts nor to defend these beliefs in any way whatsoever, beyond stating that this was simply how it actually was in the South back then. It is very possible that Barksdale's many public utterances in defense of slavery on the floor of Congress have deterred some would-be biographers. Indeed, a modern biographer of Jefferson Davis stated: "Though no one in his right mind can now condone what Davis believed in regard to the superiority of the white race and the value of slavery, one has to examine him as a man of his time—a time in which his views weren't at all extreme."[1] Barksdale surely merits this same consideration.

Barksdale was killed at Gettysburg—no memoirs exist. Nor does a collection of personal letters survive. Likely these circumstances account for the lack to date of any definitive biography and the paucity of published material about him. This situation has demanded painstaking research, thoughtful analysis, and careful interpretation. Opinions expressed by Barksdale's contemporaries often reflected their own inherent biases. As such, although every effort has been made to present facts, events, analysis, conclusions, and interpretation in a fair, accurate, and honest manner—while being true to the spirit of the man—there is unavoidably some measure of subjectivity therein. Any errors therefore are solely the author's responsibility.

Prologue
Gettysburg, July 2, 1863, 7:30 p.m., West of Plum Run Swale

"No! Crowd them—we have them on the run. Move on your regiments!" With these fiery words 41-year-old Brig. Gen. William Barksdale spurned the frantic pleas of his veteran colonels William D. Holder and Thomas M. Griffin to halt and realign the ragged battle line of the Mississippi brigade he led. After more than an hour of desperate fighting, this valiant but now battered unit had broken two defensive lines, shattering or driving off 15 Federal infantry regiments and several artillery batteries. On horseback Barksdale could clearly see that beyond Plum Run's rocky thicket—but for a few artillery pieces—the entire Union position lay open for the taking.[1]

Barksdale, weakened by loss of blood from two leg wounds, refused to be denied his victory in this bloody twilight. The very next day on another part of the field Union Maj. Gen. Winfield Scott Hancock would observe that "There are times when a … commander's life does not count!" Instinctively, Barksdale recognized this moment as such a one. At extreme risk as the only mounted Confederate officer in the vicinity, he pressed onward as if the sheer force of his will could pierce the thin remnant of remaining Union resistance, as if he alone could procure for the Army of Northern Virginia, and the Confederacy, the great and desperately needed victory.

Amidst enemy and friendly shell bursts and fearful musketry, Barksdale's Mississippians pressed on as the sun began sinking on the western horizon behind them. Low on ammunition, the exhausted attackers finally approached the boulders and thickets of Plum Run swale. With the impetus of the attack beginning to falter, Barksdale in a frenzy of profane rage continued to exhort his bone-tired veterans forward. He wasn't stopping now. He had been in combat with the Yankees for the last 11 years: eight in the U.S. House of Representatives in Washington and the last three of bloody conflict fighting with the Army of Northern Virginia. "Brave Mississippians," he shouted out, "one more charge and the day is ours!"[2]

Within the hour the general and both his gallant colonels, Holder and Griffin, would all lie wounded on the blood soaked fields south of the once peaceful crossroads town of Gettysburg, Pennsylvania. In extreme pain and shock from a ghastly sucking chest wound, Barksdale lay sprawled motionless on his back, alone in the darkness—awaiting either assistance or death. He was thinking about his adoring wife, Narcissa, and their two young sons, Ethelbert and William, and quite possibly also of the lifelong path that had led him to this spot, this night, far from home.

One

Beginnings

Future United States Congressman and Confederate Brig. Gen. William Barksdale grew up on his father's farm near Smyrna, Rutherford County, in central Tennessee with older brothers, Harrison and Fountain, younger sister, Virginia, and younger brother, Ethelbert. To tell his complete story, requires a brief review of his ancestry.

Barkesdale, or Barksdale, derived from two of the five general classes of surnames—the first denoting the occupation of the original bearers, and the second describing their place of residence. In Medieval England, persons who tanned hides for a living were called "barkers" while "dale" indicated a geographic location containing a valley. Hence, the surname Barksdale originally described a family of tanners who resided in a valley, or alternatively denoted a valley where excellent bark existed for the tanning of hides. Either way, the first recorded use of this name in England, Thomas de Barkesdale, dated to 1332 in Hampshire. Subsequently, many of these original Barksdale's were, indeed, found to be tanners by trade.[1]

Genealogical research by Capt. John A. Barksdale published in 1940 confirmed three main branches of the family existed during the 16th and 17th centuries. They were located at Newbury in Berkshire, Oxford in Oxfordshire, and Winchcomb in Gloucestershire. All were believed to be descended from Thomas de Barkesdale.[2] No pedigree nor printed genealogy of the Barksdale Family exists in England. Captain Barksdale, "based on a process of exclusion of other possibilities, agreement of dates, and the unique and frequent occurrence of the Christian name *Nathaniel* in both English and American families," concluded that Confederate general William Barksdale descended from the Newbury Branch of the Reverend Barksdale.[3]

More specifically, the reverend's son, the Rev. Nathaniel Barksdale, married Dorothy Woodhull on November 21, 1622, and had issue of three sons, Richard, William, Nathaniel, and a daughter, Barbara. It was this second son, William, who it is believed emigrated to Virginia around 1660. Being a younger son in England, "his prospects were none too bright" and he was also estranged from his siblings. Captain Barksdale postulated that William was "exactly the sort of young man to join in an adventure to the new colony."[4] It is believed that William arrived at either Jamestown or Yorktown, Virginia. Unfortunately, no information regarding his initial activities survives as many early records of the Tidewater Counties were destroyed. As William was "undoubtedly the first emigrant of the name Barksdale to America," it may be reasonably assumed that he was also "the progenitor of the Barksdales of Colonial Virginia."[5]

However, it can be stated with absolute certainty that General Barksdale's great-grandfather, Nathaniel Barksdale, settled as the first Barksdale in Halifax County,

Virginia, in the mid–1700s. He initially served as a plantation overseer, eventually purchased land, and gradually built up an impressive estate which included 29 slaves. A prominent citizen, he served as justice of the peace in 1766.[6]

Assisted by his father, the General's grandfather, Nathaniel, Jr., also acquired land in Halifax County, and inherited two slaves upon his father's death in 1790. Nathaniel, Jr., served with distinction in the Continental army during the American Revolution. He enlisted as a private in the Virginia Militia and was later commissioned as an officer. In 1796 he qualified as ensign, and in 1799 was appointed lieutenant in the 84th Regiment, Virginia Militia. He married Anne Garden in 1784, and the couple went on to have 12 children, 11 of whom were born in Virginia—including General Barksdale's father, William. Upon his father's death, Nathaniel, Jr., continued to live as a planter in Halifax County on or near the family plantation.

In true pioneering spirit during the summer of 1808 Lt. Nathaniel Barksdale decided to relocate his expanding family in order to improve their prospects. Exhibiting strong self-reliance, a trait his future grandson would inherit, he embarked with his entire family on the hazardous journey to Rutherford County, Tennessee, some "400 miles away as the crow flies."[7] As Capt. John A. Barksdale notes:

> To those of us today, with paved roads and modern transportation, this does not appear as very much of a journey. But to those of that day it was indeed a big undertaking. With several small children, the youngest a babe in arms, their household belongings loaded on wagons drawn by oxen, they made their journey through the mountains to the new country. There were practically no roads at this time, the routes to the West were known as "traces" being old Indian trails widened by the trees and brush having been cut back to allow the passage of wagons. Nathaniel Barksdale established his new plantation and built his home place near the present town of Smyrna, where his twelfth child Julia was born three years later and where he lived for the remainder of his life.[8]

Rutherford County was a favored location due to the abundant supply of water power which "caused more good mills to be erected ... than was the case in other places."[9]

Arriving with meager resources, the Barksdales faced the formidable task of building a primitive dwelling in the wilderness before the onset of winter. Also, fields had to be cleared in time for spring planting. Assisted by his eldest son William (General Barksdale's father), Lt. Nathaniel Barksdale established his new plantation near the Stones River and Smyrna, a village just southeast of Nashville. William lived on and farmed a 51-acre tract on the northwestern corner of his father's estate. It was subsequently bequeathed to him upon his father's death in 1830.[10]

William, Sr., saw active military service during the War of 1812, enlisting as a private in the Second Regiment of Tennessee Mounted Volunteer Gunmen. He participated in campaigns in the southeast and later fought under Gen. Andrew Jackson at the battle of New Orleans.

Before enlisting however, William, Sr., wed Nancy Hervey Lester in Williamson County, Tennessee, in 1813. Her father, Henry, was a Baptist minister in Charlotte County, Virginia, and is said to be descended from the Earls of Leicester in England. Upon his return from the war, William, Sr., resumed his life as a planter. William and Nancy would eventually have four sons and one daughter, including future Congressman and Confederate general William Barksdale, who was born on August 21, 1821, near Smyrna.[11]

Described as a "farmer of moderate circumstances," William, Sr., was "highly esteemed by all who knew him for the virtues of integrity and courage"—traits for which his son and namesake would also be known throughout his life. A surviving confirmation of his father's sterling character is a letter written on behalf of the widow and three small children of a fellow soldier—William A. Purnell of the Seventh Regiment who died during the War of 1812—soliciting information regarding payments due his family.[12]

Young William came by his interest in things military honestly as a child. Doubtless he enjoyed conversations with both his grandfather and father about their military service in their respective wars. In addition, many of the old Revolutionary soldiers settled in Rutherford County—enticed by grants from the State of North Carolina after the admission of Tennessee into the Union on June 1, 1796. (Previously the Territory of Tennessee had been part of North Carolina.) Rutherford County had also furnished many troops during the Creek War of 1812–1814.[13] Thus young William would have had ample opportunities to hear old war stories and develop an abiding interest in (and perhaps a desire for) future battlefield glory.

The devastating cholera epidemics of 1832 and 1835 in nearby Murfreesboro would have been another major influence on an impressionable adolescent. According to the contemporary historian of Rutherford County:

> Men and women frightened fled from their homes as though they were pursued by a devastating army; business was suspended, relief committees were formed…. Providing coffins, digging graves and nursing the sick took all their attention. The town seemed depopulated by the disease and fright. Soon the destroying angel raised its wings and fled, but sadness was left in nearly every household.[14]

Sickness and disease would later profoundly affect William Barksdale during his military service in both the Mexican and American Civil War.

William's normal happy childhood changed abruptly in 1825 with the tragic death of his mother who was only 36 years old. His father now had to raise five children, ages one to ten, with William only four at the time. Before William's 10th birthday, his grandfather Nathaniel also died in his 70th year. Four years after Nancy's death, William's father remarried to Ann Eliza Calhoun on May 14, 1829, doubtless in part to provide a stepmother for his five young children. As his will lists an additional child, Anne, born between the dates of birth for Virginia and William, it would appear that Ann Eliza too was a widow with one daughter when she remarried.[15]

Young William spent his early years working on his father's farm and attending various local schools between 1829 and 1831. During these formative years he began to exhibit traits and acquire values which would define his character in adulthood. In 1832 he transferred to a neighboring school taught by a Mr. Silas Tucker, "a teacher of considerable note and especially known for the severity of the treatment of the boys under his tutelage." William rebelled against this harsh discipline. He considered it blatantly unfair and "an encroachment upon what he conceded to be his personal rights." The inevitable confrontations resulted in "many a stormy scene between the two." This marked a pattern throughout Barksdale's life—a quickness to resent a perceived insult or wrong contrary to his sense of fairness—but after reacting he was able to forgive and "bury the hatchet." It is recorded that William and Mr. Tucker became "fast friends" in later life.[16]

In July of 1835 tragedy once again struck the Barksdale family when William's father died at age 48 years after a "brief and agonizing illness."[17] His son and namesake was one month short of his 14th birthday. This tragic event again brought illness to the forefront as a major influence on young William. William Sr.'s last will and testament was recorded on July 7, 1834, and simply read as follows:

> To my wife Ann Eliza all the property which she has received from her father except the horse.... My sole reason for making no other provisions for my wife is that her father is sufficiently able to support and maintain comfortable if she should survive me. All my estate divided among all my children, viz., HARRISON, FOUNTAIN, VIRGINIA, ANNE, WILLIAM, ETHELBERT. I appoint my sons Harrison and Fountain, Executors. This 7th July 1834. Wit: JESSE SIKES and ISAAC.[18]

Older brothers Harrison and Fountain were young men at 20 and 19 years of age, but William and Ethelbert were still "minor heirs." Since the older boys were designated as executors the court appointed Harrison, being the eldest, as legal guardian of his two youngest brothers. Shortly thereafter in December 1835 the family homestead was broken up and sold to settle the estate. In the meantime, William sought and gained employment as a clerk in a store in nearby Murfreesboro. Subsequently, as funding from the estate became available, a trust fund was established for William's education. He attended Clinton College in Smith County for one year, followed by another year at Union Seminary near Spring Hill in Marcy County. Based on the 1940 Barksdale Genealogy it has been widely accepted that in 1837 the four brothers pulled up stakes and relocated en masse to Mississippi, gaining the sobriquet "The Barksdale Brothers of Mississippi." However, closer examination by several subsequent researchers refutes this popular claim.

William and Ethelbert didn't relocate, they continued their education. Over this period Rutherford County records confirm several considerable estate payments by Harrison as legal guardian to both younger brothers for "schooling, clothing, and boarding." University of Nashville records confirm that William pursued but did not complete a course of classical study there. School records indicate that he enrolled on August 13, 1839, but was dropped "at his own request" after only 51 days. Despite his premature exit, the university officials classified William as "moral character good." The young man had made an impression during his brief tenure, being recognized for "the facility with which he acquired knowledge—his readiness in debate—and the prominent parts he performed in the association organized by the students for social enjoyment and literary advancement."

After leaving the University of Nashville, it appears that William pursued his initial study of law by working at the legal office of Judge Edmund Dillahunt in nearby Columbia. In late 1839 he joined his older brothers, Harrison and Fountain, who had relocated to Yazoo City in Mississippi two years earlier. Younger brother Ethelbert would soon join them.[19] Thereafter all "Four Barksdale Brothers of Mississippi" would lead prominent lives of service in their adopted state—none more interesting and compelling than William.

Two

Mississippi
Land of Opportunity

So why would all four Barksdale brothers relocate to Mississippi? In a word—opportunity!

Congress had organized the Mississippi Territory in 1798, thereby opening it up for settlement. However, westward emigration of Americans had increased exponentially following the American Revolution and was especially robust during the Great Migration years, 1800–20. Before 1800 only two states, Kentucky and Tennessee, lay west of the Appalachian Mountains, but by 1820 the number had tripled with the addition of Ohio, Louisiana, Illinois, Indiana, Mississippi, and Alabama. The population of these eight Western states also skyrocketed, from 386,000 in 1800 to 2,216,000 by 1820. Mississippi was admitted to the Union as a new state in 1817, followed by neighboring Alabama in 1819.

Traditionally tobacco and rice had been staple crops for Southern farmers. However, European demand for these products decreased significantly in the late eighteenth century. Moreover, prolonged poor agricultural practices depleted the soil on traditional Southern plantations, significantly reducing yields. The invention of the cotton gin by Eli Whitney in 1794, coupled with the emerging industrial revolution in England and its burgeoning textile industry, spurred the market for Southern cotton. Mississippi's fertile virgin soil, indeed, the soil across the southern heartland, created dramatic opportunities for Southern planters. Mississippi cotton production further fueled the Great Migration. "Mississippi, with soil and climate ideally suited to cotton culture," one writer suggests, "became the center of Southern cotton production during the first half of the nineteenth century."[1]

Consequently, the cultivation and marketing of cotton determined both Mississippi's and the Deep South's future and indeed its very social, economic, and political fabric. As the state's premier historian John K. Bettersworth observed: Mississippi "had its geographical divisions—hills, lowlands, and prairies—and each ... had developed its distinctive ... character, depending largely on the amount of cotton it did or did not produce; for there was no crop but cotton, and Mississippi was its prophet." In short, by 1861 King Cotton would make Mississippi one of the most prosperous southern states in the Union; by 1865 the devastating effects of the Civil War would render it one of the poorest. In the words of Bettersworth, in Mississippi "a struggle that began as the breaking of a nation ended with the breaking of a state."[2]

The four Barksdale brothers certainly made the most of their new opportunities in

Mississippi. They achieved great personal success in several diverse fields: planting, commerce, law, journalism, and finally military service.

Harrison, the eldest of the brothers, settled in Yazoo County and soon established a prosperous cotton plantation, "Oak Valley," on the Yazoo River 10 miles south of Manchester (later renamed Yazoo City) where he lived the comfortable life "typical of the large cotton planters of the day." In 1838 he married Laura Caroline Read and together had issue of eight children including five sons. Over the subsequent 23 years of his life Harrison accumulated great wealth in both cotton and slaves. When the Civil War came, Harrison, at age 47 years, enlisted in the 30th Mississippi at Yazoo City on March 15, 1862, for three years. Subsequently he achieved the rank of 1st lieutenant in Company E. His teenage son, Lycurgus Read, also joined this same company and was later promoted to corporal. Sadly, neither would survive the war. On July 3, 1862, Harrison succumbed to camp fever at Tupelo, Mississippi, while Lycurgus died of sickness at McMinnville, Tennessee, in November 1862.

Another son, Fountain, who was 2nd lieutenant and quartermaster in Company D, 18th Mississippi, was killed at age 23 at the battle of the Wilderness in May 1864. Fountain was then fighting as part of Brig. Gen. Benjamin Grubb Humphreys Mississippi Brigade, formerly his uncle William Barksdale's command. Third son Sterling Lester survived the war in successive assignments as a private in Company K, 10th Mississippi, a corporal in Company D, 18th Mississippi, and finally as assistant paymaster in the Confederate States Navy. Harrison's fourth son, William, a 15-year-old, voluntarily left the Kentucky Military Institute to enlist as a private in Company K, Woods Regiment of Wirt Adams Cavalry. He was surrendered by Lt. Gen. Richard Taylor on May 4, 1865, and paroled eight days later at Gainesville, Alabama. Fortunately, Harrison's remaining son, James Allen, was too young to enlist.[3]

Harrison Barksdale had indeed repaid dearly any debt to his adopted state of Mississippi for all the success he had achieved, sacrificing his own life and those of two of his five young sons in her service.

The second eldest brother, Fountain, also reached Mississippi sometime in 1837 and settled in Manchester. He initially partnered with Richard Allen, one of the first merchants in the area, to form Barksdale & Allen, a widely known mercantile business in that part of the state. Reportedly "people would travel as far as fifty or sixty miles from all directions to trade with the firm." The business grew and prospered, right along with the flourishing steamboat trade. Fountain Barksdale eventually became sole owner, and the firm was renamed simply F. Barksdale. By the outbreak of the war, Fountain had built up a significant estate.[4]

Before 1861 approximately 250 steamboats operated on the Yazoo River system transporting bales of cotton and rafts of timber to faraway markets like New Orleans. They returned with manufactured goods, foodstuffs, and a myriad of luxury items for the farmers and merchants in the rich bottom lands of the Yazoo delta. Perhaps mirroring this business relationship, in 1842 Fountain married Josephine Parrisott, the daughter of John Martin Parrisott, who had been a soldier in Napoleon's Grand Armee and participated in the disastrous march on Moscow. Fountain's new brother-in-law, Sherman H. Parrisott, would go on to found the Parisot Line of steamships which included the "splendid" 155-foot *F. Barksdale* (named in honor of Fountain). This riverboat provided "regular and reliable freight service as well as the elegant passenger accommodations that had become synonymous with the P. Line." She successfully plied the river as a "favorite" for five seasons. Sadly, the *F. Barksdale* was destroyed in a tragic fire on January 4, 1889.[5]

Fountain and Josephine had six children including four sons too young to enlist. Fountain did not serve in the Confederate army. However, given his prominent position after the war, he likely contributed to "the Cause" in some other capacity. All the steamboats on the Yazoo River were destroyed within two years after the war began. Consequently, Fountain Barksdale suffered serious financial setbacks because many of his friends and customers couldn't pay their outstanding bills. A sensitive, kind, and caring individual, he found it difficult to press his debtors for payment. Not surprisingly people respected and esteemed him as a man of sterling character. Reflecting upon the death of Fountain Barksdale, "the city's oldest and most venerable citizen," on December 20, 1907, in his 82nd year, the city's mayor proclaimed that "in commemoration of his long and useful life," all business in Yazoo City be suspended during his funeral service and that "the several churches toll their bells, and the flag on the City Hall be placed at half-mast for the period of thirty days."[6] This outpouring of grief and respect had only been surpassed by that afforded his brother William in the capital city of Jackson some 40 years earlier.

Upon reaching Mississippi in 1839, 18-year-old William had settled in the recently organized county of Lowndes in the city of Columbus, formerly known as Possum Town, and decided to pursue a career in law. Undoubtedly his choice of location owed much to the reputation of the city's lawyers' bar as "one of the ablest in the South." Moreover, by this time, large plantations were proliferating in northeast Mississippi, especially around Columbus. These planters represented a wealthy clientele for a prospective young lawyer, and Lowndes County offered land opportunities aplenty for ambitious young investors seeking wealth and aspiring to status in the community.

There, with enthusiasm, persistence, diligence, and self-discipline, William set about the formidable task of teaching himself law. Although his training may have been superficial by modern standards, young William was admitted to the bar and granted license to practice law three years later, shortly before his 21st birthday. Soon thereafter he opened his own law office in Columbus and hired his cousin, John Nash Barksdale, who was already a practicing lawyer in Woodbury, Tennessee. Despite his youth, William quickly established a reputation as an effective litigator whose "eloquence and ability" gained him a significant clientele. William's keen debating skills, previously demonstrated at the University of Nashville, contributed significantly to his success as a practicing attorney. So too did his booming voice when necessary—an attribute for which he would be admired on many a future battlefield.[7]

Two years later in 1844 William purchased half interest in a local newspaper, the *Columbus Democrat*, which had begun as the *Democratic Press* in 1836. He partnered with H.H. Worthington, who was also the lead editor, and who, as owner, had renamed the paper in 1837. Much later, in 1858, it would once again be renamed, this time as the *Mississippi Democrat*. William Barksdale also became co-editor during 1844–45 and soon "acquired the reputation as an able and vigorous writer." Furthermore a Southern newspaper recorded that Barksdale "drew to himself that attention which a bold independent journalist will always attract ... when ... moved by no other conviction than that of 'the right'". Despite his obvious skills with the written word, Barksdale was driven, not necessarily by pursuit of a second career in journalism, but rather by his burgeoning and passionate interest in politics and furtherance of the principles and policies of the

Democratic party, which William avidly embraced. As was common among the newspapers of the time, news was secondary to partisan political content.⁸

As its name implies, the *Columbus Democrat* functioned to further the interests of the Democratic party. The following excerpt, likely edited by William, and republished by a sister paper in Jackson, Mississippi, reflects this reality:

> We give the following from our excellent contemporary The Columbus Democrat: Gen. Foote was introduced to the meeting by Dr. Tate, president of our democratic association and commenced his speech at 11 o'clock A.M. He continued to address a delighted audience until dinner.... After dinner they reassembled in still greater numbers.... Gen. F again took the stand and for some three hours held enchained the attention of his auditory, eliciting frequent and enthusiastic rounds of applause. Seldom if ever, has a more effective speech been delivered in our goodly city. That it told well, was evidenced as much by the elongated visages of the Whigs, as by the bright smiles and rapturous applause of the Democrats.... After a few remarks from Wm. L. Harris esq. (whig) ... Maj. Jefferson Davis was loudly called for ... Mr. Davis ... addressed the meeting in a brief, but pertinent and forcible speech ... Mr. D is certainly a very pleasing and eloquent speaker and must produce an effect wherever he addresses the people.⁹

Confederate President Jefferson Davis, Barksdale's close friend and confidant, would later write Barksdale's widow describing him as "your gallant husband, my esteemed friend ... who died as he had lived, like a patriot and a soldier" (Library of Congress).

During his two years as co-editor William frequently took the opportunity to espouse his staunch support of states' rights as guaranteed under the Constitution and "the doctrines of Jefferson and Madison." His platform at the paper served the young editor's political ambitions quite nicely. Indeed, an October 1860 treatise in *DeBow's Review* observed that "the press has furnished to Mississippi nearly all of her leading politicians" and then listed them by name, including William Barksdale. The article concluded, "These gentlemen ... will show the class of men she has trained up for the State's service."¹⁰

On January 8, 1844, William attended the State Democratic Convention at Jackson in the Hall of the House of Representatives where he participated as one of three recording secretaries. Fellow delegate Jefferson Davis gave a protracted speech in favor of John C. Calhoun of South Carolina as Democratic nominee for president and Levi Woodbury of New Hampshire for vice president. This slate countered the one recommended by the selection committee: former president Martin Van Buren of New York and Tennessee governor

James K. Polk. The convention also selected delegates, including William Barksdale, for the upcoming national convention in Baltimore in May to ratify the nominees. This was probably the first time Barksdale met with Jefferson Davis in any official political capacity, and thus was begun a close and lifelong personal friendship. Later, during their time together in Washington, Davis would place great faith in his friend's political views. This is confirmed by the many letters between them which survive in Davis' personal papers.[11]

As his professional career flourished, Barksdale "invested his capital wisely in land and slaves." Gradually, through judicious investment and borrowing, he became a planter of considerable means. By 1860 he owned a cotton plantation worth $22,000, a total of 36 slaves, as well as several "choice parcels of unimproved land in other parts of the country." His total personal estate was then valued at $44,000. In short, he became a prominent member of the South's planter class, with all its attendant social status, political power, unqualified advocacy for slavery, and ardently pro–Southern and states' rights political views.[12]

Ethelbert, like older brothers Harrison and Fountain, initially settled in Yazoo City. By 1844 at age 20 years, doubtless influenced by William, he became editor of the *Yazoo City Democrat.*

Relocating to Jackson in 1850, he purchased a controlling interest in the *Mississippian*, a semi-weekly newspaper (oldest one in the state) and the "central organ of the Democratic Party." Ethelbert remained as editor for the next decade where he earned the reputation as "the ablest paragraph writer the State has ever afforded." A piece in *DeBow's Review* published in April 1859 stated, "[The *Mississippian's*] present able editor, Major E. Barksdale has been spoken of for high official positions, but his devotion to the cause of journalism has invariably prompted him to decline." He also served as State Printer, editing the official state journal during 1854 to 1861 and later between 1876 and 1883. In September 1861 he finally relinquished his duties and interest in the *Mississippian* upon his election as a representative to the Confederate Congress where he served for the duration of the Civil War.[13]

Ethelbert had launched his political career the previous year, when as chief of the Mississippi delegation at the 1860 Democratic Convention in Charleston, South Carolina, "he had spoken so strongly." A fellow journalist in attendance noted Ethelbert "was full of fire and prone to fly off the handle ... there is a dangerous glitter in his eyes." William has repeatedly but erroneously been labeled as a "fire-eater." In fact, Ethelbert was the fire-eating secessionist of the Barksdale clan due in part to his extreme personality. A contemporary described Ethelbert as follows: "His fault was that he was too caustic and severe. In person he was small, and his manner was grave and dignified. He rarely laughed, and there was something in his smile which indicated more of malice than mirth." R.H. Henry, fellow owner/editor of the Jackson *Clarion-Ledger*, commented: "Major Barksdale had a way of doing things after his own plan with no fear of imitators. He perhaps made more editors and public men mad than any other politician in the state, and rarely was there a reconcilement, for as a rule when [Ethelbert] Barksdale crossed the Rubicon he burnt his bridges behind him." In this lack of forgiving behavior, he could not have been more diametrically opposed to brother William.[14]

Ethelbert's service in the Confederate Congress was marked by staunch support of President Jefferson Davis. Most notably on February 10, 1865, he finally introduced an exceedingly controversial bill advocating military service by negro slaves within the Confederate States of America. This bill permitted President Davis "to ask for and accept from the owners of slaves the services of such number of able-bodied negro men as he may deem expedient to perform military services in whatever capacity the General-in-chief may direct." Another key provision stipulated that nothing in the bill "does authorize a change in the relation which said slaves shall bear towards their owners as property."[15]

Ethelbert also headed up the Confederate States House Standing Committee on Printing, served on the Foreign Affairs Committee, and presented a design for the Second National Flag.[16]

Following the Civil War, he resumed editorial duties at the Jackson *Clarion* (formerly the *Mississippian*) from 1867 to 1883. During Reconstruction, Ethelbert helped to overthrow Republican rule in Mississippi in 1875. From March 4, 1883, to March 3, 1887, he served two terms as a Mississippi Representative in the United States Congress. Despite widespread support from farmers, he ran for both the U.S. Congress in 1890 and for the U.S. Senate in 1892 and lost because he supported deregulation of the railroads.[17]

Ethelbert married Alice Jane Harris in 1843 and had two sons and a daughter. The eldest son, Harris, although a lad of 16, enlisted in the Confederate army and ultimately served on General Barksdale's staff at Gettysburg. (Harris would later accompany his uncle William's body back to Jackson for burial in 1867.) Ethelbert, after his failed campaign for the senate, retired to his plantation, Gumwood, in Yazoo County and dedicated the remainder of his life to agricultural pursuits. He died on February 17, 1893, while visiting at Oak Valley and is buried with other family members at Greenwood Cemetery in Jackson.[18]

William was always much closer to his younger brother Ethelbert since they were born only a little more than two years apart. The influence William exerted over Ethelbert is striking. Emulating William, Ethelbert embarked on a career in journalism followed, albeit many years later, by political office. William also appointed Ethelbert as co-executor of his will along with his own wife Narcissa. In January 1867 William would be interred in Ethelbert's family plot in Greenwood Cemetery in Jackson.[19]

By 1845, as war with Mexico loomed, Barksdale was still shy of his 24th birthday. He had already accomplished much and his character, personality, key abilities, and goals had been established. Tall and robust like older brother Fountain, William possessed many of his siblings' key strengths and few of their flaws. Personal observation, heredity, conscious effort, or perhaps a combination of all three spawned an individual of notable character. William already exhibited the keen sense of responsibility and diligent devotion to duty his guardian

Ethelbert C. Barksdale emulated his older brother, William, becoming an accomplished editor and politician (Archives and Records Services Division, Mississippi Department of Archives & History).

Harrison had shown him. His sensitivity (especially to insult, real or perceived) and business acumen reflected older brother Fountain. William's fiery, aggressive personality and fearlessness mirrored Ethelbert but without the mean-spirited, unforgiving bent exhibited by his younger brother. Indeed, because of his forgiving nature, William repeatedly converted many from enemies to close friends throughout his life.

Perhaps William's greatest talent was his remarkable innate ability for self-learning despite little or no formal training. He had already demonstrated this ability in the reading and practice of the law, as well as his proficiency at journalism. This attribute above all would propel him to a successful military career during the Civil War. As a young man not yet 24, he had already identified politics as his life's chief interest. His visibility as a journalist and increasing wealth and status, positioned him as a prominent up-and-coming Mississippian with good chances for future political success.[20]

Buoyed by his rising political profile, and certainly not lacking in self-confidence, in late 1845 William boldly wrote to President James Polk seeking a political appointment in his administration in Washington. On November 13, he followed up with a letter to former Senator Robert J. Walker from Natchez, Polk's Secretary of the Treasury, seeking his influence. Barksdale made this brash request although he was not personally acquainted with Walker, immodestly qualifying it with the phrase "still I presume I am not altogether unknown to you by reputation." This letter indicates that William was not above using flattery to get what he wanted. Barksdale continued, "Being a member of Cabinet and wielding an immense influence with the Executive, if I could secure your influence, I would have no fear as to the result. I am aware of the inordinate amount of business, you are compelled to discharge, but I trust you can find time to make known my application to President Polk, and to state what claims you may believe I have upon him."[21] Despite William's best efforts, the desired appointment did not materialize.

But another field of endeavor and opportunity for Barksdale lay on the horizon. After a year and a half of turmoil, the United States formally declared war against Mexico on May 13, 1846. Barksdale immediately put his political aspirations on hold. Military service was beckoning, and perhaps it represented another means to further his political ambitions by achieving glory and renown on some distant battlefield—and he wasted no time grasping the prospect.

Three

Military Service in Mexico
Disease, Deprivation and Death

After Sam Houston led the Texas army to victory over Mexican forces under General Antonio Lopez De Santa Anna at the battle of San Jacinto on April 21, 1836, Texas declared itself an independent republic. Texas existed as a separate country for the next nine years, formally recognized by Great Britain, France, and the United States. From the outset Mexico disputed the boundary with Texas. With no immediate resolution this disagreement continued to fester.[1]

During this time American political writers espoused the United States possessed a "God-given right to expansion." Ardent Democrat John L. Sullivan crystallized this view in a succinct phrase when he wrote that the country "had a *manifest destiny* to overspread and possess the whole of the continent." Support for emigration to the territory west of the Mississippi River increased dramatically during the early 1840s. Just as slavery would become the *issue* (not the *root cause*) that would ignite the American Civil War in 1861, the "peculiar institution" was a key factor in the annexation of Texas by the United States in 1845 and the subsequent war with Mexico during 1846–1848. Indeed, this parallel is striking but historians have paid it scant attention.[2]

Great Britain also posed a significant threat should it try to extend its empire by acquiring a further foothold in North America via Texas. (England still professed control over the Oregon territory.) Since Britain had abolished slavery throughout its empire in 1808, should this acquisition occur, slavery would undoubtedly also be banned in Texas. The Southern states, particularly Mississippi, therefore regarded the annexation of Texas as a ready means to admit Texas into the Union as a slave state—thereby increasing their power base. Indeed, Ulysses S. Grant, a participant in the war with Mexico, later recorded in his memoirs, "the occupation, separation, and annexation [of Texas] were from the inception of the movement to its final consummation, a conspiracy to acquire territory out of which slave states might be formed for the American Union."[3]

The U.S. government's strategy for achieving its Manifest Destiny consisted of a three-pronged approach: annexation of Texas, purchase or occupation of California and New Mexico (then controlled by Mexico), and coercion of control of the Oregon territory away from Britain.[4]

By 1843 Texas actively sought annexation by the United States to gain protection and a multitude of other benefits. Texas became a major issue in the 1844 presidential election campaign. James K. Polk of Tennessee, a lawyer and slave owner who supported annexation of Texas at all costs (up to and including a war with Mexico), won the Democratic presidential nomination and was elected president on November 2, 1844. Polk, who was heartily supported by Mississippi Democrats, carried Mississippi by a margin of just under 6,000 votes. He took office in March 1845, and immediately began proceedings to formally annex Texas. This action triggered an immediate hostile response from Mexico, which broke diplomatic relations, recalled its ambassador from Washington, D.C., and threatened military hostilities against both Texas and the United States. Annexation of Texas was finalized on December 29, 1845, over the vigorous protest of Mexico.

The United States made one final attempt at a diplomatic resolution in early 1846 when Commissioner John Slidell (later to become a commissioner of the Confederate States of America) traveled to Mexico City. However, Mexican officials refused to receive him and treated him with disdain. So he returned to Washington having achieved nothing.

During this time President Polk had also sent Brevet Brigadier General Zachary Taylor (known as Old Rough and Ready) with 3,000 Regular army soldiers (subsequently increased to 4,000) to the Rio Grande River, Texas' disputed southern boundary. These troops soon faced a Mexican army numbering 5,000 on the opposite side of the river. The Mexican commander politely notified General Taylor in writing that Mexico considered that formal hostilities were already underway. By April 1846 Mexican cavalry had crossed the Rio Grande to harass and attack U.S. scouting patrols, inflicting numerous American casualties and taking several prisoners. General Taylor immediately sent an urgent dispatch to President Polk requesting volunteer regiments to augment the undersized U.S. Army that totaled only 7,000 regulars. Action was swift. At Polk's urging, on May 13, 1846, Congress formally declared war on Mexico and authorized a call for 50,000 volunteers to serve one year. Specific quotas were established for individual states.[5]

The young men of the southern and mid-western states eagerly heeded the call. Those from the northeastern states largely ignored it due to political agitation by the abolitionists. Their view that the westward expansion south of the Mason-Dixon Line was driven by "the machinations of the slave power" rendered the war effort much less popular in the northeast.[6]

Mississippi, where "war fever" was rampant, responded enthusiastically. On May 9th Governor Albert Gallatin Brown had ordered the colonels of the Mississippi State Militia "to have their men organized in companies" and to "open a list for the enrollment of such volunteers as are ready to march on twenty-four hours notice." To the great disappointment of both the governor and citizens of Mississippi, when Congress issued the formal call, it stipulated only "one regiment of infantry or riflemen" from the Magnolia State. Although 17,000 volunteers had already raced to Vicksburg to enlist in General Taylor's army, Governor Brown's published call on June 1, 1846, specified only 10 companies (1000 soldiers).[7]

By June 10, a total of 22 militia companies had reported for service at Vicksburg, including the Lauderdale Volunteers under Captain W.J. Daniel. Competition was fierce amongst the various local units and the pressure was overwhelming to be among the few selected. Ultimately those units that were earliest to "be complete and organized" gained acceptance. This formula caused bitter resentment amongst units like the Natchez Fencibles who, although one of the first companies to arrive at Vicksburg, were not selected because the unit fell short by only two or three men. When vigorous protests failed, this insult to their local pride severely dampened their martial spirit, and many of these companies essentially melted away. The Lauderdale Volunteers (of which

William Barksdale was a member) failed to be selected. However, this unit persevered and remained intact until the next call for volunteers, six months later. Barksdale's involvement with the Mississippi State Militia dated back to January 1845 when he was appointed as Inspector of the Second Brigade, under Brig. Gen. William Brown, of the Fourth Division.[8]

In response to a second requisition from President Polk, on November 27, 1846, Governor Brown called for a second regiment of volunteers to serve for the duration of the war. With the "war spirit [in Mississippi] more fully aroused than before," the complement of 10 companies was quickly filled. Twenty-five-year-old William Barksdale was among the first to enlist as a private, and was assigned to Company F of the Lauderdale Volunteers under Capt. W.F. Daniel. Like his fellow recruits William was "inspired by a combination of personal factors ranging from patriotism to martial fever." By enlisting he followed the tradition of military service established by both his grandfather and father, and fed his interest in things military, instilled during his childhood. Perhaps for a politically ambitious junior planter then ascending the social ladder, possessed of a true love of money, and already owning slaves, other less patriotic motivations were likely also in play. Having migrated westward from Tennessee to Mississippi, William recognized potential opportunities afforded by new large land tracts.[9]

In regarding the war with Mexico as an opportunity to win fame and fortune on the battlefield to further his desired political career, Barksdale was no different than other future leaders of his time. Six months earlier Jefferson Davis had left his seat in the U.S. Congress (over the strong protests of his young bride, Varina) to assume command as colonel of the 1st Mississippi Rifles. Davis confided his true motivation to his sister, "It may be that I will return with a reputation over which you will rejoice." Recognizing this truism, it has been ascribed that "[U.S.]Grant was dismayed to note that this zeal for war had less to do with right or wrong than with personal advancement and glory."

No one was more frank in his admission than Reuben Davis, soon to be elected colonel of the 2nd Mississippi Regiment. Davis allowed "the charm of novelty and adventure and excitement, which appealed to me as to all the young men of the country, and the contagion of the wild enthusiasm which was sweeping over the State,"—and the lure of

Democratic Congressman Reuben Davis of Mississippi, Barksdale's military commander in Mexico, early political rival, knife-wielding attacker, fellow congressman, and lifelong friend. Julian Vannerson photo in McClee's Gallery of the 35th Congress, 1859 (Library of Congress).

status and reputation—to cloud his judgment. Caught up in the moment, he accepted the position of colonel for which he was totally unprepared, and later wrote "from that one event, I date all the mistakes, and most of the troubles, that have been mine throughout a long and eventful life."

Finally, Charles Sheldon Coffey, future Captain of the Thomas Hinds Guards, Co. G, 2nd Mississippi Regiment, plainly revealed his motivation for enlisting in a letter to his brother: "I am Satisfide that if I Cannot Distinguish my Self in this Situation that I Cannot in any in Case an opertunity presents is self."[10]

The companies of the newly formed 2nd Mississippi gathered at Vicksburg between January 1 and 5, 1847. One week later elections were held for general staff officers. Reuben Davis was elected colonel, and young William Barksdale was elected assistant commissary with the rank of captain. His commission was duly approved in Washington City, soon thereafter. Only President Polk could appoint generals and staff officers in the volunteer regiments and these appointments then had to be approved by the U.S. Senate. In this capacity, as part of Col. Rueben Davis' staff, William would be responsible for purchasing, storing, and distributing the food, clothing, and tentage required for the entire regiment. For this service he would be paid $40 per month—the same rate as a captain in the regular army. Captain's rank was signified by shoulder epaulettes of silver with quarter-inch bullions, 2.5 inches long on the dark blue dress coat and by shoulder strops with silver embroidered edging around a dark blue background with two silver bars at each end worn on both shoulders of the dark blue fatigue frock coat. Barksdale was also authorized to carry a brass-hilted Model 1840 sword, sheathed in a black leather scabbard with gilt mountings.[11]

In these duties he would work closely with, and depend upon, Capt. Charles M. Price, Regimental Quartermaster, who was responsible for transporting these articles of subsistence. He would also work closely with, and quickly befriend, Dr. Thomas N. Love, Regimental Surgeon. Barksdale would be responsible for supplying the special nutritional needs of the soon to be overwhelming numbers of sick and dying patients. Whether his fellow volunteers in the regiment initially recognized William's inherent capacity for self-learning, mathematical skills, attention to detail, diligence and perseverance—or not—they had chosen wisely, for Barksdale would fulfill his duties admirably under the most trying of circumstances.

There can be no doubt that the

Dr. Thomas Neely Love, Regimental Surgeon, 2nd Mississippi Rifles. A native of Columbus, MS, Love became close friends with Barksdale during war service in Mexico and his diary details their shared experiences (H. Grady Howell, Jr., *A Southern Lacrimosa*).

2nd Mississippi Regiment of Volunteers fully intended to play a prominent military role in the war, and fully expected to win its share of battlefield glory and acclaim. One need look no further than its armament to see the truth of this statement. Six months earlier, Col. Jefferson C. Davis of the 1st Mississippi Rifles had insisted, over the objections of Gen. Winfield Scott himself, to arm the entire volunteer regiment with the latest Model 1841 .54 caliber percussion cap rifle instead of the old standard Model 1822 smoothbore flintlock musket used by most infantry troops. This newer weapon provided a decided advantage in reliability and killing power, increasing the effective range to one thousand yards. Jefferson Davis therefore stood his ground against the opposition of the old army officers and placed an order with the armory at New Haven, Connecticut, for these new Whitney rifles. Colonel Davis wrote: "I knew the confidence the men I was expecting to lead had in rifles, and their distrust of the muskets then in use, and therefore notwithstanding my reluctance to oppose the General [Winfield Scott] insisted upon the thousand rifles."

Based upon the successes of the 1st Mississippi Rifles under Davis at the battles of Monterrey on September 21–23, 1846 and especially at Buena Vista on February 23, 1847, this Model 1841 rifle was thereafter forever known as the Mississippi Rifle. Despite these triumphs, the War Department still intended to arm the 2nd Mississippi with flintlock muskets. But due to the strenuous efforts of Gen. Charles M. Price, editor of the Jackson *Mississippian* and father of the 2nd Regiment's quartermaster, this unit too was armed with Mississippi Rifles and authorized to carry Bowie knives.[12]

In the absence of any written accounts by Captain Barksdale concerning his Mexican War service, the diary of Dr. Thomas N. Love, Barksdale's close personal friend, provides specific details of William's duties, contributions, and experiences. Love also vividly describes the suffering and privations endured by all these volunteers during their 18 months of continuous military service. Many of Surgeon Love's recorded experiences, observations, and opinions were common to most, if not all, members of the regiment and are therefore germane to understanding this period of Barksdale's life.

The surgeon's journal begins on Christmas Day 1846 in Barksdale's hometown of Columbus, when Love's Company A, the Lowndes Guards under Capt. Andrew K. Blythe, assembled for their formal send off. His emotional descriptions are indicative of similar tearful scenes repeated in several other cities and towns throughout Mississippi, and sadly that would be repeated many times over in spring of 1861 at the commencement of the Civil War. His journal records that an honor guard was provided by the Columbus Riflemen and records: "Early the streets of Columbus were filled with people; they came to bid farewell to the Lowndes Guards, which were assembled in the [Franklin] Academy lot and were soon ordered to 'fall into line.'" The green recruits were escorted to the Musgrave Tavern where Love records: "Miss McCarthy, on the part of the fair ladies of Columbus, we had presented us a most magnificent Flag with the inscription 'The Lowndes Guards—Victory or death.'" This was followed by a luncheon in the tavern's dining room with a heartfelt toast to the Lowndes Guards. It was then time to say final good-byes.

Dr. Love continues:

> But the trying scenes were yet to come—parting of friends. Many an eye was filled with tears, which perhaps knew no tears of grief equal to these. We were now severing the ties that bound us to home, to friends and all that was near and dear upon earth.... Columbus indeed has reason for grief.... This day she has dedicated to her country many of her native sons for the perils of war, and the trials of a

soldier's life. She bids them march forth upon a long and hazardous journey. Many a beloved boy has gone forth ... to return no more....

Dr. Love concludes as follows: "The Columbus Riflemen escorted us across the bridge, and took an affectionate leave of us—there was something more solemn in this than any separation I have ever made."[13]

The volunteers then made their way under Indian-summer-like weather to Vicksburg where they mustered into service, an arrangement that Love described as being "a little like being married—easy to get into, but devilish hard to get out of—the process is very simple, yet it 'puts the clutches' on a fellow." Camp McLung (named in honor of Lt. Alexander McLung who had been severely wounded leading the charge of the 1st Mississippi Rifles against La Teneria at the battle of Monterrey) was established three miles outside Vicksburg.

This proved to be an extremely poor location being "situated upon a low bank of the river, exposed to a wide sweep of the north and west winds—very low and very damp." A combination of factors resulted in truly miserable and distressing conditions. Insufficient woolen and flannel clothing, sudden placement on a camp diet of lean beef and crackers, lack of firewood, and a dramatic onset of inclement weather on January 10, 1847 (torrential rain followed by sleet, hail, and cold north winds) took their toll on the new recruits. Thus began a nightmare of suffering, disease, and death—an ordeal which would plague the 2nd Mississippi throughout its term of service.

Some sense of the misery and desperation can be gleaned by Dr. Love's following description:

> Sunday January 10th. They were a lean, gaunt, smoky looking set of fellows—muddy up to their knees.... The camp looked indeed desolate.... O how cold—the whole camp about six inches deep in mud and water.... Some muffled themselves up in their dripping blankets and huddled together in their cold and comfortless tents; some hovered over the smoking fires, calmly submitting to the pitiless peltings of the storm, and others with their wet and frozen blankets close around them.... Language fails to give an adequate idea of the sufferings of our men. They felt as if the very marrow of their bones was congealed. [Inevitably] fatigue, exposure, insufficient food and clothing were soon followed by the most remarkable and disastrous effects—influenza, rheumatism, pneumonia, and a disease more formidable than them all—cold plague.[14]

By January 13 there were twenty cases of pneumonia, including Dr. Love himself. Conditions were so bad that members of the regiment were allowed to seek out food and shelter at their own expense within Vicksburg. Although their Mississippi Rifles had not yet arrived, under these desperate circumstances, eight companies embarked by steamboat for New Orleans on January 13–14, with the final two following on January 18.[15]

If these volunteers, including Barksdale, thought their lot in life (or the weather) would improve at their next camp several miles south of New Orleans at Chalmette Plantation—the "Old Battle Ground" (site of the battle of New Orleans during the War of 1812)—they were sadly mistaken. Despite the existence of "at least half a dozen of large brick houses entirely empty" at the nearby Federal Barracks, the unfortunate Mississippians were again forced "to lay upon the cold wet ground, the tents above them wet—their blankets wet—wading about in mud and water and dying like sheep with the rot." The Federal Government Bureau had denied both the 2nd Mississippi Rifles and the 2nd Pennsylvania Regiment access to these barracks. Although Col. Reuben Davis later refused to accept any responsibility for this dire situation, his culpability is clearly evident. When previously faced with these identical circumstances, Col. Jefferson Davis, through sheer will and aggressive leadership, had forced the issue and relocated the 1st Mississippi Rifles to these indoor quarters.[16]

Sick Mississippi soldiers were soon dispatched to various hospitals in New Orleans, filling them to capacity. The Jackson Barracks in New Orleans was also converted to a military hospital. The sick were also permitted to secure shelter in private homes and boarding houses—but only at their own expense. This extreme suffering continued unabated. On January 31st, Love made the following journal entry: "Such a scene of distress, suffering and misery, hardships, and everything else I can think of has been the misfortune of our Regiment for the last two or three weeks.... We have all seen and felt ten times the misery of a hard fought battle. Indeed, we have fought a battle—disease has been our invincible enemy." Perhaps a sergeant in the 2nd Pennsylvania summed it up the best with the following laconic entry in his diary: "January 21 Cold and clear. *Mississippians dying as usual.*"[17]

By early February, several ships had been secured for passage to Mexico and the 2nd Mississippi Rifles, imbued with renewed hope, bade an emotional farewell to New Orleans. It was not so much a farewell as "good riddance!" Surgeon Love spoke for the regiment: "I am glad to leave this place—the city has treated us badly—they have cheated us—they have slandered us—they have rejoiced at our departure—they have refused to sympathize with us in all our misfortunes." On the other hand he failed to recognize that under their severe hardships the Mississippians "were little disposed to obey the restraints of discipline" and that "not a few outbreaks were committed by such as flew to the wine cup to forget their sufferings."[18]

Their hope for improved conditions was short lived. Seasickness was soon added to their torment as the ships were tossed about on the stormy waters of the Gulf of Mexico. Men were "vomiting all over the ship" and the drinking water was so offensive that "the sick men could scarcely use it." Surgeon Love's pleas to Col. Reuben Davis to improve the filthy conditions onboard fell on deaf ears, and the miserable conditions persisted. The end result was predictable—some of those still reasonably healthy became sick, and those already sick and weakened continued to die from conditions such as "troublesome diarrhoea" and pneumonia. Dr. Love's journal describes several emotionally touching scenes of the inevitable burial at sea for these unfortunate victims.[19]

The 2nd Mississippi Rifles finally reached the mouth of the Rio Grande after a voyage of about 20 days—about the time Jefferson Davis and the 1st Mississippi Rifles were gaining fame at the battle of Buena Vista, some 200 miles away. By January 1847 Gen. Winfield Scott had pulled rank on Old Rough and Ready, and ordered nearly all General Taylor's regular army troops and officers, as well as most of his experienced volunteer regiments, south to join his own Vera Cruz invasion campaign to seize Mexico City. Only about 500 regulars and roughly 4,500 volunteers remained with General Taylor who faced up to 25,000 Mexican troops in the San Luis Potosi region. (Jefferson Davis and the 1st Mississippi Rifles were some of the few experienced volunteers retained at Taylor's specific request.)

Greatly outnumbered, General Taylor could only assume a defensive posture and hang on for dear life. As a direct result of General Scott's personal intervention—motivated in large part by his own political ambitions—General Taylor's successful northern invasion campaign was now rendered static. Taylor's much smaller army transformed into an army of occupation. William Barksdale and the 2nd Mississippi Rifles now

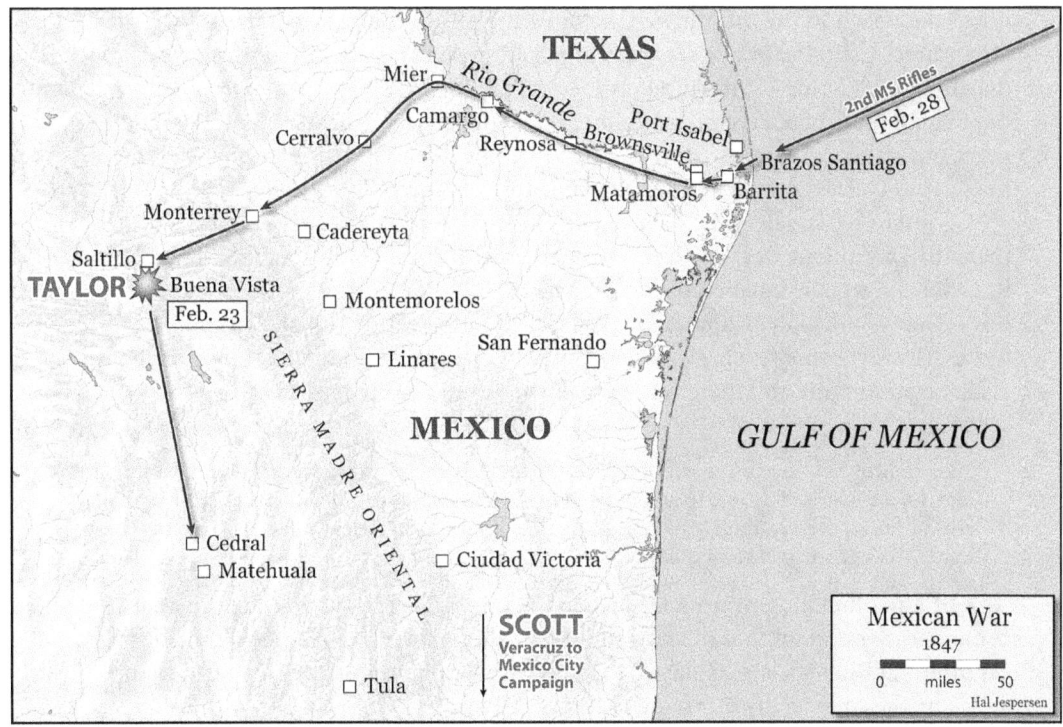

Route of William Barksdale's Military Service in the Mexican War

arrived into this drastically different scenario still imbued with their ill-fated expectations of battlefield glory.

Per orders of Col. Reuben Davis, Quartermaster Price, Assistant Commissary Barksdale, and Surgeon Love eagerly prepared for the transfer of supplies and the sick to Matamoras. Just then some convalescents from the hospital at New Orleans belonging to the 2nd Mississippi arrived, and Surgeon Love and Captain Barksdale kindly decided to remain to look after them. That evening they dined together at the Greenwood Tavern onboard a steamboat, and Captain Barksdale passed along some letters that he had received from Columbus, Mississippi, for Dr. Love.[20]

Despite the volume of U.S. government stores here at Brassos Santiago, the depot had been left virtually unprotected. Here on March 6, 1847, the first of many false alarms occurred. Dr. Love records,

> This morning at 2 A.M. Capt. Barksdale and myself were aroused from our beds by great excitement.... It was said that the Mexicans were crossing the river at [Barrita] about 2000 strong. The bell at the Q.M.'s office was ringing most furiously. Every man was rushing for a gun.... By daylight we stood behind the fortifications of meat and bread, ready in number about 400.... We flattered ourselves that we could hold the Mexicans a good fight.

Nothing transpired, so Love and Barksdale returned to the Greenwood Tavern for breakfast amidst great excitement. Three wagons and horses were provided to transport the remaining soldiers to the mouth of the Rio Grande. These two compatriots then rode together on horseback along the beach for nine miles enjoying the scenery and conversation. What a wonderful interlude it must have been after having been cooped up on a vile, stinking, disease-ridden ship for close to a month. In Dr. Love's words: "Our ride down the beach to the mouth was the most magnificent one I ever took. I was perfectly enraptured. Capt. Barksdale was very much enthused. We thought of the girls who would delight in such a ride." Unfortunately fears of a night attack by the Mexicans returned and once again "our men were put into line. We marched down under Capt. Barksdale & got guns, orders etc." Again, nothing developed. They departed by steamboat for Matamoras next day and arrived there in the early morning of March 8.[21]

Captain Barksdale must have experienced a deep sense of relief to be reunited with the entire regiment. Despite the continued hardships of soldiering, he made the best of it. Indeed, Surgeon Love recorded on March 8: "I am getting confounded sleepy—the boys (Capt. Barksdale, Capt. Price, Wilcox etc) are keeping up such a noise that I can't write." However this revelry was short lived, for about noon the next day, the bells once again began ringing and there was a great commotion in the plaza. Dr. Love described the scene:

> The Regiment had been dismissed—but were ordered to parade instantly again—Capt. Barksdale & Capt. Price came rushing into the room for guns, pistols, swords etc. I learned that 2000 Mexicans were advancing rapidly upon Matamoras. They had been seen but a few miles off—The guns had been heard. All was excitement and commotion.[22]

Absent any official communication from General Taylor's Army for the past 12 days, rumors were rampant that the outnumbered American force had been "cut to pieces and captured" at Buena Vista. Isolated, the 2nd Mississippi understandably feared imminent attack by the supposedly victorious Mexican Army.

Colonel Reuben Davis assigned each company a specific position to defend. Years later Davis would recall William Barksdale's actions that day:

> When the men were drawn up in the Plaza, I observed a tall figure without coat or vest, and with a very large sword buckled about the waist. This proved to be Captain William Barksdale, the quartermaster of the regiment. I asked him how he happened to be there in that trim, when as quartermaster, his duty did not call him to the front. He said he thought there might be some warm work presently, and it was a hot day, and he thought he could do better without his coat. Although our small force would be outnumbered, he counted on a glorious victory, and could I expect him to lose his chance of being in the thick of it? I told him to fall in where he pleased, and I hoped that he might find use for his ponderous blade before the day was over. Poor Barksdale! What a noble, generous heart beat in that broad bosom.[23]

What an overwhelming disappointment when the "dark clouds of dust that were seen to rise in the distant chaparral" turned out to be caused by a "large drove of Mexican ponies being driven into the city." The accompanying friendly Mexicans confirmed the absence of any attacking force. Unfortunately for young William, eager to join the fray, this would come as close to actual combat as he would get. However, it would not be as close to dying as he would come while in Mexico. Later that same day a cannon shot announced the arrival of a steamboat from Camargo upriver with confirmation of General Taylor's victory at Buena Vista. This prompted a wild celebration among the 2nd Mississippi Rifles at Matamoras. Col. Reuben Davis later wrote: "That was joyful news indeed. The men were fairly wild with pride and delight. They huzzaed themselves hoarse, and there were a hundred salutes fired."[24]

Several days later, on March 14, the officers and volunteers of the regiment embarked on steamboats for the voyage upriver to Camargo en route to Monterrey. Thus began a period of bad luck for Barksdale. First, his Mexican servant "gave him the slip about the time [they] were setting out" and "Capt. Barksdale was unfortunate enough to [lose] his trunk and all his clothes." Next day disease finally caught up with him. Dr. Love's journal entry for March 15, 1847, contained the following alarming statements: "Capt. Barksdale is very sick. I think he is either taking small pox or measles." Two days later Surgeon Love confirmed his diagnosis: "Capt. Barksdale is becoming dangerously ill. His case is measles. He has great difficulty of breathing which I do not like." The following day William's condition worsened: "Capt. Barksdale is exceedingly ill—gives me great trouble." However, in less than two weeks from falling ill, Barksdale recovered sufficiently to resume his duties as assistant commissary on March 27th "in a great splutter," returning with a large lot of condemned bread to Camargo. This great turnabout was undoubtedly due to the expert care and attention provided by his close friend Dr. Love, and to Barksdale's strong will and constitution.[25]

By mid–April the regiment had relocated to Monterrey, but disease continued to dog the men. Surgeon Love reported 69 cases of smallpox amongst the 85 hospital patients. Love described the depressing scenario this way:

> What a horrid scene it is to visit these poor fellows—I find this morning two men dead.... Some are delirious and have to be tied—some are being "blowed" by the flies—maggots in their eyes, nose, and in the flesh of the cheek.... Some have their faces so much swollen that they can not even see the dawn of day—others have such sore mouths that it is impossible to eat anything.

By June 1847, from an initial strength of 850 men, the regiment had lost 167 dead, 134 discharged due to sickness or accident, and 38 by desertion—a total loss of 339 men (40 percent)—all without a single shot being fired in anger! So depleted were the ranks that Capt. Charles Clark of Company G, the Thomas Hinds Guards, was ordered back to Mississippi in July to recruit replacements. This mortality rate of 20 percent due to sickness or accident in the 2nd Mississippi was double the corresponding average for all volunteer regiments combined and that for the regulars. A case can be made that the 2nd Mississippi Rifles endured twice the suffering due to disease compared to every other regiment who served in Mexico. This lends credence to Surgeon Love's belief that it was the initial exposure to extreme winter weather at Vicksburg that was the root cause of all subsequent sickness and disease within the regiment.[26]

As General Scott advanced toward Mexico City, Col. Reuben Davis and the 2nd Mississippi Rifles were ordered forward to Saltillo and then Buena Vista. Soon after their arrival here at Camp Taylor, Barksdale and others eagerly made a two-mile trek to view the Buena Vista battlefield—scene of the 1st Mississippi Rifles' victory over Santa Anna's forces. In letters back home William informed friends that "hundreds of unburied Mexicans still covered the ground."[27]

Here the regiment "suffered grievously from that terrible scourge, Mexican diarrhoea, a disease that prevails there all the year, and is almost sure to attack persons unaccustomed to the climate." This new affliction did not discriminate by military rank soon incapacitating both Col. Reuben Davis and Lieutenant Colonel Kilpatrick, subsequently forcing both to resign. This necessitated a reorganization of the regiment with Capt. Charles Clark being elected colonel and Lt. John A. Wilcox as lieutenant colonel.[28]

It was during this period in Buena Vista in the final six months of 1847 and early 1848 that William Barksdale, like many of his fellow volunteers including Surgeon Thomas Love, became a Master Mason, receiving all three degrees while in Mexico. On July 10, 1847, the Second Mississippi received a dispensation from the Grand Lodge of Mississippi and formed St. Johns Lodge, a military lodge attached to the regiment. This lodge banded together with Virginia Military Lodge No. 1 who had been presented earlier with "a copy of the Holy Scriptures, a complete set of tools and implements, jewels, regalia etc." in Richmond which they had brought to Mexico. An observer wrote at the time that "these two lodges work together in the utmost harmony and good feeling ... occupy the same lodge room, use the same furniture etc., and nothing occurs to mar the truly fraternal feeling which exists between these two bodies of men."

This observer also confirmed that, unlike many of the rank and file, no member of either lodge had been guilty of offenses such as "intemperance, disorderly conduct, insolence, and disobedience," thereby reflecting "the true character of our ennobling institution." St. Johns Lodge dissolved in 1848 at the conclusion of the war. Barksdale would remain a practicing Freemason for the remainder of his life. Upon his return to Mississippi in 1848 he affiliated with Columbus Lodge No. 5, the second oldest Masonic Lodge in the Magnolia State. Barksdale remained a member until his death in July 1863.[29]

It speaks very well of Captain Barksdale's performance as assistant commissary that he was retained in that position. Despite the inevitable intermittent shortages of provisions, potable water, etc., Barksdale performed his duties with ability and diligence so that no blame was attached to him by his fellow volunteers. Rather they recognized that he was doing the very best he could with what he had to work with, under difficult conditions often beyond his direct control. Years later, *Harper's Weekly* would record that, in Mexico, Barksdale performed "his arduous duties with recognized abilities."

Surgeon Love also appreciated Barksdale's inherent potential, writing of his friend at the time, "He is a splendid man—industrious—warmhearted—smart—tries to do well." The fact that he steadfastly remained in service with the regiment for another 14 months, with no expectation of active combat nor opportunity to win acclaim on the battlefield, demonstrated Barksdale's profound sense of duty and devotion to a cause once taken up. Barksdale would exhibit these strong character traits throughout his life.[30]

The regiment subsequently encamped near Monterrey. It remained there after Mexico City was captured by General Scott on September 14, 1847, following the battle of Chapultepec on the previous day. In April 1848, the headquarters for the 2nd Mississippi Rifles relocated to Cedras, about 120 miles south of Saltillo. Here the regiment continued to act as an occupying force and suffered the "dull monotony of camp duty" until finally returning to Vicksburg for mustering out on July 14, 1848.[31]

Captain Barksdale continued to diligently perform his duties and to impress his superiors as confirmed by his compiled service record: During October 1847 promoted to Acting Regimental Quartermaster; November 1847–Present; December 1847–February 1848—Absent on detached service by December 6th order of General Wool; March 1848—transferred to General Staff; April & May 1848—Present with 2nd Mississippi Regiment; May 21, 1848—ordered to relieve Captain W.E. Graves, Assistant Commissary Subsistence, North Carolina Regiment at Buena Vista; July 1848—Absent—ordered to report to General Brook at New Orleans by July 10th order of Colonel Charles Clark.[32]

This latter posting arose in response to a January 31, 1848, State of Mississippi Treasury Appropriation Act for $8000 "to be drawn on receipt of Captain William Barksdale Assistant-Commissary of Subsistence and Acting Assistant-Quartermaster ... for the purchase at New Orleans by him of such clothing as may be necessary to provide for the comfort of said volunteers." While Captain Barksdale's actions would have been too late to benefit his regiment in Mexico, it does indicate the level of responsibility and trust bestowed on this young man by his adopted state. This widespread trust was expressed in a soldier's letter to his wife concerning money owed him by various members of the 2nd Mississippi Rifles, including Barksdale who owed him $10. While he doubted some would pay, this soldier wrote, "I know some will, Capt. Barksdale certain, who is my friend." As a result of his detached service, Capt. William Barksdale's honorable discharge at Washington, D.C., was delayed until September 1, 1848—nearly two months after the rest of the regiment had mustered out.[33]

What conclusions can be drawn regarding William Barksdale's military service in Mexico and its influence on his future political and military careers? From a military perspective, through no fault of their own, Barksdale and his entire regiment never participated in a major battle nor even a small skirmish. Unlike many West Point graduates and future Civil War generals who experienced active combat in Mexico—and who learned tactics and maneuvers they would later use to wage war alongside or against one another—Barksdale never got close enough to the battlefield to benefit. The best training he got was an introduction to infantry drill, living the arduous day-to-day life of a soldier, a true appreciation of the importance and inherent difficulties in maintaining effective supply and logistics, and recognizing the importance of military discipline. Given his inherent ability for self-learning, these concepts were certainly not lost on him. Indeed, years later as a Confederate colonel and later a brigadier general, he would be noted for his strong emphasis on daily drill and firm discipline, and for placing the welfare of the troops he commanded at the top of his list.[34]

This lack of battlefield action became a source of bitter disappointment for the entire regiment. Surgeon Love gave voice to the universal depressing sentiment they shared: "Our soldiers have indeed had a hard time. They have endured suffering indescribable—they have met disease openly in all its terrors, and yet have had no opportunity for glory and distinction." In praising one specific soldier, Love wrote a fitting tribute for each member of the 2nd Mississippi Rifles, including Captain Barksdale: "Although he has not been in a battle, he has served his country patiently, faithfully, and with honor to himself. That we have never been in a battle is not our fault—we have always been ready—we have suffered with disease, borne privations and we are willing if an honorable peace is obtained to return to our homes quietly—with a clear conscience that we have done our duty."[35]

For Barksdale, however, his military service in Mexico would become much more than a disappointment—it would become a stinging embarrassment and a major motivator to gain military laurels on the battlefields of the Civil War. During the bitter congressional election of 1853, Barksdale's political enemies sought to publicly discredit him by cruelly and sarcastically demeaning his service in the Mexican War. An article in the Aberdeen (MS) *Weekly Independent* entitled "Who is Mister Barksdale" read in part as follows:

> Well dear Democrats, Mr. Barksdale is Capt. Barksdale; and we hope you will not offend his vanity and weakness by calling him Mr. Barksdale any more. The laurels upon his brow, like wilted cabbage leafs, forbid you calling him Mr. Barksdale. Capt. Barksdale then: That will do a little better. How Capt. Barksdale came in possession of his military title it will be interesting, perhaps, to our readers to know. Well we can't exactly inform them, and don't suppose that any person else can; but believe it was by receiving the appointment of Commissary to the 2nd Mississippi Regiment, in Mexico, where it is reported he won his military glory by feeding his soldiers on wormy bread. Nevertheless, be that as it may, don't call him Mr. Barksdale any more, but Capt. Barksdale.[36]

In the face of such personal attacks, it is not difficult to visualize Barksdale vowing to seize and pursue *any* future opportunity for battlefield glory—but he would have to wait until 1861!

Of all the influences on young Captain Barksdale during the Mexican War, perhaps the greatest was disease. He had become dangerously ill with measles, narrowly escaping death when many others did not. The ever-present sickness and death throughout his 19 months of service would undoubtedly have conjured up painful childhood memories of the cholera epidemics in Murfreesboro, and perhaps his own father's "agonizing death." It is not difficult to perceive then that Barksdale would thereafter associate military service with sickness, disease, and death. Moreover, close friend, Surgeon Love, observed firsthand that intemperance was beneficial to warding off disease, i.e., in his words "those who drank freely of ardent spirits escaped comparatively the diseases which afflicted our regiment with so much mortality." In fact, Dr. Love made a very detailed study and solicited information from the officers regarding the drinking habits of disease victims under their command. This detailed analysis confirmed his conclusion beyond any doubt as indicated in the following table:[37]

	Very Temperate	*Temperate*	*Intemperate*	*Very Intemperate*
Death Due to Disease (197)	97	61	4	5
Mortality Rate	58%	37%	2%	3%

Since they were such close friends, it is a virtual certainty that Dr. Love would have shared these findings with Captain Barksdale. This would explain, to a great extent this author believes, future drunken behavior by Colonel Barksdale after First Manassas which nearly became his undoing.

Thus ended Captain Barksdale's military service in the Mexican War. It can only be regarded as an extremely trying ordeal. Deprived of the much sought-after acclaim (through no fault of his own) he returned only with the satisfaction of a job well done and the respect of his fellow volunteers. If he regretted this service and the almost two-year forced hiatus from his personal pursuits, there is no record of it. Unbeknownst to Barksdale at the time, the fact that he had served as a general officer in the commissariat system would be enough to open the door to future service in the State Army of Mississippi and subsequently in that of the Confederacy. Unlike Gen. Zachary Taylor and Col. Jefferson Davis, William Barksdale had no martial laurels with which to propel his political career. Instead he would have to pick up where he had left off almost two years earlier and simply forge ahead undaunted—an approach which was entirely in keeping with his character.

Four

Barksdale Secures His Political Future

Twenty-seven-year-old William Barksdale returned to Columbus in late summer of 1848 and began a momentous five-year period in his life. He married Narcissa Saunders Smith, celebrated the birth of the first of their two sons, and actively participated as an elected leader in the Freemasons. Furthermore, Barksdale dramatically entered into state and then national politics, culminating in his election to the House of Representatives in Washington, D.C., during November 1853.[1]

During their service in Mexico, Captain Barksdale and Surgeon Love had often talked of love and romance, mentioning desirable girls back home by name. Barksdale mentioned Miss Martha Fort as a "romantic girl" and Love later wrote to his future sister-in-law that Capt. Barksdale "does love in my opinion a relative of yours." Instead, upon his return, young William wasted no time in courting a genteel 20-year-old Louisiana belle born and raised in West Feliciana Parish. Narcissa was the daughter of the late Courtland Smith, from Granville, Massachusetts, and Jane Boon, from Warren County, Georgia—and was the ninth of 12 siblings. Narcissa's family were well-off as evidenced by her dowry which included 20 negro slaves, horses, mules, and wagonloads of household articles. Within only 15 months of his return from Mexico, William married Narcissa in late 1849 in West Feliciana Parish (not Columbus, Mississippi, as often cited) and returned with their "property" in December to make their home at the Barksdale Plantation near Columbus.[2]

There is a dearth of written material concerning Narcissa. However, two of her private letters have survived. They were written in 1862 and 1866 to her dearest friend, Alcinda Janney, wife of the mayor of Leesburg, Virginia (and have not previously been cited in reference to William Barksdale). Together with a newspaper article written upon her death in 1875, they provide keen insight into her character. They also reflect the deep, abiding love she felt for William—which he returned to her. Her letters reveal a devout Christian woman, both kind and caring of others, and who, at times like her husband, could be feisty and independent. They undoubtedly shared a profound and unshakable devotion toward each other. Indeed, it is not a stretch to say that Narcissa adored William. They enjoyed an active social life in Columbus and were regarded as "one of the leading families of Lowndes County during the antebellum period." Separated for long periods during the Civil War, they corresponded via a steady exchange of letters. Unfortunately, none have survived. Narcissa did manage to visit with William at Leesburg during the autumn of 1861, and later pressed him to allow her to visit him in Virginia during 1862–63—alas it did not happen. Despite the correspondence between them, his absence on campaign caused her to freely express her loneliness in letters to close friends.[3]

Their marriage would produce two sons. The eldest, Ethelbert Courtland Barksdale, named after William's younger brother and Narcissa's father, was born on June 3, 1850, in Columbus. Ethel, as he was affectionately known, would grow up to be a strapping lad of six feet, similar in stature and appearance to his father. Narcissa described him as a noble boy who later became a source of great comfort to her during her husband's absence. Six years later, their second son, William, was born at Columbus. His mother described Willie, as he was affectionately known, as a "good yet wild young boy often gone all day riding and hunting." Barksdale has been described as "an affectionate yet controlling father." The fact that his final thoughts and words at Gettysburg were of Narcissa, Ethel, and Willie reflect the depth of William's love for his family.[4]

In 1849 William resumed his legal duties and plantation activities. Although active in state politics, he did not gain prominence in the public eye until the bitter debate concerning the Compromise of 1850. A prominent scholar and chronicler of Mississippi history wrote that a study of the prewar politics of secession in the Magnolia State in the 1850s "offers richer rewards in an understanding of the South as a section than would be afforded perhaps by any similar study in any other state." The opposing political views within Mississippi were complicated and confusing with subtle nuances that have been often misunderstood and misrepresented. Nowhere is this truer than in attempts by various writers to characterize and label William Barksdale's political views—and apparently contradictory positions.[5]

Surprisingly, there had been no widespread defense of slavery within Mississippi prior to the 1835 national senatorial election. Until then the Mississippi State Legislature had been quite united and vocal in supporting the Union and resisting attempts to undermine it. A February 6, 1833, resolution drafted by Mississippi in response to South Carolina preaching revolution, clearly stated "we will indignantly frown upon the first dawning of every attempt to alienate any portion of our country from the rest, or to enfeeble the ties which link together its various parts." This declaration also pledged support to the president to "maintain unsullied and unimpaired, the honor, the independence, and the integrity of the Union."

The initial challenge to the solidarity of this position, and the first hint of sectional disagreement within Mississippi, came during the 1835 senatorial campaign of Robert J. Walker. In response to the threat posed by the Northern Abolitionist Movement, Walker aroused planters and slaveholders who were located very predominantly in the western half of the state by claiming "that the North was turning its batteries against our domestic institutions." Walker won the election and followed up with a fervent appeal during his first senate speech on March 2, 1836. Walker urged the Senate to put down forever the Abolitionists whom he referred to as "fanatical incendiaries" who were threatening everything the South held dear. He then defiantly defended slavery by exclaiming, "No, our peculiar institution will yield only at the point of the bayonet."[6]

Perhaps the insertion of slavery as the major divisive issue within Mississippi was inevitable. As far back as 1820, political leaders recognized the institution of slavery was key to maintaining the balance of power within the country. The South fully recognized that as new territories of settlement inevitably became states within the Union, it was critical that the balance between slave and free states be maintained. Population determined the number of seats in the House of Representatives for each new state. However, each state controlled only two votes in the Senate. In the words of British historian John Keegan, "As long, therefore, as territories were admitted to Congress as states in which slavery was permitted, and slavery was accepted in the federal Constitution, slavery was safe in the South, since anti-slavery legislation passed in the House of Representatives could be voted down in the Senate."

After the purchase of the Louisiana Territory in 1803 and Missouri's application for statehood in 1817, the historical balance between the number of slave versus free states would be tipped, and so too would the balance of power. Thus slavery catapulted to the forefront and became the primary issue for national debate in Washington. The result was adoption of The Missouri Compromise of 1820 whereby Missouri was admitted as a slave state together with Maine as a free state at the same time, thereby retaining the slave/free balance as before. It also provided that slavery would be prohibited north of the 36° 30' latitude line.

By 1841, public opinion had evolved. Mississippi's state government stood firm, cooperating with other Southern states, to protect their rights and institutions, and voicing outrage at Northern states for refusing to return fugitive slaves. By the mid–1840s Mississippi's newspapers ardently defended slavery as a "positive good" and branded those who attacked it as "insurrectionists and incendiaries." This power struggle between North and South continued unabated and reached a new peak following the Mexican War and extension of the country's boundaries to the Pacific Ocean.[7]

Again, it was a numbers game with the South determined to carve out enough new slave states in the southwestern territory to offset the new free states in the northwestern territory. As succinctly stated by professor Percy L. Rainwater, "The acquisition of states became the leading idea on both sides of the controversy. A preponderance of political power was the object sought." On August 8, 1846, the Wilmot Proviso was introduced in the House of Representatives. Aiming to restrict slavery within its existing boundaries and "forming a cordon of free states around it," this proposed legislation prompted renewed and bitter dissension between the opposing factions. This discord finally splintered party lines in the South, especially in Mississippi, and provided the basis for a united front against the Northern free states.[8]

This struggle continued unabated until passage of the Compromise of 1850 which, although not entirely palatable to either faction, at least provided the basis for a tenuous truce which would last for ten years. Terms of the Compromise of 1850 stipulated the following:

> *California was admitted as the 16th non-slave state
> *in exchange the South was guaranteed that no federal restrictions on slavery would be placed on the territories of Utah or New Mexico
> *Texas lost its boundary claims in New Mexico but received $10 Million
> *slavery was maintained in Washington D.C. but the slave trade was prohibited
> *the Fugitive Slave Law was enacted requiring Northerners to return runaway slaves to their owners under penalty of law[9]

Such was the political climate that Barksdale faced during 1850. Mississippi in essence was a microcosm of the bitter sectional conflict and political turmoil gripping the entire nation. At this time the term "Unionist" indicated one "who supported the Union cause *and opposed secession*" (emphasis added) while a member of the "States' Rights" or "Resistance" faction described one who wholeheartedly "supported a secessionist position" of upheaval.[10] Barksdale however can only be classified as an anomaly—confirmed by his apparently contradictory positions and actions during this period.

By 1850, in response to bitter and relentless attacks by Northern Abolitionists against slavery, Mississippi became a stronghold of States' Righters who angrily voiced resentment against the North. Mississippi quickly became one of the South's leading advocates for immediate secession—a very "storm center of secession" in professor Rainwater's assessment. Barksdale's fiery temperament and strong states' rights beliefs (which he held were unequivocally guaranteed by the Constitution) made him acceptable to their cause. So, at this time Barksdale actively joined the States' Rights wing of the Democratic party. Based in Columbus, within Lowndes County, Barksdale resided in one of only five counties in northeastern Mississippi where slaves outnumbered whites, whereas in western Mississippi this was the case in all 24 counties. Barksdale was therefore a minority States' Righter in Unionist eastern Mississippi, while States' Rights support was universal in Western Mississippi.[11]

When the Compromise Measures of 1850 had been debated in Congress, it is not surprising that Barksdale had initially argued against them. However, once the Compromise had been passed, he was willing to accept these measures as long as they were all rigidly enforced. In particular, he did not feel that the risks inherent with immediate secession, and the accompanying formal challenge to the federal government, were justified under the current circumstances. This position flew in the face of the true States' Rights position which advocated for immediate secession.[12]

Not all Mississippians of course were prepared to abide by the Compromise. Soon the newly elected governor, former Mexican War general John A. Quitman, spearheaded active opposition against it. In November 1850, at Quitman's request, the Mississippi Legislature sanctioned a convention to be held one year later to consider secession. Delegates to this gathering would later be termed "the most distinguished of the antebellum assemblages." Their election would be held on the first Monday in September 1851. Not content to merely support the Compromise, Barksdale and United States Senator Henry Stuart Foote, leader of the Unionist faction in Mississippi, who had helped get it passed in Washington, embarked on a speaking tour of Mississippi in March, 1851, to extol its virtues. A contemporary wrote: "in doing so [Barksdale] separated from the main body of his former political friends, but on that occasion as on others, he had the moral principles to follow his convictions wherever they led, regardless of consequences."[13]

On March 29, 1851, the *Columbus Democrat* published a summary of William's initial speech given at Columbus. In part it read:

> Said Mr. Barksdale.... The question then presents itself, shall we join our sister southern States in acquiescing in this compromise, whatever may have been our opinions with regard to it, while it was before Congress, or shall we engage in schemes of resistance which must necessarily bring us into collision with the general government? For one, so long as the political skies remain as they now are, he was for clinging to the Union of Washington and Jefferson, and the Constitution, as it was when our fathers made it and gave it to us.... Let us then said Mr. Barksdale, stand by the Union and Constitution as they are, and if the aggressions of the north should be continued, if the voice of fanaticism should still be raised against us, if the hand of outrage should still be uplifted, if the south forced as a last resort to secede, or give up her rights and property, she will have justice on her side and the sympathies of the civilized world will be with her.

Hardly the words of a fire-eating secessionist as Barksdale has often been mislabeled. So persuasive were Barksdale and Foote that, by the time of the election six months later, the tide of popular opinion had turned back in support of the Compromise. This dramatic turnabout represents the first solid evidence of Barksdale's ability to influence popular political opinion. It certainly would not be his last.

As a result, Barksdale was selected as a Unionist delegate from Lowndes County to attend the Convention in Jackson on November 10, 1851. Despite his strong beliefs in states' rights under the protection of the Constitution, it is not difficult to perceive why he would agree to attend the convention as a Union delegate. Indeed, their platform was right in line with his own beliefs, "favorable to the compromise, yet states' rights in tone" while avoiding the secession-at-all-costs extreme adopted by Quitman and his radical followers. In part the Unionist manifesto stated "whilst we acquiesce in the enactments of the late session of Congress, and feel a strong attachment and veneration for the Union established by our forefathers, still we declare that violations of our rights may occur which would amount to intolerable oppression and would justify a resort to measures of resistance." These violations were itemized as follows: congressional interference with slavery in the states where it existed, interference with the slave trade, passage of laws to prohibit slavery in the territories, and refusal of the federal government to enforce the fugitive slave law. The Unionists dominated the Convention and adopted resolutions in accordance with their platform which essentially pledged "that the people of Mississippi while they did not entirely approve of it would abide by the congressional legislation affecting slavery as a paramount adjustment of the sectional controversy, so long as the same shall be enforced, and faithfully adhered to."[14]

Unfortunately for William, the Unionists then took things a step further and proposed a resolution concerning the abstract right of secession. It stated that secession "is utterly unsanctioned by the Federal Constitution" and "will virtually amount in its effects and consequences to a civil revolution." Since he had always publicly stated his belief that a state possessed the right to peaceably secede, this declaration was too much for Barksdale to accept. Having previously broken ranks with the States' Rights wing of the Democratic party, he now did the same with the Unionist wing. Barksdale entered a motion to strike out this resolution, but it was defeated. He then declared before all present that, while no necessity for exercise of this right then existed, "if the occasion should ever come, he would make whatever sacrifice might be demanded of him by his State to which his first allegiance was due."[15] True to his word, 13 years later William Barksdale would make the ultimate sacrifice for Mississippi at a small crossroads town in Pennsylvania.

Barksdale's rising prominence in state politics resulted in his selection as a Unionist delegate at the 1852 Democratic National Convention at Baltimore during the presidential election. Barksdale supported both the party platform and ticket. Notably, prior to accepting the offer of the Unionists, he had been acclaimed as a delegate by the States' Rights wing but had respectfully declined for undisclosed reasons.[16]

Perhaps recognizing that he had burnt too many political bridges, Barksdale, over the next two years, conducted a vigorous public speaking campaign aimed at reconciliation of the Unionist and States' Rights wings of the Democratic party within Mississippi. He argued their present conflict was extremely detrimental to the party and their future success with the electorate hinged on immediate reunification. Barksdale's efforts at these local county and state rallies—where he was often the featured speaker—kept him in the limelight, bolstered his reputation, and favorably impressed the party's powerbrokers. There is evidence during this time that he was approached by close friends to stand for state office but for reasons unknown he remained non-committal. Perhaps he simply had his political sights set higher.

In any event, on April 11, 1853, at a meeting of Lowndes County Democrats in Columbus, Barksdale was voted a member of an uncommitted delegation (free to support any candidate) to attend a convention scheduled for May 2, 1853, in Jackson to nominate both a state and national congressional ticket for the upcoming elections on November 7th. Since Mississippi's population had grown to 606,526 per the December 12, 1850, Census, the state was now entitled to one additional congressman in Washington who would be voted from the state-at-large. (Redistricting of Mississippi could not be completed by election day.) For weeks, self-professed office seekers had publicly laid claim to a nomination. Barksdale had not. Instead newspapers reported that he targeted a seat in Mississippi's State House of Representatives.

Portending what was to follow, Barksdale auspiciously called the convention to order and moved a temporary chairman be selected. Benjamin Kinyon, a Unionist Democrat, then set in motion a bizarre series of events that ultimately resulted in Barksdale's totally unexpected nomination for congressman-at-large. Kinyon opened the door by prematurely proposing three ill-advised resolutions, including one which demanded the nominations be split 50/50 Unionists/States' Righters as a price for reunification. A heated debate then ensued, including several speeches in protest—one of which was given by Barksdale. He vehemently objected that such an arrangement would be tantamount to admitting that the Democratic party was still hopelessly divided by factionalism. Instead he urged that this was the time to unite in "one solid phalanx" against their "ancient [political] foes," the Whig party. Barksdale's impassioned oratory was favorably received with partisan admiration and opened the door for his subsequent nomination.[17]

The convention adjourned in turmoil around 5 p.m. absent any decision on Kinyon's resolution. That night, a council of 75 concerned delegates met behind closed doors at the office of *The Mississippian* in an effort to salvage the convention by finding common ground. During these discussions, the pros and cons of prospective candidates were reviewed, together with their chances for success in the upcoming election. Although Barksdale had still not declared himself an aspirant for the congressman-at-large nomination, his earlier condemnation of Kinyon sparked a "spontaneous Barksdale-for-Congress movement." His earlier "defections," and, at a cursory glance, his apparent flip-flopping of sides, had been severely criticized by many. His actions had also cost Barksdale more than a few political allies and personal friends. However now Barksdale's apparently contradictory machinations would actually work in his favor. Barksdale's true political position could best be described as a cross between a limited Unionist and a restrained States' Righter, embracing most but not all planks in each platform. Since he could then be reasonably (if not completely) identified with either faction, the majority of this impromptu caucus likely decided that Barksdale would be a suitable nominee should the mood of the convention continue to demand a compromise candidate.[18]

At some time prior to the convention Barksdale had been approached by Democratic party "heavy hitters" John J. McRae, Albert G. Brown, and others, who pledged their support for his nomination as congressman-at-large provided Barksdale would return to the States' Rights faction of the party. Not surprisingly, Barksdale jumped at the opportunity and quickly agreed. In doing so, at worst, Barksdale could be accused of being a pragmatic politician to get what he wanted. Barksdale clearly recognized that the Unionist faction's dominance within Mississippi's Democratic party had ended by this time. However, there is no indication *whatsoever* that in switching factions on several occasions that Barksdale ever changed or compromised his political beliefs and principles.[19]

The following morning Barksdale's name was placed in nomination together with six others. Three immediately withdrew. Amongst the remaining four, Barksdale's stiffest competition came from his former commanding officer in Mexico, Col. Reuben Davis, who had been touted as the frontrunner by the press. Davis' political friends assured him that his nomination was a certainty. Although Davis led by a significant margin on the initial two ballots, as candidates withdrew, Barksdale steadily gained momentum and finally was declared the winner on the fifth ballot. On a motion by W.L. Harris of Warren County, the convention confirmed Barksdale as their "unanimous choice" as Democratic candidate from the state-at-large for Congress.

Barksdale then addressed the delegates to make a graceful acceptance speech. Despite this attempt at solidarity, controversy erupted immediately, and would often be Barksdale's close companion throughout his political and military careers. Davis did not take his defeat in stride. Instead in an address to the assembly that afternoon he angrily "denounced the convention for its treachery and declared [he] would contest the result before the people" as an independent candidate. The more recently organized counties in northern Mississippi, from which Davis hailed, were understandably outraged, for it was growth in their populations that had gained a fifth seat in Congress. Therefore, they felt entitled to designate the candidate for the seat-at-large. Their fierce condemnation of the convention, and bitter political campaign that followed in opposition to Barksdale's nomination, was termed the Chickasaw Rebellion. To discredit him in the eyes of the electorate, Barksdale was accused by his political enemies, both privately and publicly in many Mississippi newspapers, of "everything from chicanery to political intrigue." This criticism was based on the claim that "while he was the professed friend of Col. Reuben

Albert Gallatin Brown, antebellum governor of Mississippi, Democratic United States congressman and senator, senator in Confederate Congress, and lifelong friend of William Barksdale, organized and served as Captain, Co. H, Brown Rebels, 18th Mississippi (Library of Congress).

Davis, [Barksdale] connived at the use made of his name to defeat Davis." This was also the period when some in the press sarcastically demeaned Captain Barksdale's military service in Mexico in an attempt to further discredit him.[20]

Thus began a very acrimonious canvass of the state by Barksdale and Davis, former friends now turned bitter enemies. This contest witnessed some of the best—and worst—behavior by Barksdale. Davis' unexpected entry as an independent candidate, and the splintering of the Democratic party, induced Maj. Alexander Bradford, Mexican War hero and distinguished Whig politician from Marshal County, to throw his hat in the ring as an independent candidate for the seat-at-large. Bradford, with his illustrious reputation and magnetic personality, was generally regarded as the frontrunner, capable of drawing voter support from both Democrats and Whigs. Barksdale exhibited key political insight in recognizing that Davis represented the foremost threat to his being elected. Instinctively Barksdale realized that strategically he must first defuse the Chickasaw Rebellion before confronting Bradford.

Tackling this arduous task Barksdale entered into a series of fiery debates with Davis during the initial weeks of the campaign. These exchanges were characterized by inflammatory language, personal insults, accusations of wrongdoing, and emotionally charged rhetoric which at times bordered on character assassination. The central recurring issue however concerned the "probity of the recent Democratic convention at Jackson" versus the "origin, cause, and grounds" of the Chickasaw Rebellion. Each challenged the other's legitimacy as a candidate for the congressional seat-at-large. Barksdale adroitly argued that as he was the duly nominated candidate of the Democratic party, as a party member Davis had no right to oppose him as an independent. Again, Barksdale stressed the need for party unity to avoid another split at the polls that would result in the election of a Whig candidate. He also pointed out that he had been nominated by votes from 28 counties representing every part of the state (not just in southern Mississippi as Davis contended) whereas Davis had received support from only 20. Barksdale also made an honest and forthright defense of his actions at the convention, condemning as "false and slanderous" Davis' charge of connivery. While Barksdale freely admitted that he had preferred Davis in advance of the convention and would have supported him had Davis received the nomination, Barksdale denied ever making a pledge to support Davis "to the exclusion of all others." Furthermore, he denied charges of chicanery by stating that he had not personally made any effort to solicit the nomination at the convention nor had he agreed to use of his name against Davis despite the "great temptation" to do so. Finally, Barksdale had accepted the nomination because it represented the will of the Democratic party in Mississippi.[21]

These increasingly acrimonious encounters continued to escalate. Despite an apparent agreement that the opponents would not "go upon the stand to speak with arms of a deadly character," a violent confrontation finally erupted in Vicksburg on July 1, 1853, where they were scheduled to debate that evening. The wild melee surprisingly occurred while they were finalizing arrangements for a duel to which an exasperated Barksdale had challenged Davis—after Davis had impugned Barksdale's honor, integrity, and sense of fair play.[22]

The following account of what purportedly transpired that day is based upon a lengthy article in the *Aberdeen* (MS) *Weekly Independent* published on July 16, 1853. Earlier that morning William H. Johnson, an acquaintance of the two candidates, was privy to a conversation between Barksdale and Davis. Sometime before noon Davis requested that Johnson provide him with a certified statement of "certain portions" of the aforementioned conversation that he deemed were important "to his defence in the canvas between them." Learning of this development, Barksdale became piqued since Davis' actions "seemed to convey a suspicion, on the part of Davis, that [Barksdale] would not make the same statements at all times." Barksdale quickly decided to pursue the matter personally with Davis.

That afternoon, while Barksdale was enjoying a cup of tea with friends in the dining room of the Washington Hotel, Davis arrived and sat down at Barksdale's table. Shortly thereafter Barksdale excused himself and demanded Davis join him in his hotel room. However, since Barksdale had guests present, the two men instead went to Davis' room to pursue the matter. Having brooded over this apparent insult to his honor and integrity, Barksdale promptly denounced Davis over his clandestine actions earlier that morning. When Davis protested Barksdale's rebuke, Barksdale promptly offered Davis an opportunity for "satisfaction at short notice" across the state line in Louisiana. With tempers flaring, Davis immediately accepted the challenge to a duel but—perhaps regretting his rashness—Davis soon began to quibble over the place and time. Since they could not agree on their own, they returned to Barksdale's room to seek assistance from Barksdale's guests.

Here the argument escalated, and the fight took place. At one point, Barksdale declared that Davis had made a false statement—an action which enraged Davis. Quickly losing his self-control, Davis, in a fit of anger, struck Barksdale in the face with the back of his hand. Barksdale retaliated in kind, knocking Davis backward. Although they had both agreed before entering Davis' room not to bring any weapons, Davis had apparently forgotten about the pocketknife he carried. Enraged, Davis drew the pocketknife and struck at Barksdale. Although Barksdale was unarmed, he fearlessly pressed home his attack on Davis. Despite the efforts of Barksdale's guests to separate the two combatants, the hand-to-hand struggle continued with Barksdale landing blows while Davis lashed out with his knife. With the aid of the hotel manager the onlookers finally separated them but not before a "badly bloodied" Barksdale had suffered 10 or 11 knife cuts to his left arm, chest, and side, which fortunately for Barksdale proved to be superficial. The wounds however were severe enough to require treatment from a local doctor who ordered William to his bed. Davis emerged from the wild melee "considerably bruised and blackened." For his part, Davis was arrested and charged with "aggravated assault" by Vicksburg's Mayor, J.S. Byrne. After posting bail Davis was ordered to appear before the next session of the Circuit Court. Although Davis emerged as the villain, having attacked an unarmed man, Barksdale was also ordered by the mayor to "explain his part in the difficulty."[23]

This episode marked the first recorded evidence of Barksdale's willingness to settle matters of honor by the Code Duello—or his fists. During his lifetime Barksdale would repeat these two penchants several times. Such actions not only reflected his Southern heritage and values, but also, less admirably, his hair-trigger temper which he sometimes just could not control. Perhaps this was Barksdale's greatest character flaw. Eventually he would participate in three near-duels (though none were actually consummated) and three additional fisticuffs on the floor of the U.S. Congress. Ironically, this brawl with Davis afforded the opportunity for Barksdale to later demonstrate one of his noblest character traits—a willingness to forgive and reconcile with his enemies. Commenting on their first meeting by chance 18 months later, Davis wrote: "Our temporary irritation had long since subsided, and we grasped hands in cordial greeting, as though we had been long-parted brothers. From that hour to the day of [Barksdale's] death, the most entire friendship existed between us, and no man in the State cherished a more sincere regard for him than I did, or more profoundly regretted his death."[24]

Following his altercation with Barksdale, support for Reuben Davis waned. Recognizing the futility of continuing his political campaign, Davis publicly withdrew on September 27, 1853, under the pretext of becoming an agent for the New Orleans Railroad. However, Barksdale was still not assured of victory in the upcoming election. Opponent Bradford possessed two distinct advantages over him. First, a superior military record which would guarantee the votes of many in Mississippi, and second, Bradford's campaign was being conducted with the assistance of Governor Henry S. Foote, senatorial candidate for the Union Democrats. A combination of Unionist and Whig support could guarantee Bradford a victory.[25]

After being sidelined by an "inopportune illness" shortly after his fight with Davis, Barksdale once again resumed his state canvass. For Barksdale it must have seemed like déjà vu for the Whig press now attacked him by misrepresenting his support of the Compromise measures during 1851. Specifically, they accused him of "never [being] a Union man, and that by posing as [one] in 1851 he was guilty of the rankest deception and hypocrisy." Bradford then implored the people "not to deliver the state into the hands of secession-minded candidates on the Democratic ticket." Since Bradford refused to debate Barksdale face-to-face, William could only maintain his previous strategy by appealing to the Democrats "to stand firm in their loyalty to the state organization." However, he now astutely added a warning to Union Democrats—"do not be deceived by the Whigs [for they will] use the Union vote to elevate their party to power and then laugh ... at the folly of their dupes." Again, the broader appeal of Barksdale's less extreme position managed to gain support from both factions and "the Captain" was credited by the press with "perfecting the harmony of the party."[26]

Newspapers now predicted Barksdale would win at the polls on November 7–8, 1853. Indeed, he did, carrying 38 counties and winning by a margin of almost 5,000 votes. Barksdale's victory had been assured by a massive turnout of Democrats—both Union and States' Righters—at the polls.[27] Had Barksdale actually been a fire-eating secessionist—as he has so often been portrayed—it is a virtual certainty that he would not have received the Democratic nomination nor have been elected as national congressman-at-large.

William Barksdale had now realized his true ambition of securing a position on the national political stage in Washington City where he could espouse his views and influence public policy. In doing so he had demonstrated considerable skill as an accomplished public speaker, an aggressive and effective debater, and a masterful political strategist. With no small sense of accomplishment, on December 5, 1853, William Barksdale assumed his rightful position in the House of Representatives of the 33rd Congress of the United States.

No stranger to controversy, Congressman Barksdale would make his presence felt in the national capital with high drama during the most troubled and turbulent political period in the history of the young country.

Five

Turbulent Times in Washington City

Thirty-two-year-old William Barksdale took his appointed seat in Congress as a healthy, robust, energetic politician eager to further the interests of his constituents and his adopted state of Mississippi, and to uphold the welfare of the entire country. Standing 5-feet 11-inches tall, and weighing nearly 200 pounds, he cut an imposing figure. His background as a practicing lawyer, combined with his sharp debating skills, and knowledge of both the Constitution and the political parties of the day, rendered him a force to be reckoned with. *Harper's Weekly* would later record, "his frank manners, pleasing countenance, and social courtesy have given weight to his decided remarks." Back home Mississippians held Barksdale in such high esteem that Mississippi's 3rd Congressional District would re-elect him for three more consecutive terms. Barksdale would cast his final vote in Congress nearly eight years later, on January 7, 1861, three days before Mississippi's delegation gave written notice of their resignations.[1]

Confirmed by his subsequent words and actions, Barksdale entered the House, not as a Southern agitator fomenting dissension, but with the clear intent of improving general conditions in Mississippi. He would introduce and support specific legislation to upgrade rail and river transportation, increase pay scales for land registers and receivers, secure federal benefits such as post roads and monetary relief for settlers living on public lands, and general measures to provide economic benefit to Mississippi and the South. Barksdale was quickly appointed to serve on the Standing Committee on Roads and Canals.

Conspicuously, he rose from his seat on December 23, 1853, to announce his intention to introduce "a bill granting the right of way and making a donation of public lands to the States of Mississippi, Alabama, and Louisiana, in aid of the construction of certain railroads therein." He soon followed through by introducing said bill on January 3, 1854. Then on February 7, 1854, he introduced an amendment to increase a general appropriation bill by $55,000 to cover construction of a marine hospital building at Vicksburg on a site previously purchased for $10,000.[2]

Unfortunately, the bitter debate over the Kansas-Nebraska Bill, considered by many to "have been the single most significant event leading to the Civil War," soon sidetracked Barksdale's game-plan. Introduced in the Senate by the "Little Giant," Senator Stephen Douglas of Illinois, in January 1854, it called for the formation of two new territories in the lands between the western boundary of Missouri and the Rocky Mountains. From them two new states would be established—Nebraska to the north and

Kansas to the south. Key to this act was the concept of "popular sovereignty" whereby each territory would be "free to form and regulate their domestic institutions in their own way." Notably this included allowing or prohibiting slavery. The Missouri Compromise (banning slavery north of the 36° 30′ latitude line) had permitted a tenuous peace to exist between North and South for the past 34 years. Under provisions of this new bill, the Missouri Compromise was explicitly declared "inoperative and void." Douglas envisioned Nebraska as a free state balanced by Kansas as a slave state, thereby ensuring Southern support. Construction of a transcontinental railway passing through Chicago was Douglas' motivation for this dramatic reopening of the slavery issue. Needless to say, Douglas' actions caused a violent eruption of emotion and invective by reopening old wounds and set in motion a series of events with gigantic political ramifications for the entire nation.[3]

William Barksdale took his seat in the United States House of Representatives for the first time on December 5, 1853, and cut an imposing figure (Library of Congress).

In fact, Mississippi Senator Stephen Adams had forewarned Barksdale and his fellow Mississippi congressmen upon their arrival in Washington regarding the anticipated territorial bill in the Senate. Furthermore, Adams cautioned them to be prepared to reopen discussion in the House regarding territorial slavery. In the interim they would await official instruction from Mississippi once the bill was introduced in the Senate. It did not take long for events to unfold.

Barksdale was chosen by the others as spokesman for the Mississippi Delegation in the House. On March 20, 1854, he formally presented the Mississippi Legislature's official resolution which denounced attempts by Northerners in Congress to exclude slavery from the Kansas and Nebraska territories. Mississippi's official position clearly stated: "… the bill now pending before Congress, organizing a territorial government in Nebraska and Kansas, is in accordance with the principles of the Constitution of the United States, and in the opinion of this Legislature just and proper, and that our Senators and Representatives in Congress be instructed to support this bill by all honorable means."[4]

Nine days later Barksdale gave his first formal speech in the House. His carefully worded and thought-provoking hour-long address examined this bill, answered some objections by opponents, and declared his personal opinions regarding amendments. At the outset, Barksdale stated it was not his intention to discuss "the abstract question of slavery" as it was "not necessary that I should do so." Nevertheless he took the opportunity to state that slavery was a benefit and blessing to both master and slave, not only in the Southern states but also in the free Northern states who manufactured and consumed the articles made by slave labor. Barksdale emphasized that slavery's defense rested unequivocally under the Constitution where it was shielded. Throughout his life Barksdale believed unwaveringly that the Constitution protected the rights of slaveholders.[5]

Against the first Northern objection that this bill was premature due to insufficient population in the territories, Barksdale simply stated such claims would not stand "the test of facts and scrutiny." Since it had already been introduced, he concluded "it is our solemn duty to examine it dispassionately, to discuss it frankly, fully and freely, and to act upon it with an eye single to the best interest of the country." Barksdale realized that if Congress did not then address the issue, at some point the people in the two territories would.[6]

To the second objection that the bill would infringe on the treaty rights of "Indians" in these territories, Barksdale concluded that "full and ample provision" had been made for their protection. However, if opponents genuinely felt otherwise and "in good faith" brought forth amendments, he would personally "vote to sustain them."[7]

He then made compelling arguments that the Constitution was the preeminent "compact to which sovereign and independent States were parties and to observe which the faith of all was solemnly plighted." Barksdale quoted directly from the Constitution on the issue of slavery: "No person held to service or labor in one State, under the laws thereof, escaping into another, shall in consequence of any law or regulation therein, be discharged from such service or labor, but shall be delivered up, on claim of the party to whom such service or labor may be due." He followed up by censuring Vermont where, in defiance of the Constitution and the Fugitive Slave Laws of 1793 and 1850, it was now a penal offence to aid U.S. officers in returning runaway slaves.

Barksdale then turned his attention to objections by the North regarding repeal of the slavery restriction clause in the Missouri Compromise on the basis that the South was violating a solemn and timeless compact. To these charges he responded that no such compact was made by the Southern Representatives since they had no right to, and there was no evidence of any Southern State "ever pledging the people forever to the Missouri restriction." Quite simply he stated: "The South when overwhelmed by superior numbers, acquiesced in, but never indorsed that compromise. It was accepted as a last resort to preserve the Union, as an offering upon its altar; but its justice or constitutionality had never been acknowledged by the South." Shortly thereafter Barksdale commented wryly: "How does it happen that those who were so fierce in its denunciation then are so clamorous for its preservation now?" He considered this objection for what it was—"shameless hypocrisy!" In discussing the Compromise Measures of 1850, he went into great detail summarizing what the South had sacrificed, receiving in return only the Fugitive Slave Law. A statute Barksdale claimed "which is only valuable because of the constitutional right it was passed to enforce but which is of little practical benefit to the South" since it was being largely ignored by the Northern states.

Referring to the concept of "popular sovereignty" with which he was not entirely comfortable, he posed the question: "Does this territory belong to the States [United States of America] as described in the Constitution, or is it the property of those, who in the race of emigration, shall be the first to reach it?" Barksdale clearly declared for the former and went on to state that Congress, as the trustee, had ultimate responsibility to "administer it for the benefits of all of the people of all of the States—those for whom we hold the trust ... and that in delegating powers to the territorial governments must have due regard to the limits of the Constitution."[8]

Barksdale concluded his address with the following conciliatory remarks:

> I have frankly and freely presented my views and have not withheld those objections which I feel to some amendments incorporated into this bill; and to those who viewing this subject from a different point, find objections to the measure of a different character from those I have presented. I will say, in that kindness and comity which should animate us all, as the sons of a common ancestry and the recipients of a common inheritance, that I seek no triumph over them, and am willing to make as large sacrifices for the peace and common interests of our country as my duty to those who have honored me with their confidence and intrusted to me, in part, their interest here will permit.... I am not insensible to the appeal of those northern men, who refer to the excitement existing among their constituents, and I do not ask them to brave more than every southern man must meet who votes for this bill.

Then, with keen insight, he added the following admonition: "Who does not foresee that if this question is to be thrown as an apple of discord into popular elections, that the next Congress will assemble here with far less ability than we have to make a just and honorable settlement of this controversy."[9]

For an inexperienced congressman delivering his initial address before the House, Barksdale had certainly made an indelible impression on his colleagues. Not only had he won their respect, but he established himself as a forceful spokesman on behalf of the South and its rights under the Constitution. Barksdale would never relinquish this role. Moreover, these recorded remarks are undeniably not the utterances of a fire-eating Southern demagogue intent on destroying the national government as Barksdale has so often been portrayed over the years.

Heeding Barksdale's admonition to address the issue sooner rather than later, the Kansas-Nebraska Act was passed by the House of Representatives on May 30, 1854, despite intense opposition in the North. Politically it destroyed one of the two major national political parties of the time—the Whigs—who had formed back in 1834 in opposition to the "tyranny" of President Andrew Jackson. Northern Whigs voted against this legislation while almost all Southern Whigs voted in favor. Soon Southern Whigs gravitated to the Democratic party, while their northern counterparts joined with other non-slavery/abolitionist groups to form the Republican party. Still others joined the fledgling American party, commonly called the "Know Nothings." As a result, the Democratic party became the sole national party crossing sectional lines. The Kansas-Nebraska Act's "popular sovereignty" clause gave rise to increased immigration into Kansas by rival groups seeking to sway the slavery vote. Their actions precipitated violence, riots, and depredations, bordering on civil war in what became known as "bloody Kansas." Congress struggled to govern the nation against this churning backdrop.[10]

Just before the close of the first session, Barksdale rose to voice his opposition to "squandering the public money" via a general appropriations bill. Barksdale argued "that the Constitution does not confer upon the [Federal] Government the power to commence and carry on a general system of internal improvements." Moreover, this bill added insult to injury in Barksdale's eyes by short-changing the South. When challenged on his interpretation, Barksdale sarcastically replied: "It commences in Maine, extends throughout New England, lingers in the northern and middle states but growing small by degrees and beautifully less as it approaches the South, it grants to the State of Mississippi the enormous sum of $5000. It seems to me this is a system of internal improvements in all its length, breadth, and amplitude." Specifically, he found these improvements were not "national in character" benefitting the country as a whole but were instead local in nature and thus constitutionally fell under the purview of the state governments.[11]

The Second Session of the 33rd Congress commenced on December 4, 1854. Three days later, in keeping with his original agenda, Barksdale introduced a bill "to constitute Columbus, in the state of Mississippi, a port of delivery and for other purposes." This designation would provide federal aid and economic benefit to constituents in his hometown. On February 10, 1855, Barksdale took up Senate Bill 604 which called for renaming the American-built schooner *Henry Plantagenet* as the *A.G. Brown*, after Barksdale's friend and Mississippi senator. During this session Barksdale advocated repeatedly for passage of bills to increase the size of the standing army, to construct new ships, and to increase pay of land registers and receivers.[12]

While many of his proposed bills and amendments were parochial in nature, Barksdale never lost sight of his national responsibilities regarding the public good. For example, on February 18, 1855, he gave vent to his frustration and chided his fellow congressmen for their inaction:

> Notwithstanding the efforts of the chairman of the Committee on Military Affairs to induce the House to do so, the bill to increase the Army has not been acted upon. Our whole western frontier is defenseless, and exposed to the depredations of the Indians. Congress has been called upon by the President to increase the Army, and give the government the means to protect our citizens, but his earnest recommendations have not been heeded. The bill reported by the chairman of the Committee on Naval Affairs, to construct additional sloops of war, so necessary for the protection of our commerce, has not been disposed of. The civil and diplomatic appropriation bill has not been touched even. Very nearly

Contemporary sketch of pre-war Washington City (Library of Congress).

the whole time of the present session has been engrossed with bills of a private nature ... and the public business has been neglected—I liked to have said, shamefully neglected—to legislate upon bills to plunder the treasury.

At last, on the final day of the session, at Barksdale's insistence, the House finally took up and passed Senate Bill No. 555 to increase the compensation of land registers and receivers.[13]

Barksdale repeatedly demonstrated his persistence and bulldog tenacity in pursuing his aims as a congressman. Due in large part to his deep personal sense of responsibility and devotion to duty, his behavior also reflected his single-mindedness of purpose—once he was locked in on a task nothing would stand in his way. For future confirmation of these characteristics, one need look no further than Barksdale's stubborn day-long opposition to the Union army's river crossing at Fredericksburg, or Barksdale's Brigade's "most magnificent charge" at Gettysburg, both executed against overwhelming odds.

Having acquitted himself very well during his first term in office, Barksdale returned to Mississippi in spring of 1855 to campaign for re-election. By then Mississippi's Legislature had redefined the state congressional districts, adding a fifth "to provide a district for the floater." Barksdale was nominated as the Democratic candidate for the 3rd District which included Lowndes County and Columbus. His opponent was Joseph B. Cobb, also from Lowndes County, and a nominee of the American (Know-Nothing) party. At the spring State Convention, the Democrats from Mississippi adopted a platform "boldly denouncing Know-Nothingism" which was right in line with Barksdale's beliefs.

The canvass of the state began in Starkville where William delivered "a telling speech, fearless and strong." Mr. Crusoe of Columbus announced he would reply after supper and delivered a rebuttal that was "severe and caustic." Unfortunately, Crusoe made a critical error in judgment. In an effort to discredit Barksdale, he alluded to the fight several years before between Barksdale and Reuben Davis (who was also in attendance). Anticipating a rousing denunciation of Barksdale by Davis, Crusoe must have been shocked at the result. Davis, writing years later, described the scene:

> instead of renewing ill feeling as intended, it produced the opposite effect. Barksdale and myself had shaken hands in cordial restoration of friendship that very morning. The fact was that the hatchet had long ago been buried by both, and now we had smoked the pipe of peace, and more than renewed all the old bonds of kindliness. As I listened to Crusoe, my soul was stirred to its depths.... The moment Crusoe ceased, many voices began calling for me, and I needed no second call. I rose quickly, and poured out the words that were burning upon my brain. If ever I put my whole strength in a speech, it was that night; and as I left the stand, some of my friends called to me "You can die now Davis, for you have done your best." To this day, it gives me great pleasure to remember that an opportunity was given me to celebrate my reconciliation with my old friend, by an honest effort in his support.[14]

Throughout the ensuing campaign Barksdale continued to attack the American "Know-Nothing" party and what it stood for—and won an "impressive victory" over Cobb. In defeating his American party opponent "at the height of [Cobb's] party's influence," Barksdale played a key role in curbing the spread of the Know-Nothings' nativist principles within Mississippi. By doing so Barksdale helped to ensure the dominance of the Democratic party in his state for the balance of the 1850s.[15]

The First Session of the 34th Congress commenced on December 3, 1855, and will be remembered for three occurrences—an acrimonious, partisan, nine-week ordeal to elect a Speaker of the House, the brutal caning of Massachusetts Senator Charles Sumner in the Senate Chamber by South Carolina Congressman Preston Brooks, and Barksdale's hour-long address concerning the critical nature of the upcoming presidential election of 1856. True to his character, colorful personality, and reputation, Barksdale figured prominently in the first and third, and was erroneously later accused of participating in the second.

The make-up of the new House had changed significantly. Only seven of the 42 northern Democrats who had voted in favor of the Kansas-Nebraska Act were re-elected. As a result, the previous Democratic majority of 84 in the House had now become a minority of 75. To have any chance of organizing the House, the Democrats were forced to ally themselves with 37 Whigs and/or Americans who were pro-slavery. The bitter political polarization arising from the Kansas-Nebraska Act, and the subsequent disagreement over admission of Kansas as a free or slave state, manifested itself from the very beginning of the session. Both sides aggressively attempted to organize the House. The anti-slavery faction united behind Massachusetts Congressman Nathaniel P. Banks as their candidate for Speaker of the House. Banks had been elected to the previous congress as a Democratic/Free Soil party coalition candidate. Following the collapse of the Free Soilers he had joined the Know-Nothing party and was re-elected. (Banks would eventually join the Republican party after the collapse of the Know-Nothings.) An accomplished orator and debater, Banks' background was remarkably similar to Barksdale's.[16]

From the outset Congress struggled through repeatedly deadlocked votes for speakership. Although Banks was clearly the front-runner, he could not garner the required two-thirds majority. Even Barksdale, himself, was nominated on December 11, 1855, on the 46th ballot, but garnered only a single vote from William A. Richardson, Democratic Representative from Illinois. Barksdale steadfastly supported Richardson who ran a consistent second to Banks through most of the voting for Speaker. Anticipating this struggle, the Democratic caucus, in Barksdale's absence, had resolved that each of their member representatives would vote against all motions to adjourn until a Speaker of the House was elected. By January 9, 1856, Barksdale had enough and broke ranks declaring, "For one, I am not willing to risk the rights and interests of my constituents here upon so grave and important a matter ... upon my power of physical exertion. I admit that I am well nigh exhausted, and I advise my political friends now that I shall from this time on vote for motions to adjourn." And he promptly did just that![17]

On January 12th Barksdale led the Southern attack against Banks' nomination as Speaker by proposing the following "interrogatories" and demanding that Banks answer:

1. Was he now a member of the Know-Nothing Party?
2. Was he in favor of abolishing slavery in the District of Columbia and Federal facilities?
3. Did he believe in the equality of the white and black races?
4. Did he intend to promote that equality by legislation?
5. Did he favor the exclusion of "adopted citizens" and Roman Catholics from office?
6. Did he still support the higher tariff as he had done during the previous session of Congress?

As expected, the contentious nature of Barksdale's "inquisition" prompted heated debate. When Missouri Representative Kennett interjected to add whether each candidate believed "in a future state or not," and whether it would be "a free or slave state," the House erupted in laughter. Interpreting Kennett's comments as a personal insult, Barksdale immediately lost his temper, and amidst loud cries of "No! No!" and "Order! Order!"

from those present, retaliated with the following retort: "I would say to the gentleman from Missouri that if he intends by that interrogatory to cast any reflection upon me, either directly or indirectly—I hurl it back with all the scorn, derision, and contempt which its insolence and impudence so justly merits." True to form, several days later, after Barksdale had cooled down—and following an explanation by Mr. Kennett—Barksdale formally and "cheerfully" apologized before all present in the House, "unconditionally withdrawing the harsh language employed against [Kennett]."[18]

Attempts to elect a Speaker dragged on for nine weeks and did not bear fruit until February 2, 1856, after the 133rd ballot! The impasse had finally been broken only because the "plurality resolution" had been passed, whereby the rules for winning were relaxed from a two-thirds majority of the House to a simple majority of a quorum. Nathaniel Banks was finally elected Speaker over South Carolina Congressman William Aitken by a vote of 103 to 100.[19]

Barksdale would literally have the last word regarding Banks' performance as Speaker of the House. On the final day of the 34th Congress a little over a year later, Representative Aitken proposed a resolution of thanks to Speaker Banks "for the able, impartial, and dignified manner" in which he had performed his duties. However, Aitken certainly did not speak for all the Southern representatives. Congressman Fayette McMullin of Virginia commented: "There is much in the conduct of that gentleman which I can approve; but there is much which I am called upon to condemn." Just before the vote was taken, Barksdale stated: "while I am willing to indorse, to the fullest extent, the ability of our presiding officer, I am unwilling to say by my vote that he has acted impartially. I vote 'no.'" Despite Southern opposition, the vote of thanks passed by a count of 119 to 35.[20]

Nor was the rancor over the future admission of Kansas as a slave or free state confined to the House of Representatives. The invective was perhaps even more vehement in the Senate and reached its crescendo when Senator Charles Sumner of Massachusetts rose in the chamber at 1 p.m. on May 19, 1856, to deliver his carefully prepared and thoroughly rehearsed oration titled, "The Crime Against Kansas." Having been thwarted for almost two months in his attempts to gain the floor on this topic, Sumner now had reached a fevered pitch and held nothing back in delivering his 112-page address. In anticipation, the visitor galleries were filled to overflowing, and even the doorways were blocked by bystanders. Sumner had so thoroughly memorized his address that he scarcely had to refer to his manuscript at all. He began with a challenge to his fellow senators: "You are now called to redress a great transgression…. Seldom in the history of nations has such a question been presented." Sumner then elaborated on the crime:

> Against this Territory [Kansas], a Crime has been committed, which is without example in the records of the Past…. It is the *rape* (emphasis added) of a virgin Territory, compelling it to the hateful embrace of Slavery; and it may be clearly traced to a depraved longing for a new slave state, the hideous offspring of such a crime, in the hope of adding to the power of Slavery in the National Government…. FORCE has been openly employed in compelling Kansas to this pollution, and all for the sake of political power.[21]

Before continuing with specifics of his argument and against the advice of colleague, Senator William Seward, Sumner paused to "say something of a general character" against senators Andrew P. Butler of South Carolina and Stephen A. Douglas of Illinois whom he regarded as the ringleaders. What followed was an intensely personal attack and vicious character assassination, particularly regarding Butler, which shocked the sensibilities of most senators present, including Sumner's supporters. Worse, the aged Senator Butler was not present to defend himself; he was convalescing in South Carolina from the effects of a stroke, which had impaired his speech and saliva control. Sumner stigmatized Butler as the "Don Quixote of Slavery." He claimed that, although Butler regarded himself as a "chivalrous knight with sentiments of honor and courage," he had "chosen a mistress to whom he has made his vows, and who although ugly to others is always lovely to him; though polluted in the sight of the world, is chaste in his sight ... the harlot, Slavery." Sumner sneered, "The frenzy of Don Quixote, in behalf of his wench, Dulcinea del Toboso, is all surpassed." The Massachusetts senator simply branded Senator Douglas as "the squire of Slavery, its very Sancho Panza, ready to do all its humiliating offices." Sumner then railed against the Kansas-Nebraska Act which he termed a "swindle" by the South of the North, which word singularly could express "the meanness and wickedness of the cheat." Pacing in anger and frustration across the back of the Senate Chamber, Douglas was overheard to prophesize, "That damn fool will get himself killed by some other damn fool."[22] The oration proved to be so long that the senate adjourned after three hours and Sumner was forced to conclude the next day.

Not content with the provocative and disturbing sexual imagery of the first day's personal attacks which had shocked his listeners into stunned silence, Sumner descended even further into the depths of bad taste the next day. Making caustic references to Butler's handicap of speech, Sumner stated that Butler, "with incoherent phrases," had "discharged the loose expectoration of his speech." Sumner continued to demean Butler: "But the Senator touches nothing which he does not disfigure—with error sometimes of principle, sometimes of fact. He shows an incapacity of accuracy.... He cannot ope[n] his mouth but out flies a blunder." Sumner also ramped up his attack against Douglas, and now included Senator James Mason from Virginia, who, Sumner stated, "represents that other Virginia from which Washington and Jefferson now avert their faces, where human beings are bred as cattle."[23]

Reaction was swift. Sumner had no sooner sat down than Michigan Senator Lewis Cass, Dean of the Senate, pronounced the speech "the most un–American and unpatriotic that ever grated on the ears of the members of this high body." Even staunch Republican senators "regretted the vindictiveness of Sumner's tone." As expected, the South was outraged. A Tennessee Congressman later exclaimed, "Mr. Sumner ought to be knocked down and his face jumped into." It then became a matter of not whether Sumner would be called to account, but who would administer the blow. It fell to Butler's cousin, two-time South Carolina Congressman Preston S. Brooks, to avenge both his family's and his state's honor.[24]

Ironically, Brooks was perhaps best known for his tongue-in-cheek proposal that congressmen be mandated to deposit their firearms in the cloakroom prior to entering the House. His calm, affable demeanor belied a deep hatred of Abolitionists. His strong Southern heritage embraced the Code Duello which stipulated that "to punish an inferior, one used, not a pistol or sword, but a cane or horsewhip." Thus it was that Brooks unsuccessfully stalked Sumner the next day at the Capitol Building. On the following day, May 22, 1856, both the Senate and House adjourned early, the latter before the former. This permitted Brooks and congressmen Henry A. Edmundson of Virginia and Laurence M. Keitt of South Carolina to enter the Senate Chamber as most senators were departing. Brooks had informed both Edmundson and Keitt the previous evening of his plans to attack Sumner, so their presence was not by accident.

Brooks approached the physically superior Sumner who remained hunched over his desk franking copies of his Crime Against Kansas speech. Addressing Sumner in a low voice, Brooks snarled, "I have read your speech twice over carefully. It is a libel on South Carolina, and Mr. Butler who is a relative of mine." Before even finishing this sentence, Brooks struck Sumner on the head with the smaller end of a solid gold-headed, gutta-percha walking stick, stunning the shocked senator. Then in a total frenzy of unrestrained exhilaration, Brooks rained down a series of harder blows with the thick end. In a panicked struggle to escape, Sumner actually pulled the bolts holding his desk right out of the floor. Brooks continued his assault until his cane splintered and the bloodied Sumner began to slump to the floor. Brooks grabbed his victim by the lapels and continued raining down blows on Sumner's head until the cane disintegrated, Brooks salvaging only the gold knob. The vicious attack lasted less than a minute and encompassed about 30 "first-rate" blows.

By this time, the commotion had attracted bystanders who attempted to come to Sumner's aid. While Representative Morgan grabbed the severely injured Sumner, Representative Murray grabbed Brooks by the arm in an attempt to pull him away. At this point Kentucky Senator Crittenden approached, admonishing Brooks for the violence in the Senate Chamber and imploring Brooks, "Don't kill him!" Brooks now recovering his emotions replied, "I did not intend to kill him but I did intend to whip him." Congressman Keitt then rapidly approached down the center aisle while lifting a small cane over his head in a threatening gesture toward Crittenden, bellowing "Let them alone, God damn you!" As Brooks left the chamber with Keitt, Sumner lay unconscious in a heap on the floor, his clothes soaked with blood from two severe head wounds. Suffering significant lingering effects from his injuries, Sumner would not return to full duties in the Senate until December 1859—three and a half years later.[25]

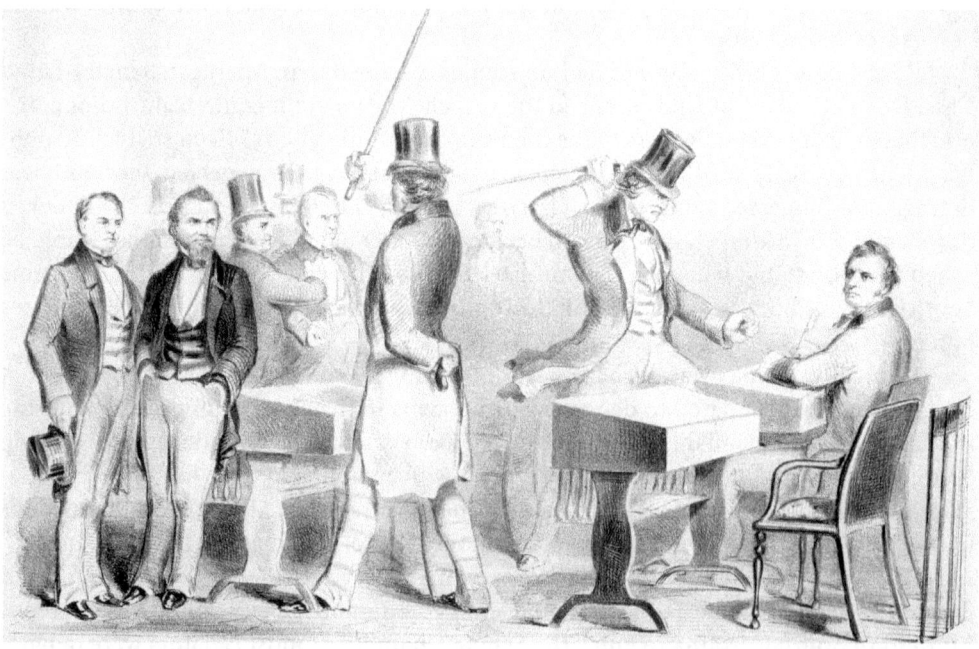

The caning of Charles Sumner by Preston Brooks on the Senate floor, May 22, 1856. Contrary to popular legend, Barksdale did not hold Sumner's friends at bay (Library of Congress).

The attack made major headlines in all key newspapers across the country. It is significant to note that all of these descriptions, including the earliest eyewitness accounts—without exception—identified Laurence M. Keitt, congressman from South Carolina (and nicknamed "Harry Hotspur of the South") as Brooks' accomplice and the only third party who actively participated. For example, the *New York Times* issue on the day after the attack stated: "[Brooks] was accompanied by Mr. Keitt of South Carolina, who attempted to prevent interference by the bystanders, in Senator Sumner's behalf." Further embellishing the story, the *Times* printed another account on the following day by its Washington correspondent who had evidently witnessed the attack: "Those who were nearest to the parties in collision seemed deterred from interference by Mr. Keitt, who with uplifted cane, and oaths upon his lips cried—'Give it to him!' to Brooks, and 'Let them alone!' to the bystanders."[26]

Although the Senate, lacking jurisdiction, took no action against Brooks, there was an extensive investigation in the House which interviewed 27 witnesses. All identified Keitt as a participant—none identified William Barksdale as even being present. Not surprisingly the result was a motion on June 2, 1856, to expel Brooks from the House of Representatives. Although supported by a vote of 121 to 95, this motion did not receive the requisite two-thirds majority. Accordingly, Brooks was not expelled and ultimately received only a $300 fine in Baltimore District Court for his brutal attack. The following day the House voted on a motion to censure both Edmundson and Keitt for their actions. Ultimately Keitt was censured while Edmundson was acquitted. Both South Carolina congressmen Brooks and Keitt responded with defiant speeches and resigned—only to be quickly re-elected.[27]

Thus, by contemporary written accounts, Barksdale played no part in this episode. How then did the myth originate that it was William Barksdale (not Laurence Keitt) who callously prevented bystanders from coming to Sumner's aid? This falsehood has persisted in print with annoying frequency until it has now taken on the appearance of truth. In his scholarly study published in May 1964, Raymond A. Tyson points the finger of "substantial" blame at *Appleton's Cyclopaedia of American Biography*, published years later in 1887. For apparently the first time, *Appleton's* asserted in its biographical sketch of William Barksdale that it was Barksdale

Laurence M. Keitt, Democratic Congressman from North Carolina. Keitt assisted Brooks in his brutal assault on Senator Sumner. He also precipitated the February 6, 1858, brawl on the House floor when Barksdale had his hairpiece forcibly removed (Library of Congress).

"who was present [at Sumner's caning] and prevented interference by bystanders." This untruth was subsequently published in later editions of *Appleton's* as well as distinguished publications including the *Biographical Directory of the American Congress 1774–1927*, issued by the Federal Government, the *Cyclopedia of American Biographies*, and *Mississippi History*. In turn these works have been referenced by many students and writers, including distinguished authors Percy L. Rainwater and John K. Bettersworth. Indeed, this myth is still being repeated today and is present on many websites and in articles on the Internet.

Although the person responsible for the original unintentional error will never be known, this untruth has done a great disservice to the reputation of an honorable man. While Barksdale later commented in Congress that Sumner had received "merited chastisement" for his "infamous libel" and slander, Barksdale's actions throughout his life demonstrated his strong sense of fairness, honor, and conscience. These moral values would certainly not have permitted him to actively assist in the continued beating of a clearly defenseless victim. Tyson concluded: "It is clear however, that this distortion of fact has appeared in a sufficient number of works and over long enough period of time to mar the record of a very gallant man."[28]

On July 23, 1856, Barksdale delivered his most famous speech to the Committee of the Whole on the State of the Union, concerning the approaching presidential election of 1856. Recognizing the bitter division within both houses of Congress, Barksdale, with passion and keen insight, began by boldly asserting his belief that the upcoming presidential election would prove to be the most critical in the nation's history. In his words the outcome would determine the "fate of the Union, the hopes of our country, the hopes of constitutional liberty" and indeed "the success of this our experiment in representative government." Then, in a reference to the issue of slavery during the upcoming campaign, he stated the viewpoint of the South in rather ironic language: "The coming conflict then ... will be for the Constitution, for State-rights, and for everything, in fact, which is dear and sacred to one half of the confederacy [i.e. Union]." Could he have seen into the future, Barksdale might well have added, "and to *all* of the *Confederacy!*"[29]

Duplicating his previous re-election campaign in Mississippi, Barksdale launched into a hostile attack against the Know-Nothing party. He condemned their secret oaths, signs, grips, and passwords as "an influence of evil" and their exclusion of foreigners and Roman Catholics from holding office as a blatant disregard of "the most sacred guarantees of the Constitution." Armed with voting statistics by party affiliation, Barksdale placed blame for electing Nathaniel Banks, a sectionalist Know-Nothing convert to the Black Republicans, as Speaker. He firmly believed they should instead have elected a nationalist candidate who represented the entire country. He then accused Banks of intentionally ostracizing all Southerners from "every committee connected, directly or indirectly, with slavery" by "arbitrary exercise of his power of appointment." Not one to mince words, Barksdale further stated this misdeed was perpetrated "in carrying out the nefarious schemes of the Black Republican Party."[30]

Barksdale moved on to present a detailed breakdown of elected Northern governors and senators by state in support of his claim that "true men of the North ... whose patriotism is broad enough to embrace ... the whole Union who have heretofore stood in the front of the battle in upholding the Constitution ... laws and sustaining rights of every section ... have nearly all been remorselessly stricken down, and disorganizing, agitating, Abolitionists [were] now filling their places." He termed passage of the Kansas-Nebraska

Bill in the House, admitting Kansas into the Union as a free state under the Topeka Territorial Constitution, as an "outrage" with no parallel which "stands alone, a monument to the infamy of those [Republicans] who passed it."[31]

While Barksdale was attacking the Know-Nothing Platform in detail, Massachusetts Senator Wilson challenged him on whether he believed the Constitution was sound on the slavery question. Barksdale replied, "I certainly do, Sir." Then whether Barksdale could find the word "slavery" anywhere within it. Barksdale responded, "I find a synonymous term—*persons held to service.*" Barksdale then added that in contrast to the Know-Nothing Platform, "[under the Constitution] I deny the power of Congress to legislate upon the subject of slavery anywhere, except to protect it. That is my position." Barksdale never deviated from this belief throughout his lifetime.

He concluded the Know-Nothing portion of his address by condemning the political record of Millard Fillmore, presidential nominee for the Know-Nothing party in the upcoming election. Fillmore had previously served as vice president under Zachary Taylor and had ascended to the presidency when Taylor unexpectedly died on July 9, 1850, of an intestinal bacterial infection after serving only 16 months in office. Barksdale reminded the House that Fillmore was "first borne into political life by the anti–Freemasonry excitement which [had] prevailed at the time." Barksdale criticized Filmore for his hypocrisy by stating: "[Fillmore] was opposed to all secret societies ... even such as were not connected with politics. Now he stands before the American people as the candidate of a secret, political, organization." After reviewing Fillmore's anti-slavery political record, the fiery Mississippian finished his attack by declaring: "Mr. Fillmore stood with the enemies of the South during his whole public career, and when he is claimed by his southern friends as true to the South, his votes in Congress, his Executive acts, rise up as a cloud of witnesses to condemn him." By careful analysis of projected electoral votes, Barksdale concluded that Fillmore could not possibly win, even if the final determination was "thrown into the House of Representatives." Barksdale declared the election would be a two-horse race with "the decision of the people ... properly between Buchanan [Democrat] and Fremont [Republican]."[32]

The fiery Mississippian then turned his attack against the Black Republican party and its "unhallowed purposes," as contained in the party platform and speeches by some of its "most distinguished champions." Chief among Republican aims was non-extension of slavery into any territory, admission of Kansas as a free state, construction of a transcontinental railroad together with immediate construction of an accompanying "emigrant road," and "appropriations by Congress for the improvement of rivers, harbors of a national character" under the Constitution. Barksdale viewed all of these as attempts to put down the South and most as contrary to the Constitution and/or infringing on state powers. He reiterated that no Southern state was "legitimately represented in the convention which adopted the platform," condemning the Republican party as purely sectional—not in the least bit national in character.

Republican senators were already on record as supporting immediate abolition of slavery, and Barksdale provided several examples. He quoted Senator Wade of Ohio: "The only salvation of the Union, therefore was to be found in divesting it entirely from the taint of slavery," and Senator Wilson of Massachusetts: "we shall overthrow the slave power of the republic; we shall enthrone freedom; shall abolish slavery in the Territories ... we shall sever the national government from all responsibility for slavery, and all connexion with it."

However Congressman Giddings of Ohio had used the most inflammatory language which Barksdale now quoted: "I look forward to the day when there shall be a servile insurrection in the South; when the black man armed with British bayonets ... shall assert his freedom, and wage a war of extermination against his master; when the torch of the incendiary shall light up the towns and cities of the South, and blot out the last vestige of slavery."

Barksdale then zeroed in on John C. Fremont, Republican nominee for president "who we are told is a southern man by birth and education" but if so "he is a traitor to the land of his birth and home of his childhood." Asserting that Fremont had no political experience nor qualifications to be president, Barksdale declared that, if elected, Fremont's first act would be to appoint a cabinet exclusively from the North. When challenged on this point, Barksdale responded "Because, sir, no Southern man, in my opinion, would dishonor himself by accepting office from him!" Barksdale's sarcastic quip elicited great applause from the galleries. When further challenged that Southern politicians "had not been in the habit of refusing office," Barksdale retorted "They have never been tendered office by a Black Republican administration, and never will be!"

At this point in his address Barksdale digressed to espouse his personal political views and to passionately draw a line in the sand:

> Sir I make no threats, but I tell the gentlemen on the other side of the House, plainly as it is my solemn duty to do so, as the representative of a hundred thousand freemen upon this floor, that we submit to no further aggressions upon us. "There is a point beyond which forbearance ceases to be a virtue" and that for the future "we tread no steps backwards." We are done, gentlemen, with compromises. All that have been made you forced upon us; and while we have observed them in good faith, you have shamelessly disregarded and trampled them under foot. I hold up before you the Constitution as it came from the hands of its immortal authors, northern and southern men—itself a compromise; we claim our rights under that and we intend to have them.

Returning to the upcoming presidential election, Barksdale switched gears to extol the virtues of the sole remaining national party—the Democratic party—which had "ever been true to the rights and interests of every section of the confederacy [Union]." Once again via the vote counts by party affiliation he demonstrated that the Democrats had passed the Fugitive Slave Law and Kansas-Nebraska Act. Furthermore, Barksdale emphasized that "in denouncing the agitation of the slavery question," those resolutions had been adopted at a National Convention where "every State in the Union was represented." He praised the political record of his party's Presidential nominee, James Buchanan of Pennsylvania, and contrasted this candidate's views with those of Fillmore and Fremont. Mr. Buchanan, Barksdale continued, "is a statesman of enlarged and elevated principles which ... will secure the rights of all and promote the onward progress and permanent prosperity of the whole people of the Republic."

Barksdale then eloquently concluded his address with strong military imagery and a stern admonition:

> I for one am proud of the leader [the Democrats] have chosen; and I have every confidence that the banner which he bears in this great conflict, upon which is inscribed in gilded capitals, State Rights, State Sovereignty, State remedies, and Civil and religious Liberty, will proudly float in triumph. But if in this I am mistaken, if these eternal principles of representative liberty and human progress are to be repudiated, if that banner is to sink in defeat, with it the hopes of the country will go down forever.

This speech was so well received and regarded that Barksdale was asked to repeat it at several key political gatherings, including a Democratic mass assembly held in Baltimore on August 18, 1856.[33]

Despite the bitter division within Congress over slavery, the House continued to function between oratorical confrontations. Barksdale continued to push on with his personal agenda by introducing bills for construction of Southern railroads (e.g. Louisville to Macon), for economic relief for his constituents (e.g. settlers and cultivators on public lands), and to safeguard the public purse (e.g. soliciting cost and construction information regarding federal building expansions). He repeatedly questioned the need and cost for government publications. These lulls even gave occasion for some humorous episodes. For example, when Representative Smith introduced a bill to prevent the introduction of "foreign criminals, paupers, lunatics, idiots, insane and blind persons" into the United States, it was Barksdale who immediately objected. Although his reasons are not recorded, it can be safely concluded that this bill contravened his personal sense of fairness. Subsequently Barksdale voted in favor of a more limited bill to restrict entry of "foreign paupers and criminals."[34]

Throughout his time in Congress Barksdale kept in very close contact with Jefferson Davis who was Secretary of War under President Franklin Pierce (1853–1856). They constantly communicated and sought opinion and advice from each other—so much so that Barksdale was sometimes questioned in the House of Representatives as to whether his positions and requests were his own or those of the Secretary of War. Davis was re-elected to the Senate in 1857 and served until January 21, 1861, when he resigned upon Mississippi's secession from the Union. Davis continued his close friendship with Barksdale throughout his senate term.

Despite their best intentions to govern in a civil manner in the House, inevitably the discussion kept returning to the volatile issue of slavery. Thus it was on December 15, 1856, near the end of the Third Session of the 34th Congress, that Representative Etheridge of Tennessee proposed the following incendiary resolution:

> Resolved, that this House of Representatives regard all suggestions and propositions of every kind, by whomsoever made, for a revival of the African slave trade, as shocking to the moral sentiment of the enlightened portion of mankind; and that any action on the part of Congress conniving at or legalizing that horrid and inhuman traffic, would justly subject the Government and citizens of the United States to the reproach and excoriation of all civilized and Christian people throughout the world.

Barksdale quickly responded "I am not in favor of reopening the African slave trade—I do not believe that any gentleman on this side of the House is. [cries of 'Order!' Order1'] But I regard the resolution of the gentleman from Tennessee as ill-timed [renewed cries of 'Order!'] out of place, thrown into the House as a firebrand, [loud cries of 'Order!' 'Order!' and great confusion] and for the accomplishment of a party purpose. I therefore vote 'No.'" Over Barksdale's vociferous objections the resolution was passed by a vote of 152 to 57.[35]

To date, in contrast to the Senate Chamber, physical violence over slavery had been avoided within the House of Representatives. Unfortunately, peace would not prevail during the upcoming sessions of the 35th Congress. True to form, fiery Congressman Barksdale would feature prominently in these altercations.

Six

Epithets, Fisticuffs and the Downward Spiral to Secession

During the next three-and-a-half years Congress vainly attempted to govern the nation efficiently. Barksdale endeavored to advance his agenda for improved conditions in Mississippi and the South, and for the nation as a whole. However, these best intentions were quickly sidetracked by "the elephant in the room"—namely, slavery! The ever-increasing vitriol of the opposing factions escalated into name calling, heated debate and shouting, and eventually erupted into physical assaults on the House floor. Congressmen, including Barksdale, even brandished weapons to make their political points. Throughout this turbulent period Barksdale resolutely stood his ground and gave as good as he got. This political struggle would finally end with the secession of his home state and the resignation of the Mississippi delegation from the House of Representatives on January 11, 1861.

The summer of 1856 had been a memorable one for the Mississippian. Barksdale had delivered his classic oration on the upcoming presidential election that brought him further national fame and recognition. Moreover, he experienced the birth of his second son and namesake, William—affectionately called Willie. The congressman had remained in Washington when Willie was born. However, the jubilant father enjoyed a grand reunion with his family when he returned to Columbus at the conclusion of the Second Session of the 34th Congress on August 30th. He returned to Mississippi to campaign for re-election—a much easier task than anticipated.

To Barksdale's delight and immense relief (as he had predicted and hoped for) James Buchanan was elected as the fifteenth President of the United States, receiving a majority of the electoral college but not the popular vote.

Barksdale actually ran unopposed in both the 1857 and 1859 congressional elections. Lack of an opponent reflected his popularity with his constituents in Mississippi's 3rd District. They appreciated his repeated efforts on their behalf and supported his positions on national issues—such as the Kansas-Nebraska Act and slavery. Barksdale also garnered support through his practice of frequently sending public documents and copies of key political speeches (including his own) from Washington to newspapers back in Mississippi for the edification of his constituents and all Mississippians. When Congress was not in session, onlookers often observed Barksdale "mingling with his constituents" and discussing political topics of interest. Although less experienced than many congressmen, by 1857 Barksdale exhibited keen political acumen. The Jackson (MS) *Mississippian* expressed voter sentiment toward Barksdale as follows:

Six—Epithets, Fisticuffs and the Downward Spiral to Secession 57

William Barksdale has shown himself worthy of the trust. Again he pledges himself to return it to you.... He is a man who is willing, in the language of his peers, to "work for you, to speak for you and if need be to fight for you." And though Mr. Barksdale has no opposition, let him have your cordial support so that his return to Congress will possess all the moral force and power of a full sanction and endorsement on your part of his bold and manly Southern rights principles.[1]

Although successful, Barksdale's bid for re-election in 1857 was not without controversy due to his fiery temper. Following the election, Barksdale angrily denounced former Mexican War general and Columbus resident, Thomas Blewett, in terms of "opprobrious language." Learning of this insult, in accordance with the Southern Code Duello, General Blewett promptly challenged Barksdale to a duel. Barksdale just as promptly accepted. They agreed the weapons would be rifles, followed by bowie knives if necessary, at a location appropriately named Dueler's Hill across the Alabama state line. However, at the appointed time the Rev. James Adair Lyon, a Presbyterian Minister, interceded at the behest of Blewett's wife, who feared for her husband's life. Lyon's persuasive words avoided actual bloodshed and Barksdale and Blewett departed Dueler's Hill with their differences resolved and their honor intact.

Unfortunately, the political consequences for Barksdale did not end there. In accepting Blewett's challenge, Barksdale had violated state law which had banned dueling within Mississippi back in 1832. State law further stipulated that a person participating in a duel could not hold nor be elected to political office. Furthermore, any votes garnered by such an individual would be considered invalid. To preserve his political career, Barksdale was forced to sheepishly request amnesty for his rash actions. Fortunately, formal amnesty was later granted—but not until November 1858.[2]

Prior to the opening of the 35th Congress on December 7, 1857, the families of Mississippi senators Jefferson Davis and Albert Gallatin Brown, and congressmen William Barksdale and Otho R. Singleton, journeyed by train to Washington City, passing through Louisville, Kentucky, on December 1st. The journey was especially arduous for Narcissa with a baby and a lad of seven in tow. A female contemporary who travelled under similar circumstances elaborated on the hardships of the trip:

Going to Washington in those days was a very different affair.... The crude railroading, the uncomfortable, barren, low berthed sleeping cars can never be forgotten. The road-beds were rough and the rolling-stock worse ... made travelling a question of physical endurance.... All trains were late, overcrowded and uncomfortable ... one suffered incessantly with either fatigue, [or] terror on account of the tortuous heights and crooked track, or suffocation from the tunnels and vile air of the cars. Eating stations were few and far between, and the improvident who had no luncheon provided had to endure the pangs of hunger.[3]

Such was Narcissa's strong desire to be with her husband that she endured this ordeal several times during William's time in Congress. Doubtless, she also took advantage of these sojourns in Washington to visit with her best friend, Alcinda Janney, in nearby Leesburg, Virginia.

Like most prominent Southern politicians in Congress, Barksdale resided at Brown's Hotel, characterized by its grandiose white marble front and located on the northeast corner of Pennsylvania Avenue and Sixth Street NW. In her 1941 landmark work, *Reveille in Washington*, Margaret Leech characterized Washington's hotels and their importance in the 1850s and 1860s this way:

The[se] large, ugly buildings were the chief attractions of the Avenue enlivening its dullness with their uniformed attendants, their ranks of hacks, and the bustle of arriving and departing guests. When

Congress was in session, their halls and parlors, dining-rooms and bars were crowded. The din was frightful, the prices were high, and the clerks were haughty and disobliging; but to see and to be seen to establish contact with the political personages of the day and feel the pulse of Government, it was necessary to go to the hotels.

Brown's Hotel's was famous for the singing of "The Star Spangled Banner" for the first time in 1814, President John Tyler taking the oath of office here in 1841 (after the sudden death of his predecessor William Henry Harrison), and Abraham Lincoln's residence here while a congressman in 1847. The wife of Congressman John A. Logan of Illinois lent a Northern perspective by her impressions of the scene at Brown's Hotel:

> This city was then dominated by the aristocratic slave-holders of the South, who looked upon the North and West as "mudsills and drudges" quite unworthy of much consideration; and far too often a swaggering manner and a retinue of colored slaves gave a man a prestige over others of scholarly attainments, simple habits, and no attendants. The hotel was quite full of the most pronounced of the aristocratic type who were then threatening disunion ... sooner or later. Daily during the dinner hour, discussions were heated and often quite boisterous. Sometimes it seemed that a collision was imminent at the table, ladies frequently appearing with secession cockades, which gave encouragement to the advocates of secession. At first I used to listen to these discussions in mortal terror, and sometimes was almost persuaded that the boasted prowess of the Southern men was a reality. I often wondered upon what they fed that they should be so boastful.

This stereotype of the aristocratic, boastful, slaveholding Southern politician would persist in the North—the Northern press reporting on General Barksdale's death at Gettysburg six years later would refer to him as that "haughty" rebel.[4]

Away from Brown's Hotel, William and Narcissa frequently attended elegant receptions and formal dinners, still very common in 1850s Washington society despite the troublesome overtones in the capital. One such pleasant Southern gathering was hosted by Congressman Roger A. Pryor (editor of the Richmond *Enquirer*) and his wife at their home in Virginia and was described by her as follows: "These suppers were very conversational and one did not mind their being so light. There would be punch and sandwiches at eleven. Such were the pleasant happenings that filled our days—clouded now by the perils which we could not ignore after the warnings to which we listened at the Capitol. We were conscious of this always in our round of visits, receptions, dinners, and balls, with the light persiflage and compliments still in our ears." Despite their best efforts at frivolity and enjoyment, it was impossible to completely escape from the threatening political undercurrents. Mrs. Pryor continued: "But when late evening came, the golden hour of our reunion in the library on the first floor of our home was marked by graver talk. There would assemble R.M.T. Hunter, Musco Garnett, Porcher Miles, L.Q.C. Lamar, Boyce, Barksdale of Mississippi, Keitt of South Carolina, with perhaps some visitors from the South."[5]

When the 35th Congress resumed, Barksdale was joined in the House by his good friend and former opponent Reuben Davis who represented Mississippi's 2nd Congressional District. Davis later recalled: "I was soon comfortably established at Brown's, then the favorite hotel for Southerners, and soon received calls from numerous Mississippians resident there. My friend, William Barksdale, came at once, announcing his intention of taking charge of me until I got fairly in harness, and in a few days I began to feel as if I had lived there always." Davis was bitterly disappointed at being named to the Committee for Post Offices and Post-Roads. Once again it was Barksdale who came to his aid. "In conversation with [Barksdale] I discovered that I was wrong in supposing I had been placed

Six—Epithets, Fisticuffs and the Downward Spiral to Secession

upon an unimportant committee.... Instead of refusing to serve, as I had fully intended, I was glad to let matters alone."[6]

During organization of the House, Barksdale was appointed to the Standing Committee on Foreign Affairs together with newly-elected Democratic Congressman Daniel E. Sickles of New York. The record does not indicate whether they were friends or merely acquaintances. However their disparate characters and backgrounds—scoundrel Sickles from the North and moralist Barksdale from the South—would suggest the latter. Although their appointments are listed side by side in the Congressional Globe, their future destiny would be as mortal enemies. Years later at Gettysburg, Union Major General Dan Sickles would face off against Confederate Brigadier General William Barksdale at the Peach Orchard. Sickles would lose his right leg—Barksdale would lose his life.

With characteristic persistence and single-mindedness Barksdale continued to push for legislation to improve conditions in Mississippi and the South. On January 4, 1858, he introduced a bill to grant lands to the states of Louisiana and Mississippi for construction of the New Orleans, Jackson, and Great Northern Railroad. He then introduced a bill to establish a federal mail route from Grenada, Mississippi, to Macon, Georgia, but was thwarted by an objection when he attempted to introduce another similar bill. Barksdale continued to support establishment and improvement of mail routes and post-roads within Mississippi throughout his tenure in Washington.[7]

Unfortunately, the "old chestnut" issue regarding the admission of Kansas, as a free or slave state, returned with a vengeance to dominate Washington politics right up until the secession of Southern states in early 1861. Although the House had passed (by a mere two votes) a Kansas Admission Bill as a free state under the Topeka Constitution back on July 2, 1855, the Senate had held it in committee. On July 8, 1855, Senator Stephen Douglas tabled a bill countering the Topeka Constitution under the "popular sovereignty" terms of the Kansas-Nebraska Act. The final decision was thrown back to the populace of Kansas Territory. This move triggered resubmission of the Topeka Constitution followed by three more—the pro-slavery Lecompton Constitution in 1857, the free-state Leavenworth Constitution in 1858, and finally the free-state Wyandotte Constitution in 1859 that ultimately prevailed in Washington on January 29, 1861. Only then was Kansas formally admitted as a free state after years of bitter political fighting in Congress.[8]

Back on December 18, 1857, the Lecompton Constitution was brought forth in the Senate for the first time and it inaugurated an even more bitter conflict within Congress. The war of words over slavery would soon escalate into physical violence in the House. On February 1, 1858, President Buchanan sent a copy of the Lecompton Constitution to the House, together with a message endorsing it. The President conscientiously advocated immediate admission of Kansas under it in order to dissipate "The dark and ominous clouds now pending over the Union" which, with further delay, "would become darker and more ominous than ever threatened the Constitution and the Union." This message threw the House "into great disorder" and significantly upped the ante for their approval.

During the night session on February 5, 1858, the intense atmosphere within the House began to take a toll on the exhausted opponents. An eyewitness recorded the scene: "It was now half-past twelve o'clock; the sofas were occupied by fatigued Congressmen while others slept in their seats. The proceedings became exceedingly dull, one-third of the members being asleep, or nodding at their desks; a few more were smoking cigars, while others were going to or returning from the restaurant, or 'hole in the wall'—a private drinking place." However, this was but the calm before the storm. Shortly thereafter the "most infamous floor brawl" and the "first free fight" on the floor of the House of Representatives suddenly erupted—not surprisingly, Barksdale was in the thick of it!

Around 2 a.m. on Saturday February 6, 1858, discussion continued as to whether this Lecompton matter should be referred to the Democratic Committee on Territories or a select committee of 15. The House was suddenly "thrown into the most violent excitement, and a fearful scene of confusion was presented." Representative Galusha Grow of Pennsylvania had casually left the Republican side of the House chamber to visit on the Democratic side in front of the Speaker's rostrum. Just at this point John A. Quitman of Mississippi requested to make a motion to which Grow objected. Keitt angrily responded, "If you are going to object, return to your side of the House," to which Grow replied: "This is a free hall and everybody has a right to be where he pleases." Whereupon Keitt attempted to seize Grow by the throat while exclaiming "Sir, you are a damned Black Republican puppy!" Grow angrily responded "Never mind what I am, no negro-driver shall crack his whip over me" and knocked Keitt's hand away. Grow then struck Keitt a "severe blow" knocking him to the floor. (Keitt later maintained that he merely stumbled while avoiding the blow.) By now "all of the sleepers were awakened to the combat."[9]

Instinctively Reuben Davis and Barksdale sprang forward in an attempt to separate

Congressional Brawl in the House of Representatives on February 6, 1858. Barksdale is visible in the lower left corner. *Frank Leslie's Illustrated Newspaper*, February 20, 1858 (Library of Congress).

the two adversaries. Davis succeeded in restraining Keitt while Barksdale attempted to usher Grow out of harm's way. Despite Barksdale's noble intention as peacemaker, he was soon drawn into the imbroglio which rapidly escalated on its own. The New Orleans *Picayune* reported what immediately followed:

> By this time quite a number of gentlemen (among whom were Barksdale of Mississippi, Craig of North Carolina, and others) rushed forward, some probably for the purpose of getting a better sight of "the ring," and others to separate the contestants. This all occurred on the Democratic side of the chamber; but when the Republicans saw so many rushing toward Grow they thought he was to be badly handled, and quick as thought started *en masse* for the scene of the conflict. Potter, of Wisconsin, a stout fellow with a fist like an ox, was foremost, and bounded into the fray like a maddened tiger. Just then Barksdale had hold of Grow, with a view of leading him out of the *melee*. Potter, mistaking his [Barksdale's] purpose, planted a "sockdolager" between Barksdale's eyes, which only had the effect of arousing his grit. Looking around, the first man he saw was Elihu Washburne, of Illinois. Supposing it was he who struck him, Barksdale sprang gallantly at him, and they exchanged a handsome little match in less than no time. Potter meantime was striking right and left at Barksdale and anybody else. Cadwallader Washburne [of Wisconsin] also came to the rescue of his brother and attacked Barksdale, who defended himself with coolness, vigor, and skill, saving his face from bruise or scratch.[10]

At this juncture the Speaker and Sergeant-at-Arms frantically attempted to restore order—but to no avail. Much to his own embarrassment, it was Barksdale who inadvertently put a comical end to the melee. As Cadwallader Washburne attempted to assist his brother who was engaged with Barksdale, he hit William a glancing blow on the forehead which knocked his hairpiece to the floor. This no doubt shocked the onlookers who were

"Scalping" of William Barksdale, February 6, 1858. Barksdale's hairpiece is knocked off by a punch thrown by Congressman Cadwallader Washburne of Wisconsin, while his brother, Elihu B. Washburne of Illinois, looks on in shock. This comical episode brought the nasty altercation to a conclusion by sustained laughter (*The Saturday Evening Post*).

not aware that Barksdale wore a wig to cover his balding head. However, when Barksdale, in his haste to replace it, repositioned it "with the wrong side foremost" (front to back) the hilarious spectacle of his undignified appearance was too much to bear. The stunned onlookers began to erupt in uncontrollable laughter. The absurdity of Barksdale's appearance effectively put an end to the fracas. The former combatants, some of whom were meeting face-to-face for the first time, summarily shook hands and returned to their seats.

Surprisingly, the session continued until 6:30 a.m. next morning with the House agreeing to defer the vote until Monday, when it was finally agreed that Buchanan's message would be referred to the committee of 15 under the chairmanship of Galusha Grow. That same day, after reflecting over the weekend, both Keitt and Grow offered contrite formal apologies to the House for their actions. Keitt admitted to being the "aggressor" and acknowledged that "whatever responsibility attaches to the act properly belongs to me alone." He offered his "profound regret" stating that "personal collisions are always unpleasant, seldom excusable, rarely justified—never in a legislative body." Grow responded that "no man can regret more than I do that there should have been any occasion for a violation of [the order and decorum of the House]."[11]

This undignified, ugly fiasco filled editorials in all the major newspapers of the day—even as far afield as London, England. Most were highly critical of the actions of the participants. One such sarcastic editorial in the Baltimore *Sun* was particularly critical of Barksdale. Already smarting from the embarrassment surrounding loss of his hairpiece and believing Potter to be the secret author of this disparaging article, Barksdale's fragile ego could bear no more. He snapped and summarily challenged Potter to a duel through his friend and second, Laurence Keitt. Although Barksdale suggested a location outside

Left: Republican Congressman John F. Potter of Wisconsin, nicknamed "Bowie Knife Potter," claimed he had "grabbed" Barksdale's hairpiece. Barksdale later forgave and befriended his former adversary. Julian Vannerson photo in McClee's Gallery of the 35th Congress, 1859. *Right:* Republican Congressman Elihu B. Washburne of Illinois. Barksdale vigorously engaged him in a "handsome little match." Julian Vannerson photo in McClee's Gallery of the 35th Congress, 1859 (Library of Congress).

Washington to avoid legal penalties, Potter would only agree to meet in a closed room inside the city. Since this was contrary to the Code Duello, Barksdale was forced to send his second to pursue and clarify the challenge. Reuben Davis acting on his friend's behalf investigated the matter. In the end Potter denied authoring the piece and agreed to publicly acknowledge he had no involvement whatsoever with the Baltimore *Sun*. This was satisfactory to Barksdale who then withdrew his demand for satisfaction.[12]

The Barksdale-Potter story did not end here. For reasons of personal safety on the dangerous streets within Washington, congressmen were obliged to leave the Capitol at night in pairs. One evening, several weeks later, Barksdale overheard Potter ask a fellow congressman to accompany him so Potter could go home for dinner. When the other fellow declined due to pressing duties, in characteristic fashion, Barksdale stepped forward and, offering his hand in friendship, agreed to accompany Potter who politely accepted. From that day forward, once again, a close friendship existed between Barksdale and another of his former antagonists.[13]

About one month later on March 29, 1858, reprising his role as ardent spokesman for Southern rights, Barksdale delivered his third major hour-long address in the House—this time concerning admission of Kansas as a slave state. While not his greatest speech, his remarks unequivocally spelled out his unqualified support for the Southern institution of slavery and identified for the record the Republican party's agenda against it. He attempted to accomplish the latter by first exposing Republican arguments against the Lecompton Constitution on the basis that this measure was not representative of the populace and therefore not "republican" in nature—a position Barksdale vehemently believed was a mere sham! In Barksdale's words, Republicans claimed "there ought to have been an enabling act and the Territorial Legislature had no right to call this convention," against which he argued that previously admitted states required no specific enabling act. Moreover, the Kansas-Nebraska Act served that purpose in this case. To the charge that the Lecompton Constitution was not "republican in nature," Barksdale argued there could be no disputing the fact that it was. He stated, "It is founded on the will of the people. Under its provisions the Governor is elected by the people; the Legislature is elected by the people; even the judiciary arte elected by the people." He continued: "Then sir I have endeavored to answer the only questions Congress ought to ask in the admission of new states; first that it is the will of the people; and next that the constitution which they present is republican in form."

Congressman Cadwallader C. Washburne of Wisconsin, who delivered the blow that separated Barksdale from his hairpiece. Julian Vannerson photo in McClee's Gallery of the 35th Congress, 1859 (Library of Congress).

Barksdale then cut to the chase— "What, then, is the ground of the opposition to the admission of Kansas? *The true ground, sir, disguise it as gentlemen may, is that its constitution recognizes slavery"* (emphasis added). Barksdale then pointedly asked nearby Republicans whether "if all the people of Kansas desired to have a pro-slavery constitution" would they vote for her admission to the Union? Giddings responded, "I will never vote to compel Ohio to associate with another slave state, if I can prevent it." Representative John Bingham, also from Ohio, replied, "Certainly not." Barksdale then asked Giddings if he spoke on behalf of the Republican party? to which Giddings quipped that he spoke on behalf of the "thinking, reflecting, humane portion of mankind generally," which elicited laughter from the House. Barksdale sarcastically responded "Black Republican mankind you mean. I have no doubt of it," eliciting more laughter.

Barksdale then proceeded to quote extensively from an inflammatory speech previously delivered on the floor of the Senate by William Seward of New York:

> Free labor has at last apprehended its rights, its interests, its power and destiny, and is organizing itself to assume the government of the Republic. It will henceforth meet you boldly and resolutely here; it will meet you everywhere, in the territories or out of them, wherever you may go to extend slavery.... The interest of the white race demands the ultimate emancipation of all men. Whether that consummation shall be allowed to take effect with needful and wise precautions against sudden change and disaster, or be hurried on by violence, is all that remains for you to decide.

Barksdale interpreted "this formal and well-considered proclamation by the leader of the Black Republican party in the Senate, reiterated by chiefs and subalterns on this floor" as "not only a declaration that no more slave states will be admitted into the Union, but that slavery must yield even in the fifteen slave states where it exists."

Congressman Barksdale concluded with an eloquent but bold admonition:

> Mr. Chairman, it is time the North and South understood each other. If this is the position of the North, we of the South desire to know it. If no more slave states are to be admitted into the Union, our people should be informed of your determination.... I too have counted the cost of this Union and I think I understand something of its value. Sir, this Union was made by slaveholders. The battles of the revolution were fought by slaveholders. A slaveholder headed your armies, and led them on to victory. Slaveholders laid deep and broad the foundations of this great Republic. The Declaration of Independence was published to the world in behalf of thirteen colonies—all of them slaveholding. The Union which they afterwards formed was a Union of equality [equal states], equal rights, and of equal privileges. If you intend to deprive the Southern States of their rights it is well for us that you have so frankly and unreservedly avowed your purpose. In every period of our history, when dangers impended over us, the South has been true and loyal to the Union. When, Sir, in the hour of danger, has she ever faltered? The bones of her sons are bleaching upon the very soil from which her people are excluded, and the achievements of her heroes adorn the brightest pages of your history. But, Sir, that same patriotic devotion which inspired them to bare their breasts, and shed their blood for our Union when it was a glorious Union of equals, will arouse their hearts and nerve their arms to resist its aggressions upon their rights and honor.[14]

By comparison Session II of the 35th Congress was much less chaotic and permitted Barksdale to pursue matters of personal interest that reflected his core values. Regarding the Mobile and Ohio Railroad, Barksdale voiced his support in the House for a bill to formally uphold the earlier federal transfer of lands to Mississippi and Alabama to protect the company and Mississippi's State government against a civil lawsuit by trespassers.

Barksdale maintained his sense of fairness and continued to exhibit the courage of his convictions. In response to an objection by Representative Garnett of Virginia to permitting Representative Morris to present Pennsylvania tariff resolutions, Barksdale intervened on Morris' behalf: "I desire to say that when a State through its legislature, desires to be heard in Congress, that request ought to be granted. I am opposed to the object of these resolutions; but it strikes me they ought to be read, and I hope my friend from Virginia will withdraw his objection." His sense of fair play in this instance is all the more impressive given the fact that Barksdale repeatedly and aggressively argued against higher tariffs advocated by the North to protect its commercial and manufactured goods since they would harm the South's agrarian economy.[15]

Similarly, Barksdale condemned the operational costs of the national postal system which were overwhelmingly skewed to the Northern states and which significantly drained the public treasury. In Barksdale's words: "the General Government does comparatively nothing for Mississippi except to furnish her mail facilities.... It was the contemplation of the framers of the Constitution that the Post Office should sustain itself, and for years it did sustain itself until the present act was passed for the benefit of the commercial and manufacturing classes to the detriment of the agricultural." Continuing the argument several days later, Barksdale argued against an amendment to a postal act:

> If this amendment be adopted, the routes which were established by Congress at its last session, and the routes which are to be established by Congress at its present session, cannot be put into operation. The constituents of the gentleman from New York may have as many mail facilities as they desire. Perhaps the constituents of the gentlemen from Virginia have all the mail facilities they want. But sir, my constituents have not adequate mail facilities. At the last session of Congress several new routes were established for their benefit, and I desire that they should be put into operation. It is important that they should be put into operation.[16]

Nor were his principles of fairness reserved only for his state. Barksdale argued fervently for a $4200 payment to the widow of Daniel S. McCauley, who had died while in office, for his judicial services rendered as the consul general to Egypt.[17]

William's involvement with the Committee on Foreign Affairs came at a very interesting time. The Louisiana Purchase of 1803 had been followed by the acquisition of West and East Florida from Spain in 1819–1821. Many in the United States felt that the purchase of Cuba should follow in a natural progression. Indeed, back in 1848 President Polk had instructed then Secretary of State, James Buchanan, to offer $100,000,000 to Spain in exchange for Cuba. The proposed purchase, or possible annexation of Cuba by the United States, was opposed by both England and France. During his presidency Buchanan renewed these efforts to acquire Cuba. Southern Democrats heartily supported this effort since slavery existed in Cuba, while Republicans naturally were opposed. Barksdale, himself a slaveholder, was eager to extend slavery into Latin America and felt the South was justified in this cause.

Barksdale also coveted Nicaragua as he thought slave labor would be very profitable there. He believed that if the North restricted the spread of slavery within the United States, expansion of the institution into Latin America would be necessary for the South to avoid being "politically bound hand and foot in Congress." Also during this time, William Walker of Tennessee led a "filibuster" of 300 men into Nicaragua and briefly seized power with the assistance of one of two warring factions there. U.S. Naval forces at Punta Arena subsequently arrested Walker and his men and returned them to America. In righteous indignation, Barksdale introduced a resolution in the House to censure Commodore Paulding for his conduct, which Barksdale claimed "was without authority of law, and meets the condemnation of this House." Personally, Barksdale believed Paulding deserved to be court-martialed and his epaulets ripped from his shoulders. The majority in the House disagreed, however, and the House formally thanked Paulding for his service.[18]

Shortly before the end of the final session of the 35th Congress, Barksdale was compelled to state his views regarding reopening of the African slave trade. The foreign importation of slaves had been banned by the federal government back in 1807. Thus Mississippi and other deep southern states were obliged to purchase slaves from the border states at higher prices. It is not difficult to understand why plantation owners would advocate reopening of the African slave trade. Surprisingly, Barksdale was opposed and said so—"I, sir, am not prepared to advocate the reopening of the slave trade...." He also vehemently opposed contemporary Northern attempts to legally brand traffickers in slaves as "pirates." By logical extension Barksdale asserted: "if the slave trade be now a crime against morality and religion, it always was, and the pirates you would hang today, stand on the same footing as my forefathers who employed and encouraged [the slavers'] predecessors.... I will never consent ... to allow this stigma to remain which degrades and puts a slur upon the people of [Mississippi]."[19]

Having been re-elected by the voters of Mississippi's 3rd Congressional District for the third consecutive term (his fourth), Barksdale returned to Washington for the opening of the 36th Congress on December 5, 1859. Thirteen months later, the vitriolic rhetoric, fierce partisanship, and complete inability to reach any hint of compromise would run their exhaustive course. Barksdale and the Mississippi delegation would officially depart the House for the last time in accordance with the mandate from their state. In a debilitating atmosphere of déjà-vu which was not lost on the participants the House again descended into a seemingly endless struggle to elect a Speaker. Barksdale was nominated as one of many candidates, garnering 15 votes (including those of the four other Mississippi representatives) on the fourteenth ballot, 10 votes on the fifteenth, five votes on the sixteenth, and only one vote on the twenty-first attempt to elect a Speaker. It is interesting to note that William did not vote for himself in keeping with the custom of the day.

Occasionally the injection of humor dissipated the tension in the House. At one point, Representative Thomas Corwin of Ohio directed the following comment toward Barksdale who had earlier suggested that the three other political parties unite against the Republicans to elect a Speaker—"The gentleman from Mississippi wants to get rid of this cumbrous business, and I will say to him that the only way to accomplish it is by voting; and I say further to him that if he should be elected [as Speaker], I will pledge him that the State of Ohio will not dissolve the Union on that account." Surprisingly, in a gesture of compromise, on the sixteenth attempt both Barksdale and John J. McRae of Mississippi voted for Congressman William B. Maclay of New York, who was a Northern Democrat. It was not until the forty-fourth ballot on February 1, 1860, eight weeks into the session, that the deadlock was broken with the election of New Jersey representative William Pennington as Speaker. A compromise Republican candidate, Pennington, garnered the minimum 117 votes out of the 233 cast to gain a simple majority by a single vote.[20]

Before this breakthrough Barksdale had risen in the House on January 23, 1860, to deliver an hour-long address regarding slavery and peaceable secession. This speech was the most revealing of his four major addresses in Congress with respect to his political beliefs and final position on secession that had evolved over his tenure in Congress. His oration, like those given by several other representatives, was meant to tackle the impasse surrounding election of a Speaker. However Barksdale used the opportunity to vigorously defend slavery, to blame the abolitionist Republicans for inciting John Brown's

Six—Epithets, Fisticuffs and the Downward Spiral to Secession

abortive October 1859 raid on Harpers Ferry arsenal to arm the slaves, and to espouse his own increasingly intransigent views regarding states' rights and secession. Most importantly Barksdale symbolically drew his final line in the sand from which there would be, for him, no turning back—the election of a Black Republican president.

The first part of this speech had a familiar ring. Barksdale stated his contempt for the Black Republican party and reiterated that the disagreement over slavery was the true cause for failure to elect a Speaker. Barksdale minced no words:

> Disguise it, as gentlemen on the other side of this House may attempt to do so, it is the agitation of the slavery question which has caused its non-organization, suspended the business of the country, fired the passions of the people, and imperiled the existence of the Union itself. Rather than the candidate of the Black Republican party should be elected, rather than my State and my constituents should be dishonored by the elevation to that chair of any one of the indorsers of the infamous sentiments of Helper—"then let discord reign here forever."[21]

Barksdale's defense of slavery under the Constitution was not new; however the depth and fervency of his white supremacist views marked an emotional escalation. He stated:

> Slavery in some form has existed in all ages of the world, and it is sanctioned by Divine authority. We believe it to be right. It is interwoven with our whole social organization, with our very existence as a people; and we are determined, at all hazards, to maintain it…. If there is any society on earth where there is the most perfect equality among white men, where labor is respected and the laborer honored, it is in the Southern States; and the reason is obvious: *there is an inferior race to do the menial service* [emphasis added].[22]

Barksdale continued:

> And now sir, we have a purely sectional party, bounded by sectional lines, and having for its object the utter subjugation and dishonor of the Southern states. Anti-slavery is now a part of the education and religion of the Northern people. It is printed in their school-books, taught in their classes and school-rooms, and thundered from their pulpits…. The Legislature of Massachusetts is carrying this doctrine into practical effect. Negro children are admitted with white children into their public schools, negroes are allowed the elective franchise, to testify in courts of justice, and to act as arbiters upon the property and the lives of white men, and by the laws, revolting as it may appear, of that State, the two races are allowed to inter-marry.

He emphasized that Republican opposition to "the acquisition of any more slave territory" extended beyond the continental United States: "They would oppose the admission of Cuba upon any terms, [even] with the consent of Spain, even though the inhabitants of that island all desired it."

Upping the ante on the House floor, Barksdale now talked openly and repeatedly about secession: "Mr. Clerk, events are rapidly hurrying to a crisis, and we are today almost in the midst of a revolution; and I deem it my duty to declare here what I have repeatedly said before, that in the event of the election of a Black Republican to the Presidency, upon a sectional and hostile platform, I am for stern, unbending resistance to his inauguration as President of the southern states." He then invoked the cause of states' rights under the Constitution to support secession: "When the compact of the Union, the Constitution, has been violated, we claim the right of peaceable secession. That was the doctrine of Jefferson and Madison. The right to judge of 'infractions of the Constitution, as well as the mode of redress' has never been delegated to the Federal Government. It is the shield of the States against the illegitimate encroachment of Federal power. We plant ourselves upon the right of peaceable secession, and there we intend to stand."

If need be Barksdale was prepared to fight for the right to secede. In response to Northern threats that the South would not be permitted to secede, Barksdale with characteristic Southern pride, indignation, and confidence responded: "How do they propose to prevent it. Sir, the army that invades the South to subjugate her will never return; their bodies will enrich southern soil."

To those historians and authors who brand Barksdale as a fire-eater, I offer in rebuttal the following words—Barksdale's own—spoken on the record in the House after serving seven years in Congress: "I have never desired a dissolution of this Union, but should the Black Republican party obtain control of the Government, I shall be for disunion." With these words Barksdale had symbolically drawn his line in the sand. And he did so with supreme confidence in the South's ability to survive and prosper on its own. In his words, "I have no fears for the South. With a territory larger than all of Europe; with our cotton now swelling up in value to more than two hundred million dollars; with our rice and sugar and tobacco; with a people united in feeling and sentiment, she has within her own borders all the elements of a splendid republic ... the South, with the strong arms and brave hearts of her gallant sons, will build up her own eternal destiny." His supreme confidence rested partly on his unqualified belief (later proven correct) that non-slaveholders in the South would rally around the cause of Southern rights should "the struggle between the sections ever come."[23]

Predictably, by this time, the atmosphere in Congress had deteriorated to the point that decorum was non-existent. The House increasingly became an "armed camp" with members openly brandishing revolvers and bowie knives, and their friends and supporters doing likewise in the galleries. More than once bloodshed on the House floor was only narrowly averted, and as expected, Barksdale, with his fiery temper, was always close to the action. On one such occasion Republican Thaddeus Stevens from Pennsylvania gave an inflammatory address ridiculing Southern threats of secession, stating they would only work on "timid" men in the North. This comment so infuriated Barksdale that he unsheathed his bowie knife and lunged at Stevens who later commented on the scene: "weapons were drawn, and Barksdale's bowie-knife gleamed before our eyes." Luckily Stevens' friends intervened to quell the altercation.[24]

Republican Congressman Owen Lovejoy of Illinois. An ardent abolitionist who participated with a station on the Underground Railroad, Lovejoy was a constant thorn in Barksdale's side. It is fair to say they despised each other. Julian Vannerson photo in McClee's Gallery of the 35th Congress, 1859 (Library of Congress).

Perhaps no Northern representative got under Barksdale's

Six—Epithets, Fisticuffs and the Downward Spiral to Secession 69

skin more than Republican Owen Lovejoy from Illinois. A very close friend of future President Abraham Lincoln, Lovejoy was a Congregational minister as well as a farmer. More importantly he was a most ardent abolitionist who actively participated in the Underground Railroad, offering his house as a station stop for runaway slaves. His eldest brother, Elijah, was also a Presbyterian Minister and editor of an anti-slavery newspaper. In 1837, as a young man, Owen had witnessed Elijah's murder at the hands of a drunken pro-slavery mob at Alton, Illinois. Barksdale and Lovejoy could perhaps be regarded as opposite sides of the same coin. Like Barksdale, Lovejoy was a big man possessed of considerable oratorical skills. He would "loose thunderbolts of moral indignation over slavery," sometimes overworking the rhetoric and appearing "too puritanically one-sided." Lovejoy is best known for introducing a bill in the House, only seven weeks before his death in 1864, which declared freedom for all slaves anywhere within the jurisdiction of the United States.[25]

During Barksdale's previous address on failure to elect a Speaker, he had castigated Lovejoy for supporting Helper's book, *The Impending Crisis of the South*. Addressing Lovejoy regarding John Brown's raid, Barksdale continued: "I say then to him, that he has taught treason and insurrection, and the country will hold him, and his party responsible, for the results. Yes sir, his doctrine, leads to treason and rapine and murder." Nine weeks later, on April 5, 1860, it was Lovejoy's turn to respond. He gave a one-hour address in the House on the slavery question and chose to refute and reject the very same arguments Barksdale had previously made in defense of slavery. Lovejoy summarized as follows: "I say therefore Mr. Chairman, that there is no justification for this practice of slaveholding from the fact that the enslaved race are an inferior race. No justification from the pretended fact that it imparts Christianity and civilization to them; and none in the guarantees of the Constitution." Barksdale shouted in reply, "The meanest slave in the South is your superior" amidst cries of "Order, Order" from the Republican side. Barksdale also proclaimed to Lovejoy "that you stand there today, an infamous perjured villain."[26]

By now these repetitive antics in Congress were wearing thin with the press, which began to publish increasingly sarcastic and derisive accounts of the goings-on in the House. An excellent example is *Vanity Fair's* description of this particular episode, entitled "The Delights of Debate," published days later:

> The art or science of conducting a clear, convincing, and intelligent debate, wherein are no unnecessary words and no irrelevant remarks, flourishes just now at our Governmental Capitol in a greater degree of perfection, perhaps, than anywhere else in the world.
>
> The dignity, manliness, and intelligence displayed in the House of Representatives on Thursday last, exemplifies this fact in a dreadfully forcibly manner. The occasion was a speech by Mr. Lovejoy, a Member of Congress and the Republican faction, and a gentleman of the most curious regard for decency, politeness, parliamentary etiquette etc.
>
> Having something to discuss, Mr. Lovejoy, put forth the theory that the people of the South, and especially their representatives there present, were "worse, more wicked, more criminal, more inglorious to man and abhorrent to God" than if they had been robbers, pirates and polygamists. This was a splendid argument, rational and clear-headed to the last degree, particularly when strengthened by Mr. Lovejoy's physical manifestations. He left his seat, pressed over to the benches of the Democratic Faction, and shaking his fists at the Southern Gentlemen, howled his words out like a first-class menagerie full of hyenas and jackalls.
>
> But, if Mr. Lovejoy is strong on discussion, so are some of his brothers on the other side. Mr. Barksdale, for instance, opposed to these chaste arguments, another, in every way worthy of them. He playfully shook his gold-headed bludgeon at Mr. L., saying "You lying scoundrel, come over here if you dare!"

Great interest now became apparent among all present, and Mr. Lovejoy continued his enunciation by asserting that nobody could intimidate him. A Gentleman from Kentucky, knowing that actions spoke louder than words, began paring his nails with an enormous bowie-knife—rather a loud action. Subsequently he told Mr. L. that he "must and should sit down," but remained standing himself, and defied the Sergeant-At-Arms to make him take his seat.

These highly effective and convincing elucidations of the question under discussion had the effect of producing—singularly enough—a little confusion; but it was partially abated, after a time, when Mr. Sherman remarked "We are all in good order now"; a proposition so obviously jocose that it was received with a universal roar of laughter, in the midst of which, according to parliamentary observance, Mr. Lovejoy continued his speech. He said that he had sworn to support the Constitution, but as his Southern friends were in the habit of beating their servants to death with handsaws, he interpreted that document in a different way from theirs.

To clear up this point, Mr. Bonham pithily remarked "You violate it sir." Mr. Ashmore added "And you perjure yourself!" Before Mr. Lovejoy could recover from the effect of this profound and astute train of reasoning, Mr. Singleton brought up a still more clinching argument: "And you are a negro-thief into the bargain!" said he. Here the discussion was terminated by Mr. Barksdale, who with equal elegance and force, asserted that he held no parley with a "perjured negro-thief."

This brilliant deduction threw much light upon the subject; and Mr. Lovejoy proceeded to bring out his reserved arguments and hypotheses. He continued, claiming that the gentlemen had murdered his brother twenty years ago, and averring that they would soon be displaced in Congress by more sensible men. Mr. Barksdale endeavored to overthrow this proposition by a few sound and telling words, saying that the meanest negro in the South was Mr. Lovejoy's superior; but Mr. L. corrected the statement by replying that Old John Brown stood a head and shoulders higher than any man there, until he was strangled. A voice assured him that the affection was not reciprocal; whereupon Mr. L compared himself to the Savior, and advised Virginia to clothe herself in sackcloth and ashes. The debate was closed by Mr. Martin who explained and settled the whole question by observing that if Mr. Lovejoy came to Virginia, they would hang him higher than they hung Old John Brown.

As not only the whole nation, but the whole civilized world, is looking pretty earnestly upon the American Republic and its Governmental Centre, we cannot but feel proud of such wit and wisdom as cluster about the House of Representatives. The only pity about us is, that these Gentlemen are such a pack of ruffianly blackguards![27]

In a follow-up article comparing a brutal illegal heavy-weight bare-knuckle prize fight held in England to the Lovejoy abolition debate, *Vanity Fair* was even more direct in its condemnation of Congress:

The demoralization of the age is increasing. The example set by the Senators and Representatives, during the present session of Congress has corrupted the whole world. Even in England, so long celebrated for Fair Play and No Favor, the ruffianly spirit has become the leading one, and the Prize Ring itself has been dishonored by an exhibition of brutal unfairness such as hardly been excelled in our House of Representatives. Neither Pryor, nor Lovejoy, nor Barksdale, nor Ashmore, nor any of the rest of that honey-tongued and creamy-tempered crew have far exceeded their transatlantic imitators and "British Sport" will soon become, no doubt, as disgraceful a title as "American Congressman."[28]

It was at this time that the Democratic National Convention took place in Charleston, South Carolina, on April 30, 1860. Ethelbert Barksdale attended as an official member of the Mississippi delegation and fervently spoke on their behalf. William attended in an unofficial but still important capacity given his political clout within the party. Even the Northern press commented upon William's presence there. The editor of the Cincinnati *Commercial* described him somewhat unflatteringly as follows:

And there is William Barksdale, the congressman from Mississippi, with his hat pulled down over his right eye. He has a way of throwing his head on one side, turning up his chin, and talking in a short sharp way, like a New York B'hoy. He is thick set, broad-shouldered and short legged. His eye is small and fierce. The whole country knows he wears a wig for Potter of Wisconsin [actually Washburne of

Illinois] knocked it off once upon a time. But as for a duel, beware of meeting Barksdale with bowie knives! He knows how to handle the implement and has handled it.[29]

The delegates were bitterly divided over the platform and its wording, particularly regarding slavery. The result—not one but two final reports. The Yancey Platform contained a plank clearly demanding protection of slavery in the territories held by the federal government. The Douglas Platform merely reasserted the policy of popular sovereignty which most Southerners now felt was totally inadequate. With William Barksdale's assistance, former congressman and Alabama fire-eater William Yancey gained the floor to deliver a rousing speech. Going even further, Ethelbert announced that Mississippi's delegation would not support Douglas irrespective of the platform. However, since Douglas' supporters were in the majority, the Douglas Platform was formally adopted. This prompted the Alabama delegation, led by Yancey, to bolt from the hall, closely followed by five other delegations. Ethelbert Barksdale headed the Mississippi delegation out the door. Following this unprecedented mass exodus, the convention had no choice but to adjourn.

A second convention met on June 18, 1860, in Baltimore with the same result. Again Ethelbert played a prominent role, and as editor of *The Mississippian*, its pages were filled with laudatory justification for the actions of the "seceding delegations." Mississippi's Governor Pettus was quoted in *The Mississippian* as saying that the action by the seceding delegations was the "first proud step that had as yet been taken by the South" and praised the Mississippi delegation with the phrase, "well done thou good and faithful servant."[30]

In the end the Democratic party totally splintered. The Democrats presented two competing presidential tickets to the nation in the fall election, thereby opening the door for a Republican victory. Southern Democrats from the seceding delegations adopted the name Constitutional Democratic party and nominated John C. Breckinridge for President, while the northern National Democrats designated Stephen A. Douglas. The moderate Constitutional Union party nominated John Bell of Tennessee, thus making it a four-way race, including the Republican candidate—Abraham Lincoln. Mississippi voted in favor of Breckinridge, giving him a sizable 15,000 vote majority over Bell, with Douglas coming in a distant third. However, on November 6, 1860, Barksdale's worst nightmare was realized with the election of Republican Abraham Lincoln as the sixteenth President. For Barksdale, this was the moment that Caesar had finally crossed the Rubicon.

Mississippi's reaction was swift. On November 14, 1860, Governor Pettus issued a call to summon the Mississippi Legislature into "extra ordinary session" on November 26th to consider "the propriety and necessity of providing surer and better safeguards for the lives, liberties, and property of [Mississippi's] citizens than had been found or was to be hoped for in Black Republican oaths."[31]

In preparation, Pettus summoned Mississippi's delegation of senators and congressmen from Washington to meet with him on November 22nd for a two-day caucus at the executive mansion in Jackson. Everyone attended except Congressman John McCrae who was absent due to his wife's serious illness. All present agreed to request the legislature to call a secession convention as soon as possible. However, there was passionate disagreement over whether Mississippi should act unilaterally or only in concert with other Southern states. Jefferson Davis, L.Q.C. Lamar, and Albert Gallatin Brown supported Mississippi's secession from the Union, but only after other states had led by example. Davis foresaw that disunion could not be "peaceably accomplished" and feared the consequences of unilateral action. Therefore, he refused Pettus' entreaties to be spokesman for "immediate, unqualified secession." Davis, Brown and Lamar voted to advise South Carolina's Governor Gist to delay issuance of an ordinance of secession by South Carolina until after Lincoln's inauguration to allow for coordinated action. However, Barksdale, Reuben Davis, and Otho Singleton voted for immediate unqualified secession by Mississippi and South Carolina. Governor Pettus cast the final deciding vote for immediate action. The three who were opposed reluctantly acquiesced thereby presenting a false impression of unanimity. (McCrae had issued a letter on November 19 declaring for secession by separate state action which Ethelbert later published in the December 5th issue of *The Mississippian*.)[32]

On November 26, 1860, the Mississippi legislature agreed to Pettus' request and authorized a secession convention. Mississippi's national representatives returned to Washington to at least give the appearance of resuming their legislative duties, although their hearts were no longer in it. On Thursday December 13, 1860, twenty Southern senators and congressmen, including Barksdale, met in the hotel room of Reuben Davis to draft a formal document which became known as "The Southern Manifesto." It read in part, "All hope of relief in the Union, through the agency of committees, Congressional legislation, or constitutional amendments is extinguished."

On December 14, 1860, six days prior to election of the Mississippi secession convention delegates, Mississippi's congressmen issued a joint communiqué to their constituents based upon the Southern Manifesto that read in part:

> We are satisfied the honor, safety, and independence of the Southern people require the organization of a Southern Confederacy—a result to be obtained only by separate State secession—that the primary object of each slaveholding State ought to be its speedy and absolute separation from the Union with hostile states.[33]

The Mississippi Secession Convention assembled in Jackson on January 7, 1861. Two days later, on January 9, 1861, Mississippi, by majority vote, became the second state to formally pass an ordinance of secession from the Union, following South Carolina's lead.

While the Mississippi Secession Convention was underway, William Barksdale appeared on the floor of the House for the last time on Monday January 7, 1861. A heated debate quickly erupted concerning a resolution by Representative Garnett B. Adrian from New York which stated in part "that we fully approve of the bold and patriotic act of Major Anderson in withdrawing from Fort Moultrie to Fort Sumter, and of the determination of the President to maintain that fearless officer in his present position." It is hard to ignore the symbolism of the scene as Barksdale struggled to explain his "No" vote over the ensuing uproar in the House. How many times had he risen before to issue dire warnings of impending conflict between North and South regarding the issue of slavery, only to have his earnestly delivered words fall on deaf ears? Describing Barksdale's last act in Congress, the *Congressional Globe* simply records: "Mr Barksdale, in giving his vote in the negative, made an explanation, amid loud and continued cries of order, which rendered his remarks entirely inaudible to the reporters"—to which may be added, and to all those congressmen present as well. Perhaps this was a fitting finale to his fruitless efforts in Washington over the previous eight years regarding the slavery question.[34]

A few days later, on Saturday January 12, 1861, with Mississippi's congressmen absent, the Speaker of the House solemnly read the following communiqué which was

Six—Epithets, Fisticuffs and the Downward Spiral to Secession

signed by Otho R. Singleton, William Barksdale, Reuben Davis, John J. McRae, and L.Q.C. Lamar:

> Sir; Having received official information that the State of Mississippi, through a convention representing the sovereignty of the State, has passed an ordinance withdrawing from the Federal Government all the powers delegated to it at the time of her admission into the Union, it becomes our duty to lay this fact before you, and to announce that we are no longer members of this body. While we regret the necessity which impels our State to adoption of this course, we desire to say that it meets our unqualified approval; and we shall return to her bosom to share her fortunes, whatever they may be.[35]

Woodcut of Congressman William Barksdale. He appeared in the House for the final time on January 7, 1861, where his impassioned words fell on deaf ears (*Harper's Weekly Journal*, February 2, 1861).

For almost eight long years on the Congress floor William Barksdale had engaged in a war of words against his Northern adversaries. Now the time had finally come to face them in a real war to be decided, not by negotiation, "but by the sword, [rifle and cannon] balls, and the bayonet!"[36] Once again Barksdale was primed for an active role of military leadership on the battlefield—and this time his ambition would be fulfilled, but at the ultimate cost of his life.

Seven

From Quartermaster General to a Combat Command at First Manassas

In Washington on January 4, 1861, a full eight days before resigning from Congress, Barksdale had already contemplated the inevitable military confrontation. That day he sent an urgent telegram to officials in Columbus, Mississippi, apprising them of the latest developments at Fort Sumter in Charleston harbor, South Carolina. Furthermore, he urged immediate preparation for military action: "The President refused to withdraw the troops from Charleston. The Commissioners regarded this as an Act of war [and] have left.... Appearances [are] warlike *and in my opinion we should be prepared to seize the forts and arsenals at a moment's warning.* William Barksdale." Events proceeded so rapidly that Barksdale entered military service a mere 20 days later.[1]

In the interim the Mississippi Secession Convention continued to meet and plan for the newly created Republic of Mississippi. As might be expected, the delegates initially passed resolutions appointing Mississippi's former United States senators and congressmen to fill these same positions in the anticipated Congress of a Southern Confederacy. However, this was not to be. A separate group of seven delegates from Mississippi was selected to attend a convention of the newly seceded states in Montgomery, Alabama, in order to establish a provisional government. Accordingly, these seven delegates, including Ethelbert Barksdale, would serve as Mississippi's representatives in the First Congress of the Confederate States of America.[2]

William would not serve the Confederacy in a political capacity as Mississippi initially intended, but rather in a military role—much to his delight. For Jefferson Davis, it was just the opposite. Desiring a position of active military leadership on the battlefield, instead he was quickly elected president of the newly formed Confederacy at Montgomery in early February. The state of flux within Mississippi's military hierarchy reflected the flurry of activity and uncertainty during this formative period.

Mississippi's Secession Convention had wasted no time in reorganizing the state military system and renaming it the Army of Mississippi on January 23, 1861. The delegates commissioned its general officers with proper rank as follows: Jefferson Davis, Major General Commanding; Earl Van Dorn, Charles Clark, James L. Alcorn, and Christopher H. Mott, Brigadier Generals. All except Alcorn were veteran officers of the Mexican War. These men, together with Gov. John J. Pettus, comprised the Military Board with full control over the army and its military property. Shortly thereafter the Board appointed Richard Griffith, former Adjutant of the Mississippi Rifles in Mexico, as

Adjutant General; William Barksdale as Quartermaster General; and Samuel G. French as Chief of Ordnance.

Barksdale's appointment doubtless resulted from his efficient performance as assistant commissary with the 2nd Regiment in Mexico, his proven leadership in Congress, and his illustrious reputation within Mississippi. Jefferson Davis, who had intimate knowledge of Barksdale's inherent abilities, also insisted upon this appointment for his close personal friend. The Board also formally adopted the following Mississippi uniform—gray frock coat and trousers with red trim for infantry, yellow for cavalry, and orange for artillery; black felt tri-parte hat with plumes for officers and horse-hair pom-pom for enlisted men.[3]

Due to election of Jefferson Davis as President of the Confederate States of America in Montgomery on February 12, 1861, the make-up of the Military Board quickly changed. Earl Van Dorn succeeded Davis as Major General of the Army of Mississippi. On March 12, 1861, in General Orders No. 1, Van Dorn made several new appointments and officially confirmed several others. Among them were the appointment of Barksdale as Quartermaster General—but now with the rank of brigadier general. Richard Griffith (whom Barksdale would later replace as brigade commander after Griffith's mortal wounding at the battle of Savage Station) was replaced as adjutant general by Beverley Matthews and was also promoted to brigadier general. When Van Dorn and Clark subsequently accepted commissions in the Confederate States army, Barksdale's friend, Reuben Davis, was appointed supreme leader of the Army of Mississippi as Major General on July 1, 1861.[4]

As had been the case with the Mexican War, an overwhelming flood of volunteer 12-month enlistments occurred within Mississippi. However, there were simply too many volunteers and not enough weapons. This dire shortage resulted despite Governor Pettus' earlier efforts (as far back as May and November 1860) to procure arms from federal arsenals in the South as well as manufacturers in the North. The mounting frustration arising from the enforced inactivity of the volunteers very nearly cost Pettus his re-election as governor in 1861. Indeed, some overly keen volunteers even vented their extreme dissatisfaction regarding lack of equipment and delays in their deployment, in personal letters to Pettus. At the same time these young men expressed their unbridled patriotism for the Southern cause: "There are fifty in the company now, as enthusiastic as those who love freedom should be. We are perfectly willing to buy our uniform and everything else that is necessary.... If the state does not reject us.... We can have a splendid company.... Cruel and mortifying indeed would it be to cast us out.... Our motto is 'Ducit amor Patriae'—'the love of my country leads me.'"[5]

The inability of the fledgling Confederate States army to assimilate those companies who had already been successfully organized and equipped further exacerbated the situation. Following his inauguration on February 22, 1861, President Davis on March 9th called on Pettus for 1,500 troops to be sent to Pensacola, Florida, and on April 8th for 3,000 more. After the Confederate firing on Fort Sumter on April 12, 1861, Davis called for 5,000 additional Mississippians—all for 12-month enlistments. Not until June 29th did a general call come for 30,000 soldiers to be mustered in at Corinth, Mississippi, for the duration of the war.[6]

Under such trying circumstances one can only imagine the gargantuan challenge Barksdale and his quartermaster department faced to procure and then distribute the necessary supplies and equipment. Furthermore, Barksdale was required to maintain sufficient and accurate documentation for a myriad of transactions under chaotic conditions. Driven by his extreme sense of duty, and summoning all his self-discipline, determination, and perseverance, he set about his thankless—yet critically important—task. For a combination of reasons Barksdale's tenure as Quartermaster General of Mississippi lasted for only two months before he abruptly—and uncharacteristically—resigned.

His decision did not result from the difficulty of the task he had been assigned. On the contrary, Barksdale quickly became deeply offended and piqued that his integrity was constantly being drawn into question by the governor, who was a stickler for detail. Moreover, Barksdale profoundly resented being held to a much higher standard of accountability than Pettus himself. Even worse, Pettus' repeated nitpicking was transpiring at a time when there were insufficient hours in the day, resources, and trained personnel to complete Barksdale's designated duties. In his words, Barksdale could not be "showing accurately and correctly where every tin cup, spoon, canteen, knapsack etc. has gone." It was bad enough during these critically busy times that formal detailed audits were being conducted for transactions involving the treasury funds allocated to Barksdale. However, harassment over personal expenses for as little as $70 (covering lodging in Jackson, and firewood for Barksdale and the slave with him between February 24, 1861, and May 30, 1861) was simply too much for Barksdale's personal sense of honor to bear.[7]

During his tenure as quartermaster general, Barksdale received $113,761.50 from the State Treasury to procure and distribute property, arms, equipment, and supplies. He was answerable to Governor Pettus, the Military Board, and the Mississippi Legislature. In his multi-page report to Pettus, dated July 26, 1861, Barksdale presented a very detailed summary of his receipts and disbursements down to the cent and offered numerous specific explanations and clarifications. In many cases Barksdale had been compelled to rely on railroad receipts as vouchers instead of documentation from the parties to whom the property was actually furnished. In particular he cited the inexperience of his staff: "The duties of this department were entirely new to those employed as assistants and therefore, a strict and systematic rule has not been pursued in all instances in the distribution of property." Due to their lack of familiarity quantities which should have been expressed in "round numbers" were simply shown on receipts as "boxes, barrels etc."

Barksdale also mentioned a situation in which a number of vouchers were destroyed by accident and subtly gave vent to his frustration with the audit process. He continued: "After the accident occurred the fragments of the vouchers were collected by Maj. Joseph Bennett, the Clerk in the Quartermasters Department under me, and have by him been preserved, but they are so badly torn that it is utterly impossible to arrange and paste them together again without great patience, and labor, and without consuming more time than I have at present to spare." He even went to the trouble of obtaining sworn affidavits from Major Bennett and Captain McMannus "testifying to the fact of their existence and destruction, and also to the justness of Said vouchers against the State and to their having been paid by me as Quartermaster General."

The die had been cast—and Barksdale summarily resigned as Quartermaster General of the Army of Mississippi. Colonel Madison McAfee (who had just run unsuccessfully against Pettus for governor) replaced Barksdale.[8]

Despite Barksdale's frustration and the validity of these reasons for his resignation, there is another motive which, although not voiced at the time, cannot be ignored. There is a very distinct possibility that Barksdale intentionally used his open criticism against Governor Pettus, at least in part, as justification to resign in order to secure a field command in the Confederate army. Resigning his post as quartermaster general (and foregoing his rank of brigadier general) would, at last, almost certainly afford Barksdale the opportunity to gain glory on the battlefield, secure his military reputation, and refute the stinging criticism leveled during his earlier electoral campaigns in Mississippi regarding his military service in Mexico. Irrespective of his motives that is precisely what would transpire. It was also a decision that would ultimately lead to Barksdale's death on the battlefield.

After the firing on Fort Sumter, federal mobilization, and Confederate President Davis' call for 5,000 additional Mississippi troops, Governor Pettus finally dispatched numerous companies from the Army of Mississippi to Corinth under Brig. Gen. Charles Clark. On May 14, 1861, the 13th Mississippi Regiment was formally organized at Corinth from 10 existing companies as follows:

Company A—Alumutcha Infantry (E)   Company F—Kemper Legion (C)
Company B—Winston Guards (A)   Company G—Lauderdale Zouaves (F)
Company C—Wayne Rifles (B)   Company H—Pettus Guards (K)
Company D—Minute Men of Attala (I) Company I—Secessionists (G)
Company E—Newton Rifles (D)   Company K—Spartan Band (H)[9]

On that same day, Barksdale was summarily elected as regimental colonel by the enlisted men. Mackerness Hudson Whitaker, a 26-year-old married lawyer, born in Louisiana, who lived in Marion, Mississippi, was elected as lieutenant colonel. Isham D. Harrison, a 40-year-old married lawyer, born in Alabama, who then lived in Columbus, Mississippi, was elected major. Nine days later the 13th Mississippi was formally mustered into service for 12 months within the Army of the Confederate States of America, and soon afterward was ordered to report to the Camp of Instruction at Union City, Tennessee, under Maj. Gen. Leonidis Polk.[10]

For veterans of the Mexican War like Barksdale, the war fever, excitement, and tearful goodbyes of 1861 rekindled their past. The young soldiers left their homes, many for the first time—and many more for the last time. Most of these young boys and men found this forced parting from family and friends overwhelmingly difficult. One young Mississippi soldier described the experience as "the battle of leaving home, bidding farewell to all we hold dear—father, mother, wife, little ones" and considered it "the hardest battle ever fought by a Confederate soldier." He later wrote: "Gettysburg, Chickamauga, and Shiloh were pretty tough places, but I believe that this was the hardest struggle of the war!"[11]

Typical of the formal send-offs was that of the Caledonia Rifles, Company D, 24th Mississippi. The "fair daughters of Lowndes County" had hand made a beautiful silk First National (Stars and Bars) Confederate Flag and chose Miss Annie Vaughn, one of their group, to formally present it. In her recorded remarks, Miss Vaughn spoke for all women of the South:

> Upon [this beautiful banner] you behold the stars representative of the galaxy of Confederate States, and its broad bars, emblematic of faith, purity, and fidelity. Preserving all that was glorious of our old national flag, the Stars and Stripes, we have remodeled and improved it. When we behold the stars we are reminded of the standard under which our ancestors fought the battles of the Revolution of '76, and when upon our own banner we see the stars in the beautiful field of blue we are inspired with faith to engage in battle and achieve the victories of the revolution of eighteen hundred and sixty-one, the second war of independence.... In the name and by the authority of the ladies of this neighborhood,

now before me, I present you this flag. Conscious of the justness of our cause, assured of the unwavering courage, the eternal patriotism of the Caledonia Rifles, we still feel secure in our homes and safe by our firesides when we know we are protected by such brave and gallant sons of our soil. Now that the ruthless invaders have dared to pollute our soil with their hostile tread, we bid you go forth to meet them—go under this banner—and if it shall be necessary to strike in defense of our sacred rights and liberties, bear your ensign aloft. As you look upon it streaming in the breeze, remember those by whom it was made, be encouraged by their universal good wishes and their love; be strengthened by their prayers, then strike for your homes and your sires, your altars and your fires, God, and your native land.

Her speech was followed by "an old fashioned barbeque and basket dinner."[12]

Near Sarepta, in Calhoun County, Mississippi, 20-year-old student Ezekiel Armstrong, who had joined the Magnolia Guards, soon to be mustered in at Corinth as Company K, 17th Mississippi, bade an emotional farewell to his "mother & kind brothers and sisters." In his diary Armstrong recorded these poignant details: "I with heavy heart took leave of them perhaps for the last time. I braved the storm with great courage until I mounted my steed and ma burst into tears. This stirring my poor heart through and through & almost congealed the blood that darted through my veins.... As my old and dearly loved home disappeared in the distance it seemed to me that all the friends & all that were dear to me on the earth were gone." Sadly Armstrong would never pursue his dream of studying literature and law, as his promising life abruptly ended a year-and-a-half later during the defense at Fredericksburg under Barksdale's command.[13]

A similar touching scene played out at Clinton Station, Mississippi, near the college campus as the Mississippi College Rifles departed for Corinth to become Company E of the 18th Mississippi under Colonel Erasmus R. Burt. While the band played "Dixie" and "Bonnie Blue Flag," a participant later recorded: "mingling with laughter and glad young voices was the sound of bitter weeping as the last good by was said. The long train pulled out from the station, the flag was unfurled, gray caps were flung in the air, and the boys cheered wildly midst the shrill notes of fife in 'The Girl I left Behind Me.'"[14]

Recently several historians have declared that the root cause of the Civil War was slavery—that the Confederacy merely fought to keep African American slaves in bondage while the Union simply fought to free the slaves. If so, then why did Barksdale correctly espouse in Congress his prediction that, if and when conflict came with the North, non-slaveholders in the South, with no personal stake in slavery, would rally to the cause and fight? The truth lies in the fact that, although the institution of slavery was the *issue* that sparked the conflict, it was not the underlying root cause. The Civil War was fought for two reasons—the same two reasons all wars are fought—power and money. More precisely the political power heretofore exercised by the aggregate of individual slaveholding states and whether this exercise of power would continue—and equally important, the economics of slavery.[15]

By 1861 the institution of slavery had become so intricately interwoven into the fabric of Southern society that Southerners, slaveholders and non-slaveholders alike, realized that their entire Southern culture, social order, and economy, were dependent on the continuation of slavery. Indeed, their entire way of life as they knew it required the "peculiar institution." On the Union side, there can be no doubt that at the outset, Northern soldiers volunteered to fight and if necessary to die not to free the slaves, but to preserve the Union and its federal democratic principles established by the Founding Fathers. It would not become evident until later in the war that preservation of the Union could only be accomplished through the elimination of slavery.[16]

Original sketch of "A Slave Auction at the South," *Harper's Weekly Journal,* **July 13, 1861 (Library of Congress).**

Indeed, the following figures confirm the extent to which slavery dominated the economy of the South and accounted for its wealth. In 1860 there were four million slaves with a market value of $3 billion which far exceeded the value of land or cotton in the South, as well as the total capital invested in both railroads and manufacturing in the entire United States.[17] The common Confederate soldier recognized this economic reality and often expressed it in his letters and diaries. David Holt, a Mississippi private, recorded:

> Father was a strong pro-slavery man. However neither Joe [brother] nor I believed in the institution of slavery.... We both declared that we would never own slaves, yet at the same time, we denounced the fanatical ideas of the North as unjust and unfair. The abolitionists never showed a way to get rid of slavery.... We did not invent the institution of slavery but inherited it, with protection of the Constitution and recognized by law. No means was offered to relieve us of the burden which would enable us to realize even a part of the money invested in slaves. Great Britain had already freed her slaves, but there the property loss was divided between owners and the government.[18]

Another Confederate soldier, William L. Nugent, wrote to his wife in 1863: "I own no slaves and can freely express my notions, without being taxed with any motive of self-interest. I know this country without slave labor would be totally worthless, a barren waste and desolate plain—We can only live & exist by this species of labor: and hence I am willing to continue to fight to the last. If we have to succumb we must do it bravely fighting for our rights."[19]

By 1861, the United States had evolved into two distinct and disparate nations. A clash between them became inevitable. Republican Senator William Seward expressed this sentiment in a famous speech referring to the struggle between North and South as "an irrepressible conflict between two opposing and enduring forces." An Ohio congressman went further, claiming the conflict was "between systems, between civilizations."[20] Indeed, by 1860, not only were the North and South different on many levels, but they continued to diverge at an ever-increasing rate. The North was urban in nature, manufacturing-based, capitalistic, embracing of change and modernization, and supportive of a strong federal government. In contrast, the South was rural, agricultural-based, traditional, largely threatened by change (some would say backward) and favored limited federal powers. Renowned British historian John Keegan, in his excellent book *The American Civil War—A Military History*, expressed this dichotomy simply and eloquently with these words: "It would become a war of peoples, and those of each side, who had hitherto considered themselves one, would henceforth ... consider their differences more important than the values that since 1781, they had accepted as permanent and binding."[21]

Writing of the final outcome and the transforming nature of the Civil War, historian James McPherson succinctly summarized the synthesis of this long and bloody conflict as follows: "In the process of preserving the Union of 1776 while purging it of slavery, the Civil War also transformed it. Before 1861 the words 'United States' were a plural noun: 'The United States *are* a large country.' Since 1865 'United States' has been a singular noun. The North went to war to preserve the *Union*; it ended by creating a *nation*."[22]

While at Corinth, the fledgling 13th Mississippi began to take shape under their newly commissioned colonel. In the wry words of one private at Camp Corinth: "we procured tents, cooking utensils, and other necessaries and soon were initiated in all the pleasures and conveniences of camp life." On May 16, 1861, the regiment drew their arms and were soon "generally drilled in the School of the Soldier and in tactics generally though we acquired but little proficiency as our preceptors knew as little as we did ourselves." The process of electing officers in these volunteer regiments has been severely criticized—even termed "inane" by distinguished historian Robert K. Krick. The sad reality, however, was that there were just not anywhere near enough professionally trained officers and soldiers available to command these units. Even worse, as late historian Glenn Robertson highlighted, the war departments, both North and South, never sanctioned an official program for the training of volunteer officers. Perhaps the only positive for the practice of electing officers by the men in the ranks: It did ensure their confidence in those elected, even if they were not necessarily the best qualified fighting men.[23]

Equipped with only his copy of Hardee's *Rifle and Light Infantry Tactics*, and whatever knowledge he had acquired while serving in Mexico, Barksdale set about the task of learning the manual of arms, marching commands, and rapid deployments (e.g. quickly changing from column of fours into a two-rank battle-line, as well as changing front to make or receive an attack). Barksdale also struggled to impart all of this newly gained knowledge to his subordinates and non-commissioned officers. Once again, his mastery of self-instruction, coupled with his single-minded determination, proved invaluable. Barksdale would achieve a level of success on future battlefields rarely matched by a volunteer regimental or brigade commander.

Under his watchful eye and steady hand, the nine days at Corinth were "passed in drilling and preparing the organization for efficient and active service in the field." Despite any initial shortcomings, Barksdale made a favorable first impression on his men as evidenced by the following diary entry by 18-year-old Private Thomas D. Wallace of Company Q, Winston Guards: "William R. Barksdale is our Colonel. He is a brave man." The regiment left Corinth on Saturday morning May 25, 1861, headed for the Camp of Instruction at Union City in the northwest corner of Tennessee. For Private Wallace it was none too soon. He wrote: "It [Corinth] is the meanest place that I ever saw. When we heard that we had to leave to go to Union City we was the best pleased people that I ever saw."[24]

The train carrying the 1,000 men of the regiment pulled into Jackson, Tennessee, about 8 p.m. Saturday evening where a very large crowd, including many local ladies, greeted them. Recognizing the inherent dangers of travelling at night in the pitch dark, Colonel Barksdale exercised his authority and prudent judgment by refusing to go any farther that night. Although many soldiers were miffed at having to spend the night in the uncomfortable baggage cars on temporary wooden plank benches, most recognized the soundness of Barksdale's decision based upon the very real "fear of being thrown off the track" or "fear of the bridges being out." Moreover, many enlisted men had chosen to travel "perched on the roof" of the cars "scarcely heeding the many bridges that jeopardized their heads or the uneasy and dangerous rolling of the overloaded and ill constructed cars."[25]

Resuming their journey in broad daylight next morning, the regiment arrived safely at Union City that afternoon. They pitched their tents a few miles above the town near the Mobile and Ohio Railroad (for which Barksdale had procured land while in Congress). Initially all seemed well. In the words of Pvt. Albert Wymer Henley of Company K, the Spartan Band: "Our campground was an excellent one and the tents being arranged and in perfect regularity presented a pleasing and imposing appearance, besides being floored with plank, they added no small degree to our comfort and convenience, rations of the best quality and in great abundance were regularly issued so that so far as living was concerned we had no cause to complain." Despite Henley's claim, the complaints quickly surfaced as conditions, particularly the quality of drinking water, rapidly deteriorated.[26]

As the name implies, Camp of Instruction meant drill and discipline—for the next seven weeks. These independent and self-reliant Southern-born-and-bred young men, balked at the harsh military discipline immediately imposed upon them—especially at the hands of men whom they often viewed as equals. Nor was it something they were accustomed to. As might be expected, the men in the ranks initially resisted being ordered about and confined. Some became increasingly resentful of their so-called "superior" officers. Not surprisingly some at first even viewed army life as a form of slavery and freely expressed such sentiments: "It grinds me to think that I am compelled to stay here.... I've got a dozen masters who order me about like a negro."[27]

Over time, however, these Mississippi Confederates—some more begrudgingly than others—gradually became "depersonalized." They relinquished their individualism and replaced it with a fervent devotion to the common cause for which they fought—and, in many cases, for which they died. Like it or not, they soon realized that an army simply could not function—let alone succeed—without discipline. A typical day at the Camp of Instruction was as follows: 5 a.m. reveille, roll call; 7 a.m. breakfast; 8 a.m. surgeon's call; 9 a.m. guard mounting; squad drill or drilling in the manual of arms until 10 a.m.; company drill to 11 a.m.; recess—lunch at 12 noon; 2–4 p.m. company and regimental drill which generally was prolonged to 5 p.m.; 6 p.m. dress parade; 7 p.m. supper; 9 p.m. Taps. A Confederate soldier recorded: "Camp life grows monotonous in a short time. The novelty soon wears off and its routine duties become tiresome indeed.... Thus the days came and went, and our military education progressed."[28]

Colonel Barksdale imposed strict and sometimes harsh discipline which prompted Private Henley to comment: "our Colonel though generally respected was nevertheless regarded as a would-be tyrant and despot.... It was not wondered that under such a man ... the military law could be enforced with stringency and rigidity." Men could under no pretense whatever leave camp without written permission from their commanding officer. "Sentinels were posted day and night and no one was allowed to pass unless they provided the countersign which changed nightly. Several were found asleep, reported, and punished according to the will of the officers." One such 18-year-old Confederate who was found asleep on guard duty was subsequently court-martialed and sentenced to double duty. When he was again caught sleeping on his next posting as sentinel, fearing he would be shot, he quickly deserted. His fellow members of the Winston Guards were "glad to get rid of him."[29]

However, Barksdale knew when to draw the line regarding punishment for misconduct. One evening, Company D, the Minute Men of Attala, refused to carry out "some orders that we could not obey because they were given as though we were a set of fools." Soon the officer of the day with a complement of 20 men appeared to arrest the ringleaders, but the entire company "rose as one man and told them we would die before we would submit to the guard house." The arresting party then departed empty handed. Faced with this partial mutiny, Colonel Barksdale had the Minute Men drawn up the next evening and "made a few remarks in a very gentlemanly manner and thanked [us] for our kind attention [and] said the Minute Men would do." Such were the growing pains during the Camp of Instruction.[30]

The monotony and daily routine continued for several weeks with no major distractions until the evening of June 7, 1861. That night the camp was put on high alert, apparently anticipating a potential surprise Union attack (or as claimed by some a simulated defense drill ordered by Barksdale). Either way, for the first time, after evening roll call, the entire regiment was issued three cartridges and percussion caps, and the sentinels instructed to remain extra vigilant. Private Joseph Eastis of Company E described what happened in a letter written from Camp Barksdale, Union City: "About 2 oclock two of the sentinels fired the alarm. We were all called to arms in less than no time and formed in line of battle. Now I tell you, there was a great many who was scared. But, it all proved to be a false alarm." Another distraction occurred on Independence Day when the regiment "celebrated by target firing by file" which a participant observed was "generally speaking ... very well executed."[31]

BRIG.-GEN. WM. BARKSDALE.

Brig. Gen. William Barksdale, Civil War engraving. Unfortunately, no photographs of Barksdale in uniform are known to exist (author's collection).

Drilling remained the one constant—repetitive and physically demanding. Henley recorded: "Great attention was paid to drilling by both company and battalion. This was by no means an agreeable task as the weather was hot and the double quick, the most admired movement."[32]

Good water, initially plentiful, soon ran out due to the huge demand from the various regiments who were encamped within only a few hundred yards of each other. Attempts to overcome the shortage by digging wells in other locations proved to be insufficient. As a result, the soldiers were forced to rely on increasingly brackish water sources for drinking. By early July sickness and disease became so rampant, and deaths so numerous, that Colonel Barksdale travelled to Corinth on July 7 to seek permission from Maj. Gen. Charles Clark to relocate the camp to near Jackson, Tennessee. One soldier wrote: "[Barksdale] will be back tonight, I suppose. I hope he will succeed." At dusk four days later the 13th Mississippi departed Union City by train, arriving in Jackson next day. Commenting upon his last night at Union City, another Confederate recorded in his diary: "I could hear nothing but the rattling of the bells in the far-off fields and the sound of the hammer on the coffins they were making for the dead that were in the camps.... We did not have good water there so the Colonel got us off as soon as he could."[33]

Their sojourn in Jackson ended almost as soon as it began. After leaving the train station one soldier recorded, "we went about a mile from town to camp and before we got our tents up we heard we had to go to Richmond, Va. The cheers that were given could have been heard 2 miles [away]."[34]

The following morning the regiment began a grueling 10-day-and-night rail journey from Jackson to Lynchburg, Virginia, during which the soldiers scarcely ate or slept. This harrowing rail odyssey of approximately one thousand miles passed through Iuka and Corinth, Mississippi; Tuscumbia, Decatur, Huntsville, Stevenson, and Bridgeport, Alabama; Chattanooga, Cleveland, Knoxville, and Bristol, Tennessee; Lynchburg, Gordonsville, Virginia. The 13th Mississippi arrived at Manassas Junction, Virginia, on the eve of the first great battle in the east. The necessity of transferring between many different train cars on various rail lines of differing gauge rendered this exhausting journey even more aggravating. Nor was it made without risk. On the first evening of the trek, tragedy struck when a young member of the Winston Guards was killed while attempting to board the moving train at Iuka, Mississippi. Private Wallace noted the heartrending details in his diary:

> [Private] Warner saw some of his friends and jumped out of the cars and went to tell them howdah, the cars was going slow and started off pretty fast and he ran to get on when he jumped between the cars his foot slipped and he fell under the cars. One of the boys saw him fall and jumped to the forepart of the cars and let them loose so the cars that we were on was stopped. Some of the boys went back to see what had become of him. They found him all cut to pieces. They picked him up and carried him into a house. They left him for his friends to bury him in good style. So the engine came back and hitched to the cars that were loose and we went on [35]

On July 18th President Jefferson Davis telegraphed Brig. Gen. Pierre G.T. Beauregard to advise him that "Barksdale's Mississippi Regiment goes to you from Lynchburg." This arduous journey ended when the train pulled into Manassas Junction around midnight on Saturday, July 20th. The exhausted soldiers unloaded their belongings from the rail cars, laid their rubberized groundsheets and blankets on the ground, and quickly went to their well-earned sleep without even pitching their tents.[36]

Sunday morning July 21, 1861, dawned clear and very warm. Members of the

13th Mississippi awakened to "the booming of the cannon and the rattle of musketry" announcing "the opening of the first great battle between the belligerents." The fortunate few who had enough cooked food remaining from the train trip managed to gulp down a quick breakfast before Colonel Barksdale formed the regiment into line where each soldier was issued about 50 cartridges. Others, who had begun to cook breakfast that morning, unfortunately did not have time to eat it, and marched off in the stifling heat and dust with empty stomachs and dry canteens. Private Henley recorded that "by alternate quick and double quick movements [we] started for the scene of action [and] after marching about six miles we reached a pine thicket where we halted and having received no orders as to which point we should proceed, rested for about two hours."[37] As might be expected, with two massive armies comprised of soldiers "green as grass" and commanded by inexperienced officers, the scene was one of utter confusion.

Barksdale's newly-arrived regiment had been assigned to Brig. Gen. James Longstreet's brigade on the right center of the Confederate battle line near Blackburn's Ford across Bull Run. The 13th Mississippi arrived at the pine thicket in the reserve area behind Longstreet's brigade. However, Longstreet's command had already crossed Bull Run and engaged with Union artillery and infantry of the Federal 1st Division under Brig. Gen. Daniel Taylor. Earlier that morning Longstreet had requested that Col. Jubal Early (who was also located in the reserve area behind these same pine woods north of the McLean house) relinquish one regiment, and then later a second one, from his 6th Brigade. Early promptly complied.

Longstreet's brigade was part of the attack planned by supreme Confederate commander Gen. Beauregard—launched from the Confederate right against the Federal left flank. Unbeknownst to Beauregard, Union commander Brig. Gen. Irvin McDowell had already ordered an attack by the Federal right against the Confederate left flank. This Union attack was now finally starting to materialize. All morning Early had made a series of frustrating and unproductive marches and countermarches in the locale of the Confederate right-center. Finally about 1 p.m., Early received instructions to support the extreme Confederate left flank, held by Col. Nathan B. "Shanks" Evans, which was under threat of imminent Union attack. In response, Early requested that Longstreet return the companies transferred earlier from his 6th Brigade. Instead, applying sound military logic, Longstreet replied as follows according to Early:

Gen. James Longstreet, ca. 1860s. His decision to swap Col. Barksdale's 13th Mississippi for another regiment in his lines thrust the Mississippians into a prominent role at First Manassas (Library of Congress).

The messenger sent to General Longstreet returned and informed me that [Longstreet] said there was a regiment in the pines to my left which had been ordered to report to him and that I could take that regiment instead of the companies of my own, to save time and prevent the exposure of both to the fire of the enemy's artillery in passing to and from Blackburn's Ford. In this arrangement I readily concurred and soon found to my left in the pines, the 13th Mississippi Regiment under Colonel Barksdale, which had very recently arrived. The Colonel consented to accompany me, and as soon as the command could be got ready it was started on the road to Mitchell's Ford.[38]

Longstreet's decision thrust Barksdale and the 13th Mississippi into a prominent role approaching the climax of the battle. Early, irascible by nature, was understandably displeased. Greatly disappointed at having achieved nothing meaningful that morning, and deprived of his own familiar troops, he chafed at being saddled with these unproven Mississippians. Early later vented his frustration, in part against the 13th Mississippi: "the day was excessively hot and dry.... Barksdale's regiment an entirely new one, had just arrived from the south over the railroad, and was unused to marching. Our progress was therefore not as rapid as I could have wished, but we passed on with all possible speed in the direction of the firing, which was our only guide."[39]

Barksdale quickly called the regiment into line and instructed the men to leave their knapsacks behind. The Mississippians hurriedly hung them on nearby bushes. Then, "moving mostly in old and open fields under a burning sun, inhaling volumes of dust at every breath and unable to assuage [their] thirst which raged with almost unendurable violence," Barksdale swept the regiment along "in a run about 10 miles a while before [they] got to where the fighting was going on." Many soldiers fell out along the way, collapsing from the effects of fatigue, exhaustion, and heatstroke. However, the majority persevered. In the words of Private Henley: "But still as if actuated by a strange fatality or strengthened and supported by a higher power—onward we pressed. The roar of artillery and discharge of musketry at every step.... We rushed and resolved should the odds be against us to turn it in our favor." All the while "Col. Barksdale rode along the line exhorting us to fight and if need be to die in sustaining the high reputation Mississippians had so richly and so dearly earned on every battlefield [heretofore]."[40]

Gen. Jubal Early. Lee referred to the irascible and profane Early as "my bad old man." Early was critical of Barksdale on several occasions and they engaged in a prolonged war of words in Southern newspapers following the Chancellorsville Campaign (Library of Congress).

There was however an additional contributing factor to their delay—the temptation to forage.

The lure of fresh fruit on the vine proved too much for these famished Mississippians and so "every berry bush passed was stripped." When they finally got within sight of the Federal troops about a quarter-of-a-mile off, Barksdale formed them into a battle line, ordered them to fix bayonets, and to advance at the double quick. Although beyond range of their own smoothbore muskets and shorter-barreled Mississippi rifles, the Union skirmishers opened up on the Mississippians with their longer-barreled Springfield rifles. One Confederate later recorded: "The bullets of the enemy were whizzing past or knocking up dirt in our front."

This Mississippian then went on to document an amusing but embarrassing incident involving Barksdale. As they advanced through a pasture, the hungry Mississippians spied some bushes laden with ripe persimmons. Unfortunately, the bushes concealed a wasp nest. He continued:

> The boys were hot and the wasps easily angered, and instantly at least fifty men broke ranks and were running in every direction, fighting this new enemy with their hats. Our Colonel seeing this panic rushed into the breach, and at once the wasps attacked his horse, and soon the performance was at its height. The Colonel, being a large portly man, although a fine lawyer, was a poor horseman. The scene was ludicrous to the extreme … it beat a circus.[41]

Quickly regaining his composure, Barksdale restored order and immediately realigned his command that was flanked on his right by Colonel Hays' 7th Louisiana and Colonel Kemper's 7th Virginia. Together these three regiments now overlapped the enemy's right flank. A rebel private in the 13th Mississippi recorded "The Federals ran up several flags in front, a distance of about three hundred yards." By this time to Kemper's right, Col. Arnold Elzey's brigade—the final troops from General Johnston's army to be deployed—mounted a frontal charge. Interestingly enough, according to a soldier in the 1st Maryland, this attack and subsequent pursuit was also delayed somewhat as these famished men (who hadn't eaten in 36 hours) paused to grab handfuls of ripe blackberries in a sprawling patch—much to the consternation of their frustrated officers.

Perhaps wanting to make up for lost time and to regain some measure of favor under Early's critical eye, Barksdale "ordered his Regiment to engage, leaving the other two Regiments [Hays and Kemper] behind." Private Ellis continued: "The Federals, on hearing the command, 'Charge!' given by Col. Barksdale, stampeded, and the Thirteenth arrived at the summit of the hill, where they expected to meet the enemy, and were agreeably surprised to find [the Federals] had fled." Private Wallace added these comments: "our artillery was playing on them all the time as our Colonel gave the command 'charge bayonets.' When we started toward them, they ran like turkeys. When we got to the top of the hill they were about a half a mile from us. Our artillery still firing on them as they ran." Sergeant William H. Hill, the 20-year-old regimental quartermaster clerk, nonchalantly recorded the event in his diary as "arrived on the field in time to put the enemy to flight and fire a few rounds at the enemy." The cost to the regiment was only six wounded. The 13th Mississippi participated in the half-hearted pursuit of the fleeing Federals for several miles until exhaustion compelled them to halt. Returning to their lines, the men simply stacked arms and collapsed to the ground without eating. Exhausted, they fell asleep that night on the damp ground without benefit of blankets or shelter.[42]

The critical importance of this combined attack on the Union right flank cannot be overemphasized. Even General Beauregard acknowledged it in his official report:

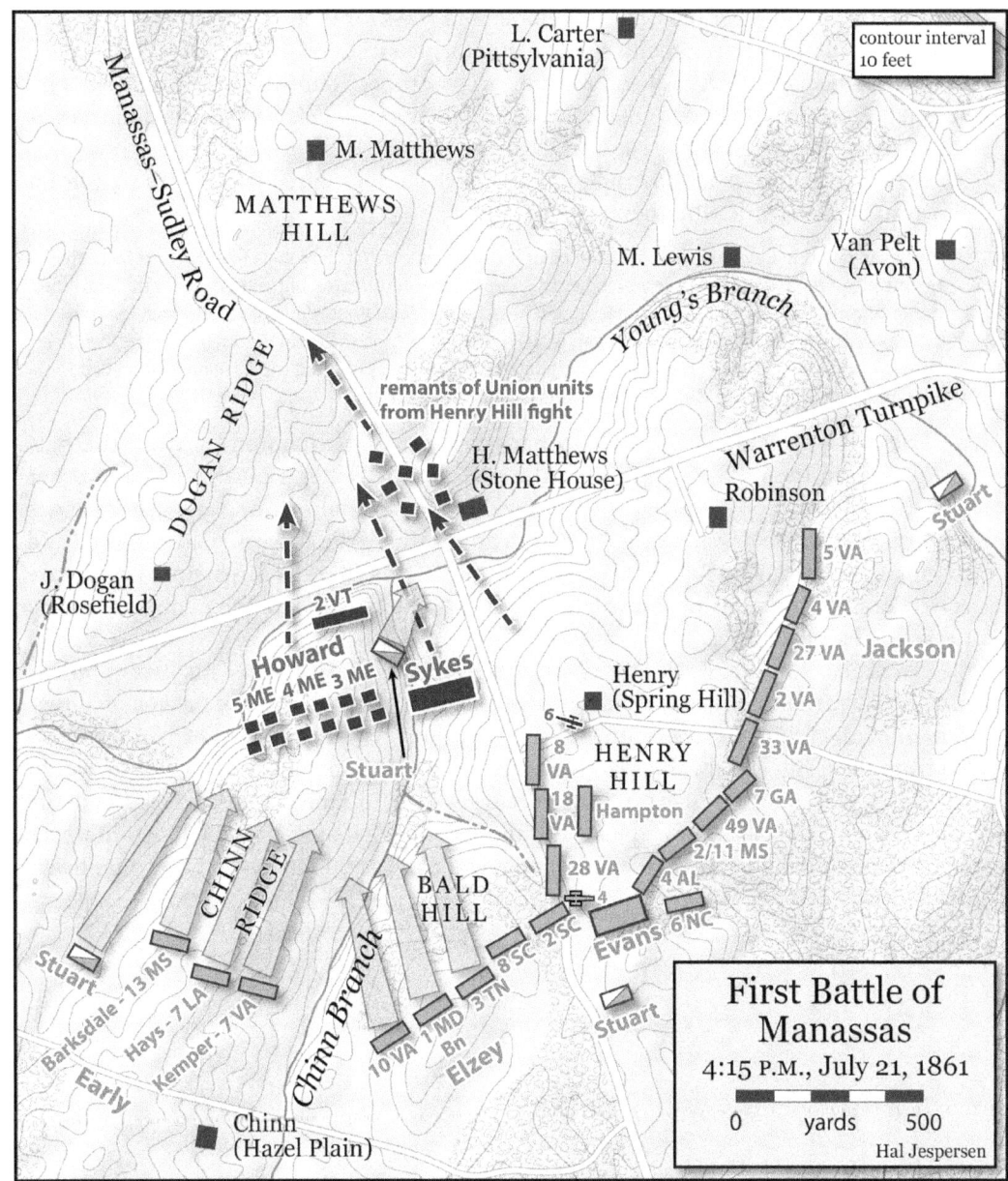

First Battle of Manassas, July 21, 1861: Action of Col. William Barksdale and 13th Mississippi

At this time the enemy had formed a line of truly formidable proportions. The woods and fields were filled with their masses of infantry and cavalry. It was a magnificent spectacle as they threw forward their cloud of skirmishers on the slopes of the ridge for another attack. But as Early formed his line Elzey's brigade and other regiments advanced, almost simultaneously, with great spirit from their various positions. At the same time, too, Early resolutely assailed their right flank and rear. Under this combined attack, the enemy was soon forced, ... rearward in extreme disorder, in all available directions toward Bull Run. The rout had now become general and complete.

In his official report Jubal Early did not acknowledge Barksdale's personal contribution to the overwhelming success of the 6th Brigade at the battle of First Manassas (Bull

Run). Early did however praise both Kemper and Hays for their "great coolness and gallantry in front of their regiments while being formed under a galling fire." Fortunately, Barksdale's decisive role has been recognized by others. Renowned historian Douglas Southall Freeman concluded that "all three of Early's Colonels had behaved like veterans—James L. Kemper, Harry Hays and William Barksdale."[43]

Military historian and instructor Steve Hawley underscored Barksdale's significant efforts in his first battle with these words:

> Early's advance, led by Barksdale at the head of his regiment with its bayonets fixed, precipitated the beginning of the federal disaster which began as an orderly withdrawal but soon degenerated into the panic commonly associated with the federal side of the battle of First Manassas.... Barksdale's resolution overcame the fog or friction of war, which in this case took the form of foraging, heat, shell fire and wasps, to bring his regiment to the designated place at the appointed time. He had succeeded in accomplishing his first mission despite an inadvantageous start....[44]

Next day President Davis, who had arrived from Richmond during the battle, addressed the 13th Mississippi in the presence of General Beauregard and other high-ranking officers. Private Henley quoted Davis as "complimenting us on the glorious achievements of the day and exhorting us to be faithful to the cause we had espoused and to which on that day we had done so much honor." Days later the Mississippi Legislature issued a resolution praising Barksdale and the 13th Mississippi on their conduct during the recent battle.[45]

Barksdale's military career was off to a promising start. In this, his first opportunity to lead men under fire, he had performed admirably in the face of the enemy under very difficult circumstances. With characteristic bravery and courage, he had fearlessly led from the front—establishing an aggressive personal leadership style which he would continue to exhibit without exception. He had also won the admiration and respect of the regiment who had "seen the elephant" for the first time—if only briefly. Yet within weeks of this sterling debut, a serious lapse in judgment cast his military career into significant doubt.

Eight

Charges of Drunkenness, Redemption at Edwards Ferry and a Court of Inquiry

Following the battle of First Manassas, the 13th Mississippi encamped near the Stone Bridge on the battlefield as "the dead and wounded and prisoners [continued] to arrive." These Union prisoners, some 1,200 in number, would soon depart for Richmond "with their own hand cuffs on" to the delight of the victorious Confederate soldiers. The Federal army had brought some 35,000 pairs with them into Virginia intending to take Beauregard's entire army prisoner, but the Confederates had quickly turned the tables. Following a torrential downpour, the day after the battle, the ground remained very wet and muddy, and many men began to fall ill from exposure. Within days a full-fledged measles epidemic set in together with cases of typhoid fever and pneumonia. Twenty-five-year-old Pvt. John Alemeth Byers from Company H, 17th Mississippi, described the scene in a letter to his sister: "There are at least fifteen hundred sick or wounded soldiers here. Four or five die every day, the herse [sic] is continually on the go." At the same time many new recruits arrived from Mississippi to join the 13th.[1]

On July 25, 1861, Beauregard reorganized his Army of the Potomac. Although Col. Nathan G. Evans retained command of the 7th Brigade, it was now comprised of the 13th, 17th, and 18th Mississippi Regiments under colonels William Barksdale, Winfield Scott Featherston, and Erasmus R. Burt respectively, the 8th Virginia under Colonel Eppa Hunton then at Leesburg, six guns of the Richmond Howitzer Battalion under Captain Robert Stiles, and four companies of Virginia cavalry under Lt. Col. Walter H. Jenifer.

Barksdale did his best to maintain discipline by continuing two-a-day drill sessions until sickness finally overtook his regiment. To boost morale, on the evening of August 4th he assembled the entire regiment and read the recent resolution from the Mississippi Legislature praising the 13th Mississippi for their role in the battle on July 21st. The camp was relocated to Centreville six miles away where daily drill continued with a dress parade in the evening. So many were absent that one soldier recorded that the regiment "looked like we had but one company." By the sixth day of August absenteeism from sickness reached alarming proportions with nearly 600 out of 900 incapacitated. With so many absent, either sick or tending to their prostrate comrades, even posting of guards was suspended.[2]

Private Henley provided insightful analysis: "It was now that the ten days ride on the cars, the fatigue and hardship of the 21st and the drenching rain of the 22nd began to show the injuries wrought. The deaths in the regiment approximated a hundred." Private

Wallace recorded: "All of our regiment is sick at this time. Now we have the name of 'the sick regiment.'" Their predicament was further exacerbated by numerous cases of venereal disease that had been contracted during stopovers on the ten-day rail trip to Manassas. In a letter to brother Ethelbert regarding the epidemic, William confided that "measles and improper sexual indulgence accounted for most of the cases."[3]

Fearing attack by Federal forces, Beauregard ordered the 7th Brigade to Leesburg on August 9th to take up defensive positions some 30 miles above Washington. The 13th Mississippi obeyed but left 260 sick men and 100 horses behind—among them Private Wallace, too sick to travel, and Sergeant Hill as Acting Quartermaster. Colonel Barksdale would remember events of the following day for the rest of his life. His recollections of August 10, 1861, would be painful ones.

Despair over the deaths of so many young men due to sickness was now taking a toll on the mood of the officers as well. It is not hard to imagine how Barksdale would have thought that a little insobriety on his part would help to lift his spirits and dull anguished memories of suffering and death from the cholera epidemics of his childhood, from the camps at Vicksburg, New Orleans, and Mexico during 1846–1848, and his own near-death experience there from measles. Moreover, the words of his friend, Surgeon Love, resonated in support—consumption of alcohol would likely ward off any potential sickness of his own. Accordingly, in a very serious lapse of judgment, Barksdale decided to imbibe on the march to Leesburg. The situation soon got out of hand with catastrophic consequences for the colonel.

Private Henley recorded the embarrassing details:

> [Barksdale] imbibed too freely, on that occasion having taken on more than he could possibly carry. While under its influence he "bucked and gagged" a man who was generally regarded as half a fool, and then he gave the order "route step" while informing them that did not necessarily release them from keeping the step. But worst of all he impeached the honesty of his men by asserting that they would all steal while he avowed the officers would sanction the act by simply winking at the deed. Soon after which the liquor producing a drowsy feeling, he at last dismounted and laying his bald head on a rock he proceeded to sleep off the intoxication.

Colonel Evans was a reputedly heavy drinker himself. Nevertheless, upon ascertaining the particulars, Evans summarily took Barksdale's sword and put him under arrest—where he remained until September 6th. In the interim Lt.-Col. Mackerness Hudson Whitaker assumed command of the regiment. Private Henley commented that the regiment "could easily have overlooked the whole affair but for one thing, [Barksdale] had denounced them as thieves and though they could ill brook the insult, they had none the less no means of avenging it." It is interesting to note that charges had already been prepared against Maj. Isham Harrison for getting drunk and cursing the men while at Stone Bridge. Although the enlisted men had no means of redress, the officers certainly did. Under the leadership of Mack Whitaker, they immediately exercised it.[4]

The officers filed charges against Barksdale on the same day his transgressions took place. They indicted Barksdale "for drunkenness, for abusive and insulting language to officers and men, and for other military derelictions." Evans forwarded their protest to Beauregard who demanded that these charges be "drawn up formally and returned [to him]." It is not known specifically what, if any, discussions took place thereafter, or by whom. Whitaker simply recorded later that these charges were refused, and Barksdale was restored to command over the officers' protests against "this illegal act." As a last resort, with the support of the enlisted men, "almost without a dissenting voice," the

Eight—Charges of Drunkenness, Redemption and Court of Inquiry

officers petitioned Barksdale directly to resign. When he refused, 32 of 40 officers tendered their resignations through General Evans on September 5th. However, according to Whitaker, these resignations were not accepted due to "some alleged informality."

Undeterred, on September 19 these officers again submitted their resignations. Having received no formal reply, Whitaker wrote directly to President Davis on October 15th. Whitaker summarized in chronological detail all that had transpired since the incident on August 10, and re-emphasized—in forceful language—the legitimacy of their actions. Despite knowing that Barksdale and Davis were close personal friends, Whitaker pulled no punches in his condemnation of Barksdale's conduct, and came close to suggesting Davis and/or his administration were exercising favoritism. The following excerpts convey Whitaker's tone:

Brig. Gen. Nathan G. Evans, nicknamed "Shanks" due to his spindly legs. Reputedly a heavy drinker himself, Evans placed Barksdale under arrest for drunken behavior but restored him to command before the Battle of Leesburg (Library of Congress).

> All efforts having failed, we tendered our resignations. Those who suppose us disposed to abandon the cause of Southern independence and to rest quiet at home, do us great injustice. Perhaps we shall be in active service long after some of the pitiful office seekers who have upheld Col. Barksdale in this wrong have sought safety in the department of peace.... The truth is however, that the Col. whom we elected to rule over us, did get beastly drunk and did take advantage of his position as a superior officer to abuse the officers and privates of his command in a most insulting manner. We know very well what penalty the law attaches to this crime; we have seen the penalty of this offence inflicted upon privates. Shall it be said that our Col. is above the law of the Confederate States which in its provisions seems to apply to every man, applyed to Col. Barksdale when he should become an officer—and believing too as volunteer soldiers we were entitled to its protection, we enlisted among our country's defenders and chose him as our leader. Finding however that this law does not embrace Col. Barksdale in its provisions nor protect us from wrong and insult when our Col. is the aggressor we have no course left but to seek relief from his command—we are willing and anxious to remain in the Service but not willing to sacrifice pride and honor for the sake of preserving our officers, nor are we willing to be made tools to support the profanity of Col. Barksdale.

This damning letter bore the signatures of all 32 supporting officers. In his endorsement written upon it, President Davis acknowledged the legitimacy of "the appeal from the decision of the Commanding Gen'l [Beauregard]" but noted "it should not have been accompanied by a tender of resignation, at least until after the unquestionable right exercised had been exhausted." Davis concluded that "As the charges referred to are not presented in specific form it may be better to order a Court of Inquiry to examine into the case."[5]

Irrespective of his motives, and with no way of knowing it at the time, Davis had provided the one precious commodity that might save his friend Barksdale—time! By chance, the delay would provide Barksdale the opportunity to prove his worth. In the interim Barksdale decided to be on his best behavior through a combination of contrition, conscientious effort, and perhaps a little flattery thrown in for good measure. However, Barksdale would eventually survive the crisis by demonstrating his sound military leadership when it counted most. Fate would smile on William Barksdale by providing a significant battle—one that would erupt largely by chance at the ideal time.

Of all their postings during the war, Leesburg would be, by far, the favorite of these young Mississippi troops. Virginia's Richmond Howitzers shared this sentiment. A member of the 17th Mississippi recorded that "Leesburg is in God's country and the boys still having their negroes and having their camp chests and plenty of money, lived on the best of the land." Another Confederate from the 18th Mississippi remembered "the beautiful hills and fertile valleys, the crystal springs and clear running streams, the fresh baker's bread and clover fed beef, and the milk and honey of old Louden [County]." The Brigade would remain there through the winter of 1861–62, taking full advantage of the bounty of the land, and the warm hospitality of the residents.[6]

In particular, these youthful soldiers courted the young maidens of "the good little burg." Seventeen-year-old Pvt. William Meshack Abernathy of the 17th Mississippi, years later, would bemoan the fact that he was the only member in Company B who did not have a local sweetheart while at Leesburg. He attributed this forlorn status to his tender age. Comrades were so smitten that they swore to return after the war to marry and settle down there. These sentiments were echoed by the well-educated artillerymen of the Richmond Howitzers. Captain Stiles fondly and eloquently summarized their feelings post-war:

> Leesburg, the county seat of Loudoun, was at the time, perhaps the most desirable post in our lines on account of the character both of the country and its people—the former beautiful and rich, full of everything needed by man and beast, and the latter whole-hearted and hospitable, ready to share with us all they had.... During the war ... our thoughts would often turn fondly back to our bucolic Loudoun paradise ... "when this cruel war is over" more than one of our boys went back there to "get the girl he left behind him" from '61 to '65 but would never leave again; and today many a grizzled, wrinkled, burdened man feels his heart grow young again and breaks into sunny smiles when a comrade of long ago slaps him on the back and reminds him of the good times we had at Leesburg.[7]

Despite the idyllic surroundings, the 7th Brigade had been deployed at Leesburg for a military reason. A prosperous town of about 4,000 residents, Leesburg occupied a strategic position between low rounded Catoctin mountain range to the west and the Potomac River to the east, which flowed southeasterly to Washington. Harpers Ferry lay about 25 miles upstream to the northwest. In the Leesburg sector the gentle rolling farmland gives way to wooded hills and deep ravines near the Potomac and abruptly ends at Ball's Bluff—a steep cliff towering a hundred feet above the narrow riverbank. Directly opposite the bluff in mid-river is Harrison's Island—500 acres of flat farmland fringed by woods. Although a bridge at Berlin had been burned earlier by Confederate cavalry, two ferries between the Virginia and Maryland shores still operated in the area—Conrad's Ferry near the northern end of the bluff, and Edwards Ferry five miles to the south where Goose Creek empties into the Potomac. Since the Potomac River delineated the boundary between the Confederacy and Union each side patrolled its shore opposite the enemy.

Evan's brigade with a strength of approximately 2,800 was tasked with occupying the

Leesburg area. This force protected the nearby fords and ferries as well as the turnpikes linking Leesburg with Alexandria, and Alexandria with Winchester, which intersected in town. Evans constructed a substantial trapezoidal earthwork, named in his honor, which enclosed one-and-a-half acres near the Edwards Ferry Road, two miles northeast of town. Two additional earthworks, Forts Johnston and Beauregard, were also begun during the summer but, unlike Fort Evans, were not completed until after the battle.

A Union division headquartered at Poolesville, Maryland, under the command of recently appointed Major General Charles P. Stone, opposed Evans. This Union force consisted of three brigades under Brigadier General Willis P. Gorman and Brigadier General Frederick W. Lander, and sitting senator from Oregon, Colonel Edward D. Baker. Two unassigned infantry regiments, five companies of cavalry, and three batteries of artillery rounded out this division of some 11,000 men. Evans was naturally apprehensive given this disparity in strength, coupled with the fact that the nearest Confederate reinforcements were at Centreville—some 30 miles away. This was the backdrop during the late summer and early autumn. Both sides warily kept an eye on each other across the Potomac River on the left flank of the Confederate forces in Northern Virginia. Each commander contemplated his next move while his uneasy troops conducted reconnaissance patrols.

Meanwhile, as Whitaker chafed, Barksdale was restored to command of the 13th Mississippi on September 6th. He promptly used battalion drill that evening "to openly acknowledge his error and [make] all the necessary apologies." He concluded by asking for his soldiers' forgiveness and by "assuring them that in the future he would give no cause to complain of him." Although Barksdale's contrite apologies satisfied many of the men, most reserved judgment and would require more evidence and confirmation of his sincerity. Shortly thereafter they indicated their displeasure when "some scamp cut [Barksdale's] horse's tail off last night."[8]

Undeterred the colonel resumed his duties by conducting several scouts with Companies F and G in the Goose Creek sector. By mid–October Evans expected a Union attack somewhere along the front and put the entire 7th Brigade on high alert. On October 16th, on his own authority, Evans began evacuating Leesburg in order to form a new defensive line about eight miles south on the Old Carolina Road at Carter's Mill on Goose Creek. This unexpected move vexed Beauregard who reminded Evans that the Leesburg fortifications were strong and more easily defended. Although falling short of formally ordering Evans back to Leesburg, Beauregard insisted that one regiment (Hunton's 7th Virginia) remain in Leesburg. The 13th Mississippi relocated to Carter's Mill on Goose Creek about 12 miles southeast of Leesburg.

After the Union debacle at Manassas in July, Major General George B. McClellan replaced Major General Irvin McDowell as supreme commander of Union forces in the east. Washington increasingly pressured the new commander to take action. Evans' withdrawal from Leesburg did not escape McClellan's notice and prompted him to set in motion a series of events that would culminate in the battle of Ball's Bluff (known in the South as the battle of Leesburg). This engagement was a relatively small affair in terms of numbers engaged and casualties compared to the slaughter of later large-scale battles. However, this encounter took on huge importance due to the personages involved and the resultant political fallout in the North.

McClellan ordered Major General George McCall's 12,000-man division to perform a reconnaissance near Dranesville, several miles below Edwards Ferry, to map the area, and possibly to "shake the enemy out of Leesburg" without a fight. McClellan visited McCall in Dranesville on the evening of October 19th and ordered him to continue mapping the area and reconnoitering toward Leesburg. He also ordered McCall's division to return to Langley, near Washington, by October 21st. McClellan's adjutant advised Maj. Gen. Stone of McCall's activities at Dranesville, adding: "The General desires that you keep a good lookout upon Leesburg, to see if [McCall's] movement has the effect to drive [the enemy] away. *Perhaps a slight demonstration on your part would have the effect to move them*" (emphasis added). Modern historian James Morgan III has correctly concluded that "this suggestion, seemingly almost an afterthought, led to the unintended battle that occurred the next day."[9]

The same evening that McClellan visited McCall in Dranesville, a local plantation owner visited Barksdale's camp and informed him that a Yankee army was then advancing along the Alexandria Road only eight miles away. Barksdale immediately doubled his pickets on all nearby roads and dispatched a courier to inform Evans (who had already begun to transfer the brigade back to Leesburg). Finally, Barksdale ordered the 13th Mississippi to sleep on their arms and to be ready to move on a moment's notice.[10]

At 4 a.m. next morning the long roll roused the camp. By daybreak on October 20th the regiment was on the march, reaching Leesburg in about an hour and a half. Shortly thereafter, while en route back toward Goose Creek, the 13th Mississippi encountered commander Evans who exhorted them to be "valiant, heroic, and brave." In response Colonel Barksdale "proposed three cheers for the South and three more for General Evans, both of which were cheerfully given." Fortuitously, that morning Evans had captured a courier from McCall bearing dispatches to Brigadier General George Gordon Meade, one of his brigade commanders. Evans knew then that McCall and his 12,000 troops had already been ordered back to Langley and would not be advancing to Leesburg. One overwhelming Union threat had disappeared. Ironically, no one apprised General Stone of McCall's orders to withdraw—a very critical oversight.[11]

In the meantime, Stone interpreted McClellan's "suggestion" as an order. Accordingly, Stone set the wheels in motion about noon on October 20th to launch the desired "slight demonstration." He dispatched the 1st Minnesota, 2nd New York State Militia, 7th Michigan and two troops of the 3rd New York Cavalry to Edwards Ferry under Brig. Gen Gorman. Here they joined Battery I, 1st U.S. Artillery, already in position. Gorman marched his forces conspicuously on the Maryland side in full view of Barksdale's pickets. Federal artillery shelled the supposed Rebel positions in the woods all afternoon. Just before sundown, per orders from Stone to feign an attack, Gorman crossed two companies of the 1st Minnesota to the Virginia side in flatboats. After a brief time, he returned them to their camp on the Maryland shore for the night.

While this diversion unfolded, Stone ordered the 20th Massachusetts, along with four companies of the 15th Massachusetts, to join the Union pickets on Harrison's Island, and to demonstrate opposite Ball's Bluff. Lastly, Stone deployed the 42nd New York and part of the 1st Rhode Island Light Artillery in full view opposite Conrad's Ferry several miles upriver. Had Stone simply called it a day at that point he would have satisfied McClellan's intentions without precipitating a Union disaster that ultimately destroyed his own promising military career.

McClellan's original orders to Stone back in August had been discretionary—"should you see the opportunity of capturing or dispersing any small parties by crossing the river, you are at liberty to do so." Although leaving the decision to Stone's best judgment, McClellan had added a cautionary comment—"though great discretion is recommended." On his own initiative Stone sent a small scouting party of 40 men across in three flatboats at Harrison's Island. Undetected, they approached to within about two miles of Leesburg and later reported seeing what appeared to be an undefended Confederate camp in the moonlit shadows. These purported tent rows were actually neatly dispersed haystacks.[12]

Stone immediately decided to exploit this apparent advantage and dispatched five companies of the 15th Massachusetts, some 400 men, under Colonel Devens, together with two 12-pdr mountain howitzers to cross under cover of darkness around midnight. Requiring about 15 roundtrips by boat, this attacking force finally assembled atop Ball's Bluff around 4 a.m. on October 21st. By 7 a.m. they began to take fire from Confederate pickets of Company K, 17th Mississippi, under Capt. W.L. Duff. By this time Stone had instructed Gorman to cross the river again at Edwards Ferry and probe toward Leesburg. Under artillery support from the Maryland side Gorman crossed a force of cavalry reinforced by two companies from the 1st Minnesota.

By mid-morning, this Union feint was well underway. Barksdale deployed the 13th Mississippi in a blocking position southeast of Leesburg, opposite Fort Evans, on the Edwards Ferry Road. A masked (hidden) battery of the Richmond Howitzers supported the Mississippi defensive line. (It should be recognized that early in the war masked batteries of artillery represented a powerful deterrent to attacking cavalry and infantry due to the fear engendered by the psychological component of the unidentified threat.) Throughout the ensuing battle, commander Evans would remain at Fort Evans with the majority of his brigade in reserve. From here, Evans deftly parceled out his units to threatened positions as the conflict escalated. At 1:30 p.m. he ordered Barksdale's Mississippians to advance toward Edwards Ferry to "ascertain the position and number of the enemy."[13]

That morning Stone had "upped the ante" by empowering Col. Edward Baker to cross at Ball's Bluff with his entire brigade plus reinforcements in support of Devens' raiding party—or to withdraw all Federal forces—at Baker's sole discretion. Stone would forever regret this action. (Command of this force should have fallen to Brig. Gen. Frederick W. Lander but, unfortunately for Stone, Lander was absent in Washington.)

Baker was also a career politician and an accomplished orator, like Barksdale. He had served two terms as an Illinois congressman before his election as U.S. senator from Oregon. Baker had served credibly in the Mexican War, but, unlike Barksdale, saw action as an infantry commander of the 4th Illinois Volunteers. Baker's martial experience should have imparted a distinct military advantage. Baker was also a very close friend of President Lincoln going back to their early days as young lawyers in Springfield. They were so close in fact that Lincoln named his second son Edward Baker Lincoln, in his honor. Baker and Barksdale owned similar backgrounds. Here at Leesburg each received their first somewhat "independent" command requiring them to exercise discretion and make crucial decisions on their own while several miles removed from the careful watch of their commander. A comparison of Baker's and Barksdale's military leadership and performance at Leesburg offers a striking contrast.

A detailed description of the episodic and confusing main action at Ball's Bluff is beyond the scope of this book and is not salient to Barksdale's story. The reader is directed to the excellent works of James A. Morgan III, Kim B. Holien, and the late Bryon Farwell for full particulars. Suffice it to say that this action has been aptly described as a series of sporadic skirmishes or "bushwackings" which steadily grew in magnitude and intensity over 12 hours. Evans and Baker continually threw in more troops—the former with steady coolness and efficiency, the latter with recklessness and little forethought. The nature of the terrain, combined with the lack of combat experience of the "green" troops, magnified the growing confusion. This chaos often resulted in vicious hand-to-hand fighting and use of the bayonet.

Baker's actions were consistent with his bombastic nature but contrary to his written orders. It appears he had made up his mind from the outset to push as many troops across the river as possible and to engage whatever Confederate force he might encounter. Assuming a function he should have immediately delegated, Baker wasted precious morning hours on October 21st assembling and managing his inadequate supply of transfer boats. He even neglected to observe the situation atop the bluff for himself as he continued to cross troops below. When he finally did arrive atop the bluff after 2 p.m., Baker carelessly deployed his forces without even personally inspecting Devens' forward position.

Furthermore, Baker sometimes ignored the advice of more experienced subordinates. The senator eagerly continued the fight based upon the unrealistic expectation of being reinforced by Gorman's forces approaching from Edwards Ferry. Some described Baker as then being in a state of euphoria as he reveled in the greatest moment of his life. His moment in the sun would end quickly. Colonel Edward Baker was shot in the head at close range by a member of the 18th Mississippi—and died instantly. His written order from Stone, which Baker carried folded in his hat, was later retrieved—stained with his blood. Upon hearing by telegraph of Baker's death, President Lincoln openly wept. (Baker was the only sitting U.S. senator killed in action during the Civil War.)

Col. Edward Baker of Oregon. Despite their similar backgrounds, Baker performed poorly at Leesburg in contrast to Barksdale. Baker was killed near Ball's Bluff and President Lincoln openly wept at news of his death (Library of Congress).

In his formal report Stone would later blame Col. Baker for this Union fiasco with these stinging words: "The plain truth is that this brave and impetuous officer was determined at all hazards to bring on an action, and used the discretion allowed him to do it." A major in the 8th Virginia present that day later wrote, "Without reconnoitering ... [Baker] pushed forward into the fight in total disregard of Stone's precautionary orders.... He had conspicuous personal bravery, but in all other qualities of a commander, as shown by this battle, he was totally lacking." Moreover, because Baker neglected to report frequently to his superior (as ordered) Stone was unaware of his perilous situation and thus made no attempt to render assistance.[14]

Confederate regimental commanders on the other hand, without exception, performed very well at Ball's Bluff—colonels Eppa Hunton, Walter Jenifer, and Erasmus Burt, who was mortally wounded "while cheering on the four right hand companies [of the 18th Mississippi] in their headlong massacre of the enemy." Burt died several days later in Leesburg. Near dusk, Col. Winfield Scott Featherston mounted the final charge of the day at the bluff. Leading the 17th Mississippi, assisted by the 18th Mississippi, Featherston rallied his men with the admonition: "Forward Mississippians and drive the Yankees into the Potomac or into Hell!"[15]

Panic stricken, the defeated Federal soldiers by the hundreds jumped and scrambled down the steep bluff and into the frigid waters and swift current of the Potomac. All the while the victorious Confederates fired into the fleeing Yankees—like shooting fish in a barrel. Many Federals drowned while desperately trying to swim the 50 yards to safety on Harrison's Island. Hopelessly overloaded, one of the few transfer boats capsized, disgorging its terrified occupants into the swirling waters; only one man survived. A Union officer, Captain Francis Young, recorded: "All was terror, confusion, and dismay ... the shrieks of the drowning added to the horror." Hundreds more, fearing death in the water, hugged the narrow shoreline in the growing darkness and were captured. For weeks afterward the bloated corpses of Union soldiers washed up downriver along the shore at Washington, a sickening reminder of the Union debacle at Ball's Bluff.[16]

Seeking a scapegoat, the Lincoln administration, led by Senator Baker's colleagues in the Senate, formed the Joint Committee on the Conduct of the War. This political body proceeded to "skewer" Stone (not Baker) as the responsible party. In 1862 Stone was arrested and imprisoned for 189 days without any formal charges. Despite later reinstatement within Major General Nathaniel P. Banks' headquarters staff in 1863, Stone was sickened by this relentless personal attack and resigned from the military on April 14, 1864. These developments enhanced the prominence of the battle of Ball's Bluff and exaggerated its importance out of all proportion to its strategic consequences.

What of Barksdale's and the 13th Mississippi's participation at Ball's Bluff and Edwards Ferry? Around noon, as ordered by Evans, Barksdale dispatched Company D, the Minute Men of Attala, under Captain L.D. Fletcher, to Fort Evans. Evans then ordered Fletcher and his 90 men "to advance and skirmish a skirt of woods opposite and near to" the Jackson house. Flanking the enemy position Company D "put them to flight, killing or wounding 7 or 8 of their number." Ordered then to join in the main action near the bluff, these Mississippians joined with the 8th Virginia and part of the 18th Mississippi and "quite a spirited and hot contest ensued, in which [Fletcher's] company acted a conspicuous part." This combined force successfully charged the Union position and captured a battery of howitzers. Fletcher proudly reported "several of my men [were] among the first to reach the guns and take part in their removal." Company D lost one killed and four wounded.[17]

Union forces had crossed the Potomac at Edwards Ferry in strength during the morning of October 21st. This contingent included a detachment of the 3rd New York Cavalry, Gorman's three infantry regiments, two howitzers, and Lander's 7th Michigan—a force which outnumbered Barksdale's by more than four to one. Per Evans' instruction, Barksdale advanced around 1:30 p.m. toward Edwards Ferry with the remaining nine companies of the 13th Mississippi. They halted in the vicinity of the Daily

House. Exercising due caution, Barksdale deployed skirmishers from Company I's Secessionists in the woods to his front and from Company C's Wayne Rifles near the river to his left. Both quickly reported large numbers of the enemy on the Virginia side of the Potomac just beyond the Daily house.

Displaying his characteristic aggressiveness, Barksdale "immediately ordered the regiment to advance, and when near the house a number of shots were fired by the advanced guard on both sides, killing one man of [the 13th Mississippi] regiment" and an unascertained number of the enemy. While Barksdale was reforming the regiment to continue his attack, he received orders to return to support the rest of the brigade in the conflict now raging at Ball's Bluff two miles away. Leaving Company K, the Spartan Band, to observe the enemy near Edwards Ferry, Barksdale immediately commenced a double-quick march toward the sound of the guns. His pulse quickened at the thought of joining the main action. However, this hope was quickly dashed when he received "two peremptory orders from [Evans] to return to the vicinity of Fort Evans, which was accordingly done." Barksdale wisely left two additional companies, Company H, The Pettus Guards, and Company I, The Secessionists, in the vicinity of the masked battery between the Daily house and the fort to prevent any advance of the enemy from Edwards Ferry.[18]

However, Barksdale's fears of a Union attack in his sector were unfounded. Learning of Baker's ignominious defeat and death around dusk, the Union High Command were in no mood for further offensive operations but rather feared an attack by the victorious Confederates. Instead the Federals dug extensive earthworks and rifle pits and reinforced their position on the Virginia side at Edwards Ferry. Two regiments from General Bank's division also crossed in the wee hours of October 22nd. By sunrise Barksdale's three companies near Edwards Ferry faced some 4,500 Union troops supported by artillery on both sides of the river.

General Barksdale.

Woodcut of Brig. Gen. William Barksdale (Frazar Kirkland, *Pictorial Book of Anecdotes and Incidents of the War of the Rebellion*, 1866).

Next morning, exhibiting confidence in Barksdale's judgment, Evans issued a discretionary order (similar to the one Stone had issued to Baker). Barksdale later referenced this directive in his battle report: "On Tuesday morning I was ordered by [General Evans] to reconnoiter the enemy at Edwards Ferry, and attack him if in my judgment his numbers and position would warrant me in doing so." Accordingly, Barksdale advanced with the entire regiment to the forward positions of the previous day and threw out skirmishers. Based upon his personal observation, Barksdale believed the Federals were planting a battery at the edge of a woods in a field to the right of the Daily house. True to form, the aggressive Barksdale determined to attack and

Eight—Charges of Drunkenness, Redemption and Court of Inquiry 99

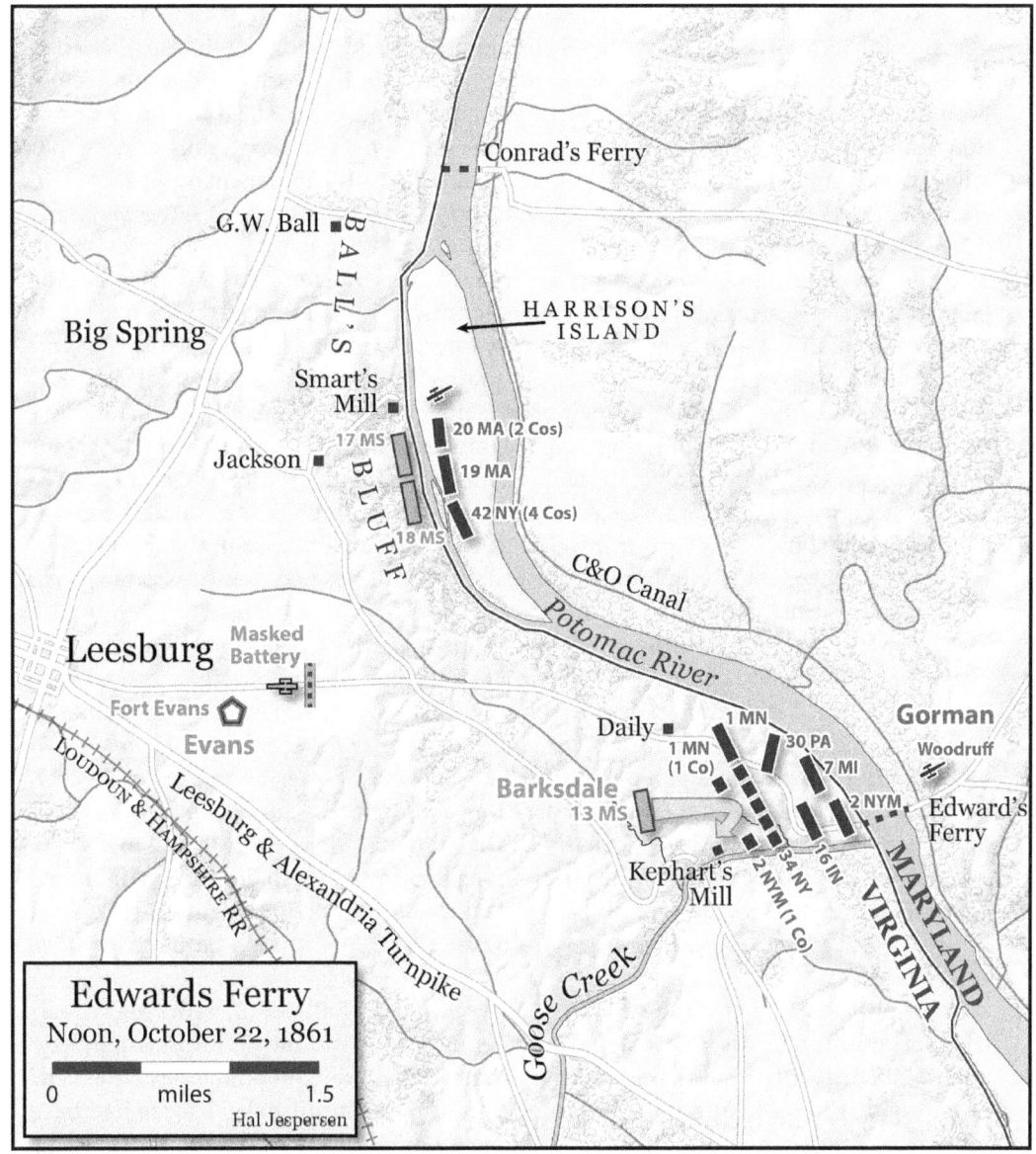

Leesburg (Ball's Bluff) Theater of Operations and Action at Edwards Ferry, Oct. 22, 1861

capture this artillery. Barksdale ordered Captain W.J. Eckford to advance with his Wayne Rifles and Captain McElroy's Spartan Band to attack "several companies of [enemy] pickets which were stationed along the field." With the Union skirmishers removed, Barksdale ordered the entire regiment forward. Barksdale recorded that "the engagement in a moment became general." Another Confederate noted that these Mississippians "assailed [the Union line] with such fury that [the enemy] broke and ran ... through the ploughed fields, over their breastworks, and past their guns," 400 yards to their entrenchments alongside the river. All the while these Confederate attackers remained under heavy artillery fire from both sides of the river. A Mississippian concluded that "the guns would have been brought in, but being so far from all support, the men fell back without them."[19]

However, unlike Baker, Barksdale kept a cool head and, did not panic. Instead, recognizing the 13th Mississippi was greatly outnumbered and facing multiple artillery batteries, he instinctively decided to break off his attack. In his words, "I did not deem it proper further to continue the assault, and hence withdrew the regiment to its position near Fort Evans, which I reached some time after dark." Barksdale's losses were four killed, two wounded and one missing. During the night, still apprehensive of a Confederate attack, these Federal forces re-crossed the Potomac to the safety of the Maryland side.[20]

The next morning General Evans ordered his "very much exhausted brigade ... to fall back towards Carter's Mill to rest," while leaving "Colonel Barksdale, with his regiment, with two pieces of artillery and a cavalry force, as a grand guard."[21]

In his after-action report General Evans praised Barksdale, stating that "He gallantly attacked a much superior force in their entrenchments, driving them to the bank of the river, killing 30 or 40 and wounding a considerable number. About sundown, the enemy being strongly reinforced and stationed in rifle-pits, Colonel Barksdale wisely retired with his regiment to Fort Evans, leaving a guard of two companies to watch the movements of the enemy...." Any prior misgivings Evans, or anyone else in the 7th Brigade, may have harbored regarding Barksdale's leadership abilities had now been quickly and completely dispelled.[22]

Nor was General Evans the only one to appreciate Barksdale's contribution to the Confederate victory at Leesburg. Colonel Elijah V. White, Virginia cavalryman and local guide during the clash, later wrote a brief history of the battle which he stated "would be sadly incomplete if the operations of *the game old Colonel Barksdale and his noble regiment, the Thirteenth Mississippi, were omitted, because only by their splendid work in holding Gorman's brigade quiet at Edward's Ferry was Confederate victory made possible at the Bluff*" (emphasis added). Albert Gallatin Brown wrote that "here the 13th had the post of honor, because it was eminently the post of danger; and right well did they maintain it." Brown continued, "Barksdale boldly sallied back and forth and impudently attacked the [Union] force. Of course, if they had known his real strength they would have walked right over him."[23]

Major R.W. Hunter of the 8th Virginia, eyewitness at Ball's Bluff, wrote many years later concerning "the essential role" of Colonel Barksdale and the 13th Mississippi Regiment: "Whenever Gorman's skirmishers advanced they were met in fierce contest and promptly driven back, and he was thus kept 'bottled up' until Baker's force had been routed and captured." In his official battle report Barksdale stated he was satisfied that the presence of his command in position at Edwards Ferry had prevented the advance of a large column of the enemy intended to reinforce General Baker's command. Hunter later wrote that he regarded this statement by Colonel Barksdale as "ample testimony to the great value of the service here rendered, and *also to the modesty and valor of this noble Mississippian*" (emphasis added). Another Virginian, cavalry commander Col. Walter H. Jenifer (while discounting the contribution of Captain Fletcher's Company D), also credited Barksdale in his official report: "[Barksdale's] regiment, though not in the engagement on the 21st, held one of the most important positions and prevented the enemy from flanking us."[24]

Barksdale received one final honor several days later when he was given command of the large honor guard which escorted the body of Colonel Burt of the 18th Mississippi out of Leesburg.[25]

Eight—Charges of Drunkenness, Redemption and Court of Inquiry 101

For his part, Barksdale bestowed credit for the success of the regiment upon his men. In his battle report Barksdale stated that "Every order I gave during both days was obeyed with promptness and alacrity, and the engagement on Tuesday [Oct. 22, 1861] was marked by the greatest possible zeal, courage, and enthusiasm on the part of both officers and [enlisted] men." This established a pattern that he followed throughout the war. Without exception, in his after-action reports, Barksdale praised the efforts of his subordinates and attributed victory to the men in the ranks, never once referencing his own personal contributions—however significant they may have been.[26]

All of the Mississippi regiments engaged in the battle now basked in the afterglow of praise for this lopsided Confederate victory. It stunned the North, already reeling from the ignoble Union defeat at Manassas only one month before. Colonel Eppa Hunton considered Ball's Bluff "the most complete victory of the war, considering the numbers engaged in it."[27]

The only negative aspect resulted from an attempt by Colonel Walter Jenifer, commander of the Confederate cavalry present, to self-aggrandize. Jenifer stated in his official report (and in newspaper accounts) that he had exercised overall command on the battlefield, issuing orders to all of the Mississippi and Virginia regiments present, including Barksdale's. In response—to a man—these commanders all denied ever having received any orders whatsoever from Jenifer. General Evans issued a supplemental report refuting Jenifer's claims, and the matter was closed.[28] However, this would not be the last time that Barksdale would tangle with a commander from Virginia over battle claims.

The grateful citizens of Leesburg, who regarded the Mississippians as their protectors, shared with them all that they had through the winter encampment that followed. Such was the depth of their affection that the ladies of Leesburg had even delivered supper to them on the battlefield following Baker's repulse on the evening of October 21st. Many a Mississippian recorded a description of the happy times spent here fraternizing with the pretty ladies. A marker in Leesburg today contains the following inscription attributed to the Richmond Howitzers—"Leesburg—paradise of the youthful warrior; Land of excellent edibles and beautiful maidens."

Before Barksdale could enjoy this quiet, pleasurable period, the repercussions from his bout of drunken behavior of August 10th had to be addressed. Enlisted members of the regiment now recognized they would be better off under Colonel Barksdale's leadership, and freely expressed their forgiveness in letters and diaries. For example, a private in the Wayne Rifles, in a letter to his father, dated November 1, 1861, stated, "I am proud to say that the whole regiment has become reconciled to Col. William Barksdale. Those who were once his enemies are now ashamed to acknowledge it."[29]

However the hackles previously raised by Lt. Col. Whitaker and the officers were still unresolved. Barksdale's Court of Inquiry, mandated earlier by the Secretary of War per President Davis' recommendation, finally convened on November 5, 1861, at Leesburg under General Order No. 68. It was presided over by Col. Eppa Hunton with Sgt. William Hill appointed as official recording secretary. Over a period of four days the Court summoned witnesses and questioned them under oath to fully investigate "certain allegations and complaints made against Colonel Barksdale."

At the conclusion, the Court rendered the following opinion:

> In view of all the facts in this case and the further facts that Colonel Barksdale is now in command of his regiment which is daily improving under his training; that he together with his whole command behaved most gallantly upon the battle-field on the 21st and 22nd of October last; that he has given a

solemn pledge to abstain from the use of intoxicating liquors; that no useful end is to be subserved by ordering a Court Martial in this case, but that much injury may result to the service therefrom: The Court is unanimously of the opinion, and most earnestly recommend, that no further proceedings be had in the premises.

The opinion was forwarded to and approved by both the Secretary of War and President Davis, and the Court of Inquiry dissolved. The entire matter was issued as Adjutant & Inspector General's Office (A.I.G.O.) General Order No. 19 on November 26, 1861, and closed.[30]

While it certainly did not hurt Barksdale's cause that he was a close personal friend of President Davis, this outcome was not an exception but the norm. In his in-depth study of the Confederate States' military justice system, author Jack Bunch made the following observations: "The indiscretions of anyone with merit were overlooked again and again. And in the final analysis such action was justified.... It is hard to imagine how the Confederate cause could have been improved by the loss of Lafayette McLaws, William Barksdale, William E. 'Grumble' Jones and others who might have been dismissed from the service."[31] Simply put, the Confederacy needed leaders who could fight, and Barksdale filled the bill. Barksdale's subsequent exploits on many a battlefield while serving with the Army of Northern Virginia certainly vindicated Eppa Hunton's decision to prolong William's military service.

One final comment regarding this matter is in order. It is logical to conclude that Lt. Col. Whitaker's persistent efforts to discredit Barksdale and remove him from command were simply motivated by self-interest. Whitaker stood to gain the most from Barksdale's dismissal. Indeed, Whitaker surprisingly remained with the regiment for another six months, under what must have been very uncomfortable conditions. Whitaker did not leave until reorganization in April 1862 when he was defeated by Barksdale in the election for colonel. Whitaker was held in high regard by the enlisted men—both as a Christian and a gentleman. He subsequently transferred to the 1st Confederate Engineer Troops where he displayed an unblemished record of service and promotion until the war's end. Fairness therefore dictates he be given the benefit of the doubt that his actions against Barksdale were prompted

Col. Eppa Hunton, commander of the 8th Virginia. Hunton presided over Barksdale's Court of Inquiry, which unanimously recommended no further action be taken (Library of Congress).

Eight—Charges of Drunkenness, Redemption and Court of Inquiry

solely by the gravity of the charges that conflicted profoundly with his deep personal sensibilities.

Through fortuitous circumstances Barksdale had successfully restored his reputation and preserved his military career. Now Colonel Barksdale could concentrate on other organizational matters and enjoy a period of relative calm as the opposing armies settled in for the winter.

Nine

The Seven Days Battles
Barksdale Commands the Mississippi Brigade

November 1861 brought significant organizational changes. President Davis, as Commander-in-Chief, ordered the brigade structure in the eastern theater be reorganized based upon state of origin. With some justification Gen. Joseph E. Johnston defiantly resisted. He argued this would destroy the cohesion within the existing brigades and would present severe logistical challenges. Davis would not relent. Thus, on November 12th, the 21st Mississippi arrived to replace the 8th Virginia, thereby creating a new Mississippi Brigade of four regiments—13th, 17th, 18th, and 21st. Colonel Benjamin Grubb Humphreys, 13 years Barksdale's senior, commanded the 21st Mississippi. Humphreys had entered West Point back in 1825 together with Joseph E. Johnston and Robert E. Lee. He was expelled two years later, along with 38 other cadets, for his participation "in a Christmas [drinking] spree ending in a riot." Humphreys later lamented his military education being cut short—"I have ever regretted my error and regard it as one of the greatest misfortunes of my life."[1]

Due to his excellent performance at First Manassas and Leesburg, Shanks Evans was promoted. Governor Pickens successfully petitioned President Davis to transfer Evans to his native state of South Carolina. Brigadier General Richard Griffith assumed command of the new Mississippi Brigade. Although born in Philadelphia and a graduate of Ohio University, Griffith had relocated to Vicksburg, Mississippi, where he taught school. He served as adjutant to Jefferson Davis and the Mississippi Rifles during the Mexican War. Most recently Griffith had commanded the 12th Mississippi in northeastern Virginia after First Manassas. Rounding out the new upper echelon appointments, Maj. Gen. Daniel Harvey Hill was appointed Division Commander in the Leesburg sector. Hill's insistence that some members of Griffith's brigade must train as artillerymen would result in dire consequences for eight of them years later while serving the guns at Gettysburg.

Parting was bittersweet for Shanks Evans. A deep personal bond had been established with these Mississippi soldiers—a bond which time and distance would not sever. Writing months later to his wife, Evans confided: "My old brigade the Mississippians flocked to greet me and begged me to come back to them…. I do wish I had them as I know they *will* fight. I have applied for them." The Mississippians, upon hearing of Evans' promotion, drafted a congratulatory letter which read in part, "We would fail to do justice to the feelings of those whom we represent, if we did not attempt to express our regret at this separation and to tender to you our most cordial wishes for your success in every field of action to which you may be called." Indicating the depth of their affection, several Mississippians applied unsuccessfully for positions on Evans' staff as late as June 1863.[2]

In a grand personal gesture, Evans, at his own expense, commissioned a new battle flag sewn by the ladies of Richmond, for each regiment in his former 7th Brigade. He personally presented these banners to each colonel during General D.H. Hill's review of the entire brigade at Camp Carolina. During this ceremony General Griffith formally took command of the new Mississippi Brigade. General Evans made a short speech which was answered in turn by the colonel of each regiment. Each colonel then made a brief speech to his own regiment while entrusting the new flag to the care of its color guard. Evans then departed and the brigade passed under the review of Generals Hill and Griffith.[3] Diarist Sergeant Hill recorded that General Griffith and his staff, together with Colonels Featherston, Thomas M. Griffin, and Humphreys, then dined with Colonel Barksdale at his headquarters. Hill emphasized that Barksdale was now "as popular with the men as he was previous to getting drunk on the 10th of August!"[4] Barksdale chose to show acts of kindness toward the men. For example, he lent his horse to Private Nash so he could visit a friend on picket duty four miles away at Edwards Ferry.[5]

Col. Benjamin Grubb Humphreys. Expelled from West Point in 1827, and 13 years Barksdale's senior, Humphreys served reliably as commander of the 21st Mississippi. Upon Barksdale's death, he assumed command of the Mississippi Brigade (Library of Congress).

During December, William received a brief visit from brother Ethelbert who was now serving in the Confederate States Congress in Richmond. To mark the occasion the regimental band conducted an evening serenade. Following this musical interlude Ethelbert delivered a near 15-minute speech to the crowd in front of Colonel Barksdale's tent.[6]

Despite the absence of campaigning during this period, activity abounded. Initially the enlisted men constructed winter quarters at Camp Carolina on Catoctin Mountain, about a mile-and-a-half from Leesburg. Many constructed wooden huts, while others persevered with tents heated by handmade rock stoves with chimneys. On November 15, the Mississippians were finally paid for their service during July and August. The men could now purchase food items to augment rations issued by the Confederate government. For example, Pvt. Newton Nash wrote his wife that he had bought a goose for 75 cents, and interrupted his letter writing to enjoy a dinner of "baked goose, ham, biscuits, and sugar." He added that they received "plenty meal, flour, beef, sugar, rice, and hams every three days—So you see we are faring better than common." In part to retain discipline, there was the ever-present drilling which, included firearms inspection on Sundays. At the insistence of General Hill significant energy was also expended toward completing earthen forts Johnston and Beauregard. During this period many members of the Mississippi Brigade described a common distraction from this drudgery. Their diaries repeatedly mentioned the ascension of Union observation balloons at several locations, including Edwards Ferry. The fair maidens and ladies of Leesburg also made frequent visits to the Confederate camps.[7]

In a symbolic gesture on Christmas morning, Colonel Barksdale shared eggnog at his headquarters with the officers of the 13th Mississippi—the same officers who had only months before submitted their resignations, not once but twice, in protest of his conduct. While Barksdale was on his best behavior, many enlisted men in camp were not. In celebration of the season, many over-indulged in the spiked eggnog. In the words of one private, "several boys [got] a little tight in camp & some have been sent to the guardhouse." The eventful year 1861 closed out with a Grand Review and inspection of the entire division, including cavalry and artillery, by General Hill near Fort Evans on December 31st. A private recorded that although the weather was "disagreeable yet many of the fair sex honored us with their presence which added greatly to the delight of the souldiers." He then confessed, "I think our lines would have been much straighter had we not had to look towards them."[8]

Per orders from General Hill, the next two wintry months witnessed increased activity toward completing earthen forts Beauregard and Johnston. With the already completed Fort Evans, these earthen defenses, sitting on three prominent hills, formed a triangle which enclosed Leesburg. Fort Evans commanded the Potomac and approaches from Edwards and Conrad's Ferry. Fort Beauregard to the south covered the approaches from Goose Creek. Fort Johnston to the west protected the approaches from Lovettsville and Snickers Gap. These formidable bastions each contained numerous mutually supporting artillery positions. These cannons covered the gaps between the forts except for a three-quarter mile space between Forts Evans and Johnston. In the event of a Federal attack, Barksdale and the 13th Regiment would occupy Fort Beauregard. Featherston and the 17th Mississippi would defend Fort Evans. Griffin and the 18th Mississippi would hold Fort Johnston. Humphreys and the 21st Mississippi would defend the space not covered by artillery and support the forts as emergency demanded. General Hill was so popular with the Mississippians that Colonel Humphreys remarked that these men worked "so cheerfully day and night in construction of fortifications and carrying out all his plans for the defense of his portion of the Confederate lines."[9]

Hill's clever plans included training 20 of these Mississippi infantrymen to serve as artillerymen under the direction of Captain Stiles and the Richmond Howitzers. The eager recruits received instruction on three large siege cannons, as well as two light field guns, in Fort Johnston. Hill instructed Stiles to adapt the light artillery drill to the heavy siege pieces, and then teach the manual to the Mississippians. The end result, in Captain Stiles' words, was that "all of us could work effectually all the pieces in the fort." Stiles pronounced the exercise a resounding success: "The Mississippians were glad to come. They liked the noise and smoke and uproar of the guns. There never were two such field artillery detachments as they made after a brief period of drill." In fact, these recruits were so eager, Stiles continued, that "We passed a good deal of time running up and down the river with the field pieces … firing across at the railroad trains and canal boats on the other side. On two or three occasions we stirred up a hornet's nest in the shape of Federal batteries which happened to be drilling on the other side, and [we] were compelled to withdraw with more speed than dignity." Artillery service was not without its risks—Sergeant Hill noted in his diary that on February 25th "one of the largest cannon in Fort Evans burst today and killed and wounded four men."[10]

Hill also recorded that Colonel Barksdale departed for Richmond on February 17th and did not return until nine days later. It is very likely that William went to meet Narcissa, Ethel and Willie at Richmond for a happy reunion. They had now been separated for over nine months. Barksdale returned with his family to Leesburg on February 26th. Narcissa later wrote fondly of this visit and the happy times spent with William and her best friend, Alcinda Janney, whose husband, John, was mayor of Leesburg. She later referred to "my sojourn in Leesburg" as the "one bright spot in the past to refer to, and one gleam of hope in the future." Concluding the letter, Narcissa lamented, "Having to leave my husband and friends was a great trial to me." She departed for Mississippi before the Confederates withdrew from Leesburg on March 7, 1862.

Shortly thereafter, Federal forces, under Col. John W. Geary, occupied Leesburg and promptly arrested prominent citizens, including Mayor Janney, for their strong secessionist activities. In her letter Narcissa railed at this outrage against Mr. Janney and opened up to her best friend Alcinda: "I wish I could have obtained the cap of invincibility and the sword of sharpness that I might have avenged his wrongs. The only weapon a weak woman has is prayer and my heart is so wicked I fear my prayers will not be acceptable to our Heavenly Father."[11]

While enjoying this pleasant reunion with his family, Barksdale had been occupied with pressing organizational matters—the most important of which was re-enlistment. Unlike members of the 21st Mississippi who had enlisted for the duration of the war, enlistments of soldiers in the 13th, 17th, and 18th regiments were for only 12 months and were due to expire at the beginning of May. Continuation of the existing brigade structure depended upon sufficient numbers within each company re-enlisting for three years or the war. Therefore, all officers, from Brigadier General Griffith on down, tried to persuade the enlisted men to rejoin. Barksdale took his turn on March 2 when he assembled the 13th Mississippi. In Private Henley's words, "for the purpose of exhibiting his oratorical powers on the subject of re-enlistment," urging its "propriety and necessity." Others, including the indefatigable Lt. Col. Whitaker and Maj. Harrison, also addressed the regiment on this subject. Later that day some of the Mississippians, perhaps to relieve the tension surrounding this issue, engaged in a lively snowball fight. This campaign for re-enlistment would continue intermittently in some form, and would dominate conversation, for another eight weeks.[12]

Confederate army commander Gen. Joseph E. Johnston had never felt confident regarding the defensive line along the Potomac River in Northern Virginia. In mid–February, before the anticipated spring campaign commenced, Johnston had decided to abandon this position and retire to a stronger one south of the Rappahannock River. Under a cloak of secrecy in preparation for the evacuation, military stores and supplies were stealthily transferred to the rear for several weeks "without exciting suspicion" of either the enemy or the Confederate troops. The evacuation of Leesburg was set to begin with daylight on March 7th. Everything that could not be carried was destroyed. Sergeant

Hill recorded that "we burned all the cabins.... General Hill had all the corn and wheat and mills burned and blew up the Forts."

By 5 a.m. the Mississippians were on the march, but with heavy hearts and feelings of guilt which they freely expressed. Eighteen-year-old James Dinkins, a private in Company C of the 18th Mississippi, wrote, "The parting of the brigade from the Leesburg people was sad and touching. The citizens felt that their defenders were being taken away, and the soldiers were not forgetful of the many kindnesses they had received at their hands." Speaking for all, Captain Stiles expressed the depth of their sadness and regret: "and a sad leave-taking it was, for some of these dear people had treated us as no strangers were ever treated before; and besides, we all felt not only the pain of parting but also something akin to the disgrace of desertion." Heading for Culpepper to link up there with Johnston's army they marched about 14 miles that day and camped at Dover in sight of Manassas Plains.[13]

Griffith's Mississippi Brigade reached Culpepper Court House on March 13th where it joined Johnston's forces. By March 20, the brigade had fallen back to the south side of the Rapidan River and camped near Orange Court House on the Orange and Alexandria Railroad. On April 8, the Mississippians boarded a train for Richmond where they arrived well before dawn. Later that day, the 13th Mississippi boarded the steam ship *Curtis Peek*, which transported the regiment south to Kings Mills on the James River on Virginia's Peninsula near Yorktown. The regiment then marched overland to Lee's Mills on the Warwick River where they went into camp on the right flank of Major General "Prince John" Magruder's Yorktown defensive line. Magruder utilized the trenches dug years earlier by the British alongside the Warwick to defend Yorktown during the Revolutionary War. These defenses certainly impressed Private Henley who described them as follows: "Our lines extended from the York to the James rivers and mostly running along the banks of the Warwick River, a small stream having on either side an almost impassable swamp and crossable at only two points. Large dams had been thrown up accumulating the water and placing a sheet of the dimensions of a lake between the opposing armies. On either side were high banks, all strongly fortified."

Pvt. James Dinkins, Co. C, 18th Mississippi. Seen here in his cadet uniform at the North Carolina Military Institute in 1860, Dinkins enlisted at sixteen and was befriended by Barksdale, whom Dinkins described as "brave, patriotic, and kind" (James Dinkins, *1861 to 1865, By an Old Johnnie*, 1897).

These obstructions must also have greatly impressed Union commander Maj. Gen. George B. McClellan. He arrived on the Virginia Peninsula in early April with an army of 100,000 men, intending to march on Richmond. Despite initially facing only 11,000 troops under General Magruder, "Little Mac" McClellan exhibited the trepidation that he soon would become infamous for. Instead of attacking, he decided to lay siege and simply waited for additional heavy artillery to arrive.[14]

It was here at Barksdale's camp at Lee's Mills on April 21 that Ethelbert visited his brother for a second time. Ethelbert was accompanied by John J. McRae, a fellow CSA Congressman, and former Mississippi Governor and U.S. Congressman. The following evening both gentlemen addressed the regiment. Unfortunately, as recorded by diarist Sgt. William Hill, "Major Ethelbert Barksdale ... used some language intended in jest but [which] gave great offence to the soldiers [as] the remark was very ill-timed." Fortunately, both speakers departed later that evening without further incident—much to the relief of Colonel Barksdale. On April 26, 1862, the Mississippi Brigade was reorganized for the remainder of the war. The election of commissioned officers was conducted by each company while, as one officer remarked, "under fire of the enemy." Despite his brother's earlier offending remarks, William Barksdale was re-elected as colonel of the 13th Mississippi. Barksdale easily defeated his nemesis, Mack Whitaker, who soon transferred out of the regiment along with Isham Harrison who failed to be re-elected as major.[15]

Since the battle of Ball's Bluff, Barksdale had diligently worked to improve the military efficiency, discipline, and morale of his regiment. Colonel Humphreys of the 21st Mississippi described this period as "toiling through the drudgery and privations of 'Winter Quarters' in the frosts and snows of Virginia." He considered it as their "initiation into the practical workings of war's demands that developed those high qualities of the soldier and established that 'esprit de corps' that signalized their valor and daring on so many bloody fields to the close of the war."[16]

By early March Colonel Featherston had been promoted to brigadier general for his performance at Ball's Bluff. He left the 17th Mississippi in early April to command another brigade in General D.H. Hill's Left Wing at Yorktown.

In recognition of Barksdale's abilities and contributions, a campaign was mounted for his promotion to brigadier general. On March 29, 1862, Albert Gallatin Brown sent a letter to President Davis seeking this honor for Barksdale. Seven additional Mississippi senators and congressmen endorsed this recommendation. Brown praised Barksdale's "conduct as an officer ... skill in command and courage in battle" displayed at both Bull Run and Leesburg, where "[Barksdale] was distinguished for [his] skill and daring." Generals Beauregard and Evans had both mentioned Barksdale's leadership in their official reports.

On April 15, a second shorter letter was sent to Davis and copied to brigade commander Richard Griffith. This letter was forwarded from Lee's Mills and was signed by a total of 39 officers from the brigade's original three Mississippi regiments. They recommended Barksdale for appointment as brigadier general, based on his "high capacity for [this] position." By recommending the advancement of "this efficient officer" they also sought "the advancement of our cause."

On April 25th, Brigadier General Griffith provided his own endorsement from Lee's Mills when he wrote to his close personal friend, President Davis. This letter read in part:

> If our gallant State is entitled to any more, I feel it my duty as well as pleasure to recommend to your most favorable consideration Col. Wm. Barksdale for the position of Brigadier. I understand an

application has already gone forward in his behalf, and I can but add my testimony *to his worth and qualification as a man, a soldier, and an officer*.(emphasis added) For nearly five months past Col. Barksdale has been under my command and it is due him to state that in every position and in all circumstances he has proved himself iminently worthy of command—*ever prompt, active, energetic and efficient* (emphasis added)... His appointment at this time would be extremely gratifying to his numerous friends, and greatly serve the public cause; and whilst I regret his loss from my command, I must hope you will not hesitate to give him this deserved appointment & oblige.[17]

Despite these several earnest appeals on Barksdale's behalf, Davis failed to intercede for his friend, and took no action. Perhaps Davis, who was well known to be very sensitive to criticism, did not wish to be accused of showing any favoritism to his friend and fellow Mississippian, especially since Barksdale's Court of Inquiry had concluded only five months earlier. Or perhaps Davis did not wish to feel pressured to make such a move, or it was simply that an opening to command a brigade did not then exist. Regardless, with Colonel Burt's death at Ball's Bluff, and Featherston's promotion and transfer, Barksdale now became the senior ranking colonel within the Mississippi brigade. Ironically, it would not be Griffith's eloquent words which would gain Barksdale's much sought after promotion—but rather Griffith's mortal wounding weeks later on the battlefield. In the meantime, Barksdale would have to be satisfied with commanding a single regiment—the 13th Mississippi.

The siege of Yorktown continued for 30 days. Johnston's army was recalled from the Rapidan toward Richmond in early April, to reinforce Magruder's greatly outnumbered defensive line along the Warwick River. This would be Magruder's finest hour—some termed it a theatrical performance. Using a combination of deception, clever ruses such as "Quaker Guns" (logs painted black to simulate cannons) and highly visible demonstrations, Magruder bluffed McClellan into thinking he faced a superior Confederate force. Finally, on May 3rd, Johnston ordered Magruder to quietly withdraw toward Richmond via Williamsburg. Next morning the Union army awoke to discover the Confederate defenses were silent and apparently abandoned.

Magruder had one more infuriating surprise for McClellan and his men. As the initial Federal cavalrymen entered the Confederate lines along the roadways, a violent explosion suddenly erupted which, uplifted both horses and riders. This was soon followed by another "stunning report" that left a large smoking hole with acrid black powder fumes, surrounded by several wounded and mangled soldiers. Lack of any accompanying cannon report, nor whizzing of an artillery projectile, mystified the onlookers. The Union soldiers soon confirmed the report of a Confederate deserter who had entered Union lines earlier that morning. These were torpedoes (termed land mines and booby traps today) which had been planted virtually everywhere. These explosive bombs were triggered by pressure-sensitive percussion fuses or concealed trip wires. The Confederates had placed them near wells, springs, flagstaffs, powder magazines, telegraph offices, in carpetbags, barrels of flour, even rigged to coffee pots. They posed a significant psychological deterrent due to the overwhelming "fear of a weapon [the enemy] could not see or hear, a weapon that lay dormant and concealed, causing death at the slightest touch."

McClellan, outraged at this "most murderous and barbarous conduct" by the Confederates, immediately ordered that Rebel prisoners must locate and remove these "infernal machines." Once identified, torpedoes were marked with small red flags and sentries were posted to keep marching columns clear. This innovation of "sub terra shells" was the creation of General Gabriel Rains who commanded a brigade at Yorktown and who had experimented with these torpedoes 22 years earlier during the Seminole War in Florida. Although killing or wounding perhaps only "three dozen men," by McClellan's own admission, these torpedoes definitely slowed the Union pursuit.[18]

McClellan's very tentative pursuit was fortuitous for Griffith and his Mississippi Brigade who formed the rearguard for the Confederate withdrawal toward Williamsburg. Despite being called into battle formation several times, the brigade saw no action. Magruder had previously designated Williamsburg as his fallback position and had completed a large earthen redoubt, named Fort Magruder, to protect the intersection of the Yorktown and Lee's Mills Roads. Thirteen additional small redoubts and redans defended the narrow three-mile line. College and Queen's Creeks covered its flanks. Johnston chose to defend this strong position in order to buy additional time to evacuate his supply trains and artillery to Richmond on the single muddy road leading out of Williamsburg. Here on May 5th the forces of Generals Longstreet and D.H. Hill fought a sharp delaying action, and then slipped away overnight toward Richmond.

By May 25th McClellan cautiously advanced to Fair Oaks Station on the Richmond-West Point Railroad only seven miles east of Richmond. Church steeples within the Confederate capital were now within sight. Lincoln had finally agreed to McClellan's long sought demand to release General McDowell's force at Fredericksburg (now numbering 40,000 men) to reinforce his army. Accordingly, McClellan positioned his forces to cover McDowell's approach and to be aligned to immediately attack Johnston when these reinforcements arrived. (Ultimately, McDowell's force would be withheld from McClellan due to the threat posed to Washington by Maj. Gen. Thomas J. "Stonewall" Jackson's force in the Shenandoah Valley.)

McClellan positioned three corps north of the Chickahominy River and one corps south of it, with another also south but in a reserve position well to the rear. Due to heavy spring rains, the Chickahominy was in flood and un-fordable. However, three bridges were located in the immediate vicinity. Splitting one's force in the face of the enemy, with an un-fordable stream in between, is never militarily sound. Johnston recognized this opportunity. On May 31st, before McDowell's expected arrival, he decided to attack General Keyes' isolated IV Corps south of the Chickahominy near Fair Oaks Station. Again, although under enemy shelling, Barksdale's men did not actively engage the enemy.[19]

Due to poor coordination the Confederates attacked piecemeal and failed to break the Union lines. This battle, known in the South as Seven Pines, became famous for another reason. Attempting to personally intervene late in the day, Johnston was shot in the shoulder and hit in the chest by a shrapnel fragment which knocked him from his horse. Evacuated to Richmond, he would survive but would not return to military service for six months.

President Davis was desperate to appoint a competent successor. He immediately turned to his personal military advisor, General Robert E. Lee, who assumed command the following day—June 1, 1862. Lee renamed his army the Army of Northern Virginia. For the next three years, mostly against overwhelming odds, under his leadership this army would establish an unsurpassed reputation as one of the greatest fighting forces in military history.

Despite numerical superiority McClellan was simply content to passively entrench and pursue a strategy of laying siege to Richmond. In contrast Lee soon aggressively seized the initiative by launching a fierce counteroffensive which became known as the Seven Days battles. Major General Stonewall Jackson had just completed his brilliant

Shenandoah Valley campaign. His 4,200 man "foot cavalry" (subsequently reinforced to 17,000) had defeated four superior but separate forces comprising some 70,000 troops under four different Union commanders. Lee now directed Jackson to covertly and rapidly join him via rail at Ashland Station north of Richmond. Jackson left behind only a single detachment in the Shenandoah Valley.

Ironically, the Seven Days battles commenced with a Union attack on June 25, 1862, to capture high ground at Old Tavern near the center of the Confederate line south of the Chickahominy. This indecisive battle was known as Oak Grove or White Oak Swamp. Lee aggressively attacked the Union right north of the Chickahominy at Mechanicsville (Beaver Dam Creek) on the following day but was repulsed with heavy losses. Next day, June 27th, Lee and Jackson combined to attack and defeat Gen. Fitz-John Porter's V Corps in a bloody battle at Gaines' Mill on the Union right flank. Gaines' Mill proved to be the largest and bloodiest battle of the entire Seven Days engagements with the attacking Confederates suffering 7,885 killed and wounded to 4,008 for the Union defenders.

McClellan had seen enough. Having suffered a major defeat, he still erroneously insisted the Confederates outnumbered his Union forces. So McClellan decided on a full retreat. He informed his corps commanders of his intent to abandon his base at White House Landing where the Richmond and York River Railroad crossed the Pamunkey River, and to withdraw to the shelter of Federal gunboats on the James River. Throughout the night, Union soldiers north of the Chickahominy trudged across the bridges to the south side. Last to cross were General Sykes' regulars who burned the bridges behind them at daybreak. This Federal retreat set the stage for the battle of Savage Station two days later. This clash would prove to be crucial for Barksdale, tragic for Griffith, and the 21st Mississippi's baptism under fire.

The battle of Gaines' Mill gave rise to a myth involving Barksdale. Brigadier General John F. Reynolds, who commanded a brigade in General McCall's Pennsylvania Division, was exhausted after two days of continuous service and sought to catch some sleep in a supposedly secure location. Somehow, he was overlooked during the retreat across the Chickahominy River and was captured on the morning of June 28th by some of D.H. Hill's men. Having served with Hill in Mexico, Reynolds confided his mortification at the circumstances of his capture. Hill reassured Reynolds of his reputation as a good soldier, stating: "Reynolds, do not feel so bad about your capture, it is the fate of wars." Subsequently Reynolds was confined in Libby Prison at Richmond for six weeks until he was exchanged for Brig. Gen. Lloyd Tilghman. Tilghman had been captured during the fall of Fort Henry in Tennessee, and subsequently imprisoned at Fort Warren. Unfortunately, during the July 1, 1899, dedication ceremonies for the equestrian statue of Major General Reynolds at Gettysburg, Col. Henry S. Huidehoper of the 150th Pennsylvania recounted this episode incorrectly. In his oration Huidehoper erroneously stated that Reynolds "was exchanged for General Barksdale, who afterwards was killed at Gettysburg." Regrettably this obvious error has been preserved for posterity in Volume 2 of the three-volume published series, *Pennsylvania at Gettysburg*.[20]

Saturday, June 28, 1862, has been referred to as "the eye of the hurricane." The preceding three days had been marked by three battles of escalating ferocity, as would the next three—but this day would be very quiet in comparison. Since McClellan had disengaged, it would take Lee this entire day to discern McClellan's intentions. Though Lee did not know it, McClellan had already begun the general withdrawal, leaving three corps—Brig. Gen. Edwin V. Sumner's II Corps, Brig. Gen. Samuel P. Heintzelman's III Corps, and Brig. Gen. William B. Franklin's VI Corps as a rearguard west of Savage Station on the Richmond and York River Railroad. Having personally departed for the James River, McClellan strangely did not designate an overall commander for this delaying force. This critical oversight precluded a coordinated defense. Sumner objected to any retreat at all and reluctantly withdrew his corps from their fortifications that night. He proceeded only as far as Allen's farm and Orchard Station on the railway two miles short of Savage Station, the newly designated Union headquarters per McClellan's orders.

Savage Station was a depot on McClellan's line of supply and the site of a Union field hospital now filled with 2,500 wounded from the battle of Gaines' Mill. By dusk, Lee used various pieces of intelligence to correctly divine McClellan's intentions. Lee immediately issued orders in the hope of engaging and destroying this retreating Federal army. Lee's plan called for Magruder's division, which included Griffith's Mississippi Brigade, to attack the Union rearguard. Magruder's attack would be supported by Major General Benjamin Huger's division to the south, and Jackson's from the north. Simultaneously the divisions of Longstreet and A.P. Hill would march from the left flank, behind Magruder, to the right flank near Glendale, in an attempt to cut off McClellan's line of retreat. Theophilus Holmes' division would march to the extreme Confederate right flank at Malvern Hill to assume a supporting position.

At 9 a.m. on Sunday June 29, Brig. Gen. George T. "Tige" Anderson's Georgia Brigade attacked and dislodged Sumner's forces in the peach orchard of the Allen farm after a bitter two-hour action. It was here, near Orchard Station, that Fate once again intervened to further Barksdale's military career. What letters of recommendation could not accomplish, a stray Union artillery shell could—and did! During this morning action, Griffith's Mississippi Brigade had been held in reserve and occupied the defenses just vacated by Sumner's Union men. Three eyewitnesses recorded what must be considered a bizarre occurrence of destiny—in modern parlance, a tragic "fluke." Private James Dinkins of the 18th Mississippi recalled: "As we stood in the fort and ditches ... suddenly the enemy's batteries, a mile off began shelling our line.... While waiting the order to advance, a wicket shell struck the railroad section house just in our front and exploded, a piece of which we distinctly saw pass over our heads. In falling it struck General Griffith on the thigh, tearing the flesh down to his knee, while he was sitting on his horse near the fort just in our rear." Captain Stiles, an artilleryman, was more specific and recalled that "at least half a shell from a three-inch rifled gun lodged in [Griffith's] body," and Stiles marveled that he did not die instantly. Stiles vividly remembered the "desperate clinch of [Griffith's] fingers and the pallor of his face as he clasped his hands back of his head after he had fallen from his horse." Major Joseph Brent, Magruder's aide, remarked that this Union artillery fire was completely harmless save for this one maverick projectile. He candidly pondered the strange twist of fate that had "only singled out the General for death."[21]

As senior colonel within the brigade, Barksdale immediately assumed command—and never looked back. In his after action report Barksdale referenced this personal milestone with these simple words: "The brigade was at once ordered in line of battle and while gallantly executing this order General Griffith fell mortally wounded, and was borne from the field ... when command devolved upon me." Barksdale's first order as brigade commander was to dispatch Majors Watts and Hawkins of Griffith's staff to accompany the critically wounded general back to Richmond, where he died later that evening.[22]

Despite Lee's order to attack the Union rearguard, Magruder found himself outnumbered 26,000 to 14,000. Magruder did advance—but very slowly. Understandably he hesitated throughout the day to aggressively push forward. Instead Magruder preferred to await the arrival of Jackson's force on his left and Huger's on his right. Unfortunately, Huger was not where Magruder expected him to be. Worse, due to confusion and delays in rebuilding the Grapevine Bridge over the Chickahominy River, Jackson would not arrive until the next day. Adding to Magruder's difficulty was a bout of severe indigestion for which his personal physician dispensed morphine. This narcotic rendered the naturally high-strung Magruder even more intensely anxious and agitated, as noted by many who were present.

On this day Magruder received a powerful new weapon—the "Land Merrimac." Another first in military history, it consisted of a rifled 32 pounder Brooke naval gun mounted on a railway flat car. Protected in front by a sloped casemate of eighteen-inch thick timbers covered with four inches of iron plating through which the gun protruded, it was pushed from behind by a steam locomotive whose cab was protected by a surrounding wall of cotton bales. Lee, had anticipated that McClellan would advance along the Richmond and York River Railroad. So, weeks earlier, Lee had requested that the Confederate navy construct such a weapon based on Lt. John M. Brooke's design of the ironclad, CSS Virginia (converted from the fire-damaged hull of the USS Merrimac). Now it had finally arrived, much to Magruder's relief, and to the delight of the men in the ranks. Once Federal obstructions placed on the tracks near Orchard Station had been removed, the Land Merrimac went into action and triggered an artillery duel which lasted throughout the day.[23]

A member of Kershaw's Brigade in the Confederate vanguard commented on the service rendered by this 60-ton leviathan and its crew: "Nor was the railroad battery idle, for I could see the great black, grim monster puffing out heaps of gray smoke, then the red flash, then the report sending the engine and car back along the track with a fearful recoil." A Union signal officer remarked, "the range and service of the piece were splendid, and its fire most annoying." A Union prisoner estimated this lethal oddity had killed or wounded one hundred men and 30 horses. However, the locomotive, protected only by cotton bales over the cab, was its Achilles heel. Once Federal artillery found the range, the Land Merrimac had to back off and could not advance any closer.[24]

By mid-afternoon Magruder received confirmation that neither Jackson nor Huger would be supporting his attack. On the Union side, in the absence of an appointed supreme commander, General Heintzelman unilaterally decided to withdraw his corps without informing Sumner nor Franklin. Magruder wisely decided to keep Barksdale's Mississippi Brigade in reserve. He ordered Toomb's and Cobb's brigades to advance into the woods north of the railroad tracks, and Kershaw's and Semmes' brigades to advance into the woods south of the tracks. While supporting Cobb's brigade, Barksdale was ordered to reinforce the attack by Kershaw and Semmes on the right. In his first tactical decision as brigade commander, Barksdale prudently chose to send forward the two regiments least affected by recent changes in command structure, namely the 17th and 21st Mississippi. He put both under the control of reliable Col. Benjamin Humphreys. Barksdale remained behind with the 13th and 18th Mississippi Regiments in support of Cobb.[25]

Throughout the day the Union forces had been burning and destroying supplies, arms, and equipment at Savage Station to prevent them from falling into Confederate hands. It was here that Sumner decided to turn and fight so the Federals could complete

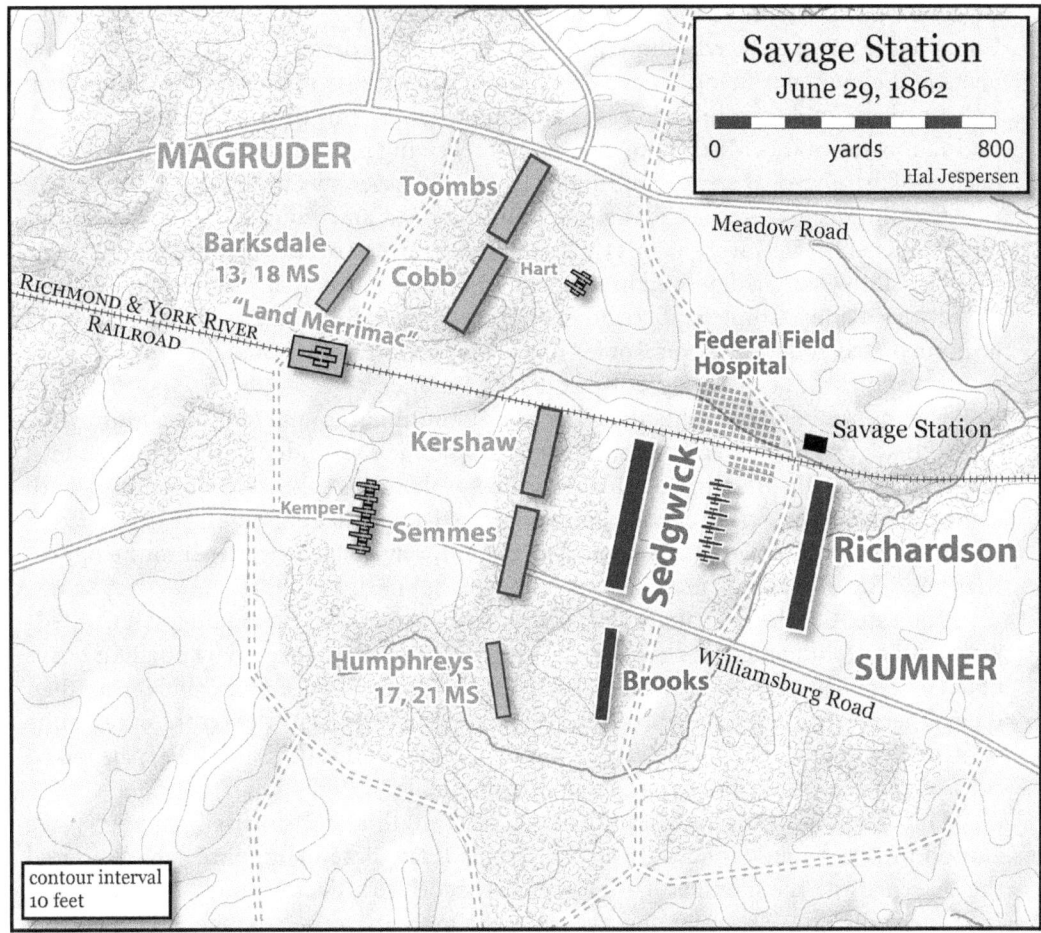

Battle of Savage Station, June 29, 1862—Action of Barksdale's Brigade

their task. Sumner was now on his own, since Franklin's VI Corps was already well to the rear. Magruder's attack on the right began in earnest about 5 p.m. and continued until darkness when a severe thunderstorm terminated the contest. All but a few of the Union cannon were masked which made the task much more difficult for the attacking Confederates.

Humphreys later described the 21st Mississippi's baptism of fire in "a sure enough fight" against General Brooks' Vermont Brigade: "Our brave boys charged forward with a wild rebel yell but the Green Mountain boys stood their ground manfully.... It certainly changed the opinion of many of the 21st regiment as to the feasibility of one southern man whipping and running five Yankees, and I am certain that it was the most stubborn, unyielding, and defiant line I ever encountered in an open field."[26]

In the lengthening shadows and chaos, Humphreys halted his line at the edge of the woods and fired across a ravine at the Yankees. In his words "the firing was incessant and telling on both sides." Suddenly a courier rode up on horseback imploring Humphreys to cease firing as they were shooting into a regiment of Georgia troops. Although Humphreys immediately complied and ordered his men to lie down, the opposing line continued to target his men. Captain Kemper of Kemper's Virginia battery, who had been engaged with, this same enemy line, raced to Humphreys exclaiming that it was indeed a Union battle line they faced. Humphreys had no sooner ordered his regiments to fix bayonets and commence firing, than a second mounted officer in a Confederate uniform rode up again imploring him to cease firing into friends. This time Humphreys refused, stating that unless his Mississippians stopped receiving fire, he would drive the opposing line off by a bayonet charge. The line in front soon gave way due to the Mississippians' rifle fire and disappeared—leaving one hundred dead and wounded *Yankees*. (Humphreys did believe however that his rightmost company had overlapped and fired into the left of the 10th Georgia deployed in the ravine.) Upon hearing that Humphreys had supposedly fired into a Confederate regiment killing 60 men, Barksdale was so annoyed that he immediately rode with several of his officers to investigate. Much to the relief of all, he confirmed that the 60 dead bodies were, in fact, Federals.[27]

Having accomplished his delaying action, Sumner completed the Union withdrawal that night. However, he abandoned 2,500 sick and wounded soldiers to their fate. Although the battle of Savage Station had been prolonged—and at times vicious—both commanders had exercised caution. Sumner engaged only 10 of his 26 II Corps brigades, while Magruder released only two-and-a-half of his available brigades into the fight—Kershaw's, Semmes,' and half of Barksdale's Mississippi Brigade.

The extent of the destruction of war materiel astonished the bedraggled Confederates. Stiles commented wryly: "there must have been acres covered by burning boxes of bacon, crackers, and desiccated vegetables—'desecrated vegetables' our boys called them. There were other mementoes of their stay and of their hasty departure ... not quite so attractive or appetizing—the ghastly leavings of numerous field hospitals; pale naked corpses and grotesque piles of [amputated] arms and legs."[28]

One final vignette related to the attack of the 17th and 21st Mississippi at Savage Station involved Gen. Stonewall Jackson the next day. When Humphreys had ordered the ceasefire and the men had laid down, they received a deadly volley from the supposed friendly line. An eyewitness recorded the macabre scene next morning as members of the 21st Mississippi retrieved the bodies of their fallen comrades: "Almost every man struck was killed, and every man killed was shot through the brain ... as soon as it was light [we] brought out the bodies and laid them in rows, with hands crossed upon their breasts but eyes wide-staring.... Every eyeball was strained upward toward the spot where the bullet had crashed through the skull and every forehead stained with the ooze and trickle of blood." As comrades silently bent low trying to identify their friends among these distorted countenances, Stonewall Jackson halted in the roadway not 50 feet away. Mounted on Little Sorrel "Old Jack" was dusty, bone-weary and careworn. The rest of his staff lagged 150 yards behind. The eyewitness continued, "He sat stark and stiff in the saddle. Jackson glanced a moment toward this scene. Not a muscle quivered. 'Eyes Front' and he resumed his steady gaze down the road toward Richmond. He was the ideal of concentration—imperturbable, resistless."[29]

Humorously, Humphreys later referred to this action as his stint serving as "a newly made half brigadier" and freely admitted it had unsettled him. Withdrawing his 21st Mississippi back along the Williamsburg Road, he completely forgot their sister 17th Mississippi Regiment, who remained on the battle line. Humphreys added self-deprecatingly "to be cared for by their gallant Colonel Holder, who doubtless thought he could do as well without me as with me."[30]

The entire brigade slept on the battlefield that night. It must have been a hectic one for Barksdale as he struggled with his new responsibilities. Next day dawned clear and warm. Magruder wisely kept Barksdale's Mississippi Brigade as his reserve while the Confederates pursued the retreating Federals eastward toward the James River. This reserve position afforded Barksdale the opportunity to acclimatize to his new role as brigade commander. In a less stressful environment, Barksdale could familiarize himself with Griffith's staff, and transition to the mastery of directing and issuing orders to four regiments rather than leading only one.[31] The entire day was spent on the march, attempting to catch up with the retreating enemy. That day the forces of Longstreet and A.P. Hill unsuccessfully tried to penetrate the Union defensive line at Glendale and Frayser's farm. The Mississippi Brigade did not reach the battlefield until 10 p.m. that night—too late to participate. One Mississippi private recorded that for the second consecutive night Barksdale and his men "slept among the dead and wounded who were so numerous that it was difficult to walk in the dark—the scene was horrifying."[32]

The following day, July 1, 1862, afforded Barksdale his first opportunity to lead his entire brigade in combat at the bloody battle of Malvern Hill—later described by General D.H. Hill as "not war but murder!" It would be here that Barksdale, his officers, and enlisted men would do their whole duty and prove themselves "worthy of the name of Mississippians."[33] Here, Barksdale would also earn the direct praise of General Lee for individual gallantry under fire.

Ten

Malvern Hill

Barksdale Exhibits
the Highest Qualities of the Soldier

Since assuming command of the Army of Northern Virginia on June 1, 1862, Gen. Robert E. Lee had lifted McClellan's siege of Richmond. By repeated attacks, launched in rapid succession, he had beaten back the Army of the Potomac in a series of bloody battles. However, Lee had not achieved his ultimate goal—to destroy or capture this invading Union army. Now, Lee believed he had one final chance to do so by unleashing another all-out assault before McClellan reached the protection of Union gunboats on the James River.

Tuesday July 1, 1862, dawned hot and humid. The sun soon transformed into a yellow fireball in a cloudless sky of blue on this sultry morning. Before departing for Harrison's Landing McClellan had ordered a defensive line to be formed in order to protect Union wagon trains and reserve artillery already en route to the James River. Accordingly, the triumvirate of Brig. Gen. Fitz-John Porter, Chief Army Engineer John G. Barnard, and Army Artillery Reserve Commander Henry J. Hunt established a very strong defensive position across Malvern Hill. (Some Confederates would later call it impregnable.) This prominence was an open plateau, oriented north-south, that towered 80 to 100 feet above the surrounding countryside. One-and-a-quarter miles long, and three-quarters of a mile wide, it was flanked on both sides by creeks flowing in deep ravines. The frontal approach to the Union defenses consisted of a wheat field, devoid of cover, about a half-mile long that gradually sloped down to a swamp, barely passable at only a few places. Further south, Malvern Hill became a series of marshes, and finally terminated in dense woods. Hunt had assembled over 100 artillery pieces, lined up virtually hub to hub across the crest, supported closely behind by infantry. These Union cannons commanded this entire approach including the Confederate assembly area in the distant woods. Indeed, it is hard to imagine a more formidable, natural defensive position than that presented to Lee and his generals on this day.

Moreover, faulty maps, poor communication, flawed and inadequate staff work, and the extreme fatigue resulting from the sustained attacks of the past week all conspired to confound Confederate leadership. The inevitable confusion and chaos would culminate in a series of uncoordinated, unsupported, piecemeal frontal attacks. The result—a horrendous casualty tally and the senseless sacrifice of so many young Confederates. The battle of Malvern Hill would clearly not be Lee's finest hour and would bear a striking number of similarities to another future Confederate disaster—the battle of Gettysburg, exactly one year later.

Lee had ordered Magruder to march his division via the Quaker Road to a position near the Confederate right flank. Uncertain as to the correct road to take, Magruder advanced in the wrong direction until he encountered General Longstreet, who redirected him to take another road. Thus it was not until about 2 p.m., as Barksdale later recorded, "By [Magruder's] orders, given to me in person, the brigade was formed in the woods in front of the enemy and in range of his fire both from his batteries and gunboats in [the] James River, about 14 miles distant." Here the Mississippians endured constant shelling for the next four hours until ordered to attack and participate in the carnival of death already well underway.[1]

The command structure of Barksdale's Mississippi Brigade suffered under a severe state of flux. Like Barksdale himself, clearly half of the regimental commanders were facing combat in their new position of leadership for only the second time. Lieutenant Colonel James W. Carter, a 32-year-old farmer from DeKalb County, Mississippi, now commanded Barksdale's old regiment, the 13th Mississippi. Major Kennon McElroy, a 22-year-old farmer from Lauderdale County, Mississippi, and an 1861 graduate of the University of Mississippi, seconded Carter. McElroy was one of seven brothers who served in this regiment.

The 17th Mississippi fell under command of Col. William Dunbar Holder, a 38-year-old planter and prewar U.S. Marshal and State Legislator, from Pontotoc County, Mississippi. Holder was seconded by 27-year-old Lt. Col. John Calvin Fiser, (like Barksdale) another native Tennessean. Reared by an uncle in Panola County, Mississippi, Fiser became a prewar merchant in Memphis.

Lt. Col. William H. Luse, 18th Mississippi. Captured at Second Fredericksburg, when Barksdale's thin line was breached at the stone wall, Luse was paroled only to be recaptured during the repulse of Barksdale's Charge at Gettysburg (Library of Congress).

Forty-six-year-old Col. Thomas M. Griffin continued to command the 18th Mississippi. Griffin was a prewar planter from Madison County, Mississippi, who had succeeded Colonel Erasmus Burt who was mortally wounded at Ball's Bluff. Second in command of the 18th was Lt. Col. William H. Luse, a 25-year-old farmer from Midway, Yazoo County, Mississippi, former captain of Co. B, the Benton Rifles. Luse would become famous after the war for having escaped from the Johnson Island federal prison camp.

Reliable Col. Benjamin Grubb Humphreys was absent in a Richmond hospital due to a severe case of his "old enemy the flux," during both the battle of Malvern Hill as well as Lee's subsequent invasion of Maryland. Therefore command of the 21st Mississippi reverted to crusty, gray-haired 62-year-old Lt. Col. William L. Brandon, a planter from Wilkinson County, Mississippi, who stood six-feet-two-inches tall, weighed 200 pounds, and who had three adult sons serving in the regiment. Major Daniel N. Moody, a 39-year-old jeweler and watchmaker from Vicksburg, Mississippi, was this regiment's second in command.[2]

This bloody battle at Malvern Hill would be the most catastrophic for the leadership of Barksdale's Mississippi Brigade until Gettysburg. All four regimental commanders, plus one of their subalterns, became incapacitated with serious battle wounds. Some would not return to active duty for many months. Amazingly, despite being in the thick of the action, Barksdale did not become a casualty.

Having assembled in the woods within reach of the Federal guns, the Mississippians hunkered down as best they could and endured hours of indiscriminate shelling with little protection and no means of fighting back. For many, passively surviving this artillery hell with no opportunity to retaliate was more frightening and nerve wracking, and required more courage, than charging a strong enemy line. This sentiment was freely expressed in soldier diaries throughout the war—by Johnny Reb and Billy Yank alike. As an example, Private Dinkins provided the following description at Malvern Hill:

> Barksdale's brigade reached a position in front of the enemy's lines, screened from view somewhat by small pine trees. We lay down and waited for the command to move forward. Large shells from the gun-boats and from land batteries, also, were tearing and literally smashing everything in reach. The Camden Rifles, a company of the Eighteenth Mississippi, lay under a large oak tree. A ten inch shell struck it about ten feet above the ground, cutting off the entire top. This fell on the Camden Rifles, killing several men and creating a worse panic than if ten times the number had been killed by bullets.[3]

To say that confusion reigned supreme within the Confederate High Command that day is a gross understatement. General D.H. Hill recognized that the Federal position was simply much too strong to be attacked. During a conference that morning, he somewhat impudently advised Lee, "If General McClellan is there in force, we had better let him alone," to which General Longstreet laughingly replied "Don't get scared, now that we have got him whipped."[4]

According to Hill it was Lee's mistaken belief that the Union army was completely demoralized that made him risk an all-out attack. Although there is some disagreement as to how the final attack was initiated, and whether Lee tried to amend his original battle plan at the last minute, the generally accepted version of events is as follows. At some point Longstreet identified a position on the Confederate right where he believed 60 cannons could be brought to bear on the Union position. If supported by enough artillery pieces on Jackson's front on the Confederate left, an effective crossfire could result in a successful frontal assault by infantry. Lee acquiesced to the plan around 1:30 p.m. when his chief of staff, Lt. Col. Robert H. Chilton, issued the following garbled order—amazing for its lack of detail and clarity: "Batteries have been established to rake the enemy's lines. If it is broken, as is probable, [Brig. Gen.] Armistead, who can witness the effect of the fire, has been ordered to charge with a yell. Do the same. By order of General Lee." On the Confederate left D.H. Hill received a note from Stonewall Jackson at about 2 o'clock with Chilton's order enclosed. Confirming his understanding Hill later stated "[Armistead's] shout was to be the signal for a general advance, and all the troops were to rush forward with fixed bayonets."[5]

Unfortunately, in reality, the terrain precluded getting sufficient numbers of cannon into position to provide the desired firepower. Instead the Confederate guns could be brought into position only a few at a time—to be quickly destroyed by the massed Federal batteries. Three of these unfortunate Confederate field pieces belonged to the battery of the Richmond Howitzers under Captain Stiles who provided the following vivid description of their very brief action and subsequent obliteration:

> I never conceived anything approximating the shower and storm of projectiles and the overwhelming cataclysm of destruction which were at once turned upon our pitiful little popguns. In the short time they existed as effective pieces they were several times fired by fragments of Federal shell striking them after the lanyard was stretched and before it was pulled; and in almost less time than it takes to tell it the carriages were completely crushed, smashed and splintered and the guns themselves so injured and defaced that we were compelled to send them to Richmond, after the battle, to be remoulded.

As for the artillerymen, many were killed outright. Stiles, greatly shaken but alive, wondered that any had survived and attributed this outcome to the fact that the guns had been put out of action so quickly. Nor were the unsettling effects of the artillery barrages confined to the Confederate side. A Union infantryman supporting the Union guns on the crest of Malvern Hill commented after the battle, "the din of the engagement was still in my ears, and kept up a perpetual buzzing that I could not drive away. I had a bad headache, my throat was parched, my eyes were aching. I could not sleep."[6]

At approximately 4 p.m. the situation began to unravel for the Confederates as events seemingly took on a life of their own. The hoped-for concentration of Confederate artillery fire had not been achieved on either flank, and Brig. Gen. Lewis Armistead had not yet attacked to signal a general advance along the entire Confederate line. General Hill complained to Jackson "that the firing from our batteries was of the most farcical character." Jackson simply reiterated "[Lee's] order for a general advance at the signal of the shouting from General Armistead." While conferring with his brigade commanders Hill recorded, "shouting was heard on our right, followed by the roar of musketry. We all agreed that this was the signal agreed upon, and I ordered my division to advance." However, Hill had misinterpreted the action in front of Armistead's brigade on the right and his division advanced alone. Hill later bitterly commented, "neither Whiting on the left, nor Magruder and Huger on the right, moved forward an inch" and concluded "The division fought heroically and well, but fought in vain."[7]

Shortly thereafter, Magruder, who was in command of Lee's entire right wing, became agitated and impatient while in position behind Wright's and Armistead's brigades. Even though Armistead was still pinned down by Federal artillery, Magruder received a subsequent order from Captain A.G. Dickinson of Lee's staff:

> General Lee expects you to advance rapidly. He says it is reported the enemy is getting off. Press forward your whole line and follow up Armistead's successes....[8]

No doubt perplexed and unnerved, the high-strung Magruder lost his self-control and ordered a general assault. Soon thereafter piecemeal and uncoordinated attacks by individual brigades commenced in the confusion—first by Wright and Armistead, and when they were repulsed, by the brigades of Semmes, Kershaw, Mahone, and Cobb of Magruder's own division. All of these subsequent attacks were beaten back with heavy losses.

At approximately 6 p.m., in front of the Crewe house, it was Barksdale's turn to actually lead his Mississippi Brigade into battle for the first time. His "litmus test" could not have been more difficult for he was tasked with leading the entire brigade, as part of Magruder's second echelon, in a full frontal, unsupported assault against a virtually impregnable defensive position. This situation would pose a daunting task even

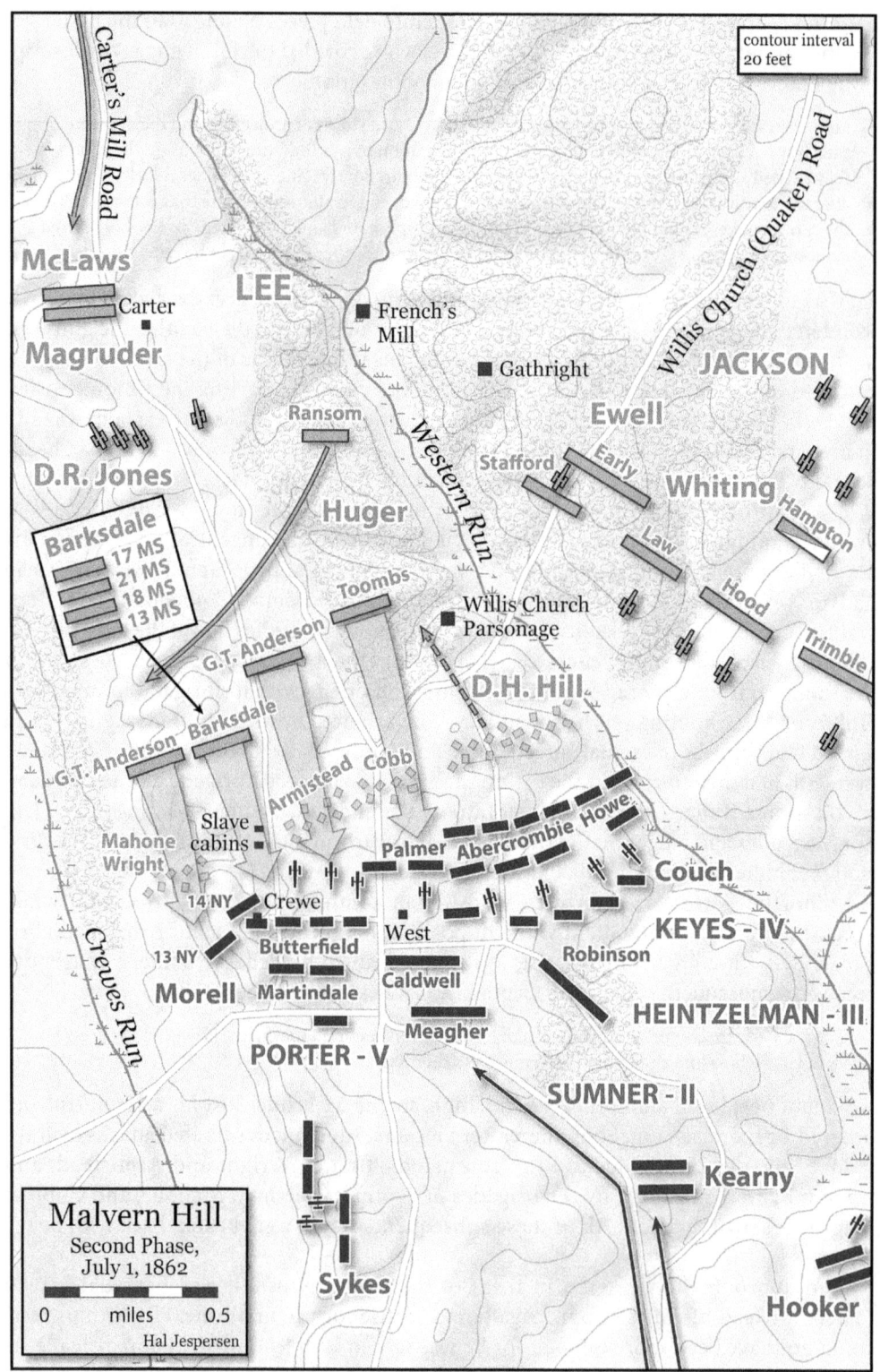

Battle of Malvern Hill, July 1, 1862—Attack by Barksdale's Brigade.

for a veteran brigade commander with a professional soldier's background. It must have seemed an overwhelming challenge for a newly acting volunteer one like Barksdale.

Although Barksdale did not mention it in his own after-battle report, Magruder stated that, while dispatching staff officers with instructions for other brigades, he personally supervised Barksdale's initial advance after issuing orders for the Mississippians to press forward in support. This likely reflects lingering concern Magruder harbored regarding Barksdale's lack of experience at brigade-level command. Magruder didn't worry for long, later confirming in his official report: "This gallant brigade, not quailing for an instant, advanced steadily into the fight!"[9] Unlike Georgia's Robert Toombs, another prominent national politician turned brigadier general in D.R. Jones' division who performed poorly at Malvern Hill, Barksdale again provided strong, effective leadership as a volunteer officer.

Barksdale later wrote: "The order was promptly obeyed. The brigade was formed in the open field, and advanced upon the enemy under a terrible fire of shell, grape, canister and Minie balls and continued the assault until night closed the scene." Barksdale wisely advanced the brigade in column of fours formation to maintain order over the rough terrain. As was his custom, he led from the front, accompanying his old 13th Mississippi Regiment who were in the lead—followed by the 18th, 21st, and 17th Mississippi.[10]

Upon reaching a point within about 300 yards from the enemy line, the 13th Mississippi halted, formed into a double battle line while under fire, "promptly dressed [the line] without confusion, and when the command forward was given [by Barksdale] advanced in splendid style to within 100 yards of the enemy."[11] It was during this advance that Barksdale, in General Lee's own words, "displayed the highest qualities of the soldier—personally seizing the colors himself and advancing under a terrific fire of artillery and infantry."[12]

Private Thurman E. Hendricks attested to this fact in his diary: "We had not gone far before the shot and shell began to thin our ranks at a fearful rate. Three color bearers were killed or wounded. Col. William Barksdale took the flag up in his own hands and advanced at least some fifty yards and asked his men to form on it, which they promptly did, but it was apparent that we could not advance [farther] on that line and live.... Within thirty minutes we had lost nearly half our men—killed or wounded."[13] For those members of his brigade who witnessed it, this act of bravery on Barksdale's part did more to validate his position of leadership than anything he could ever say to them.

Meanwhile the 18th Mississippi, now under command of Lieutenant Colonel Luse, (Colonel Griffin having been wounded and already carried from the field) left obliqued and took up a battle position about 200 yards to the left and commenced firing. An eyewitness later recorded the action and the death of a comrade:

> On July 1, just before sundown, the brigade under Col. Barksdale was ordered to attack a powerful battery of ten or twelve guns, advantageously posted upon a hill difficult of approach, and strongly supported by infantry. The Eighteenth Mississippi Regiment boldly advanced and formed in beautiful order under a fearful fire of shell.... Our colonel had now fallen, and many of our brave men were fast marking the deadly line where we stood.... The order was given to "forward" and up through the dark carnage of death, the fearful sweep of grape, canister, and rifle shot our heroic boys pressed on over the bodies of our slain with a steadiness of tread that may well fill the heart of our chivalrous State with a lofty pride in her sons. We neared the battery in line as perfect as I ever saw at evening drill ... and here where the destruction was awful, as death was reaping our ranks, your noble son, my beloved friend, reeled from his place, fell and died as only the bold hearted can die, with the lines of calm strength and Christian hope on his face.[14]

Likewise, the 21st Mississippi, under command of Lt. Col. William L. Brandon (Major Moody having been wounded earlier while in the woods during the initial shelling) formed line of battle to the left of the 18th Mississippi at about 800 yards from the enemy line. They subsequently advanced under heavy fire to within 200 yards of the Federal batteries. Without support on either flank, Brandon soon ordered the 21st Mississippi to retire, during which movement he was severely wounded above the ankle by a grapeshot. Sitting up, while holding a handkerchief as a tourniquet above his wound, Brandon waved his revolver and refused to be evacuated—shouting "Tell the 21st they can't get me til they take those guns!" Brandon had also witnessed his youngest son take a Minie ball in the leg. Now, under command of Capt. William C.F. Brooks of Company C, the 21st Mississippi regrouped in a shallow depression which offered some protection at the base of Malvern Hill.[15]

The 17th Mississippi, being the rearmost regiment in the advance of the brigade, did not fare as well. Colonel Holder, its commander, fell severely wounded during the advance "while gallantly leading his men into action through a shower of grape and shell."[16] Having deployed into line of battle under second-in-command Lt. Col. John C. Fiser, the regiment crested a hill only to find their front masked by several regiments and scattered fragments of other regiments. Despite maneuvering to their right, amidst the obvious chaos and approaching darkness, they were unable to acquire an open field of fire. Fiser later lamented, "Finding that impossible.... I ordered my men to lie down for protection from the grape and canister, which was raking the field in front and the air above."[17]

Despite Barksdale's best efforts, this initial assault by the Mississippi Brigade actually consisted of three staggered regimental attacks proceeding from right to left—with the fourth regiment failing to participate at all. In Barksdale's defense, Magruder's divisional assault was really no different consisting of a multitude of disjointed attacks by individual brigades with little or no mutual support. Throughout the battle, Barksdale earnestly attempted to control and coordinate attacks by all four of his regiments via orders issued through Major Inge and Captain Costin of the brigade staff. Barksdale graciously acknowledged the contribution of these two staff officers in his battle report. Major Inge's efforts in disseminating Barksdale's orders to his regimental commanders were also recognized by both Fiser and Luse via favorable mention in their regimental reports.

Never one to even consider throwing in the towel, Barksdale valiantly attempted to orchestrate a second assault of the Federal position. The amazing fact is not that three of his regiments failed to mount this attack, but rather that Barksdale was successful in his efforts to have the 21st Mississippi actually launch this assault at all—under their third commander of the afternoon, Capt. C.F. Brooks, and under the most trying conditions. Scarcely catching their breath, again the 21st Mississippi charged back up the hill to within about 150 yards of the enemy line when they were stopped dead in their tracks by a murderous fire of "grapeshot, canister, and small arms." Again, finding no support on either flank, they soon abandoned the effort.

While withdrawing, these gallant Mississippians retrieved Brandon, who by now had fainted from loss of blood. This game old Confederate would have his wounded leg amputated below the knee in a Richmond hospital the next day. The failure of the remaining three regiments to launch a second attack, as ordered by Barksdale, is readily explained by the cumulative effects of "enemy fire, casualties in the chain-of-command,

and other elements of friction." Specifically, in the words of military historian Steve Hawley, "the 18th Mississippi was undergoing what amounted to consolidation and reorganization, while the 13th Mississippi's route was masked by the advancing 21st, and somewhere on the right, the 17th Mississippi remained unresponsive to Barksdale's desires."[18]

As darkness fell on the battlefield, mercifully bringing the slaughter to a close, Barksdale reluctantly ordered the brigade to fall back. During this withdrawal, one final devastating blow to the command structure within the Mississippi Brigade occurred when Lt. Col. James W. Carter, commander of the 13th Mississippi, was severely wounded and carried from the field. Command of the regiment then devolved upon Maj. Kennon McElroy.[19] Carter would be incapacitated for six months and would not return until the battle of Fredericksburg.

Tactically, the battle of Malvern Hill had been a disaster for Lee and the Army of Northern Virginia. Lee ultimately failed to achieve concentration of both artillery fire and infantry force at the point of attack. Poor reconnaissance, shoddy staff work, issuance of an abysmally written attack order by his chief of staff, and lack of cohesion and coordination by the attacking elements resulted in a bloodbath with unacceptable casualties— while failing to capture or destroy any significant portion of the Army of the Potomac.

Strategically this battle ended successfully with the complete withdrawal of all Federal forces from the Virginia peninsula, thereby relieving all threat to the Confederate capital of Richmond. The importance of this development cannot be overstated. However, the salient point is that this outcome had already been guaranteed by General McClellan's earlier decision to retreat to the James River as a means of escape. This strategic Confederate victory could have been achieved without the bloodletting and severe losses to the Army of Northern Virginia had Lee not attacked so aggressively at Malvern Hill.

Instead, the Confederates suffered over 5,000 casualties while inflicting about 3,000 on the Federals. It has been said in describing Barksdale's first opportunity to lead the Mississippi Brigade in battle, that this brigade advanced as far, and endured as long, as any other such Confederate unit on that bloody battlefield. This statement is borne out by the fact that the 13th, 18th, and 21st Mississippi Regiments comprised three of the seven Confederate regiments which suffered the highest casualties.[20]

After what must have been an unimaginably traumatic and nightmarish experience, Barksdale, in his unassuming manner, simply summarized his brigade's performance this way: "The entire command, although one-third of its number fell upon the field, maintained its ground with undaunted courage, and dealt bravely terrible blows upon the ranks of the enemy, as his dead and wounded in front of our lines the next morning clearly proved."[21]

Never one to take credit for himself, he made no mention in his after-action report concerning his personal role in gallantly seizing the flag and rallying the regiment, at extreme personal risk while under fire. Barksdale was no doubt aware that it was not uncommon for multiple color bearers to be shot down or killed in rapid succession during a battle. But he also recognized the importance of the colors as a visual rallying point when verbal commands could not be heard above the deafening noise of battle. Although not expected of a brigade commander, this courageous and selfless act by Barksdale was a reflection of both his strong leadership skills and his total commitment to gaining victory for the cause.

Perhaps Maj. Kennon McElroy, erstwhile commander of the 13th Mississippi, penned the most succinct and eloquent assessment of the contribution of these Mississippi soldiers at Malvern Hill—"I will simply say that both the company officers and men did their whole duty and *proved themselves worthy of the name Mississippians*"[22] (emphasis added).

Private Dinkins of the 18th Mississippi sadly despaired, "Brigade after brigade was sent against [the enemy's] lines and were slaughtered.... It was impossible to reach the top of the hill, and yet the charge was renewed time and again. Barksdale's brigade lost a great many good men. The horrors of Malvern Hill can never be known and hardly even imagined by those who were not there."[23]

However the most famous quote regarding Malvern Hill, and indirectly the most glowing tribute to Barksdale's and the other brigades of Magruder's Division was made by General D.H. Hill—"I never saw anything more grandly heroic than the advance after sunset of the nine brigades under Magruder's orders. Unfortunately they did not move together, and were beaten in detail. As each brigade emerged from the woods, from fifty to one hundred [artillery] guns opened upon it, tearing great gaps in its ranks; but the heroes reeled on and were shot down by the reserves at the guns, which a few squads reached.... *It was not war—it was murder*"[24] (emphasis added).

On July 2, 1862, McClellan withdrew his army to Harrison's Landing on the James River and entrenched under the watchful eyes of the Confederates. Barksdale's Brigade spent the next several days burying the dead, caring for the wounded, and guarding the large number of prisoners who were being brought in daily. After conferring in person with President Lincoln, McClellan soon began withdrawing most of his force from the Virginia peninsula in an attempt to join with the Army of Virginia. This latter force was newly consolidated from the various commands in the Shenandoah Valley and was placed under command of the over-confident Maj. Gen. John A. Pope. By July 8 Lee correctly concluded McClellan no longer posed a threat to the Confederate capital and therefore marched his exhausted army back to the Richmond defenses.

While the weary soldiers enjoyed a brief well-earned rest, Lee reorganized the structure and leadership of his army, breaking up the cumbersome independent commands, and reassigning them into a more streamlined and efficient command system. Major General Magruder, piqued by this turn of events, promptly sought a transfer to the Trans-Mississippi Department. Lee, who perhaps directed an unfair portion of the blame toward Magruder for the fiasco at Malvern Hill, readily concurred, and promptly relieved Magruder of his official duties on July 3rd.

The brigades of William Barksdale and Robert Toombs were reassigned to the division of Major General Lafayette C. McLaws as part of Lieutenant General James Longstreet's newly formed First Corps. This triumvirate of Barksdale-McLaws-Longstreet would actively participate in every campaign of the Army of Northern Virginia for the next 12 months, including Gettysburg, with the sole exception of Second Manassas. (Longstreet personally would miss the battle of Chancellorsville while on detached service near Suffolk.) Although effective militarily, relations amongst these three were not always harmonious. Their strong personalities, coupled with their high sensibilities regarding Southern honor, sometimes resulted in expressions or acts of pettiness, rancor, or animosity toward one another.

One of McLaws' first official duties was to formally recommend Barksdale for promotion. On July 8,1862, noting Barksdale's service in leading the brigade at Savage Station and Malvern Hill just days before, and recognizing "it is highly to be desired that a brigade should be commanded by a Brigadier General," McLaws wrote Barksdale: "I take the liberty of recommending you for the appointment." In his endorsement, McLaws acknowledged that his personal judgment of Barksdale's "fitness for this position is endorsed by the brigade which regards you as the officer to whom the honor should be confirmed."

McLaws then extolled the virtues of the Mississippi Brigade—"for there is no command that stands higher in good conduct everywhere, whether as individuals, as companies, as regiments, or as a Brigade, and now more distinguished for that unexceptionable, undisputed courage which requires no hurrah to urge it to their highest acts of daring." He concluded by claiming that no brigade "has dared more and done more."[25]

Maj. Gen. Lafayette McLaws. This burly Georgian commanded a division within Longstreet's First Corps, which included Barksdale's Mississippi Brigade. Stolid and defensive-minded, McLaws did not always appreciate Barksdale's aggressive leadership and often failed to give him due credit (Library of Congress).

Such high praise is even more impressive considering it came, not from a fellow Mississippian, but rather from a native-born Georgian, and a professional, career soldier as well who acknowledged a personal bias against political appointees to the military. Lee endorsed Barksdale's promotion, citing his gallantry in personally "seizing and advancing the colors himself under terrific artillery and infantry fire," thereby "displaying 'the highest qualities of the soldier.'" Jefferson Davis also formally endorsed Barksdale's recommendation for promotion two days later—this time without any hesitation. Barksdale's promotion to brigadier general was officially confirmed on August 12, 1862, as was Kennon McElroy's to lieutenant colonel of the 13th Mississippi—based largely on Barksdale's recommendation.[26]

Barksdale, indeed, was very fortunate to command such a fine body of men as the 3rd Mississippi Brigade, for a commander can only be as great as the troops he leads into battle. McLaws was by no means the only one to recognize and appreciate the character and stature of these Mississippians. Virginia artilleryman Capt. Robert Stiles knew them intimately. Having campaigned alongside them for the past year, Stiles believed there were none better:

> This Mississippi Brigade was, in many respects, the finest body of men I ever saw. They were almost giants in size and power. In the color company of the Seventeenth Mississippi Regiment ... there were thirty-five men more than six feet one inch high, and in the Twenty-First there was one man six feet seven inches in height.... They were healthy and hardy, even ruddy, which was surprising, coming as they did from a region generally regarded as full of malarial poison. They were bear hunters from the swamps and cane brakes and naturally enough, almost without exception fine shots.... As a body, they

were very young men and brimful of enthusiasm, equally for play and for fight. The laugh, the song, the shout, the yell of the rebel charge burst indifferently from their lips; but in any and every case the volume of sound was tremendous.... At times they seemed about as rough as the bears they had hunted, yet they were withal simple-minded and tender-hearted boys....[27]

Barksdale was a born leader of men and clearly understood the character and motivation of these volunteer soldiers. After all, Barksdale himself was a volunteer officer. Now nearing age forty-one, and in charge of young men mainly in their teens and twenties, it has been stated quite correctly that command brought out Barksdale's strong paternal instincts. Many contemporary descriptions of "Old Barks" couch him in terms of a father-figure to his troops, while numerous firsthand accounts reference Barksdale's concern for their well-being, and cite personal acts of kindness on his part toward his men. W. Gart Johnson of the 18th Mississippi wrote post-war that "we loved Gen. Barksdale because we knew he was proud of us, and would do anything in his power for our welfare."[28] For the next year, until his mortal wounding at Gettysburg, Barksdale's Mississippi Brigade would put their trust in their fearless leader, and he in them, repeatedly leading them into battle—always conspicuously from the front.

Following the short rest outside Richmond, Lee quickly departed with the Army of Northern Virginia. He headed northward in an aggressive move to intercept and defeat Pope's Army of Virginia before it could link up with McClellan's force, not yet fully removed from the Virginia peninsula. Since McClellan had left a small force at Harrison's Landing, Lee chose to leave McLaws' Division, together with two brigades under Missouri-born Brigadier General John G. Walker, behind to defend Richmond against any possible Union counterattack.

McLaws' division consisted of one brigade of South Carolinians under Brigadier General Joseph Brevard Kershaw, two Georgia brigades under Brigadier Generals Paul J. Semmes and Howell Cobb (who would be replaced by Thomas R.R. Cobb and then William T. Wofford after Thomas Cobb's death at Fredericksburg) and Barksdale's Mississippi Brigade. None of these brigadiers had professional military training nor experience. Army of Northern Virginia authority Robert K. Krick has noted that, while most divisions within the army contained a mix of about one-half professionals among the brigades, McLaws' Division was the only one to operate for a prolonged period with completely volunteer leadership at brigade level. This fact renders McLaws' solid performance as a division commander all the more impressive. Furthermore McLaws, by his own admission, loathed the "very many politicians who are seeking military promotion," including the two Cobbs, fearing they would undeservedly be promoted ahead of him.[29]

On July 5th the Mississippi Brigade went into camp about four miles outside Richmond on the York River Railroad at Camp Holly. This location had been one of General Washington's winter campsites during the Revolutionary War. The Confederates still closely identified their cause with that of Washington's army causing Colonel Humphreys to record, "Here the victorious rebels of Lee drank from the same spring and bathed in the same waters used by the victorious rebels under Washington."[30]

On July 14th, a clear and warm Monday afternoon, the entire Mississippi Brigade was formed up by General Barksdale and reviewed for the first time by Major General McLaws near the Fairfield Race Course. Of their time spent here, one private recorded, "They are giving us short rations and drilling us very hard though we live pretty well by paying out our own money. We send a wagon to Richmond every other day to buy vegetables and such things as the regiment wants ... but we pay awful prices: a head of cabbage $1; onions

$2 a dozen; butter $1 per lb...." A private in the 13th Mississippi complained that their newly appointed commander, Kennon McElroy, was being too strict: "I tell you he is the tightest wad yet. There is more discipline in our Regt than ever before."[31]

The daily routine was abruptly interrupted on August 10th when the remaining Union force advanced from Harrison's Landing and feigned an attack on Richmond. In response, McLaws ordered Barksdale forward to meet them, while holding the other brigades in reserve. During this maneuver, Company I of the 13th Mississippi formed the vanguard with a regiment of Confederate cavalry. In response to Barksdale's rapid approach, the enemy quickly withdrew, unwilling to engage. During pursuit of the Federals, Company I "captured five horses, one mule, and provisions, camp equipage etc. in abundance." Barksdale wisely allowed the men to keep their spoils of war, much to the delight of Private Newton Nash who sold a fine four-year-old horse to a sutler for $100.[32]

Otherwise this march was only noteworthy for a macabre scene "of indescribable horror" encountered on the site of the battle of White Oak Swamp, six weeks earlier. Several hundred Federal soldiers had been killed along a plank fence and had been overlooked by the burial parties. A member of the 18th Mississippi described what he saw: "Some were killed while in the act of climbing, while others lay on both sides of the fence. The buzzards had torn their clothing nearly off and stripped the flesh from their bones. They were scarcely any thing but bones and rags when we saw them. The skulls with hair on them looked horrible." Exhibiting a sense of decency, and out of respect for their fallen foe, Barksdale ordered a long ditch to be dug and the ghastly remains were buried.[33]

One final more pleasant diversion was a visit by Barksdale's old friend and fellow Mississippi politician, Senator Albert G. Brown, who delivered a brief address to the brigade during the evening of August 20th.[34]

Two days later Lee ordered McLaws to rejoin the main body near Manassas and Barksdale's brigade departed on the Virginia Central Railroad for Hanover Junction which they reached at midnight. Then, after a series of long forced marches over several days, on September 1st, they arrived at the site of Lee's victory at the battle of Second Manassas the previous day. Here the forces of Stonewall Jackson and Pete Longstreet had routed Pope and his Army of Virginia. Passing through this battlefield the Mississippians were again greeted with the unnerving spectacle of bloated, decomposing Yankee dead. A horrible stench accompanied these unburied and ghastly corpses. This somber scene stretched out for five or six miles along the roadway and in the neighboring fields and woods. One Confederate commented, "It almost sickens the army to pass through such a place of carnage."[35]

Continuing to march northward the brigade reached their former stomping grounds at Leesburg on September 3, 1862, much to the delight of the townspeople. Leesburg's thankful citizens were elated to see the return of their defenders to deliver them from Yankee rule. Without exception, the Mississippians recorded in their diaries details of this most happy reunion. Many of the local inhabitants greeted the brigade several miles outside Leesburg with a "cordial welcome home," throwing open their dwellings to every soldier and providing them supper. One private recorded, "It was a scene never to be forgotten, and from which it was difficult to stir the men. All order and formation were discarded and officers and men mingled among the throng with natural expressions of pleasure." Barksdale's brigade happily reoccupied Camp Carolina, their old campground near Double Springs, for the next two days. When it came time to depart on September 6th, understandably, the soldiers were reluctant to obey. Private Dinkins elaborated: "It was difficult to get Barksdale's brigade to move. Beautiful women, married and single, hung around them, recalling the happy associations of the previous winter."[36]

Heading north toward Maryland with the rest of the Army of Northern Virginia, McLaws' division crossed the Potomac River at Cheats Ferry near Point of Rocks. They pitched camp within a mile of the river on the Maryland side after a march of 18 miles. Next day they reached the outskirts of Frederick City, Maryland, and encamped once again. Here the entire division remained for the next two days.

Lee's invasion of Maryland had begun!

Eleven

Harpers Ferry and Sharpsburg
Brigadier General Barksdale Front and Center

Lee invaded Maryland with high expectations of receiving 20,000 to 30,000 new volunteers from the Old Line State. However, this anticipated surge in support for the Southern cause did not materialize. Lee penned an eloquent open letter "To the People of Maryland" which explained his Confederate army was present to restore the rights, freedoms, and sovereignty which the Union had usurped. Lee would allow them "to decide [their] destiny freely and without constraint" and would "respect [their] choice whatever it may be." However, Lee's plea fell on deaf ears. Colonel Humphreys described it this way—"Alas! Alas! If the hopes of [Lee's] invasion rested on the basis of a Secession uprising among the people of Maryland, it was delusion and was doomed to sad disappointment." Speaking of Confederate efforts to persuade Marylanders to join their cause, a disgruntled Texan commented, "It was like singing psalms to a dead horse." Although there were a few enlistments, and a few citizens waved handkerchiefs in support, many Mississippians mentioned that Union sentiment was very strong here. However, the chief complaint among Barksdale's soldiers was their inability to purchase any goods in Frederick or nearby Middletown. Private Hubbert of the 13th Mississippi made the following entry in his diary: "The stores were all closed and people, on no terms, would accept our [Confederate] money for anything."[1]

Undaunted, Lee boldly issued Special Orders No. 191 on September 10, 1862. He would audaciously divide his army into four parts, capture the 11,000-man Federal garrison and arsenal at Harpers Ferry, and reunite before McClellan could react to attack and defeat the scattered Confederate forces in detail. Lee's strategy called for a three-pronged pincer movement against Harpers Ferry under overall command of Stonewall Jackson. Simultaneously Longstreet would push north to Boonsboro, and then Hagerstown, with the rest of the army and its supply trains to await developments.

The Federal stronghold at Harpers Ferry was situated at the convergence of the Potomac and Shenandoah Rivers at the site of a Baltimore and Ohio Railroad bridge and a canal. It was critical for Lee to control this strategic location to maintain his line of supply from Virginia. Harpers Ferry is surrounded by Maryland Heights rising 1,000 feet above the town to the east, Loudoun Heights rising some 560 feet to the south, and Bolivar Heights rising 300 feet to the west. The key to capturing Harpers Ferry therefore lay in taking Maryland Heights on the Maryland side of the Potomac River, and placing artillery there which would command the town. Lee gave this task to McLaws who, in turn, entrusted it to Kershaw's and Barksdale's Brigades—the two brigades in whom he possessed the greatest confidence. Kershaw, as senior brigadier, would be in overall command. Major General Richard H. Anderson's Division, augmented by Brig. Gen. Cadmus Wilcox's three brigades, was also assigned to McLaws, boosting his column to almost 18,000 men with nine batteries of artillery.[2]

General Walker and his 5,000 troops were tasked with crossing the Potomac into Virginia, ascending to Lovettsville, and occupying and placing cannon on Loudoun Heights. The Federals had decided to leave Loudoun Heights undefended, deeming the terrain too rugged for emplacement of Confederate artillery. Finally, Stonewall Jackson, with the third pincer, would occupy Bolivar Heights and attack from the west, thereby completing the encirclement of Harpers Ferry and its garrison.

Time was of the essence. McLaws was allotted only three days (i.e. until September 13th) to capture Maryland Heights, bombard Harpers Ferry, and capture the enemy arsenal there. On the morning of September 10, in compliance with Special Orders No. 191, McLaws and his enhanced division marched via Burkittsville through Crampton's Gap in South Mountain, and reached Pleasant Valley the following day. Pleasant Valley, running north-south, is about three miles wide, bounded to the east by South Mountain of the Blue Ridge, and to the west by Elk Ridge whose southern terminus is Maryland Heights overlooking Harpers Ferry.

Brig. Gen. Joseph Breverd Kershaw commanded a South Carolina brigade in McLaws' division. Kershaw and Barksdale fought together as equals except for Maryland Heights where Barksdale was under Kershaw's command as his commission predated Barksdale's by two months (Robert U. Johnson and Clarence C. Buel, *Battles & Leaders of the Civil War*, Vol. 3, 1887).

On the morning of September 12, 1862, Kershaw, with Barksdale's Brigade in reserve, proceeded from Brownsville via a dirt road through Solomon's Gap—a slight depression ascending to the narrow summit of Elk Ridge leading to Maryland Heights. At this point, further progress became an ordeal for these South Carolinians and Mississippians. In the words of one of Kershaw's men, not only did they have to "pull themselves up precipitous inclines by the twigs and undergrowth that lined the mountainside, or hold themselves in position by the trees in front," but they also encountered rifle fire from Federal skirmishers and several volleys from three companies of Union cavalry. Deploying skirmishers, Kershaw's force beat off this Federal resistance. Then, in the words of historian Dennis Frye, these Confederates negotiated another "four miles of wilderness ... and brambles and tangled undergrowth which hindered visibility, formation and speed." Kershaw elaborated in his official report:

The natural obstacles were so great that we only reached a position about a mile from the [southern] point of the mountain at 6 o'clock pm. Here an abatis was discovered, extending across the mountain, flanked on either side by a ledge of precipitous rocks. A sharp skirmish ensued, which satisfied me that the enemy occupied the position in force. I therefore directed Major Bradley to retire his [Mississippian] skirmishers, and deployed my brigade in two lines across the entire practicable ground on the summit of the mountain.... General Barksdale's brigade immediately in rear. These dispositions being made the approach of night prevented further operations....[3]

In the oncoming darkness Kershaw could not discern that this Union defensive line was nowhere near as strong as it should have been. General McClellan appreciated the critical importance of holding Maryland Heights. Thus he had earlier recommended that Colonel Dixon S. Miles, commander at Harpers Ferry, entrench the entire garrison there and defend from the summit. Amazingly, Miles deployed only a relatively small force there.[4]

Compounding this critical misjudgment, at Miles' direction, by next morning the 126th New York comprised well over half of this defending force. This completely green and untried regiment from the Finger Lakes region had arrived by train only two weeks before as one of many such inexperienced regiments. This assignment is even more perplexing given that Miles had freely expressed his disdain for such "raw recruits" while declaring them unfit on August 27th. Miles stated "they never had a gun in their hands until the boxes were opened and the muskets issued to them yesterday," and demeaned their officers by claiming their complete ignorance of "how to drill or anything about the drill."[5]

Incredibly, Miles rationalized that combining at least one veteran regiment there, the smaller 32nd Ohio under Colonel Thomas H. Ford with one year's service, together with the "skeleton" unit of the 79th New York, would be sufficient to hold the position. Prophetically, Ford would later confirm that he had delayed in requesting that the 126th New York reinforce his line, commenting that "I would rather do what fighting I have got to do here with the little handful of men which I have confidence in, for I believe they [the 126th] would do me more harm than good."[6]

Early on the morning of Saturday, September 13th, Kershaw pushed his line forward in a sharp attack on this very narrow front, which severely restricted the number of troops engaged. On the left the 7th South Carolina, under heavy musketry fire, advanced quickly and, after twenty minutes, succeeded in dislodging the Union defenders from their abatis line. The Federals then fell back about 400 yards to their much stronger main work—a similar abatis backed by a breastwork of logs and large rocks extending the full width of the narrow crest and flanked again by precipitous ledges of rocks. By this time Kershaw's brigade was suffering heavy losses.

Barksdale's brigade had earlier deployed along the eastern summit face on these rocky ledges in order to extend the left of Kershaw's double battle line. Kershaw now ordered Barksdale to advance in order to drive away enemy sharpshooters, and to flank and gain the rear of the Union line. Sergeant C.C. Cummings of the 17th Mississippi later described their predicament:

> ...the Mississippians under the lead of Barksdale were to flank the enemy. It was the loneliest piece of flanking business that we had ever up to that time undertaken, and, withal, the least encouraging. We turned square down the mountainside to our left over rocks.... The problem was how were we to climb over these great bowlders and get up to the fort on the ridge without receiving a dose of lead? [We] soon discovered the safest place was next to the enemy. In firing down at us, almost perpendicularly, they overshot the aim, which was at those nearest, and those farthest down the mountainside caught most of the stray bullets.[7]

The steepness of this climb is confirmed by Kershaw's official report which stated that Lieutenant Dwight "was seriously injured by a fall from the rocks while communicating

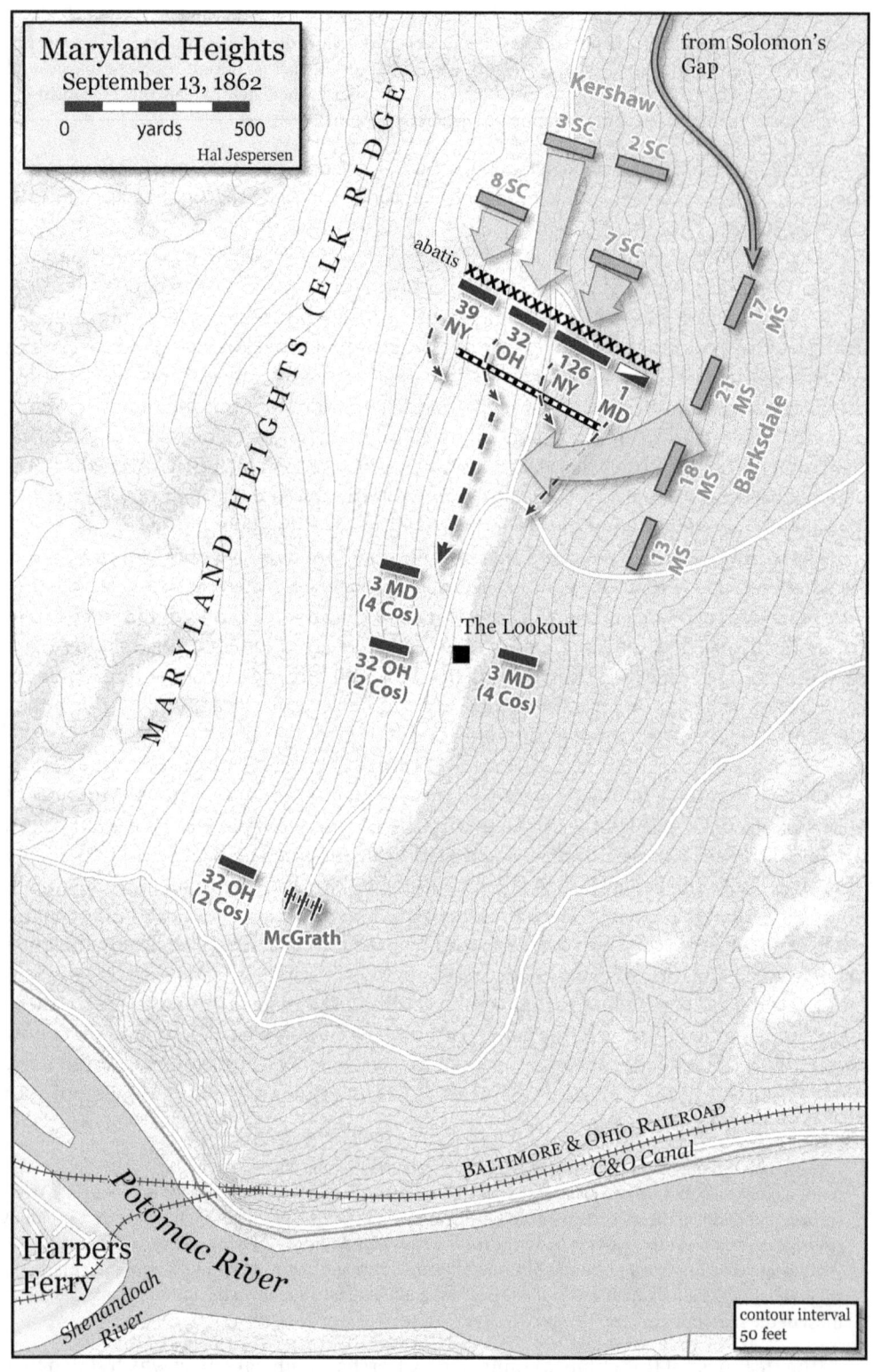

Maryland Heights (Harpers Ferry), September 13, 1862

a message to General Barksdale." Around 10:30 a.m. Barksdale sent word to Kershaw that his men were in position but could not crest the mountain as they would be in Kershaw's line of fire behind the Federals. While Kershaw endeavored to order a ceasefire by his South Carolinians, the Union line abruptly retreated in a panic. Although Kershaw attributed this rout (and subsequent escape of the Federals) to a volley from Colonel Fiser's 17th Mississippi on the right of Barksdale's line, it was actually prompted by the grisly wounding of Col. Eliakim E. Sherrill, commander of the 126th New York. Sherrill received a rifle ball through his lower jaw fired by Kershaw's own troops farther along the line to his right. This gruesome spectacle precipitated an inglorious stampede to the rear by these green recruits from New York. In their defense, it is very probable that even a veteran regiment would have broken and run in the face of enemy fire from the front, right, and rear. However, this disgraceful, panicked flight to safety earned the 126th New York the stinging sobriquet of "Harper's Ferry Cowards." These unfortunate New Yorkers would bear the shame of this moniker for the next 10 months until redeeming their reputation at Gettysburg where they would exact revenge against Barksdale and his Mississippians.[8]

When the 126th New York pulled out, the entire Union line collapsed. Barksdale's Mississippians followed closely on the heels of the fleeing Federals. Private Dinkins later recalled that the "18th and 21st Regiments in the center, as if by common impulse, raised a yell and dashed forward. The 17th on the right and the 13th on the left opened fire and joined in the charge. The enemy broke in disorder and ran down the narrow defiles leading to the river." The Union forces stampeded down the mountainside, then across a pontoon bridge into Harpers Ferry.[9]

Everything was abandoned to the Confederates, including three spiked cannon part way down from the crest on the Harpers Ferry side. The famished Rebels who had subsisted only on green apples and corn for the past several days quickly devoured the meager captured foodstuffs. These parched Confederates had also remained without fresh water which was nowhere to be found on the heights.

However, there were still no Confederate cannon on Maryland Heights. McLaws' quartermaster supervised construction of a road next morning, and, by early afternoon, fire from four Parrot guns was being directed at Harpers Ferry under General McLaws' personal direction—with telling effect. Artillery fire also came from General Walker on Loudoun Heights and Stonewall Jackson from the direction of Bolivar Heights. However, the Harpers Ferry garrison had not yet capitulated, and already five days had elapsed since McLaws had set out on his three-day mission. By this time McLaws' Confederates had exhausted the four days of rations brought from Frederick. McLaws' predicament soon became significantly more perilous due to the actions of McClellan's army to the east.[10]

The same day that Kershaw and Barksdale stormed Union defenses on Maryland Heights, McClellan entered Frederick to a thundering ovation from its citizens. In one of the greatest strokes of good fortune in the annals of military history, a member of the 27th Indiana, while making camp in an area previously vacated by Confederate troops days earlier, found a copy of Lee's Special Orders No. 191. McClellan soon had in his hand Lee's entire plan detailing his widely scattered deployments. Armed with this knowledge, McClellan with uncharacteristic boldness (which puzzled Lee and his subordinates at the time) soon pressed his army forward to force the mountain passes at Fox's Gap, Turner's Gap, and Crampton's Gap to the south on Sunday September 14, 1862. McLaws now faced a Union threat in his rear, as well as facing enemy troops in front at Harpers Ferry who might strike out in an attempt to escape and rejoin McClellan via Pleasant Valley.

In a display of decisiveness he seldom if ever equaled, McLaws, on this same day about noon, dispatched Cobb's Brigade to join Brig. Gen. William Mahone's Brigade and some of General J.E.B. Stuart's cavalry at Crampton's Gap about five miles away. Simultaneously McLaws ordered Semmes' Brigade, then at Solomon's Gap, to report to Cobb there. Cobb's Brigade arrived in the nick of time and, despite losing half its strength in killed, wounded and captured, somehow stemmed the tide against vastly superior numbers. Later that night, Cobb and Semmes were ordered to withdraw about a mile to the south near Brownsville, where they formed a new defensive line under command of General Anderson. This impromptu battle line was cobbled together with troops from the brigades of Mahone, Wilcox, Kershaw and Barksdale—minus the 13th Mississippi under Lt. Col. Kennon McElroy who remained with two artillery pieces atop Maryland Heights.[11]

Surprisingly, Maj. Gen. William B. Franklin's Union VI Corps did not advance southward from Crampton's Gap during the next day to attack this makeshift Confederate defensive line. Instead, Monday, September 15, would be remembered for another reason—the surrender of the Harpers Ferry garrison. Under severe pressure from Stonewall Jackson, who realized that every minute would count for Lee to reunite his scattered army, the entire Federal force surrendered early in the day. When this news was communicated by signal flag to the Confederate forces near Brownsville, General Barksdale, in a moment reminiscent of his days in Congress, seized the opportunity to gallop along the front of his Mississippi Brigade and, with booming voice, to personally convey the news to each regiment: "Boys—Harper's Ferry has surrendered!" Instinctively, the Mississippians let out a tremendous Rebel yell which Dinkins clarified "was a part of their daily exercise which never failed to give the enemy the shivers." With Franklin showing no indication of any aggressive move, McLaws soon ordered this Confederate force near Brownsville to withdraw toward Harpers Ferry. Although the Federal cavalry "made a show of dogging the rear," a well-aimed volley from the 18th Mississippi, acting as rear guard, "sent them scurrying back."[12]

The following day 11,000 Union prisoners were paroled in Harpers Ferry by General A.P. Hill. Stonewall Jackson had already departed with his corps to rejoin Lee at Sharpsburg, Maryland. McLaws gradually withdrew his forces from Pleasant Valley while maintaining a defensive perimeter around Maryland Heights and the Maryland side of the Potomac. About 2 a.m., once his supply trains had crossed, the infantry followed suit, entering Harpers Ferry. The Confederates also captured 72 artillery pieces, 12,000 rifled muskets, horses, wagons, munitions, and "supplies in abundance."

As Jackson's men had been the first to enter the town, and oversaw the surrender, they were the first in line to partake of the spoils of war—much to the chagrin of Kershaw's South Carolinians and Barksdale's Mississippians who firmly believed they were entitled to first "dibs." One of Kershaw's men complained, "Jackson's troops fairly swam in the delicacies, provisions, and 'drinkables' constituting a part of the spoils taken. While Kershaw's and all of McLaws' and Walker's troops, who had done the hardest of the fighting, got none. Our men complained bitterly of this seeming injustice." A Mississippian later lamented, "We received small rations of beef, no salt or bread ... after noon we received three hardtacks to the man, which was a poor return for the desperate work of the last three days."[13]

Once again William Barksdale and his Mississippi Brigade had performed

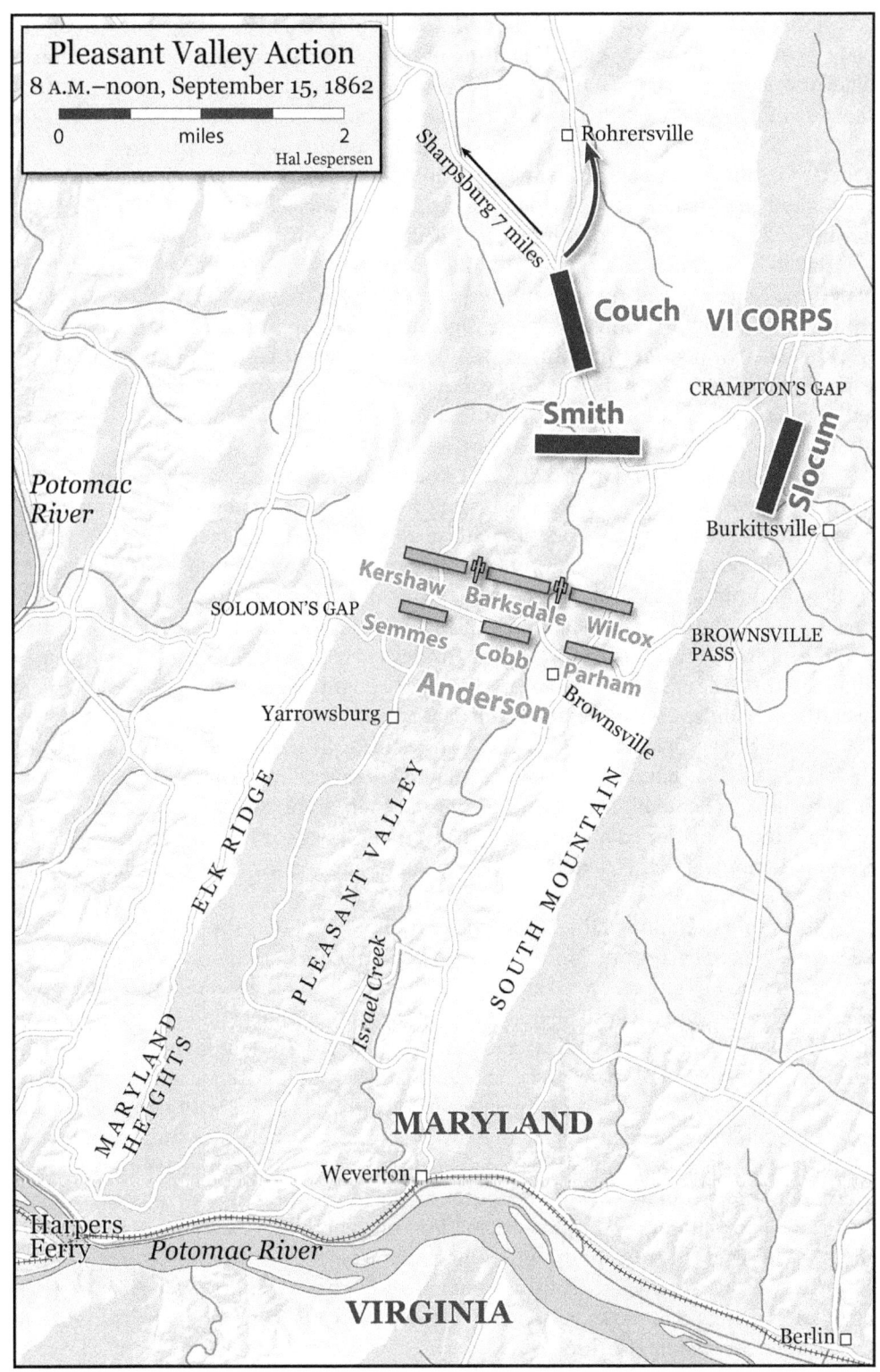

Pleasant Valley Action (Harpers Ferry), September 13, 1862

admirably under extremely difficult conditions, albeit in a supporting role. In his official report, Kershaw, while complimenting his entire combined force, singled out Barksdale for praise: "The conduct of the whole command, contending as they were against the most formidable natural obstacles, without water, which could not be obtained nearer than the foot of the mountain, and encountering an enemy most strongly posted and superior in numbers to all that could be brought into position against him, is worthy of the highest commendation. *To General Barksdale I am much indebted for his hearty cooperation and valuable insight*"[14] (emphasis added).

Likewise McLaws recorded that, "the troops that were engaged in the attack and capture of Maryland Heights are entitled to especial commendation, as they were laboriously employed for two days and one night along the summit of Elk Ridge, constantly working their way under fire, during the day and at night resting in position, all this time without water...." McLaws then commended Kershaw for his "great skill, coolness and daring," and mentioned "the operations of the brigade of General Barksdale which accompanied [Kershaw] and materially assisted in the capture of the place."[15]

In his astute assessment of Barksdale's performance at Maryland Heights, military historian Steve Hawley wrote, "It is a testimony to Barksdale's ability to command that he could move his men over such difficult terrain, maintain control over them, and be in an assault posture by 10:30 am [on September 13th]." With keen insight Hawley correctly points out that lack of a pre-arranged signal "for the lifting and shifting of [rifle] fire to allow Barksdale's assault across Kershaw's front is not surprising, as they were both volunteers and not professionals." Lastly, Hawley correctly concludes that any blame for allowing the Federals to escape from Maryland Heights rightly belongs to Kershaw as overall commander and originator of the battle plan.[16]

Now lack of provisions would result in dire consequences for McLaws, Kershaw, and Barksdale. McLaws halted his division at Halltown, several miles beyond Harpers Ferry, at 11:00 a.m. on September 16th and permitted them to bivouac there. Since A.P. Hill had already requisitioned all foodstuffs in Harpers Ferry for his own troops, McLaws, with his commissary chief, left for Charlestown, six miles away to seek an alternate food source—but to no avail.

Returning to Halltown, McLaws broke camp at 3 p.m. in response to an order from Lee to hasten to Sharpsburg. However this destination was not disclosed to the men on the march who joyfully set off to the south in the false belief they were returning to Winchester, Virginia, and the lush Shenandoah Valley with prisoners and captured weapons in tow. Despite their hunger and fatigue, on they marched until nightfall at a "lively gait" and singing at the top of their lungs. This all changed dramatically when they reached a fork in the road and turned to the right—back toward Maryland. Reality immediately set in as each company made the turn—they would again cross the Potomac and that meant a fight. Dinkins later described the transformation in their demeanor: "Within a half an hour not a sound could be heard, except the tramp of the column and the din of moving artillery. All the humor and bright anticipations of an hour ago were gone. The men were silent."[17] However the worst of this grueling march was yet to come.

An ever-quickening pace soon accompanied the change in direction. All during this overcast, misting night Barksdale and his mounted officers "rode along the column with words of encouragement calling on the boys to 'Close up' ... over and over 'Close up'; 'Close up.'" One Mississippian recalled, "The step grew faster and faster.... The gait continued to increase, until finally all were going in a trot, and hundreds could not keep up, but fell down exhausted by the roadside, where they remained until morning." This frantic pace was maintained for "nearly all the remainder of the night." Diarist Private Hubbert stoically recorded, "Many of our best men had given out and fell by the way during the dark and tiresome march."[18]

Marching all night, except for one rest just prior to midnight, the brigade covered about 30 miles in 14 hours. McLaws, Barksdale, and Kershaw all acknowledged this severe straggling and clearly attributed the resultant loss in manpower—not to any lack of resolve on the part of their men to continue—but instead to lack of subsistence, sleep deprivation over the past several nights, excessive fatigue, and sheer exhaustion. Kershaw felt it necessary to add that even those who arrived at Sharpsburg were "worn and jaded." Barksdale admitted very honestly in his after-action report, "that I went into the fight [at Sharpsburg] with less than 800 men"—this was less than half his normal brigade strength.[19]

Having received a second order from Lee around midnight—this time a peremptory command to join him at Sharpsburg with all haste—McLaws pulled out all the stops. His vanguard arrived at Boteler's Ford across the Potomac, just below Shepherdstown, about 2:30 a.m. on September 17th. After many hours of repeatedly exhorting his bone-weary soldiers to "Press on!" Barksdale was parched and desperate for a reviving drink of cool, fresh water. Unfortunately, as he later related to McLaws, when within a mile of the river, Barksdale was unable to locate the well in the darkness of that moonless and miserable night. It was still dark as Barksdale and his brigade waded across the half-mile of "very shoal" waters by torchlight. Even the officers, although mounted, were not exempt from the suffering and discomfort of this march which one Mississippian described as most certainly "one of the most trying and fatiguing of the war."[20]

Finally, at 9 a.m. on Wednesday September 17, 1862, Barksdale arrived in Sharpsburg with his exhausted brigade which a sympathetic old Maryland lady greeted with the blessing, "You dear dirty ragged souls you." Although the battle had already been raging for several hours, and the sounds of cannon and musketry fire reverberated from Miller's cornfield almost two miles to the north, the brigade was halted in the roadway near General Lee's headquarters. The Mississippians were allowed to rest for 30 minutes while two men from each company were detailed to fill the empty canteens.

McLaws had personally reported to General Lee much earlier that morning, in advance of his division, to report their impending arrival, and to seek deployment orders. This conversation had taken place before the battle commenced. To McLaws' amazement, Lee advised him to await further developments, having decided to keep McLaws' force as his reserve in the left-center of the Confederate line. Dumbfounded at this delay after Lee's earlier peremptory order had prompted the mad rush to Sharpsburg, McLaws took a well-deserved nap in the tall grass by the side of the road.[21]

Lee on the other hand was on pins and needles with sleep being the last thing on his mind. After serious deliberation, Lee had finally decided, only days earlier, to risk it all and turn to face McClellan and his superior numbers here along the banks of Antietam Creek. Lee gambled he could reunite his widely scattered army before the ever-cautious McClellan would attack to overpower him. Now with A.P. Hill and his brigade still en route from Harpers Ferry, Lee faced McClellan's imposing Union force of 71,500 effectives, backed by 300 artillery pieces, with less than 35,000 troops of his own. Another major concern for Lee was that, contrary to military maxims, he would offer battle with the Potomac River at his back—with Boteler's Ford his only route of escape.

In 1862, Sharpsburg, Maryland, was a quiet town of 1,300 inhabitants surrounded by picturesque farms bearing German names. However its key feature, which attracted military conflict like a magnet, was the presence of several major roadways which crisscrossed through it—a turnpike running north to Hagerstown and on into Pennsylvania, another turnpike running northwest to Boonsboro, and several lesser roads running east to Rohrersville in Pleasant Valley and south to Harpers Ferry. The contending armies travelled along these roads which brought the Civil War to this quiet town. A mile east of town Antietam Creek meandered by, sufficiently deep and wide to render it unfordable to an attacking army. The stream was spanned by four arched stone bridges where the four major roads intersected the waterway. Lee's battle line extended for about four miles parallel to the Hagerstown Turnpike. It ran from Miller's cornfield, three miles north of Sharpsburg, continued southward through the town, and terminated at steep bluffs bordering Antietam Creek, a mile south of the Rohrbach Bridge (soon to become famous as Burnside's Bridge).[22]

McClellan's battle plan called for Maj. Gen. Joseph E. Hooker's I Corps, numbering 8,600 men, supported by Maj. Gen. Joseph K. Mansfield's XII Corps, to cross Antietam Creek at the northernmost bridge opposite Pry's Mill and launch the main attack against Lee's left flank. Stonewall Jackson's corps of 7,700 men were deployed in the West Woods just north of the Dunker Church, and near Miller's 30-acre cornfield, now ready for harvesting. The Union attack was to then proceed southward along the Hagerstown Turnpike toward Sharpsburg, supported by Maj. Gen. Edwin V. Sumner's II Corps on the left, while Maj. Gen. Ambrose E. Burnside's IX Corps attacked Lee's right flank by crossing the Rohrbach Bridge. Fitz-John Porter's V Corps, together with Franklin's three divisions (not yet arrived from Pleasant Valley) would comprise the Federal reserve in the center of the Union line. As the fog lifted in the gray half-light of dawn, artillery thundered across the quiet countryside and the battle was on.

This vicious, frenzied, close-in fighting, often hand-to-hand, continued for several bloody hours and was remembered by Union and Confederate veterans of the Seven Days battles and Second Bull Run as "quite simply the worst fighting they had ever experienced." Despite a determined counterattack by Brig. Gen. John B. Hood's Texans, who were literally shot to pieces, suffering sixty percent casualties, the Confederate left was now hovering on imminent collapse. With all Confederate forces in the vicinity now engaged, Hood sent one last frantic appeal to Lee for immediate reinforcements. Lee now, at last, desperately committed his sole remaining reserve. Lee responded to Hood's courier, "Tell [Hood] I am now coming to his support," as Lee gestured toward the front of McLaws' column, then double-quicking toward the West Woods.[23]

The critical situation for the Confederate defense in the West Woods was due to the timely, but reckless, advance of Maj. Gen. John Sedgwick's lead division of Maj. Gen. "Bull" Sumner's II Corps. At 65 years Sumner was the oldest general officer in the Army of the Potomac and full of fight, as he had previously demonstrated during the Union delaying action at Savage Station. Sumner had expected to participate in Hooker's early morning attack. Instead McClellan had deliberately held Sumner back some two miles away on the far side of Antietam Creek. Before Sumner could engage, Union army engineers would need to prepare a crossing. Advancing to the East Woods around 9:30 a.m. directly opposite the West Woods 700 yards away, Sumner observed that the southern end of the West Woods was occupied by Federal troops of the 125th Pennsylvania (another inexperienced regiment seeing their first action a mere six weeks after being

Dunker Church and West Woods at Antietam National Battlefield. Barksdale's Mississippi Brigade spearheaded McLaws' flank attack against Maj. Gen. John Sedgwick's division in the West Woods (author photograph).

organized at Harrisburg). At the same time the combat between Union and Confederate forces at the northern end had somewhat subsided. In Sumner's mind, winning the battle on this front would be achieved by driving Sedgwick's division into this void to preserve the cohesion of the Union line, and by hitting the flank and rear of the Rebel line opposing Hooker's corps to the right.

Sumner arranged Sedgwick's division in column of brigades and gave orders for Brigadier General William H. French's division—somewhere in the rear—to follow closely behind. Appearing about 20 minutes after Sedgwick's division departed the East Woods, French inexplicably marched his division to the southwest in support of Brig. Gen. George S. Greene's 2nd Division, XII Corps, thereby completely abandoning Sumner and Sedgwick. Sumner's 3rd Division, under Maj. Gen. Israel B. Richardson, remained east of Antietam Creek. Sumner would personally lead the advance then of only a *single division* of the II Corps.

Throwing caution to the wind, Sumner, impatient and as belligerent as ever, disdained to either reconnoiter further or to deploy skirmishers on the flanks of his attacking column—both critical errors in judgment that would precipitate what some military historians have termed "a disaster in the West Woods of the first magnitude." McClellan had intended for Hooker to control the movements of Sumner and his corps. As historian Stephen Sears commented, "The rebel marksman who wounded Hooker [in the foot] put 'Bull' Sumner precisely where McClellan did not want him—in the field in an independent command."[24]

Brigadier General Gorman (whom Barksdale had opposed at Edwards Ferry) commanded the lead brigade of Sedgwick's division. The brigades of Brig. Gen. Napoleon

J. Dana and one-armed Brig. Gen. Oliver Otis Howard followed Gorman—the division arrayed in three parallel battle lines approximately 500 yards wide with barely 50 yards between. As Sumner had expected, the Union troops entered the West Woods against virtually no Confederate opposition. However things were about to change in very dramatic fashion, and the terrain, confusion, and fog of war were about to conspire to thwart Sumner's intentions.

By the time Gorman's lead brigade entered the West Woods, the 125th Pennsylvania had already advanced 150 yards inside. Having obliqued to the right while crossing the open fields to reach the West Woods, Gorman's brigade entered too far to the north to link up with the 125th Pennsylvania's right flank, leaving a gap of 300 yards. The 7th Michigan and 42nd New York Regiments on the extreme left of Dana's brigade were next to attempt to link up with the right flank of the 125th Pennsylvania partially filling the gap—but they were too late. The scene was set for Barksdale to hurl his Mississippi Brigade like a spearhead into the most vulnerable point of Sedgwick's formation—with devastating results.

Having double-quicked to an open field bordering the southern end of the West Woods, Barksdale rode in front of the line to briefly address his men in order to motivate and encourage them, a practice which he would follow thereafter. While Private Henley simply recorded that Barksdale spoke in "short but appropriate terms cautioning us against unnecessary excitement, reminding us of the State we represented and of [its] high honored reputation," Dinkins later attempted to recall Barksdale's exact words: "The situation is desperate. The enemy is pressing our center. We must drive them back. Stonewall Jackson and General Lee expect you to do so. I have promised that you will. I want every man to do his duty as a Mississippian. If any of you cannot—step out, and I will excuse you."[25]

Not a man moved. General Barksdale adeptly exercised his strong oratorical skills and powers of persuasion which he had carefully honed during his eight years on the floor of Congress. This technique was no doubt employed by many other officers, both North and South, but by none more effectively than William Barksdale. He clearly understood that by personalizing the upcoming fight and eliciting an unspoken pledge between each man in the ranks and his state, leaders, and comrades, everyone would be more apt to do his full duty. Barksdale then ordered his brigade to "leave everything, except guns and cartridge boxes, under that

Maj. Gen. John Sedgwick's division suffered 2,225 casualties in the West Woods. He was himself wounded three times. Barksdale's brigade would again face Sedgwick at Fredericksburg during the Chancellorsville Campaign (Library of Congress).

tree" (there were no more than 100 blankets in the brigade) and dismounted, moving quickly forward to lead the charge on foot.[26]

McLaws realized it was imperative to attack immediately before Sedgwick could redeploy his brigades which were still aligned in column formation. This represented the deepest penetration of the Confederate defensive line by Union troops that day. However the three closely spaced Union battle lines did not facilitate directional volley fire. McLaws ordered Cobb to the extreme left but, due to confusion, Cobb's brigade continued marching due north without turning eastward, thereby removing this brigade from the scene. Semmes formed to the left of Barksdale while Kershaw formed on his right. Barksdale's brigade entered what would become in minutes the killing zone through a ravine, and thus hidden from the view of Federal troops, took Sedgwick, Sumner, Gorman, Dana, and Howard completely by surprise.

The Mississippians arrived at precisely the most opportune time and exited the ravine diagonally at the most advantageous location and angle to the Union line. At the same time Early's brigade, who had marched southward, formed into a battle line facing east, opposite the 125th Pennsylvania. Early actually had to halt his advance for a time to allow Barksdale's Mississippians to pass obliquely across his front. Although Kershaw's South Carolinians were not yet fully formed into regimental lines, Barksdale realized the moment had come. Without halting, and without receiving a direct order from McLaws, Barksdale immediately formed his men into a battle line and, at short range, "unleashed six to eight devastating volleys" which tore into the right of the 125th Pennsylvania and the left of the 7th Michigan.[27]

At the same time, Early's Virginians let loose a withering fire into the 125th Pennsylvania from the front. Sensing victory, Barksdale immediately ordered a charge into the dazed and bewildered Union troops to maintain the momentum of his assault and to exploit the advantage already gained. John T. Parham of the 32nd Virginia of Semmes' brigade to Barksdale's left later described the scene:

> Looking to my right, I witnessed one of the most magnificent sights that I ever saw, or ever expect to see again. It was Barksdale's men driving the enemy up into and through a piece of woods to their front. Their fire was so steady and severe it looked like a whirlwind was passing through the leaves on the ground and woods.[28]

Another Confederate later recalled this part of the action:

> The Mississippians rushed at the enemy with yells and bayonets and almost charged into their ranks before they gave way.... At the crest of the ridge the enemy had thrown together some logs, behind which they halted for a death struggle. The woods were raked by grape and cannister, as well as rifle balls, but there was no hesitation. General Barksdale rushed to the front and said, Forward! Take the works! Barksdale's men went over the logs and shot the enemy as they ran down the slope.[29]

The Union troops being driven back belonged to the 7th Michigan and 42nd New York of Dana's brigade. They soon stampeded back through Howard's left flank regiments, causing further disruption.

Sumner had intended for Sedgwick's division to fill the gap between Hooker's I Corps brigades of Colonel William B. Goodrich and Brigadier General Marsena R. Patrick in the northern portion of the West Woods, and the 125th Pennsylvania of Greene's division occupying the southern end of these woods, to form a continuous Union battle line. However, Barksdale's unexpected thrust into the remaining gap in the Union line dashed this hope with devastating effect.

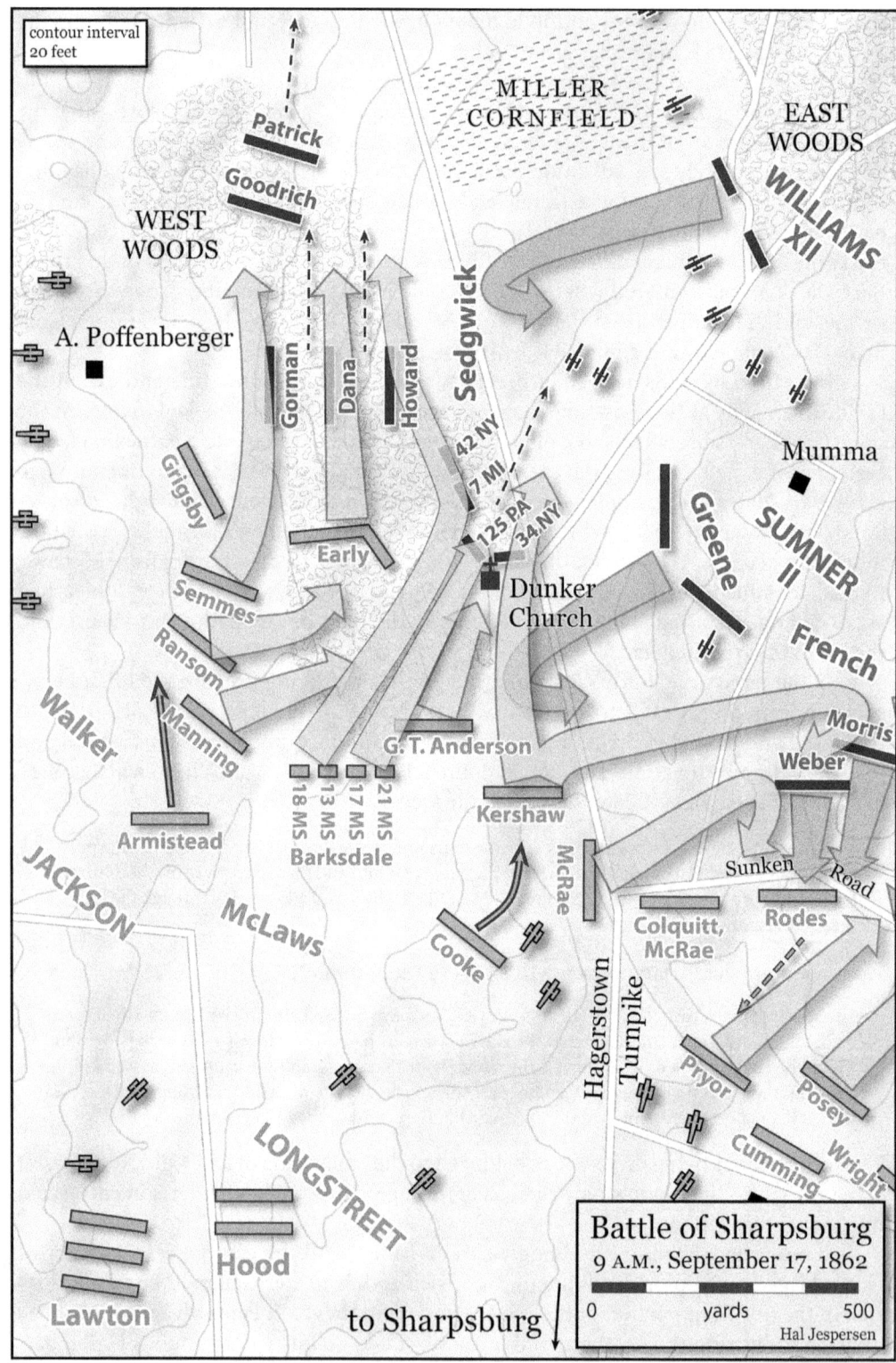

Battle of Sharpsburg, September 17, 1862—Action of Barksdale's Brigade at West Woods

Dana desperately left-obliqued his two left-flank regiments (7th Michigan and 42nd New York) to face this immediate Confederate threat—but to no avail. West Woods authority Marion V. Armstrong emphasizes that "Barksdale did not achieve this breakthrough by attacking Sedgwick's division on the flank, but by attacking frontally a weak point in the developing [Union] line." The restricted maneuverability and diminished command control resulting from the close brigade-line Federal formation ensured "the quick and complete collapse of Sedgwick's division once Barksdale's attack broke the front line of Federal regiments." Brigadier General Dana later claimed that the Confederate rifle fire here in the West Woods was "the most terrific I ever witnessed."[30]

At this point, recognizing a threat to his own left flank by a body of Union soldiers, Barksdale wheeled the 13th and 18th Mississippi to his left and drove them northward. Historian and Antietam authority Dennis Frye, describing this part of the confused action, wrote, "Barksdale's Mississippians and Early's Virginians smashed into the center and right of Sedgwick's Division, routing and pushing Howard's and Dana's brigades out of the West Woods." Historian Stephen Sears added, "the[se] regiments collapsed left to right like a stand of dominoes and streamed off to the north toward the Miller farm." At the same time the 17th and 21st Mississippi proceeded eastward, emerging out into an open pasture, while in pursuit of other fleeing Federal forces.[31]

As recorded in his official report, Barksdale, with two regiments, succeeded in putting this Federal force on his left flank to flight, and pursued them for a considerable distance into open country. However, due to lack of support, he soon prudently halted and returned to his original position at the edge of the woods. Unfortunately the 17th Mississippi, commanded by Lieutenant Colonel Fiser, and the 21st Mississippi, then under command of Captain Sims, fighting to the right alongside Kershaw's brigade, continued their pursuit across the Hagerstown Turnpike and through the open fields on the other side in the face of heavy artillery fire, which punished them severely. Finally, when confronted by Union infantry from Greene's division, these two Mississippi regiments withdrew.

Historian Robert K. Krick has termed this action in the West Woods as "the most notable Confederate tactical triumph of the day." The late Professor Joseph L. Harsh, one of the greatest authorities on the battle of Antietam, went even further in his praise, noting that the rout of Sedgwick's division, besides being a great tactical victory, "in terms of losses inflicted upon the enemy and dramatic reversal of fortunes, it was one of the greatest feats of Southern arms on any battlefield of the war." In 20 minutes, Sedgwick had lost 2,225 men (nearly 40 percent of his force) and had been wounded three times himself.[32]

But it had come at great cost to McLaws' division. Kershaw's brigade suffered 349 killed and wounded, while 290 of Barksdale's Mississippians were casualties—the majority being from the 17th and 21st Mississippi who, like Kershaw's South Carolinians, had been caught out in the open by Federal artillery. Dinkins sadly commented: "McLaws Division met General Lee's expectations, but some of the noblest men who ever lived gave their lives in that battle ... one of the bloodiest as well as one of the most stubbornly contested of the war."[33]

By 2 p.m. Barksdale repositioned his brigade along the Hagerstown Turnpike, together with the brigades of Kershaw and Semmes, in a stable defensive line while the main battle action progressed southward to the Sunken Road and Burnside's Bridge. Dinkins recorded details of a near-miss later that afternoon that potentially could have annihilated the leadership of McLaws' division and ended Barksdale's life. The 18th Mississippi were lying in an apple orchard while the "artillery on both sides was keeping up a desultory fire," with the occasional shell knocking a limb off an apple tree. He relates that Generals J.E.B. Stuart, Cobb, Kershaw, Sims [Semmes] and Barksdale were conferring together approximately 50 yards in front while observing the enemy. "Suddenly a shell exploded in their midst [and] General [Semmes] fell backward heavily to the ground." Dinkins rushed to his side and gave the general a drink from his canteen. Fortunately, although severely shaken, Semmes had suffered "only a bad powder burn."[34] This day Fate continued to smile on William Barksdale, who had just avoided the doom of his predecessor, Gen. Richard Griffith, by the narrowest of margins.

The timely arrival of A.P. Hill's Light Division later that afternoon, in the nick of time after a forced march from Harpers Ferry, allowed Lee to stave off defeat on his right flank opposite Burnside's Bridge. The single bloodiest day of the Civil War—indeed in

"Barksdale's Near Miss at Antietam." Brig. Gen. Paul Semmes was incapacitated by a shell burst while Maj. Gen. J.E.B. Stuart (far right) and Barksdale (second from right) narrowly escaped injury or death (James Dinkins, *1861 to 1865, By an Old Johnnie*, 1897).

American history, before or since—was over. The fearful tally was 2,108 killed, 9,540 wounded, and 753 missing for a total of 12,401 (25 percent) for the Union, and best estimate of 1,546 killed, 7,752 wounded, and 1,018 missing, totaling 10,318 (31 percent) for the Confederates. The 12 hours of combat on September 17, 1862, had claimed a combined total of 22,719 casualties.[35]

That night Barksdale's men rested in place along the battle line they had occupied that afternoon. Totally exhausted from a week of incessant marching and fighting, both day and night, most "dropped down where they were, and could not be roused even to take their cooked rations, brought up from our camp in the rear." Even the pitiful cries of the wounded and work of the ambulance corps on this rainy night did not disrupt their slumber.

Displaying a deep concern for the welfare of his men, a characteristic he was well noted for, Barksdale, despite his own fatigue, rode over the battlefield where his Mississippians had fought, to ensure all his wounded soldiers had been retrieved to receive medical care. Under the circumstances, Barksdale could easily have delegated this onerous task, but these were *his* men and he felt personally responsible to them and for them. Nor was his compassion reserved only for his fellow Mississippians. General Walker later related that while he and Barksdale rode along a rail fence in the darkness that night, their horses nearly stepped on a wounded Union soldier from Sedgwick's division who was lying on the ground unable to move. Enemy or not, without hesitation, they "sent for an ambulance and gave orders to care for the poor fellow."[36]

The bloodied combatant armies stared each other down the following day while Union and Confederate burial parties conducted their grisly work. Well before dawn on September 19th, Lee began his retreat and was soon back across the Potomac safely on Virginia soil—much to the disgust of the Federal political and military leadership back in Washington.

On many occasions Barksdale failed to get the credit he deserved. Instead of singling out Barksdale for his superior tactical accomplishment in his battle report, McLaws simply lumped him together with Kershaw and Semmes, and stated that all three "deserve high praise for their heroic conduct in the fight and for the skillful manner their brigades were handled." This is certainly a significant oversight and would not be the last slight McLaws would make regarding Barksdale's performance on a battlefield. In this case it may reflect some degree of annoyance by McLaws with Barksdale's decision to launch his attack without waiting for any formal order from McLaws. As several contemporaries have commented, McLaws, although possessed of a keen eye for ground and brilliant mind for setting up defensive positions, was utterly lacking in aggressive tendencies, much preferring to be directed by superiors. Not merely failing to appreciate Barksdale's innate aggressiveness, McLaws may actually have resented Barksdale for this quality. McLaws did acknowledge that "the ground over which the Mississippi Brigade [General Barksdale] advanced, and to his right, was thickly strewn with the dead and the wounded of the enemy, far exceeding our own, and their dead were much more numerous than their wounded."

Similarly, Jubal Early in his report simply stated, "I take great pleasure in bearing testimony to the gallant conduct of Semmes,' Anderson's, and Barksdale's commands, whose timely arrival was of so much service to me." This was the second occasion that Barksdale had cooperated with Early on the battlefield, but it would not be the last. Next time, however, while serving under Early's direct command, a major controversy and a bitter public argument in the Richmond press would erupt between these two fiery personalities.[37]

As for Barksdale's own report, as was his practice, he acknowledged his regimental commanders, his personal staff, and regimental surgeons by name, and gave credit to the entire brigade, never making reference to his own critical part in the battle. Instead he simply concluded with the humble understatement, "I close this report with the remark that my command did its duty upon the ensanguined field of Sharpsburg." Rather it has been left to the historians of the modern era (Murfin, Harsh, Sears, Frye, Krick, Hawley, Armstrong) to fully acknowledge Barksdale's critical contribution in the West Woods at Sharpsburg.[38]

How then had Barksdale progressed in his short tenure as a brigade commander? For his part, Hawley makes the following professional assessment:

> In only three months Barksdale had demonstrated an increasing facility for command. [Regarding Sharpsburg] Barksdale had wielded his brigade in combat and maintained as much control as any commander could on that day. He had done this on the offensive after a brutal approach march, with two of his regimental commanders missing [Humphreys of the 21st(sick) and Griffin of the 18th Mississippi (wounded)].... Despite the weakened chain of command, Barksdale maneuvered and controlled his brigade in a desperate assault, where he had squeezed the utmost potential from his depleted command by his pre-battle speech and personal example.[39]

The final word regarding Barksdale's development and potential as a military commander as of September 17, 1862, belongs to Robert K. Krick, esteemed authority on the Army of Northern Virginia: "William Barksdale had been a [commissioned] brigadier for only twenty-four days when he entered Maryland, but he steadily demonstrated that he would join Maxy Gregg as that surprisingly rare creature, a fire-eating politician both willing and able to serve with distinction in the field."[40]

At the next major battle, Fredericksburg, Barksdale again would be tasked with a vital role. This time it would be on the defensive—a challenge he would meet with the same degree of determination, vigor, skill, and success.

Twelve

Fredericksburg

*Dead Yankees on the Pontoon Bridges
and in the Streets*

The weary Mississippi Brigade went into camp two miles from Martinsburg on the Pecan River on September 19, 1862. They then proceeded by way of Brucetown to Winchester, Virginia, where they encamped for several weeks to lick their wounds. In the words of one member of the 13th Mississippi, "Our army is very much worn out and that is not all, it is almost starved out." Many times while on the march they had subsisted only on green corn and apples and "were glad to get that." Even now, as Private Dinkins recorded, "the rations furnished were entirely inadequate to satisfy our [voracious] appetites." He elaborated upon their extreme hunger: "The appetite of a soldier who has passed through an arduous campaign of four weeks, over mountains and rivers, with scant rations, and in many cases without shoes, engaged almost daily in combat, has no parallel in peace[time]." During this interlude Colonel Humphreys witnessed a humorous scene which must have embarrassed General Lee. Lee noticed a soldier eating green persimmons and admonished him, saying it was improper food for a soldier, being much too astringent. This famished Confederate meekly replied, "I am not eating it for food General, I am only trying to make my stomach fit my rations."[1]

All these Mississippians, regardless of rank, were also ragged and dirty, and used this period of respite for "patching clothes, cleaning up their rags, and ridding themselves of those hideous pests sometimes called 'body companions' and sometimes 'greybacks.'"[2] There were no tents and very few blankets. Unless they could procure firewood to build log fires, the soldiers suffered through the extremely cold nights. Indeed, shortage of winter clothing soon became so critical that members of Barksdale's brigade actually petitioned General Lee to allow one man from each company to return home to resupply them. To make matters worse, smallpox soon broke out within the 13th Mississippi and, according to Private Dinkins, although cases were widespread, "the soldiers never thought much about the danger."[3]

Lee used this quiet period to recover the large contingent of stragglers and wounded, to assimilate large numbers of new recruits and conscripts, and to replace dead and wounded officers through promotion and elections. The ranks of the Army of Northern Virginia soon swelled to near 78,000 troops. Lee also formally reorganized his army by a special act of the Confederate Congress, officially dividing it into two corps—the First Corps under Longstreet and the Second Corps under Jackson. Together they comprised 43 brigades and would soon face off against a Union Army of 135,000 men, divided into

68 brigades within 8 corps—the largest army ever assembled on the North American continent—and under a new commander.⁴

However, the suffering of individual Rebel soldiers worsened as the Confederate supply system strained to keep up—but only fell further behind. As October gave way to November the weather turned wintry. General Longstreet, in response to their plight, advised the soldiers to rake away the ashes and coals from their cooking fires and sleep on that ground which would be warm and dry. According to his Chief of Staff, Moxley Sorrell, this novel routine proved to be successful. Another of Longstreet's ideas did not. On the subsequent march to Fredericksburg many of the barefooted soldiers suffered horribly from lack of footwear. In response, Longstreet ordered the men to make "rawhide shoes"—moccasin-like coverings for their feet cut from the rawhides of the beef cattle slaughtered for food. Unfortunately, these foot coverings proved too slippery in the mud and icy slush of Virginia, either sliding off the wearer's feet or causing their owners to slip and fall. The soldiers soon cast them aside, preferring to go barefoot or with their feet wrapped in rags or straw.⁵

Throughout this period the Magnolia State Brigade kept busy by drilling, normally twice per day, and by inspections and general reviews. For example, Private Moore of the 17th Mississippi recorded in his diary that on October 28th, the brigade was inspected by General Barksdale, and that same evening, the entire division was reviewed by Generals Lee, Longstreet, and McLaws. He commented that "the presence of a number of the fair sex" rendered "the ceremonies much more pleasant." Moore also recorded that the very next evening Barksdale conducted a brigade drill which concluded with a bayonet charge which was his usual custom. This entry is noteworthy for two reasons. Firstly, it indicates that Barksdale recognized the value of bayonet drill as a means to strengthen morale and engender an élan or esprit-de-corps within his brigade. Secondly, it confirms Barksdale's sense of commitment, dedication to duty, and professionalism, in that he personally conducted these drill sessions at brigade level—as dictated by Hardee's Manual—when many of his counterparts simply delegated this responsibility to subordinates.⁶ These activities distracted the soldiers from their hardships and, by keeping them occupied, severely limited their opportunity to complain and dwell upon that which they lacked. Another notable diversion for the members of the 13th and 18th Mississippi occurred on October 18th when they were detailed to tear up the tracks of the nearby Baltimore and Ohio Railroad. As Sergeant Hill recorded, the men eagerly set about "loosening up the tracks and then burnt the cross ties and bent the rails" into what would later be called "neckties" or "Sherman hairpins."⁷

Following the bloodbath at Sharpsburg, Lee was content to lick his wounds and recover back in Virginia while awaiting McClellan's next move. Little Mac, for his part, exhibited slight inclination to renew the contest and continually petitioned Washington for more troops. In early November McClellan finally advanced his army to Warrenton, Virginia, on the eastern side of the Rappahannock River, 40 miles northwest of Fredericksburg. However, since then, he had remained inactive.

In response to the Union presence at Warrenton, Lee rushed to block any potential Federal advance by positioning Longstreet's Corps at Culpepper Court House. In recognition of McLaws' earlier success in rapidly proceeding down Pleasant Valley to capture Maryland Heights opposite Harpers Ferry, McLaws' division was selected to be the vanguard and was ordered to rush ahead. Leaving the vicinity of Front Royal on October 31st, Barksdale's brigade passed through Chester Gap, reaching Culpepper on November

3rd, after covering about 70 miles. The remainder of Longstreet's Corps arrived days later having taken a more circuitous route over the mountains.[8] The Mississippi Brigade then encamped there for two weeks while keeping a watchful eye for any Federal movement. During this time daily drills and inspections were continued as the men struggled to survive the onset of snow (two inches fell on November 8th) and plunging daytime temperatures.

One memorable and comical event occurred here which, at least for a short time, took the soldiers' minds off all their concerns. There are several recorded versions which differ in the details and outcome. What they do agree on is that a red fox had the misfortune to enter the Confederate camp whereupon the soldiers immediately took up the chase, "running back and forth, throwing rocks and sticks, and yelling madly." A witness recorded that the terrified creature was "running for his life, but headed off at every turn, he jumped from place to place, dodging his pursuers." While Colonel Humphreys claims it was members of his 21st Mississippi who flushed out the fox while gathering firewood, Private Dinkins of the 18th Mississippi recorded that it was A.P. Hill's men four miles away that had aroused the fox and initiated the chase. While they both agree that all of the Mississippi regiments participated in turn, they disagreed as to the final outcome. Humphreys insisted that the frolic ended in the camp of the 13th Mississippi where the fox was finally caught and died of fright—"scared to death by the hideous yells of over 2,000 wild rebels." More credibly, Dinkins, reflecting pride in his own regiment, recounted the finale differently. Having "passed through the ranks of 30,000 soldiers successfully," when the fox finally reached the 18th Mississippi, "he was suffering, doubtless from the blows of numerous missiles, his tongue was hanging out, and he was the picture of defeat and despair." Mercifully, the fox was shot by a member of Company G, The Haymar Rifles from Yazoo County, and the pelt was "later presented to their colonel as a prize."[9]

Although McClellan had provided what Colonel Humphreys begrudgingly termed "a semblance of a victory at Antietam," that had enabled Lincoln to issue his Emancipation Proclamation on September 22, 1862, freeing the slaves within the states then in rebellion, Lincoln and his cabinet were soon running out of patience with McClellan to launch another "on to Richmond campaign."[10]

On November 7, Lincoln removed McClellan from command of the Army of the Potomac and replaced him with Maj. Gen. Ambrose E. Burnside, a 38-year-old Indiana native and 1847 West Point graduate. Having twice refused this post previously (believing he was not up to the task) Burnside reluctantly accepted this time based on the urging of close friends. Burnside was convinced that he really had no choice but to obey the assignment order. Unfortunately, for thousands of Union soldiers who would soon become casualties, Burnside, in retrospect, should have trusted his instincts and again declined the promotion. Under severe pressure from Washington, Burnside quickly determined to outflank Lee and then proceed directly toward Richmond via the shortest and most direct route—through Fredericksburg.

Lee, anticipating this Union strategy, and still smarting from his "lost order" at Frederick, Maryland, issued a short, cryptic order to Longstreet on November 13th which read, "Longstreet's Corps will be ready to move at sunrise." Longstreet alone knew the final destination and remained tight-lipped to the vexation of General McLaws, whose division once again formed the vanguard. Although these leading brigades set out in the direction of Raccoon Ford across the Rapidan, their final destination remained unknown for several days. With growing frustration, McLaws continued to receive short incremental orders, such as "move out at sunrise, go into camp on the Chancellorsville Road," followed by "Go into camp on both sides of the road." Only after McLaws had encamped at Chancellorsville did Lee finally disclose his plans. Much to the relief of McLaws and his officers, including Barksdale, Lee's order of November 18th finally solved the mystery—"Move by daylight to Fredericksburg." One Mississippi private later recorded, "Then began a race between the two great armies.... It was not a question if we could reach Fredericksburg ahead of Burnside. We were obliged to do so."[11]

In 1860, Fredericksburg was an historic city inhabited by 5,200 citizens, almost one-third being slaves, and also counting 400 free blacks. George Washington had grown up here, and his mother owned a house on Charles St. Fredericksburg was located midway between Washington and Richmond—the capital cities of the contending armies. It was situated on the banks of the Rappahannock River which served as a natural defensive barrier and supported a thriving commercial shipping enterprise. The city also straddled the Richmond, Fredericksburg, and Potomac Railroad which became a major north-south supply route for both Union and Confederate armies. It is not surprising then that, given its location, Fredericksburg and the surrounding area became a magnet for the conflict.

Four major battles between the Army of the Potomac and Army of Northern Virginia were fought in and around Fredericksburg. These bloody encounters culminated in more than 100,000 casualties and brought utter devastation to the city—and ruination to its inhabitants. Indeed it has been said that "no community in America suffered longer or more variously at the hands of civil war."[12] Barksdale would render the greatest defensive performance of his military career here, garnering universal praise from friend and foe alike, but at great cost to his Mississippi Brigade.

During the afternoon of November 17, 1862, Burnside's vanguard, troops of Sumner's Right Grand Wing of two Federal corps, arrived opposite Fredericksburg but were held at bay at the Falmouth Ford by members of the 15th Virginia Cavalry and a company from the 42nd Mississippi.[13]

However, Burnside's forces arrived without the pontoons and bridging supplies necessary to cross the Rappahannock with his artillery and supply trains. McClellan had issued orders back on November 6th to move the pontoon bridges from Berlin (near Harpers Ferry) to Washington. However, due to the confusion accompanying McClellan's removal and Burnside's appointment, "the message was laid aside or held in abeyance until the designs of the new commander should take shape," and was not received by the Engineers until six days later. Colonel Wesley Brainerd of the 50th New York Engineers (who would pay dearly in blood for this mix-up) credited this "fatal delay" for the subsequent Union disaster at Fredericksburg.[14] The arduous transfer of these pontoons from Washington via boat, and then mule train, over nearly impassable muddy roads, further delayed their arrival. These mule trains with their precious cargo of bridging components would not arrive at Falmouth, opposite Fredericksburg, until November 25th. By then it would be much too late for Burnside to take Lee by surprise. When President Lincoln had reluctantly approved Burnside's campaign plan back on November 14, General-in-Chief Henry Halleck telegraphed Burnside a cautionary message—"The President has just assented to your plan. He thinks that it will succeed *if you move rapidly; otherwise not.*"[15] Lincoln's words would prove to be prophetic.

Barksdale's Mississippi Brigade reached the hills approximately two miles west of

Fredericksburg about 4 p.m. on Thursday, November 20th, in a driving rainstorm which continued all night. On Barksdale's orders no campfires were permitted in order to conceal their presence and numbers from the Federals on the opposite shore. After dark, the 13th and 17th Mississippi were detailed to transfer army supplies from the mills and warehouses along the riverfront in Fredericksburg to the rear of the city. This task was to be completed quietly under cover of darkness under the very noses of the Union forces on the other side of the river. This subterfuge precluded the use of wagons, the sound of which might trigger Union artillery fire upon the city, its inhabitants—and the Mississippians with their valuable freight.

As related by a contemporary, this assignment once again indicated Lee's level of confidence in Barksdale's brigade "to do any duty required of it." All night long, soaked to the bone by the driving rainstorm, these gallant Mississippians trudged along like pack mules hauling flour, wheat, corn, and grain on their backs away from the riverfront to a place of safety while their brothers-in-arms slept on the surrounding hillsides. General Barksdale was everywhere that night, constantly "passing down the lines of his toiling men, encouraging them by his presence, his words, and his example."[16]

The following day Burnside demanded the surrender of Fredericksburg by 5 p.m. under threat of an artillery bombardment to begin 16 hours later. However, negotiations between Mayor Montgomery Slaughter, General Longstreet, and Union Provost Marshal Marsena Patrick persuaded Burnside to suspend both his surrender demand and bombardment threat for an unspecified period to allow for removal of Fredericksburg's non-combatants. Colonel Humphreys recorded: "Longstreet's reply was in the laconic bluntness of a soldier—'I will not occupy the city nor shall you.'"[17]

Lee wasted no time in issuing a directive that "women, children and invalids" must evacuate Fredericksburg immediately. By November 22nd most of the civilians were fleeing the city with what few possessions they could carry, devoid of any hope that their beloved homes would survive the conflagration to come. Captain Stiles commented, "I never saw a more dismal procession. Where they were going we could not tell, and I doubt if they could." Lee provided what assistance he could. As McLaws later wrote, "Our ambulances have been running all day, and are now going back and forth, carrying out the families."[18] It was the saddest of days for all involved.

However, a few stalwarts ignored Lee's directive to evacuate and defiantly remained in their homes, determined to endure whatever Fate had in store for them. A member of the Washington Artillery from New Orleans recalled one such "venerable citizen," T.S. Barton, who stated he would stay in his house and "die there if need be." Barton threw open his house to the Confederate pickets now occupying Fredericksburg and set his dining table for them with plates of "mutton, bread and butter, flanked by bottles of old wines from his ancient stock," preferring they "consume every bottle of it than let the Yankees get it." These Confederates reveled in this "patriotic idea" and did their best to fulfill Barton's wishes.[19] Others, like 47-year-old widow Jane Howison Beale, initially evacuated the city to stay nearby with friends but later returned to her house at 307 Lewis St. in downtown Fredericksburg—just in time to endure the Federal artillery bombardment of the city.[20]

While Burnside vacillated whether to proceed with his plan, Lee, Longstreet, and McLaws energetically commenced digging in and establishing artillery emplacements on the heights west of Fredericksburg. They constructed a defensive line along the base of these hills, in expectation of a potential Union crossing. By direct order of General

Longstreet, McLaws placed one of his brigades in Fredericksburg at all times to picket the river and city. On November 25th, in the words of a Confederate staff officer, "the intrepid Barksdale" and "his gallant Mississippians" assumed this critically important function. Private Dinkins regarded this assignment as a "high compliment" stating that "Barksdale was given the post of honor for the division."[21]

Uncertain as to where Burnside might choose to bridge across, McLaws picketed the entire riverfront. He placed strong detachments stretching from the dam at Falmouth, north of Fredericksburg, down past the city, to a point a quarter of a mile below Deep Run Creek, one mile to the south. McLaws excelled at the preparation of strong defensive positions, and he deserves much of the credit for the strong Confederate line here at Fredericksburg. In particular, McLaws' expertise in assessing terrain resulted in the stout defenses in the Telegraph Hill (later called Lee's Hill) sector, including the Sunken Road, as well as along the riverfront. Lee's young artillery commander, Lt. Edward Porter Alexander, recognized this fact and later lauded McLaws for "his untiring personal zeal and energy in the study of the ground around him, and in his foresight and preparation for all contingencies."[22]

With the supervision of McLaws and Barksdale, and under cover of darkness, the Mississippians secretly dug rifle-pits along the riverbank from which they could cover the river and both shorelines. They also constructed zig-zag trenches between the rifle-pits and connected them to the cellars of houses along the riverfront. These channels provided protected entry to, and exit from, these rifle-pits and cellars while under fire. Loopholes were knocked in the walls of houses just 50 yards from the river along Water Street (now called Sophia Street) to afford a clear field of fire. Still other firing positions were identified at the windows and doorways of the warehouses, mills, and shops along the riverfront. McLaws remained convinced that the Federals had no "conception of the minute and careful preparations that had been made to defeat any [Union] attempt to cross the river in my front."[23]

The geographic features of the surrounding area determined Lee's strategy for the impending battle, should it come. By far the most dominant characteristic was the commanding ridge, known as Stafford Heights, on the eastern bank of the Rappahannock River opposite Fredericksburg. From this position Union artillery commanded the river, the city, and the surrounding area, and was beyond the range of the Confederate gun positions on the hills west of the town. This dominant Union artillery position also precluded any counterattack in the event of a Confederate victory.

Lee's artillery could cover the city and the open plain to the west, but Fredericksburg's buildings obscured the line of fire to the river. Lee realized that he could not prevent a river crossing by Burnside's forces here under protection of the Union cannons on Stafford Heights—wherever the crossing might occur. However, hopefully he could delay it sufficiently to permit concentration of his widely scattered forces for maximum effect.

Accordingly, while Lee had breastworks and artillery emplacements constructed on the hills back of Fredericksburg, he employed what has been called "a mobile defense system." Lee covered only the most probable crossing sites and relied on these "first alert" forces to forestall the Union advance until he could redeploy his army. To facilitate rapid troop movements, a new military road was constructed, and telegraph lines were installed to link the scattered defenders. This system also allowed the greater part of Longstreet's Corps to remain in their camps until required—rather than continually manning the entrenchments under the debilitating winter weather.[24]

The vanguard of Jackson's Second Corps arrived in Fredericksburg on December 1st, with the rear of his column arriving two days later, after a twelve-day, 175-mile march from the Shenandoah Valley. Lee's array near Fredericksburg was now as follows: Richard H. Anderson's division covered the river north of Fredericksburg, McLaws' division covered the city down to beyond Deep Run, and together with Ransom's division also guarded the hills west of the city, while the divisions of George Pickett and John B. Hood extended the line south of Fredericksburg along Spotsylvania Heights. The balance of Jackson's corps remained spread out along the river for almost 30 miles to the south near Port Royal.[25]

During this time Burnside sought out the best locations to lay his pontoon bridges. Accordingly, Engineer Capt. Wesley Brainerd, sometimes accompanied by his superior, Brig. Gen. Daniel P. Woodbury, and Brig. Gen. Henry H. Hunt, Chief of Artillery, made several dangerous reconnaissance missions under cover of darkness across the river south of Fredericksburg. They recommended an ideal, undefended location well south of the city near Snickers Neck. On December 9th, much to Brainerd's utter amazement, Burnside finally confirmed his decision to instead "force a crossing directley in front of the town" (together with another near Deep Run). Brainerd and his fellow engineer officers soon personally reconnoitered Burnside's choices, and in Brainerd's words, "after we had pondered the situation well we all came to the conclusion that we might now return to our quarters and with great propriety execute our last Wills & Testaments."[26]

These early days of December were also marked by an uneasy calm as the opposing armies stared each other down across the icy waters of the Rappahannock. Barksdale's Mississippians remained on picket in town with the enemy's sentries on guard across the river—in one Confederate's words, "only a biscuit's throw away." By mutual agreement "there [was] no firing" but these adversaries continually hurled taunts and insults at each other—often filled with vulgarities and laced with profanity. This practice however did not preclude some limited fraternization in the form of trading goods back and forth. Usually Southern tobacco was exchanged for Northern coffee via small handcrafted sailboats floated across the river. However, the extent of this prohibited commerce was not anywhere close to that which occurred after the battle when both armies were in winter camp.[27]

The Confederates also shared in Union band music during some early December evenings. If Burnside used this as a ploy to mask the noise of Federal efforts to assemble the pontoons, lumber, and equipment preparatory to launching the bridges, it had the opposite result. McLaws later related that, two or three evenings before the Union crossing, he and General Barksdale were attracted by Union bands playing at their end of the burned railroad bridge at the lower end of town. Several "national airs" were followed by songs popular in both North and South, and the concert ended with "Dixie," which prompted cheers from both sides—followed by "much laughter." Suspicious, McLaws continued, "Surmising that this serenade meant mischief, I closely inspected our bank of the river and at night caused additional rifle-pits to be constructed to guard more securely the approaches to the bridge."[28]

This was very intuitive on McLaws' part, for it was precisely at this time on December 8th that the Union Chief of Engineers issued a memorandum outlining the bridging locations: two were to be laid at the upper end of Fredericksburg at the foot of Hawke Street, site of a rope ferry, and opposite Sumner's headquarters in the two-story brick mansion known as Chatham; one at the city wharf near the aforementioned railroad bridge at the south end of town; and two (later increased to three) more than a mile downstream just beyond Deep Run.²⁹ Two nights later on December 10, Burnside was finally ready to attempt these crossings, and the stage was set for Barksdale's finest demonstration during the war of his inherent abilities while on the defensive.

Barksdale remained on high alert throughout Wednesday December 10, 1862 having observed increased activity by the Federals during the entire day. His instincts told him that Burnside would likely attempt to cross that night. In anticipation, Barksdale had carefully established his headquarters in the three-story Market House/Town Hall and adjoining Market Square located on the east side of Princess Anne Street, between William and George Streets, only two blocks from the riverfront. At the time, the first floor was an arcade for market stalls, emptying through open archways to the Market Lot on the river side. The upper two stories comprised the Town Hall and were built of brick with numerous windows facing the river which offered a clear vantage point for a considerable distance both upstream and downstream.³⁰

Barksdale would locate his reserves in the Market Lot and feed them, as necessary, to the threatened points. In addition to the sharpshooter positions along the east side of Sophia Street, Barksdale also fortified the next two parallel streets from the river—Caroline and Princess Anne, particularly at the intersections with the streets running perpendicular from the river (i.e. Hawke, Fauquier, Amelia, William, and George).

On orders from Barksdale, Lieutenant Colonel Fiser of the 17th Mississippi deployed Company A, Buena Vista Rifles, under Capt. Andrew J. Pulliam, to the foot of Hawke Street, and Company B, Mississippi Rangers, under Capt. Andrew R. Govan near the

Former Market House/Town Hall/Market Square, with a commanding view of the riverfront in both directions. Barksdale selected this site for his headquarters and marshalling area for reserves (author photograph).

city wharves 10 blocks to the south. The remaining eight companies were stationed at the Market Lot. At the same time, the 18th Mississippi, under Lt. Col. William H. Luse, was posted along the river south of Fredericksburg, from about a half-mile above and a quarter mile below Deep Run. Barksdale deployed his 1,500-man brigade in two echelons. The 17th and 18th Mississippi comprised the front echelon. Barksdale allowed his remaining two regiments, the 13th and 21st Mississippi, which comprised his rear echelon reserve, to stay in camp west of the city behind Marye's Heights awaiting further developments.[31]

Barksdale didn't know that the Federal engineers had moved the pontoons for the upper crossings down near the river, placing them in a ravine just out of sight of the Confederate pickets. The Union engineers awaited nightfall, with launching time set for 1 a.m. on December 11. These bridging parties had "marched as quietley as possible so as not to disturb the enemy" who Brainerd remained convinced "were expecting us to strike somewhere but could form no idea of the spot."[32]

About 11 p.m. Barksdale instructed Fiser to double his pickets. Fiser immediately complied by dispatching Companies H and C to Pulliam on the left, and Companies I and K to Govan on the right—holding the three-and-a-half remaining companies of the 17th Mississippi in reserve at the Market Square. At midnight Barksdale met with Luse and ordered him to double his pickets near Deep Run and to reinforce Govan near the City Docks by releasing three companies from the 18th Mississippi.[33]

Engineer Brainerd recorded that when the bell in the tower of Fredericksburg's principal church struck one "my men were all in line and we marched towards the river." These unarmed engineers were joined by two infantry regiments as supports. They unloaded the pontoons from the wagons at the crest of a hill overlooking the river below, passed them down the hill, quickly carried them across the level ground for 150 feet, and finally placed them "into the water at a lively rate." Brainerd added that the night air was "cold and raw" and "laden with a sort of haze or fog [that] penetrated to the bones."[34] This fog grew thicker through the night and reduced visibility further as dawn grew nearer. If Barksdale couldn't see them through the thick veil of fog, by now he could definitely hear the unmistakable sounds related to their bridge building activity, as well as the rumble of artillery being placed in support along the crest.

Barksdale notified McLaws about 2 a.m. that the Union bridging had begun. In reply McLaws advised Barksdale to allow construction to proceed until the Union engineers came to within easy range. Finally, at 4:30 a.m., Barksdale, peering through the fog, could just discern that the first pontoon bridge at the foot of Hawke Street was now about half-complete, some 200 feet long, with another 200 feet to go. This was close enough for the impatient Barksdale who sent a courier off to McLaws with an updated status report confirming that his Mississippians were about to open fire. Upon receipt of Barksdale's message, McLaws gave the order for the pre-arranged signal—the firing in rapid succession of two cannons of J.P.W. Read's Battery of the Pulaski Artillery near Marye's Hill—confirming to all Confederates within earshot that Burnside's crossing of the Rappahannock had finally begun.[35]

Having accomplished his first task of alerting Lee to the time and location of the imminent crossing by the Union Army, Barksdale now set about completing his second task—to delay the crossing for as long as possible—the importance of which cannot be overstated. The success of Lee's entire battle plan now depended solely upon Barksdale's ability to delay the crossing of the Union Army long enough to allow Jackson's entire corps to concentrate on Lee's right at Fredericksburg, and for Longstreet to maneuver his divisions into their breastworks. Realizing the critical importance of Barksdale's mission, Lee, insisted upon receiving updates throughout the day at 15-minute intervals relayed through McLaws and Longstreet. Invariably Lee responded to Barksdale "to hold the enemy in check until ordered to retire." Thus, as Hawley has emphasized, in modern military parlance, "Barksdale's mission was a high risk delay to prevent enemy forces from reaching the specified area earlier than the specified time or event, regardless of the cost." Moreover, as Hawley correctly points out, Barksdale was also tasked with "disengaging his force while under combat to prevent its destruction, while at the same time not disrupting Lee's defensive fire should the Federals be right on his heels."[36]

Meanwhile, C.C. Cummings of the Mississippi Rangers, who was sergeant of the picket post at the river near the City Docks at the middle crossing site, saw the Federals noiselessly launch their first pontoon. He and his comrades raced back to report to Captain Govan who immediately sent Cummings to advise "General Barksdale at the city hall, who was up with lights expecting it." Claiming personal credit for actually initiating the fight, Cummings later stated, "My orders [from General Barksdale] were to tell Captain Govan to open fire on the pontoons which I did, and so was opened the bombardment of Fredericksburg."[37]

However, this honor actually belonged to Lieutenant Colonel Fiser who, by his own account, at about 4 a.m. was ordered personally by Barksdale at the Town Hall to "repair at once to the upper ford ... with my reserve consisting of Companies D, E, G, and part of F ... and assume command in person, you [Barksdale] having left it discretionary with me when to begin the attack." While the 3rd Georgia of Wright's brigade of Maj. Gen. R.H. Anderson's Division remained on picket duty above the upper crossing, in open country on Fiser's left flank all day, "under a most galling fire from the enemy's batteries," Brig. Gen. Cadmus M. Wilcox placed three companies of the 8th Florida, of Brig. Gen. Edward A. Perry's Florida brigade, under Barksdale's command.

At this juncture, Barksdale personally accompanied 150 of these Florida troops, under command of Captain David Lang, and directed Fiser to assist Lang in placing his battalion on Fiser's left, north of Pitt Street above the upper crossing. These Florida troops initially performed very well under Captain Lang's leadership. Barksdale had already ordered the remainder of these three Florida companies, under command of Captain William Baya, to reinforce Govan's right wing at the lower end of Fredericksburg at the city wharves. Since the ideal places of protection and concealment near here had already been taken by members of the 17th and 18th Mississippi, Govan assigned the Floridians to positions along the exposed riverbank near the wharves—over Baya's vocal protests. This difference of opinion between Govan and Baya would continue to escalate during the morning.[38]

Fiser delayed only long enough to notify those families still inhabiting dwellings along the riverfront to evacuate immediately and to "give them time to get from under range of the enemy's guns." This compassionate act having been accomplished, Fiser recorded, "about 5 am I ordered my men to fire on the bridge-builders, which they obeyed promptly and deliberately [and I think with stunning effect], the command being echoed by Captain Govan on the right in the same manner and with equal effect ... we easily swept the enemy from their bridge from above, below, and in front."[39]

Contemporary accounts all agree that Barksdale was not a passive bystander but aggressively participated in the defense all along his line throughout the day. For example, Colonel Humphreys recorded, "During the whole day Gen'l Barksdale was actively superintending our line and was greatly distinguished for his courage and daring."[40] But try as he might, Barksdale could not be everywhere at once, so he prudently trusted in the discretion of his capable subordinates to make tactical decisions on the spot, based upon their up-to-date information gleaned through their personal observation. This was the mark of a sound commander, and further proof that Barksdale was continuing to grow into his role as brigadier general.

On this day, Thursday December 11, 1862, there would be more than enough courage to go around—on both sides. The unarmed men of the Engineer Corps faced a daunting task. Even under ideal conditions the bridging process was arduous and required close coordination by the various teams with different specific assignments. The fact that this attempt was being made under cover of darkness, in near freezing temperatures, over frigid water with glare ice along the shorelines, and under enemy fire, rendered the effort almost impossible. Barksdale's unorthodox tactics whereby he chose to fight his brigade, not in conventional close-order battle formations with volley fire, but rather as individual snipers loosely grouped in small clusters—specifically instructed to target the unarmed engineers and officers—spelled doom for the blue-coated bridge-builders.

The bridging procedure itself was complicated enough. The 31-foot wooden boat was initially launched upstream, floated into place, and secured to the shore by stakes and lashings. Then each subsequent pontoon boat weighing 1,300 pounds was launched in succession and floated into place downstream by a winch, maneuvered into place every 13 feet and parallel to the previous one, and secured in place by five 25-foot beams, called balks, which were tied longitudinally and perpendicular to the pontoon boats. When secured in place, this floating structure was then covered by 14-foot-long flooring boards, called chesses, which were laid crosswise and secured by ropes. These individual

A section of pontoon bridging (author photograph).

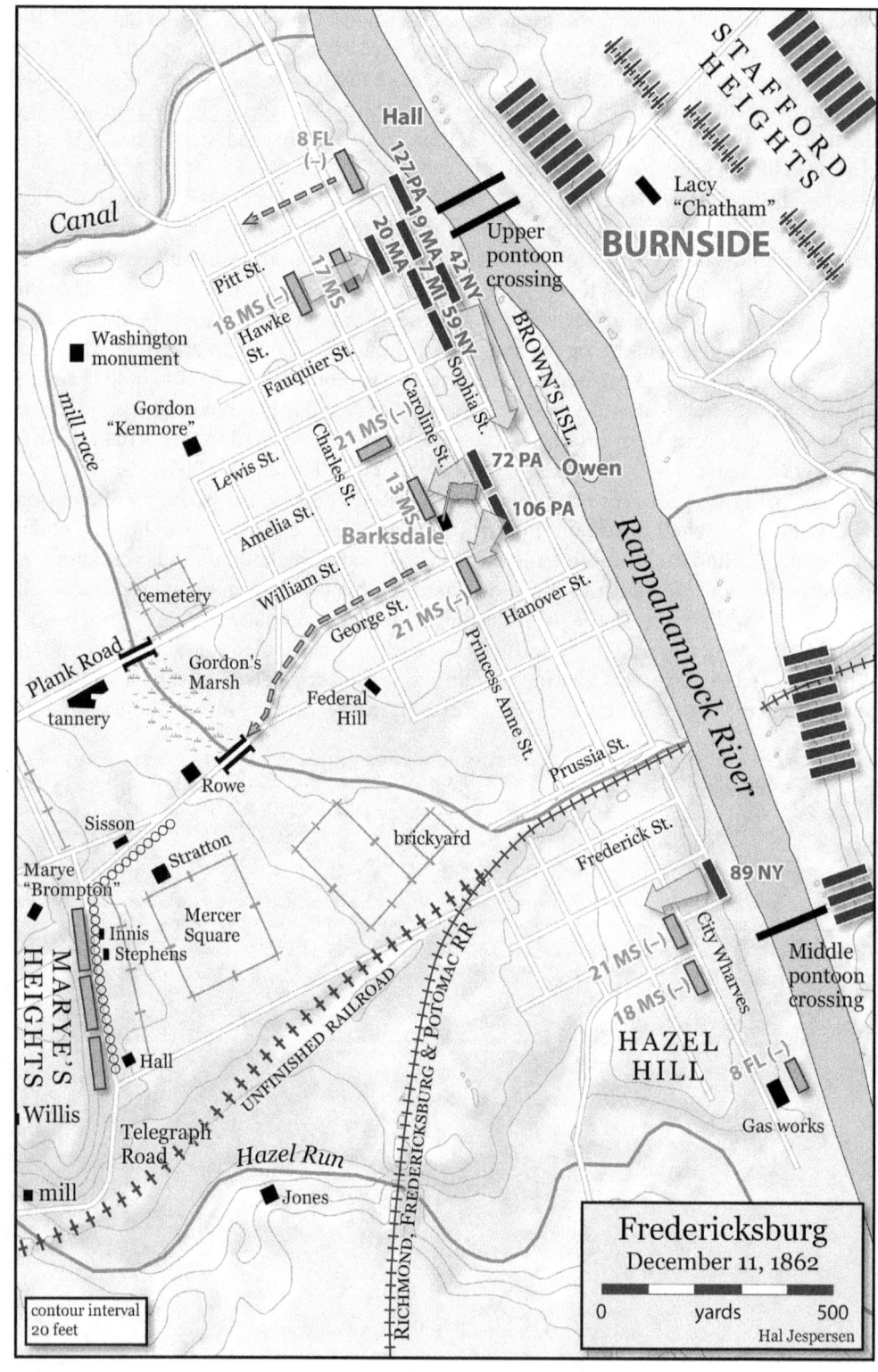

Battle of Fredericksburg, December 11, 1862

operations were performed by separate bridging "parties" known by the component which they handled, i.e., abutment, boat, balk, lashing, chess, and side-rail.[41]

By about 5 a.m., just as Fiser was about to give the command to fire, Captain Wesley Brainerd and the 50th New York Engineers found themselves in no-man's land—unarmed and poised 200 feet from the Fredericksburg shore, isolated on their half-completed bridge, peering into the shroud of lingering fog and expecting the worst at any second. Brainerd later described the scene as follows:

> I was standing at the extreme outer end of the bridge encouraging my men, when, happening to cast my eyes to the shore beyond just as the fogg lifted a little, I saw what for the moment almost chilled my blood. A long line of arms moving rapidly up and down was all I saw, for a moment later they were again obscured by the fogg. But I knew too well that line of arms was ramming cartridges and that the crisis was near.

Then came Fiser's command—"Fire!" Brainerd continued his narrative of the maelstrom that followed:

> …in an instant we were in the midst of a perfect storm of bulletts. Our Artillery on the crest of the hill in rear of us quickly responded, their shells roaring and screeching over our heads. Our Infantry on our right and left returned fire…. The bulletts of the enemy rained upon my bridge. They went whizzing and spitting by and around me, pattering on the bridge, splashing into the water and thugging through the boats … [instinctively] everyone started for the shore end of the bridge. Some fell into the boats, dead. Some fell into the stream and some onto the bridge, dead. Some wounded, crawled along on their hands and knees and in a few moments all of us were off the bridge, all except the dead. The storm of lead continued. *It was simple murder, that was all* [emphasis added].

Even back on the shoreline there was no escape, as there were no earthworks to protect either the terrified engineers nor their infantry supports. In Brainerd's words:

> We instinctively dropped upon the ground and so most of the bullets passed over us. Here we lay, our faces burried in the snow and mud while the balls whistled around like bees loose from a hive.

Desperately seeking any kind of protection, Brainerd and five companions crawled behind a bundle of lashing rods, one foot in diameter by about 18 or 20 inches long, where they remained for the next hour—"all depending upon that little bundle of rods to protect us from the bulletts which sputtered and spatted into it in the most venomous manner."[42]

Brainerd's contention that Barksdale's tactic of drawing a bead on an unarmed and defenseless enemy was tantamount to murder was shared by many under the military conventions of the time. Indeed snipers, through all wars up through the Second World War, have been universally despised, and rarely taken as prisoners. (Only in recent conflicts has sniping taken on any air of legitimacy, perhaps due to recent changes in moral values as well as the skill required given the extreme ranges associated with modern weaponry.) On this day the anger, frustration, and hatred felt by the Union soldiers toward Barksdale's sharpshooters[43] would result in extremely bitter fighting through the streets of the city, and lead one Federal commander to issue the extraordinary order that no prisoners were to be taken amongst Barksdale's men. This extreme emotion on the part of Union soldiers would also result in their subsequent wanton destruction of private property in an orgy of devastation unleashed upon Fredericksburg. Union officers scarcely attempted to restrain them.

For his part, Barksdale expressed no remorse for his methods to carry out his orders in furtherance of the Confederate cause. This is reminiscent of Stonewall Jackson's

Barksdale's Mississippians opposing the laying of the pontoon bridges (Robert U. Johnson and Clarence C. Buel, *Battles & Leaders of the Civil War*, Vol. 3, 1887).

reaction during his Shenandoah Valley Campaign to a report by Confederate Col. J.M. Patton in which the officer expressed regret at the deaths of a detachment of Federal cavalrymen who had displayed extraordinary valor and bravery. Challenged by Jackson to explain, Patton replied he thought they deserved a better fate. Jackson's terse response was "No. Shoot them all: I do not want them to be brave."[44] These were words which

General Barksdale could live by. On this particular day in Fredericksburg, he and his Mississippi riflemen did just that.

The fate of Captain Brainerd and the 50th New York Engineers was shared by the 15th New York Engineers at the middle crossing at the City Docks just south of the railroad bridge, who came under fire of Govan's right wing at the same time. Here the bridge was two-thirds completed when Govan's troops erupted from Caroline Street, rushed down the cobblestone alley known as Rocky Lane (still visible today) and sprang right onto the docks, firing point blank into the shocked construction crews. Here too, engineers fell dead on the bridge, while those still living fled for their lives. Having accurately fired their lethal rounds, these Mississippians quickly disappeared back into the warehouses, dwellings, and cellars to await the next Union attempt at completion.[45]

Despite the pandemonium around him at the riverfront, Barksdale remained calm and in control of the situation. By his prior orders, at the sound of the two signal guns at 4:30 a.m., both the 13th and 21st Mississippi had hastened to the Market House, arriving shortly after 5 a.m. to await their commander's further instructions. With the fighting already underway at both crossing sites opposite Fredericksburg, and now under Union artillery fire, Barksdale realized he could not mass all his reserves in the adjoining wide-open Market Lot. Therefore he immediately instructed Colonel Carter to deploy his 13th Mississippi along Caroline Street in support of the upper crossing defense, and await Fiser's orders for reinforcements. If Fiser could not repel the crossing, Carter was to withdraw his regiment back to the Market House. Barksdale ordered Colonel Humphreys to send half of the 21st Mississippi, the right wing under Captain Moody, to support Govan at the middle crossing, while Humphreys remained with the left wing as a half-regiment reserve at the Market House.

As the day dawned, about 70 Union cannons on Stafford Heights, together with 36 light field pieces, redeployed along the riverbank. They pounded the buildings along the riverfront in a merciless attempt to drive away Barksdale's riflemen who hunkered down as best they could. Barksdale's orders to all were to "hold the city at all hazards."[46]

Despite the onset of daylight, the fog did not dissipate, and with the added smoke from the artillery shells and rifled muskets, visibility remained greatly reduced throughout the morning—to a much greater degree for the more distant Union artillerymen and infantry supports 400 feet away. The Mississippians targeted the construction parties in the open, only 80 feet away, while remaining largely concealed themselves. Despite the ongoing noise, spectacle, pandemonium, and destruction, the Union artillery could not achieve the desired effect.

Although solid shot tore through both wooden and brick buildings, beat down walls, toppled chimneys, started fires, and rooted out some nests of sharpshooters, a Union cannoneer lamented that it was quite impossible to drive these snipers out of the dwellings because the cellars underneath afforded them protection. Each time it appeared the Mississippians had been neutralized and the Union artillery ceased firing, these Confederates re-emerged like so many rats from their holes and savaged the Union bridging parties.

Union Artillery Chief, Henry Hunt, explained to Burnside that, while his guns could destroy large troop formations within Fredericksburg, Barksdale's small clusters of snipers were exceedingly difficult to target and annihilate. A Mississippian later stated, "From their screened position, it was impossible to touch our men with gun-shot or rifle for they were scattered in all directions, in houses, barns, and every imaginable place where shelter could be obtained."

During this time the Union engineers endeavored to summon up the courage to make additional attempts. Barksdale's men were not the only ones with peremptory orders to succeed "at all hazards." Burnside relayed his message to these engineers in no uncertain terms which Brainerd paraphrased as follows: "our bridge must be completed at whatever cost and that the whole Army waited for us." Brainerd would later lament, "as there were no troops in the Army that understood our duties or that could relieve us, *there was nothing left for us but to die,* or so it seemed to me" (emphasis added).

It was during one of these subsequent attempts that this courageous captain, already resigned to his fate, took a bullet wound to his left arm which severed an artery. Brainerd staggered back along the bridge to the eastern shore, faint from loss of blood. He was assisted up the embankment by two infantrymen while bullets hissed around their heads as the Mississippians deliberately targeted this officer whose private's overcoat, having been removed, no longer concealed his rank. Brainerd reached a hospital room in the Lacy House which he described as being "filled with the wounded, dead and dying—some were crying, some were groaning, and some too far gone to do either." He noted that some of the crying were wounded officers—"crying for *grief* that their men were being sacrificed, slaughtered for *naught.*" This game of cat and mouse continued throughout the morning, with Barksdale's Mississippians thwarting nine separate and desperate attempts by the Federal engineers to complete these upper and middle bridges.[47] Barksdale's unconventional tactics were succeeding beyond expectation and, with every repulse, buying Lee precious time.

Meanwhile the situation at the lower crossing was the polar opposite. Luse with his pickets and marksmen from the 18th Mississippi heard the unmistakable sounds of the 15th New York Engineers launching their pontoons in the predawn darkness and thick fog near the mouth of Deep Run. Accordingly he anticipated the crossing would occur at this location. Confident that his forces were correctly positioned to repulse the imminent Union bridging attempt, Luse simply waited for daylight, not thinking it necessary to alert the Confederate forces along the river, south of Deep Run.

However he failed to realize that the Union engineers, per normal practice, actually launched the pontoon boats upstream of the chosen site and floated them downriver into position about a quarter-mile "below and out of range from Deep Run." In the absence of any prepared rifle-pits or trenches in this vicinity, and now recognizing his oversight in the naked light of day, Luse was forced to shift his forces southward on the open plain devoid of any natural cover. Luse's two companies of sharpshooters managed to deliver an initial volley which scattered the bridge-builders. However, when the Union artillery along Stafford Heights opened up on his exposed position, the 18th Mississippi was forced back a considerable distance from the riverbank, taking refuge in a ravine. Despite Luse's later claims that his forces were near enough to observe and oppose any further attempts at crossing, a myriad of Union eyewitnesses and participants confirmed that the initial bridge was completed by about 8:15 a.m., with no further opposition.

The second bridge further to the south was finished by Regulars of the U.S. Corps of Engineers at about 11:00 a.m. despite some resistance from Hood's Texans. Luse remained passively in position for the remainder of the morning, being reinforced at 11 a.m. by the 16th Georgia and 15th South Carolina regiments sent by McLaws who anticipated an immediate crossing by Union infantry. General Kershaw soon arrived and ordered all three regiments back to the Bowling Green Road to protect them from the Federal artillery fire. Barksdale, learning of this withdrawal, in full view of the enemy, immediately rushed with one of his staff along the River Road to this site, a mile-and-a-half away. Upon arriving, he instructed Luse, in no uncertain terms, that the 18th Mississippi "must not recede an inch." Barksdale and Kershaw agreed to hold this position, and Barksdale immediately returned to his headquarters on Princess Anne Street.

Barksdale must share in the blame for this weak resistance at the lower crossing since he did not insist that Luse dig any entrenchments to provide cover for the defenders anywhere along this sector. However, it is fair to say that, unlike Fiser and Govan who performed very aggressively and effectively at Fredericksburg, Luse, even considering the handicap of terrain, did not, and to a considerable degree fell short of the level of trust Barksdale had placed in him. Fortunately for both Luse and Barksdale, although Union Major General Franklin could have easily crossed his entire Left Grand Division during the morning, thereby forcing Barksdale out of Fredericksburg, Burnside refused Franklin's request to cross over here pending completion of the upper and middle bridges. This decision would prove very costly for the Union forces engaged opposite Fredericksburg.[48]

The only other hint Barksdale gave during the battle regarding his status as a volunteer officer—and not a professional soldier—occurred when Fiser requested artillery support. In response Barksdale ordered that two light fieldpieces from the Richmond Howitzers be placed near the foot of Hawke Street. Stiles later stated these two guns would have been obliterated by the Union artillery on Stafford Heights in a matter of minutes. Captain Stiles attributed the General's granting of Fiser's request to "Old Barksdale's" pluck and fighting spirit (which even exceeded that of Fiser.) Barksdale issued the imprudent order and the gun crews actually started out from Marye's Heights. Fortunately for all involved, McLaws intercepted the two gun crews, and upon learning of their destination, immediately countermanded Barksdale's order. Learning of McLaws' action, Barksdale swallowed his pride and quickly rescinded his ill-considered directive.[49]

Meanwhile back at Fredericksburg, Barksdale's stubborn defense continued to stymie Union efforts to complete their bridges. The cycle repeated itself hour after hour until Burnside finally reached his boiling point. Around noon he instructed Hunt to train all 150 Union artillery pieces directly on Fredericksburg in a final attempt to drive out—or annihilate—Barksdale's defenders. Hunt reluctantly obeyed. At 12:30 p.m., in an unprecedented act during the Civil War, artillery hell was unleashed upon Fredericksburg and all therein, and continued unabated for nearly two hours. Soldiers' diaries, those of both Southerners and Northerners, expressed their shock, amazement, and in many cases their contempt at the ferocity of the bombardment and extent of devastation in this historic city once home to George Washington. A Union infantryman later described the horrific scene this way—"…beginning on the right the whole 150 pieces would hurl their misles of death into the doomed city, *it was a grand but terrible* sight." Private Dinkins later commented that "no tongue or pen can describe the dreadful scene," then he made the following attempt:

> Hundreds of tons of iron were hurled against the place, and nothing in war can exceed the horror of that time. The deafening roar of cannon and bursting shells, falling walls and chimneys, brick and timbers flying through the air, houses set on fire, the smoke adding to the already heavy fog, the bursting of flames through the housetops made a scene which … was appalling and indescribable, a condition which would paralyze the stoutest heart, and one from which not a man in Barksdale's Brigade had the slightest hope of passing through.

Dinkins was correct—many did not. A Union veteran would later report that scores of Confederate dead lay "in every part of town, lying where the deadly bullet or the ragged shell had struck them ... [including] a [young] boy from Mississippi whose head had been carried away by a round shot." Another Yankee recorded "the Rebs lay thick along the fence just as they had fallen. Killed by our round shot and shell. Some with heads off, others arms and legs off, and some mutilated in a horrible manner." Indeed the destruction was so severe that one Union soldier later observed, "the town could not boast of a whole window [and] the bodies of cats and dogs were scattered through the streets, in the yards, inside the houses and ... on the doorsteps of their masters' houses." For the few citizens still trapped in Fredericksburg the terror was almost unbearable. Years later a young girl who had survived the ordeal recalled, "My aunt was cowering inside the [fireplace], and every time a [cannon] ball would roll through the house or a shell explode she would draw herself up and moan and shiver."[50]

Even during this intense and sustained bombardment Barksdale and his men remained active. Falling debris, especially from chimneys, was a constant hazard. While Barksdale and a dozen of his couriers, staff officers, and men at the Market House were enjoying a snack of hardtack sopped in a honey bucket which courier Pvt. James Branch had rescued from a burning building, a large Parrot shell dropped in their midst and spun crazily around on the ground. Luckily for Barksdale and his comrades the fuse had been extinguished and it did not detonate. However, Barksdale did not escape unscathed. This shell had passed through the slate roof overhead, dislodging a large piece which struck Barksdale on the shoulder, leaving him badly bruised but otherwise unharmed. Others, like Col. David Lang, were not so fortunate. He was struck on the head by a brick from a falling chimney, rendered unconscious, and eliminated from the fight—with dire consequences for the Floridians he commanded at the upper crossing. Private William L. Davis recorded that Joe. A. Harris of the 13th Mississippi, who was with Barksdale at another time, "was struck in the back of the neck by a brick from a chimney overhead" while "the color bearer and several others had their skulls broke at the same time."[51]

While at his headquarters Barksdale also had to contend with a woman whose bravery in Captain Stiles' estimation surpassed even that of the Mississippians. Stiles, who had been sent into Fredericksburg with a message for Barksdale, arrived at his headquarters at the same time as this woman approached unconcernedly from the opposite direction demanding to speak with General Barksdale. A young staff officer replied this was not possible but she persisted: "General Barksdale is a Southern gentleman, sir, and will not refuse to see a lady who has called upon him." Stiles later recorded their meeting as follows:

> Seeing that he could not otherwise get rid of her, the General did come to the door, but actually wringing his hands in excitement and annoyance. "For God's sake, madam, go and seek some place of safety. I'll send a member of my staff to help you find one." She again smiled gently while Old Barksdale fumed and almost swore—and then she said quietly: "General Barksdale, my cow has just been killed in my stable by a shell. She is very fat and I don't want the Yankees to get her. If you will send some one down to butcher her, you are welcome to the meat."[52]

After an estimated 9,000 rounds had rained down on Fredericksburg, near 2:30 p.m. the barrage slackened, and the engineers resumed their bridging activity at both upper sites—only to be driven back once again by Barksdale's marksmen. Barksdale sent off a courier to enquire whether his men should attempt to extinguish the fires in the city. Longstreet answered abruptly, "You have enough to do to watch the Yankees." Receiving positive reports from both Fiser and Govan, Barksdale sent off another messenger to relate, "Tell General Lee that if he wants a bridge of dead Yankees, I can furnish him with one!" Not one to display emotion, Lee, as described by his biographer Douglas Southall Freeman, reacted this way—"each time Barksdale proudly announced that a new attempt had been beaten off, Lee's countenance lighted up."[53]

At Fiser's request shortly after 2 p.m. Carter sent 10 sharpshooters from the 13th Mississippi to the upper crossing site. Barksdale also ordered Humphreys to send his three reserve companies of the 21st Mississippi, then at the Market House, to the same location. These reinforcements were guided too far to the left by several hundred yards into a very exposed position where they were raked by heavy Union artillery fire and forced to return to the Market House. Fiser's request for reinforcements was due to the casualties he had suffered and the poor performance of the 8th Florida after Lang became incapacitated. With Lang sidelined, Fiser stated, "I received but little aid from the [Florida] regiment, as it seemed troubled and in want of a commander." Fiser also felt compelled to report that "a certain [Florida] lieutenant (whom Fiser did not mention by name) so far forgot himself as to draw his pistol and threatened to kill some of my sharpshooters if they fired again as it would draw the enemy's fire on his position."

The performance of the contingent from the 8th Florida under command of Captain Baya at the middle crossing was also severely criticized by Captain Govan, who was in overall command there. Govan reported that these Florida troops "failed repeatedly to obey my commands to fire on the bridge-builders" and were "so silent … that I scarcely knew [Baya] was in position." (Their fear of drawing enemy artillery fire on their exposed position here may have been at least partially vindicated by Humphreys' aforementioned experience with the 21st Mississippi reserve when caught in the open above the upper crossing.) Twenty-two of these Floridians, including Baya, would be captured when Govan's Mississippians finally withdrew.

Despite two later attempts by Colonel Lang to salvage the reputation of Baya and his men, the stigma remained. Even modern authors Zack C. Waters and James C. Edmonds in their detailed history of the Florida Brigade, *A Small but Spartan Band*, were forced to conclude that "Baya's contingent certainly set no standard for heroism" and to reluctantly agree that these Floridians "added no luster to their record" here at Fredericksburg.[54]

Burnside, his bombardment having failed, raged at Hunt, his Chief of Artillery—"The army is held by the throat by a few sharpshooters!" and sought another solution. Hunt proposed to fill the remaining pontoon boats not yet positioned with infantry and dash to the other side, land, and attack Barksdale's defenders—thereby establishing what would be known today as a bridgehead. Other boats would simultaneously be rowed into position and the bridges completed by the engineers. This novel idea of an amphibious landing under fire had actually been suggested to Hunt earlier that morning by Maj. Ira Spaulding of the 50th New York Engineers. Burnside agreed—but only if volunteers could be garnered amongst the infantry for this untried and dangerous mission. After Col. Henry Baxter volunteered to go across with his 7th Michigan, Col. Norman J. Hall, commanding the 3rd Brigade in Maj. Gen. Oliver Otis Howard's 2nd Division, offered up his entire brigade. The 7th Michigan, supported by the 19th Massachusetts (and later the 20th Massachusetts) would cross at the upper bridge site while the 89th New York would do the same at the middle bridge and cooperate with the 15th New York Engineers who had been recalled from the lower crossing.[55]

As the Union artillery suddenly ceased firing, the 7th Michigan piled into the empty "bateaux" and set out for the other side of the Rappahannock. Most hunched down to avoid the rifle fire from the Mississippians which erupted instantaneously, peppering these craft containing 20–25 infantrymen. Under orders not to fire, other Union infantrymen concentrated on rowing and poling as fast and hard as they could to cross in the shortest time. Bluecoats were soon tumbling dead or wounded back into the boats or into the frigid water. Brave Lt. Col. Henry Baxter of the 7th Michigan took a rifle ball in the shoulder. A member of the Irish Brigade, who witnessed this spectacle of unsurpassed bravery, commented, "The Johnny fire was fatal to quite a few. It may have been the saddest sight during my life in the army. The scene forced tears from many of my comrades and me...."[56]

As the 7th Michigan approached the far shoreline, Confederate fire slackened as the steep riverbank obscured the invasion craft. The 70 Wolverines in this first wave briefly regrouped in the relative safety of the water's edge, and then rushed up toward Sophia St. overrunning the rifle-pits as successive waves made the crossing behind them. They raced across the intersection of Hawke and Sophia Street and, with a frenzy, went at the Mississippian sharpshooters stubbornly remaining in the severely damaged dwellings here.

This was the first opportunity for the Union soldiers to exact revenge against Barksdale's snipers whom they despised with a passion. Major Thomas J. Hunt, now in command of these 7th Michigan Wolverines, in an uncontrolled fit of anger, ordered his men to take no prisoners. While most refused "for humanity's sake" to obey this unheard of command, others were not so forgiving and bayoneted the trapped Mississippians

The first amphibious crossing under fire in American military history (Library of Congress).

without mercy. A Union engineer later commented, "It was fiendish work but the provocation was a strong one." Within about twenty minutes Major Hunt's force had also captured 35 prisoners, contrary to his instructions. The thousands of Union soldiers on Stafford Heights who witnessed this amphibious crossing considered it "the most gallant charge of the war."[57]

A similar scenario played out at the middle crossing with the 89th New York piling into the remaining pontoon boats which were paddled furiously across by members of the 15th New York Engineers while under fire of Govan's defenders. As the 89th New Yorkers jumped out onto the City Docks and raced ahead, Govan withdrew his combined force of Mississippi regiments to Caroline Street—leaving Baya and his Floridians to their fate.[58] From this new position Govan's wing then fought determinedly to contain this second Union bridgehead.

The battle of Fredericksburg at this stage had already established itself as unique in the annals of American military history. Not only had it witnessed a formidable defense against a river crossing by an army, the Federals without realizing it had become the initial American forces anywhere to successfully conduct an amphibious landing and to establish the first bridgeheads while under fire. The battle would soon witness another milestone—the first occurrence of large-scale urban warfare in America. In the expert opinion of historian, author, and Fredericksburg authority Francis A. O'Reilly, this battle "set the stage for the way modern armies would fight from then on."[59]

To contain these two Federal bridgeheads and defend the streets of Fredericksburg, Barksdale was forced to rely on his own instincts, resourcefulness, and ingenuity. There was no manual of tactics in existence to address these scenarios (not even Hardee's) as there had never been any need. As Fiser fell back into the yards in rear of Sophia Street fighting a delaying action against the growing Union column advancing up Hawke Street, he petitioned Carter to send forward two companies of the 13th Mississippi. While en route, Carter encountered Fiser who was already withdrawing.

Ordered by Barksdale to defend the next street parallel to the river—Caroline Street—Carter found the roadway already occupied by Federals from the 20th and 19th Massachusetts who had soon followed the 7th Michigan across the Rappahannock in pontoon boats. A member of the 20th Massachusetts recorded that his regiment overcame their initial trepidation, "remembering the experience in crossing the Potomac a year previous at Ball's Bluff," and recognizing this crossing as "one of apparent greater difficulty and danger." However he confirmed that their hesitation "was instantly dissipated as the men cheerily jumped into the boats and put a trackless path between them and the Stafford Shore." Another soldier of the 20th then described the bitter and frustrating struggle that ensued along Caroline St.

> Think of it, a company of about sixty men advancing up a street with no protection whatever and two or three hundred of the enemy sheltered completely and pouring a murderous fire upon you from every window, door, and behind every fence. They would even poke their guns around the corner of the houses and fire into us at close range.... Platoon after platoon was swept away but the head of the column did not falter. Ninety-seven officers and men were killed or wounded in the space of about fifty yards. In no battle of the war in which we were afterwards engaged did we lose so many men in so short a time.

Carter then withdrew to the next parallel street—Princess Anne—and continued his defense there "so as to command as many streets running at right angles as [he] possibly could" in accordance with Barksdale's instructions. Barksdale issued similar orders to

Humphreys who deployed the reserve companies of the 21st Mississippi at the intersections of Princess Anne Street with William, Amelia, and George Streets.[60]

From these positions Barksdale' Mississippians battled on for another three hours in a vicious and bloody contest, frequently hand-to-hand, through the streets, yards, and alleyways of the city. Here again Barksdale's decision to fight his riflemen individually or in small groups from doorways and windows, behind barricades, and shielded by cover of any sort proved very effective. These concealed Mississippians inflicted extremely high casualties on the Union forces whose officers foolishly chose to employ close order formations in the narrow streets—over the protests of the men in the ranks. A corporal in the 19th Massachusetts described this "useless slaughter of gallant men":

> The first reinforcements I saw were the 20th Massachusetts Infantry, who, to our horror and against the outcries of the 7th Michigan and the 19th Massachusetts, made their disastrous advance. Instead of skirmishing warfare and fighting from house to house, as we advised, the advance was in mass with no enemy in sight on whom to fire.... Thrown into platoon fronts I saw the 20th make this desperate march, with no definite end in view as far as anyone could see.... Marching 'into the jaws of Hell' the 20th lost within ten minutes and in the distance of one [city] square of ground ninety-seven killed and wounded.

Private Dinkins elaborated on another stratagem inflicted upon the advancing Federals: "Whole companies of Barksdale's men were concealed in cellars where they

Street fighting through Fredericksburg. Barksdale planned and directed the defense of the city in the first instance of large-scale urban warfare in American military history. Alfred R. Waud woodcut (Library of Congress).

remained [hidden] even after the enemy had passed, and emerging, fired into the rear of the Federal line from behind corners of houses and stone walls."[61]

Although Longstreet had advised Barksdale "before noon that the army was now in position and that he could withdraw his troops at any moment," Barksdale's fighting blood was up. Longstreet stated, "At four o'clock, when the landing was made by the boats, [Barksdale] thought the city safe against artillery practice, and was pleased to hold til night could cover his withdrawal." The soundness of Barksdale's decision to await the cover of darkness was also recognized by Colonel Humphreys. Longstreet called Barksdale's Mississippians "Confederate hornets" and offered that they "were stinging the Army of The Potomac into a frenzy."[62]

This prolonged and spirited defense of Fredericksburg undoubtedly was due, in no small part, to the Mississippians' strong desire to exact further retribution against these blue-coated invaders for destroying the homes and property of Fredericksburg's citizens whom they regarded with the same degree of affection as the townsfolk of Leesburg. McLaws, now believing Barksdale's position to be untenable, sent his aide with a written order to withdraw immediately. In response, Barksdale boldly put the note in his pocket and battled on to hold the high ground upon which his headquarters rested at the Market House. Shortly after 7 p.m., no doubt piqued at Barksdale's refusal, McLaws sent his brigadier a second—and this time peremptory—order to withdraw.

With the onset of darkness, during a lull in the fighting as the Federals withdrew to the battered houses along Caroline Street, Barksdale initiated the withdrawal of his remaining Mississippians from Fredericksburg. He also sent orders to Luse, near Deep Run, to fall back with his 18th Mississippi troops and regroup with the others along the Sunken Road at the foot of Marye's Heights—a position previously assigned to Barksdale by McLaws. Having ordered Colonel Humphreys and the 21st Mississippi to cover the withdrawal from the city, Barksdale himself wearily departed for the Sunken Road behind the stonewall.[63]

For the first time that day Humphreys formed a regular battle line along Princess Anne Street, and the contest appeared to be winding down when a fierce firefight erupted on Humphreys' left flank. Lieutenant Lane Brandon (son of Colonel Brandon of Malvern Hill fame), learning from Union prisoners that he was facing the Harvard Regiment of the 20th Massachusetts commanded by his former Harvard classmate and close friend, Capt. Henry L. Abbott, refused to yield. Losing his head completely, Brandon impulsively ordered an attack. Humphreys thereupon ordered Brandon to break off the engagement, and when he refused, summarily placed Brandon under arrest and had him escorted out of the city.[64]

At this point, the ruined city of Fredericksburg was abandoned to Burnside's Union army who soon completed their devilish work of sack and plunder, the extent of which even shocked the sensibilities of many Federal compatriots. A Southern correspondent bitterly described the aftermath:

> What shot and shell had spared; the ruin and deliberate thieving of the Yankees had finished.... What cannot be carried away is destroyed, pianos, bedsteads, bedding, and even the playthings of children are broken into fragments and hurled into the middle of the street. It seems as if there had been a carnival of madmen, a Pandemonium of destroyers.[65]

The extent of this wanton vandalism was prompted to some extent by the scenes of slaughter of Union soldiers in the streets, completely visible next morning in the naked

Sacking of Fredericksburg by Union soldiers. The extent of wanton destruction even shocked the sensibilities of many Union troops. Arthur Lumley pencil sketch (Library of Congress).

light of day. To a member of the 116th Pennsylvania Regiment of the famed Irish Brigade walking near the city wharves it was obvious that Barksdale's Mississippians had also paid a high price:

> Numbers of Barksdale's men lay where they had fallen whilst disputing the passage of the river. One group had an almost fascinating interest to the young men of the Regiment, because every one of the party was boyish and handsome. They had fought in a garden by the riverside ... and had died just where they had been placed. There was not a sign of a struggle near the spot, and singular to say, no indication of blood or wounds. They had all been shot through the body, and each had quietly dropped as he fired. The bodies were frozen hard, and all retained the appearance of life—eyes were open, faces placid and calm; and one bright looking youth seemed to smile in his sleep.

Deeply affected, this Irishman mused upon "the mournful Christmas there would be in many a far off Mississippi home whose soldier lad would never return again."[66]

The following morning around 10 a.m. Barksdale's brigade was ordered back in rear of Marye's Heights for rest and food. As they marched to their camp "carrying their guns at right shoulder, cheer after cheer rang out from along the [Confederate] line." Their comrades-in-arms, struck with amazement that any had survived the "dreadful bombardment" of the city, and overcome with admiration for their pluck and courage exhibited throughout the previous day, "felt a pride in their [Mississippi] comrades which they [simply] could not conceal." McLaws then reassigned the Sunken Road position (which would become a major focal point on the next day) to General R.R. Cobb's Georgia

Dead rebel pickets of Barksdale's Mississippi Brigade at Fredericksburg. Alfred R. Waud pencil drawing (Library of Congress).

Brigade, with Kershaw's, and then Barksdale's, brigades extending McLaws' defensive line to the right.[67] Later this day Barksdale's brigade constructed numerous abatis and rifle-pits in Bernard's Woods in preparation for the coming battle on the morrow.

Saturday, December 13, 1862, saw the culmination of the largest battle (in numbers engaged) fought during the Civil War—some 120,000 Union troops versus over 78,000 Confederates. Due to mismanagement, poorly worded orders, and the "fog of war," General Franklin's Left Grand Wing attacked the right of the Confederate defensive line held by Stonewall Jackson's corps, with only one division, that of General George Gordon Meade, and was repulsed. Sumner's Right Grand Wing, in what was originally intended by Burnside to be a diversionary and supporting action, launched a series of suicidal attacks into Lee's well-prepared defensive lines, expertly backed by deadly artillery emplacements along Marye's Heights. The result was a senseless Union bloodbath, marked by unsurpassed courage on the part of the Union attackers.

The opposing armies warily faced each other the following day, with Lee, still occupying his formidable defensive positions, hoping that Burnside would renew the contest. By nightfall the next day, Monday, December 15, 1862, Burnside, having quietly evacuated his wounded, ordered the silent withdrawal of his forces back across the Rappahannock River under cover of darkness, and then removed the pontoon bridges. A member of the 57th Pennsylvania Veteran Volunteers lamented, "the [Regiment] with shattered ranks, reoccupied its old quarters, the empty tents and broken messes being sad reminders of the horrors of war, and the uncertainty of the soldier's term of life."

7th Michigan monument at the Upper Crossing Bridge site at the foot of Hawke Street (author photograph).

Another member later accurately bemoaned Burnside's battle plan this way—"after reckless delays ... a movement which at first would have been a surprise, conceived in the very genius of war, [had become] mere mid-summer madness."[68]

Next day Barksdale's Mississippians again took up picket duty in Fredericksburg, while Union burial parties crossed under a flag of truce and interred the Federal dead—a task which took two and a half days.[69] Barksdale and McLaws rode near enough to observe these Union burial parties, which prompted some of these gravediggers to comment disparagingly that these Confederate officers were "dressed in old clothes and looked shabbily enough."[70]

But clothes don't make the man, and Barksdale had just given a brilliant defensive performance unique in the annals of American military history up to that time. He and his men were acknowledged for their actions in the official reports and later writings of the Confederate high command—as well as by military historians right up to the present day. Lee formally declared that Barksdale had "bravely resisted [the Union] advance into the town" and was recalled only when "the necessary time for concentration [had] been gained." Similarly, Longstreet wrote in his battle report: "Brigadier-General Barksdale with his brigade held the enemy's entire army at the river bank for sixteen hours, giving us abundance of time to complete our arrangements for battle. *A more gallant and worthy service is rarely accomplished by so small a force*" [emphasis added]. Longstreet's Chief of Staff considered the defensive stand by Barksdale's brigade as "one of the finest acts of heroism and stubborn resistance in our military annals." Even President Davis was heard to commend Barksdale, commenting that he "performed that service [at Fredericksburg] with his well-known gallantry."

Major General Lafayette C. McLaws was the only superior officer whose praise for

Barksdale was somewhat muted, and not at all commensurate with Barksdale's undisputed and unequalled defensive accomplishments at Fredericksburg. McLaws officially praised the soldiers and officers of the Mississippi Brigade with these words: "The brigade of General Barksdale, I consider did their whole duty, and in a manner highly creditable to every officer and man engaged in the fight. An examination of the positions they held shows that no troops could have behaved more gallantly." However, McLaws scarcely acknowledged Barksdale's personal leadership, determination, and efficiency, merely commenting: "General Barksdale commanded his fine brigade as it should have been commanded, and added new laurels to those gained on every other previous battlefield." Given the extraordinary circumstances of the river crossing, amphibious landing, and urban warfare through the streets of Fredericksburg, this was faint praise, indeed. Barksdale's leadership on the defensive had been nothing short of phenomenal. Adding insult to injury, McLaws actually wrote in much more glowing terms of General Kershaw: "He possesses military talents of a high order, and unites with them that self-possession and daring gallantry which endears him to his command, and imposes confidence which but increases as the danger grows more imminent."[71]

There are several likely reasons for this slight—none of which reflect well on McLaws. Firstly, he was miffed that Barksdale did not file his own official after-action report—a fact which McLaws felt compelled to note in his own report with a hint of irritation. "I inclose reports of the several brigade commanders, except General Barksdale, who, receiving leave of absence, went away without rendering his report, those of his regimental commanders, are, however, inclosed." Secondly, McLaws was undoubtedly peeved that Barksdale had seen fit to defy his immediate commander's first order to withdraw from the street fight in Fredericksburg. However, given Barksdale's level of success, McLaws could exact no measure of redress for Barksdale's insubordination (no matter the strong justification for Barksdale's refusal to obey). Lastly, given McLaws' innate dislike toward "political generals," especially one so naive as to order field pieces to the riverbank where they would certainly have been destroyed in a matter of minutes, here was Barksdale receiving virtually all of the credit for a defense that McLaws himself had, in no small part, helped to design. This was especially true with respect to placement of rifle-pits and earthworks.

Years later, perhaps regretting his earlier slight, McLaws, to his credit, would finally give Barksdale his due, albeit posthumously, when he wrote, "I think the defense of the river-crossing in front of Fredericksburg was a notable and wonderful feat of arms, challenging comparison with anything that happened during the war."[72] Modern historian Francis O'Reilly, with keen insight, has noted that it was not only Barksdale's "cleverness and fearlessness" but, to a great extent, his "unique ability to experiment under extreme duress" which earned the Confederate victory. Indeed, O'Reilly continues "[Barksdale's] fallback positions and overlapping fields of fire in downtown Fredericksburg" were proof positive that his defense was no accident but carefully planned ahead of time.[73]

If recognition of your prowess by your enemy is the true measure of military acumen, then perhaps the two greatest tributes to Barksdale at Fredericksburg came from Burnside and his Union Engineers. In his official report dated December 17, 1862, Burnside wrote, "if not for the fog and unexpected and unavoidable delay in building the bridges which gave the enemy twenty-four hours more to concentrate his forces, we would almost certainly have succeeded." Captain Brainerd of the 50th New York Engineers simply wrote, "Our experience at Fredericksburg had taught us a lesson: not to attempt to lay a bridge in the face of an opposing force until they were driven from their position."[74] Never again during the Civil War would a pontoon bridge be laid without first controlling the riverbanks at *each* end.

Barksdale departed on December 21, 1862, on a well-deserved 40-day leave of absence[75] destined for Columbus, Mississippi, and a heartfelt reunion with his beloved family, whom he had not seen since the spring at Leesburg. And he left with his head held high, secure in the knowledge that he was universally acclaimed throughout the Army of Northern Virginia—and beyond. Barksdale had superbly executed his novel battle plan to delay the crossing of the Rappahannock River by the Union army and had thwarted their subsequent advance through the streets of Fredericksburg in the debut of urban warfare. By doing so he and his gallant Mississippi Brigade had enabled General Lee to win a great one-sided victory at Fredericksburg, thereby protecting Richmond from an invading Union army once again.

Within five months the Army of Northern Virginia would return to Fredericksburg to engage the Army of the Potomac during the Chancellorsville campaign. Again, Lee would win a major victory—the greatest of his brilliant career. Again, Barksdale would be called upon to defend at Fredericksburg against overwhelming odds—but this time Barksdale's line would not hold.

Thirteen

Second Fredericksburg (Chancellorsville)

"We must make the fight whether we hold it or are whipped"

The active campaigning over the last year and a half had taken a heavy toll on Barksdale and his brigade. These Mississippians had played a prominent role at Leesburg, Harpers Ferry, Sharpsburg, and particularly at Fredericksburg—where Barksdale had been injured by falling debris and had sought medical attention. A period of respite now commenced prior to the expected spring campaign and resumption of hostilities.

Immediately following the battle and Burnside's retreat back across the Rappahannock, Barksdale's brigade once again picketed Fredericksburg. In recognition of their gallantry in defending the town, McLaws directed that these Mississippians make their winter quarters in Fredericksburg, where Colonel Humphreys confirmed "we found comfortable vacant houses to occupy, and spent the winter most comfortably, alternating the duties of the soldier with local pleasures and recreations."[1] Even Private Dinkins expressed surprise that the army "had settled down to a normal condition" merely two weeks after "they had fought with such desperation and seen so many of their friends killed and wounded by their sides."[2]

With his brigade settled into winter camp under the watchful command of Colonel Humphreys, and with little or no expectation of further combat, Barksdale eagerly set off on December 21st to Columbus, Mississippi, for a well-deserved rest and a joyful reunion with his devoted wife, Narcissa, and young sons, Ethel and Willie—his pride and joy.

Unlike other large towns and cities within Mississippi, Columbus was never attacked by Union forces and escaped the ravages of war. This is very surprising given that the city, as described by an eyewitness, had been "a continued scene of the organization, equipment, drill, and departure of soldiers" and more so since the Confederate government soon "established an immense arsenal for the manufacture of arms and the munitions of war [where] a thousand or more artisans were engaged in casting cannon, manufacturing and altering small arms, making cartridges, fuses, percussion caps." In April 1862, after the battle of Shiloh, Columbus was transformed into a hospital center with all hotels, concert halls, fairgrounds, and major buildings converted into treatment centers for the wounded and sick from the Armies of Mississippi and Tennessee.[3]

Unfortunately, details of Barksdale's blissful visit home have not survived—and all too soon the General's allotted absence neared its end. It was time for him to bid his family a tearful farewell. This was a poignant moment. Little did they know that this would be the last time Narcissa would embrace her loving husband, and his young sons would hug their devoted father. Narcissa would later admit, "the sun of my life set at Gettysburg" with her husband's mortal wounding just six months hence.[4]

Whether officially summoned, or just taking advantage of the opportunity, while returning to Fredericksburg, Barksdale stopped in at Richmond on January 27 for a meeting with President Davis. During their discussions Davis expressed optimism that 1863 would hopefully "close the war."[5] This meeting between two former Mississippi politicians and close friends was memorable for another little-known reason—one which could have potentially saved Barksdale's life.

At this meeting Jefferson Davis formally offered his friend a transfer to serve the Confederacy in Mississippi. Surviving records do not indicate whether any change in rank was associated with Davis' overture. However, Barksdale demurred, requesting some time to think it over, and returned to his brigade at Fredericksburg the following evening with the matter still undecided. For the next week Barksdale mulled over the offer, torn between the desire to be closer to his family and in a better position to directly protect them, and his loyalty to his Mississippi Brigade—Barksdale's Brigade—and to the Army of Northern Virginia. Barksdale also recognized along with Lee, Longstreet, and McLaws, they might soon have an opportunity to actually end this war. Concern for their families back home in Mississippi was an important consideration for Barksdale's soldiers, and one which they frequently commented upon in their diaries and letters.

After a one-week deliberation, and much soul-searching, Barksdale made his official reply to Davis in the following letter:

> Fredericksburg
> Feb 5th 1863
>
> Sir,
>
> Upon reflection I must decline your offer to transfer me to Mississippi.
> Since I entered the service, my fortunes have been connected with this Brigade, and I feel satisfied that the sentiment of an overwhelming majority of the Brigade officers and men is averse to any change in command.
> Under these circumstances I desire very much to remain in my present position.
>
> Very Respectfully
> Your Obt Servt
> Wm. Barksdale[6]

Barksdale and his brigade had simply been through too much together, and his sense of duty and obligation toward his men was simply too strong for him to abandon them now. This was especially so considering their accomplishments together, and Lee's great victory at Fredericksburg. Barksdale's decision was his—and his alone. There is no evidence that William ever mentioned this matter to Narcissa. However, in deciding to stay with Lee and the Army of Northern Virginia, as subsequent events would unfold, Barksdale had sealed his fate by declining the sole opportunity which might have preserved his life.

Barksdale returned to duty only three days after Burnside's ill-advised and abortive attempt to maneuver upstream, cross the Rappahannock at United States Ford, and turn Lee's left flank. However, the Confederate High Command had already determined "the quicksands along the flats, made especially protective by the winter rains" would not permit a winter campaign.[7] Although Burnside initiated the move on January 20,

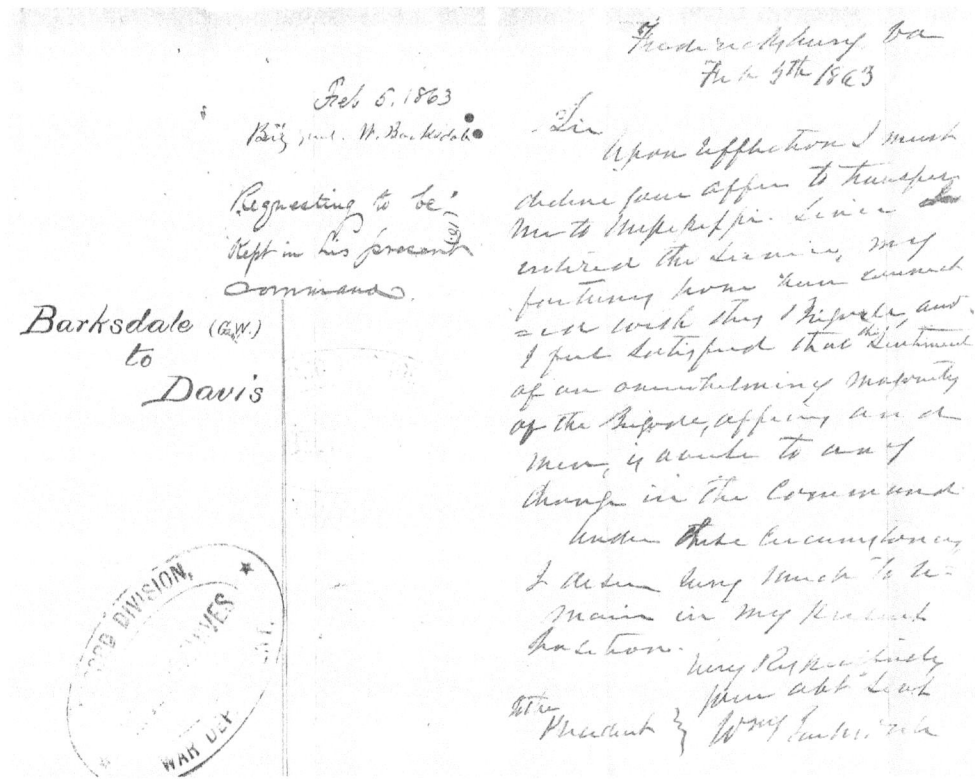

Barksdale's handwritten letter refusing President Davis' offer of transfer to Mississippi (National Archives, War Department Collection of Confederate Records, Record Group 109, Jefferson Davis Papers, 1861–1865, Entry 1).

1863, during a period of mild weather when the roads were somewhat dry, it soon began to drizzle and quickly escalated into a downpour which lasted for several days. The hapless Union columns of infantry, artillery, and supply wagons were soon hopelessly bogged down in the quagmire—much to the amusement of the delighted Confederates who hurled taunts at their struggling foe across the river.

    On the third day Burnside issued liquor to his troops in a vain attempt to improve their sagging morale. Alcohol only exacerbated the situation by fomenting drunken brawls between regiments. With all hope of surprise and success gone, Burnside, on January 23rd, aborted his campaign which forever would be known as "Burnside's Mud March." Two days later Lincoln relieved Burnside of command of The Army of the Potomac and replaced him with 49-year-old Maj. Gen. Joseph E. Hooker. A West Point graduate and Mexican War veteran, the supremely confident Hooker hailed from Massachusetts. Lee concluded that the only remaining potential threat to Richmond would be an attack from the east, south of the James River. Accordingly Lee ordered Longstreet with the divisions of Hood and Pickett to move south to Petersburg and Suffolk to block this possibility.[8]

    With Barksdale back in command, the Mississippi Brigade settled into its duties of picketing the river, garrisoning the town, and serving as Provost Guard to maintain order within Fredericksburg. These Mississippians also assisted and protected those citizens who had bravely returned to the city. However, this special duty did not absolve them from participating in regular parades, drills, reviews, and inspections designed to maintain discipline. Despite the winter weather, now began a very pleasant three-month period for "Barksdale's Boys"—second only to their earlier sojourn at Leesburg. Able to relax, these soldiers took full advantage of the great number of distractions from army life now available to them and took an active part in improvising new amusements.

Almost immediately, these fun-loving Confederates descended on a ten-pin bowling alley in town which had survived the bombardment. Quickly they repaired and fitted up the theater in Fredericksburg and formed several performing groups to provide entertainment and to generate profits for donation to benevolent purposes. "McLaws Minstrels" played three times per week to large audiences, while the Barksdale Euterpian and Thespian Club, comprised mainly from members of the 13th Mississippi, put on plays such as Shakespeare's *Julius Caesar*, together with orchestral concerts under the direction of Professor Timothy Nutting who was Leader of the Mississippi Brigade Band. This drama club was assisted by the Howitzer Glee Club, formed by members from the 1st Company of the Richmond Howitzers, who gave concerts at various locales including the City Hall. Colonel Humphreys recorded that "the theatre was crowded every night by officers of high and low rank" with "soldiers and citizens all merrily enjoying this interlude between the sad hours of war."[9]

The changeable Virginia weather, alternating between milder temperatures with rain and frigid temperatures with significant snowfalls, provided another diversion—snowball fights! Beginning as good-natured contests between small groups, these altercations steadily grew into friendly struggles between companies and regiments—finally escalating into full-fledged "pitched battles" between entire brigades for bragging rights.

One member of the 17th Mississippi, who missed one such contest due to provost duty, proudly recorded a description in his diary—"The boys had another big fight today with the 21st [Mississippi Regiment] snowballing—they fought about two hours when the 17th come off victorious again." A member of Wofford's Georgia Brigade described one such formal "pitched battle" against Kershaw's brigade of South Carolinians, replete with color parties and mounted line officers. In a letter home he described the spectacle: "Great God, I never saw snow balls fly so in my life.... I tell you it beat anything.... There was 4000 men engaged on both sides, and you know it was something!"[10]

Barksdale's men also took advantage of what one of his officers called "a most commendable sentiment [that] prevailed between the two opposing armies on the subject of picket firing," whereby "each picket walked his line and watched the enemy unmolested on either side." This informal truce was predicated on the belief that shooting a picket while in winter quarters would be considered as murder since no military advantage could be gained. This armistice gave rise to an unprecedented degree of fraternization between the opposing lines, unsurpassed during the remainder of the war. Although technically the soldiers were allowed to use the river only to procure drinking water, what Colonel Humphreys termed "a species of contraband traffic" was soon flourishing. Handcrafted sailboats "were running almost as regular as packets voyaging across the Atlantic," exchanging Northern coffee, sugar, etc., for Southern smoking and chewing tobacco. A closely guarded "flag of truce station" was also established in Barksdale's sector where crowds of soldiers from both armies gathered to buy and exchange the latest newspapers from both North and South.[11]

For a time, the officers tolerated this level of fraternization, but it soon escalated to the point that soldiers were visiting the opposing camps to socialize and even dine together. A member of the 17th Mississippi, while washing his face along the riverbank, struck up a conversation with the adjutant of the 89th New York. Upon receiving an invitation, this Mississippian was transported across in a rowboat where he enjoyed a "good breakfast of hardtack, bacon, and United States coffee." His Irish benefactors returned him to Fredericksburg where a crowd of his comrades awaited. This Confederate later wrote that upon disembarking, "I promptly placed myself under arrest for disobeying orders, but General Barksdale just laughed."[12] Lee, fearing that this widespread fraternization "might be prostituted to the purpose of spies" by his enemy (who vastly outnumbered his army), soon forbade the practice—and it quickly stopped.[13]

This period of calm also witnessed a great Christian revival throughout the Army of Northern Virginia. Nowhere was it more pronounced than in Barksdale's Mississippi Brigade. The Rev. J. William Jones, Corps Chaplain for Longstreet, and dubbed "The Fighting Parson," in his post-war book, *Christ in the Camp*, wrote extensively regarding the religious renewal of these Mississippians. He described Barksdale's soldiers returning from dress parade in Fredericksburg one evening at sundown: "…and at the command 'Break ranks,' the streets were filled with soldiers eagerly running in a given direction." "Ask the reason," he continued, and the reply was "We are trying to get into the church before all of the seats are taken." Church services were held morning and evening on the Sabbath, with sermons also preached on Wednesday evenings. The "voice of prayer and praise" could also be heard every night coming from the soldiers' tents. As the Reverend Jones deduced, the battle carnage of the Seven Days, Second Manassas, Sharpsburg, and Fredericksburg "very decidedly improved the religious tone of the army." He insightfully reckoned that "As men stood amid the leaden and iron hail of battle, saw comrades fall thick and fast around them and were made to feel 'There is but one step between me and death,' they were brought to serious reflection and solemn resolve."[14]

Even bouts of harsh winter weather could not stifle this outburst of religious fervor and, although hampering outdoor services (before chapels could be built) it did not preclude them. It was a common scene in other less fortunate brigades encamped outside the city to see soldiers being preached to while standing in several inches of snow—some barefooted and with "scores whose shoes afforded very little protection from the snow."

The Rev. William B. Owen, Methodist Chaplain of the 17th Mississippi, directed the revival within Barksdale's brigade. Jones greatly admired Owen and described him as "one of the most devoted, laborious and efficient chaplains we had in the army … and [who] held a warm place in the hearts of the soldiers." The Reverend Owen's efforts were so successful that the meetings were moved from the Presbyterian Church to the larger Methodist Church, then subsequently to the Episcopal Church in Fredericksburg to accommodate the ever-increasing congregations. Assisted by the chaplains of the other regiments within the brigade, as well as visiting ministers, Owen conducted up to three revival meetings per day. At one point he had continued for 21 consecutive days, with hundreds becoming Christian converts. That night Barksdale's brigade received marching orders for the next day, to which Brother Owen prophesied that "the Lord would not let them leave while the interest in the meeting continued so deep." Whether by intercession on Barksdale's part or not—Barksdale attended as regularly as his duties would permit—the orders were countermanded, and the meetings were permitted to continue.

All told, over 500 soldiers were converted to Christianity through this revival in Barksdale's brigade, many being visitors from other commands. During Sunday services the sacraments of baptism, the Lord's Supper, and first communion were freely celebrated.

The revival would be interrupted by the battle of Chancellorsville at the beginning of May but would resume in earnest until the march to Gettysburg in mid–June. Following the battle of Gettysburg, the revival resumed along the Rapidan River in August 1863 and continued to some degree right up until Lee's surrender at Appomattox.

President Davis declared Friday March 27, 1863, as a day of fasting, humility, and prayer. The previous evening an order from General Lee was read to each regiment during Dress Parade "commanding that all kind of duty be suspended [tomorrow] and that the Chaplains hold public worship in their respective Regiments and advising all of the troops to the strict observance of the day." Sergeant Hill recorded that most of the soldiers complied.[15]

Another significant initiative was taken within Barksdale's brigade during this winter encampment which would have very beneficial effects for the remainder of the war. On March 3, 1863, 40-year-old Pvt. Lewis L. Liebenfeld, a prewar merchant and now a butcher in the Commissary Department, left on furlough for Mississippi. He carried a formal written request from Barksdale and the Masons within his brigade to seek a dispensation from the Grand Lodge of Mississippi to open a Masonic Lodge in camp. Liebenfeld returned on April 7th having successfully procured permission to open an army Masonic Lodge in Barksdale's brigade. The "William Barksdale Lodge of Mississippi" was established at Fredericksburg and immediately held regular meetings, initiated and raised new members, and conducted Masonic funerals. Since these circumstances mirrored William Barksdale's own experience with Freemasonry during the Mexican War, and because the new Lodge bore his name, one can only assume that the idea most probably originated with the General himself. At the very least he would have fully championed the concept and used his status as a Third Degree Mason—together with his personal reputation—in support. Only nine days later Sergeant Hill, Company Clerk of the 13th Mississippi, proudly recorded in his diary, "I was made a Master Mason last night in the room of the Fredericksburg Lodge #4 by William Barksdale Lodge of Mississippi." Hill then proudly added that this was the same location where George Washington had become a Freemason.[16]

Renowned professor and pre-eminent historian, the late Bell Irvin Wiley—who documented the life of the common soldier of the Civil War in his definitive works, *The Life of Johnny Reb* and *The Life of Billy Yank*—described music as "perhaps the favorite recreation of the Confederate Army."[17] Whether it was on the march, in camp around the wood fire, during drill sessions, or listening to evening serenades, Johnny Reb found comfort in the sentimental melodies and maudlin lyrics of the contemporary songs—or was stirred by the martial airs and marches of the time. Regimental and brigade bands played a key role in this diversion, so much so that Lee, after enjoying a brass band serenade, was heard to remark, "I don't believe we can have an army without music."[18]

Barksdale's Brigade was blessed with three excellent regimental bands. On March 6 the band of the 13th Mississippi gave a party and concert in Fredericksburg for General Barksdale and several other officers of the brigade accompanied by 25 ladies. Sergeant Hill recorded, "All had a very pleasant evening." Ten days later, under direction of Professor Nutting, this same regimental band serenaded Fredericksburg's Mayor Slaughter at his residence in celebration of his re-election for a fourth term. The Mayor rewarded these musicians with "a drink of good whiskey with him."[19] The band of the 17th Mississippi had been formed back in August 1861 at Leesburg when each company had appropriated $50 to purchase instruments. After two months of practice this band made its debut during an evening dress parade on Sunday, November 10, 1861. The 21st Mississippi Regimental Band was universally recognized as "a very fine brass band," from the time the regiment had joined the brigade back in November of 1861.[20] A member of Kershaw's Brigade agreed that "Barksdale had a magnificent brass band" while he lamented that these South Carolinians "had only a fife corps." However, perhaps rationalizing the omission, he added, "The music of fife and drum while it may not be so accomplished, gives out more inspiring strains for the marching soldier than any brass band." When combined under the leadership of Professor Nutting, Barksdale's Brigade Band was a force to be reckoned with.

The situation was not much different in the Army of the Potomac where Union brass bands staged concerts almost every evening. When possible, such as here at Fredericksburg, in response, Confederate bands would often join in. Soldier accounts agree that the majority of these evening concerts began with Northern anthems like "Yankee Doodle," "The Star-Spangled Banner," and "Rally Round the Flag" played by Union bands. The Confederate bands would respond with songs like "Bonnie Blue Flag," "Lorena," "All Quiet Along the Potomac Tonight," and the immensely popular "Dixie," which elicited "wild Rebel yells from one end of Fredericksburg to the other." These concerts would inevitably conclude with both sides playing "Home Sweet Home," which normally filled the soldiers' eyes with tears on both sides of the Rappahannock.[21] Generals Barksdale and McLaws would often stroll to the riverbank together to enjoy these evening band concerts—mirroring their behavior prior to the Fredericksburg battle.

Barksdale was kept busy with his official duties which now also included picket and provost duty within Fredericksburg. These responsibilities were in addition to normal regimental and brigade parades, drills, reviews, and inspections, conducted regularly throughout this occupation. In typical fashion Barksdale took these new duties very seriously. Although one prominent citizen in Fredericksburg criticized Barksdale's efforts to adequately control his men, another action he took bespoke his diligence. Once the snow had melted and spring was approaching, Barksdale decided it was time to clean up the town. A reporter for the *Richmond Daily Dispatch* filed the following laudatory report on April 20th (which also reflected the racial biases of the time):

> A considerable number of free negroes, who have been vegetating for some time doing nothing ... have been impressed by the Provost Guard, under an order from Gen. Barksdale, and put to work repairing the streets and cleaning the town. It is a fine field for these sable scavengers, who were a little taken by surprise when the order was given them, but soon fell to work in earnest, and have, so far, greatly improved the appearance of the streets and contributed to the health of the citizens and soldiers by removing not a little of the filth accumulated during the visit of the Yankees before and after the battle.[22]

The onset of spring-like weather afforded the men more sporting opportunities. Popular recreations were pitching quoits, playing baseball, and especially fishing. Unfortunately, even these pleasurable activities sometimes had their downside. For example, playing baseball on the Sabbath brought the participants into conflict with many of their devout Christian brethren. Private Joseph Miller of the 17th Mississippi freely expressed his consternation in his diary—"I think the autorities ought to put a stop [to] the desecration of God's holy day." These objections were quickly upheld, for Miller soon recorded a serious altercation in another regiment—the 21st Mississippi—who played baseball on Sunday evening against orders. Miller related that the Provost Guard from the Panola Vindicators, Co. H of the 17th Mississippi, under command of Provost Marshal Capt.

Frank Middleton—perhaps over aggressively—tried to end the ballgame. The 21st Mississippi players and supporters resisted, and it was soon necessary to summon the entire guard—and finally all of Company H—to quell the melee. Miller wrote "several were taken to the guardhouse, a good [many] wepons were drawn, but no blood spilt."[23]

The repercussions arising from fishing were quite another matter. By the beginning of April 1863 soldiers of Barksdale's brigade were eager to fish the cold waters of the Rappahannock—both for the sheer fun and enjoyment, but also to tap into this alternate food source. Private Newton Nash wrote to his wife on April 5 that "Gen. William Barksdale [has] given us permission to fish as much as we want." Nash went on to relate that he had crafted a fish basket out of white oak "but have not got a minnow for my trouble." The favored method of catching fish was by "seining" with large nets which the individual soldier companies purchased from merchants in Fredericksburg. This method proved overwhelmingly successful

Barksdale's Mississippians at Railroad Bridge. Mississippi veterans stare defiantly across the ruined railroad bridge at Fredericksburg, prior to the Chancellorsville campaign. A. J. Russell photograph (Library of Congress).

as the soldiers' diary entries for April and May attested. Nash recorded that "one company in the 17th Regt. caught over seven hundred at one drag," while Sergeant Hill of the 13th Mississippi wrote, "The soldiers of this brigade are catching large quantities of fish with seines, more than they can consume." Hill identified the numerous species as "White Shad, Mullets, Sturgeon, Herring, Catfish, Rockfish Carp, and Perch." It is hard to believe that such a joyous pastime could result in sadness and death, but that is just what soon transpired. An unfortunate private from Company E, 13th Mississippi, drowned while seining, and another private from the 21st Mississippi shared the same fate the following morning when he became entangled in the net at the same location.[24]

Even when not actively campaigning, death was never far away from these soldiers. It resulted from sickness, disease, and firearms accidents. A member of the 17th Mississippi recorded just such an accident which occurred on April 7—"yesterday evening, just as our co. was forming to go out on dress parade, one of the provost guard accidentally shot himself, close to our quarters, the ball went in neare his abdemen and lodged in his side." Unfortunately, all too frequently "Old Barksdale" had to preside over funerals for young soldiers in his brigade. A private described one such typical funeral procession for a soldier from the 13th Mississippi: "the band of music was in front playing a melancholy dirge, then followed the corpse boarne by six men, then came the company to which the deceased belong[ed] performing a slow march, with inverted arms, it was quite an imposing scene."[25]

On April 1st Lee prepared for the oncoming spring campaign by issuing orders to send all "extra cooking utensils" and "baggage that could possibly be spared" to Richmond. During the upcoming march only one wagon would be allotted per every 100 men. During the latter part of April, Barksdale sensed that active combat would soon resume and addressed his own personal salvation. "Old Barks" made a concerted effort to attend as many of Chaplain William B. Owen's prayer meetings and church services as possible. He attended on the morning of Tuesday, April 14th, until he was called away. At Sunday service on April 19th Barksdale was overheard to praise Brother Owen's effort with the comment, "That was a very good sermon wasn't it."[26] Another evening, while enjoying "an admirable military band attached to Barksdale's Brigade," the Rev. M.D. Hoge, Minister at the Second Presbyterian Church in Richmond—and later recognized in both America and Europe as "one of the greatest pulpit orators of the age"—had occasion to be introduced to General Barksdale. During their conversation, Hoge later recorded that Barksdale "said his men were never more comfortable, never in such health, and never so eager for the fray as now."[27] They would not have long to wait.

General McLaws echoed Barksdale's sentiments regarding the morale of his Mississippians at this time in a letter to his wife. McLaws commented in regard to an evening visit to Barksdale's headquarters in Fredericksburg, "[I] found the command there, all in good spirits. The men were playing ball, the band playing. Some fishing, and all as unconcerned about the enemy as if there was no war, no enemy within a thousand miles...."[28] However the Union High Command were acutely aware of the presence of their enemy, and were keen to resume hostilities.

Just days before the Chancellorsville campaign began, Confederate Senator Albert G. Brown and Confederate Congressman Ethelbert Barksdale came to visit General Barksdale and the Mississippi Brigade on April 26th. The following evening, as had been the custom during previous visits, the guests were serenaded at the General's headquarters by the brass band of the 13th Mississippi—Barksdale's old regiment. Afterward Senator Brown responded with "a very appropriate speech and was repeatedly cheered by the large crowd in attendance." Representative Ethelbert Barksdale "then spoke for a short time after which General Barksdale was called for and spoke for a few minutes." According to one Confederate soldier present, the General "got up and gave us a very interesting 'family talk' as he called it." This same soldier felt compelled to add, "he is very much attached to the boys, as the boys are to him."[29] Sadly this would be the last time Ethelbert would see his older brother and closest sibling alive.

For "Fighting Joe" Hooker the time to act finally came on April 27th. Hooker silently initiated a march of his army past Lee's left flank outside Fredericksburg. He concealed this move by leaving a force of 30,000 Union troops under Gen. John Sedgwick opposite Fredericksburg. By the time Lee discovered this Union maneuver on April 29th, Hooker had already crossed the Rappahannock with his army at United States Ford and established his headquarters at Chancellorsville nine miles to the west. Having surprised Lee, Hooker boasted in a general order to his troops, "…our enemy must ingloriously fly, or come out from behind his defenses and give us battle on our own ground, where certain destruction awaits him."[30] Hooker had accomplished what his predecessor, Burnside, had repeatedly failed to do—stolen a march on the "Gray Fox." Lee's accomplished young artillery commander, Col. Edward Porter Alexander, was so impressed that he would later write: "On the whole I think this [Union] plan was decidedly the best strategy ever conceived in any of the campaigns ever set foot against us."[31]

At first light on the morning of April 29th, under cover of thick fog, Union forces south of Fredericksburg applied the earlier successful tactics of first securing a bridgehead by rowing assault parties across in pontoon boats to drive off the Confederate pickets. The Engineer Brigade at Deep Run quickly constructed three pontoon bridges opposite Bernard's cabins at the same location as General Franklin's previous crossing six months earlier. They were completed by 9:45 a.m. with the loss of only one Federal soldier killed and 10 wounded.

A second crossing was attempted one mile further south at Fitzhugh's Crossing after the fog had lifted. In the face of significant opposition by Confederate infantry, Union artillery had to be employed to effect the construction of two more pontoon bridges that were not completed until noon. Casualties here were much higher on both sides, including 108 Confederate prisoners who were captured in their rifle-pits from behind by Union soldiers who had encircled them.

In a short time two entire Federal divisions with their artillery had streamed across, linked up, and dug in. They formed one continuous heavily defended Union bridgehead almost three miles long on the west bank of the Rappahannock River. Barksdale's pickets at the Fernahough house, south of Fredericksburg, were soon alerted to the Federal crossing. Immediately the alarm bell at Fredericksburg was sounded, followed closely by the long roll, which promptly brought Barksdale's entire brigade into line.[32]

No Union crossing had yet been attempted directly opposite Fredericksburg. At this point, not sure if the crossings south of Fredericksburg signaled another oncoming battle here, Lee concentrated Jackson's Corps opposite the lower crossing sites, maintained McLaws in position opposite the town, and summoned his artillery from their winter encampments. Lee also beseeched President Davis to immediately return Longstreet's two divisions from Suffolk. Uncertain of Hooker's intentions, Lee simply awaited further developments. However, Lee felt it necessary to visit McLaws' Headquarters around noon to give the Georgian a "pep talk."

In Longstreet's absence, McLaws reported directly to Lee. In a letter to his wife written that same day, McLaws confided that Lee "was very confident of his ability to beat back the enemy should our troops behave as well as they have usually done." Then echoing the words of Col. William Travis at the siege of the Alamo (strangely prophetic considering Barksdale's soon-to-be defense of Marye's Heights against overwhelming odds) Lee admonished him to inspire his men—"General McLaws, let them know that it is a stern necessity now, it must be Victory or Death, for defeat would be ruinous."[33] This same day, in a telegraphed message from General J.E.B. Stuart, his cavalry commander, written the previous day, Lee learned for the first time of the presence of Union infantry to the west at United States Ford. This unsettling news, no doubt, greatly deepened his concern.

Reacting to this new situation on April 30th, Lee issued orders to Stonewall Jackson to designate a single division from his corps to remain at Fredericksburg while he readied the remainder of his corps to rush to Tabernacle Church, near Chancellorsville, on the morrow. At the same time, Lee issued similar instructions to McLaws to do the same with his division, i.e., designate one brigade to remain as pickets at Fredericksburg while moving the remainder of his division to Tabernacle Church "as soon as possible." In this initial order to McLaws, Lee indicated *his personal preference to designate Barksdale's brigade* to remain at Fredericksburg.

Jackson lost no time in selecting Major General Jubal Early to remain. Early's division was already picketing the river at Hamilton's Crossing and was furthest away from Chancellorsville. Incredibly, McLaws demurred, and even more implausibly requested that Lee himself issue "positive orders" for the selection of one of McLaws' own brigades to report to General Early. In doing so, McLaws exhibited the type of lackluster leadership and lack of initiative that would later result in Longstreet launching court-martial proceedings against him in 1864, during the failed Knoxville campaign in Tennessee. In his written reply to McLaws—the second formal order he issued to McLaws that day—Lee adamantly refused, simply explaining himself as follows: "I suggested Genl Barksdale as the officer to be left, believing from his qualifications and knowledge that he would be able to render valuable service, and that by his remaining, the trouble of withdrawing pickets from the front would be diminished. You can designate any brigade to remain that you think best."[34]

This bizarre episode must also have raised doubts in Lee's mind regarding McLaws' lack of decisiveness. McLaws never revealed his reasons for hesitating. It may have been due to lingering resentment against Barksdale, stemming from the battle of Fredericksburg five months earlier when Barksdale had refused to retire from the town when ordered to do so by McLaws. Or Barksdale's subsequent request for a leave of absence. Or perhaps Barksdale's failure to submit an after-action report. Alternatively, it may have arisen out of concern for slighting the "gamecock," General Kershaw, whose commission as brigadier general predated Barksdale's by six months. Lastly, with his own strong aptitude for assessing defensive positions, perhaps McLaws foresaw that this reduced "holding" force was totally inadequate to successfully resist Sedgwick's superior horde of three Union corps, and thus sought to avoid any future blame or censure for a potential rout. Maybe all of these considerations resulted in McLaws' recalcitrance.

In any event, in the end, McLaws was intelligent enough not to buck Lee's stated preference, and wisely decided to make the only logical choice and designate the Mississippi brigade to form part of the Confederate rear guard. The men in the ranks heartily applauded Barksdale's selection for the task at hand. Private Joseph C. Lloyd of the 13th Mississippi later commented: "General Lee knew his men. He selected two of his best brigadiers [Barksdale and Georgia's John B. Gordon] to keep [Sedgwick's] force quiet, knowing they would hold their positions as long as possible. And they held them to the last minute, even to the danger of capture."[35]

Hooker was en route to Chancellorsville and expected to arrive during the night of April 30th. With three Federal corps already concentrated there, General Meade urged an immediate attack to close the vise on Lee. However, Hooker insisted on delaying until the arrival of two additional Federal corps, the II and XI, already underway from Fredericksburg. Astoundingly Hooker instructed Meade to prepare *defensive* positions.

Hooker's instructions to Sedgwick at Fredericksburg for May 1st were to "Be observant of your opportunities, and when you strike let it be done to destroy." Sedgwick, who was "careful, cautious, and conservative" by nature, like Lafayette McLaws, disliked discretionary orders. Sedgwick strongly preferred to execute direct commands.[36] Thus, while both Hooker and Sedgwick hesitated on May 1st, Lee rushed the remainder of his army toward Chancellorsville and soon gained the initiative against Hooker's forces there.

Meanwhile on May 1st at Fredericksburg, Early was left, by his own estimation, with a total force of 9,000 men plus 30 artillery pieces, to face Sedgwick's force of 40,000 infantry and vastly superior artillery resources. Before departing, Lee gave Early specific instructions which Early recorded as follows:

> ...to watch the enemy and try to hold him; to conceal the weakness of my force, and if compelled to yield before overpowering numbers to fall back towards Guiney's depot where our supplies were and to protect them and the railroad; and I was further instructed to join the main body of the army in the event that the enemy disappeared from my front or so diminished his force as to render it prudent to do so, leaving at Fredericksburg only such force as might be necessary to protect the town against any force the enemy might leave behind.

Barksdale was ordered to retain his position in Fredericksburg and on the heights in rear with a portion of General Pendleton's Reserve Artillery posted on Marye's Heights and Telegraph Hill (subsequently known as Lee's Hill).[37]

There was no firing on May 1st, and in Barksdale's words, "appearances indicated that the enemy were leaving their encampments on this side of the river and were marching to reinforce Hooker [at Chancellorsville]."[38]

The following morning saw much the same Union activity, with Federal infantry and artillery abandoning the lower Fitzhugh Crossing site and disappearing under the near bank of the river. A short artillery duel then followed as Early probed the Union positions. These new developments caused Early to consider the possibility of sending part of his force to assist Lee. While he was deliberating this move, Early received a message from Barksdale and Pendleton who from their vantage point believed Sedgwick might be initiating a pontoon crossing at Fredericksburg preparatory to an attack on the Confederate left. In response, Early rode to Lee's Hill to see for himself, and was soon joined by Barksdale and Pendleton. This trio then speculated on the Union plan.

It was during this discussion about 11 a.m. that Early was confronted by Col. Robert Chilton, Lee's Chief of Staff, who had been sent by Lee with peremptory verbal orders. Lee's intent was merely to repeat and reemphasize the third of his previous discretionary orders, i.e., should the enemy withdraw and move upriver, Early was to join the main body at Chancellorsville with as much of his command as could be spared from the defense of his lines. Unfortunately, Chilton completely misconstrued Lee's verbal directive and formally notified Early that he was to move *unconditionally* at once, leaving only one brigade and a few guns to keep the Union force in check. Though astounded, Early felt he had been left no discretion and promptly set about complying. He decided that Hays' Louisiana Brigade would remain and relieve Barksdale's position on the hills behind Fredericksburg, and that Barksdale would detach one regiment (21st Mississippi presently deployed within Fredericksburg) to remain as pickets along the river from Falmouth to the southern end of Fredericksburg. General Pendleton would supervise withdrawal of the reserve artillery.[39] Chilton's mammoth blunder would very nearly result in the complete unraveling of Early's rear-guard defense.

Under no misapprehension concerning their predicament, Barksdale soon gave Colonel Humphreys the following orders for the 21st Mississippi: "Watch your flanks, hold the picket-line as long as you can, then fall back along the Spotsylvania Courthouse Road, and hunt for your brigade." Years later, Humphreys reflected upon the personal anxiety and dread he felt at that moment—"I cannot well describe my feelings when I found my regiment thus left alone, stretched out three miles long, with only a small river between us and thirty-thousand well armed and hostile men, purposely displayed to magnify their numbers on Stafford Heights, with balloons and signal corps observing and reporting our weakness." He also described the palpable tension exhibited by his men in the ranks as they awaited their fate—"Of course every man in the Twenty-first regiment felt his loneliness and danger, and was on the 'qui vive,' watching front, flank, and rear, with his gun loaded, his knapsack on his back, and rations in his haversack." Despite this sense of isolation and foreboding, there was still room for gallows humor when Colonel Holder of the 17th Mississippi quipped, as he marched off with the brigade, "Tell [Colonel Humphreys] farewell; the next time I hear from him will be from Johnson's Island."[40]

Having to exercise extreme caution "so as to attract as little attention as possible," Early's division did not actually depart until late afternoon. Barksdale's three regiments marched at the tail end of the column. This unfolding drama then took a sudden turn when Early received another message from Lee, who had now learned of Chilton's debacle upon Chilton's return to Chancellorsville later that day. This time, leaving no room for misinterpretation, Lee provided Early with written orders confirming his earlier instructions that removal of any troops from Fredericksburg was to be at Early's discretion. The march away from Fredericksburg continued for another mile while Early agonized over whether he should turn the column around. He finally concluded, "I had proceeded so far that I determined to go on."[41] It would be the bold actions of Barksdale, *taken solely on his own initiative, without orders,* that would change Early's mind and trigger his decision to return his division to defend at Fredericksburg.

As evening approached, and while the sounds of the battle that had been raging at Chancellorsville all day continued to be heard at Fredericksburg, General Barksdale received a message delivered by an officer belonging to General Pendleton. The artillery commander confirmed that the enemy were now advancing toward Marye's Heights in considerable numbers. In the opinion of both General Hays and Pendleton, without immediate support, all the artillery pieces Early had left them would soon be captured. That was good enough for Barksdale. Without hesitation, and despite risk of court-martial for acting contrary to orders, Barksdale immediately ordered his three Mississippi regiments to rush back toward Fredericksburg. Without delay Barksdale dispatched a courier to inform Early of his actions, trusting that he had made the correct decision under these dire circumstances.

While en route at dusk, Barksdale encountered Colonel Walton and cannon of the Washington Artillery moving toward Chancellorsville under previous orders from Pendleton. According to an eyewitness, Barksdale then inquired, "Col. Walton, you are not going to desert me, are you?" Walton replied, "General I am the last man in the world to desert you or anybody else. I am acting under orders." Barksdale responded, "Then will you obey an order from me?" When Walton replied in the affirmative, Barksdale issued the following directive: "Then reverse your column and come back with me to Fredericksburg. We must hold this point to the last."[42]

When Barksdale's courier reached Early, the commander was forced to reconsider. While Early deliberated, General Gordon rode up and gallantly volunteered to rush his Georgia Brigade to the aid of Hays and Barksdale. Realizing that he must keep his division united to stand any reasonable chance of success either way, Early quickly decided upon a retrograde movement to secure his former positions and protect Lee's rear. Early then sent a messenger to Barksdale to confirm his formal approval of the Mississippian's countermarch already underway, and a second courier to Lee advising of his decision to stay and fight at Fredericksburg.[43]

Barksdale's three regiments were the first to arrive back at Marye's Heights after nightfall, joining with Hays' Louisianans who occupied the trenches. Barksdale, in order to bluff the enemy that the Confederate line had been re-established and heavily reinforced, ordered innumerable campfires to be set along the heights. This was a welcome sight for all the Confederates who had stayed behind, none more so than Colonel Humphreys and the 21st Mississippi. During the interim, they had been ordered to "hold the city until forced out of it." Fearing a flanking movement from the Federals already across the Rappahannock south of Fredericksburg, the men of the 21st considered themselves as "rats in a rat-trap." When news of Barksdale's return reached them, cheers of "Bully for Barksdale! Bully for Hays! Bully for the Washington Artillery! Bully for Old Bob [Lee]" were shouted and passed down the picket line.[44]

Humphreys soon reported to Barksdale at Marye's Hill, updated him on the situation within Fredericksburg, and received Barksdale's approval of his own instructions to the pickets to oppose any crossing as best they could, and then to consolidate and slowly withdraw through the town if pressed.

Concerned that Early did not intend to defend Marye's Heights, Barksdale soon departed for a conference with his commander at Hamilton's Crossing, and to receive his orders. Around midnight, Humphreys returned to Barksdale's bivouac on Lee's Hill to learn the outcome. Discovering his leader "wrapped in his war blanket, lying at the foot of a tree," Humphreys politely inquired, in a subdued voice, as to whether the General was asleep. Barksdale's gruff reply—"No sir; who could sleep with a million of armed Yankees all around him?"—conveyed his foul mood arising from his earlier discussion with Early. It had turned out to be a "good news/bad news" scenario. On the positive side it was relayed by Barksdale that "it was determined by General Early to hold Marye's Hill at all hazards"; while on the negative side, "that [Barksdale's] brigade and a portion of the Washington Artillery had to do it"—alone.

Barksdale and Early clearly did not see eye to eye regarding the location of Sedgwick's imminent attack. Such disagreements amongst the Confederate High Command regarding strategy and tactics were not unusual. Early believed Sedgwick would attack on the Confederate far right, opposite Franklin's Crossing site, and that any observed Union movements toward or near Fredericksburg were simply feints to disguise this fact. Barksdale, for his part, remained firmly convinced the Federal assault would be aimed directly at his isolated and undermanned position along Marye's Heights—just as it had been five months earlier. (Subsequent events the next day would prove Barksdale correct.) When Humphreys concurred that Barksdale did not have enough men to hold the position, Barksdale responded with emphasis and resignation: "Well, sir, we must make the fight, whether we hold it or are whipped."[45] During the night, Hays' Louisianans returned to their former position with Early's division on the extreme right near Hamilton's Crossing.

In the aftermath of Stonewall Jackson's surprise attack on the Union right flank at Chancellorsville that afternoon, Hooker sent Staff Officer Gouverneur K. Warren to Fredericksburg that night with peremptory orders to ensure that Sedgwick would attack next morning and then rush to fall on Lee's rear at Chancellorsville. This order dictated that Sedgwick must move west toward Marye's Heights, not south toward Hamilton's Crossing. Hooker much later reemphasized the criticality of Sedgwick's mission when he stated this order "would have justified [Sedgwick] in losing every man of his command in its execution."[46] Sedgwick's time for uncertainty was now over—he now had the direct order he desired.

That night Union troops moved up from Franklin's Crossing and forced the pickets of Humphreys' 21st Mississippi to make a fighting withdrawal out of Fredericksburg (as previously agreed). Having heard the preparations being made for pontoon crossings at Fredericksburg, Humphreys assumed these Union troops had crossed over these completed bridges and so informed Barksdale. (These bridges were actually finished much later, closer to daybreak, and the Union troops which drove out the Confederate pickets had simply moved up from the southern bridgehead below Fredericksburg.)

Barksdale rode personally to Early's headquarters to update his commander and to urgently request reinforcements once again. Despite Barksdale's entreaties, Early was only willing to release a single brigade, Hays' Louisianans. Expressing confidence in Barksdale's abilities, Early "direct[ed] General Barksdale to post the brigade where it was needed, as he understood the ground thoroughly."[47] Rushing back to the left-center of the Confederate defensive line, Barksdale deployed his 1,500 man Mississippi Brigade along a three-mile front as follows: the 21st Mississippi was posted on the left between the Plank Road and Marye's Hill (three companies would later be shifted southward to support the left of the 18th Mississippi's line), the 18th Mississippi was stationed behind the stone wall along the sunken road in front of Marye's Hill in the center, the 17th Mississippi was deployed in front of Lee's Hill to the right, and the 13th Mississippi was deployed still farther to the right in front of Howison's Hill.

When Hays' brigade arrived later, four regiments were deployed to the left of Marye's Hill, with a single regiment, the 6th Louisiana, posted to the right of the 13th Mississippi on the extreme right. Four artillery pieces were placed at the Marye House and the balance on Lee's Hill and Howison's Hill. Barksdale established his headquarters at Lee's Hill. In his official report, Barksdale concluded this was "the only disposition of the small force at my command which, in my judgment, would prevent the enemy from passing the line." Edward Porter Alexander later confirmed Barksdale's assessment when he wrote—"the length of line held by Barksdale had stretched out his brigade more than double the distance it should have had to hold."[48]

Next day, Barksdale would receive support on the extreme left from an unexpected source. Brigadier General Cadmus M. Wilcox's Alabama Brigade of Richard H. Anderson's division had been guarding Banks Ford to the northwest without incident and was preparing to march to Lee's support that morning. When Sedgwick's artillery opened on Early's position at first light Wilcox marched instead toward the sound of these guns and soon encountered Barksdale and Hays. Responding to Barksdale's anxiety regarding the northern end of his defensive line, Wilcox, on his own initiative and in the nick of time, hurried his brigade into line in front of Taylor's and Stanbury's Hills. This deployment

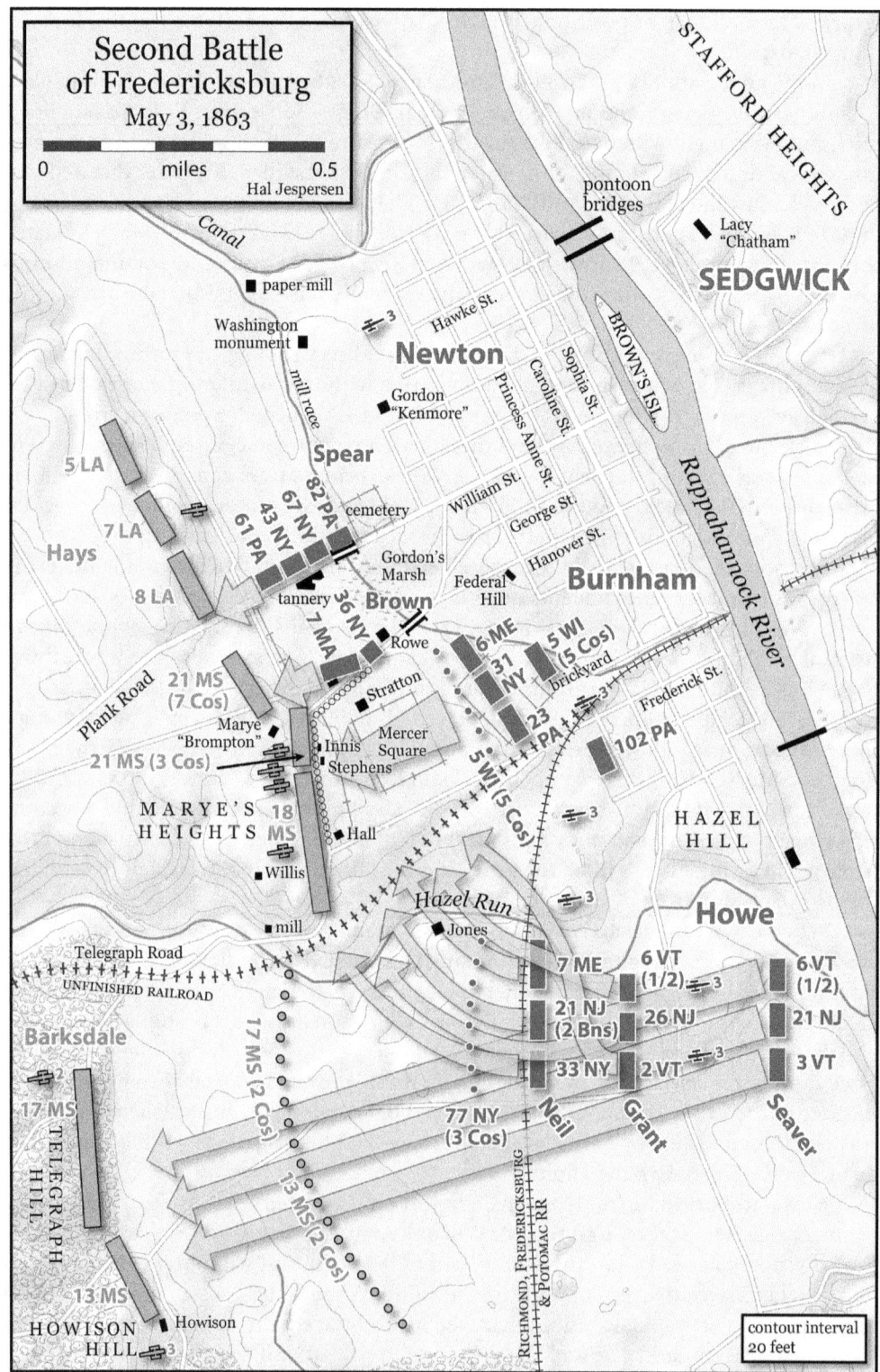

Second Battle of Fredericksburg, May 3, 1863 (Chancellorsville Campaign)

extended Barksdale's line and blocked the River Road leading west to Chancellorsville. When Brig. Gen. John O. Gibbon's division of the Union II Corps advanced out of Fredericksburg shortly after dawn they were impeded at once by a 30-foot-wide canal and millrace. While Gibbon's men were attempting to skirt around the Confederate left flank, it was Wilcox and Hays, assisted by the 21st Mississippi, and backed by the Washington Artillery on the heights, who stubbornly turned them back while inflicting significant losses.[49]

According to both Barksdale and Early, Sedgwick probed along the entire Confederate defensive line at dawn with both artillery and infantry. This activity included two separate assaults launched very early that morning against Marye's Heights by New York and Pennsylvania regiments of Maj. Gen. John Newton's division. Barksdale later reported that both Union attacks were "signally repulsed." According to a member of Sedgwick's staff, the first assault, launched out of the fog, actually "closed to within twenty paces of the stone wall" when a fierce Rebel volley erupted followed by Confederate artillery fire. Early stated the first of these was made prior to Gibbon's advance from Fredericksburg. Early also claimed later that, in messages sent by both Barksdale and Pendleton throughout that morning, both generals repeatedly expressed their belief they could hold their position. Such optimism flies in the face of Barksdale's new request for additional troops to bolster Thomas M. Griffin's position behind the stone wall. A request that Early refused. Barksdale's official report also refutes Early's claim. Barksdale stated, "With a line as extended as this, and in consideration of the small number of forces at my disposal, and the uncertainty as to the point against which the enemy would hurl the immense force he had amassed in town, I deemed it proper that the regiments should remain as they were and await the happening of events."[50]

It was at 9:30 a.m., according to eye-witness Capt. William B. Owen, that 47-year-old Col. Thomas M. Griffin, veteran commander of the 18th Mississippi behind the stone wall, injudiciously, and without authorization from Barksdale, accepted a Federal flag of truce requesting a cessation in order to remove Union wounded. Barksdale was then located on Lee's Hill far to the rear on the right. Griffin, whom Barksdale termed "a brave and gallant officer," in a spirit of "generous chivalry characteristic of that battle-scarred veteran" (according to Colonel Humphreys), refused the Federal request, but "imprudently" allowed the truce party to approach to within 100 yards of his line. Unfortunately, this was close enough for these Yankees to observe just how thin Griffin's line of Confederate infantry actually was, and how few the number of supporting artillery pieces. (Ironically, only days before, on April 28, 1863, Barksdale had submitted a letter to Secretary of War Seddon recommending Griffin for promotion to brigadier general. This recommendation also bore the signature of each senior field officer from each regiment within Barksdale's Mississippi Brigade.) Since a general Federal assault was soon mounted between 10 a.m. and 11 a.m., the Confederates believed this flag of truce had been a ruse or "Yankee trick." However, judicious study of the official Union records indicates that the plan for this final attack on the Confederate center had already been set in motion prior to this act.[51]

In all likelihood, the reconnaissance value of the truce party merely lay in increasing the morale of the attacking Union columns. It was perhaps because of this new intelligence that just after 10 a.m. Sedgwick sent a dispatch to Hooker (then being severely pressed by Lee) stating that "three strong columns of attack" were being launched against Marye's Heights. Sedgwick added confidently, "I have good prospects of success." To discourage Early from reinforcing the Marye's Heights sector, Union demonstrations were made along the entire Confederate line.

To defend his entire six-mile front Early had 12,700 infantry (including Wilcox's brigade) and 46 cannon. Unfortunately, his force was concentrated at the southern end near Hamilton's Crossing where he expected the Union attack to fall. This left only approximately 1,200 infantry and only eight cannon to defend the immediate stone wall/sunken road location and surrounding Marye's Heights sector. At the previous battle of Fredericksburg, this area had been defended by two full brigades supported by considerable reserves and 32 artillery pieces. Although additional reserve artillery was available to the rear, Pendleton failed to bring it forward as requested by Barksdale.

Against this meager defense Sedgwick launched three fast-moving, compact, attacking columns covered by the sustained fire from 40 Union artillery pieces posted in Fredericksburg and along Stafford Heights. These lines comprised of four men abreast totaled some 20,000 men from the Union VI Corps. The northernmost column from Newton's division attacked from William and Hanover Streets out of Fredericksburg along the Plank Road. The center column, comprised of men from five regiments of the Light Division under the command of Col. Hiram Burnham of the 6th Maine, was aimed directly at the stone wall. This spearhead was protected on its left flank by a third column to the south composed of one-and-a-half brigades from Brig. Gen. Albion Howe's division directed against the 17th and 13th Mississippi along the valley of Hazel Run in front of Lee's Hill. To maximize their chances of punching through the thin Confederate line these Union attackers had been ordered to make the charge without percussion caps on their rifles, but with bayonets fixed, and at the double-quick (at a fast trot).[52] The stage was then set for some of the most brutal, desperate, hand-to-hand combat of the entire war.

The suddenness of the Union onslaught was described by Colonel Humphreys this way—"three columns of infantry seemed to rise out of the earth, and rushed forward with demoniac shouts and yells." Though surprised, and greatly outnumbered, Barksdale's Mississippians gave a good account of themselves. The northernmost column attacking along the Plank Road was checked by rifle fire from the 21st Mississippi, as well as cannon fire from Captain Miller's single gun of the Washington Artillery. This Federal assault column was beaten back twice with heavy loss. At the outset, Col. George Spear of the 61st Pennsylvania, who led the first assault, had been killed instantly by a shell fragment to the head. His absence contributed significantly to a loss in Union momentum. At the same time the southernmost column from Howe's division was held in check by the combined rifle fire of the right wing of the 18th Mississippi and two companies each from the 17th and 13th Mississippi, plus artillery fire from the heights in rear. The middle attacking column was spearheaded by the 5th Wisconsin of Burnham's Light Division. As they stepped off, their leader, Col. Thomas Allen, steeled their nerve with the following instruction—"Boys, you see those heights. You have got to take them. You think you cannot do it but you can and you will. When the signal 'Forward' is given you will start at double-quick—you will not fire a gun—and you will not stop until you get the order to halt. You will never get that order."[53]

These Union soldiers surged on in a mad rush for the stone wall. During the previous battle of Fredericksburg, the stone wall had been defended by Kershaw's South Carolinians in closed formation four ranks deep. Muskets had been loaded by the rear ranks and passed forward to the front rank to maintain a sustained heavy volume of rifle fire—with deadly effect. Now this wall was defended only by Colonel Griffin's 400 men who were necessarily spread out in one sparse line. These riflemen were spaced from four to six paces apart (as evidenced by Alexander Gardner's iconic photo of the Rebel slain here taken immediately after the attack). This thin Confederate line was supported by three companies of the 21st Mississippi, and three guns of the Washington Artillery on the heights above. Despite heavy casualties, the Union attacking column rushed forward like an irresistible tide and soon reached the wall as the Confederate fire slackened abruptly.

Colonel Allen, sword in one hand and revolver in the other, led the advance and was the first to jump up and over. Immediately scores of Union infantrymen from Wisconsin, Maine, Pennsylvania, and New York vaulted over the wall and viciously stabbed the defenders with their bayonets or crushed their skulls with their rifle butts. Typical was Pvt. George Brown of the 6th Maine who bayoneted two Mississippians and then clubbed a third with his rifle butt. Adjutant Charles A. Clark of the 6th Maine claimed that, by actual count, 40 Mississippians were bayoneted here. Private Joseph C. Lloyd of the 13th Mississippi, who witnessed the Union breakthrough from a distance, recorded that "from our position we could see it all and reasonably concluded the 18th was about annihilated." Lloyd was not far off in his assessment—losses in the 18th Mississippi totaled 68 killed or wounded, 226 captured (including Colonel Griffin and Lieutenant Colonel Luse) and loss of its regimental flag.

In this frenzied melee, and in the subsequent overrunning and capture of the

18th Mississippi dead at the Stone Wall, where Barksdale's thin line was broken. Iconic photograph by A.J. Russell taken during the Battle of Fredericksburg, May 3, 1863 (Library of Congress).

artillery on the heights, many Mississippians were actually shot down while surrendering—and in some cases murdered in cold blood after they had. This led to claims by some, like Colonel Humphreys, that many of the Union soldiers were intoxicated. These charges were later vehemently denied. Commenting upon this savagery, Capt. John A. Barksdale, Adjutant to General Barksdale, later stated, "It was I think done in the excitement and heat of battle when men's passions set all restraint at defiance and was not the result of a deliberate determination to give no quarter."

Buoyed by their success, and with the remnant of the 18th Mississippi and the three detached companies from the 21st Mississippi now scrambling to escape, the Union attackers raced up the steep slope of Marye's Hill to seize the artillery emplacements. Federal support from the other two assault columns now converged toward the gap in Barksdale's line to exploit the breakthrough. Despite resolutely resisting to the last, which cost many a brave cannoneer his life, the guns were quickly captured. The Union conquest of Marye's Heights was signified when Color Sergeant John Gray of the 6th Maine was first to plant the Union colors on the crest amidst great cheering by the Union troops all the way back to Fredericksburg.[54]

Observing these developments from his vantage point on Lee's Hill, Barksdale issued orders for Lieutenant Colonel Fiser to rush reinforcements from the 17th Mississippi to Griffin at the stone wall. But it was too late, and Barksdale immediately canceled the order. The rapidity of the Federal breakthrough similarly precluded any assistance from Hays' and Wilcox's forces on the extreme left. In a display of his courage, leadership—and more importantly of his growing confidence in his own martial abilities—Barksdale did not panic. Instead he coolly and methodically first consolidated the 17th and 13th Mississippi and the 6th Louisiana in a defensive position atop Lee's Hill to prevent the Federals from gaining the rear of his line. Once Marye's Heights had fallen, Barksdale attempted to rally the fleeing remnant of the 18th Mississippi and subsequently the 21st Mississippi, who, in turn, were compelled to retire to avoid being surrounded and captured. It was during this frantic effort that Private Lloyd acknowledged that Barksdale "came near being captured." When questioned by artilleryman William M. Owen at this time whether a battery then on Lee's Hill firing at the victorious Union forces on Marye's Hill was still in a safe position, Barksdale calmly answered, "Our center has been pierced, that's all; we will be all right in a little while." This was the mark of a professional officer. As military historian Stephen Hawley has noted, "Such imperturbability in the face of adversity is contagious and a good combat commander can use it to steady a shaky command, as Barksdale did here."[55]

Having rallied his brigade, Barksdale deployed them in a battle line across the Telegraph Road and, in Early's words, "made obstinate resistance to the enemy's advance ... falling back gradually before the large force opposing him." Two miles back, at the intersection with Mine Road, Barksdale linked up with Early and his division. The Confederates deployed in line of battle and were not challenged. Instead, the bulk of the Union forces pressed westward toward Chancellorsville along the Plank Road further to the north. Wilcox and Hays rushed westward along the River Road, halted at Salem Church about five miles from Fredericksburg, turned, and repulsed Sedgwick's vanguard at sundown. With the onset of darkness, Confederates and Yankees bivouacked for the night.[56]

Earlier that afternoon Lee, having learned of events at Fredericksburg, immediately dispatched McLaws' division, along with two brigades from Anderson's division, from Chancellorsville to Salem Church. Lee also approved Early's plan to retake possession of Marye's Heights next morning, and then march to Salem Church to attack Sedgwick from the rear—taking precautions to bottle up any remaining Federal force still in Fredericksburg.[57]

This simple act of regaining Marye's Heights and reoccupying the entrenchments at the stone wall would soon become a major point of contention prompting a bitter public dispute between Early and Barksdale in the Southern press only days later. Accordingly, next morning, per Early's instructions General Gordon informed Barksdale "that orders were for us to retake the positions lost the day before." When Gordon advised Barksdale that his Georgia Brigade was to take the lead with Barksdale's Mississippians in support, Barksdale erupted—strenuously objecting.

Since he had lost the positions the day before, Barksdale insisted Southern honor demanded that he and his Mississippians be in the forefront to retake them. Private Lloyd, who witnessed the altercation, reported "they had quite a scrap over it, Gordon reminding Barksdale that he (Gordon) was ranking officer, and [Barksdale] would have to obey." They proceeded first to Lee's Hill where, according to Early, Barksdale halted without orders. In the meantime, Gordon's brigade proceeded to reoccupy Marye's Hill which was "defended" only by a few women from Fredericksburg on a mercy mission searching for Confederate wounded. However, Gordon was soon forced to battle a small Federal force along the Plank Road immediately to the northwest which was protecting a Federal supply and artillery wagon train. By the time Barksdale's Mississippians reached Marye's Hill and the stone wall along the Sunken Road, Gordon was nowhere to be seen.

Ordered by Early to occupy his old position, Barksdale was also directed to advance rapidly into Fredericksburg. If the city was not too heavily defended, Barksdale should capture the pontoon bridge and a wagon train then visible at the south end of town. Soon, observing the wagon train departing across the bridge, an impatient Early sent a courier to repeat the order to Barksdale. Upon his return, this courier advised Early that Barksdale was then preparing to advance a skirmish line. In an ironic reversal of roles, Barksdale soon discovered that the 20th Massachusetts was now defending Fredericksburg against his Mississippians from rifle pits dug across the streets. Gibbon's Union division was present there in force with supporting artillery on both sides of the river. When apprised of this information, Early countermanded his former order and directed Barksdale to assume a defensive position to repel any Federal advance westward out of Fredericksburg.[58]

That same afternoon near Salem Church, poor coordination between Early and McLaws, coupled with McLaws' very lackluster performance as senior Confederate commander on-site, robbed Lee of a decisive victory over the still cautious Sedgwick. McLaws' performance was so poor in fact that Lee had to personally intervene in the battle. That night Sedgwick's force escaped back across the Rappahannock via Bank's Ford, and Gibbon evacuated Fredericksburg and dismantled the pontoon bridges. Barksdale reoccupied Fredericksburg on the following morning and captured 40 additional prisoners. On this day, Tuesday, May 5th, Lee once again unsuccessfully attempted to annihilate Hooker's army at Chancellorsville. During the night Hooker and the Army of the Potomac also withdrew across the Rappahannock at United States Ford and headed back to its old campground at Falmouth.

Lee had successfully beaten back a vastly superior force from a decidedly inferior tactical position—and gained his greatest victory. In the face of the enemy, Lee had boldly divided his army, not once, not twice, but three times to secure the triumph—but it had cost him dearly. Several days later, Stonewall Jackson (Lee's "right arm") died of pneumonia after being wounded by his own men during a night reconnaissance immediately following his devastating flank attack at Chancellorsville.

Regarding the rearguard action at Fredericksburg, Lee was quick to credit Early for a job well done, stating in his official report that Early had "performed the important and responsible duty entrusted to him in a manner which reflected credit upon himself and his command."[59]

Barksdale and his Mississippi Brigade had actually borne the lion's share of the fighting at Fredericksburg. While losses in Early's division had been few during the Federal attacks of May 3rd, Barksdale had lost 226 killed or wounded with an additional 350 taken prisoner. Although Lee applauded Early's efforts, many other Confederates believed the Federal capture of Marye's Heights at Fredericksburg—and the missed opportunity at Salem Church—significantly detracted from Lee's brilliant victory at Chancellorsville—what historian Gary Gallagher has aptly termed "unfortunate brush strokes on an otherwise perfect canvas."[60] Indeed, both at the time and since, the events at Fredericksburg in May 1863 have been completely overshadowed by those at Chancellorsville.

From Barksdale's vantage point it was crystal clear. Despite yielding Marye's Heights to the enemy, his Mississippi Brigade had performed valiantly against vastly superior numbers—inflicting nearly 2,000 Union casualties. He said as much repeatedly in his official report—"It will thus be seen that Marye's Hill was defended by but one small regiment, three companies, and four pieces of artillery. A more heroic struggle was never made by a mere handful of men against overwhelming odds." Barksdale continued, "After a determined and bloody resistance by Colonel Griffin and the Washington Artillery, the enemy, fully twenty to one, succeeded in gaining possession of Marye's Hill; at all other points he was triumphantly repulsed."[61]

What Barksdale could not say in his official report (although it is difficult to believe he did not harbor deep feelings of resentment) was that this predicament resulted through no fault of his own. Rather, over his personal objections, his valiant Mississippians had paid the price for the indifference, negligence, and incompetence of his Virginian superiors, Early and Pendleton. Had he not correctly pointed out to Early that the Union attack would be directed at his center (precisely where it came) rather than near Hamilton's Crossing where Early had stubbornly concentrated his forces? Had Early not repeatedly refused his requests for additional reinforcements from Early's front where they were never substantially engaged? Had Pendleton not inexplicably refused to bring forward at least some of the 20 guns from the reserve artillery which remained idle throughout the whole engagement? It was all so clear in Barksdale's mind. Had these reasonable requests been granted, this Union breakthrough of his line—the sole blemish on the sterling reputation of Barksdale's Mississippi Brigade—undoubtedly would have been averted.

Other participants, both Northern and Southern, did openly express such views. A Louisiana artilleryman, lamenting the loss of his gun on Marye's Heights, was heard to bitterly complain, "I reckon now the people of the Southern Confederacy are satisfied that Barksdale's brigade and the Washington Artillery can't whip the whole Yankee army." Even Union General Newton later wrote, "If there had been one hundred more men on Marye's Hill, we could not have taken it." At least one Confederate officer put the blame on Early, postulating eight days later that Lee's victory at Chancellorsville would have been even greater if Early had "managed better below at Fredericksburg."[62]

To add insult to injury, Early rubbed salt in the wound by taking a verbal swipe at Barksdale in remarks he made immediately after the battle, and also by claiming in his May 7th Battle Report that Gordon's Brigade of his own division had "recaptured" Marye's Hill. Colonel Humphreys recorded that "this fling aroused the fiery spirit of Barksdale" and touched off "an unpleasant controversy between General Early and General Barksdale, immediately after the battle, that all their mutual friends deeply deplored." Barksdale countered with proof that a celebrated scout, named Roberts, from Company K, 21st Mississippi, known throughout the brigade as "Yankee Hunter," had passed over Marye's Hill after dawn on May 4th and found it unoccupied except for a few ladies from Fredericksburg seeking out wounded Mississippians. Roberts added that, when Gordon's brigade finally arrived there, Barksdale's aide, nephew Harris Barksdale, and Lieutenant Ramseur, Company B, 17th Mississippi, together with six advanced pickets, were already present on Marye's Hill.[63] The matter should have ended there.

However, Early chose to make their bitter disagreement public in a letter to the *Richmond Enquirer* printed on May 13th. A correspondent for the *Enquirer* had previously published an account concerning the Union capture of Marye's Heights which Early perceived was prejudicial to him. Early's inflammatory response began by referencing "the statements of correspondents ignorant of the real facts, *or writing in the interests of particular commands*" (emphasis added), which all but accused Barksdale of exerting undue influence upon the press. Having defended his command decisions, Early then closed with a thinly veiled smear on Barksdale and his Mississippians by writing, "Without meaning to cast censure on Barksdale's brigade, even by implication, I will state that my division did not lose Marye's Hill, but one of my brigades [Gordon's] recaptured it before 9 o'clock on the next morning." Early ended this emotionally charged epistle by relating that it was three of his own brigades who "bore the brunt of the fight when the enemy was driven back across the river" while Barksdale's brigade had been left in a supporting role "to keep the enemy in check in the direction of Fredericksburg."[64]

Early's public challenge was like a gauntlet slap across the face for the fiery Barksdale. In some respects, it was surprising that Barksdale did not demand satisfaction according to the Code Duello with which he was all too familiar. However, since the insult was not only against himself but against the men of his beloved Mississippi Brigade, and since the challenge was already public, Barksdale would refute it in the same manner—in the press.

Barely restraining his anger, Barksdale boldly responded two days later in his own letter to the *Enquirer*. Barksdale flatly denied any coercion of the press. In reference to Early's insinuation that correspondents reported "in the interest of particular commands," Barksdale stated, "if intended for this brigade [this charge]is gratuitous and unfounded." Barksdale then took his own backhanded swipe at Early by confirming that he had been unaware that his commanding officer's "conduct in the late engagements around Fredericksburg had been made the subject of newspaper censure until I saw it announced over his own signature."

Quoting extensively from his own official report, Barksdale then carefully pointed out several key inaccuracies in Early's previous account. Barksdale's defensive line, what Early had described as a "comparatively short line," was actually "not less than three miles" in length. Secondly, Barksdale confirmed that "Marye's Hill was defended by one small regiment, three companies, and four pieces of artillery, and not the entire brigade" as asserted by Early. Thirdly, Barksdale forcefully set the record straight regarding the "recapture" of Marye's Heights. Contrary to the impression that Gordon's brigade had forced the enemy from a position the Mississippians had relinquished the previous day, Barksdale carefully affirmed, although "I would scorn to detract from the well-earned reputation of [Gordon's] brigade and its gallant commander, but the truth is, the enemy had abandoned Marye's Heights and Gen. Gordon took possession without opposition." Always the protective father figure when it came to his men, Barksdale closed with a statement of support for his "boys": "My brigade needs no defense at my hands. Its reputation, won upon many battlefields, is well established." However, Barksdale could not resist one last swipe at Early: "This communication is not written for that purpose but to correct erroneous impressions which Gen. Early's publication was calculated to make."[65]

On this same day, May 15, 1863, a different account of the recent battles was published in the *Richmond Enquirer* by another special correspondent. This report supported Barksdale's version of events and was critical of Early, as evidenced by the following excerpts regarding the defense at the stone wall: "Thus the enemy, throwing ten regiments against one, carried the crest.... I cannot perceive that anything but praise attaches to the Mississippi brigade for the part which they bore in these ever more memorable battles. History records Leonidis and his Spartan heroes though overpowered at Thermopylae, and the men of Mississippi [who] clubbed muskets with the enemy even after they had been flanked and the foe had turned their own guns upon them." Reference was made to the heights being retaken "without the firing of a gun on Monday morning, by Gordon's Brigade with charged bayonets."

Finally, commenting on the Early-Barksdale feud then playing out in the press, this reporter apparently condemned both participants—"This is no time for bickerings and newspaper controversies among our braves in the field. There is too strong a disposition—and I speak of it with regret—on the part of some who are attached to one command in this army to speak of the achievements and results of those connected with other command somewhat disparagingly." The next day, the correspondent, whose column had precipitated Early's original letter, responded. He directed his criticism pointedly at Early, who he asserted "has shown his strategy by poking his nose into a hornet's nest." The reporter then stated Early's claims were both "unworthy of himself" and "unnecessary to deny." Declaring "it is no time for Confederates to quarrel," he concluded by saying, "I have not censured him. So much for Early."[66]

Several days elapsed, but Early could not refrain from responding on May 19th to Barksdale's rebuttal. Professing he would not permit himself to be drawn into a controversy "which accords neither my taste nor sense of military propriety," Early then reiterated his claim that Barksdale, shortly before Marye's Hill fell, "had previously no uneasiness about the safety of his position, as he deemed it impregnable," but expressed "a good deal of anxiety about my position which had been threatened all morning." Early finished by claiming that on May 4th, Marye's Hill "was *retaken* by Gordon's brigade ... from a superior force drawn up in line behind the plank road" (emphasis added).[67] Barksdale's inevitable response was dated May 31st. In it he flatly refuted Early's claims regarding Barksdale's assessments of the relative strengths of his position versus Early's. Barksdale also asserted that he then had "the amplest testimony in my possession ... that Marye's Hill had been abandoned, and that whatever engagement Gen. Gordon may have had with the enemy on Monday morning, was beyond the plank road."

Barksdale also took this opportunity to publicly absolve Colonel Griffin of any blame for the loss of Marye's Hill. Although Barksdale had seen fit to previously make mention in his official report of Griffin's unauthorized acceptance of the Union flag of truce on May 3rd, he now stated unequivocally that "It is proper for me to say in justice to a gallant officer, that I am satisfied from his statement, that the enemy gained no advantage from the flag of truce which was granted by Col. Griffin."[68] Barksdale's assertion is borne out by the fact that Griffin retained his command of the 18th Mississippi, and was never disciplined for his unauthorized action. While reflecting Barksdale's life-long propensity for forgiveness, his value of loyalty, and his sense of fairness, his action in this instance also bespeaks his unequivocal belief that the collapse of his defensive line was attributable directly to lack of manpower and not to Griffin's momentary lapse of judgment.

Lee too had read and heard enough. Before Early could respond to Barksdale's second rebuttal, Lee intervened and reprimanded Early (the senior commander) for airing differences in public. As historian Gary Gallagher has noted, Early reminded Lee after the war of his chastisement at Lee's hand concerning this whole episode—"You gave me a mild rebuke for that and I never repeated the offence," while the record is silent as to whether Barksdale was ever called on the carpet for his actions.[69]

By mid–May Lee's Army of Northern Virginia and Hooker's Army of the Potomac were once again in their old camps and facing each other across the Rappahannock at Fredericksburg. And once again Barksdale's Mississippi Brigade occupied the town in their familiar roles as pickets and Provost Guard. The monotony was broken by three significant events. The first occurred on the evening of May 10th when Barksdale, having already advised Hooker of his readiness to exchange the Federal wounded prisoners in Fredericksburg and the surrounding vicinity, supervised their transfer across the Rappahannock River under a flag of truce.[70]

The second occurred on May 16th when a dark bay-colored horse belonging to a Yankee officer broke free and swam across the river. This fine mount was soon claimed as "the spoils of war" by General Barksdale who refused to return it despite numerous requests from its previous owner who alleged it was private property.[71] (Barksdale would be mounted on this horse when he received his mortal wounds at Gettysburg seven weeks later.)

The third joyous event occurred on May 26th when Colonel Griffin and Lieutenant Colonel Luse, along with other members of the 18th Mississippi, returned to their regiment at Hamilton's Crossing after being formally exchanged. Following their capture on May 3rd, they had been incarcerated at Old Capitol Prison in Washington City. Surprisingly, Griffin and Luse had been very well treated and acquired near-celebrity status as the following report in the *Washington Star* confirms: "Colonel T.M. Griffin of the 18th Mississippi regiment was permitted, with another rebel officer captured at Fredericksburg, to visit various places of business on the avenue yesterday, under guard, to make purchases of clothing, exchange money etc., etc. He is a large sized, powerful-looking man, and attracted a crowd wherever he moved."[72] They were both subsequently paroled on May 18th and exchanged eight days later.

By the beginning of June, McLaws' Division had been reunited at Fredericksburg under General Longstreet who had finally returned from Suffolk. Back on May 3rd, when their line had been breached, one of Barksdale's men had given voice to their despair in a letter home: "The Mississippi Brigade had never been whipped before, and felt mighty bad." Now reunited with the brigades they had "fought side by side [with] for over twelve months," the morale of Barksdale's brigade soared once again. In Colonel Humphrey's words, "Such was the confidence in each other they deemed the Division invincible when fighting together."[73] This feeling of invincibility was shared by Lee and would soon be put to the test at a sleepy crossroads town in southern Pennsylvania.

Fourteen

Gettysburg
A Grim Determination to Do or Die

True to form, Lee wasted no time in seizing the initiative. He immediately travelled to Richmond to attend a series of meetings with President Davis, Secretary of War James J. Seddon, and the Confederate Cabinet to make his case for another invasion of the North. While Davis favored sending reinforcements from the East to Lt. Gen. John C. Pemberton at Vicksburg, Lee argued convincingly that by striking north into Pennsylvania, possibly even capturing the state capital of Harrisburg, the Army of Northern Virginia would threaten major Northern cities—including Baltimore, Philadelphia, and Washington. This bold move would not only force the Army of the Potomac to relinquish its strong positions and supply bases near Fredericksburg and deter Union reinforcement of Maj. Gen. Grant at Vicksburg, it would compel Hooker to wage combat at a favorable location of Lee's choosing. Furthermore, engaging on Northern soil would eliminate the need for Virginia to sustain his army, permit a normal harvest there, and free the Old Dominion state from further Yankee depredations.

Lee had gained no meaningful advantage from his victories in Virginia. However, a decisive victory on Northern soil might facilitate a negotiated peace and/or formal diplomatic recognition of the Confederacy by England and/or France. Lee's aide-de-camp, Col. Charles Marshall, summarized the strategic alternatives this way: "So if General Lee remained inactive, both Vicksburg and Richmond would be imperilled, whereas if he were successful north of the Potomac, both would be saved." In a post-war oversimplification Lee, himself, reportedly stated that his strategic choices were only two—"[to] retire on Richmond and stand a siege … or to invade Pennsylvania."[1]

Stonewall Jackson's death on May 10th at Guinea's Station forced Lee to reorganize his army once again. From the former structure of two corps of eight divisions, Lee created three new corps of three divisions each. While Longstreet retained command of First Corps, most of Jackson's former corps comprised the new smaller Second Corps under newly promoted Lt. Gen. Richard S. Ewell. This Virginian, West Point graduate, and Mexican War veteran was returning to duty after losing a leg nine months earlier at Groveton, one day before the battle of Second Manassas. The Third Corps was put under command of another newly promoted lieutenant general, Ambrose Powell Hill. Hill was another career soldier. A native Virginian, he had graduated from West Point and served in the Mexican War.

This reorganization meant that two-thirds of Lee's army now served under commanders who had never directed so many troops in battle. Moreover, unlike Longstreet's

First Corps which retained three experienced divisional commanders—Hood, McLaws, and Pickett—only three of the divisional commanders in the other two corps had previous experience in leading a division. In addition, neither Ewell nor Hill had previously served directly under Lee, and they were unaccustomed to Lee's command style of issuing discretionary orders. Even more importantly, the officers within the existing inadequate staff organization would now be dispersed among generals with whom they were not personally acquainted. In turn, these generals commanded unfamiliar troops in many cases. These significant shortcomings rendered this new army structure a significant liability which would result in serious consequences at Gettysburg. Indeed, renowned historian Douglas Southall Freeman termed this reorganization "one of the major tragedies of the Confederacy."[2]

Late on June 2nd, Barksdale's brigade marched out of Fredericksburg along Telegraph Road and camped four miles out of town. They spent the following day cooking three days' rations in preparation for the march westward toward the Shenandoah Valley. Toward sunset the brigade took up the march, arriving near Chancellorsville at 11 p.m. after a trek of 10 miles. Thus began Lee's invasion into Pennsylvania with his 75,000-man Army of Northern Virginia. With Barksdale's brigade leading the march, McLaws' division formed the vanguard of Longstreet's corps, with Hood's and Pickett's divisions following next day. Ewell's corps then broke camp and joined the march on the next day while A.P. Hill's corps remained at Fredericksburg to observe Hooker's forces.

On June 4th Barksdale's brigade marched 23 miles, passing through Chancellorsville early that morning. Sergeant Hill felt compelled to record, "the country around is completely devastated for several miles and the stench from the dead bodies of men and horses is intolerable."[3] After resting on June 5th, the brigade again took up the march, crossing the Rapidan River at Raccoon Ford and continuing westward to the outskirts of Culpepper Courthouse after a march of 16 miles. A series of shorter marches and countermarches near Culpepper followed over the next several days as General Lee concentrated his forces west of the town.[4]

In order to screen this movement, Lee had placed General J.E.B. Stuart's cavalry near Brandy Station, several miles east of Culpepper, to protect against any Federal advance. During this lull of several days, Barksdale's brigade was called upon to march to nearby Stevensburg and form into line of battle to fend off an incursion by Federal cavalry.[5] However the flamboyant "Beau Sabreur" Stuart was more concerned with staging a grand parade to impress the local citizens and to boost morale than remaining vigilant. On June 9th Union cavalry commander Brig. Gen. Alfred Pleasanton split his force and stealthily crossed the Rappahannock River at Beverley's and Kelly's Fords. Pleasanton attacked Stuart in a pincer movement and caught the Confederates completely by surprise. With a combined total of nearly 20,000 cavalrymen engaged, the battle of Brandy Station constituted the largest single cavalry engagement in the history of the Western Hemisphere. Although Stuart eventually managed to rally his forces and desperately beat off the Federal attack, the myth of the invincibility of the Southern horsemen had been forever dashed. Thereafter the effectiveness of the Confederate cavalry as a fighting force steadily declined while that of the Union rapidly ascended.

On June 15th Hooker finally started the Army of the Potomac northward from Fredericksburg in response to Lee's march. This Union move, in turn, prompted Hill's Third Corps to vacate the Fredericksburg defenses and march westward to fall in behind Ewell's and Longstreet's corps. For the next two weeks the Union army moved north while remaining east of the Blue Ridge Mountains, thereby interposing Federal forces between Washington and Lee's army in the Shenandoah Valley. After remaining in the Culpepper area for several days, Barksdale's brigade was ordered on June 15th to cook three days' rations—a clear indication that a long march would ensue on the following day. The long-awaited campaign to, once again, invade the North had now begun in earnest. Quartermaster Clerk, Sergeant Hill noted that "the subsistence trains will carry 10 days rations additionally"[6]—another clear indication of the grueling campaign to come. Over the next several days Barksdale and his Mississippians continued their march northwestward, passing through Woodville and Sperryville en route to the Shenandoah Valley. Lee would march his army northward down the Shenandoah and Cumberland Valleys all the way to Pennsylvania. Sheltered by the mountain ranges to his right, the Gray Fox secured his lines of supply and communication. By defending the east-west mountain passes, the Confederate commander kept his location and intentions away from the prying eyes of the Federal cavalry.

Unfortunately, the march had barely begun when the weather turned "intensely hot—as hot as I ever saw in Mississippi" according to Private Newton Nash of the 13th Mississippi. After daily marches of 18–22 miles, the extreme heat took its toll on the weary, dusty infantrymen. Their diaries contain numerous entries confirming that "a great many fainted in the road with heat [exhaustion] and several died 'due to sunstroke and overheating.'"[7] Despite widespread hardship, suffering, and several deaths—straggling within the Mississippi Brigade was all but eliminated by Barksdale's judicious implementation of effective control measures. This was a dramatic turnaround from the march from Harpers Ferry to Sharpsburg a year earlier which saw a 50 percent reduction in manpower due to straggling. Under Barksdale's leadership the logistical organization within the brigade had also improved considerably.

While Barksdale cannot take credit for devising the countermeasures to prevent straggling, there can be no doubt that he vigorously adopted and oversaw their implementation. Observing Semmes' and Barksdale's brigades later on the march through Maryland, Col. Arthur J. Freemantle of Great Britain's Coldstream Guards commented, "They marched very well and there was no attempt at straggling.... All were well shod and efficiently clothed. In rear of each regiment were from twenty to thirty negro slaves, and a certain number of unarmed men carrying stretchers and wearing in their hats red badges of the ambulance corps—this is an excellent institution, for it prevents unwounded men falling out on pretence of taking wounded to the rear." Gettysburg historian Harry W. Pfanz added that these ambulance corps men were accompanied by a field officer and a surgeon who examined each "casualty" and issued a pass to those legitimately disabled. In addition, trailing each brigade were 20 wagons under command of a staff officer with a surgeon who re-examined each straggler and signed the passes of legitimate candidates as confirmation.[8] With such extensive safeguards in place it is not surprising that Barksdale quickly recovered any men he lost along the way, and that his brigade went into battle at Gettysburg at full strength.

Again, on June 21st Barksdale's brigade was called upon to assist Stuart's cavalry—this time in defending Ashby's Gap against Union cavalry attacks. Subsequently the Mississippi Brigade crossed the Shenandoah River at Upperville where the water was up to Private Abernathy's mouth. In a gesture of kindness which Abernathy related, "Barksdale always ready to do something, took Fox Moore up behind him on his horse," thereby sparing the shorter soldier the trauma of crossing on foot.[9]

On June 23, on McLaws' direct order, the division washed in the waters of the Shenandoah River and fell in for a dress parade in the evening. Next day the march resumed northward through Winchester with the brigade reaching Martinsburg on the following day. On June 26, McLaws' division crossed the Potomac River into Maryland at Williamsport—a memorable event for an unexpected reason. McLaws later related that the Potomac was quite deep and the wading across difficult, with his men becoming very wet. A large quantity of whiskey had been confiscated in the city, and McLaws ordered that a "gill apiece [be] given to each man that wanted it." McLaws proudly proclaimed, "in justice to my division I will assert that I never heard of anyone refusing it." McLaws also asserted, "the consequence was that the men were all in good humor." This sentiment was echoed by Private Abernathy of the 17th Mississippi who described McLaws' Confederates at that moment as "about a lively set of men as ever tramped up that pike."[10]

By this time Ewell's corps, which now formed the vanguard, had already crossed into Pennsylvania and had advanced to occupy Chambersburg. Ewell's march soon took on the appearance of a masterful raid with large quantities of livestock and supplies seized and immediately dispatched southward. His corps soon fanned outward with Early's division crossing South Mountain and marching east through Gettysburg and York until reaching Wrightsville on the Susquehanna River. At the same time Rode's and Johnson's divisions continued marching northeastward via the Cumberland Valley to Carlisle.

On June 27th Barksdale's brigade left their camp near Williamsport at sunrise, passed through Hagerstown at 9 a.m., and crossed the Pennsylvania state line at Middleburg at 1 p.m. The Mississippians passed through Greencastle during the mid-afternoon. A teenage girl at the time recalled many years later the impression made upon her as Lee and his army marched past her house for 10 consecutive days. Sometimes leaning from a second story window she would inquire of the Confederate guard posted at the front door as to the identity of the generals as they approached at the head of their brigades. She recorded: "one day, noticing an unusually fine looking man, I inquired who he was, and learned that he was General Barksdale of Mississippi." It was here that Barksdale's quartermasters and commissaries began to appropriate "a large number of horses, mules, wagons, beef cattle, sheep, forage etc." for their own use, paying in Confederate currency. If the owners refused, then "a receipt for it to be paid at the end of the war" was issued instead. One member of the 13th Mississippi noted in his diary that "A large number of citizens have fled, leaving their homes unprotected." That night the brigade camped at the village of Marion, having marched 21 miles.[11]

It was here that Col. John Logan Black of the 1st South Carolina Cavalry unexpectedly reported to General Barksdale's headquarters. Black had taken command of three cavalry companies and Hart's Battery of field artillery, who had been separated and cut off from Stuart's command while crossing the mountains. Black now sought Barksdale's assistance in locating General Lee's headquarters. Colonel Black recorded: "I was very courteously received by General Barksdale & invited to breakfast with him. By that time a rumor came that Yankee Cavalry were in our rear & by Gen'l Barksdale's sanction, I moved several miles to the rear, sent out scouts but soon learned it was a kind of straggler's dispatch & without foundation." Thus Barksdale, always willing to accept additional responsibility, temporarily assumed command of Black's cavalry and artillery contingent. This arrangement lasted until Black reached Lee's headquarters at Chambersburg when

Lee personally took command of this orphaned group. Subsequently Lee assigned Black and his contingent to special duties under direction of General Longstreet.[12]

Later this same morning Barksdale's men passed through Chambersburg after a short march of about 10 miles. They soon halted, and went into bivouac just outside town. These Mississippians were decidedly impressed with Chambersburg and the lush beauty of the surrounding Pennsylvania countryside. Invariably they made complimentary notations in their diaries and letters. Sergeant Hill considered Chambersburg "a very pretty town" while another private recorded that "Chambersburg is quite a little city ... a great many fine looking ladies." Private Newton Nash wrote "[this] is the richest and most beautiful country I ever beheld. I hate to see such a fine looking country in the possession of such people." Private Clendenen Black of Company I, 13th Mississippi elaborated further—"This is the most beautiful country I ever saw, the houses are all fine, the barns are more magnificent than the dwelling houses."[13]

These haggard, dusty, Mississippians also made a profound impression on the Pennsylvania citizenry. Eyewitness Jacob Hoke, a local merchant, later recorded his detailed observations:

> The Confederate infantry, as they marched through Chambersburg, presented a solid front. They came in close marching order, the different brigades, divisions, and corps, all within supporting distance of each other. Their dress consisted of nearly every imaginable color and style, the butternut largely predominating. Some had blue blouses, which they had doubtless stripped from the Union dead. Hats, or the skeletons of what had once been hats, surmounted their partly covered heads. Many were ragged, shoeless, and filthy, affording unmistakeable evidence that their wardrobes sadly needed to be replenished. They were, however, all well armed and under perfect discipline.... Those from Mississippi and Texas were more vicious and defiant than those from other parts of the South.[14]

In a familiar role, the 18th Mississippi was detached to garrison Chambersburg for two days. Barksdale's brigade settled in for a pleasant sojourn, "living on the fat of the land" in the words of Private Nash. Private Moore of the 17th Mississippi documented his joy at partaking of "chicken pie, molasses, buttermilk, pork etc." Their enjoyment was diminished only by the disdain openly expressed by the local citizenry toward these invaders. Although one Confederate recorded "[the locals] say we treat them much better than expected," Sergeant Hill commented "the people are very much depressed and uneasy on account of our invasion of their state and express their dislike for us on all occasions." General Lee issued specific orders that were read to all his troops—"No private property shall be injured or destroyed." Lee took extra measures such as posting sentries at private dwellings and restricting the men to camp, as well as instructing them to treat the citizenry courteously. However, invariably, as Private Moore acknowledged, "the souldiers are committing some depredations on private property."[15] By this admission members of the Mississippi Brigade undoubtedly participated in these transgressions despite the best efforts of General Barksdale and his officers to prevent this behavior.

While Barksdale's brigade remained in and around Chambersburg on June 28th, a momentous change occurred in the Army of the Potomac that would alter the outcome of the forthcoming battle at Gettysburg and affect the fortunes of Barksdale and his men. Lincoln unexpectedly removed Fighting Joe Hooker and replaced him with 47-year-old Maj. Gen. George G. Meade, then commanding the V Corps. Meade was an 1835 West Point graduate, topographical engineer, Mexican War veteran, and career professional soldier. He was a steady, no-nonsense commander with a somewhat crusty personality. In deportment Meade was the complete antithesis of the cocky and flamboyant Hooker.

It is difficult to conceive of a leader assuming overall military command under more trying circumstances. Meade's promotion unfolded only three days before the largest three-day battle ever fought on the North American continent. Not surprisingly, Meade assumed command amidst self-doubt which he expressed in a hurried letter to his wife: "...it remains to be seen whether I have the capacity to handle successfully [such] a large army." Indeed, British historian Richard Holmes perhaps summed up Meade's sudden predicament best—"And if George Gordon Meade did not have the real opportunity of winning the war for the Union in July 1863, he had every chance of losing it." Lee, on the other hand, when soon learning of Meade's appointment, gave the new Union commander more credit. Lee prophesized, "General Meade will commit no blunder in my front, and if I make one he will make haste to take advantage of it."[16]

Meade concentrated his army of 95,000 men, divided into seven corps, near Frederick, Maryland, on June 29th. Next day he started marching them northward into Pennsylvania. In contrast, Lee's forces were widely separated. With Stuart's cavalry—who were normally the eyes of his army—away on an ill-timed and ill-advised raid around the Union army, Lee did not know the precise location of the large Union force to the east. Wisely he chose to quickly consolidate his army. Accordingly, on this same day, Ewell, who was then poised to seize the Pennsylvania capital of Harrisburg, received Lee's order to immediately rejoin the main army near Gettysburg.

June 30th saw Lee move his headquarters and march McLaws' and Hood's divisions 10 miles east to Greenwood. Lee left Pickett's division to hold Chambersburg. (The absence of Pickett's division at Gettysburg on July 2nd would have deadly consequences for Barksdale.) Barksdale's Mississippi Brigade reached Greenwood by 2 p.m., cooked three days' rations, and camped there for the night. They expected a relatively short march on the morrow over South Mountain to Cashtown or Gettysburg—only 15 miles away. Although McLaws had his division ready to start by 8 a.m. on July 1, 1863, Longstreet ordered them to wait for the passage of Johnson's division of the Second Corps, followed by Ewell's entire wagon train—some 14 miles long. As a result, McLaws' division did not get underway until 4 p.m. and slowly trudged along in a frustratingly slow stop-and-go fashion. They tramped along within a cloud of dust over a roadway liberally decorated with the excrement of thousands of horses and mules which had preceded them. McLaws' Confederates did not fall out to rest until midnight when they reached Marsh Creek about four miles west of Gettysburg.

By this time the first day's battle at Gettysburg was over. The battle had been heralded by the boom of artillery as Barksdale's brigade crested the mountain pass earlier that day about 5 p.m. The most significant result of this action was the manner in which it set the opposing battle lines which, in turn, determined Lee's battle plan for the next day. This battle plan, flawed from the outset, and executed with poor coordination, would seal Barksdale's fate.

The previous day had witnessed the sole occurrence of the destruction of personal property by the direct order of a Confederate officer—and it held significant meaning for William Barksdale. Another old nemesis in Congress, abolitionist and Radical Republican Thaddeus Stevens—against whom Barksdale had once angrily brandished his bowie knife on the floor of the House—owned a large ironworks a few miles west of Gettysburg. Called "Caledonia," it consisted of a large charcoal furnace, forge, rolling mill, coal house, shops and workers' houses. After confiscating all Stevens' horses and mules, Maj. Gen. Jubal Early, on his own initiative, ordered the entire facility (except for the workers' homes) to be put to the torch in retaliation for Stevens' virulent admonition to confiscate the property of slave owners in the South. According to contemporary newspaper reports, the damage inflicted exceeded $50,000. When the Mississippi Brigade marched past, all that remained were ashes and smoldering ruins. Despite his strong sense of fairness and capacity for forgiveness, it is not difficult to conclude that the wanton destruction of Stevens' treasured foundry, and the accompanying deep financial loss inflicted on this despised Black Republican abolitionist, would have elicited a strong sense of satisfaction and vindication within William Barksdale.[17]

The second day of battle at Gettysburg would exhibit amazing similarities to the bloody Confederate repulse at Malvern Hill suffered one year earlier. About 5 a.m. on July 2, the Mississippians were again on the march. McLaws, at the head of his division, arrived early that morning at Lee's headquarters on the Chambersburg Pike overlooking Gettysburg. Shortly thereafter Colonel Black rode along, passing "the brave General Barksdale sitting on a fence waiting for his brigade to come up." Recognizing Black, Barksdale offered his hand in friendship. In response to Black's cordial salutation, Barksdale replied that "he was unwell and felt badly," although the nature of his ailment that day remains unknown.[18] Whatever Barksdale's affliction that day, the exhilaration of combat would soon overcome its symptoms. Indeed, within hours Barksdale would rally to lead what eyewitnesses, both Confederate and Union, would invariably describe as "the most magnificent charge of the war." This attack would be perhaps Barksdale's finest moment as a commander—most certainly while on the offensive.

It was during these morning hours prior to 11 a.m. that Lee formulated his battle plan for the coming day. This late timeframe is indicative of the extreme state of flux and uncertainty surrounding the battle lines—a situation exacerbated by the absence of Stuart's cavalry. As additional infantry corps and artillery batteries from both armies continued to arrive from several directions and to deploy, Lee struggled to assimilate new information from several sources including his own personal observations. However, by default, he was forced to place his greatest confidence in the reconnaissance report of his engineer, Captain Samuel Johnston, whom he had dispatched with a few others to scout the enemy lines south of town before dawn.

The two armies had stumbled into one another by accident the previous day when Maj. Gen. Henry Heth's division of A.P. Hill's Third Corps had approached the crossroads town from the west. These Confederates were confronted by dismounted Union cavalrymen under command of Brig. Gen. John Buford. Although Lee had wished to avoid a general engagement before his entire army was concentrated, the arrival of Ewell's corps from the north in time to support Hill's attack from the west had presented the aggressive Lee with an opportunity he just could not pass up.

Despite Lee's initial misgivings, the engagement had soon escalated into a full-scale battle as additional units arrived and joined the fray. Despite having been driven back through the town in full retreat, the Union forces had rallied a defense on the high ground east and south of Gettysburg under the guidance of Maj. Gen. Winfield Scott Hancock. They dug in on Cemetery Hill and Culp's Hill and along a low crest—Cemetery Ridge—which extended some two miles south. This ridge terminated on two additional prominences—Little Round Top and the more heavily wooded and higher Big Round Top. This Union defensive line took the shape of a giant fishhook with Culp's/Cemetery Hills forming the barb and curve, Cemetery Ridge the shank, and the Round Tops the eye. Lee's forces were arrayed along a parallel ridge one mile to the west—Seminary Ridge—and extended around Culp's Hill on the extreme left of the Confederate line.

Located midway between the rival lines at the Union left/left-center—opposite the Confederate right flank—was the farm of Joseph Sherfy. It included his brick farmhouse, large barn, and, most importantly, his sizable peach orchard. Soon to become famous as "*The* Peach Orchard," this mature four-acre orchard was located southeast of the intersection of the Emmitsburg Road and Millerstown Road (subsequently known as Wheatfield Road). From a military perspective, the orchard's pre-eminent feature was that it sat on a knoll or elevated plateau some 20–30 feet higher than the surrounding countryside— with a commanding view in all directions. In short, the Peach Orchard comprised an excellent artillery platform—an attribute not lost on either army. For this reason it may be argued that the Peach Orchard more significantly influenced the manner in which the second day's battle unfolded than any of the other much more famous landmarks such as Little Round Top, Devil's Den, the Wheatfield, Culp's Hill, and Cemetery Hill. In short, this terrain feature essentially determined the battle plans and the location/direction of the opposing battle lines. To a great degree the Peach Orchard influenced nearly all phases of the battle that day.[19] It was precisely against this position that Barksdale launched his relentless attack.

Captain Johnston had reported back to Lee that morning that there were no Union troops present on Little Round Top or on Cemetery Ridge opposite the Sherfy farm. This clearly could not have been the case as Union troops had encamped in the fields near the Weikert farm northwest of Little Round Top during the previous night and continued to arrive from the south. Johnston's failure to observe any Union presence here remains a mystery. Based upon this faulty information, Lee concluded incorrectly that the Union left flank was "in the air" somewhere along Cemetery Ridge, or nearer the Emmitsburg Road, just south of Cemetery Hill.[20]

Thus, based upon a fallacy—and recognizing that by occupying the Peach Orchard "it was thought our artillery could be used to advantage in assailing the more elevated ground beyond, and thus enable us to reach the crest of the ridge" on Cemetery Hill—Lee decided to focus the main Confederate attack against this apparently unprotected Federal left flank. Simultaneously Ewell's corps would launch a diversionary assault against the Union right on Culp's and Cemetery Hills. Two divisions of Longstreet's corps would attack up the Emmitsburg Road in a perpendicular line, stepping off near Sherfy's peach orchard and driving northward. McLaws' division would initiate the attack, followed by Hood's division in support. When this assault reached the southern end of A.P. Hill's line along Seminary Ridge, the brigades of Maj. Gen. Richard H. Anderson's division would launch a frontal assault due eastward. (Anderson's division replaced Longstreet's absent division under Pickett who had remained behind at Chambersburg to secure the Confederate rear and had not yet arrived at Gettysburg.)[21]

From the very outset there was confusion amongst the Confederate high command regarding Lee's intentions. Lee reviewed his plan with McLaws around 11 a.m. As McLaws later related, Lee pointed out McLaws' assigned position with the instruction, "General, I wish you to place your division across this road ... and I wish you to get there if possible without being seen by the enemy." For emphasis in a later narrative McLaws added "and the line [Lee] marked out on the map for me to occupy was one *perpendicular* to the Emmitsburg Road" (emphasis added). McLaws offered to personally reconnoiter for a preferred route of march but was quickly overruled by Longstreet who was nearby and abruptly intervened with the words, "No, sir, I do not wish you to leave your division." Longstreet then pointed to the map and added, "I wish your division placed so—running his finger in a direction [*parallel* to the Emmitsburg Road] perpendicular to that pointed out previously by General Lee." Lee immediately corrected Longstreet, stating "No, General, I wish it placed just perpendicular to that, or just the opposite." At this point, perhaps attempting to diffuse the situation, McLaws reiterated his offer to scout a "hidden" path to the Sherfy peach orchard, but "General Longstreet again forbade it," preferring to rely solely on Captain Johnston. For the second time this day Lee's Engineer officer would fail miserably in his assigned task. McLaws saw fit to add the comment, "General Longstreet appeared as if he was irritated and annoyed."[22]

Barksdale's brigade spent the morning resting with their sister brigades of McLaws' division. They were stretched out in a long column, in-line with Hood's division, on Herr Ridge near Black Horse Tavern. Longstreet's temporary headquarters was close by, somewhere adjacent to the Fairfield Road. Under Barksdale's direction early that morning each of his Mississippians had been issued 20 extra cartridges. As veteran soldiers, they spent the balance of the morning eating from their haversacks, and in anticipation of the upcoming "bloody fray," cleaning and then clearing their rifles by discharging a percussion cap without a black powder load.[23]

After awaiting arrival of Brig. Gen. Evander M. Law's brigade of Hood's division, sometime between noon and 1 p.m. Longstreet finally ordered the march toward Sherfy's farm. McLaws rode at the head of the column with his assigned guide—the ubiquitous and failure-prone Captain Johnston who had been tasked by Lee to determine a line of march hidden from the enemy's view. With Kershaw's brigade in the van of McLaws' division, followed by Hood's division, they crossed the Fairfield Road and proceeded southward. The march progressed smoothly until they approached the crest of a hill on a road leading southeasterly to the Pitzer Schoolhouse. If the column continued on this route it woud be visible to Union signalmen on Little Round Top. The formation halted while Johnston and McLaws frantically sought a viable alternate route—but to no avail. The general became so frustrated that, in the words of one Mississippian within earshot, "McLaws was saying things I would not like to teach my grandson to repeat."[24]

By this time, the impatient Hood had overlapped the front of his column with the tail end of McLaws', intermingling the two divisions. The agreed upon solution was a time-consuming and vexatious countermarch back to where they started, followed by a more circuitous "hidden" route suggested by McLaws. However, instead of just reversing the column to put Hood's Division in the lead, McLaws stubbornly insisted that his division retain the honor of forming the van and later leading the attack. Somewhat surprisingly, Longstreet refused to overrule McLaws. Having already disagreed with Lee on strategy, Longstreet may simply have been reluctant to countermand Lee's direct instructions. Perhaps Hood had not been briefed in detail by Lee on the attack plan as thoroughly as McLaws had been. Some modern historians have even suggested that Longstreet believed that the delays incurred as these two divisions sorted themselves out and backtracked might become sufficient justification for his cancellation of the attack altogether.[25] Regardless, Longstreet's two divisions did not reach their assigned position until 4 p.m.—more than three hours later. The final irony is that Porter Alexander, who had moved Longstreet's artillery to the same position earlier that day along the same initial route, had avoided the crest of the hill simply by marching around it overland—in Alexander's words, "by turning out through a meadow."[26]

During this delay, the military situation near the Peach Orchard knoll had completely changed, giving rise to the well-known Meade-Sickles Controversy. That morning Meade had ordered Maj. Gen. Daniel E. Sickles, Commander of the III Corps, to extend the Union defensive line southward along Cemetery Ridge. Sickles' right flank would link with the left flank of General Hancock's II Corps immediately south of Cemetery Hill, while his left flank would be anchored on Little Round Top. Forty-three-year-old Daniel Sickles, a lawyer and prominent politico from New York's Tammany Hall, was the highest-ranking political general in the Union army and a force to be reckoned with. This was despite his being, in the words of one modern historian, "by the standards of any age, a shameless scoundrel."[27]

From his personal observations that morning, Sickles immediately concluded that his assigned position was a poor one for a variety of reasons. His utmost concern emanated from "the commanding ground" along the Emmitsburg Road Ridge, and particularly the Peach Orchard Knoll. If occupied by Confederate artillery, Sickles reckoned that Confederate cannon fire from the Peach Orchard platform would render his designated position untenable. Although Sickles was a political appointee and not a professional soldier, like Lee, he had made the same military assessment of the Peach Orchard as the ideal artillery platform.

Sickles had been unable to meet with Meade despite several attempts that morning. By 1 p.m., on his own initiative and in violation of his direct orders from Meade, Sickles decided to advance his III Corps with its artillery forward from Cemetery Ridge three-quarters of a mile to occupy the high ground along the Emmitsburg Road.

When completed, this maneuver resulted in an unorthodox and vulnerable defensive line as follows: The left flank rested at the boulder-strewn rock outcrop known as Devil's Den. The line then ran diagonally in a northwesterly direction along Houck's Ridge through the Wheatfield to the Peach Orchard. This half of the line was held by Maj. Gen. David B. Birney's 1st Division. At the Peach Orchard salient the line made a 90 degree turn and ran along the Emmitsburg Road connecting with the 2nd Division under Brig. Gen. Andrew A. Humphreys north of the Sherfy farm buildings. Humphreys' line then extended northward along

Maj. Gen. Daniel E. Sickles' decision to move his III Corps to the high ground at Sherfy's peach orchard confounded Lee's battle plan at Gettysburg on July 2, 1863, resulting in Barksdale's "most magnificent charge of the war" (Library of Congress).

the roadway with its right flank "in the air" near the Klingle house (unconnected to Hancock's left flank well to the rear along Cemetery Ridge).[28]

The relative merits and shortcomings of Sickles' action are still hotly debated by military historians. Despite strong arguments to the contrary based upon sound military principles, this author agrees with British historian John Keegan who concludes that Sickles deserves "much of the credit" for "blunting the whole Confederate offensive that was intended to collapse the Union line" on July 2nd. Keegan termed the resultant "deepening [of] the Union line precisely at the point where Lee planned to breach it" as "creative disobedience [on Sickles' part] since it frustrated a most dangerous stroke by the enemy."[29] Perhaps Sickles, himself, while later testifying before the Joint Committee on the Conduct of the War in 1864, stated it best—"It was either a good line or a bad one, and, whichever it was, I took it on my own responsibility...."[30] Maybe the most accurate assessment is that tactically it was an unsound line; however, strategically, its very presence both confounded Lee's attack plan and thoroughly disrupted Longstreet's attempt at its execution.

Expecting to be well beyond the Union left flank and thus facing no opposition whatsoever, McLaws' Confederates, with Kershaw's brigade in the lead, followed by Barksdale's Mississippians, were shocked at what they saw upon emerging from Pitzer's Woods. McLaws later wrote, "...the view presented astonished me, as the enemy was massed in my front, and extended to my right and left as far as I could see." Colonel Humphreys of the 21st Mississippi described the scene this way—"...it was unmistakably anything but the [enemy] flank. It was a formidable compact line of frowning artillery and bristling bayonets." McLaws continued: "Thus was presented a state of affairs which was certainly not contemplated when the original plan or order of battle was given, and certainly was not known to General Longstreet a half hour previous."

Coming under immediate artillery fire, instead of proceeding in columns of companies to mount the intended attack, McLaws' lead brigades sought shelter along Warfield Ridge (the southern extension of Seminary Ridge). McLaws later elaborated: "Kershaw, a very cool judicious and gallant gentleman, immediately turned the head of his column and marched by flank to the right, and put his men under cover of a stone wall" while "Barksdale, the fiery, impetuous Mississippian following, came into line on the left of Kershaw, his men sheltered by trees and under a gentle declivity."[31]

Almost immediately McLaws received a message via courier from Longstreet with a peremptory order to attack without delay. McLaws refused and sent for Longstreet who was not yet aware of the new circumstances. Observing the situation for himself, Longstreet immediately cancelled the attack order. Longstreet was under immense pressure to get the battle underway after a delay of at least five hours. He now desperately attempted to modify Lee's original battle plan according to these new developments while endeavoring to retain its essential components and intent. In an effort to reach the actual Federal left flank, he directed Hood's Division to proceed farther south along Warfield Ridge, past McLaws' position, and to initiate the attack toward Devil's Den and Little Round Top. This assault would be followed up, somewhat later, by McLaws' division at the Rose farm, the Wheatfield, and the Peach Orchard, thus transforming it from a mere flank attack into an *en echelon* offensive.

Using a prize-fighting metaphor, the attack would be a series of "right hooks" designed to draw Union defenders from their right to left against the point of attack until the Union line was sufficiently weakened to permit a Confederate breakthrough. At this point a "straight left" in the form of a frontal assault by Maj. Gen. Richard H. Anderson's division of Lt. Gen. A.P. Hill's corps would fully exploit the piercing of the Union defensive line. However, the attack would now be mounted from a battle line *parallel* to the Emmitsburg Road and not *perpendicular* to it as originally envisioned by Lee. Furthermore, Longstreet modified this offensive from en echelon by *division* to one by *brigade*—a change which would have very disastrous results for both Kershaw's South Carolinians and Barksdale's Mississippians.[32]

Lee's original plan of attack had been based on faulty reconnaissance and clearly could not be executed to the letter given the Union defensive line now visible to Longstreet. Coupled with vocal opposition from both Hood and McLaws, a strong case can be made that Longstreet (even despite Lee's direct order) would have been justified in postponing the attack and conferring with Lee. Post-war, McLaws made a compelling argument for this alternate course of action.[33] The decision to stubbornly proceed—albeit on a revised basis—is likely the worst error in judgment of many Longstreet made this day. Longstreet's determination to launch the attack anyway doomed hundreds of Confederates in his First Corps, including Barksdale.

It was obvious to both sides that the Peach Orchard salient was the key to the impending action. As such, Meade now sought to bolster its defense by directing his Chief of Artillery, Brig. Gen. Henry J. Hunt, to post additional artillery support there. Similarly, Colonel Alexander was ordered by Longstreet to deploy his artillery pieces to neutralize the Union cannon at the salient and to support the eventual infantry attack there. Given the clear lines of sight, and the relatively short range of approximately 500–800 yards, this prelude soon erupted into what is considered the greatest artillery counter-battery "gunfight" of the war—eclipsing the "artillery hell" of Sharpsburg. Close enough to aim, fire, actually hit each other and see the effects, battery targeted battery—while any unfortunate infantry units hunkered down nearby endured horrendous casualties as part of the collateral damage.[34]

Unfortunately for the Mississippians, Barksdale's brigade suffered this consequence in the extreme. McLaws had instructed Alexander to position Cabell's Battery south of the Millerstown Road *between* Kershaw's and Barksdale's brigades. When Longstreet arrived on the scene, he ordered that two batteries be placed close to and *directly in front of* Barksdale's position. McLaws immediately protested to Longstreet—"General, if a battery is placed there it will draw the enemy's artillery [fire] right among my lines formed for the charge, and will of itself be in the way of my charge, and tend to demoralize my men."[35] However, Longstreet insisted, and soon Capt. George V. Moody's four 24-pounder howitzers of Louisiana's Madison Light Artillery, and to its left, Lt. S. Capers Gilbert's four 12-pounder howitzers from South Carolina's Brooks Artillery, were placed directly in front of Barksdale's right wing.

As anticipated by McLaws, the devastating result was instantaneous and was later described by a survivor from the 21st Mississippi: "I remember vividly the effects of the first shot from the [Union] battery in our front…. The shell exploded in the ranks of my company near me. J.T. Worley was killed and Captain H.H. Simmons, John H. Thomson and John T. Neely each lost a leg but survived the war. By the same shot, there were other casualties but I did not recall the names and companies of those killed and wounded." The Union battery inflicting this damage was Battery E, First Rhode Island Light Artillery under command of 1st Lt. John K. Bucklyn, a future Medal of Honor Winner. Bucklyn deployed his six bronze Napoleons along the Emmitsburg Road among the Sherfy farm buildings approximately 150 yards north of the Wentz log house and farmyard at the road intersection.[36]

The severe pounding in front of Barksdale's position soon took its toll on the Confederate artillery posted there—with repercussions for eight members of the 17th Mississippi. Alexander later related, "so accurate was the enemy's fire, that two of my guns were fairly dismounted, and the loss of [artillery]men was so great that I had to ask General Barksdale whose brigade was lying down close behind in the wood, for help to handle the heavy 24-pounder howitzers of Moody's battery. He gave me permission to ask for volunteers, and in a minute I had eight good fellows of whom alas! we buried two that night and sent to the hospital three others mortally or severely wounded." Private Abernathy provided names of four of these volunteers in his memoir.[37] It is most probable that these eight volunteers were members of the 17th Mississippi who had been trained on the heavy siege guns within the earthen forts at Leesburg under direction of Captain Stiles almost two years earlier. Losses in Gilbert's Battery, just to the left, were the highest on the battlefield with 40 artillerymen killed or wounded of the 75 manning the guns.[38]

The Confederates were not the only ones to suffer under the intense bombardment. Union diaries and regimental histories invariably echo the universal sentiment of the infantryman. The 57th Pennsylvania was lying prone in a field a few rods in back of the Sherfy house east of the Emmitsburg Road—the 105th Pennsylvania to its right and the 114th Pennsylvania to its left. Their regimental chronicle read in part: "For two hours we lay here under the hottest fire of artillery we had as yet been subjected to. The enemy had some thirty pieces of artillery planted on the ridge to the south and west of us, hurling their missiles toward us as fast as they could work their guns ... but to stay there so long under that howling, shrieking storm of shot and shell was more trying to the nerves than to be engaged in close action with the enemy." Even the batterymen were impressed by the pandemonium created by the combined total of over 80 guns. Bugler Charles Reed of the 9th Massachusetts Battery, one of five deployed in a line along the north side of the Wheatfield Road facing south, wrote, "...such a shrieking, hissing, seething I never dreamed was imaginable ... it seemed as though it must be the work of the very devil himself ... their fire about this time was tremendous ... the roar of which was deafening." One observer recorded a bizarre occurrence which added to the surrealism of the scene: "When the cannonade was at its height, a Confederate band of music ... began to play polkas and waltzes, which sounded very curious, accompanied by the hissing and bursting of the shells."[39]

Union shells continued to explode within Pitzer's Woods, shearing off tree limbs, which inflicted further casualties amongst the Mississippians lying upon the ground. Barksdale seethed at their predicament and sought permission to remedy it. Twice before, at Malvern Hill and again at Fredericksburg, his brigade had endured severe artillery fire with no recourse. However this scenario was different. Bucklyn's Battery—the source of their misery—was clearly visible only some 600 yards away and, in Barksdale's mind, was his for the taking. Two or three times Barksdale approached McLaws with the entreaty, "General let me go; let me charge!" McLaws later recorded: "But as I was [a] waiting General Longstreet's will, I told General Barksdale to wait...."

Unfortunately, as a result of McLaws' lackluster performance and dearth of leadership during the Chancellorsville campaign—especially at the battle of Salem Church— Lee had lost confidence in McLaws and (unbeknownst to McLaws) had directed

Longstreet to personally supervise his division this day. McLaws chafed under Longstreet's close oversight, regarding it as unmerited interference. In a rare exhibition of emotion five days later, in a letter to his wife, McLaws vented his spleen against Longstreet's' heavy handedness—"During the engagement [Longstreet] was really excited giving constantly orders to everyone, and was exceedingly overbearing. I consider him a *humbug*, a man of small capacity, very obstinate, not at all chivalrous, exceedingly conceited, and totally selfish."[40] Such was the level of dysfunction amongst the Confederate High Command on this day.

When Longstreet came near while inspecting the Confederate line, the aggressive Barksdale seized his opportunity and boldly petitioned Longstreet directly—"I wish you would let me go in General; I would take that battery in five minutes." An eyewitness, Capt. William M. Owen of the Washington Artillery, recorded Longstreet's brief response—"Wait a little, we are all going in presently." Dismayed, Barksdale turned to Owen, shook his hand, and in reference to their earlier action at Second Fredericksburg, coolly commented, "I hope we have better luck this time with your guns than we had on Marye's Hill."[41]

By this time Hood's division, still not beyond the Union left flank, began their assault towards Devil's Den and Little Round Top. This advance prompted Union artillery posted along Wheatfield Road (Captain Judson Clark's 1st New Jersey long-range Parrot rifled guns, Patrick Hart's 15th New York Independent Battery, Captain Charles Phillips' 5th Massachusetts Battery, Capt. John Bigelow's 9th Massachusetts Battery, and Capt. James Thompson's Pennsylvania Batteries C & F) to switch targets to Hood's infantry ranks. One licensed Gettysburg Battlefield guide asserts it was a shot from Clark's battery—some 1,400 yards away—which disabled General Hood—one round of 1,342 that the battery fired this day.[42]

Longstreet allowed Hood's attack to proceed on its own for almost one hour with no support from McLaws' division. Unfortunately for both Hood and later McLaws, Alexander failed to achieve his primary task of neutralizing the Union artillery prior to the Confederate infantry attacks. Alexander failed despite several key advantages—converging and flanking fire, superiority in number of guns available, and close proximity of reserve ammunition. Alexander came close to admitting as much in a postwar summation of this action:

Col. Edward Porter Alexander, artillery battalion commander in Longstreet's First Corps (Francis T. Miller's *Photographic History of the Civil War*, Volume 2).

I had hoped with my 54 guns & close range to make it short, sharp & decisive. At close ranges there was less inequality in our guns, & especially in our ammunition, & I thought that if ever I could overwhelm and crush them I would do it now. But they really surprised me, both with the number of guns they developed, & the way they stuck to them. I don't think there was ever in our war a hotter, harder, sharper artillery afternoon than this.[43]

Now Longstreet's infantrymen would pay a heavy price in blood for Alexander's shortcomings this day.

During this time some of Barksdale's Mississippians filled canteens from a little stream in rear of Pitzer's Woods while others sampled cherries from numerous trees nearby. Each regiment piled their blanket rolls in a heap and posted a single guard.[44] Barksdale, for his part, took this opportunity to say what he probably believed would be his final prayer. This is not surprising given the situation he faced that afternoon. In a very short time, his brigade would emerge from the edge of Pitzer Woods and charge the line of Union infantry and artillery at the Peach Orchard salient. By order, all field officers below the rank of brigadier general (excepting personal aides and couriers) would be dismounted due to the difficulty of replacing horses killed. Thus the few mounted officers, which included Barksdale, became more conspicuous targets—Barksdale especially so since he would lead in advance of his Mississippians.[45]

A Georgia private from Wofford's brigade observed Barksdale's simple act of petition behind the Confederate line and later described the scene:

> General Barksdale came back to near where I stood, hidden by the undergrowth, and stepping behind a large white oak tree, uncovered his head, and with his right hand and face lifted up, began his silent prayer. I could see his lips move, but heard no sound. Before his devotions were ended a courier came with an order. One of his aides went to him and touched him and gave him the message. He replaced his cap, walked rapidly to his horse, mounted, and gave the order.[46]

For a few brief moments Barksdale had sought God's blessing on both the Confederate cause this day for a victory that might very well win the war, and for the contribution he would make to achieving it. No doubt he also prayed for the continued safeguarding of his beloved wife and two sons back in Mississippi. Having made his peace with God, Barksdale now resolutely set his mind to the daunting task at hand.

It is important to understand the mindset of Barksdale's brigade and its leader that day in order to explain their almost superhuman effort and accomplishments against overwhelming odds. The morale and confidence of the Army of Northern Virginia had never been higher as reflected in the opinions recorded by numerous participants and observers of Lee's invasion. Alexander wrote that "[Lee] carried the best and largest army into Pennsylvania that he ever had in hand" and further observed that this deepest penetration of the North now put them "somehow nearer the enemy's heart than we had ever been before." He continued, "There seemed to be a prevalent feeling that fortune now favored us and that victory or defeat depended solely on ourselves."[47] Arthur J. Freemantle, a visiting captain from Britain's Coldstream Guards, present on July 2nd, commented, "the universal feeling in [Lee's] army was one of profound contempt for an enemy whom they have beaten so constantly, and under so many disadvantages."[48] A member of the 21st Mississippi later wrote of Barksdale's Mississippians at this moment, "Never was a body of soldiers fuller of the spirit of fight, and the confidence of victory."[49]

In reference to Barksdale's remarkable attack at Gettysburg, British historian Richard Holmes has insightfully observed that battles are not always decided by "the inevitable supremacy of sheer numbers" because combat is "an affair of the human spirit, played out in an environment characterized by chance and uncertainty."[50] The importance of visible, unflinching leadership, amidst the confusion and chaos on the battlefield, cannot be overstated. William Barksdale demonstrated just such superb leadership on this day.

There was one other primary motivation here at Gettysburg, unique to Barksdale and his brigade within the Army of Northern Virginia. These Mississippians still smarted from the breaching of their line two months earlier at Marye's Heights. Moreover, Barksdale yet chafed at the personal criticism and accusations leveled at him by Jubal Early during their bitter public quarrel in the press. For Barksdale, his officers, and the men in the ranks, restoration of their collective reputation weighed heavily on their minds. It was of paramount importance now and drove them on with a burning passion to prevail in what was generally regarded by these Confederate soldiers to be "the decisive battle of the war … [one which] would be stubborn and bloody." Not surprisingly then, when Private John Seymour McNeily of Co. E, 21st Mississippi later recalled his last view of Barksdale riding along the battle line he focused on Barksdale's grim demeanor, writing, "impressions of his appearance are indelible. Stamped on his face, and in his bearing, as he rode by, was determination 'to do or die.'"[51]

McLaws' division was arrayed in a double line, with Kershaw's Brigade (2,200 men) on the right backed up by Semmes' Georgia Brigade (1,330 men) while Barksdale's Brigade (1,420 men) fronted the left with Wofford's Georgia Brigade (1,630 men) in support, 150 yards behind.[52] Thus Longstreet's intent was to attack in a battle line two brigades

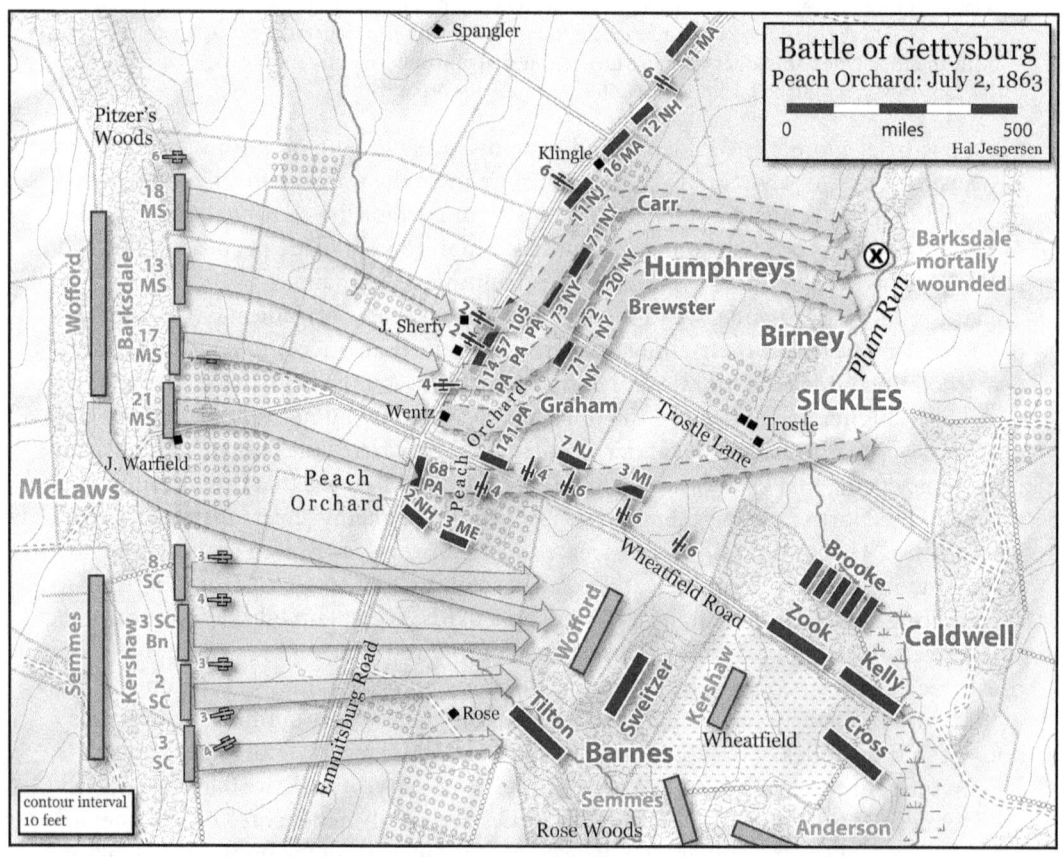

Gettysburg, July 2, 1863—Barksdale's Charge at Peach Orchard

deep along the entire front. According to postwar writings by Kershaw, it was his clear understanding from "instructions received in sundry messages from both General Longstreet and McLaws, and in part by personal communication with them," that McLaws' entire division would advance simultaneously and that "Barksdale would move with me and conform to my movement; that Semmes would follow me, and *Wofford follow Barksdale*" (emphasis added). However, this is clearly not how events unfolded.

Sometime after 5 p.m. Cabell's artillery paused and then fired three guns in rapid succession—the prearranged signal for Kershaw's South Carolinians to step off followed by Semmes' Georgians. According to numerous eyewitnesses including Kershaw, "Longstreet accompanied me in this advance on foot, as far as the Emmitsburg Road." At this point, Kershaw later recorded, "I heard Barksdale's drums beat the assembly" and much to his dismay, "knew then that I should have no immediate support on my left" which soon came under "severe fire from Union artillery and infantry at, and in rear of, the Peach Orchard."[53]

This delay of Barksdale's advance has puzzled historians to this day and is mystifying in view of Barksdale's impetuous nature and his repeated requests (up to an hour earlier) for permission to charge Bucklyn's Battery. Possible explanations have included Barksdale being unaware of the signal guns, a decision by Longstreet to delay, "the absence of a controlling hand," or some unknown mischance. What is known for certain is that at least part of this delay was due to Barksdale's (and then Wofford's) brigade becoming entangled with the artillery batteries placed in their front by order of General Longstreet. Just as he had predicted, McLaws later related, "[These two brigades] had been mixed up with the batteries which had been placed among their lines, and were temporarily delayed in extricating themselves." He added that one of Wofford's regiments was so detained that it fell behind the rest of the brigade by "about one hundred yards."[54]

Hawley also makes a plausible argument that further delay was caused in merely attempting to get Moody's and Gilbert's Batteries from Alexander's Artillery Reserve (a separate command from Cabell's First Corps artillery) to cease their firing after Cabell's prearranged signal. Ultimately both Hawley (and Alexander before him) attribute this costly lack of coordination to a breakdown "in the command and control arena." Hawley blamed McLaws. Alexander blamed Longstreet and the lack of an adequate staff organization within Lee's army with the stinging indictment, "Few battles can furnish examples of worse tactics."[55]

To the rousing cheers of the Confederate artillerymen Barksdale's brigade eventually stepped out of the woods and over the stone wall, forming in line with the regiments arranged from left to right as follows: 18th, 13th, 17th, and 21st.[56] After his brief prayer Barksdale rode behind the entire line from left to right, thereby signaling the regimental commanders to get ready for action. As he rounded the right end, Barksdale called out to remind Colonel Humphreys to move forward and "swing to the left." Barksdale then continued to canter down the line facing his men until he stopped in front of the 13th Mississippi. It was Barksdale's custom to lead his brigade into battle from a position in close proximity to the 13th Mississippi—his old regiment. Barksdale immediately barked out the following command: Halt! Front! Order Arms! Load! Fix Bayonets!

Then, as he had done so effectively at Sharpsburg, Barksdale again attempted to motivate his troops through his oratorical skills and powers of persuasion. One of his veterans later recalled the General's brief address: "The intrenchment 500 yards in front of you and the red barn and that park of artillery ... and besides that entrenched line there is another 200 yards beyond which we are also expected to take. This is a heroic undertaking and most of us will bite the dust making this effort; now if there is a man here that feels this is too much for him just step two paces to the front and I will excuse him." Then switching to the tactics to be employed, Barksdale stated, "We will proceed to within 75 yards of the entrenchment, withholding our fire. There you will receive the command, halt, ready, fire! Then without command you will charge with the bayonet."[57]

Only Barksdale's Mississippians charged that day in close order formation (i.e. shoulder to shoulder) on a narrow 350-yard front, bounded on the brigade's right by the Peach Orchard (targeted by the 21st Mississippi) and on the left by the Sherfy house and barn (targeted by the 18th Mississippi). The 13th and 17th regiments struck the "intermediate line" of the enemy in between. Thus Barksdale willingly exchanged a higher initial casualty rate for maximum shock value at the point of impact in order to break the Union line at the salient.[58]

Barksdale had always exhibited a tall and robust physique. However, now six weeks shy of his 42nd birthday—with fair complexion, clean shaven, bald on top, and thin sandy hair now turned pure white and flowing down to his shoulders—Barksdale exhibited a middle-age spread such that a contemporary kindheartedly described him as being "large, rather heavily built." As noted previously, Barksdale was not graceful when mounted in the saddle. However, a member of the 21st Mississippi noted "[Barksdale's] forward, impetuous bearing, especially in battle, overshadowed and more than made up for such deficiencies."

In describing Barksdale's appearance on July 2, 1863, Private McNeily stated, "he had a very thirst for battlefield glory, to lead his brigade in the charge."[59] This statement has perhaps been the most often quoted reference to Barksdale, and (unfortunately) continues to be so. It is this author's considered opinion that McNeily's misinterpretation of Barksdale's true motivation has led to a popular misconception of Barksdale as being vainglorious—in the same way George Armstrong Custer is viewed by most. However, Barksdale's actions throughout his life are at odds with this inference. Barksdale clearly was not seeking personal glory nor fame this day. Rather—like the rest of his brigade—he was seeking a major Confederate victory which in the minds of many (including Barksdale himself) might very well end the war and gain independence for the Confederacy. In leading his soldiers to victory he would also restore the illustrious reputation of Barksdale's Mississippi Brigade that had been tarnished at Second Fredericksburg three months earlier.

In fact, he was already well known—most would say famous in the South, infamous in the North—as a result of his active and vocal participation in Congress on behalf of states' rights and slavery. Moreover, it was clearly not in his nature to self-aggrandize his personal accomplishments including those of a military nature. In all of his after-action battle reports there is not a single instance where he took personal credit or embellished his own actions (although there were many instances where he could have done this if so inclined—Malvern Hill, Sharpsburg, Fredericksburg come to mind). Instead, Barksdale invariably gave credit to the officers and enlisted men of his beloved brigade of Mississippians, often singling them out by name. Personal aides, couriers, and surgeons often merited special mention in his reports. Had he survived Gettysburg, his after-action report would have been no exception.

Another one of "Barksdale's Boys" pointedly contradicted McNeily's assertion in a post-war magazine article. This member of the 18th Mississippi characterized Barksdale as "Just as far removed from military hauteur as one could imagine. He was not a military man, but was a pure type of genuine southern chivalry, a southern gentleman of the old school." In support this soldier cited the following occurrence: "We were in camp, it was one summer evening. Gen. Cobb, of Georgia, his old friend and former fellow Congressman, had dined with [Gen. Barksdale]. We were drilling, when the two Generals, arm in arm, coats off, came walking out to look on. It reminded me very forcibly of two farmers in antebellum days taking an afternoon stroll through the farm to look at the crop."[60]

The formidable Union defensive line of Sickle's III Corps here at the Peach Orchard was comprised of the six Pennsylvania regiments of Brig. Gen. Charles K. Graham's First Brigade of Birney's 1st Division who were now defending the soil of their home state—always a great motivator. They were arrayed from south to north along the east side of Emmitsburg Road as follows: 68th Pennsylvania (south of the Wheatfield Road intersection), 114th Pennsylvania, Collis' Zouaves, 57th, 105th, and finally the 141st Pennsylvania as a reserve in rear along the north side of Wheatfield Road. The 63rd Pennsylvania were deployed as skirmishers in the open fields on the west side of Emmitsburg Road.

Sickles had hurriedly dispatched reinforcements to this sector, taking Col. George C. Burling's 3rd Brigade out of Brig. Gen. Andrew A. Humphrey's 2nd Division line to the right of Graham's position along Emmitsburg Road and putting them at Birney's disposal. Thus the 2nd New Hampshire joined the 68th Pennsylvania at the left of the line in the Peach Orchard, while the 7th New Jersey joined the 141st Pennsylvania in the rear reserve. Birney also placed the 3rd Maine from Brig. Gen. J.H. Hobart Ward's 2nd Brigade from his own 1st Division as skirmishers in the Peach Orchard.

Thus Barksdale's four Mississippi regiments, totaling 1,420 men, were initially assaulting nine Union regiments comprising about 3,000 infantry who were supported by two-and-a-half artillery batteries (10 cannon) along the Emmitsburg Road facing west (Captain Ames' 1st New York, Captain Bucklyn's 1st Rhode Island, and two guns of Captain Thompson's Independent Pennsylvania Artillery).[61] If numbers alone dictated the outcome, Barksdale's assault would be quickly repulsed. However, Barksdale's "fiery mettle flamed high" and with his "forward, impetuous bearing" as the "guiding spirit of the battle," seemingly 50 yards in advance of his line, the Mississippi juggernaut was about to finally kick the door in along the Federal left at the Peach Orchard.[62]

Anyone—whether Confederate or Union—who witnessed the charge of Barksdale and his Mississippians that day never forgot it. With the indelible memory imprinted on their minds invariably they spoke of it in glowing terms. A senior staff officer with Barksdale confirmed that he wore "a Confederate gray uniform and [carried] a soft black felt hat [and] he rode a bay horse," while another veteran, T.M. Scranton, later recalled that "[Barksdale] had a bright red sash around his waist four inches wide" under his sword belt.

When Longstreet finally released Barksdale from his torment under Bucklyn's cannonade, McLaws dispatched his aide-de-camp, Georgia Capt. G.B. Lamar, with the order to attack. Lamar later recalled:

> When I carried [Barksdale] the order to advance his face was radiant with joy. He was in front of his brigade, hat off, and his long white hair [shoulder length] reminded me of the "white plume of Navarre." I saw him as far as the eye could follow still ahead of his men, leading them on.... I had witnessed many charges marked in every way by unflinching gallantry—but I never saw anything equal to the dash and heroism of the Mississippians.[63]

Similarly, Pvt. George Clark of Wilcox's Alabama brigade, positioned north of Barksdale's left flank, recalled the scene in a post-war article in the *Confederate Veteran* magazine:

"…Barksdale threw forward his Mississippians in an unbroken line in the most magnificent charge I witnessed during the war, and led by the gallant Barksdale who seemed to be fifty yards in front of his brave boys—the scene was grand beyond description." These Alabamians were ordered "to move rapidly by the left flank … at full speed until space was cleared sufficient for the Mississippians … then with right face the brigade moved forward to the assault."[64]

Even amongst the opposing Union defenders, this assault by Barksdale's Mississippi Brigade was so impressive that its memory remained fresh long after the war. Typical of their recollections was a quote by a Union colonel stationed at the Peach Orchard who commented many years later at a Gettysburg Reunion: "I am sure it was the grandest charge that was ever seen by mortal man. Nothing we could do seemed to confuse or halt Barksdale's veterans.… You just came on, and on, and on … the carnage you inflicted on us boys in blue would be impossible to detail.… I would like to shake the hand of every member of the Barksdale brigade who is here today, and I now and here pass this encomium upon them, that they are the bravest men I ever met or ever expect to meet."[65]

Private McNeily described the scene: "Next came the ringing command—'Double quick charge,' and at top speed, [shrieking the Rebel Yell] at the top of their voices, without firing a shot, the brigade sped swiftly across the field and literally rushed the goal." Now these Mississippians began to take dreadful casualties from rifle and cannon fire. A Union infantry officer later recalled their bravery and discipline under fire—"…besides the mischief done by the sharpshooters and pickets the 10 guns were hurling missiles of death into your ranks and swept gaps through them all the way across the field, and when a solid shot tore a gap in your ranks, it was instantly closed up, and the brigade came on in almost perfect line." In the words of a Confederate contemporary, the Union skirmish line, then aligned along a rail fence several hundred yards west of the Emmitsburg Road, was immediately "[swept] before them like chaff before a whirlwind." The 63rd Pennsylvania, who formed this skirmish line, having exhausted their ammunition, was unwisely sent to the rear.[66] When in range, the Mississippians leveled their rifles and delivered a devastating volley into the Union ranks and batteries all along the line. For Barksdale the time for retribution against Bucklyn's Battery had now arrived.

Targeted by both Alexander's Confederate cannon and now Barksdale's infantry, Bucklyn and his batterymen had taken a beating and now feared being captured. Bucklyn made a direct appeal to their infantry support—Collis' 114th Pennsylvania who were in rear of the guns—to advance across the Emmitsburg Road and meet the 17th Mississippi head-on in order to allow the battery to escape. The advance was bravely and quickly made while Bucklyn's guns limbered up and began to withdraw. But this thorn in Barksdale's side paid a heavy price that day—29 officers and men were killed or wounded along with 40 horses lost—highest casualty rate within Sickles' III Corps artillery. Bucklyn, who had two horses shot beneath him, and who suffered a shrapnel wound to his left shoulder which would incapacitate him for six months, later bitterly commented, "My battery [was] torn and shattered and my brave boys have gone never to return. Curse the Rebs." Seeing their sister regiment advance, the 57th Pennsylvania and 105th Pennsylvania also crossed to the west side of the Emmitsburg Road to contest the advance of the 13th and 18th Mississippi. This move not only protected the right flank of the 114th Pennsylvania but gained these two regiments better cover and firing positions amongst the Sherfy house and farm buildings and shielded Federal cannon positions near the house.[67]

The 18th Mississippi under Colonel Griffin engaged the Federal forces in and around the two-story brick Sherfy house and barn. Members of the 57th Pennsylvania took up firing positions within the house and "kept up a steady fire from the west windows … and for a while … had the best of the fight owing to [their] sheltered position." However, as the Mississippians closed in their fierce fusillade had a telling effect. A Union veteran remembered, "Every door, window, and sash of the Sherfy house was shivered to atoms." The adjacent barn became "riddled like a sieve from base to roof, and cannon shot at every instant split its boards and timbers into showers of kindling wood."

To Griffin's right, the 13th Mississippi advanced in line against the Collis Zouaves. A Mississippi private later stated: "Some of us scaled the fences and some tore them down. Both fences and Zouaves disappeared quicker than I could possible give an account of it." However, upon reaching the Emmitsburg Road the scene changed drastically. This soldier continued: "Oh that Turn Pike, that death trap, a perfect torrent of death racing down it. Our losses were very heavy there. Our Col. [James W.] Carter was killed in it while urging his men not to stop in it, but to cross over into the field beyond." Carter was struck by four rifle balls. In postwar letters to Gettysburg historian John B. Bachelder a captured member of the 114th Pennsylvania, Pvt. William A. Boggs, misidentified Carter as General Barksdale. This error caused some confusion as to the location where Barksdale received his mortal wound.[68]

Meanwhile on Barksdale's extreme right, Kershaw's South Carolinians had suffered mightily under the Union cannon firing southward from the Wheatfield Road. From the vicinity of the Rose farm these South Carolinians fired upon the 3rd Maine and 2nd New Hampshire defending the south end of the Peach Orchard. As part of Barksdale's assault Col. Benjamin Humphreys and the 21st Mississippi attacked the 68th Pennsylvania defending the Peach Orchard along the east side of the Emmitsburg Road. At the same time the 17th Mississippi assaulted the 68th Pennsylvania's right flank and the pressure became overwhelming. Captain Nelson Ames' 1st New York Light Artillery Battery, having exhausted their ordnance and fearing imminent capture, quickly withdrew as other nearby batteries prepared to evacuate. Unleashing deadly volleys at close range, and sounding the high-pitched Rebel Yell, the 21st Mississippi surged forward. With understatement, Colonel Humphreys described this critical action with these few words—"The 21st regiment struck the Peach Orchard and forced its way through passing over and leaving behind artillery caissons, six in number, and emerged into the open field." This brief description belies the ferocity and critical importance of this action.

Most Union troops courageously mounted a fighting withdrawal, rallying at the midpoint and then the eastern edge of the orchard. They absorbed severe casualties in the process. The 2nd New Hampshire suffered 193 killed, wounded, or captured out of 380 engaged. The 141st Pennsylvania, detached from its brigade, received no order to withdraw and finally stood alone. In the words of its commander, Col. Henry John Madill— "[We] suffered a devastating volley from one of Barksdale's Mississippi Regiments and after a brief resistance withdrew towards Cemetery Ridge." This regiment suffered 149 casualties (71 percent)—including the entire color party—amongst the 209 men present for duty. General Graham suffered a severe shoulder wound but initially refused to abandon the field and was soon captured.[69]

At the same time, the 17th Mississippi struck the left flank of the 114th Pennsylvania at the Wentz farmhouse near the road junction and broke through the Union defenses. This now placed Confederate infantry from both the 21st and 17th Mississippi in the left rear of the Union line along the Emmitsburg Road. Barksdale, in accordance with his general instruction to his regimental officers earlier that day to "swing to the left," commenced a left wheel up the Emmitsburg Road (as per Lee's original battle plan). Barksdale's shrieking Mississippians swept toward the remaining regiments of Graham's brigade which soon "tumbled like dominoes" in the words of historian Stephen Sears. Captain Edward R. Bowen now valiantly tried to rally the 114th Pennsylvania Zouaves—but to no avail. Bowen described the action: "as the enemy had already advanced so quickly and in such force as to gain the road and, pouring a murderous fire on our flank, threw the left wing of the regiment on to the right in much confusion ... my men falling in such numbers." In reference to the gaudy zouave uniforms, a Confederate officer celebrated the collapse of Sickles' line here in a disparaging tone—"The volleys from the 18th and 13th [Mississippi] literally covered the plain with *red breeches*" (emphasis added) while "the 17th regiment moved directly on in hot pursuit of the luckless 'skedadlers' and closed up on the right of the 13th regiment."

During this action Major Gerald led members of the 18th Mississippi in assaulting the Sherfy barn occupied by riflemen of the 114th Pennsylvania. Gerald later recalled, "[My men] followed me with a rush and I forced the door open, and within less than two minutes we had killed, wounded or captured every man in the barn." (Next day a Union shell would set the barn ablaze and it burned to the ground, incinerating the unfortunate Union wounded and dead still trapped inside.) The Union collapse here was so sudden that members of the 57th Pennsylvania posted inside the Sherfy house (despite attempts by Captain Nelson to order them to fall back) "kept on firing from the windows" after their comrades had withdrawn until "they were summoned to surrender by the rebels who came up the stairs in their rear."[70]

Graham's remaining regiment, the 105th Pennsylvania "Wildcats" next in line to the north, changed front 90 degrees, deploying across the Emmitsburg Road. Assisted by the six Napoleons of Lt. Francis W. Seely's 4th United States Battery positioned further north at the Trostle Lane, they attempted to stem the Mississippi tidal wave. Earlier Sickles had also hurriedly dispatched the 73rd New York Fire Zouaves from Andrew Humphreys' 2nd Division to bolster Graham's line. They were deployed in the open field east of the Emmitsburg Road one hundred yards in rear of the 114th Pennsylvania's position. Captain Frank E. Moran of the 73rd New York observed that the 114th Pennsylvania Collis Zouaves "though fearfully exposed on that deadly crest were bravely disputing the ground with the Mississippi brigade, which came swarming up the slope, yelling like devils and led by Barksdale." Having to withhold their fire for what must have seemed an eternity until the fleeing Zouaves cleared their front, these New York firemen unleashed "a volley at the [Mississippians] who fell in scores among the dead and wounded Pennsylvanians." Staggered by this "fresh fire," Barksdale's men "waved their flags, cheered, and returned [the] volley." This supporting Union line was soon ordered to fall back as "[Union] wounded in hundreds went streaming back over the Emmitsburg Road." Unfortunately Captain Moran had been wounded and could not withdraw—"...I waited in a tornado of bullets and shells on my one good leg and my painful eye, until the 13th Mississippi, came over me cheering and firing ... as [they] passed over me a fresh and terrible volley hissed through them from the front ... and scores of [Rebels] went down."[71]

The 105th Pennsylvania put up a valiant defense across the turnpike and actually countercharged to stop the Mississippians in their tracks. The impetus of this counterattack temporarily pushed Barksdale's Mississippians back to near the Sherfy house. In the

Joseph Sherfy house. Soldiers of the 57th Pennsylvania fired at the onrushing 18th Mississippi from upstairs windows (author photograph).

words of their colonel, the Wildcats had "fought like demons," rallying numerous times under their battle cry of "Pennsylvania!" Despite this momentary setback, all the hours of drilling over the past two-plus years under Barksdale's strict code of discipline would now pay great dividends. Catching their breath, and under close supervision of their line officers, Barksdale's men regained their momentum. The Mississippians soon overlapped both flanks of the 105th Pennsylvania and sent the Union survivors scurrying to the rear.

Barksdale and the hard driving 18th, 13th, and 17th Mississippi Regiments now enveloped the exposed left flank of Brig. Gen. Andrew A. Humphreys' 2nd Division of Sickles' III Corps held by Brig. Gen. Joseph B Carr's 1st Brigade. Humphreys was a no-nonsense 53-year-old West Point graduate and career soldier who had little use for Dan Sickles—and even less for his tactics on this particular day that Humphreys termed "disgusting." It was around this time that Sickles was struck in the right leg by a solid shot which would necessitate its amputation above the knee. An officer from the II Corps wryly commented, "The loss of [Sickles'] leg is a great gain to us, whatever it may be to him." Andrew A. Humphreys no doubt fully agreed with this assessment. Command of the III Corps then evolved to General Birney, but soon at Meade's insistence, was transferred to Maj. Gen. Winfield Scott Hancock, commander of the II Corps. For the first time this afternoon, command of the entire Union left wing was consolidated under one senior (and outstanding) officer—with telling effect.

With several of his regiments having already been drawn off to bolster Sickles' line to the left, Brig. Gen. Andrew A. Humphreys was now called upon to "refuse the flank" in order to stop Barksdale's advance northward. He turned the 11th New Jersey ninety degrees to occupy the orchard to the left and rear of the Klingle farm—facing south, perpendicular to the Emmitsburg Road. Colonel W.R. Brewster's Excelsior Brigade of Humphrey's Second Division composed of the 71st, 72nd, 73rd, 74th and 120th New York sustained this new line in a south westward diagonal north of the Trostle lane. Nineteen-year-old Pennsylvanian Jesse Bowman Young, an officer on General Sickles' staff and an eyewitness, later described the scene:

> [General Humphreys] had to manoeuver to meet this new attack, and in the heat of battle performed a task hardly ever undertaken on the field under fire: changing front by wheeling a part of his line to the left and rear, so as to face the new antagonist, Barksdale, who the embodiment of an ancient warrior, sword waving in the air, his hair, prematurely white, streaming in the wind, his words of cheer sounding through the smoke, was leading his men.

At this juncture the Alabamians of Brig. Gen. Cadmus M. Wilcox's brigade and the Floridians of Perry's small brigade under command of Col. David M. Lang advanced eastward against Humphreys' main Union line facing west along the Emmitsburg Road. These latest Confederate attackers belonged to Maj. Gen. Richard H. Anderson's division of A.P. Hill's Third Corps.

Professional soldier that he was, Andrew Humphreys recognized his situation was now critical. His division was being assaulted from both the front and the left flank, and he had no reserves to draw upon. Humphreys later commented, "For a moment I thought the day was lost ... so far as I could see, the crest in my rear [Cemetery Ridge] was vacant...." He also realized that any withdrawal would have to be slow and deliberate to avoid a total collapse. As for staff officer Jesse Young, he feared the worst: "When our division began to fall back under the awful pressure which was incumbent from three directions it seemed to my distracted boyish vision that the Union was going to pieces, and that Lee was winning a decisive victory on the soil of my native State."[72]

As a result, some of the most desperate fighting of the day occurred here as attested to by the horrendous casualties within A.A. Humphreys' division—2092 killed, wounded and missing (42.5 percent), third highest for any division within the Army of the Potomac. On the flip side, an entire company from the 11th New Jersey was directed to bring down a Confederate officer mounted on a white charger. Conspicuously he wore a red

Brig. Gen. Andrew A. Humphreys. A West Point graduate, civil engineer and "no nonsense" career soldier, his tenacious fighting withdrawal against Barksdale bought Hancock precious time to reinforce the Union line at Gettysburg (*Library of Congress*).

fez captured from a 114th Pennsylvania Zouave. This unidentified officer—later claimed erroneously by some to be Barksdale—paid the ultimate sacrifice for his indiscretion—his body was pierced by five rifle balls.[73]

Under the unrelenting pressure from Barksdale's three Mississippi regiments Humphreys calmly directed a fighting withdrawal. Observing this orderly maneuver Lieutenant Young regarded the division commander as "without a superior on the field of battle, full of fire and yet in absolute equipose." For his part Humphreys later stressed the deliberate nature of this retreat—"Twenty times did I bring my men to a halt & face about" to fire upon the onrushing Confederates.[74]

Miraculously, despite presenting a conspicuous target—on horseback and sporting a red sash under his waist belt—Barksdale had escaped injury. However, it is generally accepted that during this action immediately east of the Emmitsburg Road, Barksdale suffered two serious wounds to his left leg. Whether by grapeshot or rifle fire, these wounds were severe enough to fracture the limb and result in serious blood loss. Barksdale "reeled" in the saddle "but did not halt" and, although becoming increasingly weak from loss of blood, continued to lead the onslaught with the exhortation "Forward, men, forward!"[75] But where was the 21st Mississippi? More importantly, what had become of Wofford's Georgia brigade that had been designated to follow in support of Barksdale?

Colonel Benjamin G. Humphreys related that when the 21st Mississippi emerged from the Peach Orchard, the rest of the Mississippi Brigade had already wheeled far to the left along the turnpike. The 21st on Barksdale's right flank became exposed to an enemy battery on its right. These Union cannoneers rallied and fired into Kershaw's South Carolinians who were then advancing from the south. Humphreys instantly recognized this threat to Barksdale's right flank and rear. This wily Confederate commander also immediately recognized the glorious opportunity to capture prized Federal cannon then unsupported by infantry. The cool-headed Humphreys immediately wheeled his regiment to the right and moved directly to capture the six bronze Napoleon guns of Capt. John Bigelow's 9th Massachusetts Battery which was seeing action for the first time. By this move however, the 21st Mississippi separated from their three sister regiments and would thereafter advance alone. This loss of manpower diminished the strength of Barksdale's attack up the Emmitsburg Road by one quarter—a significant reduction.

Lieutenant Colonel Freeman McGilvery—who had been tasked by Brig. Gen. Henry Hunt with shoring up the artillery defenses—now ordered Bigelow to "hold his position as long as possible at all hazards" near the Trostle house. Bigelow's desperate delaying action bought time for the remaining batteries to withdraw and allowed McGilvery precious minutes to cobble together a makeshift artillery line east of Plum Run. Since the Mississippians targeted the horses, several batteries were forced to cut their traces and retreat by prolonge (utilizing the recoil together with guide ropes to withdraw the guns). Captain Bigelow "received two serious wounds and his horse was shot under him." Two lieutenants received mortal wounds, six of the seven sergeants and a third of the enlisted men were killed or wounded. Some members of the 21st Mississippi vaulted onto the limber chests and shot the artillerymen still manning their guns. Bigelow recorded that normally only several rounds of canister were sufficient to thwart a charge. This day however his battery "fired 92 out of 96 rounds of canister they had ... mostly into close ranks of [the enemy]." Despite the best efforts of the batterymen many Union guns ultimately were abandoned.[76]

Two survivors from Bigelow's Battery described this furious action. Batteryman

Levi W. Baker—shot twice in the hip and shoulder this afternoon—later wrote in the official history of the battery: "As we commenced retiring, Barksdale's brigade emerged from the Peach Orchard about 400 hundred [sic] yards on our right and halted to reform their lines. [Captain Bigelow] directed the left section to keep back Kershaw's skirmishers with canister, and [the right section] to throw solid shot into Barksdale's lines." Then referencing the advance of the 21st Mississippi, Baker continued, "As soon as the enemy appeared over the ridge they were received with a vigorous fire, some of which was with double canister; but they were too near the prize to be stopped, and pressed on and received our fire not six feet from the muzzles of our guns. Then our cannoneers were driven at the point of the bayonet, and were shot down on the limbers."

Cannoneer David Brett, manning another gun in the battery, gave this description in letters to his wife: "…we fought at our guns until they got within two rods of us … the bullets flew thick as hailstones—it is a wonder we were not all killed … 4 or 5 fell within 15 feet of me … we fought with our guns until the rebs could put their hands on the guns.… I hope never to see another such a time … we have lost so many officers and men it does not seem like the same battery.…"[77] The battery lost four guns captured.

As soon as the 21st Mississippi had cleared the Peach Orchard of Union defenders, Colonel Alexander rushed forward six Confederate batteries in an "artillery charge" and "went into action again at the position the enemy had deserted." Alexander later described his feelings at this moment:

> I can recall no more splendid sight, on a small scale—and certainly no more inspiring moment during the war.… An artillerist's heaven is to follow the routed enemy, after a tough resistance, and throw shells and canister into his disorganized and fleeing masses. Then the explosions of the guns sound louder and more powerful, and the very shouts of the gunners, ordering "Fire!" in rapid succession thrill one's very soul. There is no excitement on earth like it.… Now we saw our heaven just in front, and were already breathing the very air of victory.

At this juncture, Alexander shared Barksdale's optimism, writing, "When I saw their line broken & in retreat I thought the battle was ours." He exclaimed to his batterymen that they would "finish the whole war this afternoon."[78] Indeed, they very well might have done so had it not been for one critical factor—*Barksdale received no support from Wofford's brigade*—contrary to Longstreet's battle plan. Exactly why this deviation transpired remains steeped in mystery as Confederate official reports failed to address this matter. (More on this in Chapter 15.)

When Barksdale's brigade initially stepped off, Wofford's brigade was behind and slightly to their right. During the initial advance Gettysburg historian Harry Pfanz concludes that "at least half of Wofford's line must have been deployed south of the Wheatfield Road," with its right flank passing through Taylor's and Parker's Batteries. Longstreet's battle plan in this sector unfolded as designed up until the Peach Orchard was cleared of Union resistance by the 21st Mississippi. A member of Wofford's brigade confirmed this much in a letter to the *Richmond Enquirer* one month after the battle: "When the command 'forward' was given, Wofford's brigade was formed immediately in rear of Barksdale's Mississippi brigade to support it, and in this order the two columns advanced until the enemy was driven from the orchard."

By Longstreet's own admission he personally rode out in advance of his fellow Georgians to lead them on. His "gallant and inspiring" example elicited a cheer from Wofford's men which Longstreet quickly stopped with the rebuke, "Cheer less, men, and fight more." McLaws believed Longstreet personally intervened because "he was very much disconcerted and annoyed" with the manner in which his entire battle plan was unfolding. Longstreet's aide, Alabamian William Youngblood, recognized the danger of being shot by their own men and cautioned Longstreet who then reined in his horse and allowed Wofford's Georgians to pass by.

Like Barksdale, 39-year-old Brig. Gen. William T. Wofford was a prewar lawyer and had been a captain during the Mexican War. However, unlike Barksdale, Wofford had seen significant combat in Mexico. McLaws described Wofford as "very ambitious of military fame and one of the most daring of men," while Col. Benjamin Humphreys commented that "we all know that [Wofford] was but too prone to go forward ... even into disaster." Kershaw, desperate for assistance in his attack through the Rose farm against the Stony Hill, observed "Wofford riding at the head of his fine brigade, then coming in, his left being in the peach orchard, which was then clear of the enemy."[79]

At this juncture there was a critical decision to be made by Wofford and/or Longstreet—either to direct the Georgia Brigade forward in support of Kershaw (and Semmes)—or to turn it northward to the left in support of Barksdale as per the Lee/Longstreet battle plan.

According to Kershaw, Col. Jno. D Kennedy, commanding the 2nd South Carolina, upon falling back from the Rose woods, encountered Wofford, "who pointed to his fresh troops and called upon them to go [forward] with him, which they did." Kershaw continued, "I saw Wofford advancing splendidly, he was then in the field to our right of the Peach Orchard. His line of march was in the direction of Round Top ... [Wofford's] movement was such as to strike the stony hill on the left, and thus turn the flank of the troops that had driven us from that position."[80]

Thus it would appear this decision was made spontaneously by Wofford, as Gettysburg ranger/historian and author Eric A. Campbell concludes, "in reaction to swiftly changing events." In support of this belief, author Noah Trudeau suggests that "Wofford apparently lacked specific orders to keep station with Barksdale, who in turn seems to have made no attempt to coordinate with him." However, since Longstreet, at Lee's request, was personally micromanaging deployment of McLaws' division this afternoon, either Longstreet had already instructed Wofford to make this move or—if not—tacitly accepted it to reap the benefits, thereby abandoning his initial battle plan.[81] Either way, final responsibility surely rested with Longstreet. Kershaw's gain would be Barksdale's loss—and this lack of promised support precluded a

Brig. Gen. William T. Wofford. Contrary to the battle plan, Wofford's Georgia brigade supported Kershaw's attack on Stony Hill. Thus unsupported, Barksdale's lone brigade was unable to exploit its piercing of the Union line (Library of Congress).

successful follow-up to the imminent breaching of the final Federal line by Barksdale's lone brigade.

Earlier, when the Mississippians initially broke through Graham's defensive line along the Emmitsburg Road, Barksdale must certainly have noticed the absence of any supporting troops following behind. According to Adjutant Edwin P. Harmon of the 13th Mississippi, Barksdale subsequently sent back twice for reinforcements—but to no avail. When Barksdale swung to the left attacking up the Emmitsburg Road with three of his regiments (rather than proceeding due east with Kershaw followed by Wofford) it appears Longstreet and his courier Youngblood misinterpreted Barksdale's maneuver. (Confusion reigned supreme within the Confederate command structure this day.)

Youngblood later described the situation and their conversation:

> The Union army was found between [us] and the peach orchard upon a road [Emmitsburg] along which they had piled rails and whatever else ... that would aid in making a breastworks and were lying behind these rails awaiting our attack. The peach orchard was on Wofford's left and Barksdale's right ... the Union forces had fallen back beyond the orchard; our people were driving them, but General Barksdale's Brigade had halted behind the small breastworks which the enemy had abandoned, while Wofford's men had gone on. I called General Longstreet's attention to this, and said, "Do you want General Barksdale to halt?" He turned his head and said "No; go tell him to retake his position in the line!"

Dashing to Barksdale, Youngblood later related, "I found General Barksdale on his horse standing behind a brick milkhouse and giving him the order from General Longstreet he put his spurs to his horse, dashed a little way along his line, giving the order to charge at double quick."

Although the precise time this order was delivered is extremely difficult to pinpoint, it remains significant (in view of later statements by Longstreet) for it confirms that the only recorded communication received by Barksdale from Longstreet during this battle action was to continue his attack.[82]

With the Alabama brigade of Wilcox and the small Florida brigade of Lang (from Anderson's division of Hill's Third Corps) now bearing down perpendicularly on his left, Barksdale changed direction. He wheeled his battleline to the right heading east past the Trostle farm toward Cemetery Ridge and into the ever-widening gap in the Union line. Despite their valiant fighting withdrawal, the portion of Andrew A. Humphreys' Union line facing Barksdale finally began to give way and stampede to the rear. It was about this time that Colonels Holder and Griffin implored Barksdale to halt to reform his ragged line which had already advanced close to a mile under fire. A Mississippi veteran later recorded: "But [Barksdale's] fighting blood was up. 'No,' he replied, Crowd them—we have them on the run. Move on your regiments." In reference to Barksdale's grim determination and personal example, one Mississippian later recalled, "these veterans, now covered with dust and blackened with the smoke of battle, with ranks depleted by shot and shell, and faint from exhaustion, responded with cheers to the clarion call of the intrepid Barksdale as he moved bravely on."[83]

Barksdale sensed the moment of victory was at hand. The only opposition he could see was a few artillery batteries, completely unsupported by any infantry, some 400 yards to his front. These isolated Federal guns stood defiantly on the opposite slope behind the bushy thicket along Plum Run ravine. It was most likely at this time that Barksdale made his final desperate request for support—but in the glum words of Adjutant Harmon, "the asked for reinforcements were never sent."

At this same moment Col. B.G. Humphreys and the 21st Mississippi seriously contemplated rejoining Barksdale's line, visible several hundred yards to the left. However, as Humphreys later recalled, "just then another battery of 5 guns was seen three hundred yards off [to the front] beyond the [Plum Run] ravine." McGilvery had succeeded in cobbling together a weak artillery line—the so-called "Plum Run Line"—from the remnants of the Peach Orchard batteries plus additional ones from the Reserve, II Corps, and V Corps Artillery. Covering a front of 400 yards, these batteries were from left to right: Lt. Malbone Watson's 5th U.S, Lt. Edwin Dow's 6th Maine, three remaining guns from Captain Phillips' 5th Massachusetts, and two from Captain Thompson's Independent Pennsylvania Light Artillery.

So once again the 21st Mississippi charged forward, and quickly overran Watson's Battery of four three-inch rifles. Humphreys recalled that "one poor gunner lay dead at the muzzle of his gun with the charge rammed halfway home." In so doing the 21st Mississippi crossed over Plum Run, the only Mississippi regiment to do so that day. Like Barksdale, Humphreys now believed victory was within the Mississippi Brigade's grasp— "No other guns or a solitary soldier could be seen [directly] before us. The Federal Army was [cut] in twain."[84]

However, Barksdale and Humphreys were not the only ones to exhibit brave and courageous leadership under fire this day. On the Union side, Col. Freeman McGilvery's quick thinking, determined effort, perseverance, and skillful action were for a time the difference in preventing a breakthrough at the gap in the Union infantry line. For close to an hour in the gathering twilight it was McGilvery's thin unsupported Plum Run artillery line—at one point reduced to just seven fieldpieces—that alone confronted, disrupted, and held at bay the hard charging brigades of Barksdale and Wilcox. Wilcox himself reported, "From the batteries on the ridge ... grape and canister were poured into our ranks," while one member of the 21st Mississippi recalled, "thinned by the storm which swept down with such terrific fury from the ridge, the advance line staggered and began to waver; the awful crisis of that awful day had come."[85] But McGilvery's rag-tag artillery line had held on just long enough to permit infantry support to arrive in the nick of time.

Consolidation of command of the entire Union left under Maj. Gen. Winfield S. Hancock earlier that afternoon was now to pay huge dividends. In another example of superb leadership, Hancock now rushed forward the only available reinforcements from Cemetery Hill on the Union right and threw them into the breach at the Plum Run swale at a critical moment. In doing so Hancock also precipitated one of the most amazing twists of fate of the entire war—what has been termed "the redemption of the Harper's Ferry Cowards."

It will be recalled that almost nine months earlier the green 126th New York had been stampeded off Maryland Heights by Barksdale and his Mississippians. The Northern press blamed the collapse of this inexperienced regiment for the subsequent capitulation of the entire garrison and loss of the Harpers Ferry Arsenal. Immediately surrendered and paroled, the 126th New York made the arduous and ignominious journey by ship to Baltimore, and hence to Chicago by boxcar. Here they awaited exchange while being billeted in the barracks at Camp Douglas, a prison camp for Confederate officers. Along the way, as their regimental historian later commented, "Every newspaper they saw libelled and slandered them [for] cowardice on Maryland Heights." On November 19, 1862, these unlucky and much maligned troops were finally exchanged and proceeded to Washington, D.C. Here they were re-armed and then deployed to Union Mills near Centreville,

Virginia, to guard the approaches to the Federal capital. Now at Gettysburg, Fate placed their future in Hancock's hands—their moment of vindication had arrived at last.

Thirty-five-year-old Col. George L. Willard, a Mexican War veteran and regular army officer from New York City commanded this brigade of four New York regiments—the 125th NY, 126th NY, 111th NY, and 39th NY. This brigade, now at full strength, belonged to Brig. Gen. Alexander Hays' 3rd Division of Hancock's II Corps. These fresh reinforcements fixed bayonets, marched rapidly southward for a mile, and "then were faced westward toward a shallow ravine grown up with trees and bushes through which were flying the routed Excelsior Brigade driven by Barksdale's Brigade."

Captain Benjamin W. Thompson, Co. F, 111th New York, described the scene as follows: "The Third Corps were pouring through the gap to the rear closely pursued by a line of rebel infantry who were firing rapidly. It was difficult to keep a line in the face of these squads of flying men who were not moved by Hancock's shouted orders or his blistering curses." With no time to lose and without hesitation, the 125th, 126th and 111th "were formed in line, and with shotted guns and gleaming bayonets, charged down the slope into the bushes swarming with triumphant foe." Another Union veteran simply recalled, "Into this hell of destruction we were ordered to charge ... [and] pushed through the Plum Run thicket of alders...." One Union officer later described this "swale" as being "12 or 15 rods wide grown up to thick bushes and in some places were old stumps and large rocks or rough boulders." Soon "death volleys" erupted from both lines "which withered before that consuming fire." These New Yorkers then "pressed on till they passed through the low woods and bushes to the open space beyond, where the enemy made his most desperate effort to repel our advance."[86]

Maj. Gen. Winfield S. Hancock. Assuming command of the Union left wing at Gettysburg, Hancock's superb leadership in quickly rushing forward the only available reinforcements to plug the gap saved the day (Library of Congress).

A post-war account by William A. Love, a Mississippi Confederate veteran, described Barksdale at this juncture: "Mounted and with sword held aloft 'at an angle of forty-five degrees,' he exclaimed: 'Brave Mississippians, one more charge and the day is ours!'" According to Love, these desperate and exhausted veterans "responded with cheers to the clarion call of the intrepid Barksdale...."[87]

What happened next is reminiscent of a scene from a Hollywood movie script—but sometimes truth really is more unbelievable than fiction. Here at this swale two of the most highly motivated brigades on the entire battlefield crashed headlong into each other—both supremely determined to prove their mettle and thereby restore the luster of their tarnished reputations. The moment of redemption for the Harpers Ferry Cowards also marked the climax of Barksdale's "most magnificent charge." The regimental historian of the 126th New York fervently described the scene as follows:

> At this critical moment our line wavered, when a voice that our boys had heard before was heard cheering on the enemy. It was BARKSDALE, the same whom they fought on Maryland Heights, who now, with oaths and imprecations, was urging on the rebels. A low cry, "Remember Harper's Ferry!" was heard in our ranks, and swelled into a shout from hundreds of voices. Remember Harper's Ferry! rose above the roar of musketry and the clang of arms. The venom of that old taunt, "Harper's Ferry cowards!" which had so long burned in the veins of this noble Regiment, now excited them to fury.

Captain Charles A. Richardson of the 126th New York described the vicious fight as this Union regiment continued to press forward:

> A short but terrible contest ensued in the bushes in the swale, but the brigade continued to advance till they reached the open field on the other side, where we had come so persistently on the enemy who had contested every inch of ground ... large numbers of them at the very points of our bayonets threw down their arms and lay down in ranks over whom we advanced scarcely able to step without treading upon them.

Richardson also wrote several postwar letters to refute the "many absurd statements [that] have been made about the killing of Gen. Barksdale." Stating, "what can be proved beyond question if need be," Richardson continued:

> Gen. Barksdale was trying to hold his men, cheering them and swearing, almost frantic with rage, directly in front of the left of the 126th near the right of the 125th who both saw and heard him as they emerged from the bushes and immediately several from both regiments fired at him and he fell hit by several bullets, and a corporal in my company which was next to the left passed over his body while advancing up the hill.

Former Adjutant John F. Randolph of the 126th New York later professed to being that soldier—"Some writers claim that Genl. Barksdale met his death at the hands of some other regiment. I only know that there were no Union troops ahead of us, and that I stepped over his bleeding body as our line advanced."[88]

Confederate eyewitness accounts tell essentially the same story. Private Joseph C. Lloyd of the 13th Mississippi described the scene this way—"Then still on to Plum river. And did our gallant Barksdale ride into our midst and still say, 'Forward through the bushes.' Did I hear him make a sound and see men rush to him. I turn again to the front and see the enemy bursting through the bushes and firing on us." When Barksdale was hit and tumbled from his horse, he was accompanied only by a courier, Pvt. Jackson Boyd, who tried with the help of a few others nearby to drag Barksdale to the rear. Due to Barksdale's corpulent stature (he weighed 240 pounds) and the very painful nature of his chest wound and fractured left leg, the General begged them to leave him there. In shock, and believing death was imminent, Barksdale implored Boyd: "I am killed; tell my wife and children that I died fighting at my post." At this time Boyd received a leg wound himself from the Union infantrymen who were "not more than twenty yards distant."

Captain John A. Barksdale, the brigade's assistant adjutant general, whose horse had been shot from underneath him minutes earlier, gave the following account. General Barksdale had ordered him to go back to one of Alexander's batteries, some 250 yards behind, and order it to the front. Captain Barksdale quickly returned but stated "when within forty yards of the brigade I saw General Barksdale's horse galloping over the field without a rider, and the men falling back while the enemy was advancing—To go to him was impossible." As a contemporary lamented, "Their General had fallen, and they [fell] sullenly backward, contesting every inch of ground til they reach[ed] the [Emmitsburg] turnpike."

During this fighting withdrawal Colonel Griffin assumed command, but soon received a painful wound to the leg. Colonel Holder suffered a critical wound to the abdomen which required him to hold in his protruding entrails. Lieutenant Colonel Fizer (head wound) and Major Pulliam of the 17th Mississippi were also both wounded during the retreat, while Lieutenant Colonel Luse of the 18th Mississippi (previously captured at 2nd Fredericksburg and subsequently paroled) became a prisoner for the second time. As author Phillip Thomas Tucker has noted, the "true high water mark of the Confederacy" had been reached this day by Barksdale's brigade who had advanced over one mile, fighting furiously all the way for two hours in the twilight and approaching darkness.

However, in the absence of the promised support by Wofford's brigade, the noble sacrifice of these Mississippians could not be exploited, and their bloody effort was ultimately in vain. Private Moore of the 17th Mississippi summarized it this way—"Drove [the enemy] before us for 1¼ miles but were forced to fall back *for lack of support*" (emphasis added).

Soon thereafter, Private Lloyd—who suffered a severe wound to his left arm at Plum Run swale that necessitated its amputation on the following day—somehow evaded capture in the thicket as the Union line surged forward. Hearing "a weak hail to my right and turning to it, I find General Barksdale," Lloyd later wrote. He attempted to give his fallen leader a drink of water but as he held his canteen to the general's parched lips, Lloyd later expressed his bitter disappointment at discovering "a ball had gone through and let it all out." Lloyd was the last member of the Mississippi Brigade to see Barksdale alive.

Willard and the 125th, 126th, and 111th New York Regiments continued their advance but were beaten back by the Confederate batteries that Alexander had advanced to the commanding Peach Orchard knoll. During the subsequent Union withdrawal Willard was killed instantly when a piece of shrapnel inflicted a ghastly head wound which carried away a portion of his face.[89]

Barksdale's Mississippians and the Harpers Ferry Cowards both succeeded this day in restoring their combat reputations—sadly neither Barksdale nor Willard survived to bask in the glow of their accomplishment.

Hancock, in complete desperation, also ordered a suicidal charge by the 1st Minnesota to beat back Wilcox's Alabamians to Barksdale's left. The valiant 1st Minnesota succeeded but at a cost of 82 percent casualties—highest of any regiment on any battlefield during the entire war.[90]

To Barksdale's right, Colonel B.G. Humphreys and the 21st Mississippi found themselves in an untenable position. Barksdale's "three shattered regiments" were now in retreat to their left. On their right Wofford's and Kershaw's brigades were now streaming to the rear under direct orders from General Longstreet. In the face of artillery fire and the advance of the fresh 39th New York Regiment, Humphreys quickly concluded "that nothing but a rapid retreat to the stone wall in the ravine where we captured the 4 Napoleon guns [Bigelow's Battery] could save the 21st Regiment." However, game to the end, Humphreys "was confidently looking for reinforcements to enable us to again advance and complete our victory," when, "to my profound chagrin, I received orders from Longstreet to fall back to the Peach Orchard." Humphreys "demurred but in vain" as the order was imperative—he reluctantly obeyed, later remarking sarcastically, "my retreat was unmolested."[91] Darkness finally brought the bloody struggle to a merciful close. William Barksdale's ordeal would, however, continue for several more excruciating hours.

In just a little over two hours of vicious fighting, Barksdale's Mississippi Brigade had advanced over a mile. His four regiments, comprising 1,420 men, had routed or broken 14 Union regiments, totaling 4,200 men—inflicting 1,800 casualties in the process. As well, Barksdale's assault had precipitated the capture or withdrawal of eight batteries comprising 44 guns and over 800 batterymen. But this amazing accomplishment had come at a fearful price—747 officers and men killed, wounded, and missing. This casualty rate (53 percent) represented the highest loss for any brigade in Longstreet's corps that day. In terms of regimental losses, the 17th Mississippi ranked sixth highest, and the 13th Mississippi ranked thirteenth highest, of any Confederate regiment engaged throughout the three-day battle at Gettysburg. The three Mississippi regiments that wheeled to the left up the Emmitsburg Road with Barksdale each suffered greater than 50 percent casualties, while the 21st Mississippi who separated and drove generally eastward suffered significantly less at 32.8 percent.[92]

The regimental command structure within the Mississippi Brigade had been shattered—only Colonel Humphreys of the 21st Mississippi survived unscathed. Commanders of the other three regiments were either dead, wounded, or captured. Private Moore of the 17th Mississippi recorded his personal assessment of the day's action in his diary, and spoke for the entire brigade—"Every man acted the hero. Miss[issippi] has lost many of her best and bravest sons. How thankful should all be to God who have escaped. OH! the horrors of war."[93]

Fifteen

Barksdale's Death, Burials, State Funeral and Legacy

Barksdale's eventful life had come down to this depressing moment. Lying there alone in the darkness, he gasped for breath. Each painful exhalation sputtered blood from his chest wound. Colonel Wheelock G. Veazey of the 16th Vermont, as officer-of-the-day, established the Union picket line in this sector. He later described the scene as "the saddest night on picket that I ever passed ... the dead and wounded of the two armies, lying side by side, thickly strewed the ground." By a "tacit understanding" stretcher bearers from both armies were allowed to freely pass through the picket lines but, as Veazey lamented, "scores of wounded men died around us in the gloom, before anyone could bring relief or receive their dying messages." Barksdale's cries for water and help mixed with the groans and supplications of countless others to form what one eyewitness described as "a sound, low and almost indescribable ... the groaning of the wounded swelling up from field and wood and blending for miles in one low inarticulate moan." It was so mournful and unsettling that the Union bands were brought up between the troops and field hospitals and ordered to play throughout the night in order to drown out the cries from the wounded—and from the operating tables. A member of the 111th New York complained, "They played *When This Cruel War Is Over* for hours together, and while we sympathized with the sentiment, we execrated the doleful and monotonous music."[1]

Soldiers of the 126th New York, searching for members of their own regiment lying near the Plum Run swale where dead and wounded Mississippians outnumbered Union casualties two to one, were the first to come upon Barksdale. Barksdale begged Lt. Samuel Wilson of Company A to bring him off, but was rebuffed with the curt reply, "our own men must be seen to first." In a post-war letter to the *National Tribune*, a Union sergeant, who headed a squad distributing water to wounded on the field, claimed they came upon "a prominent-looking Confederate officer"—identified by an artillery officer present as General Barksdale. He was "bleeding and weak from his wounds and loss of blood. We gave him water and he drank copiously from a Yankee canteen.... We left him a filled canteen which in his weakened condition he could only thank us for with a polite nod of his head. We passed on distributing our supply of water...."[2] Barksdale would be forced to endure several more hours of agony before receiving any further assistance.

Meanwhile, back at the Peach Orchard, Colonel Humphreys was ordered by Longstreet to take command of the Mississippi Brigade. Based upon eyewitness accounts of General Barksdale's wounding and Pvt. Jackson Boyd's recounting of Barksdale's final message to his family, Humphreys and the rest of the brigade believed that Barksdale was likely already dead. A contemporary recorded: "Their grief was intense and those brave strong men wept like children ... at the loss of their beloved commander." Some volunteered to cross enemy lines to search for the General, while others advocated a night charge to retrieve his body. However, "with tears in his eyes, Humphreys informed them this could not be tried, and that their beloved leader was gone—and gone forever." Even after the repulse of Pickett's Charge on the following afternoon, in the evening some of "Barksdale's Boys" knocked on the door of Henry Garlach's house at 323 Baltimore Street and asked to use his attached cabinet shop to make a coffin for General Barksdale. Fearing the lantern light would draw fire from Union sharpshooters, Catherine Garlach directed them to Daniel Culp's nearby cabinet shop where construction of the coffin began. However, the order to retreat late on July 4th interrupted their work and these Mississippians reluctantly abandoned the unfinished coffin.[3]

Many different Union regiments claimed credit for shooting Barksdale down. Many different officers and units also purported to have found and brought him within the Union lines late on July 2nd.[4] However there is no doubt that a squad from the 14th Vermont actually recovered the mortally wounded brigadier general. Later that night Colonel William Nichols of the 14th Vermont became aware that a Confederate prisoner had reported that Barksdale lay wounded in front of his line. In response, Nichols sent out a search party from Company B under Sergeant Henry Vaughan. Private David Parker was amongst this group of volunteers and later recalled, "we searched among the dead and wounded until about 11 at night ... when we found [Barksdale] he was suffering from bleeding inwardly and suffering very much." In a letter written to his wife on July 6th Lt. Col. Charles Cummings of the 16th Vermont stated: "I assisted in bringing within our lines in a dying condition the rebel Gen. Barksdale—who was a noisy member of Congress from Mississippi."

Almost 19 years later, Private Parker finally fulfilled a promise he made to General Barksdale that night. In a letter to Ethelbert (the General's brother), Parker provided a detailed description of finding his mortally wounded brother:

> I immediately sat on the ground, took his head in my lap, and gave him coffee that I had in my canteen from a spoon as he could swallow but a small amount at a time. His mind was clear, he stated who he was and first told me we could not carry him into our lines without a stretcher and more help as he weighed 240 lbs. Two men went for more help. He commenced by telling me he was dying, that he was leaving a good and loving wife and two sons, if I remember right ages 11 and 13. Now I will use his words as near as I can remember—*O my wife, it will be hard for her. Tell her that my last words were words of love to her. But my boys, O it seems that I cannot leave them, their loss they will not fully comprehend—they need a father. Many times have I thought and planned for their future, and O I loved them, so to leave them is the hardest struggle I ever knew. But tell them all that I died like a brave man,* that I led my men fearlessly in *the fight. I was wounded by a rifle ball in my left limb above the knee but I led my men. Next I was wounded by having my left foot took off or nearly off near the arch by a cannonball. Though I was weak from loss of blood still I rode my horse and led my men in the fiercest of the charge, that we broke the lines and drove our enemy, and at the moment of success, I was pierced by a ball through the breast, knocked senseless from my horse, and left by my soldiers for dead. And tell them all, all my friends at home* (the following he repeated several times during the night) *that I never regretted the steps I have taken, and although dying, I do not regret my steps now, although it is hard to leave friends, wife, and children. I do not regret giving my life in a cause that I believe to be right. But one thing I do regret is that I could not have lived to have done more for the cause. O that I might again lead my men, but tell them I die content that my last day's work was well done. I feel that I am most gone. May God ever watch over and care for my dear wife, and O my boys, may God be a father to them! Tell them to be good men and brave, always defend the right.*

Parker then closed by saying Barksdale became unconscious while talking of his family.

Colonel Nichols soon dispatched a total of eight stretcher bearers who carried Barksdale about 400 yards east to the temporary regimental field hospital of the 148th Pennsylvania. It had been hastily set up in the small two-story house of shoemaker Jacob Hummelbaugh, a hundred yards west of the Taneytown Road. As they lifted Barksdale onto the stretcher one of the bearers picked up the General's hat and gloves and offered them to Barksdale who declined them. They were brought to Colonel Nichols who still had them in his possession in 1870.[5]

The Hummelbaugh family had vacated their house in such a rush that they left a partially eaten supper on the table. Before long all the premises including the barn floor were filled with the severely wounded, mainly from Sickles' III Corps. The overflow soon spread to the yards and surrounding spaces. When Barksdale arrived, he was placed upon a couch of blankets on the ground in the front yard of the house. Musician Robert A. Cassidy from the 148th Pennsylvania, who was assisting Regimental Assistant Surgeon Alfred T. Hamilton (the sole medical officer on-site) came upon Barksdale by accident. In the candlelight, Cassidy recognized that Barksdale was an officer of distinction and knelt by his side. At the General's request, Cassidy attempted to give Barksdale a drink of water from his canteen "but was unable to do so in consequence of his recumbent position, and the pain from his wounds was so great as not to admit of his being raised upright." Cassidy then handed the candle to another helper and, taking his spoon from his haversack, tenderly administered several spoonfuls of water to the parched Barksdale who "drank the water with feverish avidity." Cassidy summoned Dr. Hamilton who examined Barksdale's wounds and described them as "shot through the left breast *from behind,* came out above the heart (*an exit wound in the chest*) and the left leg was broken off below the knee by two missiles" (emphasis added). In response to Barksdale's repeated question, Dr. Hamilton "informed him in kind but confident terms that [his chest wound] was mortal, and that the best that could be done was to render him as comfortable as possible."

Then, in as poignant a scene as any during the battle of Gettysburg, the young musician tended compassionately to the dying Confederate general. Cassidy later recalled—

> Taking the general's right hand in my left and holding the spoon in my right I began the administration of the morphine dissolved in water. The general inquired several times—"Do you think there is no hope? How long do you think I can live?" to which I could but reply, "General, there is no hope; you are now sinking rapidly; compose yourself, we shall do all in our power to make you comfortable."

A Union officer happened upon the scene and offered up a flask of liquor to which Barksdale agreed. After sipping a small amount from the spoon he found it too strong and asked that it be diluted with water.

Even in his death throes, Barksdale's appearance, character, and muted conversation made a distinct impression upon Dr. Hamilton who later recorded his observations:

> [Barksdale] was large, corpulent, refined in appearance, bald, and his general physical and mental makeup indicated firmness, endurance, vigor, quick perception and ability to succeed whether as politician, civilian, or warrior. He desired peace, but only upon terms that would recognize the Confederacy. He said that Lee would show us a trick or two before morning; that before we knew it Ewell would be thundering in our rear. He was dressed in the jeans of their choice. His short roundabout was trimmed on the sleeves with gold braid. The Mississippi button, with a star in the center, closed it. The

collar had three stars on each side next the chin. Next his body was a fine linen or cotton shirt which was closed by three studs bearing Masonic emblems. His pants had two stripes of gold braid, half an inch broad, down each leg.

Barksdale's extreme thirst played upon his senses and soon delirium began to overtake him, interrupting the serenity of the scene. It was at this time that Joseph W. Muffly, Adjutant of the 148th Pennsylvania, approached the Hummelbaugh house in the early hours of July 3rd and stepped upon a "peculiar object" in the darkness. Upon closer examination, Muffly discovered it was an arm. He also observed the outline of a pyramid under the west window of the house which he soon confirmed was "a pile of hands, arms, feet and legs which the surgeons had thrown out in their work and which had now reached the window sill." Muffly then spied General Barksdale lying in front of the house "alternately begging for water ... and cursing the Yankees, it was a most pathetic scene." He recalled Barksdale's words—"Bring me water, cold water—when I am well I am a great lover of water, and now when I am shot all to pieces and burning with fever, I must have cold water." Then Barksdale would shout out, "yes you think you have whipped us, but wait til morning and you will hear Ewell thundering in your rear." Cassidy assured Barksdale that the water he was receiving "was as good as could be obtained," which seemed to satisfy the General. Cassidy eloquently described Barksdale's final moments as follows:

> Noticing his strength was failing rapidly, I sought to compose him, and continued to administer water, dissolved morphine and diluted liquor alternately until I saw that he was very near the verge of the dark river. I reminded him that he had but a few moments to live and that he would soon stand in the presence of the final judge. I am not certain that he made any direct reply, although incoherent utterances escaped him frequently until the last. Before I relinquished my grasp upon his hand I felt it chilling in dissolution, and having satisfied myself that I had done all that human instrumentality could accomplish to soften his fall into the arms of death, left him to perform similar offices to others, hundreds of whom, belonging to both armies lay strewn upon the ground about him.

Very soon after, Barksdale's spirit quietly slipped its bonds from his earthly body. In a post-war letter to the General's nephew and aide, Harris, Dr. Hamilton recorded the time of Barksdale's death as July 3rd at 2 o'clock a.m.[6]

Cassidy entrusted the safekeeping of Barksdale's personal effects to an individual present. These mementoes were to be returned to the General's family. However, this supposed trustee proved to be a charlatan and a "despicable vulture who made robbing the dead a business." As a result, by morning, Barksdale's collar insignia, Masonic studs, jacket buttons (save one), and other valuables were all missing. Cassidy salvaged only the lone remaining Mississippi star I button from the General's jacket and the shoulder belt for his sword for future return to the family.

Word of Barksdale's death soon spread quickly throughout the Union camps and by sunrise many were making the trek to the Hummelbaugh dooryard to gawk at his lifeless corpse. One such spectator was Lt. George G. Benedict of the 12th Vermont who was also a correspondent for the *Burlington Free Press*. Benedict later recalled, "[Barksdale's] bald head and broad face, with open, unblinking eyes, lay uncovered in the sunshine! There he lay alone, without a comrade to brush the flies from his corpse." Later that morning Barksdale's body was wrapped in a blanket and hastily buried in a shallow grave "in Hummelbaugh's garden under a cherry tree across (south of) the lane" (now Pleasanton Avenue) only "but a few feet from where he died."

A contemporary newspaper report described the battlefield grave of General Barksdale as follows:

Jacob Hummelbaugh house. Barksdale breathed his last in the front yard inside the picket fence and was soon interred across the laneway, near the tall tree visible to the left (author's photograph).

> It is a plain mound, with rough pine head and foot boards. At his head written with a lead pencil is the following inscription: "Brig. Gen. Barksdale/ McLaws' Division, Longstreet's Corps/ Died July 3rd/ Wounded in left breast—left leg broken/ Eight years a representative in Congress.' At the foot written in the same hand is 'Gen. Barksdale, CSA.'"

This article also described two additional graves of Union soldiers. "At the Confederate general's feet and almost touching him it lies so close is the grave of a slain Federal officer." His headboard identified him as Captain Robert M. Forster, Company C, 148th Pennsylvania Volunteers, and at his feet was another grave for N.M. Wilson of the 11th Massachusetts Infantry. The report concluded with the observation, "...bitter enemies during life, but [now] sleeping their last sleep together...."[7]

Thus, hours before Pickett's Charge was launched that afternoon—a forlorn hope which would forever eclipse his own "most magnificent charge of the war"—Barksdale was already dead and buried, albeit only temporarily, under the sacred soil of Pennsylvania. In another ironic twist, Barksdale's temporary grave was only a stone's throw from the headquarters of the 15th and 50th New York Engineers whom Barksdale's sharpshooters had wreaked havoc upon during the laying of the pontoon bridges at Fredericksburg. (The Engineer Brigade site is now marked by an imposing granite monument in the form of their castle insignia inset with a bronze relief plaque of a pontoon bridge.)

While the Army of Northern Virginia lacked official confirmation of Barksdale's death this was not the case within the Army of the Potomac nor the Northern press. William Barksdale's fame was such that senior Union commanders—including Generals Abner Doubleday, Winfield S. Hancock, and even Meade himself—saw fit to mention his mortal wounding and death in their initial reports, dispatches, and telegraph messages

Fifteen—Barksdale's Death, Burials, State Funeral and Legacy

late on the night of July 2nd. By July 4th Barksdale's death was widely reported in Northern newspapers such as the *New York Herald, Cleveland Morning Leader, Chicago Tribune,* and *Philadelphia Enquirer*. A subsequent account was provided in the *New York Evening Post* edition of July 7, 1863.[8]

On July 4th Meade did not counterattack following the repulse of Pickett's Charge the previous afternoon, and late that night the Army of Northern Virginia commenced its sullen retreat back into Virginia. A Union veteran of the Peach Orchard fight later rejoiced in the moment writing, "it was in true historic order ... that [the Confederacy's] decisive defeat should be secured here where literal bulwarks of upheaved slain preserved the North from the despairing foot of a traitor, *and accordingly the rebellion staggered back from Gettysburg to its grave*"[9] (emphasis added).

By July 4, Lee was convinced that Barksdale was dead and in a letter to Jefferson Davis included the statement "General Barksdale is killed." However, holding out a sliver of hope that his old friend might yet be alive, President Davis sent a telegram on July 9th to Ethelbert Barksdale—"No official intelligence received concerning your gallant brother though the report of his death comes from several sources. I still hope it may be untrue." Official confirmation was received two weeks later. This prompted President Davis to write a formal heartfelt letter of condolence to Narcissa on July 24, 1863, which read in part:

> It will hereafter be some consolation to you, as it will be a legacy of honor to his children, to be assured that your gallant husband, my esteemed friend, fell at the post to which honor and duty called him, and died, as he had lived, like a patriot and a soldier. To his country he was a great loss—to his friends, it brings enduring sorrow—to his family it is an irreparable injury—yet the blow came to him when it was most acceptable and glorious to receive it. God tempers the wind to the shorn lamb, and alone can give comfort to your mourning heart. You have my deepest sympathy; and to you and your little ones I offer my best wishes and sincerest affection.

Narcissa was completely devastated and confided to a friend, "then the sun of my life set at Gettysburg." She continued, "Oh the night of despair commenced then—I look back and wonder that my memory was not blotted out forever. For weeks my life was despaired of and Oh such gloom that entered my house which could never be a home to me again." Thenceforth Narcissa would never be the same person—her joy for life was gone. Only her maternal instinct got her through the remainder of her life—but only barely. Writing of her two sons in 1866, Narcissa confessed, "I try to be cheerful for their sakes but it is a struggle. My earnest prayer is that they may be such men as their Father."[10]

On September 4, 1863, Columbus Masonic Lodge No. 5 formally recognized Brother Barksdale's passing by adopting three resolutions. The first to record "the distinguished services of our Brother as a Statesman and Soldier" and "to bear testimony to the many moral and social virtues which adorned his character as a man and were so constantly exemplified in assemblies of our order." The second to "respectfully tender to his afflicted family our heartfelt sympathy in this their great bereavement" and to point his widow and orphans "to the only source of consolation and comfort, the promises of a merciful God as revealed in the sacred scriptures." And the third to place these resolutions permanently in the records of Columbus Lodge No. 5 and to transmit a copy of all "to the widow of our deceased friend and Brother."

On October 18, 1863—despite the absence of his remains—a memorial service for William Barksdale was conducted at Columbus, Mississippi. Reverend Phillip P.

Nealy, a close personal friend, delivered the eulogy. In his moving address Nealy earnestly and eloquently extolled in glowing terms the virtues of Barksdale's character and personality:

> As a man Gen. Barksdale was endowed with a grand nature—a nature that rose like a mountain above the ordinary level of humanity; a soul vast in its proportions—tender in its susceptibilities—gentle in its affections—strong in its sympathies—sublime in its magnanimity and in its benevolence.... He had that marvelous power which so few possess, of breathing his own soul into others and of swaying them by the irresistible might of his royal nature.... Never have we known a more perfect combination of energy and gentleness—of susceptibility to insult and of placability toward the wrongdoer—of quickness and forgiveness than met in him.... It was as a friend that his nature proved itself most loyal. He knew the meaning of the word and his life illustrated its sacredness. In this sacred relation I knew him and loved him as did many of you who hear me and if the depth of our sorrow is to be measured by the vastness of our loss, we have reason to be overwhelmed.[11]

Following the battle of Gettysburg, embalmers descended upon the battlefield to prepare bodies of Northern officers and soldiers from well-to-do families for shipment home. Dr. Cyrus B. Chamberlain was one of these "embalming surgeons" who soon arrived on the scene. He was a partner in Chamberlain & Waters Embalmers at No. 431 Pennsylvania Ave. in Washington, D.C., adjoining the funeral parlor next door at No. 433, directly opposite the United States Hotel. At the request of the Barksdale family, soon after the battle the late General's northern friends arranged for his body to be exhumed, disinfected, embalmed, and transferred to the aforementioned undertaker's. Here it was preserved—defiantly lying in state so to speak—until it was repatriated back to Mississippi. This process proved to be an extremely difficult and painful ordeal for the family and would not be completed for another three-and-a-half years. As Narcissa later bemoaned, "I tried time and again to bring Mr. Barksdale's remains home, but was denied the privilege by the Federal Government. Gen. Lee also requested that I might have his remains but the sterne hearts were too cold to relent."

The Rev. Thomas Teasdale, former Baptist Minister in Springfield, Illinois, and acquaintance of President Lincoln, now lived in Mississippi and attempted to raise funds in the North for the Orphan's Home of the State of Mississippi. Teasdale travelled to Washington in March 1865 and made inquiries regarding Barksdale's corpse. He actually saw the coffin in which it rested and wrote the General's brother that "the body is disinfected & was in a good state of preservation at the last inspection of it." However, due to military operations, Teasdale was unable to secure passage on a vessel out of New York to bring Barksdale's remains (along with orphanage goods) back to Mobile.

By then outstanding undertaking fees totaled $440 and express shipping charges were still to be determined. Although Narcissa had the financial means before the war ended to bring her husband's remains home, afterward she did not. She wrote, "After the surrender I was left in straightened circumstances and my husband's brother [Ethelbert] forsook me." Narcissa's inability to repatriate William's body due to lack of funds bothered her deeply. She wrote that it "has caused me to feel my poverty more than anything else." Narcissa's execution of William's will had further exacerbated her financial situation. Surprisingly, during the final years of the war Narcissa had been forced to pay claims lodged by the Confederate government against his estate for military expenditures Barksdale had authorized which were subsequently deemed "inadmissible and contrary to [army] regulations." She was also forced to sell property (land and slaves) to raise funds to pay off other outstanding debts William had incurred. Nevertheless, Narcissa repeatedly corresponded with the embalmers in Washington who agreed to continue caring for Barksdale's corpse.

Likely due to her bitter falling out with her brother-in-law, Narcissa gave serious consideration to burying her husband in West Feliciana Parish in Louisiana—her childhood home—"Where all love him so much." However, in deference to William's numerous friends and associates in Mississippi, she reluctantly agreed to have his remains interred in Jackson, the state capital, in the Barksdale family plot of brother Ethelbert at Greenwood Cemetery. The vexing repatriation process was not concluded until January 9, 1867. At 1 p.m. General Barksdale's body finally arrived at Jackson's train depot in company of Harris Barksdale, his nephew and former aide, who had accompanied it from Washington. The train was met by a formal committee of dignitaries. The General's remains were conducted in a solemn procession to the State Capitol to lay in state there until the appointed hour of his funeral the following afternoon.[12]

Narcissa and the immediate family desired that the ceremonies be as unostentatious as possible. However, they "yielded to the very general desire of the community" to bestow "those tokens of public respect" upon "one of the most prominent men of our state." Barksdale's body, "in an elaborately mounted coffin," lay in state in the Capitol Rotunda where thousands passed by to pay their final respects to this Mississippi statesman and soldier. At 3 p.m. the following afternoon, the religious funeral service was conducted there at the Rotunda by the Reverend Mr. Crane. Out of respect, the Mississippi High Court was adjourned and all the merchants in Jackson closed their stores for the duration of the service, the procession to the graveside at nearby Greenwood Cemetery, and the final Masonic ceremony conducted there.

Newspapers recorded the details of this elaborately organized procession under the byline *The Funeral Obsequies*: "Under direction of Col. Geo. L. Donald, Marshal, and Maj. A.J. Herod, Assistant Marshal, [it] will be formed in the following order 1.The Body 2.Relatives of the Deceased 3.State Authorities 4.Judges of the High Court 5.City Authorities 6.Survivors of the Brigade 7.Masonic Fraternity 8.Citizens." Pall Bearers included former Confederate generals Winfield S. Featherston and James B. Clark, and a second set from the Masonic Fraternity. The graveside Masonic service was conducted by Past Grand Master Col. Harvey Washington Walter from Pearl Lodge No. 28 F.&A.M. in Jackson, who "took occasion to pay a brief but eloquent tribute to the deceased" which included the following remarks:

> We are before the grave of no ordinary citizen. In all the relations of life, Gen. Barksdale challenged the esteem and compelled the respect of his fellow men. As a friend he was true and trusty; as a son, dutiful and obedient; as a husband, tender and loving; as a father, affectionate yet controlling. As a citizen, his manly frankness and sterling virtues won him friends; as a lawyer, his genial nature and commanding talents secured audiences; as a statesman his nervous eloquence, his sound counsels and incorruptible integrity reflected honor upon himself and his constituents. When the hour of peril came to the South, he sought the post of danger and the halo of heroism illumed the chaplet of the statesman. At the head of his noble Mississippians, he led the van on the ensanguined field, and wherever blows fell fastest and blood flowed freest, his manly form was seen and his clarion voice was heard. In the frightful carnival of death at Gettysburg, he yielded to that conqueror whose command is law, and his gallant spirit went home.[13]

Unfortunately William's grave is unmarked as Narcissa could not afford a headstone befitting her husband's status, and either Ethelbert was unwilling to provide one or Narcissa refused his offer given their very strained relationship. As the cemetery records for this period were destroyed in a fire, the precise location of William's grave is unknown, beyond the fact that it is within the Ethelbert Barksdale family plot in Section 4 Lot 4. The General's nephew, Harris Barksdale, is buried in a marked grave nearby.[14]

Only eight years later, his beloved Narcissa would be laid to rest beside him. She had lived modestly with her younger son, William, in Columbus during this time. Narcissa became a schoolteacher in order to make ends meet. By her own admission, at times her health was "very bad." Try as she might, Narcissa could not overcome her melancholia and grief, and constantly pined for her beloved husband. According to the Jackson *Weekly Clarion*, Narcissa died on March 23, 1875, at 3 p.m., age 41 years, at the residence of her eldest son, Ethelbert, in Holly Bend, Yazoo County. Narcissa was taken to Jackson for burial next to her husband. The *Weekly Clarion* eulogized her with touching imagery as follows:

> General Barksdale was justly proud of his wife, proud of her intellect, proud of her gentleness and grace, and above all, proud of her devotion to himself. Her life had been a very happy one until the battle of Gettysburg; but when her gallant husband yielded up his noble spirit on that blood stained field, the world had no further charms for her. The earth grew silent when his voice departed, and she dropped like a bird with a broken wing. There was no rebound under that terrible blow, and though she went through life without complaining, it was apparent that her heart was not with things of this world, and that it was yearning to be at rest by the side of him who was so long the pride and joy of her life.

At her death, by the terms of her will and an Act of the Legislature of the State of Mississippi approved on December 7, 1863, "a trusty negro servant named John," who had accompanied her husband faithfully throughout the war and who had returned home "disdaining to receive his liberty from the hands of the murderers of his master," was hereby emancipated.[15]

The Barksdales' youngest son, William, outlived his mother by only two years—dying unmarried at 21 years of age. Eldest son Ethelbert, a spitting image of his father, clerked in his Uncle Fountain's store in Yazoo City, and eventually relocated to Texas where he worked as a depot agent at Denison, Navasota, and Beaumont. Ethelbert married Miss Fern Wheeles at a young age and had two daughters and one son. When Fern died, Ethelbert remarried a much younger woman, Eliza Bennett Wellborn, in Beaumont about the turn of the century. The couple relocated to Athens, Louisiana, to engage in

Ethelbert Barksdale family plot in Greenwood Cemetery, Jackson, Mississippi. William and Narcissa Barksdale's remains lie together unmarked somewhere within this plot (author photograph).

a sawmilling operation there. They had issue of four children, only one of whom, also named Ethelbert and born in 1905, survived to adulthood. General Barksdale's son Ethelbert died in Bessmay, Texas, near Galveston, in February 1919 at age 70 years.[16]

How then has history treated William Barksdale and what is his true legacy? In the years following his death at Gettysburg and immediately after the Civil War, Barksdale was clearly a famous personage in both the South and the North—both as a politician and a military leader. As a statesman he was remembered as perhaps the most vocal and ardent supporter in Congress for states' rights and slavery. For this role Barksdale was celebrated in the South and reviled in the North. In the tumultuous years leading up to secession and civil war, Barksdale had been constantly at the center of the action. On those few occasions when violence inevitably erupted in the House of Representatives, he was always an active participant. Indeed, the image of Barksdale as the defiant Southern champion brandishing a bowie knife on the floor of Congress had been firmly established in the minds of citizens throughout the Northern states.

In many respects Barksdale's reputation as a brawler and duelist—although only partially true and greatly exaggerated—had preceded him to Washington and shaped popular opinion regarding his persona and politics. For example, an erroneous report that Barksdale had personally prevented Senator Sumner's friends from coming to his aid while Sumner was being caned into unconsciousness by Congressman Preston Brooks on the Senate floor has stubbornly persisted. Thankfully, recent scholarly works have corrected this obvious injustice to Barksdale's honorable character and legacy.

Harris Barksdale headstone in Greenwood Cemetery, Jackson, Mississippi, near grave marker in Ethelbert Barksdale family plot. Nephew Harris was on William's staff at Gettysburg, was nearby when William was mortally wounded, and years later accompanied the General's remains back to Jackson (author photograph).

As a result, Barksdale the Congressman, if remembered at all, is now mistakenly labeled as a fire-eating secessionist who campaigned for the breakup of the country throughout his time in Congress. Barksdale's own words, in speeches and debates recorded for posterity in the Congressional Globe, clearly refute this misconception. In reality, Barksdale was a true Southern patriot who, although defending states' rights under the Constitution, had worked tirelessly to address sectional differences within the framework of this document—without resorting to a break-up of the nation. Only when he believed reconciliation was no longer possible "in the event of the election of a Black Republican

President, *upon a sectional and hostile platform,*" did Barksdale throw in with the Secessionists, stating unequivocally, "*I have never desired a dissolution of this Union, but should the Black Republican Party obtain control of the Government, I shall be for disunion.*"[17]

Perhaps the fairest, most accurate assessment of Barksdale's career as politician in Congress was contained in a tribute published shortly after his death in the Chattanooga *Daily Rebel* on July 16, 1863, which stated, "During his eight years service in that body, no man maintained a more vigilant opposition to the constant and accumulating aggrandizements of Northern power than he did, nor was there any member more adept in the discharge of his representative duties, and more watchful of the public interests than him." By way of explaining the fading from popular memory of Barksdale as politician, it has also been argued that, in the aftermath of the Civil War, the popular focus was on sectional reconciliation rather than dwelling on the causes of the conflict—namely states' rights and slavery—and those personages, like Barksdale, who ardently espoused them.[18]

However, the memory of Barksdale as a soldier and commander for the Confederacy has at least prevailed to some extent through the years within military history circles—and for good reason. Barksdale was a rare exception—a so called "political general" lacking any formal military training who, despite being self-taught, steadily grew into a gifted, reliable, and successful military leader and battlefield tactician. Barksdale achieved results at the brigade level that were unsurpassed within the Army of Northern Virginia. Indeed, Barksdale's Mississippi Brigade won recognition and respect from friend and foe alike as one of the hardest fighting, most aggressive, and well-disciplined brigades within any Confederate army.

Barksdale's superb military leadership won praise from his commanders including Lee, Longstreet, McLaws; from his brothers-in-arms including artillerymen Robert Stiles, William M. Owen, Moxley Sorrell, and Porter Alexander; as well as the men in the ranks whom he commanded, including Dinkins, McNeily, and many others who left personal glowing tributes. "Barksdale's Boys" also contributed many laudatory articles concerning their beloved commander to *Confederate Veteran* magazine and submissions to the *Southern Historical Society Papers*. Upon assuming command after Barksdale's death at Gettysburg, Colonel Humphreys proclaimed that, although the brigade would henceforth be officially known as Humphreys' brigade "no other name will be more fondly cherished ... or affectionately remembered" by the men in the ranks, than *Barksdale's* Brigade.

Under Barksdale's personal leadership, his Mississippi Brigade won military laurels in virtually every battle they had fought in. However, standout performances occurred on the defensive at Sharpsburg, Fredericksburg, and Second Fredericksburg (Chancellorsville), and on the offensive at Gettysburg. Indeed noted historian Robert K. Krick and the late Professor Joseph L. Harsh have respectively termed the repulse of Sedgwick's Union attack in the West Woods at Sharpsburg (where Barksdale spear-headed the Confederate counterattack) as "the most notable Confederate tactical triumph of the day" and "one of the greatest feats of Southern arms on any battlefield of the war." (See Chapter 11.) Barksdale's tenacious resistance to the laying of Union pontoon bridges and amphibious landing together with his subsequent brilliant defense through the city streets of Fredericksburg were recognized at the time—and still are today—as key to this major Confederate victory. These actions, whereby the Union battle plan was delayed for some 16 hours, have been lauded as "one of the finest acts of heroism and stubborn resistance in our military annals." Moreover Barksdale improvised the successful defensive tactics for both of these military firsts—the initial *opposed* river crossing by an army and the first large-scale urban warfare within America. Finally, Barksdale's unparalleled attack at Gettysburg has been recognized by one modern historian and author as "the most effective brigade charge not only of this battle but of the whole war."[19]

Immediately following the war Barksdale was venerated along with other fallen Confederate leaders in a popular poem written by Fanny Downing—*Memorial Flowers*—later set to music to gain wider appeal in the South. Commemorating Stonewall Jackson, Turner Ashby, A.P. Hill, John Hunt Morgan, Patrick Cleburne, Jeb Stuart and others, the fourth verse reads:

> Let stars of Bethlehem, gleaming be,
> As pure as Barksdale's soul, which soars
> While he exclaims: "I gladly die
> In such a cause."[20]

Despite his status as one of the most prominent men in the history of Mississippi, William Barksdale never received—either during his lifetime or afterward—recognition for his accomplishments in the full measure they justly merited. In the decades following his death, while his contemporaries yet lived, a number of tributes in the form of permanent monuments to honor him were planned but sadly never came to fruition. The original concept for the massive granite carving at Stone Mountain, Georgia, outside Atlanta, comprised numerous figures representing each state of the Confederacy. Barksdale's likeness was selected to represent Mississippi, but when this towering work was finally completed in 1972 it bore only the equestrian mounted images of Confederate Generals Lee and Jackson, together with President Davis.

Similarly, by 1906, over $1,600 had been contributed to the Stephen D. Lee Chapter No. 34 of the United Daughters of the Confederacy for a monument to be placed in front of the county courthouse at Columbus, Mississippi. This statue would honor Confederates from Lowndes County and was to consist of a figure of a Confederate private atop a great shaft and, about the base, figures of the four brigadier generals from Lowndes County—William Baldwin, William Barksdale, William B. Wade, and Jacob Sharp. However, due to cost restrictions, when it was finally dedicated in 1912, this monument had been reduced to a domed temple with three uniformed Confederate soldiers—a flag bearer on top and two infantrymen on the bottom holding their rifles.[21]

Perhaps the greatest omission to Barksdale's memory has occurred at Gettysburg—scene of his "most magnificent charge of the war." Barksdale is most well known and still remembered primarily for this single event. In an address to the Barksdale Camp of the Sons of Confederate Veterans at Meridian, Mississippi, published in *Confederate Veteran Magazine* in 1901, Maj. John J. Hood read an "eloquent description of Barksdale's last charge written by Mr. Fontaine Maury." It concluded with this passage—"No shaft marks the spot where [Barksdale] fell. The Federal authorities refused to allow the point reached [by Barksdale's Mississippi Brigade] to be designated by the appropriate stones, but that gallant charge is written upon the hearts of his countrymen, and will be told in song and story as long as gallant deeds and heroism are virtues." And 21st Mississippi veteran J.S. McNeily opined in 1914, "but the glory that Mississippians achieved in Peach Orchard Hill will shine undimmed, through all time. And when the State erects a monument on the memorable field it will be placed there, *surmounted by the effigy of Wm. Barksdale*" (emphasis added).[22] This was the expectation of the survivors who reached the true high tide of the Confederacy at Gettysburg.

However, once again when the State of Mississippi's most impressive monument was finally dedicated on October 9, 1973, at the site where Barksdale's charge began, it contained no bronze statue of Barksdale. Rather it depicts the bitter hand-to-hand fighting that day and consists of two larger than life bronze castings of Mississippi soldiers. One is a prostrate color bearer who has been mortally wounded, and the other is an infantryman swinging a clubbed musket in defense of the fallen flag. Although Barksdale again does not receive his just due this author believes he would be satisfied with the result. For the Mississippi soldiers depicted here were "Barksdale's Boys" and their commander always credited *their* efforts in his after-action reports, disdaining to claim any personal credit.

For their part, his soldiers loved him like a father and were not hesitant to admit it. In an article to *Confederate Veteran* published in July 1893, W. Gart Johnson of the 18th Mississippi wrote affectionately, "We loved Gen. Barksdale because we knew he was proud of

Ceremonial Headstone for Brig. Gen. William Barksdale, Greenwood Cemetery, Jackson, Mississippi. This headstone is the sole monument in Mississippi's state capital honoring William Barksdale's military service (author's photograph).

us, and would do anything in his power for our welfare." James Dinkins expressed similar sentiments when he wrote, "…we drop a tear to the memory of heroic General William Barksdale, brave, patriotic, and kind. He was a statesman and a hero. We saw him in battle, on the march, and in camp. He felt a personal interest in every man in his brigade; he was proud of his men, and never doubted them. He believed they would follow him, nor was he mistaken."[23]

A few final comments are in order concerning the part of Barksdale's legacy pertaining to his actions at Gettysburg. Blame for the fact that this "most magnificent charge of the war" did not end in Confederate victory that day most assuredly does *not* rest with Barksdale nor the superhuman efforts of his brigade. This truth has been documented by participants, historians, and scholars ever since.[24] The absence of any supporting force—notably Wofford's brigade—to exploit Barksdale's hard won momentary breakthrough remains a critical deficiency in the execution of Longstreet's attack.

Historians have not looked favorably upon General James Longstreet concerning his performance at Gettysburg. Longstreet has been severely criticized by many historians for the significant delay in launching the attack on July 2nd—as charged by Early and Pendleton following Lee's death. However once launched perhaps Longstreet's gravest mistake was his failure to support Barksdale as initially planned. Longstreet made a truly astounding admission years later in a letter to McLaws, dated July 25, 1873. Concerning the attack on July 2nd at Gettysburg, Longstreet affirmed: "*This attack went further than I intended that it should, and resulted in the loss of your gallant Brigadier Barksdale. It was my intent not to pursue this attack if [it] was likely to prove the enemy's position too strong for my two divisions. I suppose Barksdale was probably under the impression that the entire Corps* [including Pickett's Division] *was up.*"[25]

This admission—or might it even be termed a quasi-confession—is rich coming from a commander whose only recorded communiqué via courier Youngblood to Barksdale that afternoon (in response to the latter's repeated requests for reinforcements) "was to retake his position in the line" and continue his attack. Indeed, at that time Longstreet *knew* that neither Wofford's brigade nor Pickett's division was available to reinforce Barksdale. Stephen Sears censures Longstreet with these words: "But instead of stepping in to halt the misguided operation the moment it ran into trouble, Longstreet had watched his inspired officers and men smash through the Yankee lines."[26] In other words Longstreet became a mere spectator.

Mississippi State Monument at Gettysburg National Military Park, commemorating Barksdale's Mississippi Brigade and the "most magnificent charge" by "Barksdale's Boys" on July 2, 1863 (author photograph).

Ultimately Barksdale's death may be viewed as a tragic sacrifice precipitated by Longstreet's error of omission in not supporting Barksdale's attack as originally intended. Ironically, Barksdale fell as a victim to his own success. The only logical reason for Longstreet's failure to call a halt was the dramatic triumph of the Mississippi Brigade. Instead Longstreet allowed the action to continue for as long as it did. Not wanting to draw attention to his own personal lack of direction in this regard it was not by accident that Longstreet noticeably did not commend—nor even mention—Wofford in his after-action report. Longstreet did however name Barksdale, Semmes, and Kershaw in the list of officers "most distinguished for the exhibition of great gallantry and skill." In particular, Longstreet remarked that Brig. Gen. Barksdale was mortally wounded *"while bravely leading his brigade in the assault"* (emphasis added).[27]

In his 1896 memoir *From Manassas to Appomattox* Longstreet included the following comment concerning the Peach Orchard action: "I had one brigade—Wofford's—that had not been engaged in the hottest battle. To urge the troops to their *reserve* power in the precious moments, I rode with Wofford"[28] (emphasis added). This is an interesting choice of words to say the least. Perhaps it was Longstreet's subtle attempt many years later to misrepresent Wofford's brigade as purely a *general* reserve force without any pre-assigned role—which, of course, was contrary to the initial battle plan whereby Wofford had been directed to support Barksdale.

Historian and mapmaker John D. Imhof rightfully considers the diversion of Wofford's brigade away from its supporting role for Barksdale as "one of the most important, yet least discussed, controversies of the Battle of Gettysburg." Clearly holding Longstreet responsible, Imhof speculates (correctly I believe) "that had Willard encountered Wofford after hitting Barksdale that the outcome could have been very different." Indeed, one only needs to recognize—in the words of Stephen Sears—"the particularly chilling effect" Wofford's splendid brigade had upon the Union defenders at the Stony Hill and Wheatfield. Union defenders there observed Wofford's Georgians "marching steadily, with colors flying as though on dress parade, and guns at right-shoulder-shift..." and these Yankees "were perfectly well satisfied of the impossibility of long holding their ground." One of Alexander's artillerists recorded his impression of the "aggressive" and "highly visible" Wofford also leading from the front: "Oh he was a grand sight, and my heart is full now while I write of it."[29] Had Barksdale received the benefit of such support, his breakthrough may have precipitated a Federal rout, in turn triggering a more spirited effort from the brigades of Anderson's division of Hill's corps to their left.

In some respects, it is surprising that Barksdale's last words were not a bitter condemnation of Longstreet's failure to support his brigade. Perhaps it was the shock of his mortal wounding. More probably it was a reflection of Barksdale's noble character and capacity for forgiveness—so often mentioned by his friends. Likely Barksdale was satisfied that he had done everything humanly possible to achieve a total Confederate victory that day. Thus, in a magnanimous gesture, the proud Mississippian had given Longstreet the benefit of the doubt and attributed the lack of support to the exigencies of war on the battlefield.

In the aftermath of the Confederate attack on the Union left during the late afternoon of July 2, 1863, bitter accusations soon arose as the senior officers sought to assign blame. With some justification perhaps, Longstreet pointed to "the failure of the supporting brigades of Anderson's division to cover McLaw's left flank (Barksdale) as directed...." Careful not to disparage the soldiers of the Third Corps—in reference to the separation between the brigades of Wilcox and Barksdale—Longstreet later wrote: "Those brigades acted gallantly but went astray early in the action."[30] Longstreet also owns some of the responsibility for this lack of coordination since he had not discussed details with A.P. Hill beforehand, likely believing that Lee had already done so. Furthermore, the separation was undoubtedly due in part to the alignment—once Barksdale left-wheeled up the Emmitsburg road as per Lee's battleplan, Wilcox and Barksdale were at right angles to each other. Post war, a member of Wilcox's brigade wrote: "The order was then given our brigade to move rapidly *by the left flank,* and the movement was made at full speed until space was cleared sufficient for the Mississippians, and then with right face Wilcox's brigade moved forward to the assault" (emphasis added).[31]

Major General Richard H. Anderson committed only three of his five brigades (Wilcox, Perry, Wright) into action as support. Only two regiments of Brig. Gen. Posey's Mississippi Brigade actually went forward—and only as skirmishers—with no appreciable result. Brigadier General William Mahone (who reportedly refused direct orders to advance) stated in his minuscule after-action report that "The brigade took no special or active part ... of that battle beyond that which fell to the lot of its line of skirmishers" to protect batteries on Seminary Ridge. The late Gettysburg authority Edwin B. Coddington estimates that Anderson therefore deployed only approximately 4,300 officers and men of the 8,300 available. Modern historian Chris Mackowski simply states that Hill and Anderson "did not commit timely reinforcements when and where needed, allowing the hard-fought Confederate gains to be lost." Unlike Longstreet who positioned himself near the front of McLaws' division, Anderson unfortunately established his headquarters well to the rear in the woods on the far slope of Seminary Ridge and failed to exert the necessary command and control. Bitterly, Brig. Gen. Cadmus Wilcox later commented on being "quite certain that Gen'l Anderson never saw a foot of ground on which his three brigades fought on the 2nd of July."[32] In contrast to Longstreet, sickly A.P. Hill was nowhere to be found near the front that afternoon.

Colonel Alexander was also critical of General Anderson's effort, reiterating that Wilcox's brigade had not been placed properly for the attack and "required a flank movement to the left of 400 to 500 yards over ground obstructed by stone and plank fences." Coddington asserts that "the fatal flaw in Anderson's tactical arrangements" had been correctly identified by Wilcox—namely that the brigades of Wilcox, Lang, and Wright attacked in a *single unsupported battleline*. Furthermore, as recognized by Colonel Alexander, they attacked progressively and were in turn individually driven back in sequence, thereby demonstrating "the evils of [en echelon] attacks." Alexander concluded the failure ultimately resulted from poor leadership—not from the actions of the fighting men. He wrote: "In all the reports of all the battles of the war there is no one more eloquent of fine conduct, but of poor handling, of splendid troops." In contrast to this breakdown in Confederate command, Alexander considered the Union effort that afternoon as "perhaps the best example which the war produced of active supervision and efficient handling of a large force on the defensive."[33]

For his part McLaws blamed both Longstreet and Lee. Soon after the battle McLaws confided to his wife, "General Longstreet is to blame for not reconnoitering the ground and for persisting in ordering the assault when his errors were discovered." Regarding Lee, McLaws complained: "I think the attack was unnecessary and the whole plan of battle a very bad one."[34] Suffice it to say that the events of July 2, 1863, were certainly not the finest hour for the High Command of the Army of Northern Virginia.

Commenting upon the lack of coordination within the Army of Northern Virginia at Gettysburg, McNeily wrote: "From all the counts of indictment of ineptitude and error, Barksdale's Brigade is free—it neither failed nor faltered, boggled nor wobbled. It alone did all that was required of it, and more." Taking it a step further, one modern historian has stated the following conclusion, which, although it cannot be proven, nevertheless rings true—"...but if every Confederate brigade had performed as well as [Barksdale's], this day's battle would have ended with Meade's army split in two and retreating along the diverging axes of the Taneytown Road and Baltimore Turnpike."[35] Undoubtedly, had

Barksdale survived, he would have been promoted to major general and given command of the division (especially given the strained relationship between McLaws and Longstreet).

Unfortunately for his legacy, Barksdale's remarkable and near-successful charge on July 2nd was all but eclipsed by Pickett's courageous—but disastrous—frontal assault the following afternoon. It did not help that Barksdale was dead and no Mississippi Brigade after-action report was issued. Nor did McLaws ever issue a divisional battle report—likely due to his disgust at Longstreet's overbearing interference throughout the action of July 2nd. Author Philip Thomas Tucker has observed that in the aftermath of the war, and the promulgation of the "Lost Cause" mythology championed by "the Virginia school of history," Pickett's Charge took center stage and was transformed into "the most romanticized saga of the Civil War." The flamboyant and gaudy General George E. Pickett was depicted as the very epitome of "a romantic cavalier," thereby overshadowing "the more homespun, less attractive Barksdale."[36] Thus, although not completely forgotten, Barksdale's Charge at Gettysburg slowly drifted into near obscurity and unfairly approached the status of an historical footnote.

Recognizing this unfortunate omission, eyewitness and participant McNeilly attempted to correct it by writing a 34-page account entitled "Barksdale's Mississippi Brigade at Gettysburg: 'Most Magnificent Charge of the War,'" published by the Mississippi Historical Society in 1914 upon the 50-year anniversary of the battle of Gettysburg. McNeilly declared his intention with these words:

> This narrative has been inspired by the desire of giving to Barksdale's brigade that place in Gettysburg history to which the record entitles it; and which it has not been accorded heretofore, clearly and in full in any account. It is not contended that Barksdale's men fought with more courage than any other commands. But it is maintained that, by the record, in the achievements of its almost wholly isolated attack upon the enemy's key point, it went far beyond all.[37]

In fact the entire action surrounding the Peach Orchard became arguably the most forgotten aspect of the entire Battle of Gettysburg. Union battery commander Capt. John Bigelow espoused this truth after the war when he wrote: "Many histories have been written; but in all, the fighting at the Peach Orchard, which barely escaped bringing disaster to the Army [of the Potomac], has been hardly referred to, as of any importance." Part of his reason for writing "The Peach Orchard: An Appeal" was to explain "how the individual efforts of Col. Freeman McGilvery (Comdg. 1st Vol. Brig. Arty. Res.) prevented the enemy from discovering the great opportunity for entering the lines of the army of the Potomac, offered to them." McGilvery's so-called Plum Run Line of cobbled together cannon, without infantry support, had held Barksdale's charging Mississippians at bay for at least forty-five minutes—preventing the Confederates from gaining the Federal rear—until Willard's counterattack commenced at 7:15 p.m.[38]

For those skeptics who would question the singular importance of the high ground at the Peach Orchard salient as a pre-eminent artillery platform, I would offer the expert opinions of two Union artillery commanders present that day. First Captain George E. Randolph in charge of Sickles' Third Corps artillery brigade who wrote post war: "I have always been convinced that if the Rebels had occupied the Peach Orchard without a fight, they would easily have broken the part of the main line to which the 3rd Corps was originally assigned." Second, in a post-war conversation while sitting together in a carriage at the Peach Orchard, Captain Bigelow asked General Hunt "if, with guns placed [here] could he not have swept clean the low land, in our front, where Gen. Meade had intended the 3rd Corps line to have been." The former Chief of Artillery of the Army of the Potomac replied cautiously: "I cannot afford to answer; but I will say, that, *when this advanced position was lost, the opportunity passed away for acting on the offensive after the repulse of Pickett's charge on July 3rd*"[39] (emphasis added).

However Barksdale's Charge never completely vanished from popular memory. Following the Centennial of the Civil War, author Michael Shaara included Barksdale in his Pulitzer Prize winning novel about the battle of Gettysburg, *The Killer Angels*. Shaara devoted three pages to separate laudatory references to "the famous Mississippi politician, his hat off ... waving it wildly and his white hair was flowing and bobbing, conspicuous, distinguished." Shaara stated that "Longstreet was fond of this [Mississippi] Brigade [and] privately he thought it the best in McLaws' whole Division, but of course he couldn't say so." The novelist had Barksdale on foot "going straight for the guns, running, screaming, far out in front alone ... hair streaming like a white torch." When the book was made into the hugely popular Turner Pictures movie, *Gettysburg*, in 1993, Barksdale's character was included briefly. When son Jeff Shaara wrote the prequel, *Gods and Generals*, centered on the life of Stonewall Jackson, he entitled four-page Chapter 30 for Barksdale and vividly described the Mississippians' staunch opposition to the laying of the pontoon bridges and subsequent fight through the streets of Fredericksburg. Both actions featured prominently in the subsequent movie of the same name in 2003.[40] Barksdale's role was played by Les Kinsolving, an actual blood relative and descendant of Barksdale, who bears a resemblance to the General.

Barksdale's attack through the Peach Orchard has also been featured in six extensive and very informative Gettysburg Battlefield Walks conducted since 1997 by various GNMP Park Rangers. The Pennsylvania Cable Network (PCN) has made these on-site seminars available on DVD. More recently, during the Sesquicentennial, Barksdale's star has been ascending once again. The History Channel's 2011 Civil War 150th Anniversary Edition 3-DVD Set from A&E Television Network features a 96-minute production on Gettysburg by Executive Producers Tony and Ridley Scott. This accurate portrayal is told from the perspective of the soldiers who fought there—one of whom is General William Barksdale regarding the Peach Orchard attack.[41] The release of Phillip Thomas Tucker's book, *Barksdale's Charge—The True High Tide of The Confederacy at Gettysburg* in 2013 further restored the memory of Barksdale in the public consciousness. Most recently James A. Hessler and Britt C. Isenburg have authored *Gettysburg's Peach Orchard—Longstreet, Sickles and the Bloody Fight for "The Commanding Ground" Along the Emmitsburg Road*. This book is the first detailed battle study devoted solely to the controversial and bloody action near Joseph Sherfy's peach orchard and will doubtless generate additional interest and curiosity regarding General Barksdale. Hopefully *William Barksdale, CSA* will become the definitive biography to provide details of his remarkable life.

Other available DVD productions include scenes concerning Barksdale. Historical Films Group's *Antietam*, filmed at Antietam National Battlefield and narrated by James Earl Jones, underplays Barksdale's brigade's role at Sharpsburg. However, their *Fredericksburg* production, filmed on-site, provides an accurate and impressive depiction of Barksdale's defense against the Union river crossing, and especially the street fight through the town. This DVD also includes a contemporary photo of Barksdale in civilian clothes (there are none in Confederate uniform) and an interview with park ranger, author, and authority on the battle of Fredericksburg, Frank O'Reilly. In particular he lauds Barksdale for his ingenuity in conducting the initial large-scale urban warfare. *Civil*

War Fredericksburg: Then & Now, a cooperative production of the Fredericksburg Civil War Roundtable and the Central Virginia Battlefield Trust, was also filmed on-site. This DVD includes an excellent detailed presentation concerning the role of Barksdale and his Mississippians in opposing the Union pontoon bridges and advance through the city streets. Partially narrated by a descendant of a member from the 13th Mississippi, this excellent summation is based upon his personal extensive research.[42]

In his book, *Causes, Won, Lost, Forgotten*, esteemed historian Gary W. Gallagher argues that modern understanding of the Civil War is gleaned primarily not from books, but from Hollywood and popular art. Modern artists Mort Kunstler, Don Troiani, Gary Lynn Roberts, Mark Maritato, Jaime Cooper, Bradley Schmehl, and Dale Gallon have all rendered paintings and prints depicting Barksdale and/or his Mississippians in combat. In 1990 Kunstler produced a head-and-shoulders portrait of General Barksdale in dress uniform, backed by the Magnolia Flag of the Sovereign Republic of Mississippi. This banner is emblazoned with the Bonnie Blue Flag in the upper left corner and the Magnolia Tree in the center. Two years later Kunstler issued his somewhat surreal depiction of Barksdale at Gettysburg titled, "The Grandest Charge Ever Seen by Mortal Man." That same year Troiani issued one of his most popular paintings—"Barksdale's Charge"— showing, in authentic detail, Barksdale mounted on his horse and waving his hat as he exhorts his Mississippians during their onslaught at the Sherfy farm. Similarly, artists Roberts (*The Barksdale Charge*, 2000), and Maritato (*Forward to the Foe*, 2005), depict Barksdale in action at Gettysburg, while Cooper (*General William Barksdale*, 2012) rendered a close-up in a camp scene. Schmehl (*Collapse of The Peach Orchard Line*, 1998) depicted the battle action at the Sherfy house as viewed from behind Collis' 114th Pennsylvania Zouaves. Finally, Gallon's *Essayons* (1996) depicted the laying of the pontoon bridges by the 50th New York Engineers at Fredericksburg while under fire of Barksdale's Mississippians.[43]

Finally, Barksdale's memory has been preserved in his adopted home state of Mississippi—but not to the extent and in the manner warranted by one of Mississippi's most prominent citizens. Indeed, prompted by a General Barksdale exhibit in the rotunda of the Old Capitol Building at Jackson in 1968, a Mississippi journalist opined: "It is one of the strange fates of history that a man who served his state so faithfully could be forgotten so easily."[44]

A Mississippi roadside painted metal marker was finally placed in 1973 on Mississippi Highway 182 at the intersection of Phillips Hill Road. Located about five miles east of downtown Columbus, it marks the site of Barksdale's former plantation. The marker reads: "William Barksdale—Eminent lawyer and editor. U.S. Congressman 1852–1861. Miss. Quartermaster-General, 1861. Commanding General of famous Mississippi Brigade. Killed at Gettysburg. Here is site of his plantation."[45]

The Mississippi Hall of Fame at Jackson was created in 1902 to honor individuals who have made significant contributions to the state. The Hall now contains over 100 members, with elections occurring every five years. Amazingly, William Barksdale was not even nominated until 1981. Furthermore, the person who initially placed Barksdale in nomination has been lost to history. Apparently "the effort to resurrect the memory and recognition of this great Mississippian" dated initially from the 1950s, but for unknown reasons was unsuccessful. His nomination was not reconsidered until 1986 when it received letters of support from Mr. Tip Allen, Jr., then Professor of Political Science at Mississippi State University, and from Dr. David L. Payne, then Director & Professor of Library Services at Mississippi University for Women at Columbus. Dr. Payne at that time was also Commander of William Barksdale Camp 1220, Sons of Confederate Veterans, which had been reconstituted in May 1981 at Columbus. This time Barksdale's nomination was approved, and he was finally elected to Mississippi's Hall of Fame—amazingly, 84 years after its creation. This honor clearly was very, very long overdue.[46]

It is customary that members have their portrait hung in the State Capitol. Accordingly, back in 1986 SCV Camp 1220 commissioned an oil portrait for this purpose but it never reached the Hall of Fame. Prompted by discussions with this author, Camp 1220 officers tracked the portrait down to a storage vault of the Columbus Public Library's Archives Department. Unfortunately, the quality of this piece is not considered appropriate for this purpose. As a result, at last report, Camp 1220 is considering the commission and donation of another portrait to correct this glaring deficiency.[47]

Although Barksdale's portrait has not yet graced the State Capitol, public exhibits of his surviving military memorabilia and related correspondence have been featured at the Old Capitol Museum several times. These relics continue to be exhibited in the recently completed Mississippi Museum of History in downtown Jackson, Mississippi. Items include Barksdale's sword, scabbard, and belt. Barksdale's sword was formally received during a special joint session of the Mississippi State Senate and House in February 1882. In the Hall of Representatives, Hon. Thomas H. Woods, representing Barksdale's Mississippi Brigade, solemnly proceeded down the aisle and formally presented this treasured artifact to William's adopted state. In his address Woods stated that "the Confederate armies held no truer, braver, more devoted, unselfish man than William Barksdale." In giving the "sword of this dead hero" to Mississippi, Thomas confirmed that "we do fulfill [the General's] dearest wish." Hon. William H. Luse, formerly of the 18th Mississippi and then a state senator, accepted the cherished blade on behalf of the state. In his own address, Luse asserted that the Magnolia State had not forgotten the services rendered by William Barksdale whom he characterized as "her faithful servant, her noble defender, [and] the chivalrous, heroic martyr in her cause." Barksdale's collar insignia of rank—comprised of three gold metallic thread 5-pointed sequined stars on a black felt backing, hand-stitched to his grey-blue twill wool uniform—had been donated by nephew Harris Barksdale way back on February 18, 1866.[48]

In the final analysis, William Barksdale typically reflected the social and moral values and political views of his Southern heritage. Atypically, he combined them with an indomitable and fearless spirit, a fiery and aggressive personality, nobility of character, and an extraordinary ability to succeed in any field he chose to pursue—whether as lawyer, editor, statesman, or military commander. Although he made mistakes—such as the drunken behavior and abuse of the 13th Mississippi's officers and enlisted men in August 1861—these transgressions were relatively few. More importantly, Barksdale learned from them and quickly moved on.

In the turbulent years preceding the Civil War, Barksdale's record in Congress confirms that he was perhaps the most ardent defender of states' rights under the Constitution—but most assuredly was not a fire-eating secessionist. To the contrary, Barksdale only became a last-minute advocate for secession when all hope for peaceful compromise was lost upon Lincoln's election to the Presidency in November 1860. Like many white Southerners of his generation Barksdale was a white supremacist, slave-owner, and ardent defender of slavery. These traits have undoubtedly rendered Barksdale much less appealing to modern biographers. Coupled with the lack of any memoir (due to his premature death at Gettysburg) and a general dearth of written biographical reference material, it is not surprising that a comprehensive biography has not heretofore been published. Due to these factors, Barksdale's legacy as a colorful and effective Southern politician and Congressman has been largely forgotten—except for a few scholars and academics.

However, over time the memory of Barksdale—the Confederate general—has managed to still remain in the public consciousness, albeit to a minimal degree. Although not anywhere near as prominent as Lee, Jackson, Longstreet, Pickett and many others, Barksdale's legacy as a military commander is still remembered by Civil War scholars and military historians. While these experts may still recognize and applaud Barksdale's earlier military successes at Leesburg, Malvern Hill, Maryland Heights (Harpers Ferry), and Fredericksburg, the general public only remember his military exploits at Gettysburg—if they remember at all.

Over the last two decades however there has been a resurgence in public awareness regarding Barksdale's Charge due to popular media (movies, television, DVD's, oil paintings, and books). This upsurge is fitting, since Barksdale is arguably the most successful "political general" of the Civil War—certainly at the brigade level. At Gettysburg, General Barksdale demonstrated a degree of tactical leadership that was clearly orders of magnitude higher than could be expected from a pre-war politician lacking any formal military instruction. That day, only Barksdale's Mississippi Brigade achieved the level of success envisioned by Lee. These Mississippians accomplished this by grit, courage, sacrifice and tactical direction by their line officers—all while under the exemplary generalship of Brig. Gen. William Barksdale.[49] In this author's opinion his personal bravery and courage displayed at Gettysburg on July 2, 1863, remains the equal of any officer—professional or volunteer—in Union blue or Confederate grey—throughout the Civil War.

Following his death at Gettysburg, Barksdale received many expressions of tribute from politicians, friends, and soldiers in his brigade. Many contained references to the apparent contradictions in his character. Typical is the following description of Barksdale by a member of the 18th Mississippi: "Bold as a lion, yet gentle as a lamb.... Quick to resent, and as quick to forgive, quick to punish disobedience in a subordinate, and as quick to ask forgiveness.... No truer patriot ever fell on the field of battle."[50]

However, perhaps the most fitting epitaph for Barksdale's entire life is a quote taken from a speech by the Honorable Albert Gallatin Brown. Barksdale's friend and fellow Congressman delivered this address in the Confederate Senate months after Barksdale's death when considering how to strengthen the army and improve the currency. Commenting upon whether the Confederacy shall stand or fall, Brown articulated, "If I were asked Mr. President, what the country most needs in this hour of peril, I would say patriotism; an all pervading and universal patriotism; not the babbling, noisy patriotism that prates of what it is about to do or has done, but the earnest, heartfelt, quiet, but bounding patriotism that does all things and dares all things. and *wholly oblivious to self, lives only for the cause*"[51] (emphasis added).

Throughout his life, William Barksdale was truly such a patriot—no matter the cause he chose to support.

Appendix
Previously Unpublished/Published Material Concerning William Barksdale

To date there are only two major scholarly works concerning the life of William Barksdale:

James W. McKee, "William Barksdale: Intrepid Mississippian," Ph.D. Dissertation, Mississippi State University, Starkville, 1966, 319 pages. This unpublished work presents a chronology of events in William Barksdale's life—descriptive but short on analysis particularly concerning his military exploits. However, it stands as the initial attempt to document, in detail, William Barksdale's life and service to Mississippi and to annotate many valuable references.

Steve Carl Hawley, "Brigadier General William Barksdale, CSA: A Study in the Generalship of a Volunteer Officer," Master of Arts Thesis, Texas A&M University, 1992, 191 pages. Hawley also holds a B.S. Degree from the USMA. This unpublished study constitutes an excellent detailed analysis of Barksdale's struggles to "make the transformation from civilian to wartime combat leader" and provides key insights into his military leadership and effectiveness during the Civil War.

Only for completeness do I mention a recent self-published annotated work of 137 short pages: B.J. Jordan, *One Final Charge!—The Life and Times of Mississippi's General William Barksdale CSA* (Denver: Outskirts Press Inc., 2008). This superficial treatment unfortunately includes several of the oft-repeated historical inaccuracies concerning Barksdale.

The first significant compilation concerning Barksdale's life was a 40-page "Biographical Sketch of William Barksdale" written by renowned and prolific chronicler of Mississippi history, J.F.H. Claiborne, who was a planter, politician, and contemporary of William Barksdale. This unpublished, handwritten manuscript resides within the J.F.H. Claiborne Papers, #151, Southern Historical Collection at the University of North Carolina, Chapel Hill.

Also in print is a brief three-page biographical sketch of William Barksdale supplemented with a portrait by illustrator Harry Coughlin: Clayton Rand, *Men of Spine in Mississippi* (Gulfport, Mississippi: The Dixie Press, 1940) 186–189. Rand describes Barksdale as follows: "Tall, strong and fearless, General Barksdale was the perfect soldier. He lived in fighting times and wherever he fought men sang his praise. Mississippi never produced a braver man."

Appendix

Lastly, a recent book focuses in detail on the charge by Barksdale's Mississippi Brigade launched on July 2, 1863, at the battle of Gettysburg: Phillip Thomas Tucker, Ph.D., *Barksdale's Charge: The True High Tide of the Confederacy at Gettysburg* (Philadelphia: Casemate Publishers, 2013). Tucker also touches on some aspects of Barksdale's background and persona.

Chapter Notes

Introduction

1. Civil War Book Review: William J. Cooper, *Jefferson Davis, American* (New York, 2000), www.civilwarbookreview.com accessed February 3, 2001.

Prologue

1. J. S. McNeily, "Barksdale's Mississippi Brigade At Gettysburg," Mississippi Historical Society, 1914, 14:243.
2. William A. Love, "Mississippi At Gettysburg," ibid., 1906, 9:32.

Chapter One

1. John A. Barksdale, *Barksdale Family History and Genealogy with Collateral Lines* (Richmond, VA, 1940), 4–5 (hereinafter cited as Barksdale Family History).
2. *Ibid.*, 17.
3. *Ibid.*, 26–27. Rev. Barksdale (b.1551–d.1628).
4. *Ibid.*, 19–20. Rev. Nathaniel Barksdale (b.1595–d.1633); Richard (b.c1625–d.1661); William (b.c1629–d.1694); Nathaniel (b.1631–d.in infancy); Barbara (b.?–d.1694).
5. *Ibid.*, 40–42.
6. *Ibid.*, 56–58. Nathaniel (b.1710–d.1790); Nathaniel Jr., (b.1760–d.1830).
7. *Ibid.*, 266–67; James W. McKee, "Congressman William Barksdale of Mississippi," in F. A. Dennis, ed., *Southern Miscellany: Essays In History In Honor of Glover Moore* (Jackson, MS, 1981), 44.
8. *Barksdale Family History*, 267. William Sr., (b.1787–d.1835).
9. *Rutherford County History of Tennessee* (Chicago, IL, 1887), 3.
10. *Barksdale Family History*, 268; McKee, "Congressman William Barksdale," 44.
11. *Ibid.*, 272; *ibid.*, 44. Nancy Lester (b.1789–d.1825).
12. John Francis Hamtramck Claiborne Papers, 1797–1884, *Biographical Sketch of William Barksdale*, #151, Southern Historical Collection, University of North Carolina, Chapel Hill, NC, 1 (hereinafter cited as SHC); [Compiled Service Records, National Archives, Washington, D.C.] www.fold3.com/image/#277734559, accessed 9 December 2011.
13. *Rutherford County History of Tennessee*, 4, 14.
14. *Ibid.*, 22.
15. *Barksdale Family History*, 266, 272. No mention is made of William Sr.'s remarriage, and incorrectly states that he died intestate; McKee, "Congressman William Barksdale," 44; Ancestry.com website.
16. Claiborne, "Biographical Sketch of William Barksdale," 2–3.
17. *Ibid.*; *Barksdale Family History*, 272.
18. Helen C. Marsh and Timothy Marsh, *Wills and Inventories of Rutherford County, Tennessee (1828–1840)*, 2 Vols. (Greensville, SC, 1998), 2:100.
19. *Ibid.*, 140, 162, 216; Claiborne, "Biographical Sketch of William Barksdale," 3–4; McKee, "Congressman William Barksdale," 44–45; Steve Carl Hawley "Brigadier General William Barksdale, CSA: A Study In The Generalship of A Volunteer Officer," MA Thesis, Texas A&M University, 1992, 8; www.dillahunty.com/files/Dillahunty_Master_update.pdf, accessed 10 November 2013. McKee references various Tennessee state records as well as Rutherford County deed and guardianship records. Hawley references specific University of Nashville records in the Tennessee State Library and Archives in Nashville.

Chapter Two

1. Charles Lowery, "The Great Migration To The Mississippi Territory," 1798–1819," *Mississippi History Now*, www.mshistorynow.mdah.state.ms.us/articles/169, accessed 19 September 2018.
2. John K. Bettersworth, ed., *Mississippi in the Confederacy: As They Saw It* (New York, 1970), xxxi; *ibid*.
3. Barksdale, *Barksdale Family History*, 275–76; 290–91; Dunbar Rowland, *Military History of Mississippi 1803–1898* (Madison, MS, 2003), 89, 283; H. Grady Howell, Jr., *For Dixie I'll Take My Stand! A Muster Listing of All Known Confederate Soldiers, Sailors, and Marines*, 4 vols. (Madison, MS, 1998), 1:120–21.
4. *Barksdale Family History*, 277–78; Robert

Lowery and William H. McCardle, *A History of Mississippi* (n.c., 1891), 614–15.

5. Harry P. Owens, *Steamboats and The Cotton Economy: River Trade in The Yazoo-Mississippi Delta* (Jackson, MS, 1990) 4, 9, 25–26, 36, 109, 120, 229. An interesting study attaching warranted importance on the steamboat for ensuring commercial success of King Cotton in Mississippi. Sherman Parrisot later standardized spelling of his surname to Parisot and changed his nickname to "Shum" to avoid any reminder of General Sherman who twice invaded Mississippi's waterways.

6. *Barksdale Family History*, 278–82.

7. McKee, "Congressman William Barksdale," 45; Claiborne, "Biographical Sketch of William Barksdale," 4; *Chattanooga Daily Rebel*, July 16, 1863; James W. McKee, "William Barksdale and the Congressional Election of 1853 In Mississippi," *Journal of Mississippi History* (JMH), (1972) 34:130; *Barksdale Family History*, 273, 283; James W. McKee, "William Barksdale: Intrepid Mississippian," PhD Dissertation, Mississippi State University, 1966, 12 (hereinafter cited as "Intrepid Mississippian")

8. McKee, "Congressman William Barksdale," 46, and "William Barksdale and the Congressional Election of 1853," 131; Claiborne, "Biographical Sketch of William Barksdale," 4. On the partisan press, see I. M. Patridge, "The Press of Mississippi" in *Debow's Review* (1860), 29:508. (Patridge was editor of the *Vicksburg Whig*.).

9. James T. McIntosh, ed., *The Papers of Jefferson Davis*, 14 vols. (Baton Rouge, 1987), 2:194–95.

10. McKee, "Congressman William Barksdale," 46; Patridge, "The Press of Mississippi," 509.

11. On the Davis-Barksdale relationship, see correspondence between them January 1844–July 1856 in *The Papers of Jefferson Davis*, 2: 68–76; 116–17; 5:277, 444, 472; 6:485. Later as Confederate President, Davis would also value Confederate Congressman Ethelbert Barksdale's political views.

12. McKee, "Congressman William Barksdale," 45; McKee, "Intrepid Mississippian," 12–13; 1860 Census Lowndes County, MS, www.fold3.com/image#61747472, accessed 27 Nov. 2011. Barksdale was a moderate planter, never owning more than three dozen slaves at a time; many of his slaves previously belonged to his wife.

13. *Barksdale Family History*, 287; *Jackson [MS] Daily Clarion-Ledger*, February 17, 1893; Nancy McKenzie Dupont, "Mississippi's Fire-Eating Editor: Ethelbert Barksdale and the Election of 1860,"Loyola University, New Orleans, 138, David B. Sachsman, et al., eds., *The Civil War And The Press* (New Jersey, 2000), 137–38; Partridge, "The Press of Mississippi," 507; Reuben Davis, *Recollections of Mississippi and Mississippians* (Boston, 1890), 353; *Debow's Review*, April 1859, 26:467; *Biographical Directory of The United States Congress 1774–Present, Ethelbert Barksdale*, accessed 17 October 2018; http://bioguide.congress.gov. Ethelbert was commonly referred to as "Major." However, he never officially served in the Confederate States Army. He did act as volunteer aide-de-camp on Gen. Richard S. Ewell's staff for several months in spring 1862 during recess of the Confederate Congress. (See Donald C. Pfanz, *Richard S. Ewell: A Soldier's Life*.) Since DeBow's reference predates the Civil War one must conclude that Ethelbert's salutation as "Major" derived from some earlier militia service.

14. Dupont, "Mississippi's Fire-Eating Editor: Ethelbert Barksdale," 144; *Jackson Daily Clarion–Ledger*, February 23, 1893, 1; Davis, *Recollections of Mississippi and Mississippians*, 353; R. H. Henry, *Editors I Have Known Since The Civil War* (New Orleans, 1922), 94. Henry was the owner/editor of the *Jackson Clarion-Ledger*.

15. Bruce Levine, *Confederate Emancipation: Southern Plans To Free and Arm Slaves During The Civil War* (New York, 2006), 117; "Proceedings of The Second Confederate Congress," *Southern Historical Society Papers*, 52 vols. (Millwood NY: Kraus Reprint, 1977) 52:329–30, 345 (hereinafter cited as *SHSP*)

16. "Proceedings of The First Confederate Congress," SHSP, 44:49–50,151; 49:273. Ethelbert insisted that the individual Confederate states not be represented as stars on the new flag as they were on the "Star Spangled Banner," since he believed the flags of the two countries should be as distinctly different as the character of the two societies.

17. Kenneth G. McCarty, "Farmers, The Populist Party, and Mississippi (1870–1900), *Mississippi History Now*, http://mshistory.k12.ms.us/features/featured42/populistparty.html, accessed 30 July 1999. This essay includes a photo of Ethelbert in later life. See also *Biographical Directory of The United States Congress 1774–Present, Ethelbert Barksdale*.

18. *Barksdale Family History*, 287–93; Harris Barksdale Compiled Service Record, National Archives; By-line "General Barksdale," *The Weekly Clarion*, January 17, 1867.

19. Last Will and Testament of William Barksdale, Subject File, MDAH. Ultimately Narcissa would become sole Executrix after a bitter falling out with brother-in-law Ethelbert.

20. Hawley, "Brigadier General William Barksdale CSA," 8–9. Hawley puts great emphasis on Barksdale's innate capacity for self-learning.

21. William Barksdale to Robert J. Walker, November 13, 1845, written at Columbus, Mississippi. Copy kindly provided by Brian Green, Proprietor of Brian and Maria Green Historical Autographs, Kennersville, NC. Some members of the 13th Mississippi under Colonel Barksdale's command would later accuse him of using flattery to achieve his purposes.

Chapter Three

1. Sam Olden, "Mississippi And U.S.—Mexican War 1846-1848," *Mississippi History Now*, www.mshistorynow.mdah.state.ms.us/articles/202. Texas maintained that its territory extended to the Rio Grande (Rio Bravo) while Mexico argued that it terminated miles north at the Nueces River.

2. Martin Dugard, *The Training Ground: Grant, Lee, Sherman and Davis in the Mexican War 1846–1848* (New York, 2008), 29.

3. *Ibid.*, xiii. In his introduction to *A Southern Lacrimosa* (xiii–xiv) historian Grady Howell, Jr., references Robert Self Henry's *Story of The Mexican War*, which argues the expansion of slavery as the true cause was overstated due to the proliferation of northeastern propagandists whose "views were accepted as almost undisputed truisms for more than half a century."

4. *Ibid.*, 29.

5. Olden, "Mississippi and the U.S.–Mexican War 1846–1848," 1–3; Dugard, *The Training Ground*, 29–33; Philip Katcher, *The Mexican-American War 1846–1848, Men-At-Arms Series* (London, 1976) 6. Taylor would later be elected the 12th president of the United States.

6. *A Southern Lacrimosa: The Mexican War Journal of Dr. Thomas Neely Love, Surgeon, Second Regiment Mississippi Volunteer Infantry, U.S.A.*, Grady A. Howell, ed., (Chickasaw Bayou Press, 1995), xiii–xiv (hereinafter cited as Love, *A Southern Lacrimosa*).

7. Rowland, *Military History of Mississippi*, 18–19; Dugard, *The Training Ground*, 119,151. Initially in April 1846 General Taylor directly called on Texas and Louisiana for eight volunteer regiments. General E. P. Gaines, Military Department Commander, without authority from the War Department, also requisitioned volunteers, including two regiments from Mississippi, for which he was soon relieved of command. Governor Brown was bitterly criticized within Mississippi for disregarding the Gaines requisition.

8. Rowland, *Military History of Mississippi*, 14–15, 20, 29; Chesley S. Coffey, "The Mexican War Letters of Chesley S. Coffey," Mary Ellen Rowe ed., *Journal of Mississippi History*, Vol. 44, August 1982, 235–36; *Kosciusko Jeffersonian*, January 18, 1845.

9. Davis, *Recollection of Mississippi and Mississippians*, 221; Betty C. Wiltshire, *Mississippi Soldiers—Revolutionary, 1812, Indian and Mexican Wars* (Carrolton, MS, 1998), 74, 76; McKee, "Congressman William Barksdale," 46; Love, *A Southern Lacrimosa*, 215. Dr. Love, who befriended Barksdale and who served closely with him continuously in the Second Mississippi for 18 months, wrote "[Barksdale] will some day be rich, for he loves money."

10. Dugard, *The Training Ground*, 40, 138; Davis, *Recollections of Mississippi and Mississippians*, 221–22; Coffey, "Mexican War Letters," 240, 251.

11. Claim by William Barksdale for Bounty Land, Columbus Mississippi, October 24, 1850, National Archives, Washington, D.C.; Rowland, *Military History of Mississippi*, 29–30; Dugard, *The Training Ground*, 123; William Barksdale Compiled Service Record, www.fold3.com/image/#272668668, #272668669, #272668671, #272668672; Wiltshire, *Mississippi Soldiers*, 76. Captain Barksdale's title as Assistant Commissary is chosen based upon his bounty land application which bears his signature. Rowland lists him as Commissary. Reuben Davis in his memoirs repeatedly refers to Barksdale as Quartermaster. Barksdale's compiled service record shows him as A.C.S. (Assistant Commissary Subsistence) but also indicates he served as Acting Regimental Quartermaster in October 1847 and relieved the A.C.S. of the North Carolina Regiment in May 1848. Lastly, an "Act To Appropriate Money For The Relief of The Mississippi Volunteers Now In Mexico," dated January 31, 1848, in the *Code of Mississippi*, refers to Barksdale as both Assistant-Commissary of Subsistence and Acting Assistant-Quarter-Master.

12. Jefferson Davis quoted in Dugard, *The Training Ground*, 155; Rowland, *Military History of Mississippi*, 21, 30.

13. Love, *A Southern Lacrimosa*, 1, 3–4. In contrast to Jefferson Davis, Reuben Davis was woefully ignorant of military protocol, regulations, and especially camp hygiene.

14. *Ibid.*, 17–19, 24, 255–56; Dugard, *The Training Ground*, 208–09; Davis, *Recollections of Mississippi and Mississippians*, 230. Editor Grady Howell, Jr., includes an article written by Dr. Love's third granddaughter, herself an M.D., who describes the symptoms in detail to conclude Cold Plague was meningococcal 1 infection arising from the bacteria Neisseria meningitis. See Love, 270.

15. Love, *A Southern Lacrimosa*, 25, 256.

16. *Ibid.*, 36, 41; Rowland, Military *History of Mississippi*, 30; Dugard, *The Training Ground*, 151.

17. Love, *A Southern Lacrimosa*, 32, 34–35, 181, 257. Surgeon Love believed the initial exposure at Vicksburg was the root cause of all subsequent suffering since the fatality rate was no different for soldiers cared for under the best available conditions in private homes and who hadn't been exposed to the campground at Chalmette Plantation. Excerpt from diary of Sgt. Thomas Barclay, Co. E. Second Pennsylvania.

18. *Ibid.*, 42; *Vicksburg Sentinel* quoted in Rowland, *Military History of Mississippi*, 30.

19. Love, *A Southern Lacrimosa*, 43–46. Colonel Reuben Davis' ineptitude engendered a deep-seated resentment in Dr. Love and the two entered into a prolonged war of words which continued after the war. Unfounded charges of drunkenness were brought against Surgeon Love who had partaken of brandy and wine in an effort to continue performing his duties. Love in rebuttal stated, "I do honestly believe that he [Col. Davis] is wholly unfit for the station he occupies" and later added "I do believe the man is crazy."

20. *Ibid.*, 67–69.

21. *Ibid.*, 69–75.

22. *Ibid.*, 78.

23. *Ibid.*, 78–79; Davis, *Recollections of Mississippi and Mississippians*, 233, 237.

24. Love, *A Southern Lacrimosa*, 79; Davis, *Recollection of Mississippi and Mississippians*, 234–35. Surgeon Love claims they were pack mules. He incorrectly states the victory by Taylor at Buena Vista occurred at Saltillo.

25. *Ibid.*, 83–86, 94.

26. *Ibid.*, 113; Rowland, *Military History of Mississippi*, 30; Katcher, *The Mexican-American War, 1846–1848*, 5. Total American strength reached

115,906 all ranks of which 103.8 men per thousand died of disease. Of the 42,374 regulars, 4900 died of disease or accident with 4,149 discharged due to disability, while only 930 were killed in combat. Of the 60,913 volunteers who served, 6,400 died of disease or accident, another 9,200 were discharged due to disability, and only 600 were killed in action.

27. Richard Bruce Winders, *Panting for Glory: The Mississippi Rifles in the Mexican War* (College Station, TX, 2016), 104.

28. Davis, *Recollections of Mississippi and Mississippians*, 249–51; Rowland, *Military History of Mississippi*, 31.

29. Various emails between R.W. Bro. Christopher M. Reid, Grand Librarian of the Lodge of Research for the Grand Lodge of Mississippi and this author, December 2, 2013 to July 2, 2014. Quotations taken from *Masonic Review*, Vol. 3, no. 3, Cincinnati, December 1847, 65–6, Periodical Collection, University of Minnesota; Love, *A Southern Lacrimosa*, 206.

30. "The Mississippi Delegation in Congress," *Harper's Weekly*, February 2, 1861, Vol. 5, No. 214, New York, 65–66; Love, *A Southern Lacrimosa*, 215.

31. Ibid., 194.

32. William Barksdale Compiled service record, www.fold.com/image/#2726668, #27266869, #27266871, #27266872, accessed 12 February 2012.

33. "Article 17 An Act To Appropriate Money For The Relief of The Mississippi Volunteers Now in Mexico—January 31, 1848" in *Code of Mississippi: Being An Analytical Compilation of The Public And General Statutes of The Territory And State From 1798–1848* (Jackson, MS, 1848), 370–71; Joseph Grigsby to his wife in Columbus, Mississippi sent from Comargo, Mexico, July 4, 1848. Copy in author's possession.

34. Hawley makes the distinction that, as Assistant Commissary, Barksdale was not responsible for conducting drill of line infantry. Moreover, since smoothbore muskets were the norm, and rifles the exception, Napoleonic tactics were in use. By the time of the Civil War, drill manuals would change significantly due to use of the rifled musket and minie bullet, but at least Barksdale would possess a starting point for tactical study. (Hawley, "Brigadier General William Barksdale CSA," 9–10.)

35. Love, *A Southern Lacrimosa*, 201, 219.

36. Aberdeen *Weekly Independent*, November 12, 1853.

37. Love, *A Southern Lacrimosa*, 259, 269. Excerpted from Love's detailed Table of Diseases, Habits, Ages, Deaths, etc., of the 2nd Mississippi.

Chapter Four

1. Narcissa's surname has caused much confusion. The Barksdale Genealogy lists her as Narcissa Smith while McKee records her as Narcissa Saunders. More recent genealogical research has confirmed her maiden surname was indeed Smith. A July 24, 1863 letter from Confederate President Jefferson Davis published in both the Jackson *Mississippian* and Richmond *Dispatch* concerning her husband's probable death was clearly addressed to Narcissa Smith Barksdale. It appears that Saunders was a second given name and that has resulted in confusion since there are references to both Narcissa Saunders Barksdale as well as Narcissa Smith Barksdale. William Barksdale represented Lowndes Lodge No. 114 at the 33rd Annual Communication of the Grand Lodge of Mississippi held in Natchez in February 1851. He also served on the Standing Committee on Subordinate Lodges, and was elected Grand Orator on February 4, 1851. His participation decreased as his political career escalated.

2. Love, *A Southern* Lacrimosa, 71, 215; McKee, "Intrepid Mississippian," 26; McKee, "Congressman William Barksdale,"130; Re Brig. Gen. William Barksdale of TN and MS/Civil War posted in Gen Forum of Genealogy.com; Family Search for Courtland Smith, Jane Boone, Narcissa Saunders Smith in Ancestry.com, accessed January 13, 2014. The *Barksdale Family History* incorrectly cites Columbus as the location of their marriage.

3. Narcissa Barksdale to Alcinda Janney, October 25, 1862 re visit to Leesburg etc.; Narcissa Barksdale to Alcinda Janney, April 1866 re death of William Barksdale at Gettysburg, etc., John Janney Papers, Ms2001-019 Special Collections, Virginia Polytechnic Institute and State University, Blacksburg, VA; McKee, "William Barksdale: Intrepid Mississippian," 27–28.

4. Some accounts give Ethelbert's birthday as 1849. However, his name does not appear with his parents on the December 12, 1850 Census. The 1850 birth date concurs with the July 30, 1860 Census. Narcissa Barksdale letters to Alcinda Janney; E. C. Barksdale (General Barksdale's grandson) to James W. McKee Jr., March 30, 1965, William Barksdale File, MDAH; McKee," Intrepid Mississippian," 28; David Parker to Ethelbert Barksdale, March 13, 1882, Barksdale Papers, MDAH.

5. Jackson *Mississippian*, March 31, 1849; Percy L. Rainwater, *Mississippi: Storm Center of Secession 1856–1861* (Baton Rouge, 1938), vii.

6. Rainwater, *Mississippi: Storm center of Secession 1856–1861*, 12–13.

7. John Keegan, *The American Civil War: A Military History* (New York, 2009), 26; Missouri Compromise (1820): http://www.ourdocuments.gov/doc.php?doc=22 , accessed January 13, 2014, NARA.

8. Rainwater, *Mississippi; Storm Center of Secession*, 13–14.

9. The Compromise of 1850: www.ushistory.org/us/30d.asp, accessed November 27, 2013.

10. McKee, "The Intrepid Mississippian," 32; McKee, "William Barksdale and the Congressional Election of 1853," 131–32.

11. McKee, "Intrepid Mississippian," 29–30, 32; Rainwater, *Mississippi: Storm Center of Secession*, 6. An excellent coded map gives a detailed breakdown of the distribution of slaves in each county. Slaves accounted for 71% of the total population in Lowndes County.

12. *Columbus Democrat*, March 29, 1851.

13. McKee, "Intrepid Mississippian," 31–32. Quote from Dunbar Rowland, *Official and Statistical Register of The State of Mississippi* (Nashville,1908) 197; Claiborne, "Biographical Sketch of William Barksdale," 6.

14. *Columbus Democrat*, October 27, 1851; Rowland, *Official and Statistical Register*, 244.

15. McKee, "Intrepid Mississippian," 37–38; Claiborne, "Biographical Sketch of William Barksdale," 6.

16. McKee, "Congressman William Barksdale," 48–49.

17. Quotations from the Jackson *Mississippian*, May 6, 1853. The greater substance of this Convention narrative is based upon McKee, "William Barksdale and the Congressional Election of 1853," 137–41, and McKee, "Intrepid Mississippian,"40–44.

18. Natchez *Mississippi Fur Trader*, June 7, and July 19, 1853.

19. Mc Rae had been elected to the Mississippi State Legislature in 1847 and was named Speaker of the House in 1850. He filled the unexpired term of Jefferson Davis in the U.S. Senate from December 1, 1851 to March 17, 1852, and was subsequently elected Governor of Mississippi in 1853 (being nominated at this same convention in Jackson) and again in 1855. Albert Gallatin Brown had been elected Governor of Mississippi back in 1845. He was subsequently elected to the U.S. Congress and then to the U.S. Senate in 1854.

20. Davis, *Recollections of Mississippi and Mississippians*, 332. Having publicly declared he would challenge the nomination by running as an independent in the election, Davis later declared he did so only because he "felt bound by the action of my friends and obliged to make the canvass, which I knew must end in disaster"! (333) This is much the same defense he made for his earlier failure as colonel of the 2nd Mississippi Volunteers. Quotations are from the *Columbus Southern Standard*, July 2, 1853 and June 11, 1853.

21. McKee, "Congressman William Barksdale," 54; McKee, "William Barksdale and the Congressional Election of 1853," 149–50.

22. *Ibid.*, 151–52.

23. *Ibid.*, 152–53; McKee, "Intrepid Mississippian," 47–49. Another account was published in the *Vicksburg Whig* on July 7, 1853 based on the testimony given in the court of Mayor J.S. Byrne.

24. Davis, *Recollections of Mississippi and Mississippians*, 334.

25. Jackson *Mississippian*, October 7; McKee, "William Barksdale and the Congressional Election of 1853," 155.

26. Jackson *Mississippian*, July 22; August 12, 19; September 9, 1853; Yazoo *Democrat*, August 24, 1853; *ibid.*, 156–57.

27. *Ibid.*, 157–58.

Chapter Five

1. McKee, "Congressman William Barksdale," 60–61; "The Mississippi Delegation In Congress," *Harper's Weekly*, New York, February 2, 1861, Vol. 5, no. 214, 65–66.

2. *Congressional Globe, 33rd Congress Session I*, John C. Rives, Washington, D.C., 34, 95, 114, 370.

3. "The Kansas-Nebraska Act," U.S. History Online Textbook, http://www.ushistory.org/us/31a. asp (accessed 10 February 2014); Rainwater, *Mississippi: Storm Center of Secession*, 123.

4. McKee, "Congressman William Barksdale," 62; *Congressional Globe, 33rd Congress Session I*, 678.

5. *Appendix to the Congressional Globe, 33rd Congress Session I*, 471.

6. *Ibid.*

7. *Ibid.*, 472.

8. *Ibid.*, 472–74.

9. *Ibid.* For an excellent detailed summary and analysis of this speech see McKee, "Congressman William Barksdale," 64–74.

10. McKee, "Congressman William Barksdale,"74–75;"The Kansas-Nebraska Act," The Origins of The Republican Party":www.ushistory.org/gop/origins.html; History of The Grand Old Party: www.socastee.com/politics history_gop.html, accessed 13 February 2014. In 1849 The American party emerged from secret societies formed in the 1840's in response to the influx of Irish and German immigrants. Candidates took a mandatory secret oath which included a pledge to elect only native-born citizens to public office to the exclusion of all foreigners and Roman Catholics. Sworn to secrecy, if questioned on their rituals, they were instructed to reply "I know nothing about it," hence the nickname "Know-Nothings." The Republican party was born out of two Anti-Nebraska meetings held in Ripon, Wisconsin on February 28 and March 20, 1854, attended by abolitionist Free Soilers, Northern Democrats, and Northern Whigs. They adopted the name Republicans claiming heritage from Thomas Jefferson's Democratic-Republican Party. The party name was made official at a state convention in Michigan on July 6, 1854.

11. *Congressional Globe, 33rd Congress Session I*, 1697–98.

12. *Congressional Globe, 33rd Congress Session II*, 21, 668.

13. *Ibid.*, 803, 1185, 1187, 1190.

14. All quotations are from Davis, *Recollections of Mississippi and Mississippians*, 346–49.

15. McKee, "Congressman William Barksdale," 76.

16. "Nathaniel Prentice Banks": www.archives.gov/boston/exhibits/banks, accessed 14 March 2014. Like Barksdale, Banks had been editor of several local newspapers, had studied law and been admitted to the bar at age 23, and was an accomplished public speaker. Banks would later serve as Governor of Massachusetts from 1858–1860, and would lose the Republican presidential nomination to Lincoln in 1860. Appointed by Lincoln as a major general of volunteers, he was most notable for winning the sobriquet "Commissary Banks" when soundly defeated by Stonewall Jackson during his brilliant Shenandoah Valley campaign in 1862.

17. Rainwater, *Storm Center of Secession*, 25; *Congressional Globe, 34th Congress Session I*, 16, 196.

18. *Ibid.*, 226, 231.

19. *Ibid.*, 444 (February 6, 1856).
20. *Ibid.*, 335–342; *Congressional Globe, 34th Congress Session III*, 998.
21. *Congressional Globe, Senate, 34th Congress Session I*, 529–30.
22. *Ibid.*, 530–32; David Donald, *Charles Sumner and the Coming of the Civil War* (New York, 1967) 286.
23. *Congressional Globe, Senate, 34th Congress Session I*, 543.
24. Donald, *Charles Sumner and the Coming of the Civil War*, 286, 288–89.
25. All quotations from *ibid.*, 291,294–96. Delivery of Sumner's speech and Brooks' caning of Sumner are based on Donald's detailed descriptions. See also William F. Freehling, *The Road To Disunion, Vol. II, Secessionists Triumphant*, 80–84, for a spirited, less-detailed description, and lastly Sylvia D. Hoffert, "The Brooks-Sumner Affair", *Civil War Times Illustrated*, Vol. 11, no. 6, October 1972, 35–40. It is gratifying that all three authors correctly identify Keitt as Brooks' accomplice and make no mention of Barksdale.
26. Raymond W. Tyson, "William Barksdale and the Brooks Sumner Assault," *"The Journal of Mississippi History*, Vol. 26, no. 2, May 1964,135–36.
27. Donald, *Charles Sumner and the Coming of the Civil War*, 298, 308.
28. Tyson, "William Barksdale and the Brooks Sumner Assault," 138–40. Tyson provides a more complete list of renowned authors and publications who have promulgated this unfortunate Barksdale myth.
29. *Appendix to the Congressional Globe, 34th Congress Session I*, 1177.
30. *Ibid.* Barksdale undoubtedly drew upon his personal experience as a high-degree Freemason. However, he made the distinction that these rituals were acceptable in social and benevolent institutions but definitely not in political organizations.
31. *Ibid.*, 1177–78. Barksdale contended that this state constitution was not by the populace of Kansas, but by a mere party of "adventurous traitors acting in open defiance of the law." This Kansas Bill failed to pass in the Senate thereby leaving open the question of Kansas statehood as free or slave.
32. *Ibid.*, 1178–80. Fillmore's anti-Freemasonry stance would have been particularly offensive to Worshipful Brother Barksdale. The passionate Mississippian was certainly not dissuaded in his remarks by Fillmore's status as a previous President.
33. *Ibid.*, 1180–83; McKee, "Congressman William Barksdale," 80.
34. *Congressional Globe, 35th Congress Session I*, 333.
35. *Congressional Globe, 34th Congress Session III*, 123.

Chapter Six

1. Jackson (MS) *Mississippi Semi-Weekly*, September 14, 1858; September 27, 1859; See also McKee, "Intrepid Mississippian," 51–52.
2. McKee, "Intrepid Mississippian," 53–56.
3. Louisville *Daily Journal*, December 1 and 2, 1857; *The Papers of Jefferson Davis, 6:1856–1860*, Lynda L. Crist and Mary S. Dix eds. (Louisiana State University Press, 1989), 171n2; Mrs. John A. Logan, *Reminiscences of A Soldier's Wife* (New York, 1913), 71–72.
4. Thomas J. Carrier, *Washington D.C.: A Historical Walking Tour* (Mount Pleasant, SC, 1999), 47; Margaret Leech, *Reveille In Washington* (New York, 1941), 8; McKee, "Intrepid Mississippian," 95; Logan, *Reminiscences of A Soldier's Wife*, 73; Mrs. Roger A. Pryor, *Reminiscences of Peace and War* (New York, 1904), 102–03.The hotel was sold by the Brown family in 1865 and renamed the Metropolitan Hotel, operating continuously until 1935 when it was demolished.
5. Mrs. Roger A. Pryor, *Reminiscences of Peace and* War, 102–03.
6. Davis, *Recollections of Mississippi and Mississippians*, 364, 367.
7. *Congressional Globe, 35th Congress Session I*, 31, 182. Barksdale's friend and protégé Reuben Davis served as attorney for the New Orleans, Macon, and Great Northern Railroad.
8. A detailed summary of this complicated evolution of events within Kansas is beyond the scope of this book. For a quick overview the following websites were referenced: The 2014 Kansas Directory; www.kssos.org/forms/communication/history.pdf See 22; Kansas Laws And Their Origin; skyways.lib.ks.us/genweb/archives/1918ks/v2/935.html; History of the State of Kansas; http://www.kandcoll.org/books/cutler/index.html, all accessed 25 April 2014.
9. James Dabney McCabe, *Behind the Scenes in Washington* (New York, c1873), 196–98, 200; http://artandhistory.house.gov/highlights.aspx?action=view&intID=128, accessed 5 October 2012; McKee, "Intrepid Mississippian," 93; Jeff Nilsson, Director of *Saturday Evening Post* Archives, http://www.saturdayeveningpost.com/2010/12/04/archives/post-perspective/beatings-brawl, accessed 5 October 2012; Davis, *Recollections of Mississippi and Mississippians*, 371–72. Davis supported Keitt's claim that he simply lost his balance in avoiding Grow's haymaker which did not land.
10. New Orleans *Picayune*, February 14, 1858.
11. McKee, "Congressman William Barksdale," 86; *Congressional Globe, 35th Congress Session I*, 623. No doubt frayed tempers, nervous exhaustion, and earlier consumption of alcohol by some contributed to this disgraceful exhibition. In an 1896 *Chicago Tribune* article John F. "Bowie Knife" Potter claimed that he had "scalped" Barksdale by inadvertently grabbing his wig.
12. *Ibid.*, 87–88.
13. *Ibid.*, 88.
14. All quotations taken from the *Congressional Globe, 35th Congress Session I*, 1214–16; *Appendix to the Congressional Globe, 35th Congress Session I*, 336–38. Barksdale actually took the time to revise his speech for the Appendix, adding several more paragraphs from Seward's Senate speech.

15. *Congressional Globe, 35th Congress Session II*, 450, 526.
16. *Ibid.*, 1027, 1234.
17. *Ibid.*, 1602.
18. *United States Democratic Review*, Vol. 43, April 1859, 19–34; Jackson *Mississippi Semi-Weekly*, September 14, 1858; *Congressional Globe, 35th Congress Session II*, 316.
19. *Congressional Globe, 35th Congress Session II*, 619.
20. *Journal of The House of Representatives of The United States 1789-1873*:December 20, 1859, 61–68; December 24, 1859, 79–81; *Appendix to the Congressional Globe, 36th Congress Session I*, 134; *Congressional Globe, 36th Congress Session I*, 650.
21. Hinton Rowan Helper was a Presbyterian minister from North Carolina who had written an anti-slavery book in 1859,*The Impending Crisis of the South: How to Meet It*, in which he appealed to non-slaveholders in the South to terminate slavery via political means—if unsuccessful, then by violent means. Helper also advocated that slaveholders should be banned from holding political office. Sixty Republican congressmen formally endorsed this treatise. Barksdale borrowed the discord comment from Congressman Pugh of Alabama. Quotation is from the *Appendix to the Congressional Globe, 36th Congress Session I*, 168.
22. *Appendix to the Congressional Globe, 36th Congress Session I*, 170. Barksdale's comment speaks for itself and reflects the core belief of a very large portion of society in the South. However, this view also existed in the North where some felt no differently, and said so publicly. For example, William A. Richardson, Democratic congressman, and future senator from Illinois stated in the House on January 12, 1856: "I believe that the Almighty made the negro inferior to the white man. I do not believe you can place them upon an equality, unless you bring down the white man to his level; and I am opposed to that." (*Congressional Globe, 34th Congress Session I*, 227).
23. *Ibid.*, 169–71. Contains all quotations. Barksdale had begun his political career in Mississippi initially as a Unionist, subsequently switching to the States' Rights faction of the Democratic party. Throughout he remained very proud of his American citizenship and often said so publicly. However, in the words of Dr. McKee, over his eight-year tenure as Congressman he transformed "from a moderate defender of states' rights to an avowed secessionist,"—but it must be qualified only if control of the federal government fell to the Republican party under a Republican President. (See Introduction, note 1 for a formal definition of *fire-eater*.)
24. McKee,"Congressman William Barksdale," 92; Speech of Representative Thaddeus Stevens To Congress, May 10, 1866 "On the Fourteenth Amendment."
25. Edward Magdol, *Owen Lovejoy: Abolitionist In Congress* (New Brunswick, NJ, 1967), vi–ix.
26. *Appendix to the Congressional Globe, 36th Congress Session I*, 170, 204–05.
27. *Vanity Fair Weekly Newspaper*, Vol. 10, April 14, 1860, New York, 245–49. The *Appendix to the Congressional Globe* records Barksdale's exact words as "Order that black-hearted scoundrel and nigger-stealing thief to his seat, and this side will do it."It was also recorded that 30 or 40 members from both sides of the House gathered in the area about Mr. Lovejoy and there was increased confusion.
28. *Ibid.*, May 5, 1860, 294.
29. Murat Halstead, *Three Against Lincoln*, William B. Hesseltine, editor (Baton Rouge, 1960), 15. Despite his reputation as a knife fighter, there is no recorded evidence of Barksdale actually having used a bowie knife in any of his fights or near duels. His knife fighting prowess is based solely on assumption and hearsay.
30. Pettus' quote is from the *Mississippian*, May 30, 1860; Rainwater, *Storm Center of Secession*, 125. For the larger context of the Democratic conventions see McKee, "Intrepid Mississippian," 103–04. The splitting of the Democratic party over slavery mirrored the earlier splintering of the Methodist, Baptist, and Presbyterian Churches into hostile Northern and Southern factions over negro bondage.
31. Rainwater, *Storm Center of Secession*, 167–68.
32. *Ibid.*, 168. For the caucus votes cast see Robert W. Dubay, *John Jones Pettus—Mississippi Fire-eater: His Life and Times 1813-1867* (Jackson, MS, 1975), 67–69; also James B. Murphy, *L.Q.C. Lamar—Pragmatic Patriot* (Baton Rouge, 1973) 54–55; See also Reuben Davis, *Recollections of Mississippi and Mississippians*, 390–91; McKee, "Intrepid Mississippian," 106.
33. Charles B. Dew, *Apostles of Disunion* (Charlottesville, VA, 2001) 24; McKee, "Intrepid Mississippian," 107.Secession was aided by the appointment of Secession Commissioners by the Southern states including Mississippi.
34. *Congressional Globe, 36th Congress Session II*, 282.
35. *Ibid.*, 345.
36. Woodville *Republican*, August 22, 1835; Dubay, *John Jones Pettus*, 72.

Chapter Seven

1. William Barksdale to James Blair and others, January 4, 1861, The Magnetic Telegraph Company, http://pages.cthome.net/fwc/Index.HTM , accessed 3 July 2001.
2. Edward Mayes, *Lucius Q.C. Lamar: His Life, Times, and Speeches 1825-1893* (Nashville TN, 1896), 94.
3. Claiborne, "Biographical Sketch of William Barksdale," 8; Rowland, *Military History of Mississippi*, 37. Mississippi broke with military tradition. Almost universally, blue trim designated infantry, red—artillery, and yellow—cavalry. The conventional kepi, bummer and felt slouch hats quickly superseded the tri-parte hat.
4. *The War of the Rebellion: A Compilation of the Official Records of the Union and Confederate*

Armies, 128 vols. (Washington, DC, 1880–1901), Series 1, Vol. 52, 25. (Hereafter cited as OR) All references are to Series 1 unless otherwise noted; Rowland, *Military History of Mississippi*, 38; William Barksdale Compiled Service Record, www.fold3.com/ image/#65798480/#65799280, accessed 9 December 2011.

5. Dubay, *John Jones Pettus*, 58,67; C.B.M. McCaleb to Pettus, March 22, 1861, Adjutant General's Correspondence, Mississippi Archives, Jackson, File L-75 reproduced in Bettersworth, *Mississippi in the Confederacy*, 49. In May 1860 Pettus dispatched State Adjutant General Sykes to visit several northern armories, arsenals, and factories to purchase several thousand stands of Mississippi Rifles with sword bayonets. In November 1860 Pettus ordered 9,000 rifles and muskets, 200,000 cartridges, and ample quantities of cannon powder and shot from the federal arsenal in Baton Rouge.

6. Rowland, *Military History of Mississippi*, 38–39.

7. Dubay, *John Jones Pettus*, 110; Abstract of Expenditures of Commissary Department by Col. Wm. Barksdale Q.M. Gen'l State of Mississippi, William Barksdale Compiled Service record, www.fold3.com/image/#65799162, accessed 9 December 2011.

8. William Barksdale to Governor Pettus, July 26, 1861, in Pettus papers, MDAH.

9. These are the final company designations assigned following the major reorganization in April 1862. The initial muster designations which applied for the initial twelve months of service are shown in brackets. Refer to Rowland, *Military History of Mississippi*, 66–68.

10. *Ibid.*, 69. Claiborne records that Barksdale initially enlisted as a private in the 13th Mississippi which makes sense although there is no surviving documentation supporting this fact in his compiled service record. Claiborne also maintains that Barksdale's election as colonel was unanimous.

11. LeGrand J. Wilson, *The Confederate Soldier*, James W. Silver ed., (Memphis, TN, 1973), 21. Wilson was a line officer in the 1st Mississippi and later a Surgeon in the 42nd Mississippi.

12. "Historic Event In The Days of '61," Aberdeen (MS) *Examiner*, July 29, 1937. Article describes Mrs. Annie Vaughn Parham giving this same speech under the same actual flag some 53 years after the war during the annual reunion of the Caledonia Rifles. For an excellent analysis of Southern culture and how it motivated the Confederate soldier, see Stephen W. Berry II, *All That Makes A Man: Love and Ambition in the Civil War South* (New York, 2003).

13. *To See My Country Free: Pocket Diaries of Ezekiel Armstrong, Ezekiel P. Miller, and Joseph A. Miller*, Clifton C. Valentine, ed. (Humboldt, TN, 1998), 30.

14. *Confederate Veteran*, September 1907, 413.

15. Modern scholarly works such as Charles B. Dew's *Apostles of Disunion* (Charlottesville, VA, 2001) absolutely confirm slavery was the issue that ignited the Civil War. To drill down to the root cause(s) requires additional analysis and application of specific techniques. This author's background in Quality Control and Continuous Improvement confirmed the validity of the Analyze phase of the Six Sigma Methodology developed by the Toyota Motor Corporation, popularized in the 1970's and still in use today—including the 5 Whys Determination of Root Cause. By repeatedly asking "why" up to five times, the layers can be peeled away leading to identification of the true underlying root cause of a problem or situation. In this case, "why was the Civil War fought?"

16. For an excellent analysis of the contributing causes to the American Civil War see James M. McPherson, *Drawn with the Sword* (Oxford, 1996); For preservation of the Union as the sole initial motivating force of Northern soldiers in 1861 see Gary W. Gallagher, *Causes Won, Lost, and Forgotten* (Chapel Hill, NC, 2008) 1–14, 236 n.10.

17. James M. McPherson, "Central to the Civil War," *North & South Magazine*, Vol. 10, no. 4, January 2008, 59.

18. David Holt Civil War Memoirs, *A Mississippi Rebel in the Army of Northern Virginia*, Thomas D. Cockrell and Michael B. Ballard eds. (Baton Rouge, 1995) 36, 62.

19. William L. Nugent to Wife, September 7, 1863, Howarth Letters, reproduced in Bettersworth, *Mississippi in the Confederacy*, 354. In 1833 when slavery was abolished in the British Colonies, the British government paid out a whopping 20 million pounds Sterling—the equivalent of $33,385,800 (40% of the annual Treasury budget) to 3,000 slaveholders.

20. McPherson, *Drawn with the Sword*, 9. For an excellent description and analysis of the antebellum South and its contrast to the North, see Chapter 1, 3–23.

21. Keegan, *The American Civil War*, xiii.

22. McPherson, *Drawn with the Sword*, 63.

23. Pvt. Co. H, 13th MS, Albert Wymer Henley diary, May 2, 1861, FRSNMP. See also *Official Records Of The 13th Mississippi Regiment*, compiled by Jess N. McLean Sr., ISBN 0-9722855-0-4 published independently (no city, Texas, 2001), 125 (hereinafter cited as McLean) Hawley, "Brigadier General William Barksdale, CSA," 15, 24–25; Bettersworth, *Mississippi in the Confederacy*, 177.

24. Hawley, "Brigadier General William Barksdale, CSA," 15. In 1855 William Hardee wrote the seminal manual on tactical warfare, entitled Rifle and Light Infantry Tactics For The Exercise and Maneuver of Troops When Acting As Light Infantry or Riflemen, popularly known as Hardee's Tactics. During 1856–1860 Hardee served as Superintendent of Cadets at West Point resigning on January 31, 1861 to later accept a commission as lieutenant general in the Confederate army; Pvt., Co. A, 13th MS, Thomas D. Wallace diary, Mississippi State University, Starkville, MS, May 17, 1861.

25. Pvt., Co. I, 13th MS, Newton Nash Letters, Old Courthouse Museum Collections, Vicksburg, MS, to wife Mollie, May 26, 1861; Bell Irwin Wiley

and Hirst D. Milhollen, *They Who Fought Here* (New York, 1965), 30.

26. Henley diary, May 27, 1861.

27. *The Civil War Letters of Joshua K. Callaway*, Judith Lee Hallock, ed. (Athens, GA, 1997) 16; Stephen W. Berry II, *All That Makes a Man* (New York, 2003), 176–77.

28. *Ibid.*, 177; Wilson, *The Confederate Soldier*, 30. Private Robert A. Moore of the 17th Mississippi records a very similar drill schedule—see *A Life for the Confederacy: The War Diary of Robert A. Moore, Pvt. CSA*, James W. Silver, ed. (Jackson, TN, 1959) 22, 24. Based upon personal experience as a Civil War re-enactor in the 1980s, it did not take long to buy into the camaraderie and importance of being a part of the greater whole at the expense of self. Just marching in column of fours amongst several hundred Confederate brothers-in-arms of like mind, even 120 years later, quickly established an esprit de corps that was palpable, although perhaps hard to explain.

29. Henley diary, May 27, 1861; Wallace diary, July 11, 1861. Although Henley's comments were typical of criticisms leveled against colonels of other Confederate regiments, he continually harbored a deep personal resentment toward Barksdale.

30. Newton Nash letter to Mollie, June 7, 1861.

31. Henley diary, June 7, 1861; Pvt., Co. E, 13th MS, Joseph M. Eastis to Mary, June 14, 1861, McLean, 134. Henley insisted resentfully that this was a subterfuge perpetrated by Barksdale.

32. Henley diary, May 27; July 4, 1861. Marching at the double quick was a moderate jog at about 180 paces per minute.

33. Henley diary, May 27, 1861; Pvt., Co. K, 13th MS, Wilborn P. Smith to Clay, July 8, 1861, McLean, 138; Wallace diary, July 12, 1861.

34. Wallace diary, July 12, 1861.

35. *Ibid.*, July 14, 1861. The unfortunate young soldier was six-foot Pvt. Calvin P. Warner, a 21-year-old farmer from Louisville, MS.

36. OR 2, 981

37. Henley diary, July 21, 1861.

38. OR 2, 555–56; Gen. Jubal A. Early, *Autobiographical Sketch and Narrative of the War Between the States*; Reprint of 1912 edition (Wilmington, NC, 1989), 19–20.

39. Early, *Autobiographical Sketch*, 20. Early did not mention this complaint in his official battle report. Barksdale undoubtedly would have regarded such comments as an affront to his honor and reputation of his regiment. It is also interesting to note that Early did cite the exhaustion of Hays' Louisiana troops under his command as a factor in their performance.

40. All quotations from Henley diary, July 21, 1861 except for the run of 10 miles which is from Wallace diary, July 21, 1861.

41. P. F. Ellis," Extracts from an Untitled Letter," *Confederate Veteran*, Vol. 5, December 1897, 624.

42. Account By J. F. Brown in *Confederate Veteran*, Vol. 2, November 1894, 341; *Ibid.*; Wallace diary, July 21, 1861; Sgt. William H. Hill diary, July 21, 1861, 1861–1863, 2 Vol., Z0217.00 MDAH,

Jackson, MS. References to Elzey's brigade from Bradley M. Gottfried, *The Maps Of First Bull Run* (El Dorado Hills, CA, 2009), 68. Elzey (as senior colonel) took command of the brigade when Brig. Gen. Edmund Kirby Smith was wounded. Elzey was promoted by President Jefferson Davis to brigadier general on the battlefield.

43. OR 2, 496, 558; Douglas Southall Freeman, *Lee's Lieutenants*, 3 vols. (New York, 1942), Vol. 1, 96.

44. Hawley, "Brigadier William Barksdale, CSA," 17–18.

45. Henley diary, July 22, 1861; Hill diary, August 4, 1861.

Chapter Eight

1. Letters of Pvt. J. A. Byers, 17th Mississippi, Hartman McIntosh, ed., "The Whole World Was Full of Smoke," *Military Images*, Vol. 9, no. 6, May-June 1988, 6; Hill diary, July 23, 1861.

2. Wallace diary, July 26, and August 2, 1861; Hill diary, August 4, 1861.

3. Henley diary, August 3, 1861; Wallace diary, August 6, 1861; Bell I. Wiley, *The Life of Johnny Reb* (Baton Rouge, LA, 1943, 1981 Reprint), 56, 358 n.7. The 13th Mississippi was no exception. According to Wiley the 18th Mississippi reported 25 new cases of gonorrhea in July 1861.

4. Henley diary, August 27, 1861; Hill diary, August 21, 1861.

5. Lieutenant Colonel M.H. Whitaker et al to Jefferson Davis, October 15, 1861, National Archives. Copy provided by Trevor K. Plante, July 19, 2000.

6. Confederate Memoir of William Meshack Abernathy, 17th Mississippi, typewritten copy provided in April 2002 by John W. Hoopes, Abernathy's great, great grandson. Subsequently published in *Confederate Veteran*, Vol. 2, 2003 in two parts including several photos of Pvt. Abernathy; Major W. Gart Johnson, "Barksdale-Humphreys Mississippi Brigade," *Confederate Veteran*, July 1893, 206.

7. Major Robert Stiles, *Four Years Under Marse Robert*, 1903 (Marietta, GA, 1995), 60.

8. Henley diary, September 6, 1861; Newton Nash to Wife, September 28, 1861.

9. Testimony of Maj. Gen. George B. McClellan in U.S. Congress Joint Committee On The Conduct of War—Battle of Ball's Bluff; James A. Morgan III, *A Little Short of Boats: The Fights at Ball's Bluff and Edwards Ferry* (Fort Mitchell, KY: 2004), 24, 26.

10. Hill diary, October 19, 1861; Henley diary, October 19, 1861.

11. Henley diary, October 20, 1861; Morgan, *A Little Short of Boats*, 27.

12. *Ibid.*, 34; Kim B. Holien, *Battle at Ball's Bluff* (Orange, VA, 1995), 27. Based upon alternate sources Morgan states the illusory tents were white huts for negroes and dogs near a farmhouse while Byron Farwell concludes they were only a row of trees viewed in uncertain light.

13. OR 5, 354.

14. OR 5, 302; R.W. Hunter, "Men of Virginia at

Ball's Bluff," *Times-Dispatch*, April 22–29, May 6, 1906, *SHSP*, Vol. 34, 272–73.

15. Thomas C. Caffey, *Battle-Fields of the South from Bull Run to Fredericksburg—By an English Combatant* (London, 1863), Vol. I, 150. Other political heavyweights present who gave prominence to this battle were Winfield Scott Featherston, colonel of the 17th Mississippi, a former U.S. Congressman who had served with both Baker and Lincoln; Albert Gallatin Brown, Captain of Company H, 18th Mississippi, former Governor of Mississippi, U.S. Congressman and U.S. Senator; and Otho R. Singleton, Captain of Company C, 18th Mississippi, and a former U.S. Congressman.

16. This Ball's Bluff battle summary is based largely upon Morgan, *A Little Short of Boats*, and Farwell, *Ball's Bluff: A Small Battle and It's Long Shadow* (McLean VA, 1990).

17. *OR* 5, 354–56.

18. *Ibid*.

19. *Ibid.*, 354–55; Caffey, *Battle-Fields of the South from Bull Run to Fredericksburg*, Vol. I, 151.

20. *Ibid.*, 355.

21. *Ibid.*, 350.

22. *Ibid*.

23. Colonel Elijah V. White, *History of the Battle of Ball's Bluff* (Leesburg, VA, n.d.), 21. White also stated his belief that had Evans supported Barksdale with his entire force then Gorman would have been forced to surrender; Captain A.G. Brown, 18th Mississippi, letter In Camp At Carter's Mills, November 12, 1861, reprinted in *Writing and Fighting from the Army of Northern Virginia: A Collection of Confederate Soldier Correspondence*, William B. Styple, ed. (Kearny, N.J, 2003), 67. Brown resigned shortly after Ball's Bluff and was twice elected to the Confederate senate.

24. R. W. Hunter, "Men of Virginia at Ball's Bluff," *SHSP*, Vol. 34, 264; *OR*, 5, 368. Byron Farwell recorded that under the pseudonym of "A Southern Lady," a poem entitled "The Battle Of Leesburg" was written and formally dedicated to Colonel Barksdale. However, this author has been unable to locate it.

25. Hill diary, October 27, 1861.

26. *OR* 5, 355.

27. Eppa Hunton, *Autobiography* of *Eppa Hunton* (Richmond, VA, 1933), 58.

28. *OR* 5, 352, 368–69.

29. Pvt. J. Dudley Stennis, Company C, 13th Mississippi, to his Father, November 1, 1861, McLean, 187.

30. A.I.G.O. General Order No. 19, General Orders from the Adjutant and Inspector-General's Office, CSA General Orders 1861–1862, Vol. 1, Chapter 1, 81–82, National Archives; Hill diary, November 4, 9, 18, 1861.

31. Jack A. Bunch, *Military Justice in the Confederate States Army* (Shippensburg, PA, 2000), 23, 79.

Chapter Nine

1. "The Autobiography of Benjamin Grubb Humphreys," excerpts in P.L. Rainwater, ed., *Mississippi Valley Historical Review*, Vol. 21, no. 2, September 1934, 237–38.

2. Jason H. Silverman, Samuel N. Thomas Jr., Beverly D. Evans IV, *Shanks: The Life and Wars of General Nathan G. Evans* (no city: Da Capo Press, 2002), 90–91, 106, 147–48.

3. Miss Virginia J. Miller diary, December 9, 1861, in The Glenfiddich House, 205 North King St., Leesburg, The Miles/LeHone Group Inc. http://wwwmileslehone.com/diary.html, accessed 18 September 2001; Ezekiel Armstrong pocket diary, December 8, 9, 1861, in *To See My Country Free—The Pocket Diaries of Ezekiel Armstrong, Ezekiel P. Miller And Joseph A. Miller*, Clifton C. Valentine, ed. (Humboldt, TN, 1998), 63–64. Both are eyewitness accounts.

4. Hill diary, December 9, 1861. Upon the death of Col. Erasmus Burt, 45-year-old planter Thomas M. Griffin from Madison Mississippi assumed command of the 18th Mississippi. He would later be wounded at Malvern Hill and Gettysburg.

5. Newton Nash to wife, November 10, 1861.

6. Hill diary, December 7, 1861.

7. Newton Nash to wife, December 1, 1861.

8. Hill diary, December 25, 1861; *A Life for the Confederacy—As Recorded in the Pocket Diaries of Pvt. Robert A. Moore, Co. G Confederate Guards, 17th Mississippi*, James W. Silver, ed. (Jackson, TN, 1959), 90–91; Henley diary, December 31, 1861.

9. Unpublished Autobiography of Benjamin Grubb Humphreys, Chapter VI, 25–26, MDAH. This handwritten manuscript comprising 27 chapters was donated by Humphreys great-great-grandson, Douglas More of Greenwich, Connecticut in 2001 and has never been published in its entirety.

10. Stiles, *Four Years Under Marse Robert*, 67–8. Private Moore recorded in his diary for February 5th, "Have been practicing with the artillery at Fort Johnston. Threw balls over Leesburg and Fort Evans."; Hill diary, February 25, 1862.

11. Narcissa Barksdale to Alcinda Janney, October 25, 1862, John Janney Papers; Hill diary, February 17, 26, 1862.

12. Henley diary, March 5, 1862; Hill diary, March 2, 1862; Moore, *A Life for the Confederacy*, 105.

13. Humphreys, Autobiography, Chapter VIII, 2; Hill diary and Henley diary, March 7, 1862; Captain James Dinkins, *1861 to 1865, By an Old Johnnie—Personal Recollections and Experiences in the Confederate Army* (Cincinnati, OH, 1897; Reprint 1975), 28 (hereinafter cited as *By an Old Johnnie)*; Stiles, *Four Years Under Marse Robert*, 72.

14. Hill diary; Henley diary; Pvt. Michael Hubbert, diary, Co. I,13th Mississippi, University of Texas, Austin, TX—various entries March 7, 1862 to April 14, 1862.

15. Hill diary, April 25, 1862; Brig. Gen. G. Moxley Sorrel CSA, *Recollections of a Confederate Staff Officer* (no city, 1959), Reprint Wilmington, NC, 1995, 57; Rowland, *Military History of Mississippi*, 70; Pvt. Wilborn P. Smith to brother Clay, April 27, 1862, Mclean, 242. Smith was a close personal friend of Whitaker and freely expressed dismay at

Barksdale's re-election which he claimed was only by 157 votes. This margin appears strikingly low and must be considered suspect. See Mclean 240–41 for other officers elected.

16. Humphreys, Autobiography, Chapter VIII, 27–28.

17. A.G. Brown et al to His Excellency Mr. President March 29, 1862, NA; Officers of 13th, 17th, 18th Mississippi Regiments to Honorable Jefferson Davis, President of the Southern Confederacy April 15, 1862, Compiled Service record of William Barksdale, NA; Brig. Gen. R. Griffith, to Honorable Jefferson Davis, President, April 25, 1862, NA.

18. For a concise description of the siege of Yorktown see Stephen W. Sears, *To the Gates of Richmond: The Peninsula* Campaign (New York, 1992), 40–62; Milton F. Perry, *Infernal Machines: The Story of Confederate Submarine and Mine Warfare* (LSU Press, 1965), 20–25; James M. Martin et al, *History of The Fifty-Seventh Pennsylvania Veteran Volunteers* (Kearney, NJ, 1995), 25. Description and effect of Confederate torpedo operations at Yorktown is based upon Perry and Sears, 66–67. Learning of Rains' torpedo activity at Yorktown, Longstreet commanded Rains to cease on May 11, 1862, deeming this not a proper or effective method of warfare. Rains objected, claiming they were as proper as ambuscades, masked batteries, and (tunnel) mines. The Confederate High Command debated the ethics of Rains' infernal machines. Eventually the matter was closed when, at Lee's request, Rains was transferred to the James River defenses where in Sear's words "his particular talents could be applied to the more acceptable activity of blowing up Yankee warships."

19. Wallace and Hill diaries, entries for May 1–2, 1862.

20. Sears, *To the Gates of Richmond*, 252; *Pennsylvania At Gettysburg*, 3 vols. John P. Nicholson, Secretary of Commission (Harrisburg, PA, 1904) 2:1091–92; Kennedy Hickman, "Major John F. Reynolds—To The Peninsula" website http://militaryhistory.about.com/od/UnionLeaders/p/American-Civil-War-Major-General-John-Reynolds; also "Confederate General Lloyd Tilghman at http://www.bryansbush.com/hub.php?page=articles&layer=a0605; both accessed 9 April 2013; Mark M. Boatner III, *Civil War Dictionary Revised Edition* (New York, 1988), 694, 839–40. This untruth that Reynolds was exchanged for Barksdale was also repeated in *The Twentieth Century Biographical Dictionary of Notable Americans* in its entry for John Fulton Reynolds.

21. Dinkins, *By an Old Johnnie*, 44; Stiles, *Four Years Under Marse Robert*, 95; Joseph L. Brent, *Memoirs of the War Between the States* (New Orleans, 1940), 180. See also Jack D. Welsh, *Medical Histories of Confederate Generals* (Kent, OH, 1995), 89. Welsh states this wound was on the inside of Griffith's thigh. Diarists Hill, Henley, Hubbert, and Thurman E. Hendricks of the 13th Mississippi all made entries regarding Griffith's mortal wounding. Hendricks stated, "I was standing thirty feet away from him when he was struck."

22. *OR* 11/2:750.

23. Robert R. Hodges Jr., *American Civil War Railroad Tactics* (New York, 2009), 17–20; Caffey, *Battle-Fields of the South from Bull Run to Fredericksburg*, Vol. II, 163–64; Stiles, *Four Years Under Marse Robert*, 95; Humphreys, Autobiography, Chapter IX, 13; Sears, *To the Gates of Richmond*, 269–70. It has been suggested that this Land Merrimac was the intended target of the artillery shell that mortally wounded General Griffith. This may have been the case since Humphreys recorded that the "Little Merrimac" arrived at the same time as Griffith's wounding while Caffey claimed Griffith was conversing with the engineer when he was struck.

24. D. Augustus Dickert, *History of Kershaw's Brigade* (Dayton, OH, 1976), 129; Hodges, *American Civil War Railroad Tactics*, 21.

25. *OR* 11/2: 750; Humphreys, Autobiography, Chapter IX, 15.

26. Humphreys, Autobiography, Chapter IX, 15.

27. *Ibid.*, 15–16; "The Late Colonel William Inge: His Remarkable Military Career," *Confederate Veteran*, January 1901, 20.

28. Stiles, *Four Years Under Marse Robert*, 94–95.

29. Address by Major Robert Stiles at the Dedication of Monument to the Confederate Dead at the University of Virginia, June 7, 1893, *SHSP*, 21:22–23.

30. Humphreys, Autobiography, Chapter IX, 17.

31. Hawley, "Brigadier General William Barksdale CSA," 37.

32. Hubbert diary, June 30, 1862.

33. *OR* 11/2:752.

Chapter Ten

1. *OR* 11/2:751.

2. Bruce S. Allardice, *Confederate Colonels: A Biographical Register* (Columbia, MO, 2008); Charles A. Ears, "The Seven McElroy's of the Thirteenth Mississippi Infantry CSA," *Confederate Veteran*, September-October 1993, 36–42; Jeff T. Giambrone, "Like A Cane Brake On Fire—The 21st Mississippi Infantry At Malvern Hill, "*North & South Magazine*, Vol. 8, no. 2, 25.

3. Dinkins, *By an Old Johnnie*, 48–49.

4. Lieutenant General Daniel H. Hill, "McClellan's Change of Base and Malvern Hill," *Battles and Leaders of the Civil War*, Robert U. Johnson and Clarence C. Buel, eds., 4 vols. (New York, 1887–88), 2:391 (hereinafter cited as *B&L*)

5. *OR* 11/2: 628, 677; Robert E. L. Krick, "Malvern Hill: Portrait of a Battlefield," *Civil War Magazine*, Issue 73, April 1999, 21–23. This entire issue is dedicated to the battle of Malvern Hill and is an excellent reference with numerous photos.

6. Stiles, *Four Years Under Marse Robert*, 104; Lieut. Thomas Evans, 12th U.S. Infantry, "At Malvern Hill," *Civil War Times Illustrated*, December 1967, 40.

7. *OR* 11/2: 628.

8. *Ibid.*

9. *Ibid.*, 670; Alexander S. Webb, *The Peninsula:*

McClellan's Campaign of 1862 (New York, 1992), 63; Hawley," Brigadier General William Barksdale CSA," 44–45.

10. *OR* 11/ 2:751.

11. *Ibid.*, 752.

12. *Barksdale Family History*, 284. Captain John Barksdale cites Lee's personal endorsement on McLaws' July 8, 1862 recommendation of William Barksdale's promotion to Brigadier General; Douglas S. Freeman, *Lee's Lieutenants*, 3 vols. (New York, 1943), 2: 332.

13. Hendrick's diary, July 1, 1862, McLean, 275.

14. David S. Goodloe, "Tribute to Green B Crane," *Confederate Veteran*, March 1901, 128.

15. Stiles, *Four Years Under Marse Robert*, 15; Giambrone, "Like a Cane Brake on Fire," 28–30.

16. *OR* 11/2:753. This entire battle account is derived from the four regimental reports and Barksdale's brigade report, Hawley's analysis, as well as Joseph P. Cullen's, "At Malvern Hill: 'It Was Not War—It Was Murder'," *Civil War Times Illustrated*, May 1966, 4–14; "Rediscovering Malvern Hill," various authors, William J. Miller ed., *Civil War Magazine*, Issue #73, April 1999, as well as Sears, *To the Gates of Richmond*.

17. *OR* 11/2:753.

18. Hawley, "Brigadier General William Barksdale CSA," 43.

19. *OR* 11/2: 752.

20. Hawley, "Brigadier General William Barksdale CSA," 44; 65–66; n67; Clement A. Evans ed., *Confederate Military History* 12 vols. (Atlanta, 1889), 7:117; Charles E. Hooker, *Confederate Military History of Mississippi Reprint* (Pensacola, FL, 2003), 80; "Griffith's Brigade," *American Citizen*, Canton, MS, August 15, 1862; Giambrone, "Like A Cane Brake On Fire", 29.

21. *OR* 11/ 2:751.

22. *Ibid.*, 752.

23. Dinkins, *By an Old Johnnie*, 49–50.

24. D. H. Hill, *B&L*, 3: 394. In his after-action report Hill opined: "The battle of Malvern Hill might have been a complete and glorious success had not our artillery and infantry been fought in detail." Uncoordinated attacks would later be blamed by many Confederate commanders for defeat at Gettysburg.

25. Lafayette McLaws to Colonel Barksdale, July 8, 1862 in Compiled Service Record of William Barksdale, NA.

26. *Ibid.*

27. Stiles, *Four Years Under Marse Robert*, 64–65.

28. Jackson *Weekly Clarion*, January 17, 1867; McKee," Intrepid Mississippian," 161; W. Gart Johnson, "Barksdale Humphreys Brigade," *Confederate Veteran*, July 1893, 206.

29. Robert K. Krick, "Lafayette McLaws," *The Confederate General*, William C. Davis, ed., 6 vols. (Washington D.C., 1991),4:128–131; John C. Oeffinger, ed., *A Soldier's General: The Civil War Letters of Major General Lafayette McLaws* (Chapel Hill, NC, 2002), 27, 98 (hereinafter cited as *McLaws Civil War Letters*).

30. Humphreys, Autobiography, Chapter X, 9.

31. Hill diary, July 14, 1862; Wilborn P. Smith to Brother Clay, July 27, 1862, McLean, 285.

32. Newton Nash to Molly, August 19, 1862.

33. Dinkins, *By an Old Johnnie*, 51–52; Captain James Dinkins, "Griffith-Barksdale-Humphrey Mississippi Brigade and Its Campaigns," *SHSP*, 32: 253.

34. Hill diary, August 20, 1862.

35. Hubbert diary, September 1, 1862; Dinkins, "Mississippi Brigade," 254.

36. Dinkins, *By an Old Johnnie*, 53; Dinkins, "Mississippi Brigade," 254.

Chapter Eleven

1. Humphreys, Autobiography, Chapter X, 21–22; 24–25; Hubbert diary, September 10, 1862; Hill and Henley diaries, September 10, 1862.

2. Although they would fight side by side until Barksdale's death at Gettysburg, this was the only time it was not as equals. Kershaw's commission as brigadier general dated from February 13, 1862, six months earlier than Barksdale's on August 12, 1862—See Philip Katcher, *The Army of Robert E. Lee* (London, 1994), 49–50.

3. Joseph L. Harsh, *Taken at the Flood* (Kent, OH, 1999), 158–63; 201–03; Dickert, *History of Kershaw's Brigade*, 148; Dennis E. Frye, "Drama Between The Rivers," *Antietam: Essays on the 1862 Maryland Campaign*, Gary W. Gallagher ed. (Kent, OH, 1989), 19; *OR* 19/1:863. An abatis is a defensive structure comprised of felled trees with their limbs cut off about two feet from the trunk and sharpened.

4. R. L. Murray, *The Redemption of the "Harper's Ferry Cowards,"* (Walcott, NY, 1994), 19.

5. Frye, "Drama Between the Rivers," 18.

6. Wayne Mahood, *Written in Blood: A History of the 126th New York Infantry in the Civil War* (Highstown, NJ, 1997), 32.

7. C.C. Cummings, "Capture of Harper's Ferry, "*Confederate Veteran*, April 1897, 174; Harsh, *Taken at the Flood*, 202.

8. *OR* 19/1: 864. Cummings asserted that it was the rifle fire of the gallant South Carolinians, "led by their gamecock Kershaw," which caused the rout. (See "Storming Maryland Heights", *Confederate Veteran*, March 1915, 124) and is supported by the analyses of historians Dennis Frye and Stephen Sears.

9. Dinkins, "The Mississippi Brigade," 258. In her Regimental History of the 126th New York Infantry, Mrs. Arabella Willson offers a spirited and compelling defense of this regiment, attributing the collapse of the Union's defensive line on Maryland Heights instead to a verbal order "to withdraw in good order from the breastworks," delivered by an acting aide to Colonel Ford, "who was nowhere to be found." (See A.M. Willson, *Disaster, Struggle, Triumph: The Adventures of 1000 Boys in Blue* (Albany, NY, 1870), 55–76.

10. Hill and Hubbert diaries, September 12, 1862; *OR* 19/1: 854; Harsh, *Taken at the Flood*, 223.

11. *OR* 19/1: 854.
12. *Ibid.*, 855–56; Dinkins," Mississippi Brigade," 258–59.
13. Dickert, *History of Kershaw's Brigade*, 150; Dinkins, "Mississippi Brigade," 259.
14. *OR* 19/1: 864.
15. *Ibid.*, 856.
16. Hawley, "Brigadier General William Barksdale CSA," 48.
17. *McLaws Civil War Letters*, 32; Harsh, *Taken at the Flood*, 365; Dinkins, "Mississippi Brigade," 260.
18. Dinkins, "Mississippi Brigade," 260; Dinkins, *By an Old Johnnie*, 56–57; Hubbert diary, September 16, 1862.
19. McKee," Intrepid Mississippian," 182; *OR* Battle Reports for Maryland Campaign from McLaws, Kershaw, Barksdale, previously cited. A case for lack of shoes as a contributing factor can also be made. Barksdale has been criticized for not better addressing these logistical supply issues given his previous experience. (See Hawley, 47; 49–51; 57–60.) However, this author believes Barksdale's prior commissary service in Mexico and particularly as quartermaster general of Mississippi gave him a true appreciation of the overwhelming challenges of supply and distribution, and therefore a clear realization of his inability to personally alleviate the resultant shortages. This assessment is supported by Colonel, and later Brig. Gen., Benjamin G. Humphreys who wrote post-war, "Unmistakable evidences of want and distress were exhibited in every command, through the defective administration and scanty supplies in the Quartermasters, Commissary, Ordnance, and Medical Departments. But for the self-sacrificing spirits of the Confederate soldier, and for the liberal contributions from private sources, the task would have proved too Herculean for the limited resources of the Government." (Autobiography, Chapter VI, 9.)
20. McLaws to General John B. Hood, May 31, 1863, *McLaws Civil War Letters*, 183; Dinkins, "Mississippi Brigade," 260. Company C, 18th Mississippi to which he belonged started out with 58 officers and men but only 1 officer and 16 enlisted men arrived to fight at Sharpsburg.
21. *OR* 19/1: 857, 883; quotation from Abernathy Memoir, 17; Dinkins, *By an Old Johnnie*, 58; Harsh, *Taken at the Flood*, 366–69.
22. Derived from Sears, *Landscape Turned Red: The Battle of Antietam* (New Haven, CT, 1983), 167–76.
23. *Ibid.*, 202, 214.
24. Marion V. Armstrong, *Disaster in the West Woods* (Sharpsburg, MD, 2002); Harsh, *Taken at the Flood*, 387; Sears, *Landscape Turned Red*, 220.
25. Henley diary, September 17, 1862; Dinkins, *By an Old Johnnie*, 58; Dinkins, "Mississippi Brigade," 261. The wording of Dinkins' two accounts varies somewhat. The author has used a combination from each version.
26. Dinkins, *By an Old Johnnie*, 58–59; Dinkins, "Mississippi Brigade," 261–62. For Barksdale's motivational technique See Hawley, 52.
27. Despite Kershaw's claims to the contrary, Augustus Dickert, historian of Kershaw's Brigade, recorded, "Barksdale [was] moving in action before our last regiment came fairly in line." (See Dickert, *Kershaw's Brigade*, 155; Armstrong, *Disaster in the West Woods*, 50.)
28. John T Parham, "Thirty-Second Virginia Infantry at Sharpsburg," *SHSP*, 34: 252, and 35: 350.
29. Dinkins, "Mississippi Brigade," 262–63; Dinkins, *By an Old Johnnie*, 60.
30. Armstrong, *Disaster in the West Woods*, 50–51. Armstrong considers other historians' views that this action was a simple flank attack as "at best gross over-simplifications of a complex and fluid situation." Bradley M. Gottfried, *The Maps of Antietam* (El Dorado, CA, 2012), 174.
31. Dennis Frye, *Antietam Revealed* (Collingswood, NJ, 2004), 96; Sears, *Landscape Turned Red*, 226.
32. Robert K. Krick, "Army of Northern Virginia," *Antietam: Essays on the 1862 Maryland Campaign*, Gary W. Gallagher, ed. (Kent, OH, 1989), 48; Harsh, *Taken at the Flood*, 387; Frye, *Antietam Revealed*, 96–97.
33. Dinkins, *By an Old Johnnie*, 60.
34. *Ibid.*, 61.
35. Sears, *Landscape Turned Red*, 294, 296.
36. John G. Walker, "Sharpsburg", *B&L*, Vol. 2, 681.
37. *OR* 19/1: 858–59; 971.
38. *Ibid.*, 884.
39. Hawley," Brigadier General William Barksdale CSA," 57.
40. Robert K Krick, "Army of Northern Virginia," 48.

Chapter Twelve

1. Hubbert diary, September 19, 1862; Dinkins, "Mississippi Brigade," 265; Humphreys, Autobiography, Chapter XI, 10–11.
2. Humphreys, Autobiography, Chapter XI, 9.
3. Moore, *A Life for the Confederacy*, 114,120; Pvt. William Little Davis to Honorable S. W. Smythe, December 11, 1862, MDAH; Dinkins, *By an Old Johnnie*, 64.
4. Francis A. O'Reilly, *The Fredericksburg Campaign: Winter War On The Rappahannock* (Baton Rouge, 2003), 7,10 (hereinafter cited as O'Reilly, *The Fredericksburg Campaign*).
5. Dinkins, "Mississippi Brigade," 265; Sorrel, *Recollections of a Confederate Staff Officer*, 125–26; Moore, *A Life for the Confederacy*, 118; Henley diary, October 29, 1862.
6. Moore, *A Life for the Confederacy*, 113–14; Hawley, "Brigadier General William Barksdale CSA," 72–73.
7. Hill diary, October 18, 1862; Webb Garrison, *The Encyclopedia of Civil War Usage* (Nashville, 2001), 225–26.
8. Moore, *A Life for the Confederacy*, 114; O'Reilly, 11.
9. Humphreys, Autobiography, Chapter XI, 13; Dinkins, "Mississippi Brigade," 266–67.

10. Humphreys, Autobiography, Chapter XI, 12.
11. *Ibid.*, 15–16; Dinkins, "Mississippi Brigade," 267; O'Reilly, *The Fredericksburg Campaign*, 34.
12. John Hennessy, "Fredericksburg in the War," *Blue & Gray*, Vol. XXII, Issue 1, Winter 2005, 6–7; Fire In The Streets: "A Civil War Walking Tour of Fredericksburg," http://www.nps.gov/frsp/fire.htm, accessed 30 July 1999.
13. O'Reilly, *The Fredericksburg Campaign*, 16, 30–31.
14. Colonel Wesley Brainerd, 50th New York Volunteer Engineers, *Bridge Building in Wartime*, Ed Malles, ed. (Knoxville, 1997), 92–93, 97, 365 n18, 366–67 n6.
15. O'Reilly, *The Fredericksburg Campaign*, 25.
16. Abernathy Memoir, 19–20; Moore, *A Life for the Confederacy*, 117; Henley diary, November 22, 1862; Claiborne, "Biographical Sketch of William Barksdale," 15–16.
17. Noel G. Harrison, *Fredericksburg Civil War Sites*, Vol. Two: December 1862–April 1865 (Lynchburg, VA, 1995), 55–56; Humphreys, Autobiography, Chapter XI, 16.
18. Hennessy, "Fredericksburg in the War," 14; Moore, *A Life for the Confederacy*, 117; Stiles, *Four Years Under Marse Robert*, 128; O'Reilly, *The Fredericksburg* Campaign, 37.
19. William Miller Owen, *In Camp with the Washington Artillery of New Orleans* (Baton Rouge, 1999), 176.
20. *The Journal of Jane Howison Beale 1850–1862* (Fredericksburg, 1995), vi, 124–34.
21. Dinkins, "Mississippi Brigade," 269; Dinkins, *By an Old Johnnie*, 67; Sorrel, *Recollections of a Confederate Staff Officer*, 124; Hill diary, November 25, 1862.
22. Edward Porter Alexander, *Fighting for the Confederacy*, Gary W. Gallagher, ed. (Chapel Hill, 1989), 170.
23. Lafayette McLaws, "The Confederate Left at Fredericksburg", *B&L*, Vol. 3, 86; O'Reilly, *The Fredericksburg Campaign*, 64–65.
24. *The Wartime Papers of Robert E. Lee*, Clifford Dowdey and Louis H. Manarin, eds. (New York, 1961) 368; George C. Rable, *Fredericksburg! Fredericksburg!* (Chapel Hill, 2002), 148, 159–60; Hawley, "Brigadier General William Barksdale CSA," 75. Private Moore recorded that on December 6, 1862 the ground was covered with three inches of snow and it was very cold all that week. (See *A Life for the Confederacy*, 120.)
25. O'Reilly, *The Fredericksburg Campaign*, 42–43.
26. Brainerd, *Bridge Building in Wartime*, 98–107.
27. Owen, *In Camp with the Washington Artillery*, 176–77; Rable, *Fredericksburg! Fredericksburg!*, 147; Abernathy Memoir, 20.
28. McLaws, "The Confederate Left at Fredericksburg," 86.
29. Rable, *Fredericksburg! Fredericksburg!*, 155.
30. O'Reilly, *The Fredericksburg Campaign*, 64; Rable, *Fredericksburg! Fredericksburg!*, 160; Harrison, *Fredericksburg Civil War Sites*, Vol. 2, 52;

Hennessy, "Fredericksburg in the War," 57. This building now serves as the Fredericksburg Area Museum and Cultural Center.
31. *OR* 21, 601, 604; Rowland, *Military History of Mississippi*, 82–84, 86; Hawley, "Brigadier General William Barksdale CSA," 80.
32. Brainerd, *Bridge Building in Wartime*, 106–09.
33. *OR* 21, 601, 604.
34. Brainerd, *Bridge Building in Wartime*, 110–11.
35. McLaws, "The Confederate Left at Fredericksburg," 86.
36. Claiborne," Biographical Sketch of William Barksdale," 20; Hawley," Brigadier General William Barksdale CSA," 76–77.
37. C.C. Cummings, "The Bombardment of Fredericksburg", *Confederate Veteran*, Vol. XXIII, 1915, 253. Perhaps in his zeal to claim credit, Cummings stated that the firing commenced about 3 a.m. which is about two hours earlier than numerous other eyewitness accounts.
38. *OR* 21, 601, 603, 617; Zack C. Waters and James C. Edmonds, *A Small but Spartan Band* (Tuscaloosa, AL, 2010), 43.
39. *OR* 21, 602.
40. Humphreys, Autobiography, Chapter XI, 20.
41. Hawley," Brigadier General William Barksdale CSA," 79; Brainerd, *Bridge Building in Wartime*, 293. For an excellent assessment of Barksdale's unconventional defense at the river crossings and through the streets of Fredericksburg, see Frank O'Reilly's presentation at the Battle of Fredericksburg's 150th Anniversary Event on November 17, 2012 at www.c-span.org/video/?309487-3/battle-fredericksburg-leaders-commanders, accessed 15 September 2014.
42. Brainerd, *Bridge Building in Wartime*, 111–12.
43. Commonly referred to as sharpshooters by members of both opposing armies, Barksdale's Mississippians, although expert marksmen, were not officially designated as sharpshooters within the Army of Northern Virginia which comprised only a few specialized battalions raised mainly after 1863. See Philip Katcher, *The Army of Robert E. Lee*, 123.
44. Frank Vandiver, *Mighty Stonewall* (New York, 1957), 268.
45. O'Reilly, *The Fredericksburg Campaign*, 66.
46. *OR* 21, 600, 605; Humphreys, Autobiography, Chapter XI, 17.
47. Richard F. Miller and Robert F. Mooney, "The 20th Massachusetts Infantry and the Street Fight for Fredericksburg," *Civil War Regiments*, Vol. 4, no. 4, 106, 109; O'Reilly, 68; Caffey, *Battle-Fields of The South*, Vol. II, 383; Brainerd, *Bridge Building in Wartime*, 113–15; *OR* 21, 602.
48. *OR* 21, 604–05; McLaws, "The Confederate Left at Fredericksburg," 88–89; O'Reilly, 70–73; Claiborne, "Biographical Sketch of William Barksdale," 21; Hawley, "Brigadier General William Barksdale CSA," 80–81, 87; Rable, *Fredericksburg! Fredericksburg!*, 156–57.
49. Stiles, *Four Years Under Marse Robert*, 129.

50. Sergeant Josiah F. Murphy, Co. I, 20th Massachusetts Volunteers, "Reminiscences," Boston Public Library, 23-24; Dinkins, "Mississippi Brigade," 270; Brev. Col. George A. Bruce, *The Twentieth Regiment of Massachusetts Volunteer Infantry* (Boston,1906), 208-09; George C. Rable, "Fire In The Streets," *North & South*, Vol. 3, no. 6, 82: Hennessy, "Fredericksburg in the War," 14-15.

51. Claiborne," Biographical Sketch of William Barksdale," 23; O'Reilly, 78; Pvt. William L. Davis to Honorable S.W., December 16, 1862, MDAH. Fiser was also injured by a collapsing wall but maintained his command. See O'Reilly, 78 and McLaws, *B&L*, Vol. 3, 87.

52. Stiles, *Four Years Under Marse Robert*, 133. Stiles met this woman years later when giving a Confederate Memorial Address at Fredericksburg. After relating this story, she was formally recognized "and the entire audience rose and gave her three deafening cheers."

53. Freeman, *Lee's Lieutenants*, Vol. 2, 336; Owen, *In Camp with the Washington Artillery*, 180; Freeman, *R.E. Lee: A Biography* (New York, 1934), Vol. 2, 446.

54. *OR* 21, 600, 603-05; Waters and Edmonds, *A Small but Spartan Band*, 43-44.

55. O'Reilly, *The Fredericksburg* Campaign, 78-80; Richard F. Miller and Robert F. Money, "The 20th Massachusetts Infantry and the Street Fight for Fredericksburg," 111-12.

56. Private William McCarter, *My Life in the Irish Brigade*, Kevin E. O'Brien, ed. (Campbell, CA, 1996), 150-51.

57. O'Reilly, *The Fredericksburg Campaign*, 83; Brig. Gen. George H. Brown, Adjutant General, *Record of Service of Michigan Volunteers in the Civil War* (Detroit, Reprint, N.D. (1903)), 123.

58. O'Reilly, *The Fredericksburg Campaign*, 85.

59. Ibid., 100-01.

60. Bruce, *The Twentieth Massachusetts*, 199; Murphy, "Reminiscences", 30-31; *OR* 21: 600-01, 605.

61. A.W. Greely, *Reminiscences of Adventure and Service* (New York, 1927), 84-85; Dinkins, "Mississippi Brigade," 272. For a detailed description of the fight through the streets of Fredericksburg see O'Reilly, 85-98 and Miller and Mooney, 115-22.

62. James Longstreet, *From Manassas to Appomattox* (New York, Reprint 2004 (1896)), 254-55; idem., "The Battle of Fredericksburg," *B&L*, Vol. 3, 75; Humphreys, Autobiography, Chapter XI, 19.

63. Stiles, *Four Years Under Marse Robert*, 129; O'Reilly, *The Fredericksburg Campaign*, 97-98; McLaws, *B&L*, Vol. 3, 8. Hawley considers Barksdale's initial refusal to withdraw "a prudent military decision" worthy of a trained professional, and even more impressive given that "the decision was made in the heat of a vicious urban battle." See Hawley, 92-94, for a thorough military analysis.

64. O'Reilly, *The Fredericksburg Campaign*, 98; Richard F. Miller, *Harvard's Civil War: A History of the Twentieth Massachusetts Volunteer Infantry* (Lebanon, NH, 2005) 204.

65. Tivoli, "Sacking of Fredericksburg," *Atlanta Southern Confederacy*, January 7, 1863, reproduced in William B. Styple, ed., *Writing and Fighting From The Army of Northern Virginia* (Kearny, NJ, 2003) Vol. 3, 177.

66. St. Clair Mulholland, *The Story of the 116th Regiment, Pennsylvania Volunteers* (New York, 1996), 36.

67. Dinkins, "Mississippi Brigade," 272: McLaws, *B&L*, Vol. 3, 88. Had it not been for this redeployment it would have been Barksdale's Mississippians who would also have gone into the history books (instead of Cobb's Georgians and Kershaw's South Carolinians) behind the stonewall at the Sunken Road, for repulsing the many near suicidal charges by units of Sumner's Grand Right Division next day.

68. Various Compilers, *History of The Fifty-Seventh Regiment, Pennsylvania Volunteer Infantry* (Kearny, NJ, 1995 Reprint), 69, 187.

69. Hill diary, entries for December 16; December 17; December 18, 1862. This task was made much more arduous as the corpses were frozen to the ground. The rock-hard earth necessitated that the burial trenches be very shallow.

70. O'Reilly, *The Fredericksburg Campaign*, 459.

71. *Wartime Papers of Robert E. Lee*, 369; *OR* 21, 571; Sorrell, *Recollections of a Confederate Staff Officer*, 129; Jefferson Davis, *The Rise and Fall of the Confederate Government* (New York, 1881) Vol. 2, 353; *OR* 21, 579, 582.

72. McLaws, *B&L*, Vol. 3, 89.

73. O'Reilly, Presentation at the Battle of Fredericksburg's 150th Anniversary Event on November 17, 2012 (available on C-span).

74. Rick Britton, "Hornets in the Basements: Barksdale's Brigade at Fredericksburg," *Civil War Magazine*, Issue 66, February 1998, 39; Brainerd, *Bridge Building in Wartime*, 152.

75. In accordance with Confederate Army Regulations, Barksdale's Leave of Absence was granted because the Army of Northern Virginia had gone into winter camp and was no longer on active campaign duty. It was granted by Lee based upon the endorsement of both McLaws and Longstreet. Leaves for the enlisted men were called furloughs and were tightly controlled, usually allowing only two men from each company to be absent at one time and drawn by lot unless dire personal circumstances of individual soldiers prevailed.

Chapter Thirteen

1. Humphreys, Autobiography, Chapter XI, 22.

2. Dinkins, *By an Old Johnnie*, 70.

3. Dr. W. L. Lipscomb, *A History of Columbus Mississippi During the 19th Century* (Birmingham, AL, 1909), 122, 125-26. This arsenal was later relocated to Selma, AL for greater safety. Narcissa cared for wounded Confederates at the Barksdale plantation house.

4. Narcissa Barksdale to Alcinda Janney, April 1866.

5. Joseph F. Sessions to Lida Sessions, January 28, 1863, Joseph F. Sessions Papers, MDAH.

6. Brig. Gen. Wm. Barksdale to President Davis, February 5, 1863, Jefferson Davis Papers 1861–1865, National Archives. Barksdale's reasons for declining the transfer were substantially the same as Lee provided for declining Davis' proposal to transfer him to the western theater of operations. See *Wartime Papers of Robert E. Lee*, 637.

7. Longstreet, *From Manassas to Appomattox*, 273–75.

8. *Ibid.*, 275.

9. Joseph A. Miller pocket diary, *To See My Country Free*, 170; Humphreys, Autobiography, Chapter XI, 23; Hill diary February 21, 1863, February 23, 1863;March 13, 1863; Sears, *Chancellorsville* (Boston: Houghton Mifflin Company, 1996), 40. Humphreys referred to McLaws Minstrels as "Ethiopian serenaders" in obvious reference to their "blackface" minstrel performances which were commented upon in a February 25, 1863 letter from Lt. M. A. Martin, Company I, 21st Mississippi. Professor Timothy Nutting was a prewar professor at the Illinois Conservatory of Music who was residing in Jackson, Mississippi, in 1861. He was conscripted into Confederate service and put in charge of Barksdale's Brigade Band where he served until escaping to the North in 1864. He had a very distinguished post-war career in music.

10. Joseph A. Miller pocket diary, *To See My Country Free*, 173; Jim Mobley to his Brother, February 1, 1863, Sears, *Chancellorsville*, 39.

11. Humphreys, Autobiography, Chapter XI, 24–25.

12. C.C. Cummings, "The Bombardment of Fredericksburg," *Confederate Veteran*, Vol. XXIII, 1915, 253–54. Cummings was not always the most reliable witness. He places this story on Christmas Day. If so, then Barksdale was clearly not present as he had already departed for Mississippi. For Barksdale to have participated, this event would have had to occur before December 21, 1862, or much later, after January 28, 1863.

13. Humphreys, Autobiography, Chapter XI, 25.

14. Reverend J. William Jones D.D., *Christ in the Camp*, 1887 (Harrisonburg, VA, 1986), 242–43, 266, 272–73.

15. *Ibid.*,245, 248–49, 293, 296–98, 301; Hill diary, March 27, 1863.

16. Hill diary: March 3, 1863; April 7, 1863; April 16, 1863; April 22, 1863; May 9, 1863; June 1, 1863.

17. Bell Irwin Wiley, *The Life of Johnny Reb*, 1943 (Baton Rouge, 1981), 151.

18. *Ibid.*, 157.

19. Hill diary, March 6; March 16, 1863.

20. Moore, *A Life for the Confederacy*, 54, 77–78. No diaries consulted mention a regimental band for the 18th Mississippi.

21. Dickert, *History of Kershaw's Brigade*, 225; Wiley, *The Life of Johnny Reb*, 151–58, 317–18. Some accounts state that only Union Bands played all these numbers. Quotation from Humphreys, Autobiography, Chapter XI, 26; Dinkins, *By an Old Johnnie*, 76.

22. Robert K. Krick, "Under War's Savage Heel," *The Quarterly Journal of Military History*, Autumn 2002, 93; Harrison, *Fredericksburg Civil War Sites*, Vol. Two, 22; Hill diary, March 12, 1863.

23. Humphreys, Autobiography, Chapter XI, 23; Joseph A. Miller pocket diary, *To See My Country Free*, 192–93.

24. Newton Nash to Wife, April 5, 1863; Hill diary, April 23, May 14, May 15, 1863; Privates Miller and Moore also made several diary entries regarding fishing by members of the 17th Mississippi. The two drownings actually occurred shortly after the battle of Chancellorsville when seining resumed.

25. Joseph A. Miller pocket diary, *To See My Country Free*, 190.

26. *Ibid.*, 194, 196.

27. Jones, *Christ in the Camp*, 264–65, 305.

28. Lafayette McLaws to Wife, April 13, 1863, *McLaws Civil War Letters*, 176.

29. Hill diary, April 26, April 27, 1863; Joseph A. Miller pocket diary, *To See My Country Free*, 200.

30. Huntington W. Jackson, "Sedgwick At Fredericksburg and Salem Heights," *B&L*, Vol. 3, 224.

31. Edward Porter Alexander, *Fighting for the Confederacy*, Gary W. Gallagher, ed. (Chapel Hill, NC, 1989), 195.

32. Sears, *Chancellorsville*, 154–59; Early, *Autobiographical Sketch*, 193–94; Gen. Benjamin G. Humphreys, "Recollections of Fredericksburg," *SHSP*, Vol. 14, 415.

33. Sears, *Chancellorsville*, 160–61; Lafayette McLaws to My Dear Sweetheart, April 29, 1863, *McLaws Civil War Letters*, 179.

34. *Wartime Papers of Robert E. Lee*, 447–48.

35. Joseph C. Lloyd, "The Battles of Fredericksburg," *Confederate Veteran*, Vol. XXIII, 1915, 500.

36. Sears, *Chancellorsville*, 178–79, 187, 249.

37. Early, *Autobiographical Sketch*, 196–98.

38. OR 25/1, 839.

39. Freeman, *Lee's Lieutenants*, Vol. 2, 606–07; Early, *Autobiographical Sketch*, 199–203; *Wartime Papers of Robert E. Lee*, 465–66; *ibid*. Written orders concerning tactical developments were very seldom issued during the Civil War.

40. Humphreys," Recollections of Fredericksburg", 416. Johnson's Island was a notorious Union prisoner of war camp for Confederate officers off Sandusky Bay in Ohio along the Lake Erie coastline.

41. Freeman, *Lee's Lieutenants*, Vol. 2, 610; Early, *Autobiographical Sketch*, 203.

42. *Ibid.*; *Ibid.*; Owen, *In Camp with the Washington Artillery*, 211–12.

43. Freeman, *Lee's Lieutenants*, Vol. 2, 611–12. It is interesting to note that in his official report written on May 15, 1863, several days after his public quarrel with Early had erupted in the Southern press, Barksdale simply stated that "General Early ordered the entire command to return to its former position." While technically true, this simple summary statement gave no indication that Barksdale's actual return was not authorized by Early at the time it was initiated. Bearing in mind the resentment harbored by McLaws over Barksdale's previous refusal to obey his direct order to withdraw from the streets

of Fredericksburg, Barksdale, ever the pragmatic lawyer and politician, would not provide any written statement that could possibly be used against him later should charges of insubordination be laid by Early.

44. Owen, *In Camp with the Washington Artillery*, 212; Humphreys, "Recollections of Fredericksburg," 417–18.

45. Humphreys, "Recollections of Fredericksburg," 418.

46. Sears, *Chancellorsville*, 308.

47. Humphreys, "*Recollections of Fredericksburg*," 419; Early, *Autobiographical Sketch*, 204.

48. OR 25/1, 839; Alexander, *Fighting for the Confederacy*, 211. Hawley has criticized Barksdale for attempting to defend his entire line rather than employing a reserve force to be rushed to the point of breakthrough. In the opinion of this author, Barksdale's line was already too weak to preclude depleting it any further to hold back even a small reserve that would probably have been insufficient to make a difference anyway.

49. Sears, *Chancellorsville*, 349–51.

50. *Ibid.*, 347; Early, *Autobiographical Sketch*, 205–06; OR 25/1, 839–40; Humphreys, "Recollections of Fredericksburg," 421.

51. Owen, *In Camp with the Washington Artillery*, 215; OR 25/1, 840; Humphreys, "Recollections of Fredericksburg," 421; Early, *Autobiographical Sketch*, 207; Thomas M. Griffin, Compiled Service Record, FOLD.COM, page #27, accessed 10 January 2015; Chris Mackowski and Kristopher D. White, *Chancellorsville's Forgotten Front* (California, 2013), 200–01,203; Sears, *Chancellorsville*, 353, 552 n15. Much controversy and conflicting testimony surround this flag of truce, especially concerning its timing, intent, and result. William Owen's account, which provides the most detail, including the specific time of 9:30 a.m., as well as the names of individual soldiers detailed to receive it, is considered to be most reliable by this author. Sears also concluded it was received early on the morning of May 3, rather than immediately before, or even during, the final Federal assault which some other historians assert. Griffin was never promoted to brigadier general.

52. Sears, *Chancellorsville*, 349–50, 352. For a detailed account of these attacks, as well as detailed maps delineating the regiments involved, see Mackowski and White, *Chancellorsville's Forgotten Front*, 189–224.

53. Humphreys, "Recollections of Fredericksburg," 422; Mackowski and White, *Chancellorsville's Forgotten Front*, 195; Sears, *Chancellorsville*, 355.

54. Lloyd, "The Battles of Fredericksburg," *Confederate Veteran*, Vol. XXIII, 1915, 500–01; Mackowski and White, *Chancellorsville's Forgotten Front*, 206; Humphreys, "Recollections of Fredericksburg," 422; Sears, *Chancellorsville*, 356–57.

55. Owen, *In Camp with the Washington Artillery*, 217–19; Early, *Autobiographical Sketch*, 208–09; Lloyd, "The Battles of Fredericksburg," 502; Hawley, "Brigadier General William Barksdale CSA," 106–07.

56. Early, *Autobiographical Sketch*, 208; Humphreys, "Recollections of Fredericksburg," 424–25.

57. *Ibid.*, 220–22; *ibid..*, 425.

58. *Chancellorsville—The Battle and Its Aftermath*, Gary W. Gallagher, ed. (Chapel Hill, NC, 1996) 54–56; Lloyd, "The Battles of Fredericksburg," 500; Early, *Autobiographical Sketch*, 224–25; OR 25/1, 841; Sears, *Chancellorsville*, 394–95.

59. *Wartime Papers of Robert E. Lee*, 470.

60. Gallagher, *Chancellorsville*, 53; Casualty figures from Mackowski and White, *Chancellorsville's Forgotten Front*, 223.

61. OR 25/1, 840–41. Mackowski and White list the Union casualties as Newton 400; Light Division 600; Howe 798; Total 1798 (See 223).

62. Humphreys, "Recollections of Fredericksburg," 423; Owens, *In Camp with the Washington Artillery*, 221; Gallagher, *Chancellorsville*, 53.

63. Humphreys, "Recollections of Fredericksburg, from 29th April to 6th May,'63," *The Land We Love*, Vol. 3, May-October 1867, 457–58.

64. Jubal A. Early to the Editors of the *Richmond Enquirer*, May 11, 1863 reprinted in the *Richmond Daily Dispatch*, May 13, 1863.

65. William Barksdale to the Editors of the Enquirer, May 13, 1863 reprinted in the *Richmond Semi-Weekly Enquirer*, May 19, 1863 and in the *Richmond Daily Dispatch*, May 21, 1863.

66. *Richmond Semi-Weekly Enquirer*, May 15, 1863; *Richmond Daily Dispatch*, May 15, 1863.

67. Jubal A. Early to the Editors of the *Enquirer*, May 19, 1863; *Richmond Semi-Weekly Enquirer*, May 27, 1863.

68. William Barksdale to the Editors of the *Enquirer*, May 31 1863 reprinted in the *Richmond Daily Enquirer*, June 15 1863. This author is indebted to Gary W. Gallagher for providing a copy of each of these newspaper accounts.

69. Gallagher, *Chancellorsville*, 57–58. McLaws confirmed post-war that Barksdale refused to serve under Early or to obey his orders. See Glenn Tucker, *Lee and Longstreet at Gettysburg*, p. 244.

70. McKee, "Intrepid Mississippian," 261; Hill diary, May 10, May 17, 1863. The last of the Federal wounded were returned one week later.

71. Hill diary, May16, 1863.

72. Hill diary, May 26, 1863; Thomas M. Griffin, Compiled Service Record, FOLD.COM, page #18, accessed 10 January 2015; *Washington Star* Report reprinted in the *Boston Traveler*, May 7, 1863; Wm. H. Sheldon to Bro. Elizur, May 17, 1863 in author's possession.

73. Charles W. Squires, memoir, *Civil War Times Illustrated*, Vol. 14, no. 2, May 1972, 22; Humphreys, Autobiography, Chapter XIII, 35.

Chapter Fourteen

1. Edwin B. Coddington, *The Gettysburg Campaign: A Study in Command* (New York, 1968), 6–9; Keegan, *The American Civil War*, 186–87; Alan T. Nolan, "General Lee," *Lee the Soldier*, Gary W. Gallagher, ed. (Lincoln, NB, 1996), 255. The shortage

of food within the ANV has been understated. Maj. Gen. Henry Heth wrote post war that Lee said to him, "The question of *food for this army gives me more trouble and uneasiness than everything else combined....*" Heth elaborated further: "It is very difficult for any one not connected with the Army of Northern Virginia to realize how straightened we were for supplies of all kinds, especially food." *SHSP,* vol.4, 153.

2. Harry W. Pfanz, *Gettysburg: The Second Day* (Chapel Hill, NC, 1987), 5,7; Douglas Southall Freeman, "Why Was Gettysburg Lost?" *Lee The Soldier,* 459-60.

3. Dickert, *Kershaw's Brigade,* 226; Hill diary, June 3, June 4, 1863; Moore, *A Life for the Confederacy,* 149.

4. Hill diary, June 6, June 7, 1863; Moore, *A Life for the Confederacy,* 149.

5. Claiborne, "Biographical Sketch of William Barksdale," 28; Hill diary, June 9, 1863.

6. *Ibid.*, June 15, 1863. This measure represented a paradigm shift in Confederate logistical supply compared to the Harpers Ferry and Sharpsburg Campaigns when Barksdale's troops were forced to subsist on apples and green corn.

7. Newton Nash letter to Wife, June 21, 1863; See also Hill diary, June 16, June 17, 1863; Moore, *A Life for the Confederacy,* 151; Wilborn P. Smith to Clay June 22, 1863, McLean, 431.

8. "The Gettysburg Campaign," A.J.L. Freemantle diary, *Two Witnesses At Gettysburg: The Personal Accounts of Whitelaw Reid and A. J. L. Freemantle,* Gary W. Gallagher, ed. (St. James, NY, 1994), 96-97; Pfanz, *Gettysburg: The Second Day,* 10.

9. Claiborne, "Biographical Sketch of William Barksdale," 28; Abernathy Memoir, 30.

10. Abernathy Memoir, 31-32; Moore, *A Life for the Confederacy,* 151; McLaws, "Gettysburg," *SHSP,* Vol. 7, 65.

11. J. H. Fletcher, "How Lee and Barksdale Looked To A Girl In Her Teens," *The Philadelphia Times Public Ledger,* Sunday March 12, 1911, copied at GNMP; Hill diary, June 7, 1863.

12. *Crumbling Defenses or Memoirs and Reminiscences* of *John Logan Black, Colonel CSA,* Eleanor D. McSwain, ed. (Macon, GA, 1960), 32, 36, 37.

13. Hill diary, June 28, 1863; Private Clindenen Black to Mother, June 28, 1863, in Bettersworth, *Mississippi in the Confederacy,* 163.

14. Jacob Hoke, *The Great Invasion of 1863* (Dayton, OH, 1887), 208-09.

15. Hill diary, June 28, 1863; Newton Nash letter to Wife, June 28, 1863; Moore, *A Life for the Confederacy,* 152-53.

16. For the circumstances surrounding Hooker's removal see Pfanz, 1-3; Hugh Bicheno, *Gettysburg* (London, 2001), 13, 37; George Cary Eggleston, *A Rebel's Recollections* (Cambridge, 1875), 145. Lee's quote on Meade was uttered to a personal friend of Eggleston's serving as an aide to Lee.

17. Pfanz, *Gettysburg: The Second Day,* 4-5, 12, 22-23; Freeman, *Lee's Lieutenants,* Vol. 3, 49; Hawley, "Brigadier William Barksdale CSA," 122; "The Rebels In Pennsylvania: BURNING OF THE FURNACE OF HON. THADDEUS STEVENS," *Chambersburg Repository,* reprinted in the *New York Times,* July 26, 1863; Steve Moyer, *Remarkable Humanities Magazine,* Nov/Dec 2012 Vol. 33, No. 6; Hill diary, July 1, 1863; McKee, "Intrepid Mississippian," 274.

18. Logan, *Crumbling Defenses,* 38.

19. Eric A. Campbell, "The Key to the Entire Situation: The Peach Orchard, July 2, 1863," "*The Second Day at Gettysburg,*" 2006, Gettysburg National Military Park Seminar (Gettysburg: GNMP, 2008),147-48. A second six-acre peach orchard with less mature trees was located directly north of Wheatfield Road and has recently been replanted.

20. Pfanz, *Gettysburg: The Second Day,* 106-07; E.P. Alexander, *Military Memoirs of a Confederate* (New York, 1907) Da Capo Reprint, 391; Campbell, "The Key to the Entire Situation," 150-51.

21. *OR* 27/2, 308; Bicheno, *Gettysburg,* 83; Campbell, "The Key to the Entire Situation," 149.

22. McLaws, "Gettysburg", *SHSP,* Vol. 7, 68.

23. Pfanz, *Gettysburg: The Second Day,* 116; J.W. Duke, "Mississippians At Gettysburg," *Confederate Veteran,* May 1906, 217; Logan, *Crumbling Defenses,* 38.

24. Abernathy Memoir, 35.

25. Chris Mackowski, Kristopher D. White, and Daniel T. Davis, *Don't Give an Inch: The Second Day at Gettysburg* (California, 2016), 22.

26. Pfanz, *Gettysburg: The Second Day,* 116-21; McLaws, "Gettysburg", *SHSP,* Vol. 7, 69; Alexander, *Military Memoirs of a Confederate,* 391-92. It has been postulated by Pfanz that Alexander may have benefitted from the presence of young Henry Wentz, ordnance sergeant of Taylor's Virginia Battery, who was a native of Gettysburg whose father's log cabin was located adjacent to Sherfy's Peach Orchard. For a map of the countermarch route, see Pfanz, 120.

27. Bicheno, *Gettysburg,* 82.

28. Campbell, "The Key to the Entire Situation," 153-54.

29. Keegan, *The American Civil War,* 195.

30. Campbell, "The Key to the Entire Situation," 152.

31. McLaws, "Gettysburg", *SHSP,* Vol. 7, 70; B.G. Humphreys to McLaws, January 6, 1878, in McLaws Papers, Southern Historical Collection, University of North Carolina.

32. Bicheno, *Gettysburg,* 87, 112; Alexander, *Military Memoirs of a Confederate,* 393-94; Alexander was very critical of the en echelon type of attack which he characterized as progressive versus simultaneous. He stated it had been used on four occasions, including Malvern Hill, and "always with poor success."

33. Campbell, "The Key to the Entire Situation," 156; McLaws, "Gettysburg", *SHSP,* Vol. 7, 74-76. Privates James W. Duke and Woods Mears were detailed to remove the palings from a fence at the Warfield House upon request of Longstreet. Unarmed and expecting to be killed they returned safely from their task without a shot fired. Duke

claimed to have then questioned Longstreet—"General, do you think we can take those heights" to which Longstreet replied "I don't know, do you?"—adding "This is not my fight." J. W. Duke, Co. C. 17th MS, "Mississippians At Gettysburg," *Confederate Veteran*, May, 1906, 216.

34. Bicheno, *Gettysburg*, 40; Alexander, *Military Memoirs Of A Confederate*, 395; Ralph Siegel, GNMP, Gettysburg Battle Walk—The Peach Orchard Day 2, DVD, PCN, Camp Hill, Pa., 2011.

35. McLaws, "Gettysburg", *SHSP*, Vol. 7, 72.

36. Pfanz, *Gettysburg: The Second Day*, 155, 310–11; J.B. Booth letter quoted in J. S. McNeily, "Barksdale's Mississippi Brigade At Gettysburg," Mississippi Historical Society, Vol. XIV, 1914, 238; Robert L. Murray, *E.P. Alexander and the Artillery Action in the Peach Orchard* (Wolcott, N.Y, 2000), 42–43, 50. This artillery action and the infantry engagement that followed is necessarily complex in view of the large numbers of units involved on both sides. For a detailed description refer to Pfanz and Campbell. For a concise review and critique of Alexander's performance see Murray's 116-page booklet.

37. Alexander, "Artillery Fight at Gettysburg", *B&L*, Vol. 3, 360; Abernathy Memoir, 36. Abernathy lists Dundy Gunn and his brother of Company A, and Robertson and Mimms of Company B.

38. Alexander, *Fighting for the Confederacy*, Gary W. Gallagher, ed. (Chapel Hill, 1989), 240.

39. *History of the Fifty-Seventh Pennsylvania Veteran Volunteers* (Kearny, NJ, 1995), 90; Campbell, "The Key to the Entire Situation," 160; Freemantle diary, *Two Witnesses At Gettysburg*, 123.

40. Jeffry D. Wert, *General James Longstreet: The Confederacy's Most Controversial Soldier* (New York, 1993), 249–50, 463 n23; Bicheno, *Gettysburg*, 104; McLaws, "Gettysburg," *SHSP*, Vol. 7, 73; McLaws letter to Wife, July 7, 1863, McLaws Papers #472, SHC, The Wilson Library, UNC at Chapel Hill. Longstreet later disclosed he had committed to Lee to closely supervise McLaws and his division, stating in a post-war letter to McLaws "I thus became responsible for anything that was not entirely satisfactory in your command that day." No doubt Lee also remembered McLaws' protracted unwillingness to execute Lee's preference to designate Barksdale's Brigade to remain at Fredericksburg during the Chancellorsville Campaign.

41. Owen, *Washington Artillery of New Orleans*, 245.

42. Siegel, Gettysburg Battle Walk—The Peach Orchard Day 2. Brigadier General Paul Semmes soon received a mortal wound at much shorter range from this Union artillery along the Wheatfield Road.

43. Alexander, *Fighting for the Confederacy*, 239; Murray, *E.P. Alexander and the Artillery Action in the Peach Orchard*; 111–13 Murray convincingly argues that Alexander underestimated his opponent and held back more than one-quarter of his guns for an expected grand artillery charge once the Union line was broken.

44. McNeily, "Barksdale's Brigade at Gettysburg," 235, 237.

45. *Ibid.*, 237–38, 241.

46. E. H. Sutton, *Grandpa's War Stories* (Demorest, GA, 1907), 39. Elijah Henry Sutton was a private in the 24th Georgia and was captured on July 2, 1863. See also "Barksdale Remembered: A Georgia 'High Private' Reflects on Gettysburg," by Matt Atkinson, GNMP Ranger, www.npsgnmp.wordpress.com/2014/03/28/barksdale-remembered-a-georgia-high-private-reflects-on-gettysburg., accessed 15 July 2014.

47. Alexander, "Letter on Causes of Lee's Defeat at Gettysburg," *Lee The Soldier*, 436; *Idem.*, "Artillery Fighting at Gettysburg," *B&L*, Vol. 3, 357–58.

48. Freemantle diary, *Two Witnesses at Gettysburg*, 119.

49. McNeily, "Barksdale's Brigade at Gettysburg," 235.

50. Bicheno, *Gettysburg*, 13.

51. Dickert, *Kershaw's Brigade*, 235; J.S McNeily, "Barksdale's Brigade at Gettysburg", 236.

52. Campbell, "The Key to the Entire Situation," n48, 202; Hawley, "Brigadier General William Barksdale CSA," n42, 158. Brigade strengths are approximate based upon Busey and Martin, *Regimental Strengths and Losses at Gettysburg*, except Barksdale's Brigade which is based upon Colonel B.G. Humphreys' figure of 1420. Both Pfanz and Bicheno state 1400.

53. Kershaw, "Kershaw's Brigade at Gettysburg," *B&L* Vol. 3, 333–35; Campbell, "The Key to the Entire Situation," 166–67.

54. *Ibid.*, 167; Clifford Dowdey, *Death of a Nation: The Confederate Army at Gettysburg* (New York, 1958), 221; Freeman, *Lee's Lieutenants*, Vol. 3, 124; McLaws, "Gettysburg," *SHSP*, Vol. 7, 73.

55. Hawley, "Brigadier General William Barksdale CSA," 135–36; Alexander, *Military Memoirs of a Confederate*, 397; idem. *Fighting for the Confederacy*, 236.

56. McNeily, "Barksdale's Brigade at Gettysburg," 235.

57. T.M. Scranton, January 24, 1924 to *Memphis Commercial Appeal*, in *Barksdale Family History*, 285–86; E. P. Harmon to Hon. W.S. Decker, August 16, 1886, in Richardson Papers, Ontario County Historical Society, Canandaigua, New York. Barksdale's adjutant Harmon confirmed that "fence rails were used as temporary breast works along the Emmitsburg road to the south of the [Sherfy] farm house" by the Federals.

58. Pfanz, *Gettysburg: The Second Day*, 327; Humphreys, Autobiography, Chapter XIV, 12; Bicheno, *Gettysburg*, 26, 119.

59. McNeily, "Barksdale's Brigade at Gettysburg," 236.

60. W. Gart Johnson, Co. C, 18th Miss., *Confederate Veteran*, July 1893, 206. The sole personal motive might have been to expunge the long-ago unfair criticism of his Mexican War record but Barksdale's illustrious Civil War record to date had most certainly already done so.

61. Pfanz, *Gettysburg: The Second Day*, 314; Campbell, "The Key to the Entire Situation," 164–65; Bicheno, *Gettysburg*, 119.

62. Humphreys, Autobiography, Chapter XIV, 15; McNeily, "Barksdale's Brigade at Gettysburg," 236, 241, 243; Longstreet, *From Manassas to Appomattox*, 372.

63. E. P. Harmon to Hon. W.S. Decker, August 16, 1886, in Richardson Papers; "Barksdale Museum Exhibit Recalls General's Exploits," *The Clarion-Ledger*, Jackson, MS, September 22, 1968; McLaws, "Gettysburg," *SHSP*, Vol. 7, 73-74.

64. Judge George Clark, "Wilcox's Alabama brigade At Gettysburg," *Confederate Veteran*, May 1909, 229.

65. McNeily, "Barksdale's Brigade at Gettysburg," 240.

66. *Ibid.*, 236, 240; Claiborne, "Biographical Sketch Of William Barksdale," 30.

67. Pfanz, *Gettysburg: The Second Day*, 322-23; Bucklyn to John B. Bachelder, December 31, 1863, *Bachelder Papers: Gettysburg in Their Own Words*, David L. and Audrey J. Ladd, eds. (Dayton, OH, 1994) Vol. 1, 72-73. (Hereafter cited as BP.) Bucklyn's 1st Rhode Island Battery was so "badly cut up" they did not participate in the fighting on July 3rd.

68. *History of the 57th Pennsylvania*, 91; Campbell, "Hell in a Peach Orchard," *America's Civil War*, July 2003, 41; J. C. L. [Pvt. Joseph C. Lloyd] *Daily News*, Meridian, MS, April 13, 1901; Hill diary; Pvt. William M. Boggs, 114th Pennsylvania Co. F to John B. Bachelder, May 26, 1882 and May 19, 1882 in *BP*, Vol. 2, 874-76, 882-83. Lt. Col. Kennon McElroy received a shoulder wound while Maj. Bradley suffered a severe ankle wound.

69. Humphreys, Autobiography, Chapter XIV, 13; Pfanz, *Gettysburg: The Second Day*, 328-29, 335; *History of the One Hundred Forty-First Regiment Pennsylvania Volunteers*, compiled by Chaplain David Craft (Towanda, PA, 1885), 122-23; Col. Henry Madill to brother Thomas Madill, December 2, 1864. Bravely leading this initial charge through the Peach Orchard, Capt. Isaac D. Stamps, acting major of the 21st MS, fell with a mortal wound in the abdomen. Stamps who was President Davis' nephew and Col. B. G. Humphreys' son-in-law died next day in the brigade field hospital at the Crawford farm.

70. McNeily, "Barksdale's Brigade at Gettysburg," 238; Stephen W. Sears, *Gettysburg* (Boston, 2003), 299; *OR* 27/1, 503; Humphreys, Autobiography, Chapter XIV, 13; History of 57th Pennsylvania, 91-92.

71. Capt. Frank E. Moran to John. B. Bachelder, January 24, 1882, in *BP*, Vol. 2, 771-74.

72. Pfanz, *Gettysburg: The Second Day*, 331-32, 366-67; Sears, *Gettysburg*, 301; Campbell, "The Key to the Entire Situation," 188-89; Jesse Bowman Young, *The Battle of Gettysburg: A Comprehensive Narrative* (New York, 1913), 256-57.

73. James A. Hessler and Britt C. Isenberg, *Gettysburg's Peach Orchard—Longstreet, Sickles and the Bloody Fight for the "Commanding Ground" Along the Emmitsburg Road* (El Dorado Hills, CA, 2019), 218; T. D. Marbaker, *History Of The 11th New Jersey Volunteers* (Trenton, 1898), 98; Pfanz, *Gettysburg: The Second Day*, 348. Birney's First Division suffered 2011 casualties, fourth highest total. Graham's Brigade experienced 48.8% casualties—highest of the three First Division brigades. (See Hessler and Isenberg. 218)

74. Young, *The Battle of Gettysburg*, 257; *ibid.*, 215.

75. Claiborne, "Biographical Sketch of William Barksdale," 31; Joseph W. Muffley, *The Story of Our Regiment: A History of the 148th Pennsylvania Volunteers* (Des Moines, IA, 1904), 173, 245; David Parker to Any Member of the Late Gen. Barksdale Family March 13, 1882, William Barksdale subject file—Ethelbert Barksdale Papers, MDAH; Robert A. Cassidy, "Last Hours of Gen.Wm. Barksdale, *Mississippi Index*, June 13, 1866, GNMP; Campbell, "The Key to the Entire Situation," 189; *History of The 141st Pa.*, 123-24; McNeily, "Barksdale's Brigade at Gettysburg," 238. Maj. J. B. Gerald recorded this was "the only command that I ever heard [Barksdale] give after a battle commenced." As is the case for many aspects pertaining to Barksdale's life there is contradictory eyewitness testimony concerning his wounds. Union musician Cassidy who attended the dying general states only one leg wound midway between the ankle and knee. Union Private Parker quotes Barksdale describing a musket-ball impacting above the knee and a shrapnel wound to the left foot, while the Union Assistant Surgeon who treated Barksdale simply states: "left leg was broken by two missiles."

76. Humphreys, Autobiography, Chapter XIV, 13; Pfanz, *Gettysburg: The Second Day*, 342; Campbell, "The Key to the Entire Situation," 184-85; Captain Bigelow: "Account of the Engagement of the 9th Mass Battery," *BP*, Vol. 1, 177.

77. Levi W. Baker, *History of the Ninth Massachusetts Battery* (Lancaster, OH, 1996), ix, 60-61; *My Dear Wife: The Civil War Letters of David Brett 9th Massachusetts Battery, Union Cannoneer*, Frank Putnam Deane, ed., Vol. 1 (Little Rock, 1964), 60, 63.

78. Alexander, "Artillery Fighting at Gettysburg," *B&L*, Vol. 3, 360; Alexander, *Fighting for the Confederacy*, 240.

79. Pfanz, *Gettysburg: The Second Day*, 327-28; Campbell, "The Key to the Entire Situation," 185; McLaws, "Gettysburg," *SHSP*, Vol. 7, 74-75; William Youngblood, "Unwritten History Of The Gettysburg Campaign," *SHSP*, Vol. 38, 315; Kershaw, "Kershaw's Brigade At Gettysburg," *B&L*, Vol. 3, 337.

80. Kershaw to John B. Bachelder, April 3, 1876, in *BP*, Vol. 1, 471; *ibid.*., March 20, 1876, 456; Kershaw, "Kershaw's Brigade At Gettysburg," *B&L* Vol. 3, 337.

81. Campbell, "The Key to the Entire Situation," 185; Noah Trudeau, *Gettysburg: A Testing of Courage* (New York, 2002), 377; Bicheno, *Gettysburg*, 122. Bicheno has noted that Wofford "was pointedly not commended in Longstreet's post-battle report," and concludes "whether [Wofford] was at fault or a scapegoat we cannot know."

82. E. P. Harmon to Hon. W.S. Decker, August 16, 1886, in Richardson Papers; Youngblood, "Unwritten History Of The Gettysburg Campaign," *SHSP*,

Vol. 38, 316. The only possible reason for Barksdale to hesitate here was his recognition that his attack was totally unsupported by Wofford—contrary to his understanding of the initial plan of battle. It was not in Barksdale's aggressive nature to halt while attacking.

83. McNeily, "Barksdale's Brigade at Gettysburg," 243; William A. Love, "Mississippi at Gettysburg," *Mississippi Historical Society*, Vol. IX, 1906, 32.

84. Humphreys, Autobiography, Chapter XIV, 15; Campbell, "The Key to the Entire Situation," 194-96.

85. *Ibid.*, 196-97; Maj. John J. Hood, "Tribute to Gen. Barksdale," *Confederate* Veteran, November 1901, 503.

86. Robert L. Murray, *The Redemption of the Harper's Ferry Cowards* (Wolcott, NY, 1994), 73-75; Willson, *Disaster, Struggle, Triumph*, 100-106, 111, 115, 121, 142, 168; Benj. W. Thompson, "Personal Narrative of Experiences in the Civil War, 1861-1865," *Civil War Times Illustrated*, October 1973, 18.

87. William A. Love, "Mississippi At Gettysburg," *Publications of the Mississippi Historical Society*, Vol. IX, 1906, 32. Love was too young to enlist in 1863 and so was not present at Gettysburg. He later served with the 6th Mississippi Cavalry and was paroled at Gainesville, AL in May 1865. He compiled this article from multiple sources including numerous accounts from *Confederate Veteran* magazine.

88. Willson, *Disaster, Struggle, Triumph*, 168-69; Thompson, "Personal Narrative," 19; Maj. Charles A. Richardson to John B. Bachelder, May 8, 1868, in *BP*, Vol. 1, 338-40; *ibid.*., August 18, 1867, 315-16; Lt. John F. Randolph to Aldon Hays, April 21, 1890 as quoted in "General Alexander Hays and the Third Division, Second Army Corps, At The Battle of Gettysburg," compiled by George A. Hays, February 1957, Photocopy at GNMP. Musician Robert Cassidy and Pvt. Charles W. Dey asserted that Corporal Menaugh C. Van Liew, Co. C, 126th NY delivered Barksdale's mortal wound. (See "Killing of Gen. Barksdale" and "Willards Brigade," *National Tribune*, November 29, 1894; September 24, 1908) Another claim was made by a member of the 1st Minnesota Regiment in a sworn affidavit recorded on December 13, 1889 which claimed the witness, L.Z. Rogers, saw William Brown of Co. G shoot Barksdale off his horse; while John G. Sonderman of Co. A claimed it was their fire that inflicted the mortal wound. (See *National Tribune*, January 17, 1901.) In a post-war letter to John Bachelder, Col. William Colvill, commander of the 1st Minnesota, stated "General Barksdale was shot by one of my men, and taken back a few yards to a boulder, where he died." (See *BP*, vol.1, 256-57) Another version in the 1898 Regimental History of the 11th New Jersey Volunteers claimed that Barksdale was brought down by a targeted volley from the entire Company H—riddled by five bullets while riding a white horse and wearing a red fez—obviously not Barksdale!

89. McNeily, "Barksdale's Brigade at Gettysburg," 239, 243; E. P. Harmon to Hon. W.S. Decker, August 16, 1886; Captain John A. Barksdale, "General Barksdale: Circumstances Attending His Death At Gettysburg," *Mobile Evening News*, September 11, 1863, copy at GNMP; C. C. Cummings, *Daily Courier*-Gazette, McKinney, TX, August 17, 1911; Moore, *A Life for the Confederacy*, 153; Phillip Thomas Tucker, *Barksdale's Charge—The True High Tide of The Confederacy At Gettysburg, July 2, 1863* (Philadelphia, 2013), 2; Claiborne, "Biographical Sketch of William Barksdale," 32; Willson, *Disaster, Struggle, Triumph*, 170-71; Pfanz, *Gettysburg: The Second Day*, 406. Barksdale's horse would die the next day. His saddle was retrieved afterward by local citizen J. Howard Wert and formed part of his collection. Barksdale's nephew Harris also later submitted a claim for $250 to cover the loss of his horse on the battlefield that day. John A. Barksdale had enlisted at age 21 on July 1, 1861 as a private in the 21st Mississippi. Promoted he served on the staff of both Barksdale and then Benjamin G. Humphreys. Sadly he was killed on May 8, 1864 during the battle of the Wilderness.

90. Pfanz, *Gettysburg: The Second Day*, 413-14.

91. Humphreys, Autobiography, Chapter XIV, 17-18.

92. Bicheno, *Gettysburg*, 124-25; Hawley, "Brigadier General William Barksdale CSA," 151; Rowland, *Military History of Mississippi*, 71. Bicheno claims 15 Union Regiments while Hawley identifies 14 by their numerical/state designation.

93. Moore, *A Life for the Confederacy*, 153.

Chapter Fifteen

1. Howard Coffin, *Nine Months to Gettysburg: Stannard's Vermonters and the Repulse of Pickett's Charge* (Woodstock,VT, 1997), 207-08; Lieutenant Colonel Charles Cummings to Wife, July 6, 1863, *A War of the People: Vermont Civil War Letters*, Jeffery D. Marshall, ed. (Hanover, NH, 1999), 166-67; Thompson, "Personal Narrative," 20.

2. Willson, *Disaster, Struggle, Triumph*, 179; Sgt. John W. F. Williams, "Gen. Barksdale: One of the Men Who Relieved Him on the Field Heard From," *National Tribune*, February 1, 1906.

3. Claiborne, "Biographical Sketch of William Barksdale," 32-33, Gerald R. Bennett, *Days of "Uncertainty and Dread": The Ordeal Endured by the Citizens at Gettysburg* (Camp Hill PA, 2002), 65-66, 124 n23; *Gettysburg Compiler*, August 23,1905. Daughter Anna Garlach believed the coffin was finished the following day and was used to bury Jennie Wade, the only civilian killed at Gettysburg.

4. The 11th New Jersey claimed to have carried the mortally wounded Barksdale to Brig. Gen. Joseph B. Carr's headquarters. In a letter to John B. Bachelder dated May 8, 1868 Maj. Charles A Richardson claimed that Surgeon [Charles S.] Hoyt of the 126th NY "found Barksdale's body, and directed some of our officers to it, I think it was Gen. Butterfield." During the dedication of the 149th PA monument Captain Johnson stated [we] found the rebel General William Barksdale who had been severely wounded. [We] sent him into our lines and

the next day he died at the little house in the apple orchard."(Pennsylvania At Gettysburg, Vol. 2, 747.) A monument to the 90th Pennsylvania on Hancock Avenue bears a bronze plaque with the inscription: "The Confederate General Barksdale, who had fallen mortally wounded in the attack upon the 3rd Corps, was found upon the field and carried to the rear by men of this reg't." The 146th New York claimed to have retrieved Barksdale's sword found beside his dead body and sent it to General Sykes. (*New York at Gettysburg*, Vol. 3, 1902, 972.)

5. Wheelock G. Veazey to John B. Bachelder, *BP*, Vol. 1, 59; Coffin, *Nine Months To* Gettysburg, 209; *Army Life in Virginia: The Civil War Letters of George G. Benedict*, Eric Ward, ed. (Mechanicsburg, PA, 2002), 192, 201–02; *A War of the People: Vermont Civil War Letters*, 167; David L. Parker to Ethelbert Barksdale, March 22, 1882, Ethelbert Barksdale Papers, MDAH; G.G. Benedict, *Vermont at Gettysburg* (Burlington, VT, 1870), 9. Parker was prompted to finally write Barksdale's family due to a newspaper report he read regarding presentation of General Barksdale's sword to the State of Mississippi. In a post-war submission to the *National Tribune*, December 14, 1905, "Carried Barksdale From The Field," Pvt. Harlan P. Sherwin Co. H, 14th VT who was part of Barksdale's rescue party confirmed Sergeant Vaughn was killed on the following day and that "Gen. Barksdale's hat and gloves were worn by Col. Nichols through the next day's fight."

6. *The Story of Our Regiment: A History of the 148th Pennsylvania Volunteers*, written by the Comrades, Adjt. J.W. Muffley, ed. (Des Moines, IA, 1904), 172–73, 245; Robert A. Cassidy, "Last Hours of Gen. Wm. Barksdale, "*The Mississippi Index*, June 13, 1866, in William Barksdale Subject File, GNMP; A.T. Hamilton to Harris Barksdale, February 23, 1867, in Claiborne, "Biographical Sketch of William Barksdale," 35–39; diary of Dr. A. T. Hamilton preserved at GNMP. Surgeon Hamilton's description of Barksdale's chest wound as an *exit* wound from a rifle ball is the authoritative account and explains why many eyewitnesses and authors believed it was an *entry* wound caused by a much larger grapeshot. AAG Capt. John A. Barksdale in his September 8, 1863 letter to the editor of the *Mobile Evening News* stated incorrectly that Gen. Barksdale "was wounded twice, first in the shoulder and afterward in the chest." In reality, it was one wound—a rear entry in the shoulder with a front exit in the left chest. Another account simply titled "General Barksdale" incorrectly states that "he was wounded in the thigh and severely in the right ankle, and in the right breast," *BP*, Vol. 3, 1976. (For a completely different version of Barksdale's retrieval and death by General Carr and Colonel C.E. Livingston of the 76th New York, which cannot be corroborated, see "The Barksdale Episode," in *Gettysburg Star & Sentinel*, D.A. Buehler, ed., July 27, 1886, GNMP. Private Sherwin of the 14th VT pointedly refuted Livingston's claim in a letter to the *National Tribune*: "I understand Col. Livingston, of a New York regiment, claims all the credit of [Gen. Barksdale's] removal from the field, *when in fact he had nothing to do with it*" (emphasis added). See "The Rebel Gen. Barksdale," *National Tribune*, October 25, 1894.

7. Cassidy, "Last Hours of Gen. Wm. Barksdale"; Benedict, *Army Life In Virginia*, 193; Record of Confederate Burials—Journal of Doctor John W.C. O'Neal, GNMP; Gregory A. Coco, *Wasted Valor—The Confederate Dead At Gettysburg* (Gettysburg, 1990), 146–48; *Gettysburg Compiler*, July 20, 1863, as seen by Mr. Cooke, Special Correspondent of *The Age* on July 7, 1863; Gregory A. Coco, *Killed In Action* (Gettysburg, 1992), 67–68. The temporary field hospital for Barksdale's brigade was set up in the barn of the John S. Crawford farm one mile west of the Pitzer Woods. Colonel James W. Carter and Captain Isaac Stamps (son-in-law of Colonel Humphreys and nephew of President Davis) were interred here with many other members of the Mississippi Brigade.

8. *OR* 27/1, 260, 371, 596; Glenn David Brasher, "The Battle In Public: Newspaper Reports From Gettysburg," www.civilwarmonitor.com; accessed 15 November 2013. The New York Engineers were not present at Gettysburg during the battle. They remained back in Maryland maintaining the pontoon bridges over the Potomac River.

9. *History of the 57th Pennsylvania*, 184.

10. *Wartime Papers of Robert E. Lee*, 538–39; Telegram Jefferson Davis to Hon. E. Barksdale, Richmond July 9, 1863, South Western Telegraph Company, Ethelbert Barksdale Papers, MDAH; Jefferson Davis to Narcissa Barksdale, July 24,1863, *The Papers of Jefferson Davis*, Vol. 9: January-September 1863, 303–04; Narcissa Barksdale to Alcinda Janney, April 1866.

11. Claiborne, "Biographical Sketch of William Barksdale," 39–40; Minutes of Columbus Lodge #5, September 4, 1863, William Barksdale, Subject File, MDAH.

12. Robert G. Mayer and Jacquelyn Taylor, *Embalming: History, Theory and Practice* (N.C., 2005), 481; (The exact date of Barksdale's exhumation cannot be pinpointed. Musician Cassidy recorded: "[Barksdale] was buried a few feet from where he died, and a *short time subsequently was disinterred, embalmed, sent through the lines*." See "Killing of Gen. Barksdale, *National Tribune*, November 29, 1894. Private Sherwin recorded: "I understood [Barksdale] was buried near where he fell and *soon after was disinterred* and sent South." See "Gen. Barksdale," *National Tribune*, December 6, 1894); Narcissa Barksdale to Alcinda Janney April 1866; Carl Sandburg, *Abraham Lincoln: The War Years* ,Vol. 4, 127–28; Thomas C. Teasdale to Hon. E. Barksdale, May 3, 1865, MDAH; Samuel P. Taylor to Rev. T.C. Teasdale, March 28, 1865, Washington City, MDAH; www.fold3.com/image/#65799174 Claim for $191.25, accessed 10 November 2012; Narcissa Barksdale to Hon. Stephen A. Brown, Judge of probate, MDAH; "General William Barksdale," *Jackson Weekly Clarion*, January 17, 1867. William Barksdale may very well have been the first to lie in state at the Old Capitol in Jackson, Mississippi. A legend has persisted and is still repeatedly referenced today that Narcissa travelled to Gettysburg

to retrieve the General's body from its initial burial spot near the Hummelbaugh House. She was supposedly accompanied by his favorite hunting dog who became inconsolable and refused to leave, ultimately perishing from starvation and dehydration after Narcissa departed for home. According to this legend, Barksdale's loyal companion can still be heard howling at midnight on July 2nd. A great legend perhaps, but surviving written documentation regarding Barksdale's actual earlier exhumation and repatriation most certainly debunks this myth. Pvt. William Boggs, Co. F, 114th PA mentioned in a post war letter to John Bachelder, "Did you know that Barksdale's remains laid in the undertaker's shop for several years awaiting the expense of embalming, etc.," May 26, 1882, *BP*, Vol. 2, 883. Another entry by Bachelder erroneously states that "[Barksdale's] body was subsequently removed [from the Hummelbaugh yard] to *Baltimore* by friends," *BP*, Vol. 3, 1977.

13. *Jackson Weekly Clarion*, January 17, 1867; idem., January 11, 1867; *Vicksburg Daily Herald*, January 12, 1867; Harold A. Cross, *They Sleep Beneath the Mockingbird* (Murfreesboro TN, 1994), 13–14; Jeff T. Giambrone, "His Gallant Spirit Went Home: The Burial of General William Barksdale in Jackson," http://mississippiconfederates.files.wordpress.com/2013/10, accessed 02 February 2014; Special Call of Pearl Lodge No.23 F&AM, January 9, 1867, William Barksdale Vertical File, MDAH.

14. Greenwood Cemetery Brochure published by Greenwood Cemetery Restoration Association, N.D. Established in 1821 it has grown from the initial six acres to its present 22 acres and contains the graves of six Confederate generals and seven Mississippi governors. Colonel Erasmus Burt (18th Mississippi) and Brigadier General Richard Griffith, whom Barksdale succeeded, along with his close friend Governor Albert Gallatin Brown are buried here. There is a ceremonial headstone for Barksdale in the Confederate Section at another location.

15. 1870 Census for Columbus, Lowndes County, MDAH; "Died, Mrs. Narcissa L. Barksdale," *Jackson Weekly Clarion*, March 31, 1875 quoted in Cross, *They Sleep Beneath the Mockingbird*, 14–15; Laws of The State of Mississippi Passed At A Called and Regular Session of The Mississippi Legislature Held In Jackson and Columbia Dec. 1862 and November 1863 (Selma, AL, 1864), 213.

16. Barksdale Family History, 287: E.C. Barksdale (the General's Grandson) to James W. McKee Jr., March 30, 1965, William Barksdale Subject File, MDAH. The Barksdale Family genealogy omits William's son Ethelbert's second marriage and offspring and erroneously gives his date of death as July 1892.

17. See Chapter 6, note 31. Lincoln was not even on the Presidential ballot in the Southern states.

18. Evan C. Rothera, "Forgotten Fire-Eater: William Barksdale in History and Memory," Journal of Mississippi History, Vol. LXXII No. 4, Winter 2010, 401–02. In this excellent study Rothera argues convincingly that Barksdale's legacy as a soldier clearly predominates over that as a politician. He also states that in the years immediately following Barksdale's death his political career in Congress was generally remembered in the Northern newspapers and journals in the context of his "scalping" (loss of his hairpiece), as a "troublemaker," and as a "treasonous" figure.

19. Bicheno, *Gettysburg*, 80.

20. "The Poems of Fanny Downing," *Confederate Veteran*, April 1916, 38; Mendelssohn Coote and Fanny Dowding, *Memorial Flowers*, A.E. Blackmar, New Orleans, 1867, Notated Music, LOC.

21. Barksdale Family Genealogy, 285; Randy Golden, "Stone Mountain Carving," www.aboutnorthgeorgia.com/ang/Stone_Mountain_Carving, accessed 13 May 2010; "Confederate Monument, Columbus Mississippi," *Confederate Veteran*, February 1906, 57; Lowndes County Confederate Monument—Columbus; Mississippi—American Civil War Monuments and Memorials, see Waymarking.com.

22. Maj. John J. Hood, "Tribute to Gen. Barksdale," *Confederate Veteran*, November 1901, 503; idem, "Correction," *Confederate Veteran*, February 1902, 82; McNeily, "Barksdale's Mississippi Brigade At Gettysburg," 262–63. An article in *The Commercial Appeal* indicated that Fontaine Maury was a nom-de-plume for Brig. Gen. B. G. Humphreys. (Maury was his wife's maiden name and Fontaine was the name of one of his children.)

23. W. Gart Johnson, Co. C, 18th Miss., *Confederate Veteran*, July 1893, 206: Dinkins, *By an Old Johnnie*, 86. GNMP has now been closed to any additional monuments. Ironically the last two dedicated in 2000 were for the 11th Mississippi Regiment of Joseph R. Davis' Brigade who participated in Pickett's Charge. To date there is no signage at the Hummelbaugh House concerning Barksdale's death and temporary burial there.

24. For example see G.B. Lawson letter to Mr. J.B. Bachelder, August 30, 1890, *BP* Vol. 3, 1767; B.G. Humphreys to J.B. Bachelder May 1, 1876, *BP* Vol. 2, 482; McNeily, "Barksdale's Mississippi Brigade At Gettysburg," 262; Humphreys, Autobiography, Chapter XIV, 20–21; Bicheno, *Gettysburg*, 112, 122. Humphreys emphasizes Pickett's failure to arrive on the battlefield as a critical factor.

25. James Longstreet to Gen. L. McLaws, July 25, 1873, McLaws Papers, #472, Southern Historical Collection, Wilson Library, University of North Carolina, Chapel Hill.

26. Sears, *Gettysburg*, 346.

27. OR 27/2, 362. Eyewitnesses (and Wofford's biographer Gerald J. Smith) stated that Wofford was extremely angry at being ordered by Longstreet to retreat on July 2nd. Wofford believed his Georgia Brigade should have at least been allowed to attempt an attack on Little Round Top. (See Smith, *The Most Daring of Men*, 91.) Stephen Sears in his book *Gettysburg* includes the statement, "The fiery Wofford, it was reported, "shook his pistol" at Longstreet, in protest" (p. 322). Feuding with Longstreet, both McLaws and Wofford did not issue a battle report following Gettysburg. Pettiness on Longstreet's part

cannot be ruled out as a contributing factor to his omission of Wofford.

28. James Longstreet, *From Manassas to Appomattox* (New York, 2004, Copyright 1898), 316.

29. John D. Imhof, *Gettysburg: Day Two: A Study In Maps* (Baltimore, MD, 1999), 150, 203; Sears, *Gettysburg*, 302–03.

30. McNeily, "Barksdale's Brigade at Gettysburg," 242–43.

31. Judge George Clark, "Wilcox's Alabama Brigade at Gettysburg," *Confederate Veteran*, May 1909, 229.

32. *OR*, 27, pt.2, 613–14; 621–24;631–34; Coddington, *The Gettysburg Campaign: A Study in Command*, 420–26; n84, 760–61. The undersized Florida Brigade comprised only 700 men while the remaining four brigades each comprised 1800–2000; Chris Mackowski, Kristopher D. White, Daniel T. Davis, *Don't Give An Inch: The Second Day at Gettysburg* (California, 2016), 113; 125–26. Freemantle states that Hill was standing with Lee observing the battle, while Freemantle watched the combat up in a nearby oak tree. A. P. Hill's biographer, esteemed historian James I. Robertson Jr., concluded that Hill understood that Longstreet would direct Anderson's support whereas Longstreet assumed Hill would control Anderson's division. Unfortunately, Lee did not intervene and in Robertson's words, "everything quickly became a mess." See Robertson, *General A.P. Hill: The Story of a Confederate Warrior*. (New York, 1987), 218–19.

33. Alexander, *Military Memoirs of a Confederate*, 400; 403; Coddington, *The Gettysburg Campaign: A Study In Command*, 425.

34. McLaws to My Dear Wife, July 7, 1863, *McLaws Civil War Letters*, 197.

35. Sears, *Gettysburg*, 346; McNeily, "Barksdale's Mississippi Brigade at Gettysburg," 261; Bicheno, *Gettysburg*, 122; 126.

36. Tucker, *Barksdale's Charge*, 3.

37. McNeily, "Barksdale's Brigade at Gettysburg," 261. Author and Gettysburg authority the late Harry Pfanz agreed. In a telephone interview for the old Compuserve Civil War Forum the late Brian Pohanka asked: Barksdale's charge on July 2nd seems to me one of the most hard-hitting brigade actions of the war. Would you agree? To which Pfanz replied: "I hesitate to compare it with others in the entire war, but there's no doubt it was hard-hitting, *and probably the hardest hitting at Gettysburg.*" Refer to Facebook post by historian/author David Woodbury, June 30, 2019.

38. Major John Bigelow, *The Peach Orchard: Gettysburg—An Appeal* (Minneapolis, MN, 1910), 32,. Bigelow issued this booklet in an attempt to have United States Avenue (formerly Trostle Lane) renamed Hunt Avenue.

39. *BP* Vol. 2, 666; *ibid*.., 36.

40. Michael Shaara, *The Killer Angels* (New York, 1974), 203, 209, 293; *Gettysburg*, Turner Pictures, New Line Cinema Release, 1993; Jeff Shaara, *Gods and Generals* (New York, 1996), 302–05; *Gods and Generals*, Ted Turner Pictures, Antietam Filmworks Production, 2003.

41. These Battlewalks by PCN include: *The Peach Orchard—Day 2*, 1997; *Barksdale's Assault—Day 2*, 1998; *Brig. Gen. Barksdale's Mississippi Brigade at Gettysburg*, 2001; *Col. Willard vs Gen. Barksdale—Day 2*, 2003; *Barksdale's Mississippi Brigade*, 2010; *The Peach Orchard*, 2011; History Channel, *Civil War 150th Anniversary Edition 3-DVD Set*, A&E Television Networks LLC, 2011. History Channel's production accurately portrays Barksdale's mortal wounding (entry wound in the back and exit wound in the front then tumbling from his horse).

42. *Antietam: A Documentary Film*, Historical Films Group, Media Magic Productions Inc., 1998; *Fredericksburg: A Documentary Film*, Historical Films Group, Media Magic Productions Inc., 2002; *Fredericksburg: Then and Now*, Heritage Media LLC, 2009.

43. Barksdale's likeness has also been minted on a Confederate States silver dollar as part of the thirteen-coin set *Rebels of Liberty*, commemorating famous Confederate generals. Several hand-painted miniature soldiers of General Barksdale mounted with hat in hand have been issued by various manufacturers.

44. Phil Hearn, "Barksdale Museum Exhibit Recalls General's Exploits," *Jackson Clarion-Ledger*, September 22, 1968, Sec. H, 8.

45. www.mississippimarkers.com/lowndescounty.htm, accessed 02 January 2008. Also the main east-west roadway running approximately one mile through the Potomac Crossing subdivision in Leesburg, Virginia, is named Barksdale Drive.

46. This information has been derived mainly from a series of personal email messages between April 14, 2013 and April 26, 2013 with Mr. Clay Williams, then Director, Old Capitol Museum. He also kindly provided copies of key correspondence concerning Barksdale's nomination and election; David L. Payne to Hall of Fame Selection Committee, June 18, 1986; http://mdah.state.ms.us./oldcap/hof.pdf, accessed 16 April 2013.

47. *Lowndes County's Boys at Gettysburg*, booklet produced by Lowndes County Department of Archives and History and William Barksdale Camp 1220 SCV (Gulfport, MS: N.D. circa 1986). The Barksdale portrait is shown in a photo on page 4 which includes Dr. Payne and two other officers of Camp 1220. The portrait is likely based on Harry Coughlin's illustration in Clayton Rand's book *Men of Spine In Mississippi* published in 1940; Personal email communications between author and Mr. Shawn Kyzer, Adjutant, Barksdale Camp 1220 between June 6, 2013 and March 26, 2014.

48. Phil Hearn, "Barksdale Museum Exhibit Recalls General's Exploits,"; *Journal of the Senate of the State of Mississippi—Convened January 3, 1882*, J. L. Power State Printer, 424–29; Mary Lohrenz, Curator of Collections MDAH, to John Heiser GNMP, August 30, 1989 and September 6, 1989, MDAH; Mississippi State Historical Museum, Barksdale Insignia Description, Accession No. 66.5 copied at GNMP; H.T. Holmes Historian MDAH, to Cdr. Robert L. Brake dated September 11, 1974,

copied at GNMP. Mr. Holmes indicated that neither Barksdale's sword nor collar insignia have been formally authenticated although William's brother Ethelbert wrote that members of Barksdale's brigade recognized the sword as that belonging to General Barksdale.

49. For a more detailed assessment of Barksdale's leadership see Hawley, "Brigadier General William Barksdale CSA," 151–54.

50. W. Gart Johnson, "Barksdale Humphreys Mississippi Brigade," *Confederate Veteran*, July 1893, 206.

51. "State of The Country," Speech of Hon. A.G. Brown of Mississippi in the Confederate Senate, December 24, 1863, 2, *Documenting the American South*, University of North Carolina at Chapel Hill Libraries. See http://ftp.oit.unc.edu/docsouth/browna/menu.html, accessed 20 February 2001.

Bibliography

Manuscript and Unpublished Sources

Benjamin Grubb Humphreys Autobiography Manuscript.
E.P. Harmon Letter to Hon. W. S. Decker, August 16, 1886, Charles A. Richardson.
Ethelbert Barksdale Papers.
Fredericksburg and Spotsylvania National Military Park, Fredericksburg, VA.
Gettysburg National Military Park, Gettysburg, PA.
Harris Barksdale Compiled Service Record.
Henley, Albert Wymer [Pvt., Co H, 13th MS] Diary.
James W. KcKee, "William Barksdale: Intrepid Mississippian," Ph. D. Dissertation, 1966.
Dr. John O'Neal, Journal Record of Confederate Burials.
John C. Rietti Papers.
John J. Pettus Papers.
Lt. John Randolph Letter to Aldon Hays, April 21, 1890.
Joseph F. Sessions Papers.
Mississippi Department of Archives & History, Jackson, MS.
Mississippi State University, Mitchell Memorial Library, Starkville, MS.
National Archives, Washington, D.C.
Ontario County Historical Society, Canadaigua NY.
Samuel P. Taylor Letter to Rev. T. C. Teasdale, March 28, 1865.
Thomas B. Griffin Compiled Service Record.
Wallace, Thomas D. [Pvt. Co. A, 13th MS] Diary: May 11, 1861–June 17, 1862.
William Barksdale Compiled Service Record.
William Barksdale Letter to President Jefferson Davis.
William Barksdale Request for Bounty Land.
William Barksdale Subject File.
William Barksdale Vertical File.
Sgt. William H. Hill Diary, 1861–1863, 2 Vol., Z0217.00.

Papers

Duke, James W. [Pvt., Co. C, 13th MS] memoir, Brake Collection, University of Texas, Austin, TX.
Hubbert, Mike M. [Pvt., Co I, 13th MS] memoir, Center for American History.
John Francis Hamtramck Claiborne Papers 1797–1884, Texas A&M University, College Station, TX.
John Janney Papers, www.Fold3.com.
Lafayette McLaws Papers, Virginia Polytechnic Institute and State University, Blacksburg, VA.
Nash, Nimrod Newton [Pvt., Co. I, 13th MS] Letters May 16, 1861–June 28, 1963.
Old Courthouse Museum Collections, Vicksburg, MS.
Southern Historical Collection, University of North Carolina, Chapel Hill.
Steve Carl Hawley, "Brigadier General William Barksdale, CSA: A Study in the Generalship of a Volunteer Officer," Master of Arts Dissertation, 1992.
United States Army Military History Institute, Carlisle Barracks, Carlisle, PA.
Various Compiled Service Records and Documentation.

Newspapers

Aberdeen (MS) *Weekly Independent*
Boston *Traveler*
Canton (MS) *American Citizen*
Chambersburg (PA) *Repository*

Chattanooga Daily Rebel
Columbus (MS) *Democrat*
Columbus (MS) *Southern Standard*
Daily Courier-Gazette, McKinney (TX)
Gettysburg Compiler
Gettysburg Star & Sentinel
Jackson (MS) *Daily-Clarion Ledger*
Jackson (MS) *Mississippian*
Jackson (MS) *Mississippi Semi-Weekly*
Jackson (MS) *The Weekly Clarion*
Louisville (KY) *Daily Journal*
Memphis Commercial Appeal
Meridian (MS) *Daily News*
The Mississippi Index, Columbus, MS

Mobile Evening News
National Tribune
New Orleans Picayune
New York Times
Philadelphia Times Public Ledger
Richmond (VA) *Daily Dispatch*
Richmond (VA) *Enquirer*
Richmond (VA) *Semi-Weekly Enquirer*
Vanity Fair Weekly, New York
Vicksburg (MS) *Whig*
Vicksburg (MS) *Daily Herald*
Woodville (MS) *Republican*
Washington (D.C.) *Star*

Periodicals

America's Civil War
Blue & Gray
Civil War Magazine
Civil War Monitor
Civil War Times Illustrated
Confederate Veteran
DeBow's Review

Harper's Weekly
The Land We Love
Military Images
Mississippi Valley Historical Review
North & South Magazine
Quarterly Journal of Military History

Published Sources

Abernathy, William Meshack, "Confederate Memoir: Our Mess," *Confederate Veteran Magazine*, Vol. 2, 2003.
Alexander, E.P., "Artillery Fight at Gettysburg," *Battles & Leaders of the Civil War*, Vol. 3. New York: Thomas Yoseloff, 1956.
_____, *Fighting for the Confederacy*, Gary W. Gallagher, ed. Chapel Hill: University of North Carolina Press, 1989.
_____, "Letter on Causes of Lee's Defeat at Gettysburg," *Lee: The Soldier*, Gary W. Gallagher ed. Lincoln: University of Nebraska Press, 1996.
_____, *Military Memoirs of a Confederate*. New York: Charles Scribner's Sons, 1907.
Allardice, Bruce S., *Confederate Colonels: A Biographical Register*. Columbia: University of Missouri Press, 2008.
Armstrong, Marion V., *Disaster in the West Woods*. Sharpsburg, MD: Western Maryland Interpretive Association, 2002.
Baker, Levi W., *History of the Ninth Massachusetts Battery*. Lancaster OH: Vanberg Publishing, 1996.
"Barksdale Museum Exhibit Recalls General's Exploits," *Jackson Clarion Ledger*, September 22, 1968.
Barksdale, John A., *Barksdale Family History and Genealogy with Collateral Lines*. Richmond, VA: William Bird Press, 1940.
Bauer, Jack, *The Mexican War 1846–1848*. New York: Macmillan Publishing Co., 1974.
_____, *The Mexican-American War 1846–1848*. London, UK: Osprey Publishing, 1976.
Beale, Jane Howison. *The Journal of Jane Howison Beale 1850–1862*. Fredericksburg, VA: Historic Fredericksburg Foundation Inc., 1995.
Benedict, George G., *Army Life In Virginia—The Civil War Letters of George G. Benedict*, Eric Ward, ed. Mechanicsburg, PA: Stackpole Books, 2002.
_____, *Vermont at Gettysburg*. Burlington, VT: Burlington Free Press, 1870.
Bennett, Gerald R., *Days of "Uncertainty and Dread": The Ordeal Endured by the Citizens at Gettysburg*. Camp Hill, PA: Higgins Printing Company, 2002.
Berry, Stephen W. II, *All That Makes a Man: Love and Ambition in the Civil War South*. New York: Oxford University Press, 2003.
Bettersworth, John K., ed., *Mississippi in the Confederacy: As They Saw It*. Jackson, MS: Louisiana State University Press, 1961 (Reprint New York: Kraus Co. 1970).
Bicheno, Hugh, *Gettysburg*. London, UK: Cassel & Co., 2001.
Bigelow, Major John, *The Peach Orchard: Gettysburg—An Appeal*, Minneapolis, MN: Kimball-Storer, 1910
Biographical Directory of the United States Congress, 1774–Present. http://www.bioguide.congress.gov.
Boatner, Mark M. III, *Civil War Dictionary Revised Edition*. New York: David McKay Company Inc., 1998.
Boggs, William M., Letters, May 19, 1882, and May 26, 1882, in *Bachelder Papers* Vol. 3,

Brainerd, Colonel Wesley, *Bridge Building in Wartime: Memoirs of the 50th New York Volunteer Engineers,* Ed Malles, ed. Knoxville, TN: University of Tennessee Press, 1977.
Brasher, Glenn David, "The Battle in Public: Newspaper Reports from Gettysburg," www.civilwarmonitor.com.
Brent, Joseph L., *Memoirs of the War Between the States.* New Orleans, LA: Fontana Press, 1940.
Bridges, Hal, *Lee's Maverick General: Daniel Harvey Hill,* Copyright 1961. Gaithersburg, MD: Olde Soldier Books Inc, Reprint N.D.
Britton, Rick, "Hornets In The Basements: Barksdale's Brigade at Fredericksburg," *Civil War Magazine,* Issue #66, February 1998.
Brown, Brig. Gen. George H., *Record of Service of Michigan Volunteers in the Civil War,* Copyright 1903. (Detroit, MI: Detroit Free Press Reprint, N.D.
Brown, J.F., Account in *Confederate Veteran,* Vol. 2, November 1894.
Bruce, Brevet Lt.-Colonel George A., *The Twentieth Regiment of Massachusetts Volunteer Infantry 1861–1865.* Boston, MA: Houghton Mifflin and Company, 1906.
Bucklyn, John J., Letter, December 31, 1863 in *Bachelder Papers* Vol. I., David L and Audrey J. Ladd, eds. Dayton, OH: Morningside House Inc., 1994.
Buehler, D.A., ed., "The Barksdale Episode," *Gettysburg Star & Sentinel July 27, 1886,* Copy at GNMP.
Bunch, Jack A., *Military Justice in the Confederate States Army.* Shippensburg Pa: White Mane Books, 2000.
Busey, John W. and Martin, David G., *Regimental Strengths and Losses at Gettysburg.* Baltimore, MD: Gateway Press, 1982.
Byers, Private J.A., "The Whole World Was Full of Smoke," *Military Images, Vol.* IX Number 6, May-June 1988.
Caffey, Thomas C., *Battle-Fields of the South from Bull Run to Fredericksburg—By an English Combatant.* London, UK: Smith, Elder and Co., 2 vols., 1864.
Campbell, Eric. A., "Hell in a Peach Orchard," *America's Civil* War, July 2003.
_____, "The Key to the Entire Situation—The Peach Orchard, July 2, 1863," *The Second Day at Gettysburg - 2006 Gettysburg National Military Park* Seminar. Gettysburg, PA: GNMP, 2008.
Carrier, Thomas J., *Washington, D.C.: An Historical Walking Tour.* Mount Pleasant, SC: Arcadia Publishing, 1999.
Cassidy, Robert A., "Last Hours of Gen. William Barksdale," *Mississippi Index,* June 13, 1866, Copied at GNMP.
Coco, Gregory A., *Killed in Action.* Gettysburg, PA: Thomas Publications, 1992.
_____, *Wasted Valor—The Confederate Dead at Gettysburg.* Gettysburg, PA: Thomas Publications, 1990.
Coddington, Edwin B., *The Gettysburg Campaign: A Study in Command.* New York: Charles Scribner's Sons, 1968.
Code of Mississippi: Being an Analytical Compilation of the Public and General Statutes of the Territory and State from 1798–1848. Jackson, MS: Price and Fall State Printers, 1848.
Coffey, Chesley S., "The Mexican War Letters of Chesley S. Coffey," *Journal of Mississippi History,* Vol. 44, August 1982.
Coffin, Howard, *Nine Months to Gettysburg—Stannard's Vermonters and the Repulse of Pickett's Charge.* Woodstock, VT: The Countryman Press, 1997.
"The Compromise of 1850," www.ushistory.org/us/30d.asp
"Confederate Monument, Columbus Mississippi," *Confederate Veteran,* February 1906.
Congressional Globe and Appendix, 33rd Congress Session I & II; 34th Congress Session I, II, & III; 35th Congress Session I & II; 36th Congress Session I & II. Washington, D.C.: John C. Rives.
Craft, Chaplain David, *History of the One Hundred Forty-First Regiment Pennsylvania Volunteers.* Towanda, PA: Reporter-Journal Printing Company, 1885.
Cross, Harold A., *They Sleep Beneath the Mockingbird.* Murfreesboro, TN: Southern Heritage Press, 1994.
Cullen, Joseph P., "At Malvern Hill: It Was Not War—It Was Murder," *Civil War Times Illustrated,* May 1966.
Cummings, C.C., "Capture of Harper's Ferry," *Confederate Veteran,* April 1897.
_____, "The Bombardment of Fredericksburg," *Confederate Veteran,* 1915.
_____, "'Mississippi Boys' at Sharpsburg," *Confederate Veteran,* January 1897.
Cummings, Colonel Charles, Letter, July 6, 1863, *A War of the People:* Vermont *Civil War Letters,* Jeffery D. Marshall, ed. Hanover NH: University Press of New England, 1999.
Davis, Jefferson C., Letter to Narcissa Barksdale, July 24, 1863, *The Papers of Jefferson Davis,* Vol. 9, Lynda L. Crist, Mary S. Dix, Kenneth H. Williams, eds. Baton Rouge. Louisiana State University Press, 1997.
_____, *The Papers of Jefferson Davis,* 14 Vols. Baton Rouge: Louisiana State University Press, 1987–present.
_____, *The Rise and Fall of the Confederate Government.* New York: D. Appleton, 1881.
Davis, Reuben, *Recollections of Mississippi and Mississippians.* Boston, MA: Houghton, Mifflin & Co., 1890.
Deane, Frank Putnam ed., *My Dear Wife: The Civil War Letters of David Brett, 9th Massachusetts Battery Union Cannoneer,* Vol. 1. Little Rock, AR: Pioneer Press, 1964.
Dew, Charles, *Apostles of Disunion.* Charlottesville: University of Virginia Press, 2001.
Dickert, D. Augustus, *History of Kershaw's Brigade.* Dayton, OH: Press of Morningside Bookshop, 1976.
Dinkins, Captain James, *1861 to 1865, Personal Recollections and Experiences in the Confederate Army, By an Old Johnnie.* Cincinnati, OH, The Robert Clarke Company, 1897. (Reprint, Dayton, OH: Press of Morningside Bookshop, 1975.)

_____, "Griffith-Barksdale-Humphreys Mississippi Brigade and Its Campaigns," *Southern Historical Society Papers (SHSP)* Vol. 32. Richmond, VA: Southern Historical Society, 1904.
Donald, David, *Charles Sumner and the Coming of the Civil War*. New York: Alfred A. Knopf, 1967.
Dowdey, Clifford, *Death of a Nation: The Confederate Army at Gettysburg*. New York: Barnes & Noble, 1958.
_____, *Lee Takes Command: The Seven Days: The Emergence of Lee*, Copyright 1964. New York: Barnes & Noble Reprint, 1992.
Dowdey, Clifford, and Manarin, Louis H., eds. *The Wartime Papers of Robert E. Lee*. Cambridge, MA: Da Capo Press, 1987.
Dubay, Robert W., *John Jones Pettus, Mississippi Fire-eater: His Life and Times 1813–1867*. Jackson: University Press of Mississippi, 1975.
Dugard, Martin, *The Training Ground: Grant, Lee, Davis in the Mexican War 1846–1848*. New York: Little Brown & Company, 2008.
Duke, J.W., "Mississippians at Gettysburg," *Confederate Veteran*, May 1906.
Dupont, Nancy McKenzie, "Mississippi's Fire-Eating Editor: Ethelbert Barksdale and the Election of 1860," *The Civil War and the Press*, David B. Sachsman et al., eds. New Jersey: Transaction Publishers, 2000.
Early, Jubal A., *Autobiographical Sketch and Narrative of the War Between the States*; Copyright 1912. Wilmington, NC: Broadfoot Publishing Co., Reprint 1989.
Ears, Charles A., "The Seven McElroy's of the Thirteenth Mississippi Infantry CSA," *Confederate Veteran Magazine*, September–October 1993.
Eggleston, George Cary, "A Rebel's Recollections," Cambridge: The Riverdale Press, 1875.
Ellis, P.F., "Extracts from an Untitled Letter," *Confederate Veteran*, Vol. 5, December 1987.
Evans, Clement A., ed., *Confederate Military History*, 12 Vols. Atlanta, GA: Confederate Publishing Co., 1889.
Evans, Lieutenant Thomas, 12 U.S. Infantry, "At Malvern Hill," *Civil War Times Illustrated*, December 1967.
Farwell, Byron A., *Ball's Bluff: A Small Battle and Its Long Shadow*. McLean, VA: EPM Publications Inc., 1990.
"Fire in the Streets: A Civil War Walking Tour of Fredericksburg," http://www.nps.gov.frsp/fire.htm.
Fletcher, J.H., "How Lee and Barksdale Looked to a Girl in her Teens," *Philadelphia Times Public Ledger*, March 12, 1911, copied at GNMP.
Freehling, William F., *The Road to Disunion, Vol. II: Secessionists Triumphant*. New York: Oxford University Press, 2007.
Freeman, Douglas Southall, *Lee's Lieutenants*, 3 Vols. New York: Charles Scribner's Sons, 1942.
_____, "Why Was Gettysburg Lost?" *Lee: The Soldier*, Gary W. Gallagher, ed. Lincoln: University of Nebraska Press, 1987.
_____, *R. E. Lee: A Biography*, Vol. 2. New York: Charles Scribner's Sons, 1934.
Freemantle, A.J.L., "The Gettysburg Campaign," *Two Witnesses at Gettysburg: The Personal Accounts of Whitelaw Reid and A.J.L. Freemantle*, Gary W. Gallagher, ed. St. James, NY: Brandywine Press, 1994.
Frye, Dennis E., *Antietam Revealed*. Collingswood, NJ: C.W. Historicals, LLC, 2004.
_____, "Drama Between the Rivers," *Antietam: Essays on the 1862 Maryland Campaign*, Gary W. Gallagher, ed. Kent, OH: Kent State University Press, 1989.
Gallagher, Gary W., *Causes Won, Lost & Forgotten*. Chapel Hill: University of North Carolina Press, 2008.
_____, ed., *Chancellorsville: The Battle and Its Aftermath*. Chapel Hill: University of North Carolina Press, 1996.
Garlach, Anna (Kitzmiller), "My Story," *Gettysburg Compiler*, August 23, 1905.
Garrison, Webb, *The Encyclopaedia of Civil War Usage*. Nashville, TN: Cumberland House, 2001.
"General Barksdale: Circumstances Attending His Death at Gettysburg," *Mobile Evening News*, September 11, 1863, Copy at GNMP.
"General Lloyd Tilghman," http://www.bryanbush.com/hub.php?page=articles&layer=a0605
Gettysburg Battlewalks GNMP. Camp Hill, PA: Pennsylvania Cable Network (Various DVD's pertaining to Barksdale's Brigade during the Peach Orchard action).
Giambrone, Jeff. T., "His Gallant Spirit Went Home: The Burial of General William Barksdale In Jackson." http://mississippiconfederates.files.wordpress.com/2013/10.
_____, "Like a Cane Brake on Fire: The 21st Mississippi Infantry at Malvern Hill," *North & South*, Vol. 8, No. 2.
Greely, A.W., *Reminiscences of Adventure and Service*. New York: Charles Scribner's Sons, 1927.
Greenwood Cemetery Brochure, Jackson, Mississippi, n.d.
Guelzo, Allen C., *Gettysburg: The Last Invasion*. New York: Alfred A. Knopf, 2013.
Hagerty, Edward J., *Collis' Zouaves: The 114th Pennsylvania in the Civil War*. Baton Rouge: Louisiana State University Press, 1997.
Hallock, Judith Lee, ed., *The Civil War Letters of Joshua Callaway*. Athens: University of Georgia Press, 1997.
Hardee, Brevet Lieut-Col W.J., U.S. Army, *Rifle and Light Infantry Tactics for the Exercise and Manoeuvres of Troops When Acting as Light Infantry or Riflemen, Vol. II. School of the Battalion, Prepared Under Direction of the War Department*. Nashville, TN: J.O. Griffith & Co., 1861.
Harrison, Noel G., *Fredericksburg Civil War Sites, Vol. Two: December 1862–April 1865*. Lynchburg, VA: H.E. Howard Inc., 1995.
Harsh, Joseph L., *Taken at the Flood*. Kent, OH: Kent State University Press, 1999.
Hennessy, John, "Fredericksburg in the War," *Blue & Grey*, Vol. XXII, Issue 1, Winter 2005.

Henry, R.H., *Editors I Have Known Since the Civil War*. New Orleans: Press of E.S. Upton Printing Company, 1922.
Hessler, James A., and Britt C. Isenberg, *Gettysburg's Peach Orchard: Longstreet, Sickles and the Bloody Fight for the "Commanding Ground" Along the Emmitsburg Road*. El Dorado Hills, CA: Savas Beatie, 2019.
Hickman, Kennedy, "Major John F. Reynolds: To the Peninsula." http://militaryhistory.about.com/od/UnionLeaders/p/American-Civil-War-Major-General-John-Reynolds
Hill, General Daniel H., "McClellan's Change of Base and Malvern Hill." *Battles & Leaders of the Civil War (B&L)*, Vol. 2. New York: Castle Books, 1956.
History of the Fifty-Seventh Regiment, Pennsylvania Volunteer Infantry. Kearny, NJ: Belle Grove Publishing Co., 1995 Reprint.
Hodges, Robert R., Jr., *American Civil War Railroad Tactics*. New York: Osprey Publishing, 2009.
Hoffert, Sylvia D., "The Brooks-Sumner Affair," *Civil War Times Illustrated*, Vol. XI, No. 6, October 1972.
Hoke, Jacob, *The Great Invasion of 1863*. Dayton, OH: W.J. Shuey Publisher, 1887.
Holien, Kim B., *Battle at Ball's Bluff*. Orange, VA: Publisher's Press Inc., 1995.
Holt, David, *A Mississippi Rebel in the Army of Northern Virginia: A Civil War Memoir*. Thomas D. Cockrell and Michael B. Ballard, eds. Baton Rouge: Louisiana State University Press, 1995.
Hood, Major John J., "Tribute to Gen. Barksdale," *Confederate Veteran*, November 1901; "Correction," *Confederate Veteran*, February 1902.
Hooker, Charles E., *Confederate Military History of Mississippi*. Reprint, Pensacola, FL: ebooksOnDisk.com, 2003.
Howell, H. Grady, Jr., *For Dixie I'll Take My Stand: A Muster Listing of All Known Mississippi Confederate Soldiers, Sailors, and Marines*. Madison, MS: Chickasaw Bayou Press, 1998.
_____, ed., *A Southern Lacrimosa: The Mexican War Journal of Dr. Thomas Neely Love, Surgeon Second Regiment Mississippi Volunteer Infantry USA*. Madison, MS: Chickasaw Bayou Press, 1995.
Humphreys, Gen. Benjamin G.," Recollections of Fredericksburg," *SHSP*, Vol. 14.
_____, "Recollections of Fredericksburg from 29th April to 6th May '63," *The Land We Love*, Vol. III, May–October 1867.
Hunter, R.W., "Men of Virginia at Ball's Bluff." *Richmond Times-Dispatch*, April 22–29; May 6, 1906, *SHSP*, Vol. 34.
Hunton, Eppa, *Autobiography of Eppa Hunton*. Richmond, VA: William Byrd Press Inc., 1933.
Imhof, John D., *Gettysburg Day Two: A Study in Maps*. Baltimore: Butternut & Blue, 1999.
Jackson, Huntington W., "Sedgwick at Fredericksburg and Salem Heights." *B&L* Vol. 3.
Johnson, Robert U., and Clarence C. Buel, eds. *Battles and Leaders of the Civil War*, 4 Vols. New York: The Century Co., 1887–1888.
Johnson, W. Gart, Co. C, 18th Mississippi, "Barksdale: Humphreys Mississippi Brigade," *Confederate Veteran*, July 1893.
_____, Untitled Article, *Confederate Veteran*, July 1893.
Jones, Rev. J. William D.D., *Christ in Camp*. Copyright 1887. Harrisonburg, VA: Sprinkle Publications, 1986.
Katcher, Philip, *The Army of Robert E. Lee*. London: Arms and Armour Press, 1994.
Keegan, John, *The American Civil War: A Military History*. New York: Alfred A. Knopf, 2009.
Kershaw, Joseph B., Letters, March 20, 1876 and April 3, 1876. *Bachelder Papers*, Vol. 1.
_____, "Kershaw's Brigade at Gettysburg." *B&L*, Vol. 3.
Krick, Robert E.L., "Malvern Hill: Portrait of a Battlefield." *Civil War Magazine*, Issue 73, April 1999.
Krick, Robert K., "Army of Northern Virginia." *Antietam: Essays on the 1862 Maryland Campaign*. Gary W. Gallagher, ed. Kent, OH: Kent State University Press, 1989.
_____, *Civil War Weather in Virginia*. Tuscaloosa: University of Alabama Press, 2007.
_____, "Lafayette McLaws." *The Confederate General*, Vol. 4. William C. Davis, ed. Washington, D.C.: National Historical Society, 1991.
_____, "Under War's Savage Heel." *The Quarterly Journal of Military History*, Autumn 2002.
Ladd, David L., and Audrey J. Ladd, *The Bachelder Papers: Gettysburg in Their Own Words*, 3 Vols. Dayton, OH: Morningside House Inc., 1994.
Lash, Gary G., *Duty Well Done: The History of Edward Baker's California Regiment (71st Pennsylvania Infantry), Army of the Potomac Series*. Baltimore: Butternut and Blue, 2001.
"The Late Colonel William Inge—His Remarkable Military Career," *Confederate Veteran*, January 1901.
Leech, Margaret, *Reveille in Washington*. New York: Harper & Brothers, 1941.
Levine, Bruce, *Confederate Emancipation: Southern Plans to Free and Arm Slaves During the Civil War*. New York: Oxford University Press, 2006.
Lipscomb, Dr. W. L., *A History of Columbus Mississippi During the 19th Century*. Birmingham, AL: Press of Dispatch Printing Co., 1909.
Lloyd, Joseph C., "The Battles of Fredericksburg." *Confederate Veteran*, Vol. XXIII, 1915.
Logan, Mrs. John A., *Reminiscences of a Soldier's Wife*. New York: Charles Scribner's Sons, 1913.
Longstreet, James, *From Manassas to Appomattox*, Copyright 1896. New York: Barnes & Noble Reprint, 2004.
_____, "The Battle of Fredericksburg." *B&L*, Vol. 3.
Love, William A., "Mississippi at Gettysburg," *Publications of the Mississippi Historical Society*, Vol. IX, 1906.

Lowery, Charles Ph.D., "The Great Migration to the Mississippi Territory 1798–1819," *Mississippi History Now*—Online publication of the Mississippi Historical Society www.mshistorynow.mdah.state.ms.us/articles/169.

"Lowndes County Confederate Monument—Columbus, Mississippi." American Civil War Monuments and Memorials, Waymarking.com

Lowndes County's Boys at Gettysburg Booklet. Gulfport, MS: Abbey Commercial Printers, ca. 1986.

Luvaas, Jay, and Harold W. Nelson, eds., *Guide to the Battle of Antietam: The Maryland Campaign of 1862.* Lawrence: University Press of Kansas, 1996.

Mackowski, Chris, and Kristopher D. White, *Chancellorsville's Forgotten Front.* Campbell CA: Savas Beatie, 2013.

Mackowski, Chris, Kristopher D. White, and Daniel T. Davis, *Don't Give an Inch: The Second Day at Gettysburg.* El Dorado Hills, CA: Savas Beatie, 2016.

Magdol, Edward, *Owen Lovejoy: Abolitionist in Congress.* New Brunswick, NJ: Rutgers University Press, 1967.

Mahood, Wayne, *Written in Blood: A History of the 126th New York Infantry in the Civil War.* Highstown, NJ: Longstreet House, 1997.

Marbaker, T.D., *History of the 11th New Jersey Volunteers.* Trenton, NJ: MacCrellish & Quigley, 1898.

Marsh, Helen C., and Timothy Marsh, Compilers, *Wills and Inventories of Rutherford County, Tennessee,* Vol. 2, 1828–1840. Greenville, SC: Southern Historical Press, 1998.

Martin, James M., et al., *History of the Fifth-Seventh Pennsylvania Volunteers.* Kearney, NJ: Belle Grove Publishing, 1995.

Mayer, Robert G., and Taylor, Jacquelyn, *Embalming: History, Theory and Practice.* n.c.: McGraw-Hill, 2005.

McCabe, James Dabney, *Behind the Scenes in Washington.* New York: Continental Publishing Co., ca. 1873.

McCarter, Private William, *My Life in the Irish Brigade,* Kevin E. O'Brien, ed. Campbell, CA: Savas Publishing Co., 1996.

McGarty, Kenneth G., "Farmers, the Populist Party, and Mississippi 1870–1900," *Mississippi History Now.* http://mshistory.k12.ms.us/features/feature42/populistparty.html

McKee, James W., "Congressman William Barksdale of Mississippi," *Southern Miscellany: Essays in History in Honor of Glover Moore,* F.A. Dennis, ed. Jackson, MS: University Press of Mississippi, 1981.

_____, "William Barksdale and the Congressional Election of 1853 in Mississippi," *Journal of Mississippi History Volume XXXIV,* MDAH, May 1972.

McLaws, Major-General Lafayette, "The Confederate Left at Fredericksburg," *B&L,* Vol. 3.

_____, "Gettysburg," *SHSPI,* Vol. 7.

McLean, Jess N., Sr., *Official Records of the 13th Mississippi Regiment,* Published Independently, Texas, 2001.

McNeilly, J.S., "Barksdale's Mississippi Brigade at Gettysburg," *Publications of the Mississippi Historical Society,* Vol. XIV, 1914.

McPherson, James. M., "Central to the Civil War." *North & South Magazine,* Vol. 10, No. 4, January 2008.

_____, *Drawn with the Sword.* Oxford, UK: Oxford University Press, 1996.

McSwain, Elinor D., *Crumbling Defences or Memoirs and Reminiscences of John Logan Black, Colonel CSA.* Macon, GA: J.W. Burke Co., 1960.

Miller, Richard F., *Harvard's Civil War: A History of the Twentieth Massachusetts Volunteer Infantry.* Hanover, NH: University Press of New England, 2005.

Miller, Richard F., and Robert F. Mooney, "The 20th Massachusetts Infantry and the Street Fight for Fredericksburg." *Civil War Regiments,* Vol. 4, No. 4, 1995.

Miller, Miss Virginia J., Diary in Glenfiddich House, Leesburg, VA: http://www.mileslehone.com/diary.html.

Miller, William J., ed., "Rediscovering Malvern Hill." *Civil War Magazine,* Issue #73, April 1999.

"The Mississippi Delegation In Congress," *Harper's Weekly,* February 2, 1861, Vol. V-No. 214, New York, NY.

Mississippi in the War Between the States, booklet. Jackson, MS: Mississippi Civil War Centennial Commission, 1960.

"Missouri Compromise (1820)," NARA, http://www.ourdocuments.gov/doc.php?doc=22

Moran, Frank E., Letter, January 24, 1882. *Bachelder Papers,* Vol. 2.

Morgan, James A. III, *A Little Short of Boats: The Fights at Ball's Bluff and Edwards Ferry.* Fort Mitchell, KY: Ironclad Publishing, 2004.

Moyer, Steve, *Remarkable Humanities Magazine,* Vol. 33, No. 6, Nov/Dec 2012.

Muffley, Joseph W., *The Story of Our Regiment: A History of the 148th Pennsylvania Volunteers.* Des Moines, IA: Kenyon Printing Co., 1904.

Mulholland, St. Clair, *The Story of the 116th Regiment, Pennsylvania Volunteers.* New York: Fordham University Press, 1996.

Murphy, James B., *L.Q.C. Lamar: Pragmatic Patriot.* Baton Rouge: Louisiana State University Press, 1973.

Murray, Robert L., *E.P. Alexander and the Artillery Action in the Peach Orchard.* Wolcott, NY: Benedum Books, 2000.

_____, *The Redemption of the Harper's Ferry Cowards.* Wolcott, NY: Benedum Books, 1994.

Nicholson, John P., ed., *Pennsylvania at Gettysburg,* Vol. 2. Harrisburg, PA: WS Ray Printer, 1904.

Nolan, Alan T., "General Lee," *Lee: The Soldier.* Gary W. Gallagher, ed. Lincoln, NB: University of Nebraska Press, 1996.

Oeffinger, John C., ed., *A Soldier's General: The Civil War Letters of Major General Lafayette McLaws*. Chapel Hill: University of North Carolina Press, 2002.
Olden, Sam, "Mississippi and U.S.-Mexican War, 1846-1848," *Mississippi History Now Website*, Mississippi Historical Society.
O'Reilly, Francis W., Presentation at the Battle of Fredericksburg's 150th Anniversary Event November 17, 2012. www.c-span.org/video/?309487-3/battle-fredericksburg-leaders-commanders.
_____, *The Fredericksburg Campaign: Winter, War on the Rappahannock*. Baton Rouge: Louisiana State University Press, 2003.
Owen, William Miller, *In Camp with the Washington Artillery of New Orleans*. Baton Rouge: Louisiana State University Press, 1999.
Owens, Harry P., *Steamboats and the Cotton Economy: River Trade in the Yazoo-Mississippi Delta*. Jackson: University Press of Mississippi, 1990.
Parham, John T., "Thirty-Second Virginia Infantry at Sharpsburg." *SHSP*, Vol. 34.
Patridge, I.M., "The Press of Mississippi." *DeBow's Review*, Vol. 29, Issue 4, New Orleans, October 1860.
Perry, Milton F., *Infernal Machines: The Story of Confederate Submarine and Mine Warfare*. New Orleans: Louisiana State University Press, 1965.
Pfanz, Harry W., *Gettysburg: The Second Day*. Chapel Hill: University of North Carolina Press, 1987.
Pollard, Edward A., *The Third Year of the Civil War—Southern History of the Civil War*. New York: Charles B. Richardson, 1865.
Pryor, Mrs. Roger A., *Reminiscences of Peace and War*. New York: The MacMillan Company, 1904.
"Proceedings of the First Confederate Congress," *SHSP*, Vol. 44.
"Proceedings of the Second Confederate Congress," *SHSP*, Vol. 52.
Rable, George C., "Fire in the Streets," *North & South*, Vol. 3, No. 6.
_____, *Fredericksburg! Fredericksburg!* Chapel Hill: University of North Carolina Press, 2002.
Rainwater, Percy L., *Mississippi: Storm Center of Secession 1856-1861*. Baton Rouge: Otto Claitor, 1938.
_____, ed., "The Autobiography of Benjamin Grubb Humphreys," *Mississippi Valley Historical Review*, Vol. 21, September 1934.
Ranck, James Byrne, *Albert Gallatin Brown: Radical Southern Nationalist*, Copyright 1937. Philadelphia, PA: Porcupine Press Reprint, 1974.
Rand, Clayton, *Men of Spine in Mississippi*. Gulfport, MS: The Dixie Press, 1940.
"The Rebels in Pennsylvania: Burning of the Furnace of Hon. Thaddeus Stevens." *Chambersburg Repository*, reprinted in *New York Times*, July 26, 1863.
Richardson, Maj. Charles A., Letter, May 8, 1868, *Bachelder Papers* Vol. 1.
Robertson Jr., James I., *General A.P. Hill: The Story of a Confederate Warrior*. New York: Random House, 1987.
Rothera, Evan C., "Forgotten Fire-Eater: William Barksdale in History and Memory," *Journal of Mississippi History*, Vol. LXXII, Winter 2010.
Rowland, Dunbar, *Military History of Mississippi 1803-1898*. Reprint, H. Grady Howell, ed. Madison, MS: Chickasaw Bayou Press, 2003.
Rutherford County History of Tennessee. Chicago and Nashville: The Goodspeed Publishing Co., 1887.
Sandburg, Carl, *Abraham Lincoln: The War Years, Vol. IV*. London, UK: Harcourt, 1939.
Sauers, Richard A., *Gettysburg: The Meade-Sickles Controversy*. Washington, D.C.: Potomac Books Inc, 2003.
Sears, Stephen W., *Chancellorsville*. Boston, MA: Houghton Mifflin, 1996.
_____, *Gettysburg*. (Boston, MA: Houghton Mifflin, 2003.
_____, *Landscape Turned Red: The Battle of Antietam*. New Haven, CT: Ticknor & Fields, 1983.
_____, *To the Gates of Richmond: The Peninsula Campaign*. New York: Ticknor & Fields, 1992.
Shaara, Jeff, *Gods and Generals*. New York: Ballantine Books, 1996.
Shaara, Michael, *The Killer Angels*. New York: Ballantine Books, 1974.
Sifakis, Stewart, *Compendium of the Confederate Armies: Mississippi*. New York: Facts on File, 1995.
Silver, James W., ed., *A Life for the Confederacy: The War Diary of Robert A. Moore, Pvt. CSA*. Jackson, TN: McCowat-Mercer Press Inc., 1959.
Silverman, Jason H. et al, *Shanks: The Life and Wars of General Nathan G. Evans*. n.c.: Da Capo Press, 2002.
Smith, Gerald J., "One of the Most Daring of Men": The Life of Confederate General William Tatum Wofford." *Journal of Confederate History Series*. Murfreesboro, TN: Southern Heritage Press, 1997.
Sorrell, Moxley, *Recollections of a Confederate Staff Officer*, Copyright 1959. Wilmington, NC: Broadfoot Publishing Reprint, 1995.
Squires, Charles W., "Memoir," *Civil War Times Illustrated*, Vol. 14, No. 2, May 1972.
Stanley, Dick, *The Bloody Thirteenth—History of the 13th Mississippi Volunteer Infantry*. Austin, TX: Cavalry Scout Books, 2013.
Stiles, Major Robert, "Dedication of Monument to the Confederate Dead at the University of Virginia, June 17, 1893." *SHSP*, Vol. 21.
_____, *Four Years Under Marse Robert*, Copyright 1903. Marietta, GA: R. Bemis Publishing Ltd, 1995.
Styple, William B., *Writing & Fighting from the Army of Northern Virginia: A Collection of Confederate Soldier Correspondence*. Kearny, NJ: Belle Grove Publishing Co., 2003.
Sutton, E.J. *Civil War Stories*. Demorest, GA: Banner Printing Co., 1907.

Thompson, Benj. W., "Personal Narrative of Experience in the Civil War 1861–1865," *Civil War Times Illustrated*, October 1973.
Trudeau, Noah, *Gettysburg: A Testing of Courage*. New York: HarperCollins, 2002.
Tucker, Phillip Thomas, *Barksdale's Charge: The True High Tide of the Confederacy at Gettysburg, July 2, 1863*. Philadelphia: Casemate Publishers, 2013.
Tyson, Raymond W., "William Barksdale and the Brooks-Sumner Assault." *The Journal of Mississippi History*, Vol. XXVI, No. 2, May 1964.
United States Democratic Review, Vol. 43, April 1859.
Valentine, Clifton C., ed., *To See My Country Free: The Pocket Diaries of Ezekiel Armstrong, Ezekiel P. Miller, and Joseph A Miller*. Humboldt, TN: Rose Publishing Co., 1998.
Vandiver, Frank, *Mighty Stonewall*. New York: McGraw-Hill, 1957.
Veazey, Wheelock G., Letter, n.d., *Bachelder Papers*, Vol. 1.
Voices of the Civil War, 18 Vols. Richmond, VA: Time-Life Books, 1997.
Walker, John G., "Sharpsburg," *Battles & Leaders*, Vol. 2.
Walther, Eric H., *The Fire-Eaters*. Baton Rouge: Louisiana State University Press, 1992.
_____, *William Lowndes Yancey and the Coming of the Civil War*. Chapel Hill: University of North Carolina Press, 2006.
War of the Rebellion: A Compilation of the Official Records of the Union and Confederate Armies, 128 Vols. Washington, D.C.: Government Printing Office, 1880–1901.
Waters, Zack, and James G. Edmonds. *A Small but Spartan Band*. Tuscaloosa: University of Alabama Press, 2010.
Webb, Alexander S., *The Peninsula: McClellan's Campaign of 1862*. New York: Charles Scribner's Sons, Copyright 1881–1883, Archive Society Reprint 1982.
Welsh, Jack. D., *Medical Histories of Confederate Generals*. Kent, OH: Kent State University Press, 1995.
Wert, Jeffry D., *General James Longstreet: The Confederacy's Most Controversial Soldier*. New York: Simon & Shuster, 1993.
White, Elijah V., *History of the Battle of Ball's Bluff*. Leesburg, VA: The Washingtonian Print, n.d.
Wiley, Bell Irwin, *The Life of Johnny Reb*. Baton Rouge: Louisiana State University Press, 1981 Reprint.
_____, and Hirst D. Milhollen, *They Who Fought Here*. New York: Bonanza Books, 1965.
Willson, A.M., *Disaster, Struggle, Triumph: The Adventures of 1000 Boys In Blue*. Albany, NY: Argus Company, 1870.
Wilson, Legrand J., *The Confederate Soldier*, James W. Silver, ed. Memphis, TN: Memphis State University Press, 1973.
Wiltshire, Betty C., *Mississippi Soldiers: Revolutionary, 1812, Indian and Mexican Wars*. Carrolton, MS: Pioneer Publishing Co., 1998.
Woodworth, Stephen E., *No Band of Brothers: Problems in the Rebel High Command*. Columbia: University of Missouri Press, 1999.
Young, Jesse Bowman, *The Battle of Gettysburg: A Comprehensive Narrative*. New York, NY. Harper & Brothers, 1913.
Youngblood, William, "Unwritten History of the Gettysburg Campaign,." *SHSP* Vol. 38.

Internet Sources

www.dillahunty.com/files/Dillahunty_Master_update.pdf
www.fold3.com
www.mississippimarkers.com/lowndes-county.html

Index

Numbers in **_bold italics_** indicate pages with illustrations

Abbot, Capt. Henry L (20 MA) 171
Abernathy, Pvt. William Meshack (17 MS) 92, 205–206, 215
Abolitionists 32, 44, 66, 79
Alexander, Col. Edward Porter 154, 186, 191, 211–212, **_216_**, 228
Anderson, Maj. Gen. Richard H. 132, 136, 155, 251
Antietam Creek 140
Armistead, Brig. Gen. Lewis J. 120–121
Armstrong, Pvt. Ezekiel (17 MS) 78
Armstrong, Marion V. 145
Army of Northern Virginia 104, 126; morale 217; reorganization 149, 203–204

Baker, Col. Edward D. 93, 95; death **_96_**
Baker, Levi W. (9 MA Battery) 228
Ball's Bluff 92; *see also* Leesburg
band music 155, 182–183, 215
Banks, Nathaniel P. 47–48, 97–98
Barksdale, Ethelbert (brother) 10, 15–**_16_**, 17, 70–71, 104, 109, 185, 242; gravesite **_244_**
Barksdale, Ethelbert (son) 32, 107, 177, 244–245
Barksdale, Fountain (brother) 10, 12–13, 16
Barksdale, Harris (nephew) 199, 239, 243–244, gravesite **_245_**
Barksdale, Harrison (brother) 10, 12, 16–17
Barksdale, Capt. John A. (Adjutant) 196, 233–234
Barksdale, Nancy Hervey Lester (mother) 8–9
Barksdale, Narcissa Saunders (wife) 31–32, 57, 107, 177–178, 241–244

Barksdale, Nathaniel (great-grandfather) 7–8
Barksdale, Nathaniel, Jr. (grandfather) 8–9
Barksdale, Virginia (sister) 8
Barksdale, William **ii, _42, 73, 82_**; ancestry 7–8; appearance 41, 70–71, 174, 206, 220–221, 232, 238; burial 239–240, 243–244, **_248_**; childhood/education 9–10; debating skills 10, 38; defiance of authority 9, 147; devotion to duty 28, 150,-151, 220; duels 39, 57, 62–63; elected to Congress 40, 46, 56, 66; final words 237, 239; flattery, use of 17, 92, 260n21; forgiveness 9, 39–40, 46, 48; funeral 243; moral character 10, 57, 242; resourcefulness 169; self-learning 13, 17, 80; sensitivity to insult 39, 47, 48, 62; temper 39, 47, 48, 57, 62, 68; wounding/wounds 227, 233, 238
Barksdale, William, Sr. (father) 8–9
Barksdale, Willie (son) 32, 56, 107, 177, 236, 244
Baxter, Col. Henry (7 MI) 167–168
Baya, Capt. William (8 FL) 158, 167
Beale, Jane Howison 153
Beauregard, Maj. Gen. P.G.T. 83, 86, 88–90
Benedict, Lt. George G. (14 VT) 239
Bettersworth, James K. 11
Bigelow, Capt. John (P MA Battery) 257
Black, Pvt. Clendenen (13 MS) 207
Black, Lt. Col. John Logan (1 SC Cav) 206–207, 209

Black Republican Party 44, 52–54, 64, 67
Bleeding Kansas, admission under Constitutions Lecompton, Topeka, Wyandotte 59
Blewett, Thomas 57
Boggs, Pvt. William M. (114 PA) 223, 281n29
Bolivar Heights 131, 135
Bowen, Capt. Edward R. (114 PA) 224
Boyd, Pvt. Jackson (13 MS) 233
Bradford, Maj. Alexander 38, 40
Brainerd, capt. Wesley (50 NY Engineers) 152, 155, 157, 161, 163–164, 175–176
Brandon, Lt. Lane (21 MS) 171
Brandon, Lt. Col. William L. (21 MS) 120, 124
Brandy Station, battle of 204
Brett, David (9 MA Battery) 228
Brooks, Rep. Preston 49–51
Brooks, Capt. William C.F. (21 MS) 124
Brown, Sen. Albert Gallatin 19–20, **_37_**, 109, 129, 185, 256; praises Barksdale 100
Brown's Hotel 57–58
Buchanan, U.S. President James 54, 56, 59, 65
Bucklyn, 1Lt John J. (1st RI Battery) 214–215, 221–222
Bunch, Jack 102
Burnside, Maj. Gen. Ambrose E. 140, 151, 153, 163–165, 167, 173, 175
Burnside's Mud March 178–179
Burt, Col. Erasmus R. (18 MS) 89, 100; killed 97
Butler, Sen. Andrew P. 48–49
Byers, Pvt. John Alemeth (17 MS) 89

Cabell, Col. Henry C. (1 Corps Art. ANV) 214, 219

Index

Camp Barksdale 82
Camp of Instruction 81–82
Carter, Col. James W. (13 MS) 119, 125, 163, 167, 169; killed 223
Cassidy, Musician Robert A. (148 PA) 238
Chamberlain, Dr. Cyrus B. (Union surgeon/embalmer) 242
Chambersburg, PA 206–207
Chickasaw Rebellion 37–40
Chilton, Lt. Col. Robert H. (ANV Chief of Staff) 120, 188–189
cholera epidemics 9
Christian Revivals (ANV) 181–182, 185
Clark, Pvt. George W. (11 AL) 221–222
Clark, Capt. Judson A. (1st NJ Battery) 216
Coddington, Edwin B. 251
Columbus, MS (Possum Town) 13, 36, 177
Columbus Democrat 13–14, 34
Compromise of 1850 33–34, 41
Congresses: 33rd Session I 41–45, Session II 45–46; 34th Session I-III 46–55; 35th Session I 58–64, Session II 64–66; 36th Session I 57–72; as armed camp 68
congressional bills, sponsored by Barksdale 41, 44–45, 55, 59, 64–65
Congressional brawl on House Floor (February 6, 1858) 59–*60*, 61–62; scalping of Barksdale *61*–62
Congressional speeches by Barksdale: on Admission of Kansas as Slave State 63–64; on Kansas-Nebraska Bill 42–44; on Presidential Election of 1856 52–54; on Reopening of the African Slave Trade 66; on Slavery and Peaceable Secession Under the Constitution 66–68
Corinth, MS 77, 80–81
Cotton, as King 11
Court of Inquiry re charges of drunkenness 90–92, 101–102
Cuba, purchase by U.S. 65
Culpepper Courthouse 108, 150, 204
Cummings, Lt. Col. Charles (16 VT) 237
Cummings, Sgt. Charles C. (17 MS) 133, 158

Dana, Brig. Gen. Napoleon J. (AOP) 141–142, 145

Davis, Jefferson C. 20, 23 30, 55, 75, 77, 83, 88–92, 104, 109–111, 127, 182, 241; offers transfer to Barksdale 178
Davis, Reuben *20*, 23–26, 37–38, 46, 58–60, 75; fight with Barksdale 39
Davis, Pvt. William L. (13 MS) 166
Democratic National Convention of 1860: April 30th 70–71; June 18th 71
Democratic Party 35–40, 46, 54
Dinkins, Pvt. James (13 MS) *108*, 113, 126, 129–130, 135–136, 138, 142, 145–146, 149, 151, 165, 170, 177
disease 9, 23–25, 27, 30, 89; Barksdale contracts measles 27
Douglas, Sen. Stephen A. 41–42, 48–49, 59
Dow, Lt. Edwin (6 ME Battery) 231
Downing, Fanny: *Memorial Flowers* (poem/song) 247
Duff, Capt. W.L. (17 MS) 95
Dunker Church (Sharpsburg) 140–*141*

Early, Maj. Gen. Jubal A. (ANV) 84–*85*, 86, 187–194, 196–197; muted praise for Barksdale 87–88, 147; public quarrel with Barksdale 199–201, 218
Eastis, Pvt. Joseph M. (13 MS) 82
Eckford, Capt. E.J. (13 MS) 99
Edmonds, James C.: *A Small But Spartan Band* 167
Edwards Ferry 94–95, 100; battle of 97–98, *99*
Ellis, Pvt. Peter F. (13 MS) 86
Evans, Col. Nathan G. (7th Brigade) 84, 89, 90, *91*, 93–94, 96, 98, 101, 104–105; praises Barksdale 100
Ewell, Maj. Gen. Richard S. 203

Farwell, Byron 95
Featherston, Col. Winfield S. (17 MS) 89, 97, 105, 109, 243
Fillmore, Millard 53
fire-eater, definition 3; Barksdale NOT a fire-eater 42–44, 68
Fiser, Lt. Col. John Calvin (17 MS) 119, 124, 145, 156–158, 161, 165, 167, 169, 196
fishing 184–185
Fletcher, Capt. L.D. (13 MS) 97, 100
Florida troops (8FL): at Fredericksburg 158, 167; at Gettysburg 226, 230

Foote, Henry Stuart 34, 40
Ford, Col. Thomas H. (32 OH) 133
Forster, Capt. Robert M. (148 PA) 240
Fort Beauregard 93, 106
Fort Evans 93, 95, 97, 99, 106
Fort Johnston 93, 106
Fort Magruder 111
Franklin, Maj. Gen. William B. (AOP) 136, 165, 173
Fraternization: at Fredericksburg 180–181
Frederick MD 130, 135
Fredericksburg 152; battle of 158–173, *159*–*160*, *162*; first amphibious crossing *168*–169; Market Lot Headquarters *156*–157, 163, 167; picket of town 154–155, 174, 177, 179, 183–*184*, 201; Union bombardment 165–166; Union sacking of 171–*172*; urban warfare 169–*170*
Fredericksburg, second battle of (Chancellorsville) 190–191, *192*, 193–198
Freeman, Douglas Southall 88, 167
Freemantle, Arthur James Lyon 205, 217
Freemasonry: Barksdale becomes Mason 27–28, 262*ch4n*1; Barksdale Lodge of Mississippi 182; Columbus Lodge No. 5 241
Fremont, John C. 54
Frye, Dennis 132, 145

Gallagher, Gary W. 201, 254
Georgia troops: 3rd GA 158
Gerald, Maj. George B. (18 MS) 224
Gettysburg, battle of 208–235, *218*; Longstreet's countermarch 211
Gibbon, Brig. Gen. John (AOP) 193, 197
Giddings, Rep. Joshua R. 53–54
Gilbert, Lt. S. Capers (Brooks Artillery SC) 214–215, 219
Gordon, Brig. Gen. John Brown (ANV) 187, 190, 197, 200
Gorman, Brig. Gen. Willis P. (AOP) 93–94, 97, 141
Govan, Capt. Andrew R. (17 MS) 156–158, 163, 167, 169
Graham, Brig. Gen. Charles K. (AOP) 221, 223
Greenwood cemetery, Jackson MS 243–245, 248
Gregg, Brig. Gen. Maxcy, comparison with Barksdale 148

Index

Griffin, Col. Thomas M. (18 MS) 6, 105, 119, 123, 195–196, 198, 201, 222, 230, 234; flag of truce 193
Griffith, Brig. Gen. Richard (ANV) 74, 104–105, 109; mortal wounding 113
Grow, Rep. Galusha A. 60–62

Hall, Col. Norman J. (7 MI) 167
Halleck, General-In-Chief Henry W. 152
Hamilton, Assistant Surgeon Alfred T. (148 PA) 238–239
Hancock, Maj. Gen. Winfield S. (AOP) 6, 209, 225, 231–*232*, 234
Hardee's Infantry Manual 80, 150, 169
Harmon, Adjutant Edwin P. (13 MS) 230
Harpers Ferry 131; surrender 136
Harpers Ferry Cowards 135; redemption of 231–234
Harrison, Maj. Isham D. (13 MS) 77, 90
Harrison's Island 92
Harsh, Prof. Joseph L. 145, 148, 246
Hart, Capt. Patrick (15 NY Battery) 216
Hawley, Stephen A. 88, 125, 138, 148, 158, 196, 219
Hays, Col. Harry (7 LA) 86, 88, 188–191, 196
Helper, Hinton Rowan: *The Impending Crisis of the South* 69
Hendricks, Pvt. Thurman E. (13 MS) 123
Henley, Pvt. Albert Wymer (13 MS) 81–82, 85, 88–90, 107, 142
Hill, Lt. Gen. Ambrose Powell (ANV) 136, 138, 146, 203, 251
Hill, Maj. Gen. Daniel Harvey (ANV) 104–109, 112, 120; "Not war but murder" 126; trains 17 MS as artillerymen 106–107
Hill, Sgt. William H. (13 MS) 86, 89, 101, 107–108, 150, 182, 184, 204–205, 207
Hoke, Jacob 207
Holder, Col. William D. (17 MS) 6, 119, 124, 189, 230, 234
Holien, Kim B. 95
Holmes, Richard 217
Holt, Pvt. David (16 MS) 79
Hood, Maj. Gen. John Bell 140, 211, 213, 216
Hood, Maj. John J. (13 MS) 247
Hooker, Maj. Gen. Joseph (AOP) 140, 179, 186–188, 204, 207

Howard, Maj. Gen. Oliver Otis 142, 167
Hubbert, Pvt. Mike M. (13 MS) 139
Hummelbaugh House 238–*240*
Humphreys, Brig. Gen. Andrew A. (AOP) 212, 224–227, *226*, 230
Humphreys, Col. Benjamin Grubb (21 MS) 104–*105*, 115–116, 119, 131, 149, 151, 158–159, 170, 189–191, 194, 199, 202, 213, 227, 231, 234–237, 247
Hunt, Brig. Gen. Henry J. (AOP) 118, 155, 163, 165, 167, 214, 227, 252–253
Hunt, Maj. Thomas J. (7 MI) 168–169
Hunter, Maj. R.W. (8 VA); praises Barksdale 100
Hunton, Col. Eppa (7 VA) 89, 97, *102*

Imhof, John D. 250
Inge, Maj. William M. (13 MS) 124

Jackson, Lt. Gen. Thomas J. 116, 121, 135–136, 149, 155, 157, 161–162, 173, 186–187, 198
Janney, Alcinda 107
Janney, Mayor John (Leesburg) 107
Jenifer, Lt. Col. Walter H. (8 VA Cav.) 89, 97, 101; praises Barksdale 100
Johnson, Maj. W. Gart (18 MS) 128, 210–211, 220–221, 248, 256, 277n60, 283n50
Johnston, Gen. Joseph E. 107, 111
Joint Committee on the Conduct of the War 97
Jones, Rev. J. William 181

Kansas-Nebraska Act 41–44, 47, 49
Keegan, Sir John D.P. 33, 80, 213
Keitt, Rep. Laurence M. 49–*51*, 60–62
Kemper, Col. James L. (7 VA) 86, 88
Kershaw, Brig. Gen. Joseph B. 128, 131–136, *132*, 138–139, 143, 146, 164–165, 187, 211, 219, 229, 234; praises Barksdale 138
Kinyon, Benjamin 36
Klingle farm 213, 225
Know Nothing Party 46
Krick, Robert K. 80, 145, 148, 246

Lamar, Capt. G.B. (McLaws Aide) 221

Land Merrimac 114–115
Lander, Brig. Gen. Frederick W. (AOP) 93, 95
Lang, Col. David M. (8 FL) 158, 166–167, 226, 230
Lee, Gen. Robert E. (ANV) 111, 118–119, 131, 149, 153, 158, 167, 186, 188, 198, 203, 207, 209–210, 215, 229, 241; designates Barksdale to defend Fredericksburg 187; praises Barksdale 123, 174; reprimands Early 201
Leech, Margaret: *Reveille In Washington* 57–58
Leesburg, VA 92, 129–130; battle of 95–97 (Ball's Bluff); evacuation by Confederates 107–108
legacy of William Barksdale: Mississippi Hall of Fame 254–255; as patriot 256; as politician 245–246, 255; as soldier 246–250, 252–254, 256
Lincoln, Abraham 58, 71, 95, 152
Lloyd, Pvt. Joseph C. (13 MS) 187, 195, 197, 233–234
Longstreet, Lt. Gen. James *84*–85, 120, 126, 149–150, 153, 171 , 201, 203, 210–211, 213, 216, 228–230, 234, 248–251; praises Barksdale 174, 249–250
Loudoun Heights 131–132, 135
Love, Surgeon Thomas N. (2nd MS Rifles): *A Southern Lacrimosa* *21*–28, 30
Love, William A. (6 MS Cav) 232
Lovejoy, Elijah 69
Lovejoy, Owen *68*–70
Lowndes County, MS 13, 34–36
Luse, Lt. Col. William H. (18 MS) *119*, 123, 157, 164, 170, 195, 201, 255

Madill, Col. Henry J. (141 PA) 223
Magruder, Maj. Gen. John A. (ANV) 108, 110, 113–114, 117, 121, 123, 126
Maine troops: 3rd ME 223
Malvern Hill, battle of 117–126, *122*; Barksdale seizes battleflag 123; casualties 125
Manassas, battle of 83–88, *87*
Manifest Destiny 18–19
Mansfield, Maj. Gen. Joseph K. (AOP) 140
Maryes Heights 165, 172, 181–191, 194, 196–201
Maryland Heights 131–133, *134*–136
masked battery 95
Massachusetts troops: 5th

Battery (Phillips) 216; 9th Battery (Bigelow) 215, 227; 15th MA 94–95; 19th MA 167, 170; 20th MA 167, 169, 171, 197
McCall, Brig. Gen. George A. 93–94
McClellan, Maj. Gen. George B. (AOP) 93–95, 110–113, 125, 133, 135, 151
McDowell, Brig. Gen. Irvin (AOP) 84
McElroy, Lt. Col. Kennon A. (13 MS) 119, 126, 127, 129, 136
McGilvery, Lt. Col. Freeman (Reserve Artillery AOP) 227, 231, 252
McLaws, Maj. Gen. Lafayette C. (ANV) 128, 131–132, 135, 151–152, 154–155, 157, 165, 171–172, 174–175, 185–187, 197, 206, 210–211, 213, 215–216, 219, 228–229, 251; muted praise for Barksdale 138, 147, 174- 175; post-war praise for Barksdale 175; recommends Barksdale's promotion 127
McLaws' Minstrels/Barksdale Thespian Club 180
McNeily, Pvt. John Seymour (21 MS): *Barksdale's Brigade at Gettysburg* 218, 222, 247, 251–252; "a very thirst for battlefield glory" 220
McPherson, James M.: *Drawn by the Sword* 80
Meade, Maj. Gen. George G. (AOP) 94, 207–208, 212, 241
Michigan troops: MI 94, 97, 142–143, 167–168, *174*
Miles, Col. Dixon S. 133
military characteristics/traits of Barksdale: aggressiveness 96; bayonet drill 150; care of troops 83, 147; drill 81, 151; as father figure 128, 248; harsh discipline 81–82; led from front 123, 222; "pep" talks 142, 185, 219–220
military service of Barksdale: Mexican War 18–30, *25*; militia 19–20; Mississippi Quartermaster General 75; near misses 145–*146*, 166; refuses transfer to Mississippi 178–*179*; resigns 76–77
Miller, Pvt. Joseph A. (17 MS) 183–184
Minnesota troops: I MN 95, 234
Mississippi Brigade *173*; 13th MS 89, 93, 94–95, 97–100, 125, 129, 145, 153, 163, 167, 185, 191, 194, 196, 219–220, 222–225, 235; 17th MS 89, 123–125, 145, 153, 156, 158, 183, 191, 194, 196, 215, 219–220, 223, 225, 235; 18th MS 89, 97, 123, 125, 145, 157–158, 164, 170, 191, 194–196, *195*, 219–220, 222, 224–225; 21st MS 104, 123–125, 145, 163, 167, 171, 183–184, 188, 191, 195–196, 214, 217, 219–220, 223, 227–228, 231, 234–235
Mississippi military uniform 75
Mississippi Rifles (Mexican War) 1st 20, 22, 24; 2nd 21–24, 26–29
Mississippi secession 72–74
Mississippi State Monument (Gettysburg) 248–*249*
Mississippi state politics 33–38, 46
Mississippi's Southern Manifesto 72
Moody, Maj. Daniel N. (21 MS) 120, 124
Moody, Capt. George V. (Madison LA Light Artillery) 214–215, 219
Moore, Pvt. Robert A. (17 MS) 150, 207, 234–235
Moran, Capt. Frank E. (73 NY) 224
Morgan, James M. III: *A Little Short of Boats* 95
Muffly, Adj. Joseph W. (148 PA) 239
Mulholland, Col. St. Clair (116 PA) 239
myths: Barksdale's dog at Gettysburg 280–281n1; exchange for Gen. Reynolds 112

Nash, Pvt. Newton (13 MS) 105, 129, 184, 205, 207
Nealy, Rev. Phillip P. (Columbus MS) 242
New Hampshire troops 2 NH 223
New Jersey troops: 7 NJ 221; 11 NJ 225–226
New York troops: 3rd Cav. 94, 97; 15th NY Engineers 163–164, 167, 169, 240; 39th NY 232; 42nd NY 142–143; 50th NY Engineers 163, 167, 240; 71st NY 226; 72nd NY 226; 73rd NY 224, 226, 74th NY 226; 79th NY 133; 89th NY 169; 111th NY 232, 234, 236; 120th NY 226; 125th NY 232, 234; 126th NY 133,135, 232–234, 236
Nichols, Col. William (14 VT) 237–238
Nugent, Pvt. William L. (13 MS) 79
Nutting, Prof. Timothy D. (MS Brigade bandleader) 180, 182–183

Ohio troops: 32 OH 133
O'Reilly, Francis A. 169, 253
Owen, the Rev. William B. (Chaplain 17 MS) 181, 185, 193
Owen, Capt. William M. (Washington Artillery LA) 196, 216

paintings/artwork of Barksdale 254
Parham, Pvt. John T. (32 VA) 143
Parker, Pvt. David L. (14 VT) 237
Patrick, Brig. Gen. Marsena N. (Provost) 153
Pendleton, Col. William N. (Chief of Artillery ANV) 188–189, 193, 198
Pennsylvania troops: 57th PA 173, 215, 221; 63rd PA 222; 68th PA 221, 223; 105th PA 215, 221–222, 224–225 114th PA 215, 221–224; 125th PA 140, 142; 141st PA 221
Pettus, Gov. James J. (MS) 71–72, 74–76
Pfanz, Harry W. 205, 282n37
Phillips, Capt. Charles (5 MA Battery) 216
Pickett, Maj. Gen. George E. (ANV) 208, 252
Pleasant Valley (MD) 132, 136–*137*
Plum Run artillery line 227, 231, 252
Plum Run swale 230–231, 236
Polk, Pres. James J. 17, 19, 65
pontoon bridging 152, 155–157, *159*, 173, 186, 197
Potter, Rep. John "Bowie Knife" 61, *62*; Barksdale duel 63
Pulliam, Capt. Andrew J. (21 MS) 156–157

Quitman, John A. 34

Rains, Col. Gabriel J. 110–111
Rainwater, Prof. Percy L.: *Storm Center of Secession* 33–34
Randolph, Capt. George E. (1st RI Battery) 252
Randolph, Adj. John F. (126 NY) 233
Reynolds, Maj. gen. John F. (AOP) 112
Richardson, Capt. Charles A. (126 NY) 233
Richmond Howitzers 89, 106–107, 121, 165, 180
rifle pits (Fredericksburg) 154

Index

Robertson, Glenn 80
Rothera, Evan C. 246, 281*n*18
Rutherford County, TN (Smyrna) 8

Salem Church, battle of 196, 215
Savage Station, battle of 112–116, *115*
Scott, Gen. Winfield 22, 24, 27
Scranton, Pvt. T.M. (13 MS) 221
Sears, Stephen W. 141, 145, 224, 249
secession 66–68
Sedgwick, Maj. Gen. John (AOP) 140, *142*, 145, 186, 188, 193–194
Seeley, Lt. Francis W. (4th US Battery) 224
Semmes, Brig. Gen. Paul J. 128, *146*, 249
Seven Days Battles 111–126
Seven Pines, battle of 111
Seward, Sen. William E. 64, 79
Shaara, Jeff: *Gods and Generals* 253
Shaara, Michael: *The Killer Angels* 253
Sharpsburg, battle of 140; casualties 147; West Woods action 140–143, *144*, 145
Sherfy Peach Orchard action 210, 212–214, 223–*225*, 228, 252
Sherrill, Col. Eliakim E. (126 NY) 135
Sickles, Maj. Gen. Daniel E. (AOP) 29, *212*–213, 225
Sims, Capt. John (21 MS) 145
Slaughter, Mayor Montgomery (Fredericksburg) 153, 182
slavery 18, 32–33, 55, 78–*79*
snipers 161–*162*, 167–171, 272*n*43
snowball fights 107, 180
Sorrell, Adj. Gen. Moxley (First Corps ANV): praises Barksdale 174
South Carolina troops: 7 SC 133
Spaulding, Maj. Ira (NY Engineers) 167
Stafford Heights 154, 163, 165

Standing Committee on Foreign Affairs 59, 65
Stennis, Pvt. J. Dudley (13 MS) 101, 268*n*29
Stevens, Thaddeus 68; destruction of ironworks 208–209
Stiles, Capt. Robert (Richmond howitzers) 89, 106–107, 113, 121, 153, 165–166; describes MS Brigade 127
Stone, Maj. Gen. Charles P. (AOP) 93–97
Stone Mountain, GA: Confederate Memorial Carving 247
straggling 138–139, 205
Stuart, Maj. Gen. J.E.B. 187, 204–205, 208
Sumner, Sen. Charles: caning 49–52, *50*; incendiary speech "The Crime Against Kansas" 48–49
Sumner, Maj. Gen. Edwin V. 140–141, 143
Sutton, Pvt. Elijah H. (24 GA) 217

Taylor, Gen. Zachary (US Reg.) 19, 24, 26, 30, 53
Teasdale, the Rev. Thomas 242
Thompson, Capt. Benjamin W. (111 NY) 232
Thompson, Capt. James (PA Light Artillery) 216, 221
Tilghman, Brig. Gen. Lloyd 112
Toombs, Brig. Gen. Robert M. 123
torpedoes (booby traps) 110–111
Trudeau, Noah A. 229
Tucker, Philip Thomas: *Barksdale's Charge* 234, 252
Tyson, Raymond A. 51–52

Van Dorn, Maj. Gen. Earl 74–75
Vanity Fair: "The Delights of Debate" (Barksdale vs. Lovejoy) 69–70
Vaughn, Sgt. Henry (14 VT) 237
Veazey, Col. Wheelock G. (14 VT) 236
Vermont troops: 14 VT 237; 16 VT 236

Virginia troops: 8th VA 89, 97
visual media, on Barksdale (DVDs/movies) 253–254

Walker, Brig. Gen. John G. (ANV) 132, 135–136, 147
Wallace, Pvt. Thomas D. (13 MS) 80–81, 83, 86, 90
Walter, Past Grand Master Col. Harvey Washington 243
Walton, Col. James B. (Washington Artillery LA) 189
Warner, Pvt. Calvin P. (13 MS) 83
Washburne, Rep. Cadwallader 61, *63*
Washburne, Rep. Elihu H. 61, *62*
Washington Artillery (LA) 189, 194, 198
Washington City (DC) *45*, 57–58
Waters, Zack C.: *A Small But Spartan Band* 167
Watson, Lt. Malbone (5th US Battery) 231
Whitaker, Lt. Col. Mackerness H. (13 MS) 77, 90–91, 101–103
White, Col. Elijah V. (35th VA Cav.): praises Barksdale 100
Wilcox, Brig. Gen. Cadmus M. (ANV) 132, 158, 191, 196, 226, 230, 234, 251
Wiley, Bell I. 182
Willard, Col. George L. (125 NY) 232, 234, 252
Williamsburg, battle of 111
Wilmot Proviso 33
Wilson, Pvt. Nathan W. (11 MA) 240
Wilson, Lt. Samuel (126 NY) 236
Wofford, Brig. Gen. William T. (ANV) 128, 228–*229*, 234

Yorktown, VA, siege of 110
Young, 2nd LT Jesse Bowman (84 PA) 226–227
Youngblood, Pvt. William (15 AL) 230

www.ingramcontent.com/pod-product-compliance
Lightning Source LLC
Chambersburg PA
CBHW060336010526
44117CB00017B/2850